Gettysburg
and Lee's Escape to Virginia

★ Other Books by Donald S. (Don) Lowry ★

The 1863 Series

Over the River: The Campaigns of Vicksburg and Chancellorsville, March–May 1863 (2014)
". . . [E]xtremely interesting and informative . . . highly recommended to all Civil War campaign and battle enthusiasts."
– Civil War News

The Road to Gettysburg: Lee's Invasion of Pennsylvania and Grant's Siege of Vicksburg, May–July 1863 (2015)
". . . [W]eaves together a fast-paced narrative with contemporary quotations and thoughtful analysis."
– Civil War News

The 1864 Series

No Turning Back: The Beginning of the End of the Civil War, March–June 1864 (1992)
". . . [R]eveals a sure grasp of Civil War history and military strategy."
– Library Journal

Fate of the Country: The Civil War from June to September 1864 (1992)

Dark and Cruel War: The Decisive Months of the Civil War, September–December, 1864 (1993)
". . . [A] superior contribution to the narrative histories of the Civil War."
– Booklist

Towards an Indefinite Shore: The Final Months of the Civil War, December 1864–May 1865 (1995)

GETTYSBURG
and Lee's Escape to Virginia

Donald S. Lowry

Gettysburg and Lee's Escape to Virginia
Copyright 2016 by Donald S. Lowry

All rights reserved. No part of this publication may be reproduced, stored in a retrieval system, or transmitted, in any form or by any means, electronic, mechanical, photocopying, or otherwise, without the prior written permission of the author.

ISBN-13: 978-1533262769
ISBN-10: 1533262764

Cover design & maps by George Skoch, copyright 2016 Donald S. Lowry

Designed and typeset by Catspaw DTP Services
http://www.catspawdtp.com/

"Your golden opportunity is gone, and I am distressed immeasurably because of it."

– *President Abraham Lincoln, in a letter addressed to Major General George Meade – but never sent*

Table of Contents

Prologue 1

Part One   *Gettysburg: Day One* 4
Chapter 1   "Sown with Dragon's Teeth". 5
Chapter 2   "Bloody Desperate Fight". 29
Chapter 3   "Hard Times at Gettysburg!". 54
Chapter 4   "The Portrait of Hell" 80
Chapter 5   "It Is Too Late to Leave It" 106

Part Two   *Gettysburg: Day Two* *136*
Chapter 6   "You Will Be Entirely on the Flank of the Enemy" 137
Chapter 7   "The Best Three Hours' Fighting Ever Done" 178
Chapter 8   "The War Was Very Nearly Over". 216
Chapter 9   "It Is All Right Now". 238
Chapter 10   "Success That Did Not Succeed" 264
Chapter 11   "We Must Sacrifice Our Pride" 304

Part Three   *Gettysburg: Day Three* *333*
Chapter 12   "I Am Going to Take Them Where They Are" . . . 334
Chapter 13   "The Air Seemed Filled With Shells" 367
Chapter 14   "Fredericksburg on the Other Leg". 391
Chapter 15   "We Can't Expect Always to Gain Victories". 420

Part Four   *Retreat and Pursuit* *446*
Chapter 16   "Lee Must Fight His Way Through Alone" 447
Chapter 17   "Vicksburg Has Surrendered" 475
Chapter 18   "My Army Is All in Motion" 499
Chapter 19   "A Dreadful Reminiscence of McClellan" 532
Chapter 20   "If General Meade Can Complete His Work" 563

Part Five   *Escape* *600*
Chapter 21   "I Should Like to See a Clear Day" 601
Chapter 22   "Broadway Looked Like a Field of Battle" 631
Chapter 23   "The War Will Be Prolonged Indefinitely". 669
Chapter 24   "Let There Be No Compromising" 714
             Afterword. 747
             The Armies. 751
             Bibliography. 775

Gettysburg 1 July

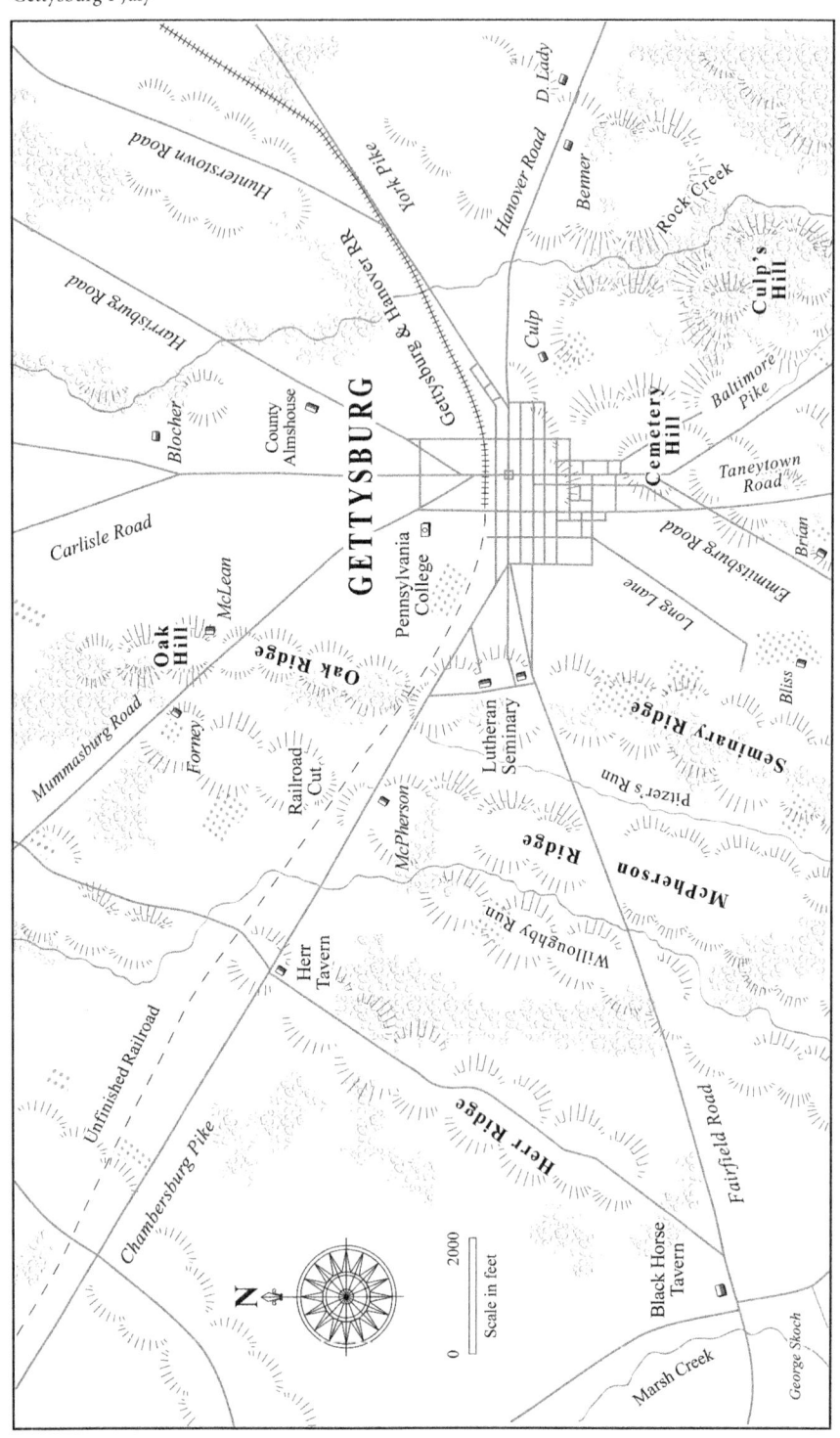

Gettysburg 2–3 July

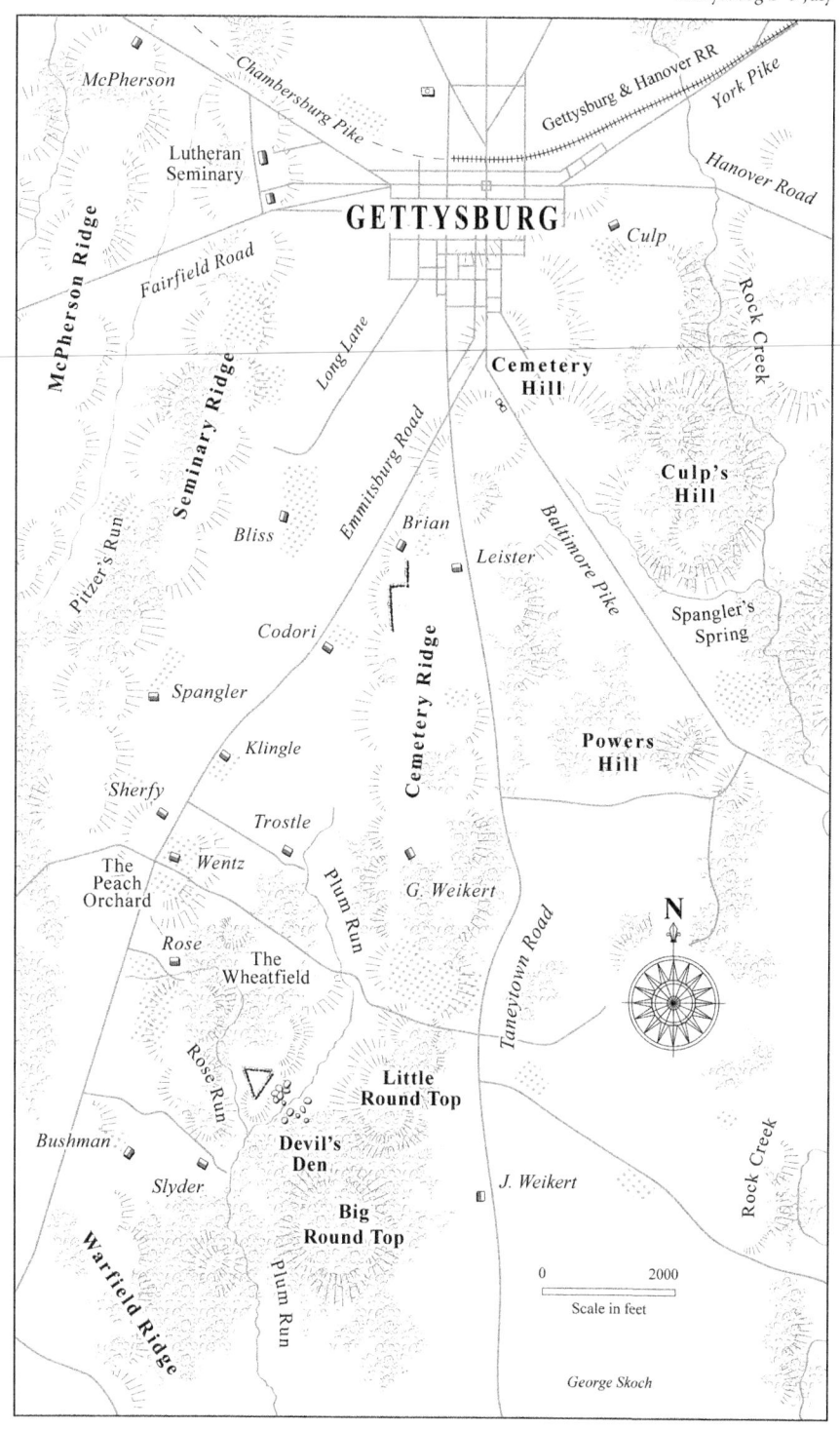

Mississippi

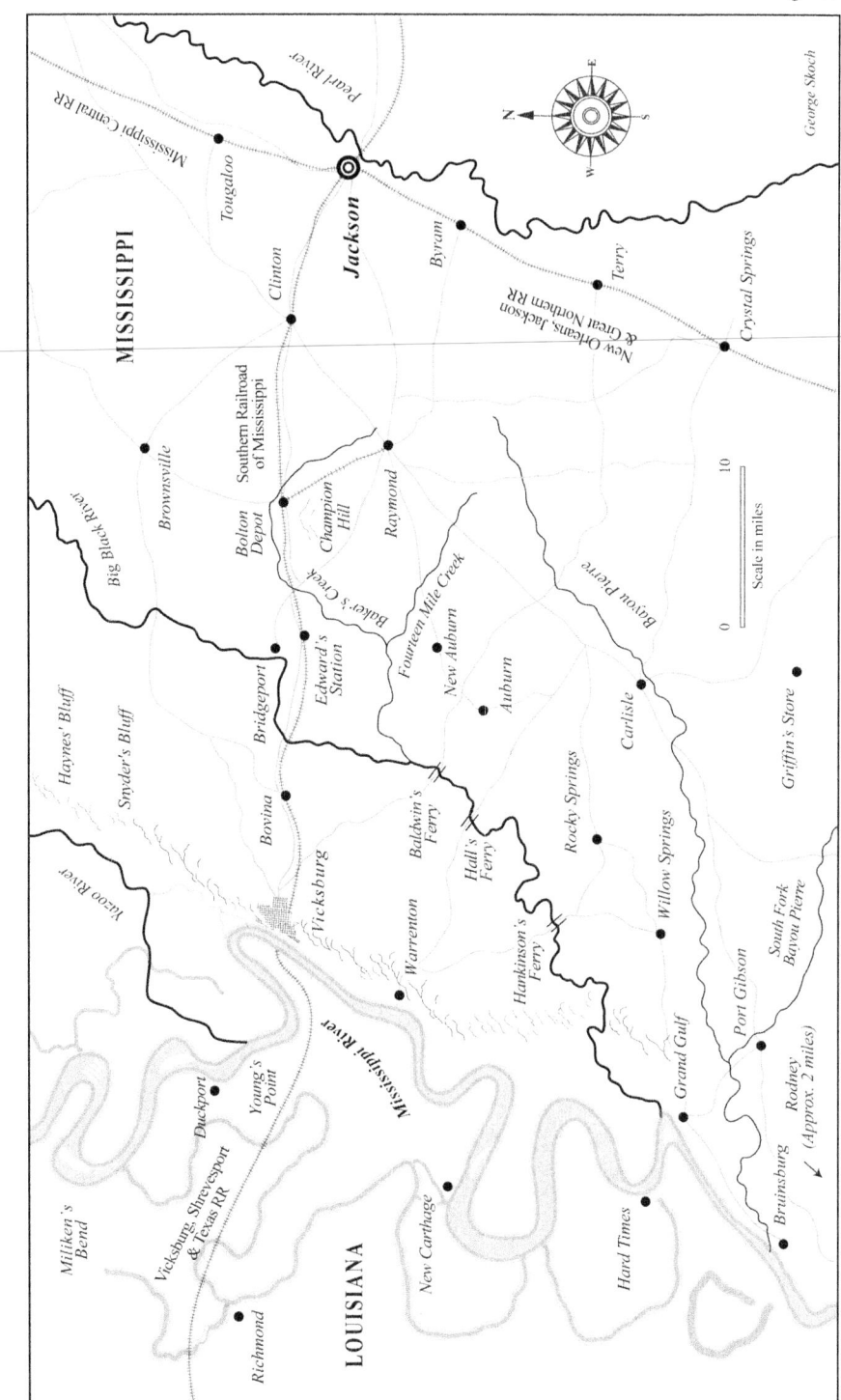

Vicksburg area

Eastern Theater of War

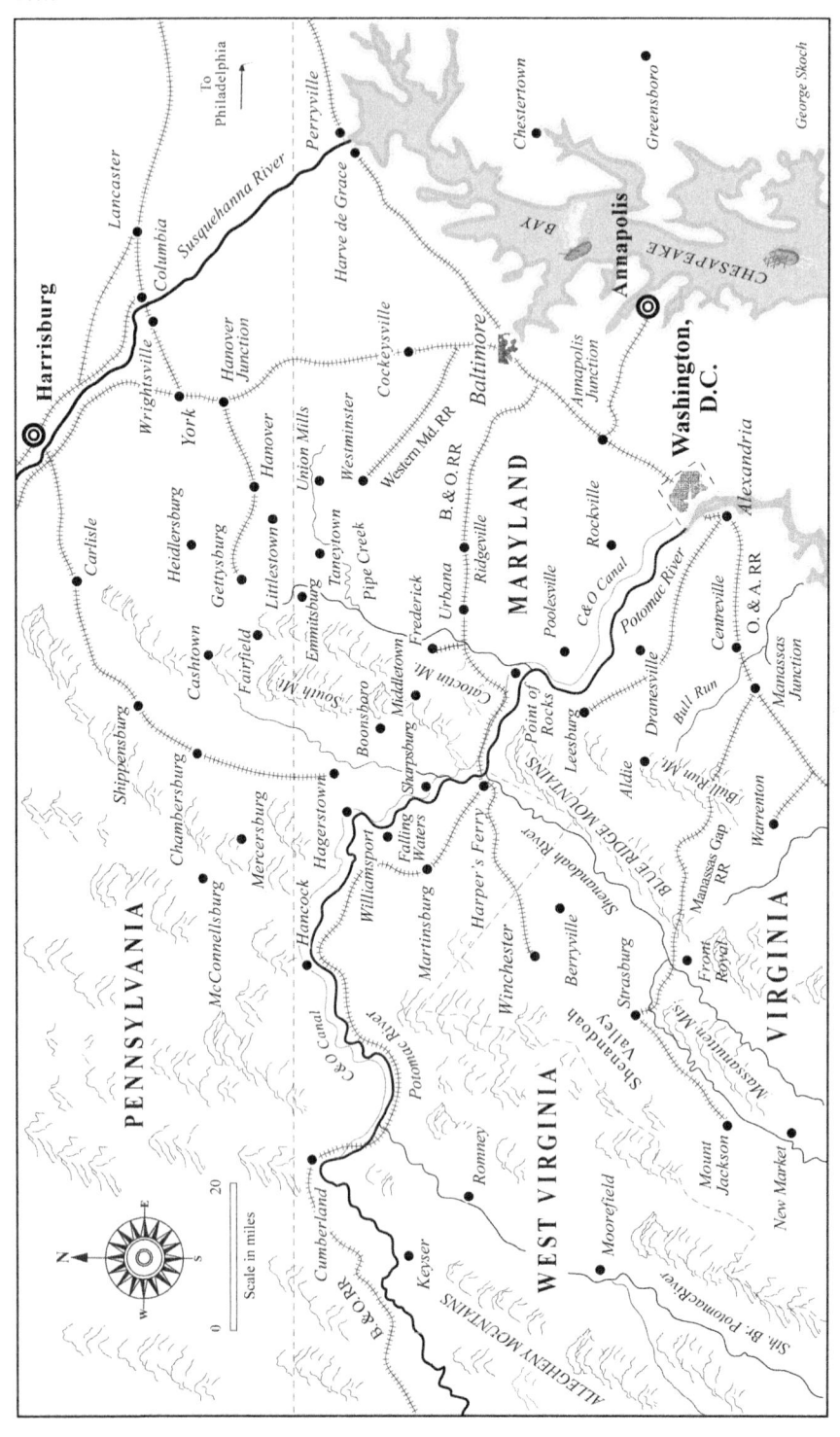

South-Central Tennessee

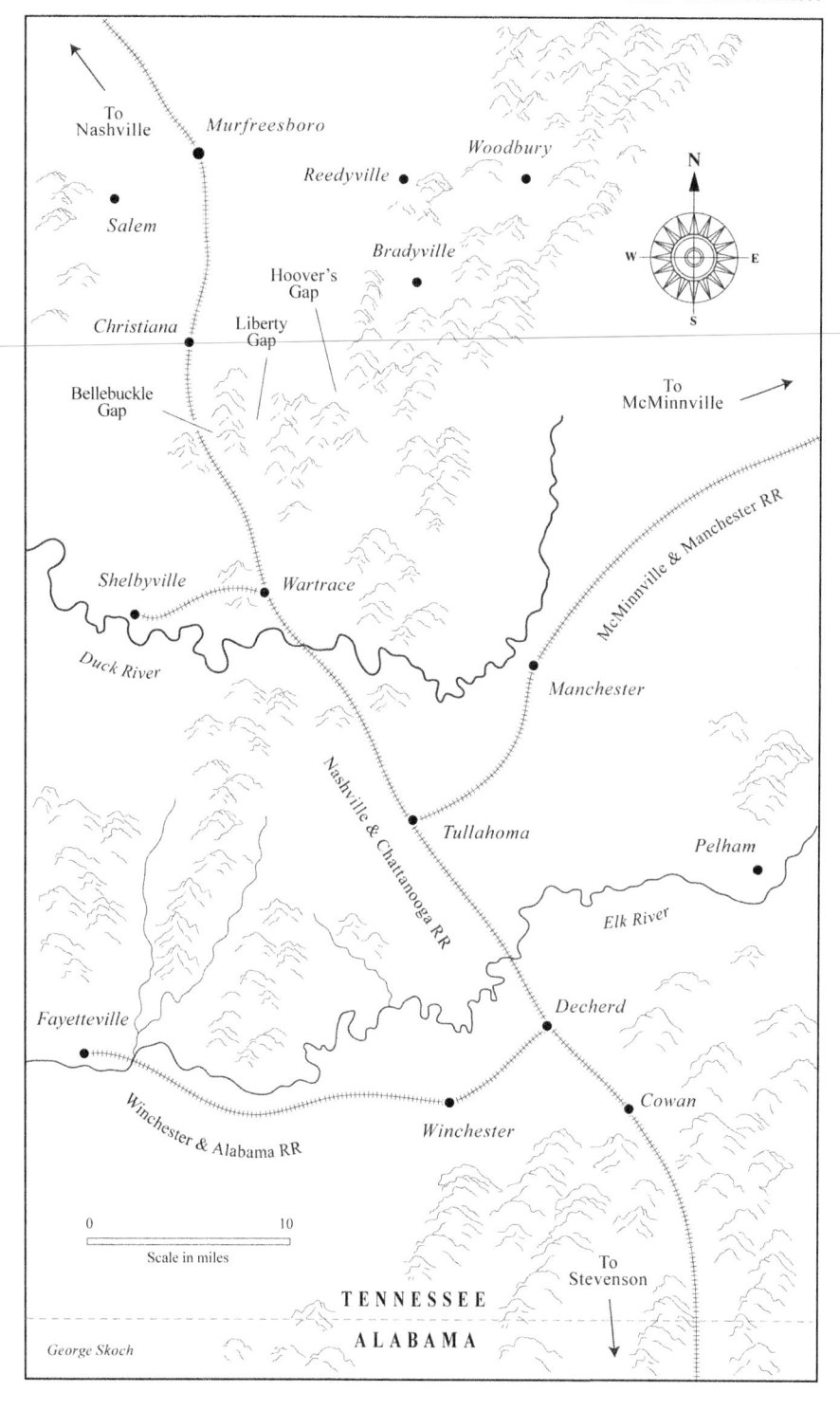

From OR I:27:I:438 – the report of Col. Norman J. Hall.

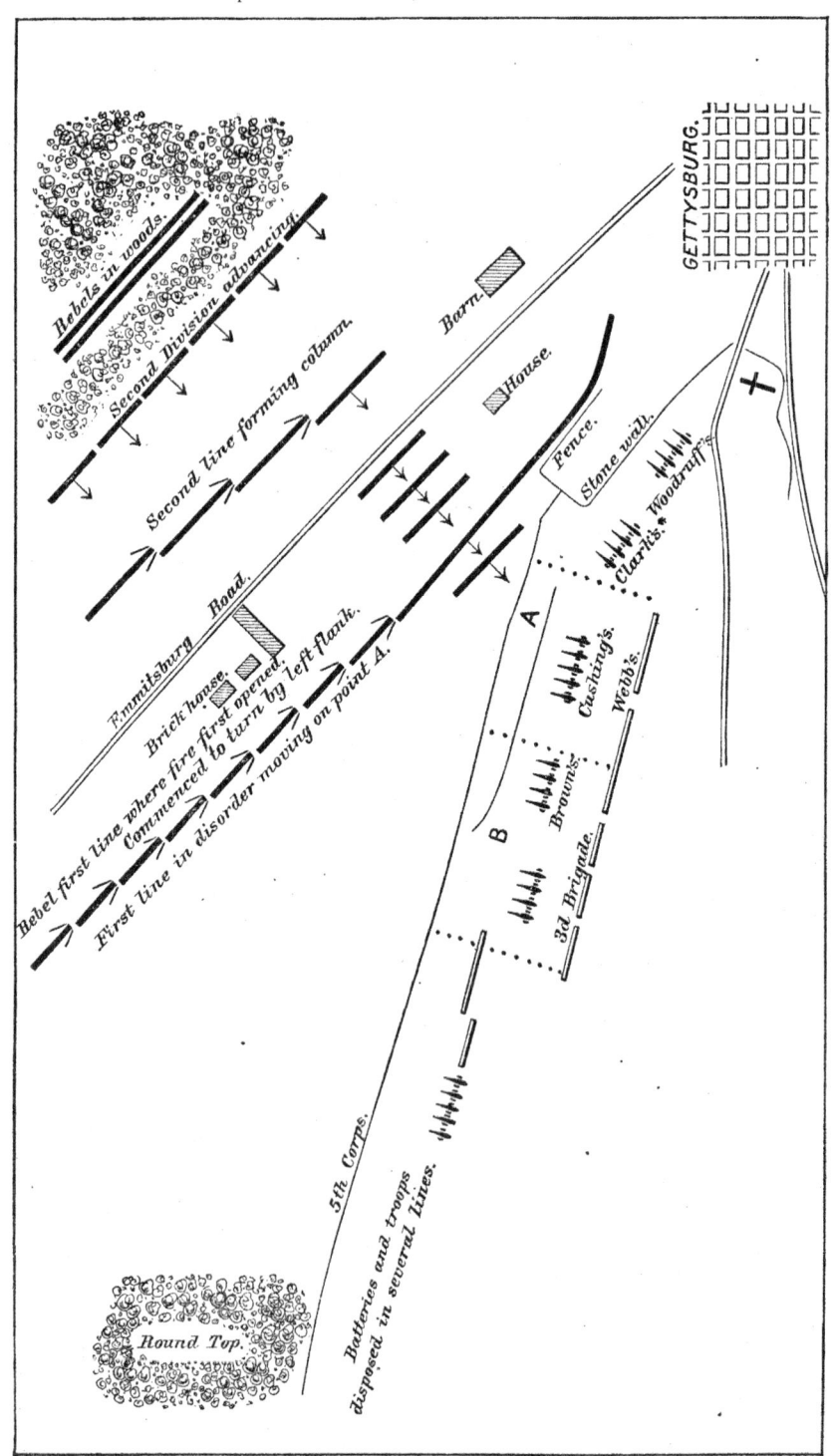

*Should be Arnold's.

East Cavalry Field

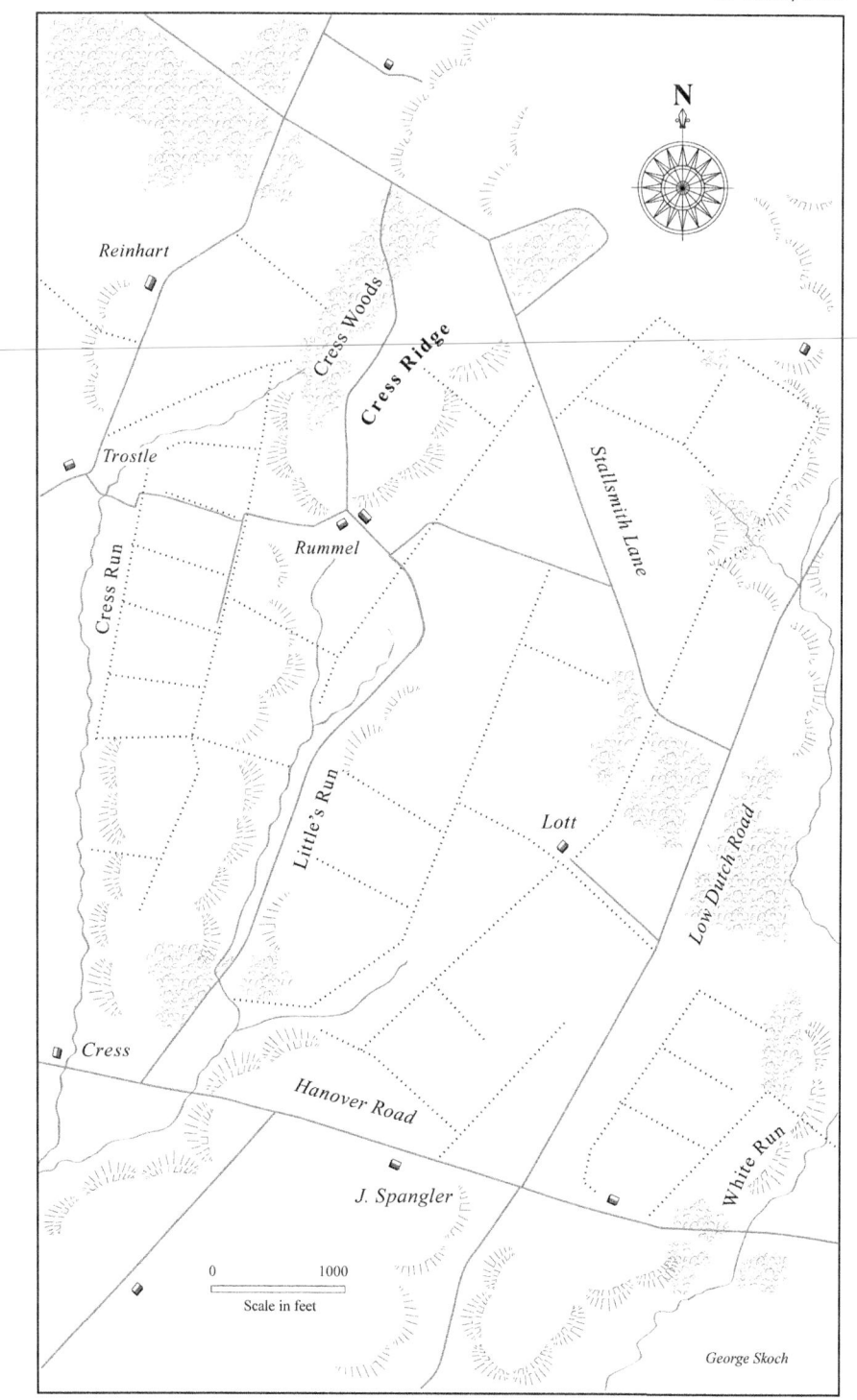

South Cavalry Field

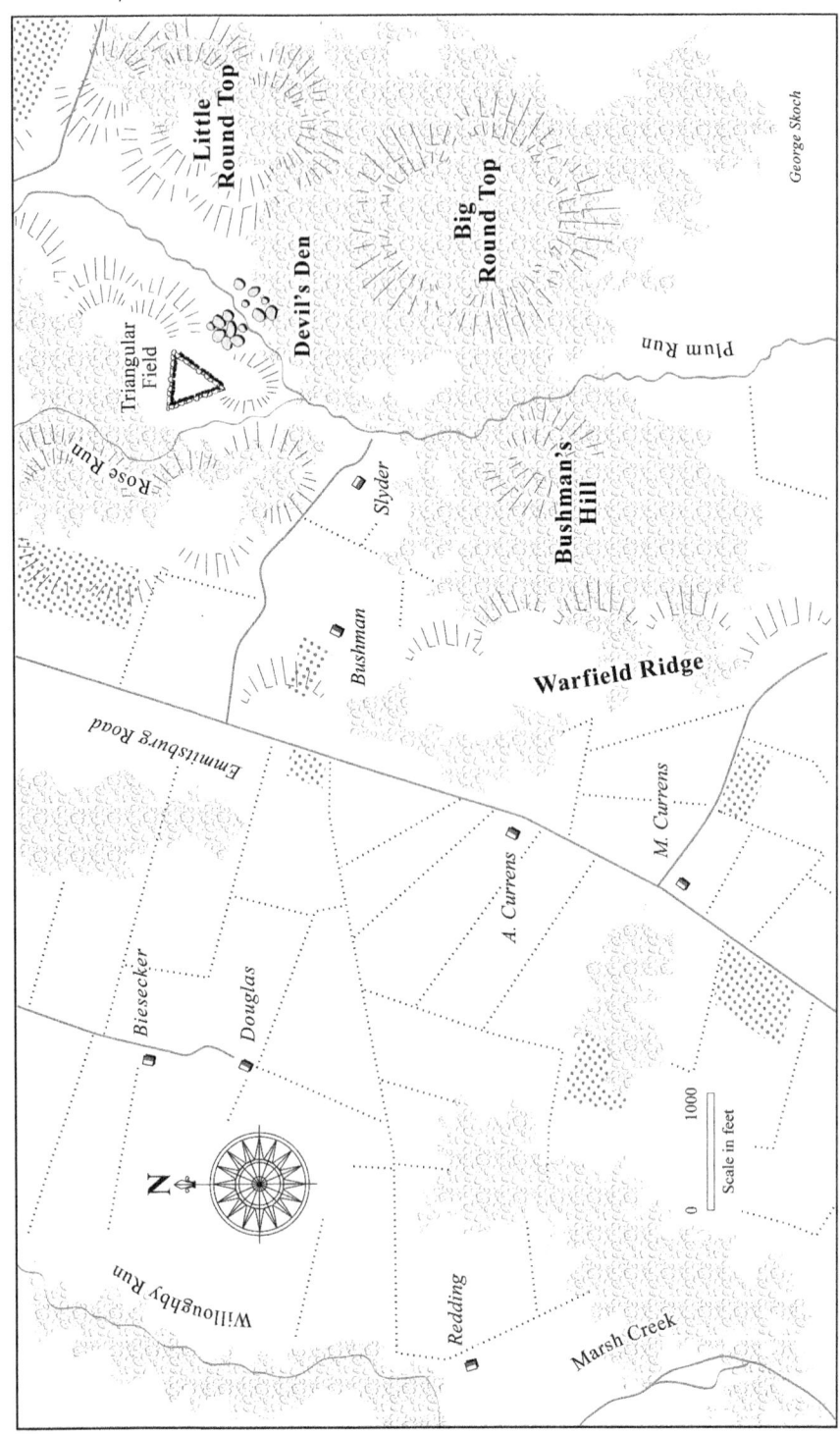

The Area of Lee's Retreat

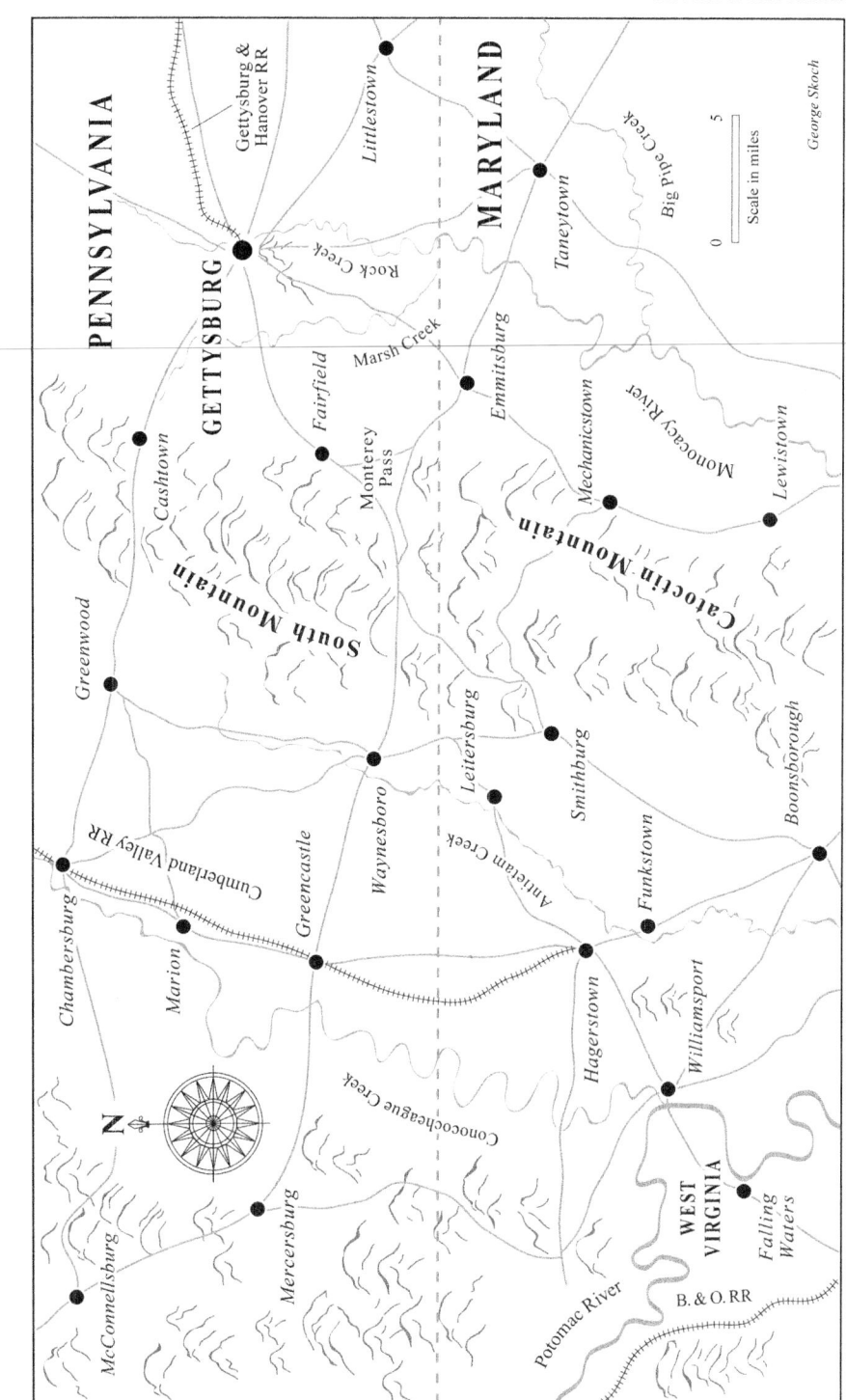

PROLOGUE
"The High Water Mark"

WARNING: DON'T SKIP over this part! It explains a lot.

History, as taught in American schools, is, or seems to be, a boring list of facts to be memorized and regurgitated on a test or two, after which most of it can be safely forgotten to make room for more interesting stuff. But it's not really like that. History is much less certain than our textbooks would have us believe. Mostly, history – real history – is an attempt by we, who weren't there, to figure out "what happened," or, all too often, "how did we get into this mess?" Much of what we learned in school was really just somebody's best guess, or somebody's repetition of what he or she learned when they were in school, which was, in turn the best guess of somebody writing generations before. However, as the song says, "It ain't necessarily so." The much-studied battle of Gettysburg, 1-3 July 1863, is no exception.

A few days after that battle ended, a 37-year-old artist and teacher from New Hampshire, named John B. Bachelder, arrived at Gettysburg, and he started making drawings and maps of the battlefield and noting down the scratchings on the numerous makeshift headboards that marked the hastily dug graves scattered all over the area. It was the beginning of his life-long fascination with the battle. By the 1880s, he was an influential director of the Gettysburg Battlefield Memorial Association, which, at that time, had charge of the site. A casual conversation that Bachelder had, during those days, with Walter Harrison, the former adjutant and inspector general of Pickett's Division of General R. E. Lee's Confederate army, has played a pivotal role in the history of that battle ever since.

"I invited Colonel Harrison to visit the battlefield with me," Bachelder later wrote, "and we spent several hours under the shade cast by the copse of trees, when he explained to me what an important feature that copse of trees was at the time of the battle, and how it had been a landmark towards which Longstreet's assault of July 3d 1863 had been directed. Impressed with its importance, I remarked, 'Why Colonel, as the battle of Gettysburg was the crowning event, of this campaign, this copse of trees must have been the high water mark of the rebellion.' To which he assented, and from that time on, I felt a reverence for those trees. . . . The thought of naming the copse of trees the 'High Water Mark of the Rebellion,' and the idea of perpetuating its memory by a monument, was mine."[1] The executive committee of the Gettysburg Battlefield Memorial Association soon unanimously passed Bachelder's proposal "that a bronze tablet be prepared, indicating and setting forth the movements of troops at the copse of trees on Hancock Avenue, July 3d 1863. . . ."[2] Soon Union veterans rushed to place monuments dedicated to their units near the indicated clump of trees, and the rest, as they say, is history. Or is it?

The trouble is that the "copse of trees" that Bachelder had preserved and protected with an iron fence, had only been a copse of bushes or saplings in 1863, scarcely noticeable from the Confederate lines. The real "landmark towards which Longstreet's assault of July 3d 1863 had been directed" was most likely two acres of woods, known as Ziegler's Grove, some three-tenths of a mile farther north along Cemetery Ridge, at the southwest corner of Cemetery Hill. But Ziegler's Grove had been cut down during the late 1870s and early 1880s, and so was no longer in existence on the fateful day when Bachelder and Harrison sat beneath a "copse of trees" and unwittingly re-wrote history.

For more than a century, most historians have followed Bachelder's lead, and described the little copse of trees as being the point for which the Confederate attack, known as Pickett's Charge, was aiming. Finally, in 1981, a senior historian at what was by then the Gettysburg National Military Park, named Kathleen Georg, wrote a paper that argued that Ziegler's Grove, not the small clump of trees that Bachelder had marked, had been the actual objective of the Confederate assault, but noted that "By the time the War Department took over administration of the Gettysburg Battlefield in 1895, the story that the clump of trees was the objective of Lee's attack on July 3 was accepted as fact and preached by the Park Commission as doctrine."[3]

In 2003, Troy D. Harman, a National Park Service Ranger at Gettysburg, expanded upon this thesis in his book *Lee's Real Plan at Gettysburg*, which opened the present author's eyes to Bachelder's and Harrison's mistake. The story of Gettysburg makes ever so much more sense in light of Georg's and Harman's thesis, and I am extremely grateful that their reasoning came to my attention just as I was embarking upon this, my own narrative of the battle. It helps to justify one more book about the most written-about battle in American history.

This book is the third in a series narrating a chronological history of the campaigns and battles of 1863, but it should be able to stand alone as a study of the battle of Gettysburg and its aftermath, and how they fit into the overall strategic situation that summer. I hope the reader gets as much enjoyment and enlightenment out of reading it as I am having in writing it, although that really seems far too much to hope for.

∽ Endnotes ∽

1   Troy D. Harman, *Lee's Real Plan at Gettysburg* (Mechanicsburg PA, 2003), 88.
2   Ibid.
3   Ibid., 89.

Part One
GETTYSBURG: DAY ONE

CHAPTER 1
"Sown with Dragon's Teeth"
1 July 1863

WEDNESDAY, THE FIRST DAY of July, 1863, was a typical summer day in the southern Pennsylvania town of Gettysburg – warm and very humid – except, of course, that in those days it was not crowded with tourists, as it would be in later years and probably will continue to be for as long as it exists.[1] The tourists would come eventually because of what happened there that day and over the two days to follow. And the town of some 2,400 inhabitants would never be the same again.

But on that morning, instead of tourists, the town was hosting two brigades of Union cavalry, who had arrived the previous morning and had made camp on a ridge just west of town, more than doubling the local population. They had arrived just in time to scare off a brigade of Confederate infantry that had been approaching from the northwest, along the road from Cashtown (though other Rebels had marched right through the town the Friday before, on their way east to York, Pennsylvania). The cavalry's commander, Brigadier General John Buford, was sure the Confederates would be back today and in greater strength, and he was right. An officer from a Union infantry division that was not far south of Gettysburg rode into town that morning and found Buford and his staff gathered in front of a tavern. "What are you doing here, sir?" Buford asked him. The officer replied that he had come to get some shoes for his division, but Buford told him to return to his command immediately. "Why, what is the matter, general?" the staffer asked. Just at that moment the distant sound of cannon fire was heard, and Buford mounted his horse, saying only, "*That's the matter*," before galloping off.[2]

What we now call the American Civil War (in those days it was just the War) had been going on for about 26 months, but it had taken a new turn a few weeks back when General Robert E. Lee's Confederate Army of Northern Virginia had begun moving into Pennsylvania. The year before, Lee had made a brief foray into Maryland, a border state of mixed loyalties, but this was the first time a sizable body of Confederates had invaded a solidly loyal Northern state. The Union's Army of the Potomac had been slow to respond, for its commander, Major General Joseph Hooker, had been unable to get reliable intelligence about just where the Rebels were and what they were up to. The cavalry of the two armies had clashed several times in the area just east of Virginia's Blue Ridge mountains, but the Federals had been unable to get past the Confederate horsemen to get a look down into the Shenandoah Valley, where Lee's army was thought to be.

In fact, the Confederates had swept down the Valley and crossed the Potomac River into the narrow part of Maryland, eventually moving on into Pennsylvania. One of Lee's three large army corps, the 2nd Corps under Lieutenant General Richard Ewell, had moved on ahead of the other two, itself splitting off one of its three divisions, that of Major General Jubal Early, to march eastward to York, and to at least threaten to cross the wide Susquehanna River toward Philadelphia, while Ewell with the other two divisions had marched up the Cumberland Valley (the Maryland-Pennsylvania extension of Virginia's Shenandoah) to threaten, and capture if possible, Harrisburg, the capital of Pennsylvania, on the northeast bank of the Susquehanna.

Hooker had already been in bad standing with the Lincoln administration because of his poor performance in the recent Chancellorsville campaign, and then his befuddlement and his quarreling with his superior, Major General Henry W. Halleck, general-in-chief of the Union Army, over what to do next had finally led to his dismissal just three days back, on 28 June. He had been replaced by Major General George G. Meade, until then commander of one of the seven small army corps of the Army of the Potomac. (For the composition of both Union and Confederate armies, see Appendix 1.)

Meade was then 47 years old; he had graduated from West Point in 1835, two years ahead of Hooker, and gone into the artillery, but had resigned his commission shortly afterwards to become a civil engineer. However, he had returned to the Army in 1842 and had served as an officer of topographical engineers in the Mexican War and in the peace-time Army. Early in this war he had been made commander of one of the three brigades in a division of Pennsylvania troops, which he had led during the Peninsula Campaign of 1862, where he was wounded, and in the Second Bull Run Campaign. He had commanded that entire division at Antietam and Fredericksburg, and he had commanded the 5th Corps during the recent Chancellorsville Campaign.

Meade now was doing a pretty good job of getting a grip on his army, which he had found camped around Middletown, Maryland, for Hooker had finally decided to move it to the north side of the Potomac River. Knowing that Confederate forces were threatening to cross the Susquehanna at Wrightsville, east of York, and at Harrisburg, Meade had promptly put the Army of the Potomac in motion, heading north. He had reasoned that his approach from the south would deter the Rebels from crossing the wide Susquehanna for fear of being attacked from behind or cut off from the rest of Lee's army, and he had been right. He had just learned the night before that his strategy had worked and that Ewell's and Early's forces were turning back, the latter heading west from Wrightsville and the former south from Carlisle. Meanwhile, less substantial or less timely information indicated that Lee's other two large corps were probably concentrated around Chambersburg, in the Cumberland Valley, with part, at least, as far east as Cashtown, about nine miles up the road from Gettysburg.

But before the information about Early and Ewell turning back had been received, Buford's two brigades (he had a third one being held in reserve down in Maryland to protect the army's rear) had been sent up to Gettysburg to scout out the area and see what was going on, and two corps of Union infantry had been ordered to follow. This was cavalry's normal role in this war. Seldom employed in dramatic mounted charges any more, the mounted arm was primarily used to find the enemy, keep the enemy from finding its own army, protect lines of supply, and occasionally to make raids deep into enemy territory.

One such raid was underway at that very time. Lee's cavalry commander, Major General J. E. B. "Jeb" Stuart, after screening the Confederate infantry's passage down the Shenandoah Valley, had found himself at the rear of Lee's army just when he was most needed up in Pennsylvania to protect the infantry's southern flank and give warning of the approach of the Army of the Potomac if and when it ever got a move on. He therefore had two alternatives: to follow after the Confederate infantry, cross the Potomac where it had crossed, and somehow try to get past the marching foot-sloggers to the head of the column; or to cross the Potomac farther east and use unclogged roads to go up into Pennsylvania and catch up with Ewell's corps. The latter seemed obviously preferable except for one little difficulty: namely the Union army, which was then camped all over northern Virginia, just east of Stuart's position.

However, Stuart's reliable scout and guerilla leader, Major John Singleton Mosby, who often slipped through Union lines, had assured him that the Federals were sitting quietly in their camps, which were widely scattered, and that Stuart could squeeze between them and be over the Potomac before the "Yankees" could do anything about it. This was probably true at the time that Mosby said it, but by the time Stuart had tried it the next day, with his three oldest and best brigades, Hooker had made his decision to move his own army to the north side of the Potomac, and Stuart had found the roads clogged with marching Union infantry. This had necessitated a wide detour to the south and then east, which was the first of several problems that had delayed Stuart's march.

On 28 June, the morning after finally crossing the river, he had come upon a long column of Union supply wagons from Washington, D.C., heading for the Army of the Potomac. Most of these were promptly captured, as both the supplies and the wagons would be valuable additions to Lee's army, but the presence of 125 wagons, as well as several captured Federals, had further slowed Stuart's progress.

On the last day of June, Stuart's column had collided with the new 3rd Division of the Army of the Potomac's Cavalry Corps at Hanover, Pennsylvania, some 12 or 15 miles east of Gettysburg. These two brigades of Union cavalry had just recently joined Meade's army, being transferred from the garrison of Washington. Their new division commander was rash young Brigadier General Hugh Judson Kilpatrick, and his two brigades were commanded by even younger (and even better) officers who had just been jumped up from captains to brigadier generals overnight: Elon J. Farnsworth and George Armstrong Custer. After an inconclusive fight, Stuart had drawn off to the east and then continued on to the north in search of Early and/or Ewell. Kilpatrick let him go, for he was more interested in finding Jubal Early's Confederate infantry.

After a long all-night ride, Stuart's weary troopers had finally reached Carlisle, Pennsylvania, where Ewell's corps was said to be, only to find that the latter had been ordered back to the south and that the town, site of a U.S. Army cavalry post, was in the hands of Union militia under the command of Brigadier General W. F. "Baldy" Smith, who had come west from Harrisburg during the day to follow Ewell's retreat. Stuart spent this first day of July in bombarding the post and the town and trying to bluff Smith into surrendering, which Smith adamantly refused to do.

While Ewell's 2nd Corps had threatened to cross the Susquehanna, Lee's 1st and 3rd corps had been concentrating around the town of Chambersburg, Pennsylvania, in the southern part of the Cumberland Valley, waiting to see what Ewell could accomplish and what the Union reaction would be. But with Stuart and his best cavalry off on what amounted to a raid, Lee had been left in the dark about where the Army of the Potomac was and what it was up to. Stuart had left two brigades of cavalry behind to cover the rear of the army and with orders to follow it north, but they had been slow to realize that it was time to do so, and they had only crossed to the north side of the Potomac on the last day of June, still well behind the main army.

Lee had just decided to send one of his two remaining corps up the Cumberland Valley to follow Ewell and to send the other eastward to follow Early when on the night of the 28th a Confederate spy, hired by the commander of Lee's 1st Corps, Lieutenant General James Longstreet, had brought the latter the important information that the Union army was north of the Potomac, had units poised in the gaps of South Mountain (the Maryland-Pennsylvania extension of Virginia's Blue Ridge) and that Meade was its new commander. Longstreet had, of course, passed the man (named Harrison) and his information on to Lee, who had, as a result, decided to change his plans. Union forces on South Mountain posed a threat to his already tenuous supply line. His men were living on food gathered from the areas through which they moved (paid for in Confederate money, or merely with receipts, or sometimes just taken, although that was against Lee's orders), but he was still dependent on Virginia for ammunition. He therefore decided, that night, to recall Ewell and Early and to concentrate his whole army on the east side of the mountains over the next couple of days in hopes of drawing the Federals away from the Cumberland Valley. He didn't know that Meade had already decided to stay east of South Mountain anyway, where he could cover both Washington, D.C., and Baltimore, Maryland, a large and important city, while threatening the rear or flank of any Confederate force that tried to cross the Susquehanna.

So the van of Lee's 3rd Corps, under Lieutenant General A. P. Hill, had crossed South Mountain through the Cashtown Gap, east of Chambersburg, and had started concentrating around Cashtown on the 29th and 30th. Hill's final division and most of Longstreet's 1st Corps were following on this first day of July. But, while waiting for the rest of the army to catch up, the commander of Hill's leading division, Major General Henry "Harry" Heth (pronounced Heath) had, on 30 June, sent one brigade, commanded by Brigadier General J. Johnston Pettigrew, down the road to Gettysburg, probably just to see what was there, although long after the war Heth claimed to have been checking out a rumor that there was a supply of shoes there. Hill and Heth both believed that the Army of the Potomac was still far down in Maryland and that the most opposition Pettigrew might run into was some home guards or militia (that's what Early had met when one of his brigades had passed through there five days before), but, just to be safe, Heth had told Pettigrew not to bring on a battle, so if he ran into significant opposition he was to turn back. Pettigrew had, of course, run up against Buford's Union cavalry (without knowing who they were, except that they behaved like experienced troops) and, following orders, he had turned back without a fight (and without the shoes, if they were indeed involved).

Hill's 3rd Corps was a new outfit. Lee's army had previously been divided into only two large corps of four large divisions each, commanded by Longstreet and Lieutenant General Thomas J. "Stonewall" Jackson. But the latter had recently died of wounds received during the battle of Chancellorsville (accidentally shot by his own men while making a night reconnaissance beyond his lines). Jackson had been Lee's strong right arm, and, unsure that any one man could replace him, Lee had decided to reorganize his army into three corps of three divisions each. He did this by transferring the division of Major General Richard Anderson from Longstreet's 1st Corps and A. P. Hill's division from the 2nd Corps and forming them into a new 3rd Corps under Hill, while placing Ewell, also a former division commander under Jackson, in command of the reduced 2nd Corps. Hill's division had consisted of six brigades, compared to the four or sometimes five of Lee's other divisions, so it could spare two, which had been stripped off and joined with two new brigades (that had just been sent up from North Carolina) to form the army's ninth division. And it just so happened that this newest division, composed of the two weakest brigades from Hill's old division and two untried brigades new to the army, was the one now commanded by Harry Heth. Like all the divisions of Lee's army, it also contained a battalion of artillery, in this case five batteries commanded by Major William Pegram.

Heth was a Virginian with good family connections, and Lee had personally requested Heth's transfer to his army from the West. It is said that he was the only one of his commanders whom Lee addressed by his first name (but presumably this doesn't count Lee's own son and nephew, both of whom commanded cavalry brigades under Stuart). And Heth was a West Point graduate, but he had graduated at the very bottom of the class of 1847. He was not, and never pretended to be, a military genius. He was imprudent, overly optimistic to the point of arrogance, and inclined to go off half-cocked, and this day he would show solid evidence of these characteristics.

That last night of June, when Pettigrew had returned to camp and reported to Heth and Hill that he had met Union cavalry outside Gettysburg, the latter had scoffed at the idea that any part of the Army of the Potomac could be that far north. Pettigrew had called upon one of his aides, Lieutenant Louis B. Young, known to Hill, who testified that the Union cavalry had certainly seemed to know its business, but neither Hill nor Heth was convinced. Hill's own scouts agreed with Longstreet's that the Army of the Potomac was still back around Middletown, Maryland. No, the Federals Pettigrew had seen must have been home guards or militia, but if it was part of Meade's army, well, that was just where Hill wanted it to be. Heth had then declared that he would take his whole division to Gettysburg the next day and get those shoes, if Hill had no objection. "None in the world," Hill had said.[3] In fact, he would send his other division that had reached

Cashtown, Major General Dorsey Pender's, to follow Heth's. However, Hill, who was "very unwell," as one observer put it, would not accompany the column but stay at Cashtown to await the arrival of Anderson's division.[4]

Lieutenant Young later said, "This spirit of unbelief had taken such hold, that I doubt if any of the commanders of brigades, except General Pettigrew, believed that we were marching to battle, a weakness on their part which rendered them unprepared for what was about to happen."[5] Hill sent word of what he was doing to both Lee, who was back up the road toward Chambersburg, and to Ewell, who was coming south from Carlisle. Lee sent his own chief of staff, Major Walter Taylor, to instruct Heth that he was "to ascertain what force was at Gettysburg, and, if he found the infantry opposed to him, to report the fact immediately, without forcing an engagement."[6]

In addition to being the newest division in Lee's army, and part of the newest corps, with a less-than-brilliant commander, Heth's division had the problem that it consisted of four very miss-matched brigades. The two veteran brigades that had been transferred from Hill's old division were very experienced but also, due to heavy casualties in previous battles, the two smallest brigades in Lee's army. One, at slightly fewer than 1,000 men, was only about half the strength of an ideal brigade. Its four Virginia regiments nominally belonged to Brigadier General Charles W. Field, but that officer had been badly wounded at the second battle of Bull Run the previous summer and was still off recuperating. Heth had commanded them during the recent Chancellorsville campaign, when they had taken heavy casualties, and it was now under the temporary command of its senior regimental officer, Colonel John Brockenbrough, an uninspiring officer of no particular ability. The other old brigade consisted of about 1,200 men in three Tennessee regiments plus a regiment and a smaller battalion from Alabama, all under the command of Brigadier General James J. Archer, a small, irascible Marylander who had not attended West Point but had served in the Mexican War and had been a captain in the pre-war Regular Army. He was suffering that morning with a fever.

Pettigrew, on the other hand, commanded four strong regiments from North Carolina. One Confederate described it as "the largest, best equipped, finest looking brigade of the whole army."[7] Pettigrew's education was for the law, not the military, but he had been active in the pre-war militia and had performed well as a brigade commander in the Peninsula campaign the year before, where he had been wounded and captured. He was the senior and the best of Heth's brigadiers, but his long absence from the Army of Northern Virginia (he had eventually been exchanged for a captured Union officer) meant that he was now an outsider there. Last, and possibly least, was a brigade of three Mississippi regiments, only two of which had seen much action (and one of those was detached this day), plus a green regiment from North Carolina. This brigade was commanded by inexperienced Brigadier General Joseph R. Davis, whose sole qualification for his position was that he had previously served on the staff of the president of the Confederate States, who was his uncle.

These four brigades of infantry and one battalion of artillery were about to run into one battery of horse artillery and two veteran brigades of Union cavalry whose men and commanders did indeed know their business. John Buford was then 37 years old – neither old nor young for the rank of brigadier general in that war. Born in Kentucky but raised in Illinois, he had graduated from West Point in 1848, one year behind Harry Heth. (He had a much older half brother, also now a Union general, who had graduated from West Point way back in 1827, when John was only a year old; he also had a distant cousin who had graduated in 1841 and was now a Confederate general out in Mississippi.) Buford had been a general for almost a year, commanding first a brigade and now a division of cavalry in the major campaigns of the Army of the Potomac. He was steady, reliable, and highly competent.

Early that morning he would have received a copy of, or

word of, Meade's order of the night before, which gave the destination that each corps of his army was to reach on this first day of July; so Buford would have known that the 1st Corps, commanded by Major General John Reynolds, was due to advance to Gettysburg that day and the 11th Corps also to Gettysburg "or supporting distance," as the order phrased it. If there had been any doubt in Buford's mind about whether he should fight to hold onto Gettysburg, that information would have dispelled it. The order also called for "Cavalry to the front and flanks, well out in all directions, giving timely notice of positions and movements of the enemy."[8] In his official report of his part in the battle, Buford said, "By daylight on July 1, I had gained positive information of the enemy's position and movements, and my arrangements were made for entertaining him until General Reynolds could reach the scene."[9]

Buford's 1st Brigade was commanded by Colonel William Gamble, a 45-year-old Irishman who had served in the dragoons of the British army and in the pre-war 1st U.S. Dragoons (redesignated the 1st Cavalry just as the war began). He had succeeded to command of this brigade only three weeks before, when its previous commander had been wounded, but he had previously done well as commander of the 8th Illinois Cavalry. He was competent, confident, and aggressive, and Buford was pleased with him so far. The 2nd Brigade was commanded by Colonel Thomas C. Devin, then 40 years old, who was another Irishman. He had been an officer in the pre-war New York militia for years and had been appointed commander of the 6th New York Cavalry in November of 1861. He had been in command of his brigade for four-and-a-half months.

Gamble's brigade was the larger of the two, containing about 1,600 troopers in two regiments and parts of two others. Buford had assigned it the job of blocking the road from Cashtown to Gettysburg, known as the Chambersburg Pike, since he knew that at least one corps of Lee's army was gathering up that way. Devin's brigade of only about 1,150 men in three regiments and a lone squadron of another was given the job of watching the northern approaches to the town, for Buford had detected a lot of Rebel cavalry up that way the day before and knew that Ewell's and Early's infantry were somewhere off in that direction. At about 7:30 that morning pickets of Gamble's brigade spotted Pegram's artillery and Archer's Alabamans, at the head of Heth's column, crossing Marsh Creek, about three miles west of Gettysburg, and fired on them. The Rebel column came to a halt and sent skirmishers toward the Union pickets, who were soon reinforced by the picket reserve, and the battle was on.

The Union pickets sent word back to their brigade camp, and Major John L. Beveridge, commander of the 8th Illinois Cavalry now that Gamble commanded the whole brigade, sent a squadron of his regiment to reinforce the pickets and sent couriers into town to alert Gamble and Buford. Gamble then sent three more squadrons to join them and form a skirmish line along a slight rise of ground northwest of Gettysburg called Herr Ridge, but the remainder of his brigade was soon deployed along another low ridge a bit closer to town called McPherson's Ridge. Gamble's right was near the line of an unfinished railroad about 100 to 150 yards north of the Chambersburg Pike, which it roughly paralleled, and his left was about a mile farther south near a road running to a small village called Fairfield. (This road was sometimes called the Hagerstown Pike because it eventually reached Hagerstown, Maryland.) Devin's brigade extended Gamble's line northward to the Mummasburg Road and then curved to the east past Oak Hill to block the road coming down from Carlisle. Both brigades were deployed dismounted, with one man out of every four holding the horses to the rear (which, of course, reduced their fighting strength by 25 percent).

Civilians living in the area soon found their farms and fields were about to become a battlefield. While Archer's infantry deployed and headed up Herr Ridge the gunners of a

Confederate battery unlimbered their cannon in someone's yard and prepared to open fire. A man rushed out of the house and yelled to them, "My God, you are not going to fire here are you?"[10] Undeterred, the Rebels continued their preparations, and the man threw up his hands and returned to the house. As Archer's Alabamans moved forward some of them shot a farmer's dog because it wouldn't stop barking at them. The farmer then came out and asked the Rebels what was going on. They informed him that a battle was about to begin between "General Lee and the Yankees." The farmer said, "Tell Lee to hold on just a little until I get my cow out of the pasture."[11] But, unfortunately for him, and probably for the cow, the war wouldn't wait.

Amelia Harmon was a teenage girl living with her aunt in a big colonial mansion known as the Old McLean Place, which overlooked a small stream called Willoughby Run, which ran to the south between Herr Ridge and McPherson's Ridge. Most of her neighbors had fled, but she and her aunt felt safe behind the mansion's thick walls and heavy shutters. When they first heard cannon being fired not far away they went to a window and saw hundreds of Union cavalrymen rushing past their house, shouting and yelling to each other, heading for some woods on the ridge to the west. "But the ridge was alive with the enemy!" Amelia later wrote. "A few warning shots from its cover sent them flying back to the shelter behind the barn, outbuildings, trees, and even the pump, seeking to hold the enemy in check...." Alarmed but filled with curiosity, Amelia and her aunt moved to a second story window on the west side of the house to watch the battle, but they only got a glance before a Confederate bullet hit the shutter close to the aunt's ear. "This one glance showed us," Amelia said, "that a large timothy field between the barn and the woods concealed hundreds of gray crouching figures stealthily advancing under its cover, and picking off every cavalryman who appeared for an instant in sight. An officer's horse just under the window was shot, and the officer fell to the ground. 'Look!' we shrieked at him, 'the field is full of rebels.' 'Leave the window,' he shouted in return, 'or you will be killed!'" They left it, but only to move to an even better vantage point in the cupola at the top of the house, from which they could see for miles. "It seemed as though the fields and woods had been sown with dragon's teeth," Amelia remembered, "for everywhere had sprung up armed men where about an hour ago only grass and flowers grew."[12]

Gamble's few squadrons were not expected to hold forever against what appeared to be an entire division of veteran Confederate infantry, and they didn't. But they delayed it for about an hour to an hour and a half, because the Rebels had to deploy from their column on the road into lines of battle and send out skirmishers to feel out the Union position. Eventually the Confederates' superiority of numbers allowed them to stretch their line far enough south to threaten Gamble's left flank, and he gave the order to fall back across Willoughby Run to McPherson's Ridge.

There was a series of these low ridges running roughly southwest to northeast, perpendicular to the Cashtown road, and Buford intended to use them, one after the other, if necessary, to delay the Confederates until Reynolds' infantry came up. On McPherson's Ridge, the next one back from Herr Ridge, Buford placed his main line and his lone battery of horse artillery. All field artillery in those days was pulled by horses, of course. The main distinguishing feature of horse artillery was that all the gunners were provided with mounts as well, so that the battery was able to keep up with cavalry on the march. In the Army of the Potomac the horse artillery consisted of some of the best units available, mostly batteries of the Regular Army. Buford's battery was Company A of the 2nd U.S. Artillery, commanded, in the absence of its captain, by Lieutenant John H. Calef. Its six 3-inch rifles were split into three 2-gun sections: one placed on each side of the Chambersburg Pike and the other farther south near the Hagerstown Pike (Fairfield Road).

Heth had deployed only parts of his two leading brigades, which he correctly deemed sufficient to drive a few hundred skirmishers before them. But upon reaching the crest of Herr Ridge, Archer's entire brigade now deployed south of the Cashtown Pike and all of Davis's (except that regiment had been left behind to guard wagons) north of it, and their combined line stretched almost a mile from end to end. Reaching the crest of Herr Ridge at about 9 a.m., Harry Heth could see Buford's main position on McPherson's Ridge a couple of hundred yards to the east and mistook the dismounted cavalrymen, or some of them, for infantry. This seemed to confirm what he had suspected all along, that the Union forces at or near Gettysburg "consisted of cavalry, most probably supported by a brigade or two of infantry."[13] This, however, was still only conjecture, so, as Heth later reported, "Archer and Davis were now directed to advance, the object being to feel the enemy; to make a forced reconnaissance, and determine what force the enemy were – whether or not he was massing his forces on Gettysburg."[14] Heth had Willie Pegram deploy his 19 guns on Herr Ridge to take on Calef's six, while his infantry moved up.

Meade, of course, was not massing all of his forces on Gettysburg that day; he had ordered only one corps to definitely go there. But John Reynolds, commander of that corps, was approaching the town just then along the road from Emmitsburg. Reynolds was 42 years of age and had graduated from West Point back in 1841. At the outbreak of the war he had been commandant of cadets there and instructor of tactics. He was a Pennsylvanian and had previously served as a brigade commander in the Pennsylvania Reserve Division, alongside now-army-commander George Meade, and the two generals were good friends. Reynolds had been offered the command of the army ahead of Meade, but he had declined it unless he could have a free hand and not be micromanaged by the authorities in Washington. He was one of the two or three best combat commanders in the Army of the Potomac; perhaps the very best. He was idolized by the men of his corps, the 1st, and one of his officers later said that he "perhaps better than any other officer in the entire army met the limitless requirements of the ideal soldier."[15]

One of his staff officers had roused him from where he had been sleeping on the floor of the Moritz Tavern, six miles down toward Emmitsburg, at 4 o'clock that morning with the order from army headquarters for him to take his corps to Gettysburg that day. He had had only four hours of sleep, but that was the longest rest he had had in several days. After having a staff officer read the order to him three times, he had risen to begin the process of putting his corps in motion. Reynolds was also in command of an informal left wing of Meade's army, which included not only his 1st Corps but also the 3rd Corps and the 11th Corps. The latter was, according to the same order, to follow the 1st Corps to Gettysburg or at least stay in supporting distance of the 1st, which meant within a few miles at most, and the 3rd Corps was to move up to Emmitsburg to replace the 11th. No particular reason was stated in the order for these moves; they were presumably part of the army's general move north in search of Lee's Confederates.

Just after 6 a.m. Reynolds had heard from Major General Oliver Otis Howard, commander of the 11th Corps, that he had also received the order from army headquarters, and Reynolds had sent back word for him to start right away and to keep his wagons out of the way of the marching troops, as he wanted to get both corps to Gettysburg by evening. Reynolds had also sent word to Major General Dan Sickles to bring his 3rd Corps up to Emmitsburg and, between 7 and 8 a.m., he had consulted with Major General Abner Doubleday, commander of the 3rd Division of his 1st Corps, who would take over the entire corps while Reynolds commanded the 3-corps wing. Doubleday was to call in the pickets around the camp and get the corps' three divisions of infantry and one brigade of artillery moving. (It being the first day of the month, the officers and sergeants of all the regiments and batteries were busy making out their monthly reports.) Colonel

Charles Wainright, commander of the corps' artillery brigade, had asked Reynolds that morning about the prospect of a battle that day but had been told that none was expected. They were just moving up to support Buford's cavalry, which was presumably going to push farther ahead. "Having given these orders," Doubleday later wrote, "he rode off at the head of the column, and I never saw him again."[16]

At around 8 a.m. Reynolds and his staff had ridden north and had soon stopped at the camp of Brigadier General James Wadsworth's 1st Division, which was the one closest to Gettysburg. There Reynolds learned that Doubleday had ordered this division to wait until the other two divisions of the corps had passed by and then to fall in at the tail of the column. It was standard practice to rotate the lead, as that was the preferred position in a column – preferable to eating the dust of those farther ahead – and Wadsworth's division had led the march the day before. However, knowing that it would be some time before Doubleday got the rest of the corps moving, Reynolds had told Wadsworth to go on and take the lead again today. Then he had ridden on ahead.

Wadsworth, then 52 years of age, was a wealthy man and a lawyer, but not a soldier. He had read law in Daniel Webster's office, been active in the anti-slavery movement, been a delegate to the peace convention that had tried to head off the war, and had been a volunteer aide de camp at the first battle of Bull Run before being appointed a brigadier general by President Lincoln. After commanding a brigade without seeing any action, he had served as military governor of the District of Columbia, and had been the unsuccessful Republican candidate for governor of New York the previous autumn. He had commanded this division during the recent Chancellorsville campaign, but again had seen little action. Other Union officers seem to have liked him and remarked on his bravery, industry and common sense, but, as Colonel Wainright of the artillery noted, he "knew nothing of military matters."[17]

It was just about 9 a.m. when, about a mile south of

Gettysburg, Reynolds was met by a cavalryman bringing word from Buford that he was under attack west of the town by Confederate infantry coming down the road from Cashtown and that he would need help if Reynolds wanted him to hold on. Reynolds send word to Wadsworth to hurry his division forward, sent a staff officer into the town to warn the civilians to stay in their houses, and rode on into town and then west out the Chambersburg Pike to the Lutheran Seminary, where, at about 10 a.m., he found John Buford. The seminary was a bit south of the pike on the next ridge east of the one where the cavalry was taking position, called, logically enough, Seminary Ridge. It was the last ridge before the town. The seminary was a multi-story building on some of the highest ground around, and it had a cupola on top that provided a panoramic view of the entire area. Buford was up there watching Heth's Confederates come on when he saw Reynolds approach. He started down the ladder and met Reynolds coming up. "What's the matter, John?" Reynolds asked. "The devil's to pay," was Buford's reply.[18]

After receiving a brief description of what had happened so far, Reynolds asked if the cavalry could hold on until the 1st Corps arrived, and Buford said he thought it could. Reynolds then turned to an aide and told him to ride quickly down to army headquarters at Taneytown, Maryland, killing his horse in the process if necessary, and tell Meade that the enemy was advancing on Gettysburg in force and that Reynolds would hold on as long as possible, even if he had to fall back through the town fighting house-to-house. An officer who had just arrived from General Howard was sent back to urge his 11th Corps forward (and, according to one witness, to form it as a reserve on Cemetery Hill, a bit of high ground at the southeast edge of Gettysburg that was the site of the town's cemetery). Other aides were sent on similar missions to Doubleday and Sickles. Then Reynolds rode south across country, his small cavalry escort knocking down fences to clear a path. In the town, thus by-passed, people milled in the streets, curious and frightened, despite efforts of both civilian and military officials to get them to stay indoors.

Coming back to the road south of town, near a farm owned by the Codori family, Reynolds found Wadsworth, riding ahead of his troops. The road to Gettysburg was muddy and rutted and ran to the northeast, whereas the troops were needed west of the town, northwest of where the two generals met, so they set their staffs, escorts and the pioneers at the head of the column to widening the gaps in the fences, and as the various regiments came up the men left their knapsacks and other impediments by the roadside and were turned off into the fields and sent toward Seminary Ridge at a rapid pace. The men could hear both cannon and rifle fire up ahead and realized they were going into a fight. Two ladies at a house they passed brought out buckets of water for the men, but this was delaying the movement too much, and an officer broke it up by kicking over the buckets and spilling the water on the ground.

Reynolds watched his men go past for a while, then turned his horse and headed back to rejoin Buford. The two generals rode west to McPherson's Ridge and found that Heth's two leading brigades (Archer's and Davis's), having caught up with their own skirmishers, were pushing across Willoughby Run. It was only knee deep with a pebbled bottom, so not much of an obstacle. At least some of the Rebels paused briefly under the cover of its bank to reform, reload, and perhaps rest a bit and get a drink, then splashed across to resume their advance. Lieutenant Calef of the Union horse artillery, which was directly in their path, said their battleflags looked even redder and bloodier than ever before. Most of Archer's Confederates entered the western end of a wood lot known as McPherson's Woods, which extended from the top of the ridge, not far south of the McPherson farm buildings, down to the stream.

Behind these Confederates, Heth's other two brigades were now also deployed, supposedly ready to support the front two, and about a half-mile farther back towards Cashtown was a large cloud of dust thrown up by more approaching Confederates (Pender's Division). If all that was not trouble enough, reports from cavalry stationed north of the town indicated that more Rebels (Ewell's) were coming down from that direction. During Reynolds' brief absence Buford had penned a quick note to General Meade at 10:10 a.m.: "The enemy's force (A. P. Hill's) are advancing on me at this point, and driving my pickets and skirmishers very rapidly. There is also a large force at Heidlersburg that is driving my pickets from that point from that direction. General Reynolds is advancing, and is within 3 miles of this point with his leading division. I am positive that the whole of A. P. Hill's force is advancing."[19]

Reynolds probably realized that his corps would be outnumbered even after they all arrived, although, fortunately for them, one of Hill's three divisions was not on hand. (There were about 15,000 Rebels in Hill's two divisions to about 8,200 Union infantry in the 1st Corps plus Buford's 2,400 cavalry, and this doesn't count any of Ewell's forces coming down from the north, which would add, approximately, another 15,000 Confederates.) The Army of the Potomac had been much reduced in recent weeks, not so much by recent losses in battle as by the expiration of enlistments. Many regiments that had originally signed up after Bull Run for two years had recently gone home, along with others who had enlisted for nine months back when Lee had crossed the Potomac the first time the previous September. As a result the 1st Corps had recently been consolidated from nine brigades down to six and was now not much larger than a single division of Lee's army. (A seventh brigade of five large 9-months regiments from Vermont had recently been assigned to the 1st Corps, but it was still on the march from the outer defenses of Washington and had not yet caught up and would not until this day's fight was over.)

Not long after rejoining Buford, Reynolds turned to find his leading brigade just filing into the Cashtown road north of the seminary, marching somewhat ahead of the rest of the corps as an advanced guard. This was the 2nd Brigade of

Wadsworth's 1st Division, commanded by Brigadier General Lysander Cutler, who, in his late 50s, was one of the oldest men in the Union army. He was not a professional soldier but had been in the pre-war militia and had demonstrated considerable talent as colonel of the 6th Wisconsin (an excellent regiment that was part of Wadsworth's other brigade) before being promoted to brigadier. His largest regiment, the 7th Indiana, was back at Emmitsburg guarding wagons, but he had with him about 1,600 men in five good regiments: four from New York and one from Pennsylvania. They were arriving in the nick of time, for Devin's men, spread thin north of the Chambersburg Pike, were just then falling back from McPherson's Ridge to Seminary Ridge, or a northward extension of it called Oak Ridge.

Wadsworth therefore sent Cutler's first three regiments north of the road and on beyond the unfinished railroad into the low ground between the two ridges to face Davis's Confederates, and then sent the other two regiments to the south side to support Gamble against Archer. Captain James A. Hall's 2nd Maine Battery (six 3-inch rifles) was the next unit to appear, and Reynolds sent it at a trot to take position just north of the Chambersburg Pike with orders to draw the fire of the Rebel artillery away from the Union infantrymen while they were deploying. The battery cut through the column of infantry that was heading to the north side of the road, causing the 147th New York to fall behind the other two regiments, the 76th New York and the 56th Pennsylvania.

General Cutler went with those two regiments after placing Colonel Edward B. Fowler of the 84th New York in charge of the two regiments sent south of the road, Fowler's own 84th and the 95th New York. (Fowler's regiment had originally been the 14th Regiment of New York State Militia, and it was from Brooklyn, still at that time separate from New York City, so its members proudly preferred to be known as the 14th Brooklyn. The men of this regiment wore a special uniform based on that of the light infantry of the French army, including short blue jackets, red caps and red trousers, and white leggings; although many of the men had apparently discarded the leggings by this time.) Reynolds sent these two regiments to a position near the McPherson farm buildings, just south of the Chambersburg Pike and north of McPherson's Woods.

Calef's horse battery, after having dueled with three times its number of Confederate guns for over an hour, was pulling out. The lieutenant had already ordered the 2-gun section down by the Hagerstown road to retire one gun at a time and join the battery's caissons near the seminary, and just as he was giving a similar order to one of the sections by the Chambersburg Pike a Rebel shell burst under the horses pulling one of the guns, killing four of them. The artillerymen were able to get the gun away, using the two remaining horses, but had to abandon the valuable harness of the dead horses left behind. As the other section was pulling out it was intercepted by Buford, who sent it to enfilade some of Davis's Confederates that were passing through a railroad "cut" – a place where a groove had been cut through some high ground for the unfinished railroad. Seeing one of these guns swing into position some of the Rebels charged it, but its crew managed to load and fire a double load of canister ammunition (large cans filled with lead or iron balls that turned a cannon into a huge shotgun) just as the Confederates closed upon it, literally blowing them away.

Meanwhile, Wadsworth sent an officer back to find his other brigade and lead it to McPherson's Woods. This brigade was one of the most famous, and arguably one the best, in the Army of the Potomac. It was composed entirely of "Western" regiments in this Eastern army: the 2nd, 6th, and 7th Wisconsin, 19th Indiana and 24th Michigan. (Everything beyond the Appalachian Mountains was still considered the West in those days.) Since the 1st Corps' recent reorganization this was now the 1st Brigade of the 1st Division of the 1st Corps of the entire Union army, and its men felt that they well deserved this distinction. They called themselves, and were called by others, the Iron Brigade, and were easily distinguished by their custom of wearing the high-crowned black hats of the pre-war regular army's dress uniform, instead of the dark blue forage caps or French "kepis" that were the common headgear in the Army of the Potomac. Many of them also wore the long, tight frock coat of the dress uniform instead of the shorter, looser fatigue blouse most regiments wore.

Wadsworth's staff officer couldn't find the brigade's commander, Brigadier General Solomon Meredith, who had been wounded by an artillery shell, but he came upon its leading regiment, the 2nd Wisconsin, just as it was reaching Seminary Ridge. This was an excellent unit, then of about 300 men, whose record went all the way back to the first battle of Bull Run, where it had been part of William Tecumseh Sherman's brigade. The staff officer led it over to McPherson's Ridge, where it deployed from column into line near the southeast corner of McPherson's Woods, then angled to its right so that it came up to the north edge of the woods, just south of Fowler's two regiments, by the McPherson farm buildings. It then followed the trees downslope, the men loading and firing as they went. The trees were tall and not tightly spaced, and there was very little underbrush, so that visibility and maneuverability in the woods were not much restricted. A volley from Archer's advancing Confederates took out about 30 percent of the regiment, killing its lieutenant colonel, and severely wounding its colonel, but it pushed on under command of its major.

Reynolds followed the regiment in, shouting, "Forward, men, forward for God's sake, and drive those fellows out of the woods."[20] At about 11 a.m., as he looked back to see if the rest of the brigade was following, a bullet struck Reynolds in the back of his neck at the base of his skull and ranged up toward his left eye. He fell from his horse and was probably dead by the time he hit the ground. His orderly and a couple of officers carried him out of the woods, then the officers rushed to give generals Wadsworth and Doubleday the horrible news: The man who had committed them to battle was gone, leaving them no hint of his plans or intentions, and they were on their own even as their men came face to face with a larger Confederate force.

∾ Endnotes ∾

1. According to Jeffrey C. Hall, *The Stand of the U.S. Army at Gettysburg* (Bloomington IN and Indianapolis, 2003), 35, the early morning was cloudy with a temperature of about 72 degrees Fahrenheit, and by 2 p.m. the temperature had risen to 76, with a slight breeze. The problem for the men fighting that day was not so much the heat as the humidity.
2. Abner Doubleday, *Chancellorsville & Gettysburg* (New York, 1908), 126n.
3. Douglas Southall Freeman, *Lee's Lieutenants* (New York, 1944), III:78.
4. Stephen W. Sears, *Gettysburg* (Boston/New York, 2003), 161.
5. Harry W. Pfanz, *Gettysburg – The First Day* (Chapel Hill NC, 2001), 51.
6. Scott Bowden and Bill Ward, *Last Chance for Victory* (Conshohocken PA, 2001), 149.
7. William Woods Hassler, *A. P. Hill* (Richmond VA, 1962), 151.
8. U.S. War Department, *War of the Rebellion: Official Records of the Union and Confederate Armies* (Washington, 1889), I:27:III:416 (hereafter cited as OR with series, volume, and part, if any).
9. Ibid., I:27:I:927.
10. Pfanz, *Gettysburg – The First Day*, 57.
11. Steven H. Newton, *McPherson's Ridge* (Cambridge MA, 2002), 28.
12. Richard Wheeler, *Witness to Gettysburg* (New York, 1987), 121-3.
13. OR, I:27:II:637.
14. Ibid.
15. Wheeler, *Witness to Gettysburg*, 135.
16. Doubleday, *Chancellorsville & Gettysburg*, 125.
17. Pfanz, *Gettysburg – The First Day*, 81.
18. Edward J. Nichols, *Toward Gettysburg* (New York, 1958), 202.
19. OR, I:27:I:924.
20. Pfanz, *Gettysburg – The First Day*, 77.

CHAPTER 2
"Bloody Desperate Fight"
1 July 1863

When the Iron Brigade collided with Archer's Confederates ("Westerners" themselves) in McPherson's Woods it was, as one Union captain described it, an "unadorned long-drawn-out line of ragged, dirty blue against the long-drawn-out line of dirty, ragged butternut, with no 'pomp of war' about it, and no show or style except our old black hats."[1] (Although Confederate uniforms were officially gray, they often had to resort to a dye that produced a yellowish color, similar to khaki, called butternut.) The Rebels soon took note of their opponents' unique headgear and one was heard to exclaim, "There are those d----d black-hatted fellows again! 'Taint no militia. It's the Army of the Potomac."[2]

While the 2nd Wisconsin advanced, the next regiment of the Iron Brigade, the 7th Wisconsin, stopped near the crest of McPherson's Ridge to wait for the other regiments to catch up. And after a few minutes so did the 2nd, although the latter was exchanging fire with the Confederates at close range. General Doubleday held back the last regiment, the 6th Wisconsin ("a gallant body of men, whom I knew could be relied upon," he later reported), placing it as a reserve southwest of the seminary, but the others soon caught up with the 7th and formed line to its left.[3]

(Doubleday was near the south end of the Union line, having been ordered by Reynolds to watch the road to Fairfield and Hagerstown, as there were reports of Rebels in that direction. Buford had brushed against two Confederate infantry regiments near Fairfield the day before.)

Archer's brigade had advanced with the 13th Alabama at the right, or south, end of its line, and the 1st Tennessee, 5th Alabama Battalion, 14th Tennessee and 7th Tennessee extending the line northward, in that order. However, the 1st Tennessee was slowed by some marshy ground near Willoughby Run, causing the line to break up, and the 13th Alabama drifted off to the south, away from the others. Archer, on foot (mounted officers were easy targets, as John Reynolds proved), hurried to that end of his command to get the wayward regiment back in line just as his other three regiments entered the west side of McPherson's Woods.

The two separated regiments went on up McPherson's Ridge through a wheat field south of the woods, and when the 2nd Wisconsin attacked the three regiments on Archer's left the 13th Alabama wheeled in that direction to enfilade the Union line. But, as Private W. H. Bird of the 13th later remembered it, "all of a sudden a heavy line of battle rose up out of the wheat, and poured a volley into our ranks...." Completely surprised by this sudden confrontation with a strong force of Union infantry that now enfiladed their own ranks, when they thought they had been fighting only dismounted cavalry or incompetent militia, the two regiments, as Bird put it, "wavered, and they charged us, and we fell back to the ravine again." The surprise had been mutual, but the Federals had spotted the Rebels first, and had fired and charged without orders. The three Union regiments had a longer line than the two Confederate ones, and the Iron Brigade's newest and largest regiment, the 24th Michigan, at the left, or south, end of the line swung inward and hit the Rebel flank while the other two charged their front and the 2nd Wisconsin charged the other Confederate regiments. Archer's Brigade simply fell apart as it turned and ran back down the hill, hotly pursued by the Federals. Bird said it seemed to him that "there were 20,000 Yanks down in among us hallowing surrender."[4]

Many of them did surrender, including General Archer, who was caught just before he reached Willoughby Run. And something like 200 of them were killed or wounded. A chaplain in Brockenbrough's supporting brigade exaggerated but said that only about a third of Archer's men returned from their encounter with the Iron Brigade. More than likely it was about a third of them who did not return. Either way, Archer's Brigade was out of the fight.

The 2nd Wisconsin lost 116 men out of 302 in that fight, but the 7th Wisconsin, 19th Indiana, and 24th Michigan did not suffer too badly, and they charged on across Willoughby Run and part way up the slope of Herr Ridge, where they stopped to round up prisoners and destroy captured rifles, undisturbed by Heth's two reserve brigades, who were taking their time about preparing to launch a counterattack.

As Archer was being led away to the Union rear he encountered General Doubleday, an old friend from the pre-war Regular Army. The latter exclaimed, "Good morning, Archer! How are you? I am glad to see you!"

"Well, I am *not* glad to see *you* by a ---- sight," the Confederate replied.[5] This was the first time one of Lee's generals had been captured on a field of battle.

While the battle was going well for the Union on this part of the field, north of the Chambersburg Pike the Confederates had the upper hand. There the 76th New York and 56th Pennsylvania of Cutler's brigade (about 625 men) encountered Davis's only veteran regiment, the 2nd Mississippi (about 500 men) in another wheat field. Men of both sides later claimed that the other had been hiding in the wheat. The two battle lines stood and blazed away at each other until the 55th North Carolina (some 640 men), at the left or northern end of Davis's line, came over the ridge well beyond Cutler's flank. Both Confederate regiments then charged the Union line. The 76th New York changed front to face the North Carolinians, but General Wadsworth sent an order for the two regiments to retreat, which they did, or the roughly 380 of them that were left did so. The Rebels paid for their success however, as the colonels of both Confederate regiments were among the casualties the Federals inflicted in this brief fight, which probably didn't last more than 20 minutes.

Davis's other regiment present, the 42nd Mississippi (575

men), at the right or southern end of his line, had, meanwhile, pivoted to its right to attack Hall's battery, which was just north of the Chambersburg Pike. It was part of this regiment that one of Calef's guns had blown away after pulling out of the position just south of where Hall's guns now stood. Hall also beat back a charge on his guns with cannister fire, in this case from four of his guns while the other two continued to duel with the Confederate artillery, and the Rebel infantry retreated to the cover of the railroad cut not far to the north. At about this time Cutler's wayward regiment, the 147th New York, which had been cut off by Hall's guns going into position, moved to the north side of the pike from where it had been sheltering behind McPhersons' barn. Captain Hall, however, was unaware of this and thought his battery stood alone against the Confederates north of the road, who now sent skirmishers forward to pick off his men and horses. This was a very effective tactic against artillery, for shooting at widely dispersed skirmishers with cannon "would be," as General Doubleday put it, "very much like fighting mosquitos with musket-balls."[6] The artillerymen could not continue such an unequal struggle for long, and, unaware of the 147th's presence, Hall decided that "if the position was too advanced for infantry it was equally so for artillery," and ordered his battery to retire one section at a time.[7]

Meanwhile an aide delivered Wadsworth's order for a retreat to the commander of the 147th just as that regiment was swinging into line with orders to "Lie down! fire through the wheat close to the ground!" at the Mississipians some 150 yards down the unfinished railroad.[8] However, just after the retreat order was delivered the regiment's commander was badly wounded and carried off the field by his frightened horse before he had passed the order on to his men. The regiment, known, perhaps not too flatteringly, as the Ploughboys, stayed put under the command of Major George Harney. These New Yorkers would lie near the highest part of the gentle ridge and fire, then crawl lower down the hill to reload under cover. But the 2nd Mississippi, having chased off Cutler's other two regiments, was now coming down on the Ploughboys' right flank. Major Harney turned three of his ten companies to face this threat, but then the 55th North Carolina came down and again extended well beyond the Union right flank, threatening to cut off the lone Federal regiment completely. General Wadsworth saw the 147th's plight and sent an aide dashing in with an order to withdrawn. Harney told his men to drop everything but their rifles and ammunition, then he gave the somewhat unorthodox order, "In retreat, double-quick, run!"[9]

Some of the New Yorkers claimed to have retreated in good order, loading and firing as they went. Another said "in getting off the field, no order or line was observed. Some kept to the north side of the old railroad over the second ridge . . . but the galling fire of the Second Mississippi and Fifty-fifth North Carolina, who were advancing from the north, drove most of them across the cut towards the Chambersburg Pike."[10] Many of them were hit when the Mississippians raked the railroad cut with rifle fire, but the rest clambered up the south side of the cut and on down the east slope of Seminary Ridge. About 75 officers and men of the 147th rallied behind Oak Ridge with Cutler's other two regiments, and Cutler later reported that the 147th lost 207 officers and men out 380 in a fight that lasted no more than half an hour. As Cutler told the survivors of the three regiments as they reformed on the back side of Oak Ridge, this battle was just like a cock fight. "We fight a little and run a little."[11] Wadsworth told Cutler to take these men even farther to the rear, and they moved down to the edge of Gettysburg, where they could rest and get water from a small stream called Stevens Run before going back into the battle.

While all this was going on, Hall's battery was still being plagued by Rebel skirmishers even as it began to withdraw. The Confederates shot down all the horses of one of the guns of the first section to pull out, and its crew had to pull it by hand. Hall had meant for this section to cover the withdrawal of the other two, but it was all it could do to save itself, and the others only escaped because they were momentarily hidden by all the smoke they had created by firing rapidly just before leaving. They were moving along between the pike and the railroad cut, and as they approached Seminary Ridge the guns had to pass through a gap in a fence and over its bottom rail. They could only get through one gun at a time, and as they did so the Rebels caught up with and captured the last piece by bayoneting all six of its horses. Upon reaching Seminary Ridge, Captain Hall met General Wadsworth, who wanted him to place his guns where they could cover a general retreat. Hall said that where they stood was a good enough place, but Wadsworth said no, they couldn't hold Seminary Ridge for long; he wanted Hall to take his guns to the high ground southeast of the town. Hall protested that he wanted to stay and recover his lost gun, but Wadsworth insisted. However, soon after he got his remaining guns into position on Cemetery Hill, an officer on Wadsworth's staff ordered him to bring the guns back to Seminary Ridge, as maybe there wouldn't be a retreat after all. Hall complied, but he had only enough men and horses left to move and man three of his guns.

There had been one more unit of the Iron Brigade following its last regiment; that was the Brigade Guard, an ad hoc collection of 100 men – 20 from each of the brigade's five regiments – whose job it was to carry and protect the brigade's triangular identifying flag (each corps, division, and brigade in the Army of the Potomac had a distinctive flag to identify it on the battlefield). The commander of the 6th Wisconsin, Lieutenant Colonel Rufus Dawes, ordered the two lieutenants who commanded the Guard to split into two companies and to position one at each end of his regiment's line. This was no sooner accomplished than the same staff officer who had delivered Doubleday's order to halt returned, saying, "General Doubleday directs that you move your regiment at once to the right."[12] Dawes shifted his now-reinforced regiment (about 440 men) into a column of fours, and it set out at the double-quick. An officer from General Meredith's staff, originally from the Iron Brigade, rode alongside Dawes explaining that Cutler's brigade was in trouble, and he was soon replaced by an officer from Wadsworth's staff with orders for Dawes to take his regiment north and form on Cutler's right flank. But as he approached the Chambersburg Pike Dawes could seen Cutler's men falling back towards the town, Hall's guns driving for the rear, and the 147th New York in full retreat with a line of Confederates in hot pursuit. Between him and them Dawes saw Union officers carrying a body across his path – only later would he learn that it was the body of John Reynolds.

The 6th Wisconsin passed behind the other regiments of the Iron Brigade as they charged and drove Archer's Rebels back to and beyond Willoughby Run. And beyond McPherson's Woods the two regiments of Cutler's brigade that had been stationed near the McPherson buildings were swinging back to face Davis's Confederates coming down from the north. But when Dawes saw the "long line of yelling rebels coming over the ridge beyond the railroad cut" he also saw an "opportunity to attack their flank." He ordered his regiment to file to the right, moving east until it was just beyond the flank of what he called the "strong but scattered line of rebels," then ordered his men into line of battle "parallel to the turnpike and R.R. cut, and almost directly upon the flank of the enemy." But, like all mounted officers, he attracted enemy fire, and just as he turned to lead his line forward to the pike his horse was hit and fell beneath him. He scrambled to his feet just as his men opened ranks to pass around him with a friendly yell. (The horse also got up and hobbled off in search of the brigade wagons; it lived for years after that, still carrying the bullet beneath its skin.) By the time Dawes was on his feet and back in action his regiment had reached the post-and-rail fence that lined the south side of the Chambersburg Pike. There it halted, and he gave the order to fire by file, sending a rolling wave of fire from one end of his line to the other. "The fire of our carefully aimed muskets, resting on the fence rails, striking their flank soon checked the rebels in their headlong pursuit," Dawes later remembered. "The rebel line swayed and bent, and suddenly stopped firing," he said, and it ran for the cover of the railroad cut.[13]

There "all the men were jumbled together without regiment or company," according to Major John A. Blair, who had succeeded to the command of the 2nd Mississippi.[14] He and Major Alfred H. Belo, who had succeeded to the command of the 55th North Carolina, were trying to get their men sorted out. They had wanted to charge the Federals to the south of them, believing that the first side to charge would win the fight, but then an order had come from the inexperienced General Davis to retreat and reform, using the railroad cut for cover. As in the wheat field south of McPherson's Woods, so here north of the Chambersburg Pike the Iron Brigade would be the first to charge.

One 6th Wisconsin soldier remembered thinking, when his regiment first encountered the Rebels, ". . . now, for once, we will have a square 'stand up and knock down fight.' No trees, nor walls to protect either, when presto! Their whole line disappeared as if swallowed up by the earth. . . . They had taken advantage of a deep railroad cut, a splendid position for them, and threatened death and destruction to any regiment that attempted to dislodge them." The 6th Wisconsin, however, was going to attempt it. Its men scrambled over the fence and reformed ranks in the road, then climbed over and/or knocked down the fence on the north side of the pike, after which they slowly advanced across a pasture while returning the fire from the cut that was decimating their ranks. (The cut was some 150-200 yards north of the pike – fairly close range for rifled muskets.) Dawes later said that "to climb that fence in face of such a fire was a clear test of mettle and discipline." The Federals were out in the open, while all they could see of the Confederates was their flag and the smoke from their rifles, but they continued to press forward. "But the rebels do not budge," a Wisconsin private remembered, "and we have no thought but to do what we set out to do. It is a terrible moment.... Our boys are dropping at a terrible rate."[15]

His line was well into the field on the north side of the road, and some of his men were calling for a charge, when Dawes noticed at least part of the 95th New York (he thought about 100 men) was forming line to his left. He didn't yet know it, but the 14th Brooklyn was also coming up farther west. Dawes, still on foot, hurried over and told Major Edward Pye of the 95th, "Let's go for them, Major!" Pye had just succeeded to the command of his regiment when its colonel had been hit, and he was unaware that Colonel Fowler of the 14th Brooklyn was planning for both of his regiments to charge as soon as they were lined up together. Pye just nodded and told Dawes, "We are with you!"[16] Swinging his sword to get attention, he ordered his men forward.

Running back to his own regiment, Dawes yelled for his men to charge, repeatedly calling on them to align on the colors because, as he explained, "Men were being shot by twenties and thirties and breaking ranks by falling or running." Not running away; running forward. One of Dawes' men later remembered that, "Up to this time our line was as straight and in as good order as any line of battle ever was, while under fire. After that, the line was not in such good order, but all seemed to be trying to see how quick they could get to the railroad cut."[17] Many of the wounded kept fighting. Some who couldn't advance could still load and fire, providing some fire support for the charge, others staggered on with wounds in various parts of their bodies. The regiment's national flag, which the men were supposed to guide on, went down three times as its successive bearers were hit, but all three times it was picked up and carried forward by other men, and the regiment, Dawes said, formed a sort of V shape, the colors at the point, nearest the enemy. The 95th New York connected to Dawes' left, or nearly so, and extended the line farther west, and the 14th Brooklyn (about 250 men) also advanced, although slightly farther behind.

As the line, or V, neared the cut the Confederate fire paused for a few seconds, and a Union sergeant later said he knew that this meant the Rebel officers were preparing their men to deliver a disciplined volley, which the sergeant said came when the Federals were within a rod (5.5 yards) of the railroad cut. He glanced down the line to the left and saw "that it seemed half our men had fallen." But the survivors rushed on with what a corporal called "yells enough to almost waken the dead." A lieutenant, a private, and a drummer all rushed forward, trying to capture the flag of the 2nd Mississippi that was planted on the edge of the cut. The lieutenant was shot in the shoulder when within 15 or 20 feet of it. He was knocked down by the impact of the bullet, tried to crawl on, but eventually gave it up. "Flag-taking was pretty well knocked out of me," he later said.[18] The private and the drummer both got their hands on the flag staff but were both shot before they could pull it free of the ground. Another Wisconsin soldier swung his rifle like a club and crushed the skull of the Rebel who had shot the private, and a fight continued to rage around the flag, with several more men going down.

By then most of Dawes' regiment was reaching the cut, the point of its V coming up to the eastern end of it. "Bayonets are crossed," one Federal remembered. "The fight was hand to hand amidst firing and smoke. The men are black and grimy with powder and heat. They seemed all unconscious to the terrible situation; they were mad and fought with a desperation seldom witnessed."[19] Some of the Federals crossed over to the back side of the cut, while many of them, now standing on the rim of the cut and looking down on their enemies, began calling for the Rebels to throw down their muskets, although one said it was "an even question who should surrender."[20] There were more Confederates on hand than Federals, but the cut that had provided the Rebels with a ready-made breastwork was now a trap. There were Federals in front of them; Federals behind them; and others in position to fire down the length of the crowded cut; while the banks, up to ten feet high at the deepest part, made it extremely unlikely that many of them could scramble out without getting shot or bayoneted. One by one they began to drop their weapons.

Dawes yelled, "Where is the colonel of this regiment?" Major Blair of the 2nd Mississippi looked up and said, "Here I am. Who are you?" Dawes pushed his way through several armed Confederates toward the major and said, "I command this regiment. Surrender, or I will fire." Without a word the Confederate handed Dawes his sword, and many of his men, on seeing this, threw down their muskets, though some, it is said, fired one last shot first. "The coolness, self-possession, and discipline which held back our men from pouring in a general volley saved a hundred lives of the enemy," Dawes later wrote, "and as my mind goes back to the fearful excitement of the moment, I marvel at it."[21]

In later years, looking back, Dawes also thought he should have been a bit more magnanimous to the Rebel major, but at the time he literally had his hands full. "It would have been the handsome thing to say, 'Keep your sword, sir,'" he admitted, "but I was new to such occasions, and when six other officers came up and handed me their swords, I took them also."[22] Major Blair was left with one consolation, however. When told that he had surrendered to the 6th Wisconsin he said, "Thank God. I thought it was a New York regiment."[23] The total number captured by the 6th Wisconsin turned out to be 7 officers and 225 enlisted men, but others did surrender to the New York regiments, both of which arrived just as the surrendering began. (Colonel Fowler of the 14th Brooklyn later claimed credit for ordering the charge by the three regiments, but Dawes said he didn't even know that regiment was on the field until the fight was over.)

Those members of Davis's Brigade who did not surrender retreated back to the north. Major Belo of the 55th North Carolina said he and his men "were able to get out of the railroad cut after a severe struggle."[24] Many of the Confederates must have retreated without weapons, for Dawes said that about a thousand muskets lay at the bottom of the cut when the fighting there was over. General Heth pulled what was left of Davis's Brigade out of the fight and later reported that "it was not deemed advisable to bring it again into action on that day."[25]

The melee over the 2nd Mississippi's flag finally came to end. The Rebel color bearer, Corporal W. B. Murphy, tore the flag from its staff when Corporal Frank Waller of the 6th Wisconsin grabbed it, but Waller was a big man and he managed to get it away from Murphy. "My first thought was to go to the rear with it for fear it might be retaken," Waller later said, "and then I thought I would stay, and I threw it down and loaded and fired twice standing on it. While standing on it there was a 14th Brooklyn man took hold of it and tried to get it, and I had threatened to shoot him before he would stop."[26] Waller later received a Medal of Honor for capturing this flag.

General Wadsworth arrived just after the surrender, and his small cavalry escort helped round up the prisoners, who were marched off under Major John Hauser, Dawes' second in command. Ten or 15 volunteers, including Corporal Waller, were sent as skirmishers to take position on the ridge north of the cut and watch for any return of the Confederates. Waller turned his captured flag over to Dawes, who tied it around the body of wounded Sergeant William Evans, who was using two muskets as crutches, with instructions to hang onto it at all hazards. Captain Hall's abandoned gun was found near the Chambersburg Pike, and a detail of men took charge of it and set off to return it to the battery, a wounded sergeant hitching a ride on the cannon as he and the other wounded men went in search of medical aid.

They found hospitals being set up in the Washington Hotel and at the courthouse in Gettysburg. Citizens of the town had set out tables and trays full of refreshments, which they offered to the wounded, and they tried to help them all they could. Sergeant Evans took refuge in the house of one Jacob Hollinger, whose daughters, "two very pretty and sensible young ladies," took care of him.[27] Later in the day, when

Rebels entered the town, the girls sewed the captured flag up inside the mattress of Evans' bed. The captured Rebel swords were also taken along and delivered to a surgeon, except for one that was retained by Dawes's adjutant.

Not all the wounded could move, of course. One Wisconsin soldier who still lay on the ground over which the regiment had charged, shot through the body and dying in agony, asked several of his passing friends to shoot him and put him out of his misery, but none of them could steel themselves to do it. Four men of the 14th Brooklyn went to rescue one of their wounded comrades, rolling him onto half a pup tent to use as a stretcher, with one man carrying each corner. But a Confederate shell hit the group, killing the wounded man and three of his rescuers and tearing a leg off the other. More Federals tried to carry this wounded man to a hospital, but he bled to death before they could reach it.

When it became apparent that the Confederates were not going to counterattack, Dawes pulled his regiment back to some woods on Seminary Ridge, east of the railroad cut, sent the members of the Brigade Guard to return to their respective regiments, called the roll, and got his companies reorganized. The roll call showed that there were over 160 men missing out of 340. Seven company commanders had been hit. How many the Brigade Guard lost he didn't know, since it had already been dismissed. (According to one member of the regiment who said he could name all the names, the 6th Wisconsin lost 40 men killed and 82 wounded between the seminary and the railroad cut.) Then Dawes took out a small journal that he carried in his pocket and started to write: "Battle Field near Gettysburg, July 1st, 1863. 2 p.m., Bloody desperate fight."[28]

By this time Gamble's cavalrymen – some of whom had stayed to fight alongside the infantrymen – had drawn off to the south to guard the Hagerstown Road and the Union left flank. But, at Wadsworth's order, Calef's battery of horse artillery returned to take position between the Chambersburg Pike and the railroad cut, where Hall's battery had been. The other four regiments of the Iron Brigade had returned from across Willoughby Run and had taken position in McPherson's Woods, with the 2nd Wisconsin at first formed in the field north of the woods, where the 14th Brooklyn had been; Cutler's three regiments that had retreated and gone to rest had returned to their former positions, reinforced by the 95th New York, while the 14th Brooklyn and 6th Wisconsin formed on their left, in support of Calef's guns.

Doubleday, who was now the senior Union officer on the field, was merely putting things back together the way they had been – or were supposed to have been – before the Confederate attack. He was a competent officer but had probably been promoted one grade beyond his aptitude. He had graduated from West Point in 1842, in the same class as Longstreet, with high enough standing to go into the artillery, and had stayed in the Regular Army right up to the beginning of the war. Today he is most famous as the supposed inventor of baseball (though he was probably just the first to write down the rules of the game), but his real claim to fame was the fact that he probably fired the first Union shot of the war when he was second-in-command at Fort Sumter in 1861. Colonel Wainwright of the 1st Corps artillery thought Doubleday was a "weak reed to lean upon," considering him to be impractical and slow on the uptake.[29] Other Union officers seem to have had similar misgivings about him. At some point he had acquired the nickname – a play on his surname – of "Forty-eight hours" Doubleday.[30] He did pretty well this day, however, given that he knew little of what Reynolds had intended or what Meade wanted done.

As the other units of the 1st Corps arrived, Doubleday fed them into his line. Colonel Roy Stone's 2nd Brigade of Doubleday's own 3rd Division arrived at about 11 a.m., after having followed the same path as Wadsworth's division, and Doubleday placed its three Pennsylvania regiments between McPherson's Woods and the Chambersburg Pike, sending the 2nd Wisconsin from there to rejoin the Iron Brigade in the woods. At about the same hour Brigadier General Thomas A. Rowley, in temporary command of the 3rd Division now that Doubleday commanded the entire corps, arrived at the south end of the Union line with his 1st Brigade. Accompanied by one battery of the corps artillery, it had followed a different road, or series of roads, than had the rest of the corps, more to the northwest. It eventually reached the Hagerstown Road, where it formed line, advanced about 200 yards north into a grove of trees, and waited for orders. There it was soon found by a staff officer sent out by Doubleday, and it moved eastward through open fields, across Willoughby Run, and over McPherson's Ridge to the low ground between it and Seminary Ridge. There its men dropped their knapsacks, and soon it was sent back over the ridge and down to the run, but this was too far forward, and eventually it settled in with one regiment at the crest of McPherson's Ridge, south of the Iron Brigade, and the other three regiments posted behind it.

Stone's brigade had been followed up the Emmitsburg Road by Colonel Wainwright with three batteries of the corps artillery. He brought them to a halt behind Seminary Ridge, leaving them in reserve there until needed, and sending the battery wagons and traveling forges to the rear, out of the way. But soon he sent one battery, the combined companies E and L of the 1st New York Light Artillery, under Captain Gilbert Reynolds, to a position 200 yards south of the seminary; then he changed his mind and sent that battery up near the unfinished railroad and replaced it with Captain Greenleaf Stevens' 5th Maine Light Battery.

The artillery had been followed by the two brigades of Brigadier General John C. Robinson's 2nd Division. Near the Codori farm they had passed a teenaged girl and her grandfather, and the latter had exhorted them to "Whip 'em, boys, this time. If you don't whip 'em now, you'll never whip 'em." The men had cheered the old man and, perhaps more enthusiastically, the young girl, whom one of the soldiers described as a "blooming lass."[31] This division was also held in reserve on the west slope of Seminary Ridge at first, but Confederates were now seen approaching from the north, and Doubleday soon ordered Robinson to send one brigade in that direction to guard Cutler's right flank. Robinson sent Brigadier General Henry Baxter's 2nd Brigade.

With his other brigade, Brigadier General Gabriel Paul's 1st, Robinson was ordered to hold the seminary. Robinson set the men of its five regiments to work building breastworks by throwing dirt over piles of fence rails. Some Confederate artillery fire was sent their way, and one overconfident soldier, despite warnings from more experienced men, gleefully stuck out his foot to stop a 12-pound cannon ball that came rolling toward him. It didn't look very big; only a little over four and a half inches in diameter. But it had plenty of momentum left, and the laws of physics do not take pity on the stupid or the ill-informed. His leg was so badly mangled that it had to be amputated.

The fortunes of war are equally unforgiving of the ignorant or over-confident. In explanation of his actions at this time, Doubleday later reported, "Upon taking a retrospect of the field, it might seem, in view of the fact that we were finally forced to retreat, that this would have been a proper time to retire; but to fall back without orders from the commanding general might have inflicted lasting disgrace upon the corps, and as General Reynolds, who was high in the confidence of General Meade, had formed his lines to resist the entrance of the enemy into Gettysburg, I naturally supposed it was the intention to defend the place."[32] Much later, when he wrote a book about Chancellorsville and Gettysburg, Doubleday expanded upon this by saying what he probably felt he could not put in his official report: "I knew that General Meade was at Taneytown; and as, on the previous evening, he had informed General Reynolds that the enemy's army were concentrating on Gettysburg, I thought it probable he would ride to the front to see for himself what was going on, and issue definite orders of some kind."[33]

Both were natural assumptions, but both were wrong.

Meade had no intention of going to Gettysburg himself that day, nor had he meant to defend the place against any sizable Confederate force. Sometime that morning his assistant adjutant-general, Brigadier General Seth Williams, wrote a long dispatch to Reynolds from army headquarters in Taneytown, in which he said, in part, "The commanding general cannot decide whether it is his best policy to move to attack until he learns something more definite of the point at which the enemy is concentrating. This he hopes to do during the day.... If the enemy is concentrating to our right of Gettysburg, that point would not at first glance seem to be a proper strategic point of concentration for this army. If the enemy is concentrating in front of Gettysburg or to the left of it, the general is not sufficiently well informed of the nature of the country to judge of its character for either an offensive or defensive position.... The movement of your corps to Gettysburg was ordered before the positive knowledge of the enemy's withdrawal from Harrisburg and concentration was received."[34]

Also sometime that morning Meade's headquarters staff finally finished copying for the various corps commanders a circular outlining what Meade wanted them to do in case the Confederates "assume the offensive, and attack." The idea was to form a long defensive line in northern Maryland behind a stream known as Pipe Creek, a tributary of the Monocacy River. "For this purpose," it said, "General Reynolds, in command of the left, will withdraw the force at present at Gettysburg, two corps [1st and 11th] by the road to Taneytown and Westminster, and, after crossing Pipe Creek, deploy toward Middleburg. The corps [3rd] at Emmitsburg will be withdrawn, via Mechanicsville, to Middleburg, or, if a more direct route can be found leaving Taneytown to their left, to withdraw direct to Middleburg."[35] There was a lot more, of course, outlining what the other corps should do, but it was all moot now. John Reynolds never received it, nor the message to him quoted above. Meade had intended for this circular to go out the previous afternoon, and he later complained bitterly about the slowness of his staff. He said he "had arranged for a plan of battle, and it had taken so long to get the orders out that now it was all useless."[36]

Sometime that morning Williams wrote to Major General John Sedgwick, commander of the 6th Corps, saying "it would appear from reports just received that the enemy is moving in heavy force on Gettysburg (Ewell from Heidlersburg, and Hill from Cashtown Pass) and it is not improbable that he will reach that place before the command under Major-General Reynolds (the First and Eleventh Corps), now on its way, can arrive there. Should this be the case, and General Reynolds find himself in the presence of a superior force, he is instructed to hold the enemy in check, and fall slowly back. If he is able to do this, the line indicated in the circular of to-day will be occupied to-night."[37]

The staff officer carrying Reynolds' verbal message to Meade reached army headquarters at Taneytown, fourteen miles from Gettysburg, at around 11:20 a.m. The general had the message, about fighting through the town house to house if necessary, repeated several times, then exclaimed, "Good! That is just like Reynolds; he will hold on to the bitter end."[38] Meade now knew that major portions of Lee's army were converging on Gettysburg and that Reynolds had also arrived there, ahead of his troops. Evidently he assumed at first that Reynolds would follow the directions given in the circular to fall back toward Taneytown, but then, perhaps after questioning Reynolds' staff officer, he realized that Reynolds had not received the circular in time and might instead be falling back towards Emmitsburg, that being the direction from which he had advanced.

That Reynolds was not falling back at all does not seem to have occurred to him. At 12:30 p.m. Meade's chief of staff, Major General Dan Butterfield, wrote to Major General Winfield Scott Hancock, commander of the 2nd Army Corps, which had reached Taneytown at 11 that morning: "The major-general commanding directs that, in view of the advance of Generals A. P. Hill and Ewell on Gettysburg, and the possible failure of General Reynolds to receive the order to withdraw his command by the route through Taneytown, thus leaving the center of our position open, that you proceed with your troops out on the direct road to Gettysburg from Taneytown. When [if] you find that General Reynolds is covering that road (instead of withdrawing by Emmitsburg, which it is feared he may do), you will withdraw to Frizellburg, as directed in the circular of directions for the positions issued this morning."[39]

But forty minutes later, at 1:10 p.m., Butterfield wrote to Hancock again: "The major-general commanding has just been informed that General Reynolds has been killed or badly wounded. He directs that you turn over the command of your corps to [Brigadier] General [John] Gibbon [one of Hancock's division commanders]; that you proceed to the front, and, by virtue of this order, in case of the truth of General Reynolds' death, you assume command of the corps there assembled, viz, the Eleventh, First, and Third, at Emmitsburg. If you think the ground and position there a better one to fight a battle under existing circumstances, you will so advise the general, and he will order all the troops up. . . ." Five minutes later Butterfield added a postscript: "Reynolds has possession of Gettysburg, and the enemy are reported as falling back from the front of Gettysburg. Hold you column ready to move."[40] A copy of this order was directed to General Howard, commander of the 11th Corps. The wording of this order is a bit vague, but Meade delivered the order to Hancock in person, and between them they ironed out what should be done. What Howard thought of it is not recorded.

Meade did not feel he could afford to leave headquarters, where he was in touch with the rest of his army, and ride off to see what a fraction of it was doing, so he still wanted Hancock to go and take charge of the troops in contact with the enemy. Hancock pointed out that General Howard, whose corps was part of what had been Reynolds' command, was senior to him (they were both promoted to major general on the same date, but Howard had been made a brigadier general earlier than Hancock, thus he had seniority by army rules). But the order that had put Meade in command of the Army of the Potomac had given him the power to appoint people to commands "as you may deem expedient." So, as Hancock's chief of staff remembered it, "he replied, in effect, that he could not help it; that he knew General Hancock, but did not know General Howard so well, and at this crisis he must have a man he knew and could trust."[41]

So at about 1:30 p.m. General Hancock rode north out of Taneytown, heading for Gettysburg. "Having been fully informed by the major-general commanding as to his intentions," Hancock later reported, "I was instructed by him to give the necessary directions upon my arrival at the front for the movement of troops and trains to the rear toward the line of battle he had selected, should I deem it expedient to do so. If the ground was suitable, and circumstances made it wise, I was directed to establish the line of battle at Gettysburg."[42] Hancock was an excellent choice. He was, to borrow Gilbert and Sullivan's phrase, the very model of a modern major general: handsome, dapper, 38 years old, a hard fighter, beloved by his men and highly respected by his fellow officers. He and his chief of staff rode north in an ambulance wagon for a while, so they could study their maps, but eventually he decided that this was too slow, and so they mounted their horses and hurried on.

Lee was just as ignorant of the situation at Gettysburg as Meade was. That morning he was in the process of moving his small headquarters from Greenwood, Pennsylvania, west of South Mountain, to Cashtown, east of it. He rode with General Longstreet, at the head of the latter's 1st Corps, for a while. When they found Major General Edward "Allegheny" Johnson's division of Ewell's 2nd Corps filing into the same road after having marched, with the corps wagons, down the Cumberland Valley from Carlisle, Lee ordered the 1st Corps to yield the right of way, so that Johnson could go on to rejoin

Ewell somewhere beyond Cashtown. But Lee and Longstreet rode on ahead, passing along Johnson's column as it toiled up into the Cashtown Gap. Soon they heard cannon fire, beyond Cashtown, and as it increased Lee decided to hurry on, leaving Longstreet to bring up his corps.

At Cashtown Lee found A. P. Hill just rising from his cot. Hill was feeling ill, but he had also heard the cannon fire, which had gotten him out of bed. Lee asked Hill what he knew about the firing in the distance, to which Hill could only say, "Nothing," but he would ride toward Gettysburg and find out what was going on.[43] Hill left in a hurry and soon came upon Pender's Division of his corps, deployed on both sides of the Chambersburg Pike and advancing toward Herr Ridge, where he ordered it to halt.

At about noon Lee called for Major General Richard H. Anderson, whose division of Hill's corps had now reached Cashtown. "I found General Lee intently listening to the fire of the guns, and very much disturbed and depressed," Anderson later told Longstreet. "At length he said, more to himself than to me, 'I cannot think what has become of Stuart. I ought to have heard from him long before now. He may have met with disaster, but I hope not. In the absence of reports from him, I am in ignorance as to what we have in front of us here. It may be the whole Federal army, or it may be only a detachment. If it is the whole Federal force, we must fight a battle here. If we do not gain a victory, those defiles and gorges which we passed this morning will shelter us from disaster.'"[44] Lee ordered Anderson to take his division forward to join the rest of Hill's corps.

While Lee was at Cashtown he was found there by Major G. Campbell Brown of General Ewell's staff. (Brown was not only Ewell's assistant adjutant-general and the son of Ewell's first cousin, but was also now his stepson, Ewell having recently married Brown's widowed mother.) Brown reported that Ewell, with Rodes' division of his 2nd Corps, coming south from Carlisle, had met up with Early's division coming west from York the previous evening at Heidlersburg, north of Gettysburg. Both divisions had started marching west that morning, on different roads, heading for Cashtown, but before reaching Middletown (later renamed Biglersville) Ewell had received word from Hill that the latter's corps was moving to Gettysburg. Therefore Ewell had turned both of his divisions to the south, heading for the same place.

Lee asked Brown, "with a peculiar searching, almost querulous impatience, which I never saw in him before and but twice afterward, whether Gen. Ewell had heard anything from Gen. Stuart." When Brown said he had not, Lee observed that Stuart had not complied with his orders to join up with Ewell and then impressed upon the young staff officer, in strong terms, "that a general engagement was to be avoided until the arrival of the rest of the army."[45] After this meeting, Brown returned to Ewell, and Lee rode on toward Gettysburg and the battle that had begun against his wishes. Sometime after 1 p.m. he passed through Pender's Division, then deployed at the western base of Herr Ridge, straddling the Chambersburg Pike, and found a place on that ridge near a couple of battalions of Hill's artillery from which to observe the situation in front of him. After receiving Heth's description of what had happened so far, he ordered the latter to keep his men under tight control until he received further orders. Not knowing how much of Meade's army was nearby, he still did not want to bring on a major battle with so much of his army strung out on various roads, many of its divisions too distant to reach the field in time to fight that day. He had hoped to create just the opposite situation, where his army would be concentrated and able to take on separate parts of Meade's army as it came in search of him. But, in the absence of his cavalry, he had no knowledge of where the various Union corps were. They might be concentrating at Gettysburg that very day for all he knew.

fact, of course, only two Union corps had been ordered to march to Gettysburg that day: the 1st and 11th. Major

General Oliver Otis Howard, commander of the 11th Corps, had received Reynolds' order to march his three divisions (six brigades) to Gettysburg at about 8 a.m. His 1st Division, commanded by Brigadier General Francis Barlow, had been camped northwest of Emmitsburg, Maryland, and it was sent, accompanied by one battery of artillery, up the same road that the 1st Corps had followed (known at Gettysburg, logically enough, as the Emmitsburg Road). His other two divisions and the rest of the corps artillery brigade had been turned off that road and moved over to the road that connected Taneytown with Gettysburg (the Taneytown Road), so as to ease congestion. After getting the troops up and on their way, Howard had ridden ahead with his staff to a crossroads by a farm owned by one J. Wintz, a couple of miles south of Gettysburg. It was an area that would soon become famous for its peach orchard. This is where Howard had planned to put his corps into camp at the end of what he had assumed would be a routine march.

However, he could hear heavy firing northwest of the town, and he sent a staff officer to try to find Reynolds and report his presence, while he and his chief of staff, Lieutenant Colonel Theodore Meysenburg, reconnoitered the area. Seeking high ground from which they could get an extended view, they came, at about 10:30 a.m., to the hill at the southeast corner of Gettysburg that held the town's cemetery. It was obvious that this hill would make an excellent position for artillery, which would dominate the town and the country to its west and north as far as Seminary Ridge. Another hill, mostly wooded, to the east (Culp's Hill), if occupied by Union troops, would protect the right flank of any forces placed on Cemetery Hill. South of the cemetery the ground sloped off as a gradually declining ridge that would protect the hill's left flank. Both officers felt that this would be an excellent defensive position for Meade's army. (Quite probably Reynolds had also seen the value of Cemetery Hill; or Buford might have pointed it out to him. Wadsworth later claimed that Reynolds had noted it, and his claim is given credence by his own action in sending Hall's battery there to cover a possible retreat.)

Howard's troops were still far behind him, so he and Meysenburg then rode into town and were invited to the top of a high building by some civilians who were watching the battle from there. "I saw firing beyond Seminary Ridge and not far from the seminary," he later reported. "Toward the right masses of cavalry were drawn up in order, to the east of the ridge and northeast of town. A portion of the First Corps, of General Wadsworth's command [its division and brigade flags would have made it identifiable], was between me and the seminary, taking position near the railroad. Another division of this corps was moving by the flank with considerable rapidity, along the ridge and in a northeasterly direction. I had studied the position a few moments, when a report reached me that General Reynolds was wounded. At first I hoped that his wound might be slight, and that he would continue to command; but in a short time I was undeceived. His aide-de-camp, Major [William] Riddle, brought the sad tiding of his death. This was about 11:30 a.m. . . . On hearing of the death of General Reynolds, I assumed command of the left wing, instructing [Major] General [Carl] Schurz [one of his division commanders] to take command of the Eleventh Corps."[46]

Like Doubleday, Howard assumed that Meade wanted the town held, and Schurz (pronounced "shirts"), who was with the troops on the Taneytown Road, was told to hurry the men forward. Howard also sent a staff officer down the Emmitsburg Road to notify division commander General Barlow and Major General Daniel Sickles, commander of the 3rd Corps, and urge them on to Gettysburg. (Sickles was told to pass the word to Meade at army headquarters in Taneytown.) Then Howard established his headquarters near the cemetery, on the highest point north of the Baltimore Pike, telling his staff, "God helping us, we will stay here until the army comes."[47]

∼ **Endnotes** ∼

1. Pfanz, *Gettysburg – The First Day*, 91.
2. Doubleday, *Chancellorsville & Gettysburg*, 132.
3. *OR*, I:27:I:246.
4. Newton, *McPherson's Ridge*, 42.
5. Ibid., 43. Italics in the source.
6. Doubleday, *Chancellorsville & Gettysburg*, 129.
7. *OR*, I:27:I:359.
8. Pfanz, *Gettysburg – The First Day*, 85.
9. Ibid., 86.
10. Ibid.
11. Ibid., 52.
12. Lance J. Herdegen and William J. K. Beaudot, *In the Bloody Railroad Cut at Gettysburg* (Dayton OH, 1990), 178.
13. Ibid., 182-3.
14. Pfanz, *Gettysburg – The First Day*, 104.
15. Herdegen and Beaudot, *In the Bloody Railroad Cut at Gettysburg*, 184-5.
16. Ibid., 186.
17. Ibid., 188.
18. Ibid., 193-4.
19. Ibid., 196.
20. Ibid., 198.
21. Ibid.
22. Ibid.
23. Ibid., 199.
24. Ibid., 205.
25. *OR*, I:27:II:638.
26. Herdegen and Beaudot, *In the Bloody Railroad Cut at Gettysburg*, 200.
27. Pfanz, *Gettysburg – The First Day*, 114.
28. Herdegen and Beaudot, *In the Bloody Railroad Cut at Gettysburg*, 212.
29. Pfanz, *Gettysburg – The First Day*, 122.
30. Patricia L. Faust, editor, *Historical Times Illustrated Encyclopedia of the Civil War* (New York, 1986), 224.
31. Ibid., 129.
32. *OR*, I:27:I:246.
33. Doubleday, *Chancellorsville & Gettysburg*, 134.
34. *OR*, I:27:III:460-1.
35. Ibid., I:27:III:458.
36. Sears, *Gettysburg*, 150.
37. *OR*, I:27:III:462.
38. Edwin C. Bearss with J. Parker Hills, *Receding Tide* (Washington, 2010), 302.
39. *OR*, I:27:III:461.
40. Ibid.
41. Sears, *Gettysburg*, 189.
42. *OR*, I:27:III:367.
43. Pfanz, *Gettysburg – The First Day*, 115.
44. James Longstreet, *From Manassas to Appomattox* (Mallard Press edition, New York, 1991), 357.
45. Pfanz, *Gettysburg – The First Day*, 150.
46. *OR*, I:27:I:702.
47. Pfanz, *Gettysburg – The First Day*, 137.

CHAPTER 3
"Hard Times at Gettysburg!"
1 July 1863

HOWARD, KNOWN TO HIS FAMILY as Otis, was ten years younger than Doubleday and had graduated from the U.S. Military Academy twelve years after him, but had already graduated from Bowdoin College, in Maine, before going to West Point. At the Academy he had graduated near the top of the class of 1854, which had included future Confederate generals Jeb Stuart, Dorsey Pender and Custis Lee (eldest son of the Confederate commander). He had gone into the small Ordnance branch of the Army and then had returned to the Point to teach mathematics. Although affable and pleasant he was unpopular with some of his fellow officers for being overly familiar with the enlisted men, and with others for being an overly pious Christian who opposed drinking and gambling. (He had studied theology with an Episcopal priest and had considered becoming a clergyman himself.) Perhaps due to some political connections in his home state of Maine, he had been given a brigadier's star early in the War (which is how he came to be senior in rank to older officers such as Hancock and Doubleday) and had commanded a brigade at the first battle of Bull Run. He had succeeded to the command of a division on the field at Antietam, and just three months back he had been appointed to command of the 11th Army Corps.

That corps was relatively new to the Army of the Potomac, although some of its units had been part of that army in its formative days, but they had missed all of its early campaigns when transferred to the area now known as West Virginia to form the core of a Mountain Department. The commander of that department, Major General John Charles Fremont, had been among the Union generals outsmarted and outmarched by Stonewall Jackson during the latter's famous Shenandoah Valley campaign of 1862. His forces, minus Fremont, had then briefly become the 1st Corps of Major General John Pope's Army of Virginia. When that army had been merged with the Army of the Potomac after losing the second battle of Bull Run, its 1st Corps had been redesignated the 11th Corps. (From that point on all Union corps were numbered consecutively throughout the U.S. Army, not as a subdivision of whatever army or department they belonged to, much as divisions have been numbered in the 20th and 21st centuries.)

The 11th Corps suffered from several morale problems. About half of the corps' regiments were composed primarily of German immigrants, most of whom had wanted a fellow German, Major General Franz Sigel, to command them, but the position had been given to Howard instead. To add to the Germans' disappointment, Howard's piety did not set well with the numerous free-thinkers among them. Then the corps' first fight as part of the Army of the Potomac had been the recent battle of Chancellorsville, where it had been its bad luck to be positioned on the army's far right when Stonewall Jackson's three large divisions had come bursting out of the almost impenetrable undergrowth of the Virginia Wilderness to fall on that very flank. The fact that many of the men had run without putting up much of a fight had not endeared them to the rest of the army, although, to be fair, the fault really lay not with the men of the corps but with Howard and with then-army-commander Hooker, neither of whom had taken proper precautions even though Jackson's forces had been seen moving toward that flank. But to the rest of the army, already somewhat prejudiced against recent immigrants, they were an unreliable bunch of foreigners. The men of the corps knew this, of course, and resented it.

General Schurz, one of the German-born officers of the corps and an influential politician (who had supported Abraham Lincoln's nomination as the Republican presidential candidate in 1860), upon receiving Howard's message, turned his division over to his senior brigade commander,

Brigadier General Alexander Schimmelfennig, and hurried on ahead of his troops to confer with Howard. On the way he passed frightened civilians fleeing from the town, one of whom yelled to him, "Hard times at Gettysburg! They are shooting and killing! What will become of us!"[1] He reached the area in time to see the ambulance wagon carrying General Reynolds' body go by on its way to Taneytown, and he joined Howard on Cemetery Hill at about 11:30 a.m. by his watch. (There was no such thing as Standard Time in 1863, so all times reported are suspect.)

The corps had broken camp near Emmitsburg at about 8 that morning (Schurz thought it was 7) and had been drenched by a local shower shortly afterwards. When they crossed the Mason-Dixon line into their home state, many Pennsylvanians had given three cheers and tossed their caps in the air. The day was hot and humid, and the condition of the Emmitsburg Road, muddy to start with, had been made even worse by the passage of the 1st Corps. The two divisions that turned off to the Taneytown Road found it and the crossroads leading to it too rocky, so the troops often marched in the fields along the edges, leaving the roadstead to the artillery and wagons. When Howard's order to hurry forward arrived, the troops tried to double-quick – a sort of jog – which caused many of them to discard extra clothing and other non-essentials to lighten their burdens. Four miles from town some of the corps artillery had their teams break into a trot, soon leaving the jogging gunners far behind as the rocky road jarred equipment and horse-feed loose from the caissons to fall in the road.

At about 12:30 p.m. Howard received a note from Wadsworth mistakenly reporting that the Confederates were retiring. However, a few minutes later a message came from Doubleday saying that he was not worried about his left but that his right was hard pressed. Looking in that direction, Howard and Schurz could see Confederates on Oak Hill, at the north end of Seminary Ridge, but in what numbers they couldn't tell. If the Rebels were few in number, Schurz later reported, then the Federals should push them "with all possible vigor," but if most of Lee's army was on hand, "then we had to establish ourselves in a position which would enable us to maintain ourselves until the arrival of re-inforcements. Either of these cases being possible, provision was to be made for both."[2] Howard knew, from the Rebels who had been captured, that the 1st Corps had been fighting part of Hill's corps of Lee's army, and Buford had sent him word that other Confederates were massing three or four miles north of the town. He told Schurz to form his and Barlow's divisions, with one battery each, on Oak Ridge, to the right of the 1st Corps, while Brigadier General Adolph von Steinwehr's 2nd Division and the rest of the corps artillery would occupy Cemetery Hill as a reserve.

At 1 p.m. Colonel Meysenburg sent a note to Major General Henry W. Slocum, commander of the 12th Corps, which was not part of the Left Wing, but was marching that day to a hamlet called Two Taverns, just five miles to the southeast down the road running over Cemetery Hill to Baltimore. The note merely said, "The general commanding directs me to inform you that Ewell's corps is advancing from York. The left wing of the Army of the Potomac is engaged with A. P. Hill's corps." Slocum, who was senior to Howard, had received the Pipe Creek Circular, and thus knew that Meade did not intend to fight at Gettysburg; so he interpreted this message as merely informational, not an appeal for help, and he did not respond.

An identical message was sent down to Emmitsburg to Dan Sickles, commander of the 3rd Corps, which was part of the Left Wing, but it was a long time in reaching him.

Meanwhile, Schurz's troops began to reach Cemetery Hill at about 12:30 p.m., out of breath and sweating from their four-mile jog. Schurz ordered Schimmelfennig to take his division through the town and deploy it to the right of the 1st Corps in two lines of battle. While passing through the town the soldiers saw many civilians "excited and scared to death, hurrying and scurrying in every direction."[3] Other citizens of the town were too frightened to venture far from their doors, but still managed to hand out food and water to some of the passing men. Anna Mary Young, a young woman who lived in the northern outskirts of the town, had gone with her family to the attic of their house to watch the distant battle, but suddenly it was not so distant anymore. "It was not until I saw the fences on our own premises torn down," she later remembered, "and cannon placed all around us, one battery just in our back yard, that I began to realize our danger. Then we shut up the house and went into the cellar, taking with us provisions to give our men, and rags for the wounded. Though the shells fell thick around us, shattering trees, knocking bricks out of the house, etc., Cousin Jennie stood on the cellar steps cutting bread, spreading it with apple-butter, and giving it to our poor men, who had been marched double-quick for miles without any breakfast. The poor fellows were so grateful, and would say, 'Courage ladies; we'll drive the rebs!'"[4]

Howard had meant for Schurz to occupy Oak Hill, a high point on Oak Ridge, which was an extension of the combined McPherson's and Seminary ridges north of the Chambersburg Pike. But when these Federals approached the high ground they found that it was already occupied by a sizable body of Confederates, so they had to deploy out in the open valley, facing northwest. Barlow's division soon arrived, and Schimmelfennig placed it to the right of his own division, its two brigades straddling the Mummasburg Road and stretching eastward to cover the Carlisle and Harrisburg roads. By then it was 2 p.m. on Schurz's watch. Among Barlow's men was Lieutenant Henry Hauschild, who had lived in Gettysburg before the war and was now returning to his old home on this the last day of his life. Confederate artillery began pounding Schurz's men as soon as they arrived.

Howard rode through the town with Barlow, sent word to Schurz to watch out for his right flank, and soon sent his brother and aide, Major Charles Howard, to find and consult with General Buford. Then he rode over to examine the 1st

Corps' position and consult with Wadsworth and Doubleday. He told the latter to watch out for his own left and that the 11th Corps would protect his right flank. He then returned to Cemetery Hill, where he remained throughout the rest of the day. Lieutenant Colonel Edward Salomon of the 82nd Illinois pointed out to Howard a sign in the cemetery that said, "Driving, riding and shooting on these grounds strictly prohibited. Any person violating this ordinance will be punished by fine and imprisonment." Just then a Confederate cannon shot struck the sign and knocked it to pieces. "Well," said the general, "the ordinance is rescinded: I think the shooting can go on."[5]

The Confederates who beat Schurz's troops to Oak Hill were part of the division of Major General Robert Rodes that Ewell had brought down from Carlisle. Rodes had been born in Virginia 34 years before, had graduated from the Virginia Military Institute in 1848 and had taught there, but he had later moved to Alabama. He had commanded an Alabama regiment at the first battle of Bull Run and a brigade through several subsequent campaigns, succeeding to temporary divisional command for the Chancellorsville campaign, in which he had performed a leading role in Stonewall Jackson's flank attack on Howard's corps well enough to earn promotion and the official command of his division. His performance this day would not be so stellar.

His division had marched south from Middletown on what, at Gettysburg, is known as the Carlisle Road, after Ewell had received word that Hill's corps was advancing to Gettysburg. Near 11 a.m., when the division had approached to within four miles of town, the sound of artillery fire could be heard by those in the column. Somewhere along the way Union cavalry videttes were encountered, who could harass the column but were far too few to stop it. When he had reached Oak Hill, Rodes could see Hill's troops to his right front, along Herr Ridge, and much of the Union 1st Corps facing Hill, but no Federal infantry facing in his direction. So, when the road descended Oak Ridge, most of the division turned to the right and followed a lesser road that ran off to the west. The last brigade in the column, some 1,400 Georgians commanded by Brigadier General George Doles, continued down the Carlisle Road and down into the flat plain and formed the left flank of the division about a mile and a quarter north of Gettysburg, with a battalion of picked sharpshooters from another brigade out front as skirmishers.

At the other end of Rodes' long line was a brigade consisting of about 1,470 men in four North Carolina regiments commanded by Brigadier General Alfred Iverson, a Georgia lawyer and railroad contractor, son of a congressman, who had served in the Mexican War and had later been commissioned as a lieutenant in the 1st U. S. Cavalry. As a captain in the Confederate Army he had been sent to North Carolina, where he had helped raise a regiment and had been elected its colonel. He had succeeded to brigade command the previous year, just prior to the battle of Antietam. Then he had made a very bad mistake. Instead of recommending one of his own officers to succeed him as colonel of his old regiment he had nominated an old friend who was then lieutenant colonel of another regiment and serving down in South Carolina. Twenty-six of his officers had signed a protest to the adjutant and inspector general of the Confederate Army. Iverson had refused to forward this document, but the officers sent it anyway. In response he had ordered the arrest of all 26 officers, but eventually he had backed down. However, by then he had earned the enmity of most of his brigade. With all of his officers ready to believe the worst of him, there were intimations of cowardice at Chancellorsville (he had been wounded while off looking for reinforcements, out of sight of his brigade) and complaints that he had recently gotten drunk up at Carlisle (which he had, but so had several other officers, including Rodes). In short, it was a brigade at war with its commander.

Rodes shifted his line so as to put it almost perpendicular

to Doubleday's line along McPherson's Ridge. Iverson's men occupied what was know as the Forney Woods, just west of the Mummasburg Road, facing south, and Colonel E. A. O'Neal's five Alabama regiments, totaling about 1,800 men, were on Oak Hill, east of the same road, behind two batteries of artillery. This left a sizable gap between O'Neal's line and that of Doles' brigade down on the plain, but Rodes' largest brigade, 2,300 North Carolinians led by Brigadier General Junius Daniel, formed a couple of hundred yards behind Iverson's brigade west of the Mummasburg Road, and, due to its size and the direction that the road ran (northwest), it extended even farther west than Iverson's line. Rodes' was one of the two divisions in Lee's army that had five brigades, but the brigade of Brigadier General S. Dodson Ramseur had been guarding the wagons at the tail end of the divisional column, and when it finally came up Rodes held it in reserve on Oak Hill.

Instead of using Ramseur's Brigade, or part of it, to fill the gap, Rodes ordered the 3rd Alabama of O'Neal's Brigade to connect with Daniel's Brigade on its right and his 5th Alabama Regiment (not to be confused with the 5th Alabama Battalion over in Heth's Division) to connect with Doles' Brigade on its left. O'Neal later reported that Rodes said he would take personal command of these two regiments, but complained that "Why my brigade was thus deprived of two regiments, I have never been informed."[6] The brigade that O'Neal commanded had belonged to Rodes himself before that officer had succeeded to divisional command, and he still kept a close eye on it. Evidently Rodes did not feel that O'Neal was well qualified to succeed him, for he had recommended that the War Department send some other officer to take over the brigade, and, possibly on Rodes' recommendation, Lee had blocked O'Neal's promotion to brigadier general.

Rodes' infantry, except for Doles' Brigade and part of O'Neal's, was deployed in woods and thus hidden from the Federals, but as soon as the two batteries were in position in front of O'Neal's line, they opened fire on Union batteries on

McPherson's Ridge that were already dueling with Hill's artillery on Herr Ridge, effectively serving notice of Ewell's arrival. Three Union batteries, including Calef's horse artillery (which Colonel Wainwright called "the crack Batt'y of the army"), moved to a swale behind McPherson's Woods that effectively divided McPherson's Ridge in two, and changed front to face north toward this new threat.[7] Wainwright eventually sent Calef's battery to rejoin Buford's cavalry, but two 1st Corps batteries dueled with Rodes' guns for almost an hour.

Some of the Union infantry also changed position. Two regiments of Stone's brigade, that had been facing west near the McPherson barn, also moved into the swale that divided the ridge and faced to the north. Cutler's three regiments that had returned to their position north of the Chambersburg Pike were in a very perilous position, with the Confederates forming to their right rear. Even if the Rebel infantry was hidden, the guns on Oak Hill were not and they could enfilade Cutler's line. He asked Wadsworth for orders and was told to take any position he thought proper. He turned his regiments to face Oak Hill but still felt exposed so he soon moved them to Sheads' Woods on Oak Ridge, less than a half-mile south of Oak Hill. Soon the six regiments of Brigadier General Henry Baxter's 2nd Brigade of Robinson's 2nd Division of the 1st Corps came up and formed between Cutler and the Mummasburg Road, facing east or northeast.

Baxter, then 42, had, as a young man, participated in the California gold rush, and without military experience, he had entered the war as a captain in the 7th Michigan. He had been wounded in the stomach during the Peninsula Campaign. Then, promoted to lieutenant colonel, he had been shot through a lung at Antietam and in the shoulder at Fredericksburg while leading an assault crossing of the Rappahannock River, and had then been jumped up two grades again to brigadier general in time for the recent battle of Chancellorsville, where, for a change, he did not get wounded, probably due mostly to the fact that the 1st Corps saw little action in that campaign.

About this time, Major Brown, Ewell's stepson, returned from Cashtown to find Ewell and Rodes both busy posting a battery near the Carlisle Road. (As historian Harry Pfanz has pointed out, neither general was an artillery specialist and both could surely have found something more useful to do at such a time.) Brown delivered Lee's admonition not to bring on a battle until the rest of the army had arrived. But, as Ewell later explained in his report, "By the time this message reached me, General A. P. Hill had already been warmly engaged with a large body of the enemy in his front, and Carter's artillery battalion, of Rodes' division, had opened with fine effect on the flank of the same body, which was rapidly preparing to attack me, while fresh masses were moving into position in my front. It was too late to avoid an engagement without abandoning the position already taken up, and I determined to push the attack vigorously."[8] Ewell evidently interpreted the arrival of Schurz's and Baxter's men as preparations for an attack upon Rodes, or at least so he and Rodes chose to present it in their reports as a justification for the attack they soon launched themselves. Ewell sent Brown and another staff officer to find General Early and have him hurry his division into position on Rodes' left, facing the 11th Corps with orders "to attack at once."[9]

Soon thereafter Ewell was found by Major A. Reid Venable of Jeb Stuart's staff, who had been sent out by the latter to find Lee's main force. Ewell sent him on to Lee, who was no doubt glad to finally learn what had become of Stuart, if not happy to learn that he was so far away. Lee sent Venable back to Stuart with orders to join the rest of the army at Gettysburg.

At about 2:30 p.m. on his watch (1:30 on some others), "Finding that the enemy was rash enough to come out from the woods to attack me," as Rodes later put it, "I determined to meet him when he got to the foot of the hill I occupied, and, as he did so, I caused Iverson's brigade to advance, and at the same moment gave in person to O'Neal the order to attack, indicating to him precisely the point to which he was to direct the left of the four regiments then under his orders. . . ." But Iverson advanced with only three regiments, as he considered both the 3rd and 5th regiments of his brigade as being detached and under Rodes' direct command, whereas Doles considered only the 5th Alabama, connecting with Doles, as detached, for he had considered the alignment of the 3rd Alabama with Daniel's Brigade "temporary and unimportant." Rodes also reported that, "Daniel was at the same moment instructed to advance to support Iverson, if necessary; if not, to attack on his right as soon as possible."[10]

His brigade commanders do not seem to have understood Rodes' orders in the same way that the latter presented them in his report. Iverson evidently thought that O'Neal was to advance first, and accordingly he sent a staff officer to watch that brigade and did not begin his own attack until O'Neal's men stepped off. These did not go far because they soon came up against three of Baxter's regiments deployed along the southwest side of an oak grove, facing north, and they also took fire from part of the 11th Corps, which enfiladed their left flank. Rodes went to order the 5th Alabama to join the rest of the brigade and found O'Neal there with this lone regiment instead of with his three attacking regiments.

The 5th went forward, detaching a company to occupy a barn to protect its left by exchanging fire with parts of the 11th Corps. But this extra regiment was not enough to turn the tide, and the Alabamans soon came to a halt, briefly exchanged fire with the Federals, and then fell back to a fence line, where they were rallied by O'Neal and Rodes. Their retreat was followed by four companies from Schimmelfinnig's brigade of the 11th Corps, sent out as skirmishers, who claimed to have captured 300 of O'Neal's men and who took temporary possession of the barn. One of the Confederates captured at the barn had a brother in the very regiment that captured him, and the two were briefly reunited for the first time since they had left Germany. But the Union brother was killed by a Rebel bullet even as his Confederate brother was being led off into captivity.

Captain Hubert Dilger's battery of the 11th Corps had found some high ground in a field and had helped to repulse O'Neal's attack. But Dilger was more interested in dueling with several Confederate batteries. His battery was from Ohio but Dilger was from Germany, where he had served in the army of Baden. He was known in the Union army as "Leatherbreeches" because of his habit of wearing doeskin trousers, and he was an excellent artilleryman. He and his battery had formed the rear guard for the entire corps when it had retreated from Stonewall Jackson's flank attack at Chancellorsville. This day the fire of his six "Napoleon" 12-pounder smoothbore cannon was tearing the Rebel 4-gun battery of Captain R. C. M. Page to pieces. Page sent word of his plight to Lieutenant Colonel Thomas H. Carter, his battalion commander, and Carter came dashing up, took in Page's situation without stopping, and hurried on to confront Rodes. He was "as mad as a hornet," he later admitted, and demanded to know "what fool put that battery yonder?" This, of course, was no way for a lieutenant colonel to speak to a major general, and Carter later said, "There was an awkward pause & a queer expression on the faces of all – Rodes included – & then he said quietly, 'you had better take it away Carter.'"[11] A staff officer quietly explained to Carter as he turned to go that Rodes had posted that battery there himself.

Iverson's brigade had advanced almost simultaneously with O'Neal's, but had to wheel to its right in order to close up with O'Neal's three regiments, which caused it to advance to the southeast, heading directly toward the field just north of Sheads' Woods. His officers, still upset about being arrested by him the year before, later blamed Iverson for misaligning his regiments so that they approached the Federal line at an angle and for not sending out skirmishers to precede the main line and warn of any surprises. There were even accusations of cowardice and drunkenness on his part. Be that as it may, the brigade had to cross about 600 yards of open fields, which exposed it to the fire of Union batteries farther south, and most of the Federal infantry they were approaching was stationed in woods, making their line hard to discern.

There were six regiments in Baxter's Federal brigade. Three of them were facing north, dealing with O'Neal's attack, but the other three were facing west. General John Robinson, Baxter's division commander, saw Iverson's North Carolinians coming and also saw that there was too large a gap between Baxter's line and Cutler's. Since O'Neal's attack had now been driven off, he ordered Baxter to move his other three regiments to face this new threat and ordered his other brigade, commanded by Brigadier General Gabriel Paul, to move up and take their place, facing north.

Although there were six regiments in Baxter's brigade, they totaled only about 1,400 men – about the same number that Iverson had. However, they had the advantage of standing still on the slightly higher ground of Oak Ridge, some with the cover of trees and fences, as the Confederates advanced across the open fields to their front "in gallant style," as one Rebel put it, "as evenly as if on parade." A Union soldier said the field was "swarming with Confederates, who came sweeping on in magnificent order, with perfect alignment, guns at right shoulder and colors to the front...."[12] The 11th Pennsylvania, at the left end of Baxter's line, opened fire, but the Confederates responded with a Rebel yell and kept coming. The next three Union regiments to the north took position behind a low stone wall, but they were so far up the slope that they soon lost sight of the Confederates as they crossed the lower ground. As one of them later remembered, the Federals "quietly awaited the enemy to come within short range." Waiting quietly for thousands of enemy soldiers to advance upon you unseen is not an easy thing to do. Baxter told them, "Keep cool, men, and fire low." (Soldiers positioned on higher ground often tended to shoot too high, for black-powder rifles were relatively low-velocity weapons that had to lob their bullets in a fairly high arc over anything but short range.)

When the Rebels were within 50 yards of the wall behind

which Baxter's men waited (not only short range but practically point-blank), the commander of the 83rd Pennsylvania shouted, "Up men, and fire." The Federals stood up and poured in a volley, and, because Baxter's line was longer and ran at a slight angle to Iverson's line, some of his men were firing into the Confederate flank. Iverson's line was brought up short and staggered under the volley, which one Rebel described as "striking down hundreds." But another Confederate proudly recorded that "the line did not recoil as O'Neal's had done." This might have been due more to the fact that it would have been almost as suicidal to retreat across the open field under such fire as to advance. A few Confederates tried to charge, but were quickly shot down, including the colonel of the 23rd North Carolina, who, lying mortally wounded, later vowed that Iverson would never command the brigade again. Those who wanted to live hit the dirt, and one Rebel recorded that "to rise from the ground meant certain death."[13] And, although some were sheltered by muddy low spots in the ground, others were not even safe lying down. One dead Confederate was later found to have five bullet holes in his head.

The 12th North Carolina, at the right end of Iverson's line, was the farthest from the Union position and was sheltered by a knoll to its front, but at the other end of the line, where the Rebels were close up to the Union wall and under a crossfire from the Federals farther north, many of them began waving handkerchiefs or anything else they had as tokens of surrender. The Federals weren't sure how to respond at first; some of the Confederates might be giving up but others were still firing back. Baxter solved the problem by shouting to his men, "Up boys, and give them steel." However, as one of his sergeants later wrote, "it was not a charge at all, only a run forward to drive in Iverson's men who were willing enough to surrender."[14] General Robinson reported the capture of 1,000 Rebels and three battleflags, but this was evidently an exaggeration; another Federal estimated the number of prisoners taken at 400, and many of those had been wounded. Even so it was a tremendous loss to Iverson's brigade, which numbered only about 1,300 men to start with. There were also, of course, many killed and probably some who were wounded but not captured. Except for the 12th North Carolina, Iverson's regiments seemed to have suffered about 70 percent casualties in less than an hour of fighting.

The Federals could not linger, however, for Confederate skirmishers in a wheatfield beside the Mummasburg Road were firing into them, and their prisoners as well, and more Rebels were approaching. Daniel's Brigade had followed about 200 yards behind Iverson's Brigade and, initially, somewhat to its right, or west. But as Iverson's line swung more to the southeast Daniel kept going south so as to come out from behind Iverson and extend his right flank. When Iverson ran into more than he could handle, he asked Daniel for help and was promised one regiment while the rest of Daniel's men would protect his right by attacking other Federals farther south. On Iverson's other flank, the 5th Alabama of O'Neal's Brigade was belatedly advancing, and Ramseur's Brigade was being sent in where O'Neal's main body had been repulsed.

Paul's Federal brigade of Robinson's division arrived at the northern end of the 1st Corps line just in time to confront this new threat. Baxter's brigade was almost out of ammunition, and most of it was withdrawn to supporting positions. Paul, who had graduated from West Point back in 1834, commanded about 1,500 men in five regiments, but early in the fight a bullet hit him in the right temple and came out his left eye socket (he survived for another twenty years, but blind), and there was some confusion about which of his colonels was now in command. However, Robinson was on hand to supervise this brigade himself. He had been five classes behind Paul at West Point and had never graduated, being dismissed for a breach of discipline. He had, nevertheless, managed to wangle a commission not long after the time when he should have graduated, and had served in the Mexican War. As a captain he had been in command of Fort McHenry, at Baltimore, when this war had begun and had successfully prevented its capture during the riots there in April of 1861. Since then he had commanded a regiment, a brigade, and now, since Chancellorsville, a division. He had horses shot out from under him twice this day but lived to win a Medal of Honor the next year at Spotsylvania.

Two of Paul's regiments, the 16th Maine and the 94th New York, took fire from Confederates in the wheat field to the north of them as they came up. These Rebels were probably skirmishers belonging to Iverson's Brigade. The Federals fixed bayonets and charged, driving the Confederates back, then fell back themselves to the woods on Oak Ridge. Colonel Adrian Root of the 94th soon discovered he was now in command of Paul's brigade, and, in such capacity, he ordered his own regiment to charge once more. It got as far as the Mummasburg Road, where it fired on a Confederate battery, but Robinson soon ordered it to return to the woods. As Root was carrying this out a shell bursting over his head stunned him and knocked him from his horse.

The 94th New York and the 16th Maine soon formed the left, or southern, end of the brigade's line. South of them, extending their left, was Baxter's brigade. Cutler's brigade had moved to the east side of Oak Ridge, in a more sheltered position, where it waited for ammunition wagons to come up. But while it waited a staff officer rode up and asked for three regiments to be sent to support the batteries near the seminary. (As the officer gestured in that direction a Confederate shell took off the pointing hand.) The 14th Brooklyn and the 56th and 147th New York were the regiments sent, and their ammunition supply was replenished at their new position. Soon Baxter's exhausted and thirsty men also made their way south, looking for ammunition, and took position south of the railroad cut in support of a battery. South of them and farther west was Stones' brigade of Doubleday's division, with two of its three regiments formed along the Chambersburg Pike, facing northeast, and the third south of the road near the McPherson house and barn, facing west.

As Daniel's Confederates moved south they started taking

fire from Stone's regiments in the pike, and Daniel realized that if he wheeled his own line to the southeast, as Iverson had done, these Federals would enfilade it. (This Union line was presenting its own flank to Hill's two divisions, farther west, but, due to Lee's restraining directive, Hill could not take advantage of this.) Consequently Daniel, who was a highly competent officer (West Point class of 1851), split his command, sending one regiment and a battalion on south to take on Stone while turning two regiments towards Oak Ridge and apparently holding one regiment in reserve. The two regiments on the left came up on the right of Iverson's 12th North Carolina, and at least one of them got to within about 50 yards of Sheads' Woods before Union fire striking both of its flanks as well its front stopped them. The colonel of O'Neal's 3rd Alabama, which had advanced along with Daniel's brigade (Rodes' order to keep contact with it not having been rescinded), sent to Daniel for orders, but Daniel, not having been told to take control of this regiment, said he had no orders to give it. The 3rd Alabama therefore went off to the east and joined up with Ramseur's brigade. Its departure further exposed the left flank of Daniel's two regiments that faced east, and at least one of these fell back another 50 yards and changed front to face south, but soon returned to near Iverson's 12th North Carolina, facing east.

Ramseur was young for his position, only 26, and had only been out of West Point a year when the war began. But in the Confederate service he had risen rapidly from captain of a battery to colonel of a regiment to general of a brigade. His men considered him "impetuous, impatient, and aggressive," noting that whenever there was a fight he wasn't happy if he was not allowed to pitch in.[15] His four North Carolina regiments, numbering only about 1,100 men, moved south along the east face of Oak Ridge but did not arrive in time to witness the repulse of O'Neal's Brigade or the virtual destruction of Iverson's. Rodes told Ramseur to send two of his regiments to the left to help O'Neal and two to the right to help Iverson. Ramseur himself went with these latter two (the 14th and 30th N.C.) and discovered that three of Iverson's regiments had been "almost annihilated" but hooked up with the 3rd Alabama, just coming up, and added it to his command.[16] A lieutenant from Iverson's skirmishers warned him of the dangers of attacking Robinson's Federals from the same direction that Iverson's Brigade had used and evidently gave him a good idea of just where Robinson's line ran. So Ramseur decided to mass his forces against the apex of the Union line, where the part that faced west met the part that faced north.

Meanwhile, some of his skirmishers, preceding his other two regiments, took cover behind a stone wall where the Mummasburg Road crossed the ridge and from there fired at the 104th New York and the 13th Massachusetts a couple of hundred yards farther south, on the part of Robinson's line that faced north. These Federals promptly charged and captured at least 60 of the skirmishers. (Some of the captured Rebels were claimed by both Union regiments.) The road at this point cut into the crest of the ridge, forming another natural trench and potential trap, like the railroad cut, and as more Rebels arrived (some Federals thought they were a whole brigade) and scrambled up the steep southern side of the road the 13th Massachusetts "let them have it" as one Bay-Stater remembered.[17] Another 132 Confederate prisoners were claimed as a result of this encounter.

About this time Robinson received orders to withdraw, the reasons for which we will see later.

Colonel Roy Stone's brigade of Doubleday's division was somewhat unique. For one thing, it contained only three regiments, but these were fairly large for that period of the war (roughly 450 men each). Little provision had been made in the Union army so far for the recruitment of replacements for old regiments, so they tended to wither away as time went by, not only due to combat losses but also, often even more so, from disease. Already, Stone's three regiments each fielded less than half their beginning strengths, but many older regiments were now down to a third or even a quarter of their initial 1,000 men. So Stone's brigade had a reasonable number of men for a brigade in 1863, which is probably why it had not been assigned any more regiments.

Another way in which this brigade was unique is that all three regiments were from the same state. (While it was Confederate policy to brigade regiments from the same state together, Union commanders preferred to mix them up, as this decreased the ability of state governors to interfere with them in such matters as selection of brigade commanders.) Two of Stone's regiments, the 149th and 150th Pennsylvania, were also known as the 2nd and 3rd Bucktails. They took this name from a famous regiment, the 13th Pennsylvania Reserve (also known as the 1st Pennsylvania Rifles or the 42nd Pennsylvania Volunteers), which had been formed in the early days of the war from among proven marksmen who wore bucks' tails attached to their caps as evidence of their prowess, and who had, for this reason, become known as the Bucktails. Because of their marksmanship they had often been used as skirmishers. Stone had been that regiment's major (third in command) until August of the previous year, when he had gone home to Pennsylvania to recruit what he had hoped would be a whole brigade of such men. As it turned out, he had only managed to fill these two regiments (though whether they were all such gifted marksman is not known), for which service he had been named colonel of the 149th. The two regiments had served in the defenses of Washington, D.C., for a while before joining the Army of the Potomac, and from that time and for the rest of the war a detachment served as guards for President Lincoln.

To fill out his brigade, Stone had been given the 143rd Pennsylvania, another relatively new regiment. The brigade had eventually been assigned to the 1st Corps and was present with it during the Chancellorsville campaign, but the corps had not seen much fighting during that time. Besides having only three regiments, and having a company down at

Washington guarding the President, the brigade was missing another company that day that was stationed south of the seminary serving as the division's provost guard (military police). Stone's effective force had been even further diminished early that afternoon when General Meredith had ordered him to send one company from each of his regiments far out to the west as skirmishers. Meredith was not Stone's division commander, nor did he have any special assignment from Doubleday to oversee this part of the field, nor did Stone, who had considerable experience with skirmishing, think he needed skirmishers out there; there was nothing to obscure his view, so he could spot any Confederate move from the west long before it came close. But a colonel must do what a general tells him to do, so he sent the skirmishers westward almost to Willoughby Run.

Stone did receive one reinforcement about noon, small in number but with high morale. "While we were watching and waiting," Major Chamberlain of the 150th Pennsylvania remembered, "our attention was called to a man of rather bony frame . . . who approached from the direction of the town moving with a deliberate step and carrying in his right hand an Enfield rifle at a 'trail.' At any time his figure would have been noticeable, but it was doubly so at such a moment, from his age – which evidently neared three-score and ten – and from the somewhat startling peculiarity of his dress. The latter consisted of dark trousers with waistcoat, a blue 'swallow-tail' coat with burnished brass buttons such as used to be affected by well-to-do gentlemen of the old school about forty years ago, and a high black silk hat, from which most of the original gloss had long departed – of a shape to be found only in the fashion plates of a remote past. . . ." This was John Burns, a cobbler and former constable, who lived in the western part of Gettysburg, a veteran of the War of 1812. He asked Chamberlain if he could fight with his regiment. The major agreed, but then referred him to his regiment's colonel, Langhorne Wister, who was just approaching. Wister questioned Burns briefly and then consented to let him fight, adding "I wish there were many more like you." But he advised Burns to go join the Iron Brigade in McPherson's woods, where he would be more sheltered from both the sun and Rebel bullets. "With apparent reluctance," Chamberlain remembered, "as if he preferred the open field, he moved towards the woods."[18]

When Stone's brigade had first taken position near the McPherson buildings almost all of it had faced west, but fire from Rodes' artillery, coming in from the north, had enfiladed that line, causing Stone to move more of his troops to face north along the Chambersburg Pike, with another company of skirmishers going farther north, probably deployed along or near the bed of the unfinished railroad. Only the 150th regiment continued to face west. But now Confederate artillery to the west could enfilade this new position along the pike, and, while Hill's infantry was being held back by Lee, no such restraint had been placed on his gunners, who could literally bowl their shots right down the turnpike. Stone countered with a simple ruse that worked: He sent the colors of the 149th to a small fort that Buford's cavalrymen had constructed earlier out of fence rails on the crest of the ridge some distance to the northwest. The Rebel gunners naturally assumed that the whole regiment had advanced and was hidden in the wheat near its colors and so changed their aiming point accordingly. The artillery fire was thus diverted, but now a new threat approached in the form of Confederate infantry.

Private Avery Harris of the 143rd was out on the north-facing skirmish line when he saw Daniel's Brigade approaching Stone's right front in well ordered formations. "Don't they do that fine?" he wrote. "But if they don't change direction, we will take them in flank. All eyes to the front now. They are swinging their right now, and that means us." But when part of Daniel's Brigade, at the extreme right flank of Rodes' Division, approached from the north, Colonel Stone sent his 149th regiment north to the unfinished railroad. As Pvt. Harris put it, "Old Roy Stone is after a big chunk of Glory for his Tails and don't intend the 143rd to have any of it."[19]

The 149th formed along the north rim of the railroad cut in a single line, with only their heads and arms exposed, the skirmishers taking position on their right, and Lieutenant Colonel Walton Dwight (the regiment's commander since Stone had been elevated to brigade command) told his Bucktails to "take deliberate aim at the knees of the enemy as he came up," but to hold their fire until they came within close range.[20]

The Rebels advanced, the second line closely following the one ahead of it, to within short range and halted at a fence that ran along slightly higher ground than that to its front, where the leading regiment fired a volley at the 149th's colors, still off to that regiment's left, and the Federals responded with a well-aimed volley as the Confederates climbed the fence. "Its effect on the enemy was terrible," Dwight reported, "he being at the time brigade *en masse*, at 9-pace interval. He now broke to the rear in great confusion. In the meantime I had ordered my regiment to load, when the enemy advanced the second time, and made a most desperate effort to carry my position by assault, in which we handsomely repulsed him by reserving our fire until we could almost reach him with the muzzles of our pieces. Again he fell back. This fight was of the most desperate character, we losing heavily, the enemy's dead and wounded completely covering the ground in our front."[21] Then the 149th also fell back, abandoning the railroad cut and returning to a dry ditch that ran along the south edge of the Chambersburg Pike, not, as Daniel believed, because of his attack, but because a Rebel battery on Herr Ridge was enfilading the Union position in the cut. Some of the Federals had a hard time climbing up the south bank of the cut where it was deepest, some were shot in the process, and some were captured when they couldn't get out before the Confederates came up again.

This second assault by Daniel's brigade consisted of the 45th North Carolina and the 2nd N.C. Battalion again attacking the railroad cut from the north while the 32nd North Carolina, which had not come up in time to participate in the first attack, was to move farther west and swing around so as to come in on the Federals' left flank. The 53rd North Carolina was to make a simultaneous assault to the east, against Oak Ridge, while Daniel's remaining regiment, the 43rd North Carolina, was held in reserve to support either attack. As they advanced, the 45th and the 2nd Battalion took several casualties from the fire of the 149th and 143rd Pennsylvania, and some of the Rebels sought cover in the railroad cut. Others got as far as the fence running along the north side of the pike before being shot down.

Many of the Rebels discovered, as others, both Federal and Confederate, had before them, that the railroad cut was a mixed blessing. An officer on Daniel's staff who had picked up a musket from a fallen soldier later recalled climbing the south embankment of the cut with considerable difficulty, taking aim at a Union officer and pulling the trigger. He didn't know whether he hit his target or not, for the recoil sent him sliding to the bottom of the cut, losing his hat and ripping his pants in the process. As he stood up a bullet or shell fragment hit him, and his contribution to the fight was over.

On the Union side, Roy Stone was wounded in the hip at about the time that his 149th regiment had abandoned the cut, and he was carried to the shelter of the McPherson barn. An officer brought word to Colonel Wister of the 150th that he was now in command of the brigade and added that a large force of Rebel infantry was heading their way. Taking note of the furious musketry all along the front of the other two regiments, Wister divided his own regiment into two battalions, intending to leave one, under his regiment's major, to hold his position facing west, and taking the other, under his lieutenant colonel, to reinforce the line facing north. But somehow his intention was not made clear, and both battalions followed him to the north, where they came up on the left of the 149th just in time to intercept the 32nd North Carolina as it came up on the Confederate right. One battalion of the Bucktails hit these Rebels with a volley at the range of only 50 yards, and it so staggered them that the Pennsylvanians were able to pour in another volley before the Confederates could respond. Colonel Wister then ordered the 149th to charge and called on the right wing of the 150th to follow him. He led it to within pistol range (say 25 yards) of the Confederates, where it fired three volleys before the surviving Rebels retreated. The 150th then fell back to the westward-facing line it had previously occupied.

The 149th was still disorganized after its retreat from the railroad cut, without its colors to rally on, and some said that Colonel Dwight was drunk. Drunk or not he was certainly wounded, having been hit in the thigh, but, using his sword as a cane, in obedience to Wister's order, he led his regiment back toward the cut, clearing the field between the road and the cut of Rebels and saving a few Union wounded who were lying there. While checking the brigade's right, Wister was shot in the mouth and, unable to speak clearly, turned over command to Colonel Edmund L. Dana of the 143rd.

Daniel had, meanwhile, pulled back his 45th regiment and 2nd Battalion to the crest of the rise where they had formed before, some 40 yards north of the railroad cut, and began to reorganize them for another attack. But this time he would not send them south against Stone's brigade but east against Oak Ridge. To keep Stone's Federals busy he would again send the 32nd North Carolina to try to take them in flank. Two things probably led to this decision: He had learned that Ramseur's Brigade was preparing to attack Oak Ridge from the north, and he wanted to hit it from the west at the same time; and he could see that Hill's troops, off to the west, were finally beginning to stir.

The 12th North Carolina of Iverson's Brigade joined in Daniel's attack, on its left flank. Its commander, 23-year-old Lieutenant Colonel William S. Davis, had only 170 men, but he hadn't seen much Union activity in his front for some time. He had heard firing off to his left and his right, and he figured the Federals had heard it too and had to be worrying about their flanks, so he reasoned that if his troops suddenly rose up with a Rebel yell and charged the woods to their front any Federals there might run away. It worked like a charm, probably because there were few Union defenders to his front, if any, as his regiment apparently struck an empty space between Paul's brigade to the north and the troops of Baxter and Cutler to the south.

Just south of Davis's small regiment, the 53rd North Carolina of Daniel's Brigade also entered the woods on Oak Ridge and then swung to the south. This regiment and the 43rd North Carolina, on its right, then advanced on Battery B of the 4th U.S. Artillery, but found their movement blocked by the railroad cut. The 45th North Carolina and 2nd North Carolina Battalion advanced to the southeast, north of and parallel with the railroad bed, and claimed the capture of 400 or 500 Federals and several flags as well as recovering the colors of the 20th North Carolina that had been captured earlier by the 97th N.Y. At the far end of Daniel's line, the 32nd North Carolina again tried to flank the northward-facing part of Stone's brigade, and, since the 150th Pennsylvania was no longer blocking its way, it was able to do so this time. It then waited until Brockenbrough's Virginians of Heth's Division came up on its right, driving Stone's skirmishers before them.

The presence of a strong Confederate force on its left flank caused the 149th Pennsylvania to swing back its left, forming a sort of diagonal line between the right of the 150th, which was facing west or northwest, and the 143rd, which was facing north or northeast. With many of the brigade's higher officers out with wounds, however, there was quite a bit of confusion in the ranks. Some men from the 149th entered the McPherson barn, which was full of wounded men, and used it as a make-shift fort, firing from its ventilation slits. But Colonel Dana, now commanding the brigade, decided that if his three regiments stayed where they were they would soon be captured or destroyed, so he gave the order to fall back, which they did in good order, though with men of the three regiments somewhat intermingled. They formed a new line in the low ground in front of Seminary Ridge, and when the Confederates who followed them crested McPherson's Ridge the Federals gave them a volley and charged them, which brought the Rebels up short. Meanwhile, the Confederates captured about 350 Federals in the McPherson barn, most of whom were wounded. The Bucktail Brigade then fell back again and took position amid some 1st Corps batteries in a peach orchard on the west slope and crest of Seminary Ridge. Nearly two thirds of its men had been killed, wounded or captured. Daniel's Brigade lost about a third of its numbers that day. General Daniel later found a hole in the crown of his hat from a bullet that had missed taking off the top of his head by about an inch.

Endnotes

1. Pfanz, *Gettysburg – The First Day*, 138.
2. *OR*, I:27:I:727.
3. Pfanz, *Gettysburg – The First Day*, 141.
4. Wheeler, *Witness to Gettysburg*, 143.
5. Gregory A. Coco, *A Strange and Blighted Land* (Gettysburg, 1995), 12.
6. *OR*, I:27:II:592.
7. Pfanz, *Gettysburg – The First Day*, 157.
8. *OR*, I:27:II:444.
9. Bowden and Ward, *Last Chance for Victory*, 163.
10. *OR*, I:27:II:553.
11. Pfanz, *Gettysburg – The First Day*, 169.
12. Ibid., 171.
13. Ibid., 172.
14. Ibid., 174-5.
15. Ibid., 190.
16. *OR*, I:27:II:587.
17. Pfanz, *Gettysburg – The First Day*, 188.
18. Wheeler, *Witness to Gettysburg*, 137.
19. Pfanz, *Gettysburg – The First Day*, 197.
20. *OR*, I:27:I:342.
21. Ibid.

CHAPTER 4
"The Portrait of Hell"
1 July 1863

WHEN HARRY HETH SAW Rodes' troops attack, and saw that attack stall, he rode to find generals Hill and Lee. "Rodes is very heavily engaged," he said, "had I not better attack?" But Lee replied, "No; I am not prepared to bring on a general engagement today – Longstreet is not up." However, when Heth returned to his division he saw that some Federals (probably Stone's brigade) that had been facing his troops were now turning to fight Rodes. "I reported this fact to General Lee," he later wrote, "and again requested to be permitted to attack. Permission was given."[1] Hill was on hand and either ordered or allowed Heth to again attack alone without waiting for Pender's Division to join in. Brockenbrough's small brigade of Virginians formed Heth's left this time, just south of the Chambersburg Pike, with Pettigrew's large brigade in the center and what was left of Archer's Brigade, about 500 men now under Colonel Birkett Fry, on the right. Davis's shattered brigade did not participate and remained north of the railroad cut.

As we have seen, Brockenbrough's brigade came up on the right of the 32nd North Carolina and helped to drive Stone's Federals from McPherson's Ridge. Opposite Brockenbrough's right and Pettigrew's left was the Iron Brigade, still occupying McPherson's woods somewhat in advance of, or farther west than, the 150th Pennsylvania's position by the McPherson buildings. This woods bordered Willoughby Run, which ran slightly east of south just there, before the high ground of McPherson's Ridge forced it to turn to the southwest near the southern edge of the woods. The 19th Indiana held the left of the Iron Brigade's line, just inside the woods on the east side of the Run just before it turned to the southwest; the 24th

Michigan, the brigade's newest and largest regiment, held the center, its line curving away from the stream; and the 7th Wisconsin held the right end of the line well back in the woods, facing northwest. The 2nd Wisconsin was in reserve behind the 7th. Doubleday regarded McPherson's woods as a key position and had told the Iron Brigade to hold it at all hazards.

It was the 7th Wisconsin that John Burns joined up with after being sent into the woods by Colonel Wister. Sergeant George Eustice of that regiment remembered that "We boys began to poke fun at him . . . as we thought no civilian in his senses would show himself in such a place. Finding that he had really come to fight, I wanted to put a cartridge box on him . . . Slapping his pantaloons pocket, he replied, 'I can get my hands in here quicker than in a box. I'm not used to them new-fangled things.' In answer to the question what possessed him to come out there at such a time, he replied that the rebels had either driven away or milked his cows, and that he was going to be even with them. About this time the enemy began to advance. Bullets were flying thicker and faster, and we hugged the ground about as close as we could. Burns got behind a tree and surprised us all. . . . He was as calm and collected as any veteran on the ground."[2] Burns went out to the skirmish line, where he took a bead on a Confederate officer who was riding straight at him at high speed. He shot the Rebel out of the saddle, and the horse ran on into the Union lines.

South of the Iron Brigade was Colonel Chapman Biddle's 1st Brigade of Doubleday's, now Rowley's, 3rd Division of the 1st Corps, but it was far back on the reverse slope of McPherson's Ridge except for the 80th New York Volunteers (20th N.Y. Militia), which was posted on the crest of the ridge but still far to the east of the Iron Brigade's left flank. Beyond Biddle's four regiments there was only Gamble's cavalry, most of which was even farther back, on Seminary Ridge, except for the 8th Illinois Cavalry, which was watching the Hagerstown Road from McPherson's Ridge, well to the south of Biddle's position.

Between Pettigrew's right and Archer's left ran the Old Mill Road, and about a quarter of a mile down that road, to the east, on a bluff overlooking Willoughby Run, sat the big brick house occupied by Amelia Harmon and her aunt. Still up in the house's cupola, they had witnessed the arrival of the 11th Corps, "a dark sinuous line winding around the distant hills beyond the town like a huge serpent." But it had not come their way. Instead, Confederate skirmishers had occupied the mansion's grounds and outbuildings but had not entered the house or bothered the women. Fire from these Rebel skirmishers was annoying the 80th New York, the only part of Biddle's brigade exposed to enemy fire, and General Wadsworth, who seems to have had skirmishers on the brain that day, ordered that regiment's colonel to send skirmishers to drive off these pesky Rebels, even though they were some 700 yards west of the regiment's line up on McPherson's Ridge. The colonel sent one company, later reinforced by another, and after a small but spirited fight they drove the Confederates away from the place.

"A sudden, violent commotion and uproar below made us fly in quick haste to the lower floor," Amelia Harmon later wrote. It was these Union skirmishers banging on the kitchen door and demanding admittance. "We drew the bolt," she said, "and in poured a stream of maddened, powder-blackened bluecoats who ordered us to the cellar while they dispersed to the various west windows throughout the house. From our cellar prison we could hear the tumult above, the constant crack of rifles, the hurried orders, and, outside, the mingled roar of heavy musketry, galloping horses, yelling troops, and the occasional boom of cannon. . . ." Some time later came a different sound: "A swish like the mowing of grass on the front lawn, then a dense shadow darkened the low, grated cellar windows. It is the sound and shadow of hundreds of marching feet. We can see them to the knees only, but the uniforms are the Confederate gray!

". . . We rushed up the cellar steps to the kitchen. The barn was in flames and cast a lurid glare through the window. The house was filled with rebels and they were deliberately firing it. They had taken down a file of newspapers for kindling, piled on books, rags, and furniture, applied matches to ignite the pile, and already a tiny flame was curling upward. We both jumped on the fire in hopes of extinguishing it, and pleaded with them in pity to spare our home. But there was no pity in those determined faces. . . . We fled from our burning house, only to encounter worse horrors. The first rebel line of battle had passed our house and were now engaged in a hot skirmish in the gorge of Willoughby Run. The second line was being advanced just abreast the barn, and at the moment was being hotly attacked by the Union troops with shot and shell! We were between the lines!"

Unable to go toward the Federal lines, they moved to the Confederate rear, where few Rebels would take time to listen to their plight and everyone told them to go farther to the rear to get away from Union cannon fire. Eventually they came to a knot of Rebel officers and newspapermen, and one of the latter volunteered to lead them to safety while listening to their tale of woe. He assured them that General Lee would punish the men who had burned their house and that they would be reimbursed for it – in Confederate money, of course. He went to see Lee himself and returned with the latter's promise to place a guard around their house while the battle lasted and to send them food, which was done. They took up temporary residence in a cottage with a Confederate guard outside. "We," Amelia later boasted, "were doubtless the only persons on the Union side who were fed from General Lee's commissary during the Battle of Gettysburg."[3]

Private Charles H. McConnell of the 24th Michigan wrote admiringly of Heth's new advance, which was being hit by artillery fire almost from the moment it stepped off. He said that the Rebels advanced as "if on dress parade, slowly, steadily, resistlessly – closing up the gaps made by our guns, the slow advance not being checked in the least – banners flying proudly, voices ringing out defiantly above the roar of artillery."[4] Private William Roby Moore of the 19th Indiana said, "They kept coming steadily on, and in as good line as ever troops did upon parade, and their muskets a glittering. It was an awe-inspiring sight to observe them." He added that "there was not a man in our ranks but realized the futility of endeavoring to turn back that horde."[5]

Biddle's brigade – actually Rowley's under Biddle's temporary command – had changed position to face north when Rodes' artillery had opened fire from that direction, then it had fallen back to the Hagerstown Road, but now, as Heth's Confederates advanced upon it from the west, it formed two lines, with two regiments in each. Both lines advanced to the north until just west of the seminary then wheeled to the left to once again take position on McPherson's Ridge. As they did so General Doubleday detached the 151st Pennsylvania from the second line and placed it in reserve at the seminary.

Coming up on the ridge, Biddle found it occupied by four guns of a Union battery that had been placed there by Colonel Wainwright, commander of the 1st Corps' artillery brigade. The infantry's move to position blocked the fire of these guns, which confirmed Wainwright's low opinion of the abilities of the infantry commanders. Seeing the large Confederate force bearing down on them, which stretched nearly a third of a mile beyond the Union left, he decided that "there was not the shadow of a chance of our holding this ridge even had our Third Division commanders had any idea what to do with their men, which they had not."[6] So when the Rebels approached to within 200 yards of his guns, he ordered them back to a stone wall about 100 yards south of the seminary. The infantry, now under Rowley's direct supervision and deprived of one regiment by Doubleday and of two companies by Wadsworth, formed a single line along the crest of McPherson's Ridge. The two companies of skirmishers that had been driven out of the Old McLean place moved south along Willoughby Run and joined Gamble's cavalry rather than climb the open slope of McPherson's Ridge under Confederate fire.

But the Iron Brigade, some 300 yards farther west, was the first Union unit to be struck by the Rebel tide, in this case the 11th and 26th North Carolina. At about the time the Confederates reached Willoughby Run these Federals hit them with a deadly fire, which, along with the rocks and brush along the stream, broke up the neat formations of the Rebels, who tended to crowd toward their colors at the centers of their regimental lines. The large 26th North Carolina (about 800 men) and the 19th Indiana each lost several color-bearers in this fight. But the Confederates overlapped the Union left flank, and the 19th Indiana's colonel ordered his men to fall back 100 yards, which they did in good order, taking cover behind trees and firing back at the Rebels as they retreated. The 21-year-old colonel of the 26th North Carolina was among those hit by this fire, taking his regiment's colors down with him.

This move by the 19th exposed the flank of the 24th Michigan, which was also soon forced to withdraw. Soon Pettigrew's men threatened the 19th's flank again, so it fell back to what was left of a fence just off the left flank of the 7th Wisconsin. The 24th also had to fall back again, but Private McConnell paused long enough to put a bullet through the lieutenant colonel of the 26th North Carolina just as he had taken the command and the flag of his regiment from its fallen colonel. General Solomon Meredith, commander of the Iron Brigade and former colonel of the 19th Indiana, suffered internal injuries when his horse was shot out from under him early in this fight. Judging by the accounts of his men, he was not sorely missed.

Brockenbrough's Virginians, numbering about 900 muskets, after appearing on the flank of Stone's brigade, veered to their right to avoid a small quarry and came up against the 7th and 2nd Wisconsin regiments on the Iron Brigade's right flank, which held them for a while, but when the 24th Michigan fell back, exposing their left, the two Wisconsin regiments had to retire as well, forming a single line adjacent to the 24th. This line was also soon threatened on both flanks, and the 7th's colonel took seven of his companies back to the crest of McPherson's Ridge, east of the woods, to avoid being turned on the right. His other three companies plus the 2nd Wisconsin stayed put and held up the Rebel advance until the regiments on their left falling back exposed their left flank again and they too withdrew to the crest of the ridge. Even this position could not be held for long, and soon the brigade formed line in the low ground between McPherson's Ridge and Seminary Ridge. By then John Burns had joined the 24th Michigan and been wounded three times, but he survived to become a local and national hero.

In the low ground between the two ridges the Iron Brigade was met by ten wagons from the division's ammunition train. After dropping off 70,000 rifle cartridges while under Confederate artillery fire, the wagons headed back toward the town, but a solid shot soon took off both hind legs of one of the mules pulling one of the wagons, and while it was being put out of its pain and cut from the harness another shot collapsed both of the same wagon's rear wheels. After handing out more ammunition to a passing regiment, the other wagons went on into Gettysburg, where they continued to hand out ammunition until eventually forced to move on.

The two regiments at the right end of Pettigrew's line, the 47th and 52nd North Carolina, bypassed McPherson's Woods to the south, and it was their presence there that threatened the flanks of the successive positions taken up by the Iron Brigade. To their right, what was left of Archer's Brigade merely swung around to face south and protect Pettigrew's own flank. But as the 52nd, at the right end of Pettigrew's line, advanced it evidently moved beyond this screen, and seeing the 8th Illinois Cavalry of Gamble's brigade off to its right it formed square for a while, the traditional formation for defense against cavalry but a difficult one to advance in. Meanwhile, the 47th North Carolina went on up the west face of McPherson's Ridge and, near the top, entered a field of breast-high wheat. These Rebels didn't see Rowley's

(Biddle's) Federals until they were within 75 yards of them. Both sides then opened fire, and the Rebels swung around to get on the Federals' unprotected southern flank. Meanwhile, the retreat of the Iron Brigade was exposing Rowley's northern flank. Seeing this, Doubleday sent the 151st Pennsylvania from its reserve position to rejoin its brigade, and it came up on Rowley's right.

At one point Colonel Biddle led the 142nd Pennsylvania in a countercharge against the 47th North Carolina, but it was cut to pieces by fire coming in from all directions. The 121st Pennsylvania, at the southern end of Rowley's line, was devastated by fire coming in on its left flank and was eventually forced to retreat to the grounds of the seminary. (It lost three fourths of its men in this day's fight.) The 80th New York, in the center of the brigade's line, thus found its own flank exposed, and it too had to fall back, but its colonel boasted that his men fought "so obstinately as they moved off that the enemy's pursuit was cautious and tardy."[7] This left the 151st exposed on both its flanks and subjected to a deadly crossfire. (It also lost about three quarters of its men that day.) Soon what was left of it fell back and took position with the rest of the brigade near the seminary.

At this point the Federals of the 1st Corps were seriously bloodied but still ready to fight, but Heth's Confederates were about played out and about out of ammunition. Heth himself received a bullet to the head as he crossed McPherson's Ridge. He was saved from death by a wad of paper he had placed inside his oversized hat, but he was knocked unconscious and stayed that way for hours. Command of his division fell to the competent but relatively inexperienced Pettigrew, who's own brigade lost over 1,000 men that afternoon, mostly from his two large regiments that had fought the 19th Indiana and 24th Michigan. One company (91 officers and men) of the 26th North Carolina had taken 100 percent casualties. Heth later reported losing 2,300 men in his division in 30 minutes of fighting. But, as Pettigrew's men scrounged among the dead and wounded for ammunition, Pender's Division passed over their lines and took up the fight on this part of the field. Anderson's Division had also arrived and was deployed either along Herr Ridge or the next ridge to the west. Its arrival is probably what allowed the use of Pender's Division, for, as Lee told Anderson, he still didn't know how much of the Union army was on hand and "a reserve in case of a disaster was necessary."[8]

However, there was yet another Confederate division coming on to the field. Major General Jubal Anderson Early was known to his troops as Old Jubilee, but General Lee called him "my bad old man."[9] He was a cantankerous, pugnacious, 56-year-old bachelor who had graduated from West Point back in 1837, three years ahead of his corps commander, Dick Ewell, who often consulted with him. He and his division of Ewell's 2nd Corps had been off on their own, trying to cross the Susquehanna River at Wrightsville, Pennsylvania, when orders had reached him to turn back to the west and rejoin the rest of the army. He had met up with Ewell and Rodes' Division the night before near Heidlersburg, and had set out this morning at about 8 o'clock heading south toward Gettysburg but intending to turn west to Mummasburg when he came to the right road. But then word had come from Ewell for him to continue on toward Gettysburg, as he and Rodes' Division were heading for the same town on a different road to meet up with Hill's 3rd Corps. About two miles north of the town officers from Ewell's staff brought word that Rodes' Division was engaged and instructions for him to hurry his march and attack as soon as his troops arrived.

Early and his staff rode to some high ground, from which they could see the town of Gettysburg in the distance and Cemetery Hill beyond it, crowned with Union artillery, and, closer, the contending lines of battle. Evidently O'Neal's attack was just going in. But the most important thing that Early could see was that the road his division was following (known locally as the Harrisburg Road) would bring it onto the field in perfect position to hit the Federals' right flank. Quickly he instructed his adjutant to tell his four infantry brigades to double-quick to the front and to open their lines so the artillery could pass through.

His leading brigade, six Georgia regiments commanded by Brigadier General John B. Gordon, soon appeared and filed off to the right into a farm lane to form line of battle facing southwest. There wasn't room for all six of them in the lane, so the last regiment, the 26th Georgia, formed line to the left of the Harrisburg Road facing the same way but a bit farther back. A battery of four 12-pounder smoothbore cannon (known as "Napoleons"), still limbered, occupied the road, ready to advance with Gordon's infantry, while the other three batteries belonging to the division unlimbered to the left of the road, extending Gordon's line.

While the guns were still unlimbering and preparing for action, Early's infantry continued to arrive. The next unit was known as Hoke's Brigade, but it was commanded in the absence of its wounded general by Colonel Isaac Avery. Its three North Carolina regiments formed line behind the artillery, while the next brigade, the five Louisiana regiments of Brigadier General Harry Hays, straddled the road, and the last brigade, three Virginia regiments commanded by Brigadier General William "Extra Billy" Smith, was placed in reserve well behind Avery's brigade with the primary duty of protecting the division's left flank from Union cavalry that was hovering off in that direction or anything else that might pop up. Seeing that the Federals in his front were still preoccupied with Rodes' Division, Early ordered Gordon's Brigade to attack at once. Gordon, as one observer later remembered, "drew his sword, the Georgians grasped their arms, and in a few minutes the line was moving through a field of yellow wheat like a dark gray wave in a sea of gold."[10]

The Federals in Early's front belonged to the 1st Division of the 11th Corps. Their division commander, Brigadier General Francis Barlow, was only 29 years old that summer and looked even younger, for in that bewhiskered age he was clean shaven. He was a Harvard man, not a West Pointer, having graduated in 1854 at the head of his class. He had been a lawyer and a newspaperman before the war, but once the war came, he rapidly climbed the ranks from private to 1st lieutenant to lieutenant colonel and colonel. While recovering from a severe wound received at Antietam, he had been promoted to brigadier general, and after commanding a brigade through the Chancellorsville campaign, where he saw little action, he had received command of this division only a few weeks back. He was energetic, enthusiastic, ambitious, brave, and devoted to duty, all admirable qualities in a commander, but he was inexperienced and unhappy with being in the 11th Corps, for he did not like or trust his German soldiers. He had told a friend that "these Dutch won't fight. Their officers say so & they say so themselves & they ruin all with whom they come in contact."[11]

Schurz's division of the 11th Corps, temporarily under Schimmelfennig, had been facing off against Doles' Brigade of Rodes' Division, with both sides content to stay on the defensive and protect the flanks of the troops actually fighting. And Barlow's division had been placed on the right of Schurz's, his 1st Brigade, under Colonel Leopold von Gilsa, on the left, and his 2nd Brigade, under Brigadier General Adelbert Ames, on the right and originally somewhat behind von Gilsa's. Ames was a year younger that Barlow but a West Pointer, having graduated just in time to command a section of artillery at the first battle of Bull Run. He had later commanded the entire battery and then had become the colonel of an infantry regiment in the 5th Corps, and, like Barlow, he was brand new to the 11th Corps. Von Gilsa had been a major in the Prussian army during its recent war with Denmark and had helped to raise the 41st New York from among his fellow German immigrants. He was popular with his men, if not with his superiors. Barlow admitted he was personally brave, and Howard said he looked good on parade and at drill, but both seem to have found it hard to work with him. At Chancellorsville his brigade had been the first one hit by

Stonewall Jackson's flank attack, despite von Gilsa's warning's to Howard.

Barlow eventually decided to move forward to occupy the best defensive position he could find anywhere in his area: a knoll on the Blocher farm near the point where the Carlisle and Harrisburg roads converged. It would possibly have been a good move if there had not been four brigades of veteran Confederate infantry coming down the Harrisburg road even as Barlow's men advanced. Von Gilsa's small brigade (about 900 men), with about half of it deployed as a skirmish line, took the knoll at the double-quick, driving off a few Rebel skirmishers, and moved on down the other side to take position facing northeast among the trees along the banks of Rock Creek, extending from the knoll as far east as the Harrisburg Road. The creek was fordable, being about 20 feet wide and only about 3 feet deep, but its steep banks and the trees along them would serve as obstacles to any Confederate attack. Von Gilsa's advance was seen by George Doles, holding the left of Rodes' line, as a threat to his own left, so he shifted his own line in that direction. This, in turn was seen by von Gilsa as a threat to his left, and he ordered his reserve, eight companies of the new, large 153rd Pennsylvania, to extend his line to the west, leaving his right – the 11th Corps' right – to be held only by the half of his brigade that was still spread out in a thin skirmish line along Rock Creek.

Four 12-pounder Napoleon guns were then placed on the knoll, from which they had a good field of fire, but they were immediately engaged by the three newly deployed batteries of Early's Division. One of the Federals' return shots struck the muzzle of a Confederate piece and knocked it out of action, but the Rebels still had about a 3 to 1 advantage in this artillery duel. The battery commander, Lieutenant Bayard Wilkerson, was hit, not long after his guns took position, by a shot that mangled his right leg and killed his horse. He applied his handkerchief as a tourniquet to the stump and amputated what was left of the leg himself. Then four of his men carried him to a nearby almshouse, where he died that night. The other two guns of the same Union battery were stationed just to the right or east of the Harrisburg Road, but farther back, to protect the 11th Corps' right flank.

Ames' brigade (about 1,200 men), stayed in place for a while but was eventually brought up to form on the left of the four guns on the knoll, with three regiments forming a line facing northwest and the fourth regiment in support behind them. Before he was aware of all this, Schurz heard the sounds of increased combat over in the 1st Corps' sector, so he rode over to a farmhouse beside the Mummasburg Road, near the left of his skirmish line, climbed onto its roof, and looked around. "The right of the First Corps seemed to be engaged in a very severe struggle," he later reported. "The enemy was evidently pressing upon that point. At the same time signs were apparent of an advance by the enemy upon my line, especially the right. The enemy was evidently stronger than he had been at the commencement of the battle, and the probability was that re-enforcements were still arriving." He fired off a request to Howard, back at Cemetery Hill, for a brigade of the corps' 2nd Division to move forward to the railroad station near the north edge of the town. "My intention was," he later reported, "to have that brigade in readiness to charge upon any force the enemy might move around my right."[12]

Howard, however, did not feel that he could send another brigade to the front. As he later reported, "I had then only two small brigades in reserve, and had already located three regiments from these in the edge of the town and to the north, and I felt sure that I must hold the point where I was as an ultimate resort. Therefore I at first replied that I could not spare any troops. . . ." He did send a third battery, which took position with Schurz's (Schimmelfennig's) division, and he ordered a battery of 3-inch rifles on Cemetery Hill to fire on a Confederate battery that he thought was only a little over a mile to the north. The Union fire fell short, however, which Howard blamed on poor ammunition. He also sent off another message to Slocum, "stating that my right flank was attacked, and asking him if he was moving up, and stating that I was in danger of being turned and driven back."[13]

Slocum was indeed moving, finally. A civilian coming from Gettysburg had informed him that a large battle was in progress there, and Slocum had sent a staff officer to investigate, who had soon returned saying he had not gone very far up the road before he could hear the sound of battle. About this time Howard's latest message arrived and the officer carrying it briefed Slocum on what he knew of the fight so far. After his columns were already on the move, Slocum received a message from Meade announcing that Hancock has been put in charge at Gettysburg and urging corps commanders to head for that town as fast as possible. So, at 3:35 p.m., Slocum sent a note to Gettysburg, addressed to "General Howard or General Hancock," saying only, "I am moving the Twelfth Corps so as to come in about 1 mile to the right of Gettysburg."[14]

With several years of hindsight, General Doubleday later wrote: "It seems to me that the Eleventh Corps were too far out. It would have been better, in my opinion, if its left had been *echeloned* in rear of the right of the First Corps, and its right had rested on the strong brick buildings with stone foundations of the Almshouse. The enemy then could not have turned the right without compromising the safety of the turning column and endangering his communications; a movement he would hardly like to make, especially as he did not know what troops might be coming up. Still they had a preponderating force, and as their whole army was concentrating on Gettysburg, it was not possible to keep them back for any great length of time unless the First and Eleventh Corps were heavily reinforced."[15]

Schurz might well have agreed with that assessment. Having returned from his look at what was going on to his left, he discovered that Barlow's division had advanced without orders, as described above, that it had lost its connection with Schimmelfennig's line, and, perhaps worst of all, that Ames' brigade was no longer where it had been, behind the corps' right flank. He immediately gave orders for Schimmelfennig to advance so as to reestablish contact between his division and Barlow's and sent an aide to keep an eye out for the advance of the brigade requested from Howard. "Soon afterward, however," Schurz reported, "about 3 o'clock, before the forward movement of the First Division could be arrested by my orders, the enemy appeared in our front in heavy masses of infantry, his line extending far beyond our right. It was now clear that the two small divisions under my command, numbering hardly over 6,000 men when going into action, had a whole corps of the rebel army to contend against. The simultaneous appearance of the enemy's battalions on so long a line led me to believe that they had been lying in position for some time behind the woods in our front, fully prepared for us, and that it was their intention, while entangling us in a fight where we were, to throw their left wing around our right, and thus to cut us off from the town. A movement to the rear became at once necessary, but before any orders to that effect could be transmitted, my whole line was engaged. . . ."[16]

Buford penned a report to Cavalry Corps headquarters, marked 3:20 p.m., saying, "I am satisfied that Longstreet [sic] and Hill have made a junction. A tremendous battle has been raging since 9.30 a.m., with varying success. At the present moment the battle is raging on the road to Cashtown, and within short cannon-range of this town. The enemy's line is a semicircle on the height, from north to west. General Reynolds was killed early this morning. In my opinion, there seems to be no directing person." In a postscript he added, "We need help now."[17]

Help was very soon on the way, but from another source, and it would take a while to arrive. Howard's messages to Dan Sickles had finally reached that general, commander of the 3rd Corps, and he replied at 3:15 p.m., "I have at this moment received a communication from an officer of your staff, and also two written communications, dated at 1 and 1.30 p.m. I shall move to Gettysburg immediately."[18] Sickles also sent a message with the same time in the heading to Seth Williams at army headquarters, informing him that he had received communications from Howard. "A large force of the enemy has engaged him in front of Gettysburg. General Reynolds was killed early in the action. General Howard requests me to support him, and I shall march with my corps toward Gettysburg immediately, moving on two parallel roads. I shall be found on the direct turnpike road from Emmitsburg." He followed this up ten minutes later with another message to Williams, saying, "I shall leave one brigade and battery on the heights beyond Emmitsburg, toward Fairfield, and another to the left and rear of Emmitsburg, commanding the approaches by way of Mechanicstown. These have orders, if unable to hold Emmitsburg, to fall back on Taneytown."[19] Five minutes after that, orders were on the way to Major General David Birney to "move your division to Gettysburg immediately, and report to Major-General Howard with the least possible delay. He is engaged with the enemy. Two batteries will join you."[20]

Confederate John Brown Gordon, a 30-year-old lawyer and graduate of the University of Georgia, had begun the war as a captain of a company, but had quickly advanced to colonel of a regiment; he was wounded at Antietam, and, since before the Chancellorsville campaign, he had been a general in command of a brigade. Like von Gilsa, he looked right for the role. A Confederate artilleryman described him as "a superb, magnetic leader," and "the most glorious and inspiring thing I ever looked upon." Another Rebel left a more colorful, if less grammatical, description of him as "the most prettiest thing you ever did see on a field of fight. It'ud put fight into a whipped chicken just to look at him."[21] But he not only looked the part, he filled it admirably, and before the war was over he would rise to corps command.

On this occasion he rode his big black stallion just behind his skirmish line so all his men could see him and so he could get a better look at what lay ahead. His men were tired after marching some ten miles or so, and he let them advance slowly until they were within 300 yards of the Union line. They were headed straight for von Gilsa's line on the knoll and along Rock Creek, but that officer was still more concerned about his left at the time, for evidently Schimmelfennig's right had not yet advanced, or perhaps it didn't stretch far enough to reach von Gilsa's left flank. So the 153rd Pennsylvania had been ordered to extend his line in that direction. But, even counting the 153rd, von Gilsa had only about 900 men to face nearly twice that many Georgians in Gordon's Brigade, and all of the Federals, except those eight companies of the 153rd, were in a thin skirmish line.

"It was upon this line, drawn up in a strong position on the crest of a hill, a portion of which was woodland, that my brigade charged," Gordon later reported. "Moving forward under heavy fire over rail and plank fences, and crossing a creek whose banks were so abrupt as to prevent a passage excepting at certain points, this brigade rushed upon the enemy with a resolution and spirit, in my opinion, rarely excelled. The enemy made a most obstinate resistance until the colors on portions of the two lines were separated by a space of less than 50 paces, when his line was broken and driven back, leaving the flank which this line had protected exposed to the fire from my brigade."[22]

Private Reuben Ruch of the 153rd Pennsylvania later remembered that just as his part of that regiment was ordered off to the left it started taking fire from its right rear. The lieutenant commanding his part of the line, thinking the fire was from other Federals, sent a corporal back to put a stop to it, but the corporal came back with the alarming news that there were no Federals back there, just Rebels who had gotten around the Union right flank. A sergeant pointed out that there were also a lot of Confederates to their front, just visible beyond the trees lining Rock Creek and coming their way. A captain came to tell the lieutenant to get his men moving to the left, but the latter convinced the former that the Rebels were about to attack, so the captain told him to get his men out however he could. Ruch said that about then the Union skirmishers were driven in by what looked like three battle lines of Confederates.

Men near Ruch began to fall, but he got off four or five shots before the lieutenant ordered a retreat, and he paused to take one more shot, hitting a Rebel who was climbing a fence only some ten yards away. As Ruch then fell back he saw Wilkerson's four guns abandoning the knoll, and as he passed the almshouse barn he looked back and saw a Confederate battle line that he estimated to be a mile long (the brigades of Hays and Avery) swing around the Union right. He also saw Colonel von Gilsa, who was on foot but calling for some men to catch a riderless horse for him, which they did. The colonel then rode up and down his line amid the flying bullets, interspersing a stream of German with cries of "rally boys."[23]

Hays's and Avery's Confederate brigades had advanced shortly after Gordon's had stepped off, through the fields east of the Harrisburg Road, with Avery's North Carolinians on the left, or east, flank. They moved slowly until they reached Rock Creek, where they came under artillery fire from the two guns of Wilkerson's battery that were stationed farther up the road to guard the Union right, as well as from rifle fire, probably from four companies that Ames had sent up the road when he had first arrived in the area. Smith's small Virginia brigade (he had left two regiments in the Shenandoah Valley) never advanced, although ordered to do so, as Smith was still worried about Devin's cavalry hovering off to the east. (When the 11th Corps' began to retreat, Buford ordered Devin's brigade to join Gamble's south of the town and west of Cemetery Ridge, a southward extension of Cemetery Hill.)

However, an addition to Early's right more than made up for this subtraction from his left: Seeing Gordon's Brigade advance, Doles, holding the left of Rodes' Division, ordered his own line forward as well. Colonel Wladimir Krzyzanowski's 2nd Brigade of Schurz's (Schimmelfennig's) division (about

1,200 men), obeying Schurz's order to close the gap created by Barlow's advance, formed line between von Gilsa's left and the Carlisle Road just as Doles' Georgians came up out of the ravine of Blocher's Run, a small west-to-east tributary of Rock Creek. "Their movements were firm and steady, as usual," a Union captain remembered, "and their banners bearing the blue Southern cross, flaunted impudently and seemed to challenge combat. On they came, one line after the other, in splendid array."[24] The Federals hit them with a volley that brought the Rebels up short, but they returned the favor, and a fire fight ensued at a range of 75 yards or less.

Krzyzanowski later said his men were "sweaty, blackened by gunpowder, and they looked more like animals than human beings." He added that "the portrait of battle was the portrait of hell."[25] The 119th New York, on Krzyzanowski's left, lost 100 men in 15 minutes, as did the 26th Wisconsin at the other end of the line; The 75th Pennsylvania lost 111 men, including its colonel, out of 194 in that same time span; the 82nd Ohio lost about 150 officers and men out of 258. The colonel of the latter regiment had his horse shot out from under him, but, despite (or perhaps because of) two leg wounds took his major's horse and continued to ride along his lines. Krzyzanowski suffered a similar fate, taking a hard, painful fall when his horse was hit, but he stayed with his brigade, conducting what was left of it to the rear, at least some of his regiments continuing to fire as they fell back. On the Confederate side, General Doles also lost his mount, although for a different reason. The horse took the bit in its teeth and took off toward the Union lines. Unable to regain control, Doles could only avoid capture by sliding from the saddle into some tall wheat when within 50 feet of the Federals. Fortunately for him, the latter didn't see him there, but he was temporarily unable to influence events.

Doles' advance hit Ames's front just as von Gilsa's retreat was exposing his right and rear. Barlow ordered Ames to meet the Rebels head-on. Ames ordered his reserve regiment, the 75th Ohio (about 160 men), to fix bayonets and counterattack. It advanced to the edge of some woods and opened fire, bringing the Rebels to a temporary halt, but both of its flanks were exposed to enfilading fire; it took dreadful losses (a third of its officers and a fourth of its men killed or mortally wounded, and half of the rest too badly wounded to fight) and soon had to fall back. And Ames' other regiments fared just as badly. The 25th Ohio was quickly whittled down from 220 men to about 60; the 107th Ohio from 434 to 171. The 17th Connecticut (minus the four companies Ames had sent up the Harrisburg Road earlier) was also badly cut up. Its commander had his brains blown out as he led his men over the knoll; they got off a few shots in return and were soon swept off the field, losing 145 men out of 386.

Barlow tried to rally his men but soon took a bullet in the side. He was able to walk at first, and followed his men to the rear, but was soon hit in the back by a spent bullet, and before long he could go no farther. He lay down, and the Rebel line soon passed him by. General Gordon later claimed to have personally ordered his Union counterpart, whom he thought to be mortally wounded, carried to a shady spot in the rear. (Eventually Confederate and captured Union surgeons dressed his wounds. They were not optimistic about his chances of survival, fearing that peritonitis would set in, but he lived to be exchanged later and to command a division in the 2nd Corps the following year.) Ames succeeded to command of the division and also tried to rally it, with little success, though von Gilsa was able to patch together a line near the north edge of the town.

Meanwhile, when he had seen Doles Brigade advance against Krzyzanowski, General Schimmelfennig had sent the 157th New York, a relatively large regiment (about 400 men) from his own brigade, to attack the Rebels' right flank. But by the time it got there, Krzyzanowski's and Barlow's lines had already given way. The regiment on that end of Doles' line, the 21st Georgia, just west of the Carlisle Road, saw these Federals coming just in time and advanced into the wheatfield to meet them, but couldn't stop them. These Georgians fell back to the north about 40 yards and laid down in a lane, out of sight, and Doles' other regiments turned to face this new threat. When they opened fire on the Federals' front the 21st stood up and hit them in the flank, and a Confederate battery also contributed to the carnage. The New Yorkers were being slaughtered by fire hitting them from three directions (they lost 307 men that day) and soon fell back, with Doles' Georgians pursuing them. The rest of Schimmelfennig's brigade helped to cover the 157th's retreat, but had to join it when they saw the 1st Corps retreating from Oak Ridge, to their left.

The two batteries that had been supporting Schurz's (Schimmelfennig's) division – Dilger's and the one sent by Howard as a reinforcement, commanded by Lieutenant William Wheeler – then had to pull out or be captured. Each detached a section of two guns to cover the retreat of the rest. One of Wheeler's 3-inch rifles was struck by a Confederate shot that knocked its barrel to the ground, and Wheeler tried to haul it off with ropes, but had to leave it behind. Eventually both batteries made their way to Cemetery Hill. The battery of the fallen Lieutenant Wilkerson, which had retreated from Barlow's knoll, stopped north of Gettysburg to replenish its ammunition from its caissons, evidently fired a few shots from the streets of the town, and also fell back to Cemetery Hill.

Gordon's advance ended near the almshouse, where it stopped to get ammunition, and Early told it to stay there. Hays's and Avery's brigades could take over now. They had stopped at Rock Creek, but Early ordered them to attack a new line of Federals that he could see forming on the north edge of the town. This was Colonel Charles R. Coster's 1st Brigade of Steinwehr's 2nd Division of the 11th Corps. After repeated appeals from Schurz, Howard had finally ordered it forward, but by the time it reached the northern edge of Gettysburg Barlow's division had fallen apart. Schurz, who had been trying to rally Ames's men, took charge of Coster's brigade and placed it behind a post-and-rail fence in the northeast part of the town, overlooking three wheatfields, with its right-most regiment straddling Stevens Run. After leaving one regiment in the town as a reserve, Coster only had about 900 men.

Captain Frederick Winkler of the 11th Corps staff, who had brought Schurz the news of Coster's advance, found about 30 men from his own regiment, the 26th Wisconsin of Krzyzanowski's brigade, retreating without officers but with the regiment's battleflag. With Schurz's permission, he took charge of these men and formed them in line in the Carlisle Road west of Coster's new line. Other remnants of Schurz's two divisions took position on both sides of that road, facing north, and another battery of the 11th Corps, commanded by Captain Lewis Heckman, unlimbered just to the northwest of, and perpendicular to, the Harrisburg Road, facing to the northeast, between the right flank of these remnants and Coster's left.

Coster's Federals were barely in position when Hays's Louisianans advanced, straddling the Harrisburg Road, heading straight for Heckman's guns and Coster's left flank. The 154th New York, in the center of Coster's line, held firm, but the 134th, at the right end, was overwhelmed by Avery's brigade coming in from the northeast with at least three times its numbers and overlapping its right flank. The 134th hit these North Carolinians with a volley at about 60 yards range, but soon had to retreat or be surrounded. It lost 40 killed and 150 wounded in the process. Its commander, Lieutenant Colonel Allan H. Jackson, only avoided capture by hiding in a house on York Street for two days before he managed to sneak through the Confederate picket line to reach Cemetery Hill.

The disorganized remnants of Barlow's and Krzyzanowski's formations soon gave way before Hays's attack and fell back through the town, and the Rebels overran Heckman's battery, capturing two of its four 12-pounder Napoleons before they could be limbered up and pulled out.

This exposed the left flank of Coster's brigade to Hays's

Louisianans just as its right was being turned by Avery's North Carolinians. The Federals were on ground that sloped up from Stevens Run on their right toward Stratton Street, and this rise may have prevented them from seeing or shooting at Hays's men coming in on their left until they were right on them. Hit on both flanks and from the front at the same time, Coster's men fell back, the two flank regiments first and finally the 154th, in the center, which was cut off and had to fight its way out. Out of its 270 officers and men, only 3 officers and 15 enlisted men made it to the relative safety of Cemetery Hill.

"About 4 p.m.," Doubleday later reported, "the enemy, having been strongly re-enforced, advanced in large numbers, everywhere deploying into double and triple lines, overlapping our left for a third of a mile, pressing heavily upon our right, overwhelming our center. It was evident Lee's whole army was approaching. Our tired troops had been fighting desperately, some of them for six hours. They were thoroughly exhausted, and General Howard had no re-enforcements to give me. It became necessary to retreat. All my reserves had been thrown in, and the First Corps was now fighting in a single line. It is stated by General Wadsworth in his official report that the portion of the Eleventh Corps nearest to us, unable to stand the pressure, had fallen back some time before this, and that our right flank was thus uncovered, so far as that corps was concerned. Biddle's brigade about this time again changed front to meet the strong lines advancing from the west. I now gave the order to fall back, this and Meredith's [Iron] brigades covering the movement by occupying the intrenchments in front of the seminary, which I had directed to be thrown up as a precautionary measure to assist in holding the new position."[26] These entrenchments were evidently not earthworks but merely piles of fence rails and debris, only two or three feet high.

Like Schurz, both Wadsworth and Doubleday had sent

requests to Howard for reinforcements, but he had none to give then without letting go of his hold on Cemetery Hill as a rallying point. He asked Schurz to send Doubleday a regiment if he could spare one, but the latter, of course, had his own problems. Otherwise, Howard's only reply was, "Hold out, if possible, awhile longer, for I am expecting General Slocum every moment."[27] At about the same hour of 4 p.m., seeing that neither corps could hold any longer, Howard sent word to both Schurz and Doubleday to fall back, fighting, to Cemetery Hill, and he sent off his brother and aide to make another appeal to Slocum, asking him to send one of his two divisions to the right of the town (to help the 11th Corps) and the other to the left of the town (to help the 1st Corps).

Major Howard found Slocum only about a mile down the road and delivered his message. That general replied that "he had already ordered a division to the right, and that he would send another to the left, as requested, but that he did not wish to come up in person to the front and take the responsibility of that fight." This seems, at first, a strange response, but it was evidently prompted by the fact that he was senior in rank to both Howard and Hancock and would, by regulations, be in command if on the field, yet he knew nothing of the situation, whereas Howard had been on the field during most of the battle, and Hancock had been sent by Meade to take charge, so for Slocum to show up might cause time-wasting wrangles about who was in charge. But the reason that he later gave to Howard was that "it was against the wish of the commanding general [Meade] to bring on a general engagement at that point."[28]

Howard also sent a request to General Buford, asking for his cavalry to make a show of force against the Confederate right, or southern, flank. "Buford," Doubleday later wrote, "was in a distant part of the field, with Devins's brigade, covering the retreat of the Eleventh Corps, and already had all he could attend to. He expressed himself in pretty round terms at the idea that he could keep back Hill's entire corps with Gamble's cavalry brigade alone."[29] Nevertheless, two of

Gamble's regiments soon trotted forward from where they had been resting south of the town. Half of them dismounted and formed line along Seminary Ridge south of Doubleday's infantry, while the other half remained mounted behind the ridge.

Gamble's other regiment, the 8th Illinois Cavalry, was still hovering off the Rebels' right flank, near the Hagerstown Road. Because of its presence there, Brigadier General James H. Lane, commanding the brigade on the right of Pender's line, had to deploy the 7th North Carolina as skirmishers to guard his right flank, just as Heth had used the remnants of Archer's Brigade to perform the same duty. (In fact, one regiment of Pettigrew's brigade was now also guarding the Confederate right against this cavalry). And as Pender's line moved farther east in pursuit of the 1st Corps it soon moved beyond this screen, and Lane had to detach a company from another of his regiments to add to the south-facing skirmish line. There was also an ad hoc force from another of Pender's brigades, known as the 1st South Carolina Sharpshooter Battalion, somewhere in this area. It reportedly drove off some Union cavalry outposts and did some foraging, making off with 30 head of cattle, a horse and a pig before receiving orders to rejoin its brigade.

When he advanced, Pender left one of his four brigades – four Georgia regiments under Brigadier General Edward L. Thomas – in reserve on the north side of the Chambersburg Pike. Brigadier General A. M. Scales' brigade of five North Carolina regiments held the left, or north, end of Pender's line, its left near the pike. (This brigade had been Pender's own before the latter had recently succeeded A. P. Hill as the division commander.) Lane's Brigade – four North Carolina regiments, not counting the one guarding the flank – had the right end of Pender's line, and McGowan's Brigade of five South Carolina regiments (minus the detached sharpshooters), commanded in the absence of its general by Colonel Abner Perrin, was in the middle. These three brigades followed Heth's advance until they came to the east crest of McPherson's Ridge, where they found Heth's men lying down. Some of Heth's officers told General Scales that they were out of ammunition. So Pender's fresh troops passed over Heth's line, halted under fire to reform in the low ground between the ridges, where there was a slight ravine holding the headwaters of Pitzer's Run, and started up the west side of Seminary Ridge. (Lane's Brigade, bothered by Gamble's cavalry on its flank, did not join this advance.) The commander of one of Scales' regiments termed the 400 yards of gently sloping open terrain the Rebels had to cross "the fairest field and finest front for destruction of an advancing foe that could well be conceived."[30]

∽ Endnotes ∽

1   Henry Heth, "Letter from Major General Heth Of A. P. Hill's Corps, A. N. V.," *Southern Historical Society Papers* (cited hereafter as *SHSP*), IV:158.
2   Wheeler, *Witness to Gettysburg*, 137-9.
3   Ibid., 143-5.
4   Pfanz, *Gettysburg – The First Day*, 280.
5. Ibid., 276-7.
6. Ibid., 278.
7   OR, I:27:I:321.
8   Pfanz, *Gettysburg – The First Day*, 320.
9   Sears, *Gettysburg*, 52.
10 Pfanz, *Gettysburg – The First Day*, 229.
11 Ibid., 223.
12 OR, I:27:I:728.
13 Ibid., I:27:I:703.
14 Ibid., I:27:III:465.
15 Doubleday, *Chancellorsville and Gettysburg*, 141.
16 OR, I:27:I:728-9.
17 Ibid., I:27:I:924-5.
18 Ibid., I:27:III:463.
19 Ibid., I:27:III:464.
20 Ibid., I:27:III:465.
21 Jeffrey D. Wert, *From Winchester to Cedar Creek*, 58; both quotes.
22 OR, I:27:II:492.
23 Pfanz, *Gettysburg – The First Day*, 243.
24 Ibid., 238.
25 Ibid., 252.
26 OR, I:27:I:250.
27 Ibid., I:27:I:703-4.
28 Ibid, I:27:I:704.
29 Doubleday, *Chancellorsville and Gettysburg*, 146.
30 Pfanz, *Gettysburg – The First Day*, 305.

CHAPTER 5
"It Is Too Late to Leave It"
1 July 1863

SCALES' AND PERRIN'S LINE stretched from the Chambersburg Pike on the north to the Hagerstown Road on the south when it stepped off. Scales' men were hit by the fire of twelve 12-pounder Napoleons and five 3-inch rifles as well as the musketry of the surviving infantry of Stone's brigade and the Iron Brigade. The colonel of the 7th Wisconsin said the Confederate "ranks went down like grass before the scythe."[1] Clouds of white smoke from the guns and muskets soon obscured the target, but the gunners and the infantrymen alike continued to load and fire as fast as they could. General Scales was hit by a shell fragment, but was able to retain command. His brigade lost its formation, and about 60 percent of its men, and ground to a halt some 75 yards short of the Union line. Some of his men returned fire, some hit the dirt, and some scattered, amid taunts from the 6th Wisconsin, supporting a battery just north of the pike, of "Come on, Johnny! Come on!"[2]

Finally the fire slackened and the smoke drifted away, revealing a field covered with dead and dying Rebels. As for the living, Scales said, "only a squad here and there marked the place where regiments had rested."[3] Pender and the wounded Scales worked to rally the 500 or so of the latter's men still able to fight (out of 1,400) and to bring up one small regiment of Brockenbrough's Brigade on Scales' left. But an officer in the 2nd Wisconsin, just after noting that his watch said it was 4 o'clock, had his attention directed to the 11th Corps sector on the far right just then, where he could see Confederate battleflags advancing and U.S. flags being carried back through the town. Obviously, things were not going so well over on the Union right. Nor were they on the Union left.

Perrin's 1,800 South Carolinians faced fewer Federals than Scales' North Carolinians and thus suffered much less, although the left and center of his left-most regiment, the 14th, took much the same kind of punishment that Scales' Brigade received, being hit by a volley from Biddle's men just as it crossed a fence some 200 yards from the Union line that Perrin called "the most destructive fire of musketry I have even been exposed to." Near the edge of some woods the 14th was hit by another volley that staggered it, and Perrin said, "It looked to us as though this regiment was entirely destroyed."[4] But while the Federals were concentrating on Scales' Brigade and the 14th South Carolina, Perrin ordered his next regiment, the 1st, to oblique to its right, beyond the end of the Union infantry line, then wheel to the left and attack its flank, while his other two regiments obliqued even farther to the right and attacked the cavalry at the south end of the Union line.

This maneuver succeeded admirably. The cavalry, hit in the front by one of Perrin's regiments and in the flank by the other, mounted up and rode back to Cemetery Ridge. Meanwhile, men of the 80th New York weren't sure whether the 1st South Carolina, moving at a strange angle across the smoke-obscured field, was friend or foe, and many withheld their fire until it was too late. When the Rebels suddenly halted, faced their way, and opened fire, the 80th headed for the rear, and soon the whole Union line began to unravel. Confederates were turning their left, the 11th Corps was retreating on their right; it was time to go. The 121st Pennsylvania of Biddle's brigade lost all formation and just ran away, possibly even before the 80th New York retreated, and soon the rest of Biddle's men and the entire Union line north of them began to retreat.

The men of the different regiments of the Iron Brigade were intermingled, but they reformed on the east side of Seminary Ridge, and the 7th Wisconsin was designated as the brigade's rear guard. As it left the ridge it had to run a gauntlet of fire from Perrin's men on one side and some of Rodes' on the other and took its heaviest casualties of the day between the ridge and the town. (The 6th Wisconsin, still detached from the brigade, had already been ordered by Wadsworth to fall back through the town to the high ground beyond.) A private in the Bucktail Brigade said that his unit retreated "without semblance of military order with every man for himself and the Rebs take the hindmost."[5] Doubleday said, in his official report, "Captain [James] Glenn, of the One hundred forty-ninth Pennsylvania Volunteers, in command of my headquarters guard, defended the [seminary] building for fully twenty minutes against a whole brigade of the enemy, enabling the few remaining troops, the ambulances, artillery, etc. to retreat in comparative safety."[6] Later, in his book, Doubleday said that Baxter's brigade of Robinson's division also helped cover the retreat. It also had the aid of a battery of artillery for a while.

General Wadsworth ordered one battery to the rear, but Colonel Wainwright, who evidently thought references to Cemetery Hill as a last refuge meant Seminary Ridge, ordered it to stay put, until someone drew his attention to troops moving south or southeast across the open plain behind them. He studied these formations with his field glasses and decided that the 1st Corps units north of the railroad cut were retreating, and so he changed his mind and ordered the guns to pull out after all. The Rebels, seeing the Federals leave, renewed their advance, and some of the Union guns got out just in time to avoid capture. Three damaged caissons and one gun, with most of its horses shot, had to be left behind. One Confederate placed his hand on a Napoleon that hadn't left yet and announced, "This gun is mine."[7] A gunner pulled the lanyard and blew him to pieces. Wainwright ordered his artillerymen to move down the Chambersburg Pike at a walk, so as not to panic the infantrymen who shared the road, but when Rebels near the seminary opened fire on the troops in the road the infantry moved farther north to the bed of the unfinished railroad, after which Wainwright ordered his batteries to trot and then to gallop.

Three guns that had been stationed north of the cut just barely got away. As they crossed the railroad bed, one of the guns got hung up on some rocks, and while the gunners struggled to pull it free Confederates not 100 yards off opened fire on them. The two other guns held the Rebels off, and, although Confederate fire wounded two of the horses pulling the stuck piece, and one of its drivers, all three guns finally got away. One of the artillerymen, Private Augustus Buell, later said, "I was astonished at the caution of the enemy at this time. He seemed to be utterly paralyzed at the punishment he had received from the 1st Corps, and was literally 'feeling every inch of his way' in his advance on our front."[8] Doubleday credited some of Robinson's men, falling back from Oak Ridge, with helping to save these guns by pausing in their retreat long enough to form line and hold off the Rebels. He also said that Cutler's brigade formed line in the railroad cut to hold off some Confederates who were pursuing the 11th Corps.

Perrin's 1st and 14th South Carolina regiments both followed the retreating Federals into Gettysburg, taking different streets, and raised a Confederate flag over the town. Pender joined them there and complimented them for their accomplishments, but soon sent them back to Seminary Ridge so they wouldn't get in the way of Rodes' Division, which was ordered to occupy the town. Lieutenant Colonel John Garnett, commander of the artillery battalion attached to Heth's Division, following up the infantry's success, remembered meeting General Lee just west of the seminary. The army commander, who had arrived at about 4:30, told him to put his guns into position there and to fire on some Union troops in the distance to disperse them or find out where they were going. Garnett did as he was told, and it was soon apparent to him that the Federals were all retreating to some high ground beyond the town: Cemetery Hill. Lee also told his chief of artillery, Brigadier General William N. Pendleton, to find positions on the right "to enfilade the valley between our position and the town and enemy's batteries next [to] the town." He found a suitable spot, but General Ramseur soon came to him and asked him not to open fire from there "as they would draw a concentrated fire upon his men, much exposed."[9] Pendleton complied with this request instead of doing what Lee had told him to do.

The 45th New York, which had been at the left of the 11th Corps' line, tried to cover the retreat, making a stand for twenty minutes near a college in the northwest part of Gettysburg, after which it fell back slowly to the town. There it came under a crossfire and broke into two segments, with six companies escaping over fences and through yards and alleys to Cemetery Hill, while the other four companies were cut off in the town, surrounded, and eventually forced to surrender at about 5:30 p.m. Their stand probably helped others get safely away. A company of the 150th Pennsylvania of Stone's brigade was intercepted as it retreated through the town by some Confederates led by a mounted officer, who ordered them to halt. One of the Bucktails shot him, saying, "We take no orders from the likes of you!"[10] And they continued on their way. A flag belonging to the same regiment was captured at the intersection of Washington and High streets by skirmishers from Ramseur's Brigade.

As parts of the 1st Corps funneled into the town from the west they collided with elements of the 11th Corps coming in from the north. A captain in the 80th New York said someone was shouting "First Corps this way" and "Eleventh Corps this way," but he couldn't see who it was or what directions were being indicated.[11] Colonel Wainwright of the artillery said that the men of the 1st Corps used one side of the street he followed and those of the 11th Corps the other side. They weren't panicky but talked and joked as they moved along. But the colonel of the 56th Pennsylvania claimed that the tail of his column was captured because the head of it was blocked by the 11th Corps.

Many units became intermixed in the confusing streets of the unfamiliar town and only got sorted out after they reached Cemetery Hill. The officers of the 19th Indiana of the

Iron Brigade couldn't form their men in the town and just let them move along as individuals. General Schurz said the worst disorder was at places where wagons (civilian as well as military) blocked the streets. One civilian, Anna Garlach, said that Baltimore Street in front of her house was so crowded with soldiers that she could have crossed the street by walking on their heads. Several Union soldiers and officers found hiding places to escape Confederate pursuit, some being provided with civilian clothes by the people of the town so as to avoid capture. Among them was General Schimmelfennig, who hid in the Garlach's yard for three days.

The 6th Wisconsin found its way blocked by a fence when it reached Chambersburg Street, which was swept by Confederate fire. But Colonel Dawes spotted a hole in the fence large enough for a man to pass through, and seizing the regiment's flag he led his men through it, although two were shot in the process. He then led his regiment to Washington Street, where he formed it in two lines across the street. While his men, tired, hot, and thirsty, were exchanging fire with pursuing Confederates, an elderly civilian brought them two buckets of water, to which they responded with a cheer. After clearing the street of pursuing Rebels they hurried on to the south and were soon further heartened to see "the colors of the Union, floating over well ordered line of men in blue, who were arrayed along the slope of Cemetery hill."[12] This was the 73rd Ohio of Colonel Orlando Smith's brigade of Steinwehr's division, which Howard had kept in reserve to hold this key position.

General Rowley evidently dealt with the misfortunes of the day by getting drunk. He threatened General Cutler, argued with Colonel Robinson of the 7th Wisconsin, and when he reached Cemetery Hill he was, as Colonel Dawes said, "raving and storming and giving wild and crazy orders."[13] The provost marshal of Wadsworth's division, a mere lieutenant, arrested him and asked Dawes to back him up, which he did. Rowley was later court-martialed and eventually resigned his commission. Howard, who had not been involved in the fighting, was calm and collected, placing regiments and batteries from his own corps into position behind fences and stone walls on the hill. A captain who had been on Barlow's staff saw him there and said watching him "taught me what a cool and confident man could do. No hurry, no confusion in his mind."[14] Soon Von Steinwehr's division held the northwest part of the hill; Schurz's division (probably no more than 1,500 men) the north end, facing the town; and Barlow's, now Ames's, on the northeast.

At Howard's request, Colonel Wainwright took command of the artillery of both corps. Wainwright took personal charge of 23 guns on the eastern part of Cemetery Hill, while Major Thomas Osborn, commander of the 11th Corps artillery, took charge of 20 guns positioned in the cemetery. Wainwright, still irked about the infantry officers' lack of understanding of artillery tactics, told his battery commanders not to take orders from anyone else, even if they had stars on their shoulders.

Hancock and Howard later gave somewhat different accounts of their meeting and how they settled on who was in charge. Hancock told Howard that Meade had sent him, but Howard evidently did not see the written order and did not realize that Meade meant for Hancock to be in command. At any rate, they supposedly agreed to divide the field, with Howard commanding east of the Baltimore Pike and Hancock to the west of it, but this didn't keep Hancock from sending troops to positions in what was supposedly Howard's sector. Brigadier General Gouverneur Warren arrived shortly after Hancock. He was the army's chief engineer, and Meade, a fellow engineer, liked him and trusted him and had, in fact, sent him to Gettysburg ahead of Hancock, but he had gone by way of Emmitsburg rather than directly, and so arrived a bit later.

In contrast to Howard's calm demeanor, Hancock, assisted by Warren, bustled about, giving orders here and there with the air of a man in a hurry who knew just what needed doing. One of the first things he did was to send the 5th Maine Battery, under Captain Greenleaf Stevens, to a knoll in the low ground between Cemetery Hill and more high ground to the east of it known to history as Culp's Hill, with orders to "stop the enemy from coming up that ravine."[15] The battery's position has been known ever since as Stevens' Knoll.

Doubleday reached Cemetery Hill at about 4:30 p.m. with fewer than 2,500 infantrymen and reported to Howard. "Our batteries were placed upon the summit of the hill," Doubleday later reported, "the First Corps having been directed to occupy the ground to the west of the road, the Eleventh Corps being on its right. A portion of the troops was placed behind the hill in reserve. Major-General Hancock now rode up, and informed me he had been placed in command of both corps. He at once directed me to send a force to support a battery which had been established on a lower range of hills, some 100 yards to the east of our position, protecting our flank in that direction."[16]

Doubleday replied that his regiments were now greatly reduced in strength and instead of a regiment sent General Wadsworth and what was left of the Iron Brigade and later added the relatively large 7th Indiana of Cutler's brigade, when it arrived from the rear where it had been guarding wagons. Years later Doubleday said that Hancock "at once brought order out of confusion and made such admirable dispositions that he secured the ridge and held it." General Schurz said that Hancock inspired confidence in the troops. "They all knew him by fame, and his stalwart figure, his proud mien, and his superb soldierly bearing seemed to verify all the things that fame had told them about him. His mere presence was a reinforcement, and everybody on the field felt stronger for his being there."[17]

Howard had, meanwhile, sent an aide to tell Buford to use his cavalry to cover the 1st Corps' retreat. Buford had scoffed at the idea that he could do much good against all those Rebels, but, nevertheless, at about 5 p.m. moved his two brigades, mounted, into the open fields west of Cemetery Hill and sent part of a regiment ahead to remove any obstacles to a mounted charge. And the mere threat of such a charge by two brigades of cavalry was enough to put an end to any Confederate pursuit through the fields south of town. As Doubleday later wrote: "The troops in front of the Seminary were stayed by the firm attitude of Buford's cavalry, and made a bend in the line, apparently with a view to form square."[18] (A square formation, having no flanks, was infantry's traditional defense against a cavalry charge.)

Northeast of Culp's Hill was a low ridge called Benner's Hill, which soon marked the far left of the Confederate army. Rock Creek, on its way south, passed between the two hills, and the road from Hannover, coming up from the southeast, ran over the northern edge of Benner's Hill just before turning due west to run the last half-mile into Gettysburg. At about 4 p.m. Brigadier General Alpheus Williams' 1st Division of Slocum's 12th Corps approached Benner's Hill on the Hannover Road, being the division that Slocum was sending to the right of the town, but Slocum soon ordered it back when he learned that the 1st and 11th Corps had retreated to Cemetery Hill south of the town. Williams took his two brigades south and put them into bivouac about a half-mile northeast of the Baltimore Pike. Slocum had his other division leave a brigade in reserve and sent the division commander, Brigadier General John Geary, with his other two brigades, to report to Howard. Geary found Hancock, instead, who told him to form his two brigades facing west along a low extension of Cemetery Hill known as Cemetery Ridge, which ran due south, getting lower the farther south it went, until it ended in a pair of higher wooded hills known to history as Little Round Top and Big Round Top.

As Doubleday later wrote, "Hancock was much pleased with the ridge we were on, as a defensive position, and considered it admirably adapted for a battle-field. Its gentle slopes for artillery, its stone fences and rocky boulders to shelter infantry, and its rugged but commanding eminences on either flank, where far-reaching batteries could be posted, were great advantages. It covered the principal roads to Washington and Baltimore, and its convex shape, enabling troops to reinforce with celerity any point of the line from the centre, or by moving along the chord of the arc, was probably a cause of our final success. The enemy, on the contrary, having a concave order of battle, was obliged to move troops much longer distances to support any part of his line, and could not communicate orders rapidly, nor could the different [Confederate] corps co-operate promptly with each other."[19]

Shortly after he arrived, Hancock had sent a staff officer back to Meade with a quick report of the situation and his estimation that the forces at Gettysburg could hold on until darkness ended the fighting for the day. At 5:25 p.m. he sent another officer with a message that said: "When I arrived here an hour since, I found that our troops had given up the front of Gettysburg and the town. We have now taken up a position in the cemetery, and cannot well be taken. It is a position, however, easily turned. Slocum is now coming on the ground, and is taking position on the right, which will protect the right. But we have, as yet, no troops on the left, the Third Corps not having yet reported; but I suppose that it is marching up. If so, its flank march will in a degree protect our left flank. In the meantime Gibbon had better march on so as to take position on our right or left, to our rear, as may be necessary, in some commanding position. General G[ibbon] will see this dispatch. The battle is quiet now. I think we will be all right until night. I have sent all the trains back. When night comes, it can be told better what had best be done. I think we can retire; if not, we can fight here, as the ground appears not unfavorable with good troops. I will communicate in a few moments with General Slocum, and transfer the command to him. Howard says that Doubleday's command gave way."[20]

It had been, of course, Howard's own corps that had actually retreated first, and Doubleday blamed Howard's accusation against the 1st Corps, evidently previously made directly to Meade by courier, for the fact that Meade that night assigned a division commander from the 6th Corps, Major General John Newton, to take command of what was left of the 1st Corps. Doubleday would return to the command of the 3rd Division of that corps, which Rowley had exercised during the day, not much mollified by the fact that he was reinforced that night by three large regiments from Vermont commanded by Brigadier General George Stannard. Their only service so far had been in the outer defenses of Washington, and their 90-days enlistments were about up. It remained to be seen whether these summer soldiers would be of any use. Any reinforcement must have been welcomed, however, for the 1st Corps had suffered well over 60 percent casualties that day, including about 2,000 men who were captured or missing. (The five brigades of the 11th Corps that had seen action that day had suffered about 45 percent casualties, including about 1,600 men captured or missing. Neither corps ever really recovered from this one day's losses, and by the spring of 1864 both had ceased to exist, their divisions and brigades being transferred to other organizations.)

When he had arranged things as best he could, Hancock sat on a stone wall near the top of Cemetery Hill with Schurz, and the two men studied the Confederates through their field glasses. They admitted to each other that they were both nervous about their situation, but Hancock said he thought their well-placed artillery would allow them to hold on until more of the army arrived. The longer the Rebels left them alone, the stronger their position would be, as the men rested and gained confidence – and the nearer the other parts of the army would be.

Considering the damage that had been done to Heth's and Pender's divisions, A. P. Hill, if he was yet conscious, was happy enough to let the Federals retreat, and did not order a pursuit, even though Anderson's fresh division of his corps had by then arrived west of the town. Ewell was somewhat more aggressive. Much of Rodes' division entered Gettysburg on the heels of the Union retreat, but Rodes, believing his division alone could not take Cemetery Hill, made no preparations for another attack. Hays's and Avery's brigades of Early's Division passed through the eastern part of the town in pursuit of the 11th Corps, but soon called a halt. A company of skirmishers from Hays's Louisianans went as far as the foot of Cemetery Hill, where they were sniped at by Union skirmishers up on the hill. Avery's Brigade, having been hit by very effective fire from Wiedrich's battery as soon as it crossed the railroad east of the town, also went as far as the foot of the hill, but Avery called a halt there in the cover of the ravine of east-west-running Winebrenner's Run. Early called for Smith's brigade to come forward while he examined the hill. He saw that it was crossed with multiple fences and stone walls that would break up any attacking formation as well as give shelter to the defenders, and that an attack from the town would require his men to form in columns in the streets, which would make them easy targets for the numerous Union guns on the hill. He quickly concluded that the hill could not be taken by an attack from the north. It would have to be hit from west of the town, but that area belonged to Rodes and to A. P. Hill.

Major Henry Kyd Douglas soon rode up and reported to Ewell that the latter's other division, that of Major General Edward "Allegheny" Johnson (which had come south from Carlisle by way of the Cumberland Valley and the Chambersburg Pike), was within an hour's march of the battlefield and ready to fight as soon as it arrived. "I gave General Ewell my message and tried to express General Johnson's earnestness as well as I could," Douglas later wrote. "When I finished General Gordon seemed to second it, saying that he could join in the attack with his brigade and they could carry that hill – pointing to Cemetery Hill – before dark. Gordon seemed to be as earnest as Johnson in the matter. General Ewell hesitated, as if in thought, and then said quietly, 'General Lee told me to come to Gettysburg and gave me no orders to go further. I do not feel like advancing and making an attack without orders from him, and he is back at Cashtown.' He then directed me to tell General Johnson, when he got well to the front, to halt and wait for orders." Then, according to Douglas's post-war memoir, Ewell's chief of staff, Major Sandy Pendleton, quietly expressed to Douglas a longing for their late commander, the highly aggressive Stonewall Jackson, saying, "Oh, for the presence and inspiration of Old Jack for just one hour!"[21]

Jubal Early, meanwhile, rode west looking for Rodes or even A. P. Hill. He encountered an officer from Pender's staff and asked him to tell Hill that if he'd send a division forward they could take Cemetery Hill, but nothing came of that. Then one of Ewell's staff officers found Early and said that Ewell wanted to talk to him about how to use Johnson's Division, but just then "Extra Billy" Smith's son and aide rode up and excitedly reported that a large Union force was approaching from the east. This might have been Williams' division of the 12th Corps, although Smith described it as being on the York road, not the road from Hannover. Early claimed later not to have believed it, but he either believed it at the time or felt he couldn't afford to take a chance, for he sent Gordon's Brigade to support Smith's, with Gordon to take overall command.

Eventually, Early, Rodes, and Ewell all came together, and the three of them agreed that they should continue the attack, if Hill's corps would join in. Ewell summoned Lieutenant James Power Smith of his staff (no relation to General Smith), who had just returned to the army after escorting Stonewall Jackson's widow and baby home and had reached Gettysburg in the company of General Lee. Since he had recently been with Lee, Ewell said, maybe he could find that general again, and instructed him to listen to Rodes and Early and then to pass on what they had to say to General Lee.

Smith found Lee with General Longstreet on Seminary Ridge, studying the Union position through binoculars. He delivered his message, saying that the three commanders of the 2nd Corps felt that "if General Lee would send troops to support them on their right, they could at once advance to occupy the cemetery hill in front of the town; and that it would be well for General Lee to occupy at once the higher ground in front of our right, which seemed to command the cemetery hill." By this they either meant the two Round Tops or, more likely, the high ground on the Emmitsburg Road that became the scene of battle the following day. Lee handed the lieutenant his binoculars and pointed to his front, saying he presumed this was the higher ground they referred to, and noted that some Federals were there already. (Smith said he saw only a few mounted men, apparently reconnoitering.) Lee added "that he had no force on the field with which to take that position; and turning to Longstreet asked where his troops were, and expressed the wish that they might be brought immediately to the front. General Longstreet replied that his leading division, Major General Lafayette McLaws', was about six miles away, and then was indefinite and noncommital. General Lee directed me to say to General Ewell that he regretted that his people were not up to support him on the right, but he wished him to take the Cemetery hill if it were possible; and that he would ride over and see him very soon."[22]

Up to this point, Lee seems to have been unsure what to do next, for Major Campbell Brown, Ewell's stepson and staff officer, later remembered carrying a message from Lee to Ewell that said, "I have not decided to fight here and may probably draw off by my right flank . . . so as to get between the enemy and Washington and Baltimore – and force them to attack us in position."[23] However, when Longstreet, according to his post-war writings, suggested to Lee that they should do just that – go around the Federals' left, or southern, flank and get between them and Washington – as he later wrote, "I was not a little surprised, therefore, at his impatience, as, striking the air with his closed hand, he said, 'If he is there to-morrow I will attack him.'" Longstreet later claimed to have replied, "'If he is there to-morrow it will be because he wants you to attack,' and queried, 'If that height has become the objective, why not take it at once? We have forty thousand men, less the casualties of the day; he cannot have more than twenty thousand.' Then it was that I heard of the wanderings of the cavalry and the cause of his uneven temper."

By this Longstreet evidently meant that Lee began his by-then-usual complaint about Stuart's absence leaving him in ignorance of where the Union army was and what it was up to, as well as complaining that Brigadier General Imboden's mounted brigade had lingered at Hancock, Maryland, thus forcing Lee to leave Major General George Pickett's division of Longstreet's corps to guard the army's rear – a job that Imboden was supposed to perform. (Sometime that evening Lee dispatched no fewer than eight couriers from the 1st Maryland Cavalry Battalion, which was attached to Ewell's corps, each of them carrying sealed orders by different roads to Stuart, instructing him to come immediately to Gettysburg.) Apparently Lee became rather heated on the subject, for Longstreet said, "His manner suggested to me that a little reflection would be better than further discussion, and right soon he suggested to the commander of the Second Corps to take Cemetery Hill if he thought it practicable...."[24]

Another verbal message was carried to Ewell by Captain Walter Taylor of Lee's staff, telling him, as Lee later wrote in his report, "to carry the hill occupied by the enemy, if he found it practicable, but to avoid a general engagement until the arrival of the other divisions of the army, which were ordered to hasten forward."[25] Lee, meanwhile, sent Colonel Armistead Long, his military secretary, a West Point graduate, to reconnoiter the Union position on Cemetery Hill. Long soon came back to report that it was occupied by the Federals in considerable force. Years after the War, Long told General Early that "an attack at that time, with the troops then at hand, would have been hazardous and of very doubtful success."[26] General Ewell, however, despite the formidable-looking array of Union guns on the hill, started making preparations for an attack, but he called them off after hearing from Extra Billy Smith about the Union force that was supposedly threatening his left flank and rear.

Taking Early and Rodes with him, he went to have a look at this situation for himself. Early claimed that, while he didn't believe in the supposed threat, Rodes did, and that Ewell was undecided. They found a place from which they could see two or three miles up the York Pike, and they saw a line of infantry, which Rodes apparently thought must be the Federals, but it turned out to be some of Smith's troops whom Gordon had ordered to move to a different location. No other sign of an enemy was apparent, yet the two brigades, half of Early's division, were, nevertheless, left guarding this road in Ewell's rear.

Meanwhile, Johnson's Division began to arrive, increasing Ewell's strength considerably, but it was nearly dark by the time its last brigade came in, and thus, despite its commander's previous boast via Major Douglas, it was too late to participate in an attack. The division halted along the unfinished railroad line, just west of the station in town. Johnson rode ahead of his column to confer with Ewell, who told him to take his division beyond the town and occupy Culp's Hill. Its mere presence there, behind the Union right and very close to the Baltimore Pike, the Federal supply line, should be enough to dislodge the enemy from Cemetery Hill without a fight. Major General Isaac Trimble later claimed credit for this idea. Trimble was another of Stonewall Jackson's former subordinates who had been laid up with a wound for some months. Lee had recently sent him to take command in the Shenandoah Valley, but by the time he had arrived there Ewell's corps (formerly Jackson's) had swept through on its way north, taking the local troops with it, and Trimble had tagged along, a general without a command. Trimble later claimed that he had spotted the importance of Culp's Hill and had urged Ewell to occupy it with a brigade, but that Ewell had replied that when he wanted advice from a subordinate he would ask for it.

Ewell, however, sent two aides to reconnoiter, and they came back to report that they had gone all the way to the top of the hill without seeing any Federals and had been able to look down on the Union position on Cemetery Hill, which, they said, would be untenable if the Confederates occupied

Culp's Hill. They had probably gone up the eastern side of the hill, where the slope was gentle, and had failed to spot the Iron Brigade on the west slope, possibly because it was hidden by some trees. (The 7th Indiana had probably not yet arrived to extend the Union line.) Ewell asked Rodes what he thought of sending Johnson's Division up there, but Rodes said the men would be tired from marching all day and didn't think "it would result in anything one way or the other." Early, however, disagreed, and later claimed to have said, "If you do not go up there tonight, it will cost you ten thousand men to get up there tomorrow."[27] Ewell agreed and thus ordered Johnson to occupy the hill, if he found it undefended. Evidently Johnson protested, and an argument ensued between him and Early, but the order stood.

Johnson returned to his division and led it off into the dusky evening, following the railroad tracks, which led it to the northeast. (Culp's Hill was to the southeast.) When these Confederates came to Rock Creek they had to ford it, because Gordon's Brigade had wrecked the railroad bridge the week before, when it had passed through on its way east. They then continued to follow the tracks to Hunterstown Road and turned right there, crossed the York Pike, and eventually, by the light of a rising moon, formed line of battle in some low ground north of Culp's Hill.

The Confederate soldiers who had fought that day, unaware of the doubts and hesitations of their officers, were confident. As seemed to be the pattern of the war in the East for over a year now, the Federals had put up a hard fight but had eventually given way; surely they would do the same tomorrow. Michael Jacobs, a professor at the local college, talked with some of Rodes' men. "They were boastful of themselves," he later wrote, "of their cause, and of the skill of their officers, and were anxious to tell us of the unskillful manner in which some of our officers had conducted the fight which had just closed. When informed that General Archer and 1,500 of his men had been captured, they said, 'Tomorrow we will take all those back again; and having already taken

5,000 (!) prisoners of you today, we will take the balance of your men tomorrow.'"[28]

In the town, as they had throughout Pennsylvania so far, the Confederates rounded up all the black people they could find. Albertus McCreary, a boy of Gettysburg, later wrote that "A number of colored people lived in the western part of the town, and . . . a great many of them were gathered together by the Confederate soldiers and marched out of town. As they passed our house our old washerwoman called out, 'Goodby; we are going back to slavery.'"[29] This particular woman managed to escape when her group passed by the Lutheran church, which was being used as a hospital and where there was a great deal of bustle and confusion. She slipped into the church and climbed up to the belfry, where she hid for two days without food or water. Most of the others were not so fortunate.

With the sounds of battle outside finally quieted, Anna Mary Young and her family emerged from their cellar in the northern part of the town after dark to find themselves in a different world. "The moon was shining brightly in the heavens," she later wrote, "while on earth, scattered everywhere, were the dead, and the wounded moaning with pain. Our yard and house were full. I actually thought I had been transferred to some strange place, so different did it seem from the home I had seen in the morning."[30]

Although maintaining his headquarters in Taneytown, Meade had decided by late afternoon on that first day of July to concentrate most of his army at or near Gettysburg, although not all of it could get there that night, and some parts were left to guard other places. At 4:30 p.m., chief of staff Butterfield wrote to Major General John Sedgwick, whose 6th Corps was the one farthest from Gettysburg, at Manchester, Maryland, and told him to move to Taneytown that night. Fifteen minutes later he wrote to Dan Sickles, commander of the 3rd Corps, that Hancock had been sent to take command of the left wing and that Sickles should leave a division at Emmitsburg to protect against a Confederate move to get around the left flank of the units at Gettysburg. However, Sickles was already on his way to Gettysburg with most of both of his divisions, but he had anticipated Meade's concern by leaving one brigade from each division to hold Emmitsburg. (Unlike the 1st and 11th Corps, each of which had three divisions of two brigades each, the 3rd Corps had two divisions of three brigades each.)

At 5 p.m., Slocum wrote to Meade from near Gettysburg: "A portion of our troops have fallen back from Gettysburg. Matters do not appear well. My Second Division has gone up to the town, and the First on the right of the town. I hope the work for the day is nearly over."[31] Meade wrote to Hancock and Doubleday (but not Howard), at 6 p.m.: "If General Slocum is on the field, and I hope he is, of course he takes command. Say to him I thought it prudent to leave a division of the Third Corps at Emmitsburg, to hold in check any force attempting to come through there. It can be ordered up tonight, if necessary. Sedgwick is moving up here, and will be pushed forward in the night, if required. It seems to me we have so concentrated that a battle at Gettysburg is now forced on us, and that, if we get up all our people, and attack with our whole force to-morrow, we ought to defeat the force the enemy has."[32]

At the same hour of 6 p.m., Meade sent a report to Major General Henry Halleck, general-in-chief of the Army, at Washington: "The First and Eleventh Corps have been engaged all day in front of Gettysburg. The Twelfth, Third, and Fifth have been moving up, and all, I hope, by this time on the field. This leaves only the Sixth, which will move up tonight. General Reynolds was killed this morning early in the action. I immediately sent up General Hancock to assume command. A. P. Hill and Ewell are certainly concentrating; Longstreet's whereabouts I do not know. If he is not up tomorrow, I hope with the force I have concentrated to defeat Hill and Ewell. At any rate, I see no other course than to hazard a general battle. Circumstances during the night may alter this decision, of which I will try to advise you. I have telegraphed Couch that if he can threaten Ewell's rear from Harrisburg without endangering himself, to do so."[33]

Slocum was informed that Hancock had orders to hand the command over to him whenever he arrived, so reluctantly he rode forward and arrived at about 7 p.m. Just then, Howard received a copy of Meade's order that had given Hancock the command. He was evidently surprised and embarrassed to learn that he had not been in command since Hancock's arrival, as he thought he had been, and he immediately wrote a message to Meade, saying he thought he had done as good a job as any of the other corps commanders could have done and that Meade's order placing Hancock over him had "mortified" him and would "disgrace" him. "Please inform me frankly if you disapprove of my conduct to-day, that I may know what to do."[34] Hancock turned local command over to Slocum and departed for Taneytown to report to Meade. Slocum, in turn, gave temporary command of his 12th Corps to Williams, his senior division commander.

By date of commission, Slocum (then 36) was the ranking corps commander in the Army of the Potomac, and had even been senior to Meade before the latter's appointment to command the army. He had graduated from West Point in 1852 at the age of 25 and had already been a school teacher before entering the academy. He had ranked seventh in his class, high enough to be commissioned in the artillery instead of the lowly infantry, and while a young officer on garrison duty he had studied law in his spare time and had left the Army in 1856 to become a lawyer and militia officer in upstate New York. He had commanded a regiment from that state at the first battle of Bull Run, a brigade and then a division on the Peninsula and at Antietam, and had been assigned the 12th Corps when its previous commander had been killed at that battle. No one seems to have expected him to succeed Hooker (whom he despised), including himself. He was considered competent and capable but not particularly brilliant. But by the fortunes of war, he was now in temporary command of about half of Meade's army.

And more of it was on the way. At 7 p.m., just as Slocum was taking command at Gettysburg, Butterfield was writing to Major General George Sykes, commander of the 5th Corps: "The major-general commanding directs that you move up to Gettysburg at once upon receipt of this order, if not already ordered to do so by General Slocum. The present prospect is that our general engagement must be there. Communicate with General Slocum, under whose directions you are placed by the orders of this morning. The general had supposed that General Slocum would have ordered you up."[35] Sykes was Meade's replacement as commander of the 5th Corps for no other reason than that he had been its senior division commander. He therefore was, at best, inexperienced at corps command, and Meade may not have considered him up to the job, for, as the message says, he had earlier placed him and his corps subordinate to Slocum, just as he had put Howard and Sickles under Reynolds.

Like the 3rd Corps, the 5th had been composed of two divisions of three brigades each, but before he had been removed from army command, General Hooker had scoured all the nearby Union garrisons for any reinforcements they could give him, and the Department of Washington, defending the nation's capital, had reluctantly parted with two brigades of the Pennsylvania Reserve Division. This entire division, originally of three brigades, was composed of regiments that had been raised in the early days of the war by the governor of Pennsylvania over and above that state's quota and had been held in state service until the first battle of Bull Run had convinced the Federal government that it needed all the troops it could get. It had originally been part of the 1st Corps, which had been left to defend Washington and northern Virginia when the rest of the Army of the Potomac had gone down to the Peninsula east of Richmond, but the division had soon been sent down as a reinforcement and had there joined the then-new 5th Corps. (Both Meade and Reynolds had been brigade commanders in that division early in the war, and each had commanded the division at one time in their careers). Upon returning from the Peninsula, it had rejoined the 1st Corps for the second battle of Bull Run, Antietam, and Fredericksburg. After the latter fight it had been sent to Washington to rest and recruit its strength, and now, minus its 2nd Brigade, still in the Washington garrison, it was back in the 5th Corps as its 3rd Division. It was composed of good troops, but after months of garrison duty they were not up to the hard marching the Army of the Potomac had been doing since leaving Virginia, and it had not been able to keep up with the other two divisions.

Those two divisions had started out that morning from Union Mills, Maryland, heading for Hanover, Pennsylvania, only some twelve miles to the north. The Reserves, now commanded by Brigadier General Samuel Crawford, had been camped a few miles father south, at Frizzelburg. At about 3 p.m., that division, at the tail of the corps' column, had crossed the Mason-Dixon line into its home state and paused to hear a patriotic speech by General Crawford before marching on. Up ahead the other two divisions passed through Hanover (where there had been a large cavalry fight the day before) with bands playing and flags flying and went into camp just west of the town. They thought they were through for the day, but they weren't. Eventually an officer arrived with Meade's order to move on to Gettysburg, some thirteen miles to the west. At about 7 p.m. they hit the road again. Somewhere along the way a rumor passed through the column, as it had through others that morning, that General George McClellan, the Army of the Potomac's first commander, was back in charge. He had been sacked several months back by President Lincoln for timidity and slowness, but most of the men still loved him, for, whatever his faults (and there were plenty of them) he had loved his army and taken good care of his men. The troops cheered this news, and perhaps it helped some of them to endure the extended march and the anticipation of a battle at its end. Sykes called a halt, however, at Bonnaughtown, four or five miles short of Gettysburg, where the first two divisions stopped for the night, and at 12:30 a.m. he sent messages to Butterfield and to Slocum announcing his presence there and his intention of resuming his march at 4 a.m. The Reserves got only as far as McSherrystown, just west of Hanover.

Dan Sickles, commander of the 3rd Corps, reached Gettysburg ahead of his troops, perhaps before Slocum assumed command, for Howard was the one to greet him, reportedly with the words, "Here you are, general, always reliable, always first."[36] Sickles and Howard were, however, very much opposites in character. While Howard was highly religious and never even used strong language, Sickles was a man of scandalous reputation. He, Butterfield and Hooker were good friends and notorious for womanizing and drinking to the extent that more fastidious generals, including Meade, were offended, and had as little to do with them, personally, as possible. Sickles was a New York lawyer and politician connected with that city's notorious Tammany Hall organization. He was most famous for having publicly shot his wife's lover, getting off of murder charges on a plea of temporary insanity (the first such in U.S. legal history), and, most scandalous of all, for forgiving his wife rather than divorcing her.

At the outbreak of war he had recruited an entire brigade from New York and had been rewarded with its command and a general's star. By the battle of Antietam, the previous September, he had risen to division command, and early in 1863 he succeeded to command of the 3rd Corps. He had no military education, but he was a fast learner. General Warren, the engineer and a future corps commander himself, later testified before Congress that Sickles, while not a soldier of the quality of Reynolds, Hancock or Meade, "did the best he could, and with the corps he had managed very well." One of his brigade commanders, French soldier of fortune Colonel Regis de Trobriand, later said Sickles was "gifted in a high degree with that multiplicity of faculties which has given rise to the saying that a Yankee is ready for everything."[37]

Shortly before dark, Sickles' first troops arrived, being two brigades of his 1st Division, commanded by Major General David Birney, with two batteries attached. His other division commander, Brigadier General Andrew A. Humphreys, however, had taken two of his brigades and one battery by a different road, roughly following the same round-about route that Rowley had taken earlier in the day. After getting lost, almost blundering into some Confederates, and backtracking part of the way, it was after midnight before they joined Birney's division on the lower end of Cemetery Ridge. Meanwhile, at 7:30 p.m., Butterfield had ordered the two brigades left back at Emmitsburg to rejoin their divisions. At the same hour he told the 6th Corps to make a forced march to Gettysburg (for a total day's march of 35 miles) and for General Sedgwick to report in person at army headquarters in Taneytown, where Meade was waiting to confer with him before going to the front.

Hancock's 2nd Corps, under Gibbon's temporary command, had set out from Taneytown at 1:30 p.m. and had marched another fifteen miles after having already gone seven that morning. Hancock, on his way back from Gettysburg, met it just south of Big Round Top sometime after dark and told Gibbon to halt there and deploy in such a way as to block any Confederate attempt to turn the army's left, or southern, flank. Hancock went on down to Taneytown to report to Meade and did not return to his corps until the next morning.

At 9:20 p.m., Slocum wrote a note to Meade saying he had received the message the latter had sent to Hancock and Doubleday at 6 p.m., the one indicating that the army was now so concentrated at Gettysburg that a battle there was forced upon it. "If you conclude to make the fight here," Slocum said, "the most of the Artillery Reserve can be used to advantage; and in that case the Fifth and Sixth Corps can be used to extend our right."[38]

Meade finally set out for the front at about 10 p.m., even though Sedgwick had still not reached Taneytown for the conference Meade wanted to have with him, and he left Butterfield and most of the staff there, taking with him only his son and aide Captain George Meade, Brigadier General Henry Hunt, his chief of artillery, Captain William Paine of the engineers, another captain, an orderly sergeant, and a local civilian to serve as guide. This group rode hard and fast, sometimes taking to the fields to by-pass the 2nd Corps troops filling the road, and it soon lost the civilian, who couldn't keep up. At about 11 p.m. it reached Gibbon's headquarters, where Meade spent about 15 minutes with that general, instructing him to bring the 2nd Corps on up at first light. A half-hour later Meade reached the gate house of Gettysburg's Evergreen Cemetery, an unusual brick building that looks much like a Roman arch of triumph, having two rooms, one above the other, on each side of the road, with an arch connecting them. There Meade met Slocum, Howard, Sickles, Warren and others. Howard asked personally what he had already put in a message – did Meade blame him for the day's reverses – and was reassured. Howard then said he was confident the army could hold this position; Slocum said that it was good for defense, and Sickles agreed that it was a good place to fight from. "I am glad to hear you say so, gentlemen," Meade replied, "for it is too late to leave it."[39]

"We lay on our arms that night," General Doubleday later remembered, "among the tombs at the Cemetery, so suggestive of the shortness of life and the nothingness of fame; but the men were little disposed to moralize on themes like these and were too exhausted to think of anything but much-needed rest."[40]

General Lee, meanwhile, had received reports at about 6 p.m. of a Union force (presumably Humphreys') approaching his right or right-rear in the vicinity of Fairfield (on the Hagerstown Road). According to Longstreet, "General Lee ordered General Anderson to put one of his brigades out on the right as picket guard. Wilcox's brigade and Ross's battery were marched and posted near Black Horse Tavern."[41] Lee then made his promised visit to his 2nd Corps, and he, Ewell, Early, and Rodes met in an arbor attached to a house in the town (quite possibly the house where Anna Mary Young lived, for her family had had tea with Ewell earlier but had declined to provide him with a couple of rooms for his headquarters). Years later General Early wrote the only surviving description of this meeting. "General Lee's purpose," Early said, "was to ascertain our condition, what we knew of the enemy and his position, and what we could probably do next day. It was evident from the first that it was his purpose to attack the enemy as early as possible next day – at daylight, if practicable. This was a proposition the propriety of which was so apparent that there was not the slightest discussion or difference of opinion upon it. It was a point taken for granted. After we had given General Lee all the information we possessed, addressing us conjointly, he asked: 'Can't you, with your corps, attack on this flank at daylight tomorrow?'"

Early later said that, as the officer most familiar with the ground, he was the one who replied first: "The purport of what I said was, that the ground over which we would have to advance on our flank was very rugged and steep; that the enemy was then evidently concentrating and fortifying in our immediate front, and by morning would probably have the greater part of his force concentrated on that flank and the position strongly fortified, as ours were the only troops then confronting him in close proximity; that we could not move through the town in line of battle, and would therefore have to go on the left of the town right up against Cemetery Hill and the rugged hills on the left of it; and that the result of an attack there might be doubtful, but if successful it would inevitably be at very great loss. I then called General Lee's attention to the Round Tops, the outline of which we could see, though dusk was approaching, and suggested that those heights must evidently command the enemy's position and render it untenable; and I also called his attention to the more practicable nature of the ascents on that side of the town, adding the suggestion that the attack could be made on that side, and from our right flank, with better chances of success.

"With these views both Ewell and Rodes coincided, and they submitted further considerations in the same direction. There was some conversation upon the several points suggested, when General Lee, being satisfied that it was not advisable to make the main assault from our [2nd Corps] flank, remarked, interrogatively: 'Then perhaps I had better draw you around towards my right, as the line will be very long and thin if you remain here, and the enemy may come down and break through it?'" Again Early made the first reply and spoke against moving the 2nd Corps from its current position. "I did not like the idea of giving up anything we had gained," he later said. He also argued that such a withdrawal would be seen by the men as a retreat and lower their morale. "Moreover, there were some of my wounded not in a condition to be removed, and I did not like the idea of leaving those brave fellows to the mercy of the enemy; and there were a great many muskets stacked in the streets of Gettysburg which I did not want to lose. So I replied at once to General Lee, and assured him that he need not fear that the enemy would break through our line, and that we could repulse any force he [the enemy] could send against us. The fact was, that on that part of the line it was more difficult for the enemy to come down from the heights to attack us than for us to ascend them to attack him, as difficult as the latter would have been.

"Ewell and Rodes again agreed with me, and urged views of their own, the fact being that I merely spoke first. I do not recollect that during all this time Longstreet's name or corps was mentioned. If it was, it was only on the assumption that he would certainly be up during the night, of which neither of us doubted. . . . The first mention of Longstreet's name in connection with the attack was in this wise: When General Lee had heard our views, both in regard to attacking from our flank and our being removed towards the right, he said, in these very words, which are indelibly impressed on my memory: 'Well, if I attack from my right, Longstreet will have to make the attack;' and after a moment's pause, during which he held his head down in deep thought, he raised it and added: 'Longstreet is a very good fighter when he gets in position and gets everything ready, but he is *so slow*.' The emphasis was just as I have given it, and the words seemed to come from General Lee with pain....

"The part we proposed to ourselves to perform in achieving ... victory, was to follow up the success that might be gained on the right, and pursue and destroy the enemy's forces when they had been thrown in disorder by the capture of the commanding positions on their left. We did not, therefore, by any means, propose to play the part of passive spectators.... We were then given to understand that the attack should begin from our right at daylight in the morning, or as soon thereafter as practicable, and that a diversion should be made on our flank to favor it, with the direction to make that diversion a real attack on discovering any disorder or symptoms of giving way on the enemy's part...."[42]

This was all post-war recollection, and therefore suspect, and certainly was not Lee's final decision at that time, for Lee later sent word to Ewell that, unless he could carry the Union position in his front, he, according to Colonel Charles Marshall of his staff, who carried the message, "intended to move Longstreet around the enemy's left & draw Hill after him, directing Genl. Ewell to prepare to follow the latter."[43] Ewell kept Marshall waiting while he had a long unrecorded discussion with Early and Rodes, then rode with Marshall on the latter's return to Lee's headquarters (a collection of tents beside the Chambersburg Pike on Seminary Ridge, just across the road from a small stone house, which happened to belong to Abolitionist Congressman Thaddeus Stevens, although rented by a Widow Thompson) and evidently persuaded the army commander that, since Johnson's Division was already on its way to occupy Culp's Hill, an act that would make Cemetery Hill untenable, his corps should remain on the army's left. This decision killed the turning movement and committed Lee's army to remaining at Gettysburg at least until Johnson's movement caused the Federals to retreat – or failed to do so. (Meade wrote, after the war, that Ewell's "occupation of Culp's Hill, with batteries commanding the whole of Cemetery Ridge, would have produced the evacuation of that ridge and the withdrawal of the troops there by the Baltimore Pike and Taneytown and Emmitsburg roads.")[44]

It was after midnight by the time Ewell got back to his own headquarters, but no word had yet arrived there of Johnson's progress, so he sent orders for that general to occupy Culp's Hill, if he had not already done so. The staff lieutenant who carried this order returned with bad news. He had found Johnson's Division in position to attack but was informed by Johnson that a reconnaissance party he had sent up the hill had found that the Federals already held it. Those Confederates had run into pickets of the 7th Indiana of Cutler's brigade, which was by then extending the Iron's Brigade's line up the west slope of the hill to its summit, and these Hoosiers had captured a Rebel officer and one soldier and driven off the rest. The reconnaissance party returned the favor on its way back down the hill by capturing a courier who was carrying a dispatch from General Sykes to Slocum in which the former said that his corps would be camping that night only four miles down the Hanover Road and would resume its march to Gettysburg at 4 a.m. Johnson sent the lieutenant back to Ewell with the captured dispatch, saying that, since the hill in question was occupied by the enemy, he would stay put until he received further orders. As Ewell later remarked in his official report of his corps' part in the battle, unconsciously echoing Meade's remark that night: "Day was now breaking, and it was too late for any change of place."[45]

∽ Endnotes ∽

1   Nolan, *The Iron Brigade*, 247.
2   Ibid., 250.
3   *OR*, I:27:II:670.

4   Ibid., I:27:II:661.
5   Pfanz, *Gettysburg – The First Day*, 316.
6   *OR*, I:27:I:251.
7   Pfanz, *Gettysburg – The First Day*, 313.
8   Wheeler, *Witness to Gettysburg*, 153.
9   *OR*, I:27:II:349.
10 Pfanz, *Gettysburg – The First Day*, 329.
11 Ibid., 323.
12 Ibid., 330.
13 Ibid., 328.
14 Ibid., 332.
15 Ibid., 336.
16 *OR*, I:27:I:252.
17 Harry W. Pfanz, *Gettysburg – Culp's Hill and Cemetery Hill* (Chapel Hill NC, 1993), 103; both quotes.
18 Doubleday, *Chancellorsville and Gettysburg*, 149.
19 Ibid., 151-2.
20 *OR*, I:27:I:366.
21 Henry Kyd Douglas, *I Rode With Stonewall* (Chapel Hill NC, 1940; Mockingbird Books paperback edition, Atlanta, 1961), 238-9.
22 James Power Smith, "General Lee at Gettysburg," *SHSP* XXXIII:135.
23 Bearss with Hills, *Receding Tide*, 323.
24 Longstreet, *From Manassas to Appomattox*, 458-9.
25 *OR*, I:27:II:318.
26 J. A. Early, "Leading Confederates On the Battle of Gettysburg," *SHSP* IV:259.
27 Pfanz, *Gettysburg – The First Day*, 347.
28 Wheeler, *Witness to Gettysburg*, 164.
29 Ibid.
30 Ibid., 164-5.
31 *OR*, I:27:III:466.
32 Ibid.
33 Ibid., I:27:I:71-2.
34 Ibid., I:27:I:697.
35 Ibid., I:27:III:467.
36 Ibid., I:27:I:129.
37 Harry W. Pfanz, *Gettysburg – The Second Day* (Chapel Hill NC, 1987), 47-48. Both quotes.
38 *OR*, I:27:III:468.
39 Pfanz, *Gettysburg – Culp's Hill and Cemetery Hill*, 107.
40 Doubleday, *Chancellorsville and Gettysburg*, 155.
41 Longstreet, *From Manassas to Appomattox*, 360.
42 J. A. Early, "Leading Confederates On the Battle of Gettysburg," *SHSP* IV:271-4. According to Longstreet (*From Manassas to Appomattox*, 363), this conference between Lee and the officers of his 2nd Corps took place the next morning, between 9 and 10 a.m., 2 July. General Trimble also remembered this conversation as taking place on the morning of 2 July. (See Douglas Southall Freeman, *R. E. Lee*, volume 3, New York, 1935, 91, note 16.) I suspect they may have been right, but at this remove it's impossible to say for sure, and it does not seem to matter much, so long as it took place after dark on the 1st and before Longstreet's attack on the 2nd.
43 Pfanz, *Gettysburg – Culp's Hill and Cemetery Hill*, 84.
44 George G. Meade, "A Letter from General Meade" in *B&L* III:413.
45 *OR*, I:27:II:446.

Part Two
GETTYSBURG: DAY TWO

CHAPTER 6
"You Will Be Entirely on the Flank of the Enemy"
2 July 1863

During the night, a light rain or heavy mist fell on the men who were lying in the fields around Gettysburg – both the living and the dead. The sun rose at around 4:15 a.m. on the second day of July, reddening the clouds that had brought the moisture. "The day . . . opened without firing," a member of the untried 2nd Vermont Brigade recorded, "save now and then a shot from the pickets, but we saw considerable moving of the troops on our side behind the low ridge which concealed us from the enemy, and doubtless the same process was going on, on their side, unseen by us. The batteries alone on the crests of the ridges menaced each other, like grim bulldogs, in silence."[1]

By 7 a.m. the temperature was already up to 74 degrees at the college, with overcast skies and a light breeze from the south. The humidity, of course, must have been very high. However, long before that hour the bugles were sounding throughout the camps, and the men were rolling out of their blankets to begin another day – the last day for many of them. Union Private Warren Goss noted that "By ten o'clock the threatening clouds vanished and the green meadows were bathed in sunlight." It was a beautiful summer day, with cattle grazing in the fields, birds singing in the trees, and not much for the troops who were already on hand to do except think about the coming renewal of the battle. Goss said, "At no time had there been such intense feeling shown among all ranks as then. It showed itself in earnest glances and tones of voice. The general feeling was well expressed by a sergeant in one of the Pennsylvania regiments who said, 'We've got to fight our best today or have those rebs for our masters!'"[2]

Besides the living and the dead there were those who

were in between: the wounded. Mrs. Joseph Bayly lived three miles northwest of Gettysburg. During the night a young Confederate had knocked on her door and asked her to hide him. He was sick of the war and never wanted to fight again. She had given him civilian clothes and a bed in her attic, and he never returned to North Carolina. When Mrs. Bayly heard that many of the men wounded in the previous day's fight were still lying unattended on the field, she packed a market basket with bread and butter, wine, bandages and pins, and set off this Thursday morning with her niece on an old blind horse. Eventually they came to where the fighting had been heavy the day before.

"Getting down into the valley," she later wrote, "I found our wounded lying in the broiling sun, where they had lain for twenty-four hours with no food and no water.... The very worst needed a surgeon's care; but, while my niece gave food to the hungry and wine to the faint, I looked after their wounds." She examined them and put fresh bandages on many. Then, hearing many cries for water, she discovered that these men had not had any for 24 hours. "I rose up in my wrath," she remembered, "and, turning to the rebels who were walking around me, I said, 'Is it possible that none of you will bring water to these poor fellows?' An officer heard me, and, finding that what I said was true, he ordered a lot of men to mount and to bring all that was necessary."[3] Evidently these were members of Brigadier General Albert Jenkins cavalry brigade, which had been attached to Ewell's corps throughout its foray in Pennsylvania. (Jenkins was on Barlow's knoll, north of the town, when he was wounded in the head at around noon that day by a fragment from an artillery shell fired from Cemetery Hill.)

Eventually a surgeon came along, who had been ordered to look after the wounded Federals. He was a German and spoke very little English, but Mrs. Bayly noted that he had a gentle touch and seemed to approve of the bandages she had administered, so she turned the work over to him. On her way home she came across a field full of Union prisoners who loaded her with letters to send to their families and friends.

The commanders of the two armies could spare few thoughts for these men who could no longer fight, for they had to plan what to do with those who still could. Before dawn, General Meade had begun a tour of his army's camps in the moonlight and, no-doubt, had noted whatever Lee's campfires had disclosed of the enemy army. Accompanied by generals Howard and Hunt, he followed Cemetery Ridge southward at first, and by the time he reached the last of the 3rd Corps camps and turned north again, if not before, there was enough light for Captain Paine of the engineers to sketch a map of the field. General Hunt later wrote a careful description of the area, beginning with Zeigler's Grove, a small wood of heavy timber near the western base of Cemetery Hill. "From this grove," he said, "the distance nearly due south to the base of Little Round Top is a mile and a half. A well-defined ridge known as Cemetery Ridge follows this line from Ziegler's for 900 yards to another small grove, or clump of trees, where it turns sharply to the east for 200 yards, then turns south again, and continues in a direct line toward Round Top, for 700 yards, to George Weikert's [house]. So far the ridge is smooth and open, in full view of Seminary Ridge opposite, and distant from 1400 to 1600 yards. At Weikert's, this ridge is lost in a large body of rocks, hills, and woods, lying athwart the direct line to Round Top, and forcing a bend to the east in the Taneytown road. This rough space also stretches for a quarter of a mile or more *west* of this direct line, toward Plum Run [a small stream running southward below the west face of the ridge]. Toward the south it sinks into low marshy ground which reaches to the base of Little Round Top, half a mile or more from George Weikert's. . . .

"Plum Run flows south-easterly toward Little Round Top, then makes a bend to the south-west, where it receives a small stream or 'branch' from Seminary Ridge. In the angle between these streams is Devil's Den, a bold, rocky height, steep on its eastern face, and prolonged as a ridge to the west. It is 500 yard due west of Little Round Top, and 100 feet lower. The northern extremity is composed of huge rocks and bowlders, forming innumerable crevices and holes, from the largest of which the hill derives its name. Plum Run valley is here marshy but strewn with similar bowlders, and the slopes of the Round Tops are covered with them. . . .

"A cross-road connecting the Taneytown and Emmitsburg roads runs along the northern base of Devil's Den. From its Plum Run crossing to the [about-to-become-famous] Peach Orchard is 1100 yards. [This is known today as the Wheatfield Road.] For the first 400 yards of this distance, there is a wood on the north and a wheat-field on the south of the road, beyond which the road continues for 700 yards to the Emmitsburg road along Devil's Den ridge, which slopes on the north to Plum Run, on the south to Plum Branch. From Ziegler's Grove the Emmitsburg road runs diagonally across the interval between Cemetery and Seminary ridges, crossing the latter two miles from Ziegler's Grove. From [the] Peach Orchard to Ziegler's is nearly a mile and a half. For half a mile the road runs along a ridge at right angles to that of Devil's Den. . . . The angle at the Peach Orchard is thus formed by the intersection of two bold ridges, one from Devil's Den, the other along the Emmitsburg road. It is distant about 600 yards from the wood which skirts the whole length of Seminary Ridge and covers the movement of troops between it and Willoughby Run, half a mile beyond. South of the Round Top and Devil's Den ridge the country is open, and the principal obstacles to free movement are the fences – generally of stone – which surround the numerous fields."[4]

Back at Cemetery Hill Meade was met by General Slocum, who was evidently concerned that the Union line ran up the west side of Culp's Hill but did not cover its east side or the space between that hill and where William's division had camped along the Baltimore Pike. Williams' men had already encountered a few Confederates northeast of them that morning. Meade told General Hunt to fill the gap temporarily with guns, and Hunt ordered some batteries of the 11th and 12th Corps posted to cover it.

Chief of Staff Butterfield finally left Taneytown at daylight, and, upon his arrival at Gettysburg, Meade told him to draft contingency orders, in case it might be necessary for the army to fall back, in which case it would take up the position Meade had outlined in his Pipe Creek circular. Evidently Meade thought it not unlikely that Lee would do just what Longstreet had suggested: try to turn his left, or southern, flank and get between him and Washington. After the war, Meade said, "Longstreet's advice to Lee . . . was sound military sense; it was the step I feared Lee would take. . . ."[5] General Warren said, in a letter written to his wife that morning, "We are now all in line of battle before the enemy in a position where we cannot be beaten but fear being turned." He added that they were all "worn down by hard marching, want of sleep, and anxiety. . . ."[6]

Butterfield later cited this order that Meade instructed him to draft as proof that Meade definitely intended to retreat rather than fight, but General Hunt later wrote that he was sure that Meade only wanted the plan drawn up as a precaution. That morning, Hunt said, Meade complained to him that one of his corps had left its artillery ammunition behind and that others were deficient in that item. "He was very much disturbed," Hunt wrote, "and feared that, taking into account the large expenditures of the preceding day by the First and Eleventh corps, there would not be sufficient to carry us through the battle." But Hunt reassured him that the Artillery Reserve, then on its way, contained enough ammunition in its wagons to supply the entire army, "but none for idle cannonades, the besetting sin of some of our commanders." Hunt later concluded that "had he at this time any intention of withdrawing the army, the first thing to get rid of would have been this Artillery Reserve and its large trains, which were then blocking the roads in our rear; and he would surely have told me of it."[7] Hunt didn't mention the possibility that this very reassurance about his artillery ammunition might have been a key factor in Meade's decision to stay and fight.

The strength or weakness of the position his army occupied would, of course, also have been extremely important in the decision. Meade, with Hunt and Howard, continued his tour that morning with a look at Culp's Hill and the area of Slocum's concern. Newspaper correspondent Whitelaw Reid witnessed Meade's reconnaissance. "He is not cheered [by the troops]," Reid noted, "indeed is scarcely recognized. He is an approved corps General, but he has not yet vindicated his right to command the Army of the Potomac."[8]

Culp's Hill was more of a ridge than just a hill. It had two peaks; the higher one rising some 180 feet about Rock Creek, which ran along its eastern side. This higher peak was some 800 yard southeast of Cemetery Hill, to which it was connected by a saddle of land that included Stevens' Knoll. But some 400 yard south of this main peak there was a second peak that rose some 80 feet above the creek and was also connected to the higher peak by a saddle of land that was somewhat higher than the surrounding area. This whole mass of high ground was rocky, and most of it, unlike Cemetery Hill, was covered with trees. The northern and eastern slopes of the whole mass, facing the Confederates, was steep, while the western and southern slopes, leading to the Union rear, were gentle, making it ideal for incorporation into the Federal defensive line.

South of the lower peak was a marshy meadow, through which a small branch ran eastward into south-faring Rock Creek. Both streams could provide a source of water for the troops, and there was also a spring, known, for its owner, as Spangler's Spring, near the southeast end of the hill. Added strength was given the position by a stone wall that began near the spring, running north along the east face of the ridge for about 100 yards before turning to the northwest across the lower hill to the saddle between the peaks, where it turned to the north again along the east face of the higher hill, then turned to the west along its north face. This fence would provide the Union troops with a ready-made breastwork. South of the little east-flowing branch was a low east-west ridge that ran between the Baltimore Pike and Rock Creek. At the eastern end of this little ridge there was an outcropping of granite boulders and a grove of trees known as McAllister's Woods, providing a strongpoint to anchor the southeast end of the Union line. To the south of this was a marshy area and a mill pond that would obstruct any Confederate attempt to get around that flank.

It is doubtful that Meade took in all of this information on his morning ride, but surely it was as obvious to him as it was to the Confederates that, should the Rebels take Culp's Hill, the Union position on Cemetery Hill (which was about 80 feet higher than the town but about 125 feet lower than Culp's Hill) would be untenable, as they would not only overlook the cemetery but also the Baltimore Pike, which ran along the southwest side of Culp's Hill. This was his army's lifeline – an improved road running southeast directly to his supply depot at Westminster, Maryland. Meade's chief quartermaster, Brigadier General Rufus Ingalls, later reported: "The wagon trains and all *impedimenta* had been assembled at Westminster, on the pike and railroad leading to Baltimore, at a distance of about 25 miles in rear of the army. No baggage was allowed in front. Officers and men went forward without tents and with only a short supply of food. A portion only of the ammunition wagons and ambulances was brought up to the immediate rear of our lines. This arrangement, which is always made in this army on the eve of battle and marches in presence of the enemy, enables experienced and active officers to supply their commands without risking the loss of trains or obstructing roads over which the columns march. Empty wagons can be sent to the rear, and loaded ones, or pack trains, brought up during the night, or at such times and places as will not interfere with the movements of troops."[9] Confederate forces interdicting the Baltimore Pike would, of course, render this arrangement hazardous at best, and, as Ingalls said, the troops had only a short supply of food on hand.

Soon Slocum's other division, Geary's, joined Williams' after spending the night on Cemetery Ridge, where Hancock had sent it. So this division was placed on Culp's Hill, to the right of Wadsworth's line, and later that morning Williams' division was used to further extend the line down to Rock Creek. Many of Meade's troops were not yet on hand, but they were arriving all during the day. The Federal 2nd Corps arose early that morning and marched up the Taneytown Road another mile or so. Meade at first placed it east of Cemetery Ridge, facing north, in position to cover a retreat down that road if necessary. Unknown to Meade, Hancock ordered all wagon traffic off of the Taneytown Road, reserving it for troop movements, which forced the Reserve Artillery ammunition train that Hunt had told Meade about to remain in its park south of Little Round Top for several hours.

At dawn, the leading two divisions of the 5th Corps continued marching up the Hanover Road after their brief stop for the night, and some time between 6 and 7 a.m. they turned right onto a farm road that led to yet another bit of high ground called Brinkerhoff Ridge, about two miles east of Gettysburg. Here they linked up with the right of Williams' division of the 12th Corps, and parts of Brigadier General James Barnes' 1st Division soon started skirmishing with some Confederates who were pestering Williams' men. Brigadier General Romeyne Ayres' 2nd Division then filled the gap between Barnes and the 12th Corps.

With Meade's right flank thus secured, the 2nd Corps, with Hancock back in command of it, was sent to extend the left flank down Cemetery Ridge. The 3rd Division of that corps, commanded by Brigadier General Alexander Hays, connected with the 1st Corps at Zeigler's Grove. Hays was an 1844 graduate of West Point, where he had been good friends with Grant, in the class ahead of him. As colonel of the 63rd Pennsylvania, he had served through McClellan's Peninsula Campaign and been severely wounded at the second battle of Bull Run. He had only been in command of this division for three days, having come, with his brigade, from the Department of Washington. As his units filed into place, they were fired upon by Confederate guns across the way on Seminary Ridge.

When the 2nd Corps moved to Cemetery Ridge, it left behind, in its reserve position, two brigades of the army's Artillery Reserve that had followed it onto the field that morning, and these were soon joined by most of the rest of the Reserve. The new position of the 2nd Corps freed Robinson's battered division of the 1st Corps to move to a reserve position on the back slope of Cemetery Hill, where it served as a support for the 11th Corps. Stannard's recently arrived brigade of nine-months men joined it there.

Even as the leading units of the 2nd Corps filed into their new positions, their skirmishers became involved in heavy fighting along and beyond the Emmitsburg Road, which ran quite close to Cemetery Ridge as it approached Cemetery Hill from the southwest. Of particular interest to the skirmishers of both armies was a sturdy stone and brick barn – a ready-made fort – owned by one William Bliss, which was about halfway between the two forces, just about due west of Zeigler's Grove. As one Union officer wrote: "We send a line of skirmishers down into the meadow among the grass and wheat fields. The enemy push out a rather stronger line from their position, and crowd our boys back. We put in a few more companies, and force them to a retrograde movement, and so the line wavers to and fro."[10]

At 7 a.m., Meade ordered Sickles' 3rd Corps to take over Geary's former position at the south end of Cemetery Ridge, facing west and anchoring the army's left flank. Returning to Cemetery Hill at around 8 a.m., just as General Gibbon's 2nd Division of the 2nd Corps was filing into position on Cemetery Ridge, to the left of Hays's 3rd Division, Meade again studied the relative positions of the two armies facing each other. General Schurz saw him there. "His long, bearded, haggard face," Schurz later remembered, "shaded by a black military felt hat, the rim of which was turned down, looked careworn and tired, as if he had not slept that night. The spectacles on his nose gave him a somewhat magisterial look. There was nothing in his appearance or his bearing – not a smile nor a sympathetic word addressed to those around him – that might have made the hearts of the soldiers warm up to him. . . . There was nothing of pose, nothing stagy about him. His mind was evidently absorbed by a hard problem. But this simple, cold, serious soldier with his businesslike air did inspire confidence. The officers and men, as much as was permitted, crowded around and looked up at him with curious eyes, and then turned away, not enthusiastic but clearly satisfied. With a rapid glance he examined the position of our army . . . nodded, seemingly with approval. After the usual salutation I asked him how many men he had on the ground. . . . 'In the course of the day I expect to have about 95,000 – enough, I guess, for this business.' And then, after another sweeping glance over the field, he added, as if repeating something to himself, 'Well, we may as well fight it out here just as well as anywhere else.' Then he quietly rode away."[11]

The arrival of Gibbon's 2nd Division of the 2nd Corps on Cemetery Ridge drew more Confederate artillery fire, so General Hancock ordered its two accompanying batteries to return fire. This drew even more Rebel batteries into the exchange, which only ended when the Union gunners ceased fire to let some infantry detachments move between their guns. When the Federals stopped firing, so did the Confederates. Gibbon's last brigade, his 1st, under Brigadier General William Harrow, was placed in reserve on the reverse slope of Cemetery Ridge, about 100 yards due east of the little copse of tree, and about 200 yards west of a little house on the west side of the Taneytown Road that would serve as Meade's headquarters. As they arrived, Gibbon's brigade commanders sent more skirmishers out to the Emmitsburg Road. Hancock's final division, his 1st, commanded by Brigadier General John Caldwell, was kept on the reverse slope of Cemetery Ridge, south of Gibbon's division, so as not to reveal itself and draw fire from the Confederate artillery across the way, its infantry brigades in columns of battalions, facing west, and its attached battery with guns still limbered.

Lee, like Meade, did not get much sleep during the night of 1-2 July, maybe a couple of hours, for he was up and busy by 3 a.m. Longstreet later remembered that the stars were still visible in the sky when he reported at Lee's headquarters for the day's orders, but Lee, he claimed, had not yet decided on a plan. A Prussian officer sent to observe this war had been impressed by Lee's "quiet self-possessed calmness" during the recent battle of Chancellorsville, but after the war he remarked that this was not in evidence at Gettysburg, where Lee "was not at his ease, but was riding to and fro, frequently changing his position, making anxious inquiries here and there, and looking careworn."[12]

At daylight, as Longstreet put it, "The enemy was found in position on his formidable heights awaiting us."[13] Evidently Lee relayed to Longstreet something of what had transpired a few hours before at Ewell's headquarters, or at least the conclusion that it was better to attack Cemetery Hill from the west or southwest than it was from the north. Longstreet then apparently renewed his argument for turning Meade's southern flank but was overruled again. Instead he was to have the leading role in attacking Cemetery Hill. (Because the attack, when it was eventually made, actually went in farther south, historians have long assumed that it was so planned all along, but at this early hour, at least, Lee's attention was still on the hill that Ewell had failed to take the previous evening.) Historians have generally accepted postwar criticisms of Longstreet by his fellow Confederates for dragging his feet during this and the subsequent day because his pet strategy had been overruled. He certainly was not in good humor at the time, but he was known to be slow even when in full accord with plans.

The report of Union troops threatening the southern flank had turned out to be a false alarm – presumably caused by the wanderings of Humphrey's division of the Union 3rd Corps. Therefore, early that morning Wilcox's Brigade was ordered to rejoin Anderson's Division.

Lee had not yet heard anything from Ewell about the fate of Culp's Hill, so he sent Major Charles S. Venable of his staff to confer with that officer. "Early in the morning," Ewell later reported, "I received a communication from the commanding general, the tenor of which was that he intended the main attack to be made by the First Corps, on our right, and wished me, as soon as their guns opened, to make a diversion in their favor, to be converted into a real attack if an opportunity offered."[14] Ewell responded by sending the same staff officer back to General Johnson again with instructions for him to be ready to attack Culp's Hill but not to actually do so, pending further orders.

Evidently one of the first things Lee did that morning was to instruct his chief engineer, Captain Samuel R. Johnston, to reconnoiter the Union position south of Cemetery Hill and find out how far it extended in that direction. Lee had often performed similar reconnaissances for General Winfield Scott during the Mexican War, and he told Johnston that "he had found that he could get nearer the enemy and do more with a few men than with many."[15] Heeding this advice, Johnston took with him only Longstreet's chief engineer, Major John J. Clarke, and two others, and headed off. After the war he said that this was at about 4 a.m., but he evidently wasn't carrying a watch that day, and this seems a bit too early. It is difficult to sort out the chronology of events during the Civil War, because Standard Time had not yet been promulgated. (The railroads eventually instigated it in order to make sense of their time-tables.) There might have been differences of an hour or more between one man's watch and another, and there is the added difficulty that in later narratives of events, memories might have been off by even more than that. But a post-war account by Major General Lafayette McLaws, one of Longstreet's division commanders, contradicts the idea that Captain Johnston departed as early as 4 a.m.

McLaws' Division followed Major General John Bell "Sam" Hood's division along the Chambersburg Pike that morning. Longstreet's third division, commanded by Major General George Pickett, had been left at Chambersburg to guard the army's rear. The day before, McLaws' Division had followed Johnson's Division of Ewell's corps and Ewell's vast train of supply wagons, which was carrying all of its plunder from scouring Pennsylvania for weeks. (McLaws timed the train's passage and estimated it as being 14 miles long). His division had stopped a little after midnight a few miles west of Gettysburg, and Longstreet at first had ordered him, McLaws said, to resume the march at 4 a.m. but had later modified that to "sunrise," which only added about a half-hour to the division's rest. Hood's Division, which took over the corps' lead on the morning of 2 July, started out at around 3 a.m. and marched past McLaws' camp for a total of only about four or five miles. Both divisions evidently halted on the Chambersburg Pike for a while and then filed off to the right onto Herr Ridge. As McLaws later remembered it, however, his division proceeded all the way to Seminary Ridge, where it stopped near Lee's headquarters.

"The march was continued at a very early hour," McLaws later remembered, "and my command reached the hill overlooking Gettysburg early in the morning. Just after I arrived General Lee sent for me – as the head of my column was halted within a hundred yards of where he was – and I went at once and reported. General Lee was sitting on a fallen tree with a map beside him. After the usual salutation, General Lee remarked: 'General, I wish you to place your division across this road,' pointing on the map to about the place I afterwards went to, and directing my attention to about the place across the country from where we were, the position being a commanding one; 'and I wish you to get there if possible without being seen by the enemy.' The place he pointed out was about the one I afterwards went to, and the line he marked out on the map for me to occupy was one perpendicular to the Emmettsburg road. He finally remarked: 'Can you get there?' or 'can you do it?' I replied that I knew of nothing to prevent me, but would take a party of skirmishers and go in advance and reconnoitre. He said 'Major [sic] Johnston, of my staff, has been ordered to reconnoitre the ground, and I expect he is about ready.' I then remarked, 'I will go with him.' Just then General Longstreet, who, when I came up, was walking back and forth some little distance from General Lee, and hearing my proposition or request to reconnoitre, spoke quickly and said: 'No, sir, I do not wish you to leave your division,' and then, pointing to the map, said: 'I wish your division placed so,' running his finger in a direction perpendicular to that pointed out by General Lee. General Lee replied: 'No, General, I wish it placed just perpendicular to that,' or 'just the opposite.' I then reiterated my request to go with Major Johnston, but General Longstreet again forbade it. General Lee said nothing more, and I left them, and, joining my command, put it under cover under a line of woods a short distance off. General Longstreet appeared as if he was irritated and annoyed, but the cause I did not ask. When I rejoined my command I sent my engineer officer, Lieutenant Montcure, to go and join Major Johnston, and gave him instructions what to observe particularly, as he was an officer in whom I had confidence, but [he] was ordered back. I then reconnoitred myself for my own information, and was soon convinced that by crossing the ridge where I then was, my command could reach the point indicated by General Lee, in a half hour, without being seen. I then went back to the head of my column and sat on my horse and saw in the distance the enemy coming, hour after hour, on to the battle ground."[16]

    It is possible that McLaws misunderstood what had been said about Captain Johnston, and that the latter had already departed when the former offered to go with him. His statement that he "then reconnoitred myself" contradicts his statement that Longstreet forbade him to leave his division. It seems likely that, like Hood, McLaws rode ahead of his division to report in and find out what was wanted of his division, and therefore reached Lee's headquarters earlier than his troops reached the field. General Hood later said that he (Hood) arrived "shortly after daybreak" and joined Lee, Longstreet and Hill in observing the Union positions.[17] "The enemy is here," Hood remembered Lee saying, "and if we do not whip him, he will whip us." Hood assumed from this that Lee was anxious to launch an attack, but he soon found that his corps commander was not. Hood later claimed that Longstreet told him at that time: "The General is a little nervous this morning; he wishes me to attack; I do not wish to do so without Pickett. I never like to go into battle with one boot off."[18] But it would take Pickett's Division all day to catch up with the rest of the army. Hood was also missing part of his command, for one of his four brigades, that commanded by Brigadier General Evander Law, had been detached to New Guilford, Pennsylvania, 24 miles away, and was at that time hurrying to rejoin its division.

Also that morning, Lee sent Colonel Long, who had scouted Cemetery Hill the previous evening, to find good positions for A. P. Hill's artillery. As Long later remembered it, Lee had decided on a general plan the night before, though not in detail: "I understood the plan of battle to be, that Longstreet, on the right, should commence the attack, while Hill, in the center, and Ewell, on the left, should cooperate by a vigorous support." He added that, "On reaching Hill's position, about sunrise, I discovered that there had been considerable accession to the enemy's forces on Cemetery Hill during the night; but it was chiefly massed to his right, leaving much of his center and almost his entire left unoccupied."[19]

Long pointed out to Colonel R. Lindsay Walker, Hill's chief of artillery, the high ground along the Emmitsburg Road, about halfway between Seminary Ridge and Cemetery Ridge, as a good place for artillery wanting to fire on

Cemetery Hill. However, General Pendleton, Lee's chief of artillery, soon appeared and took over the job of placing Walker's guns, so Long moved around to Ewell's corps. "As I examined the position of the artillery on the left," he said, "I momentarily expected to hear the guns on the right announce the opening of the battle. As the morning advanced, I became anxious lest the delay might lose us the opportunity of defeating the enemy in detail."[20]

Shortly after Long departed, Pendleton informed Lee that he and his party, while looking for positions for Hill's guns, had scouted the southern part of the field and had found no Federals there except a couple of dismounted cavalrymen, whom they had captured. Also, Captain Johnston eventually returned from his reconnaissance of the area to the southeast (McLaws thought this was at about 8 a.m.; Johnston said it was some three hours after he had departed, which would have been 7 a.m. by his reckoning) and he too reported seeing no Federals except a few cavalrymen.

Just where or how far Johnston had gone on his reconnaissance has puzzled historians every since. In a letter written to General McLaws some 29 years after the battle, Johnston claimed that he had gone up on one of the Round Tops at the south end of Cemetery Ridge, "where I had a commanding view."[21] Since Big Round Top was heavily wooded, precluding a "commanding view," it has usually been presumed that he went up Little Round Top. Had he done so at the time that he claimed, however, he surely would have seen Buford's two cavalry brigades, which, at that time, were stationed just below that hill, not to mention Dan Sickles 3rd Corps, which was also in the area. (Two regiments of Geary's division of the 12th Corps had been up on the two Round Tops all night, leaving at about 5 a.m. when that division left to rejoin Williams' division on the Union right; so if Johnston actually went up one of those hills it was certainly later than 5 a.m.) Perhaps he mistakenly went up Bushman Hill, near the Round Tops. In an earlier account (written in 1878) Johnston said, "I stood behind General Lee and traced on the map the route over which I had made the reconnaissance. When I got to the extreme right . . . on Little Round Top, General Lee turned and looking at me, said, 'Did you get there[?]'"[22] This question on Lee's part indicates, first, that Lee had not sent him specifically to look at the Round Tops, and, second, that he was surprised that Johnston got as far as he thought or claimed that he did.

In his official report of the battle, Lee said, "The enemy occupied a strong position, with his right upon two commanding elevations adjacent to each other, one southeast and the other, known as Cemetery Hill, immediately south of the town, which lay at its base. His line extended thence upon the high ground along the Emmitsburg road, with a steep ridge in rear, which was also occupied. . . . It was determined to make the principal attack upon the enemy's left, and endeavor to gain a position from which it was thought that our artillery could be brought to bear with effect. Longstreet was directed to place the divisions of McLaws and Hood on the right of Hill, partially enveloping the enemy's left, which he was to drive in. General Hill was ordered to threaten the enemy's center, to prevent re-enforcements being drawn to either wing, and co-operate with his right division in Longstreet's attack. General Ewell was instructed to make a simultaneous demonstration upon the enemy's right, to be converted into a real attack should opportunity offer."[23]

The first-mentioned hill, southeast of the town, was, of course, Culp's Hill, and the steep ridge "in rear" of the Union line was Cemetery Ridge. For, as General Hunt later pointed out in his description of the battle, "It would appear from this that General Lee mistook the few troops on the Peach Orchard ridge [along which ran the Emmitsburg Road] in the morning for our main line, and that by taking it and sweeping up the Emmitsburg road under cover of his batteries, he expected to 'roll up' our lines to Cemetery Hill. That would be an 'oblique order of battle,' in which the attacking line, formed obliquely to its opponent, marches directly forward, constantly breaking in the *end* of his enemy's line and gaining his rear."[24]

In his own report of the battle, Longstreet said, "I received instructions from the commanding general to move with the portion of my command that was up, around to gain the Emmitsburg road, on the enemy's left. The enemy, having been driven back by the corps of Lieutenant-Generals Ewell and A. P. Hill the day previous, had taken a strong position extending from the hill at the cemetery along the Emmitsburg road."[25]

From Seminary Ridge – even from the cupola of the Seminary – Lee could not have seen much of Cemetery Ridge, for the high ground upon which the Emmitsburg Road ran would have blocked his view, although he could see the higher Round Tops, farther south.[26] The Emmitsburg Road ran at an approximate 45-degree angle to Cemetery Ridge, following the high ground that General Hunt called the Peach Orchard ridge, then declined as it continued to the northeast, before rising to cross over Cemetery Hill itself and joining up with a north-south street at the south edge of Gettysburg. The heavy skirmishing between his own forces and those of the Union 2nd Corps, around the Bliss farm west of the Emmitsburg Road, where that road ran across lower ground, probably helped to convince Lee that the left of Meade's line ran along that road. Two regiments of the Union 3rd Corps were also serving as skirmishers along, or west of, the Emmitsburg Road, almost down to the Wheatfield Road, backed up by two more regiments sent out early that morning. Many of the Union troops on Cemetery Ridge were hidden from Lee's view behind stone walls, or small irregularities of ground, and Gibbon's reserves and all of Caldwell's division were on the reverse slope of the ridge. So, from Gibbon's left on south, only the troops at or near the Emmitsburg Road were visible.

Moreover, Pendelton's and Johnston's reports indicated to Lee that there were few Union troops in position to prevent a Confederate force from forming on the high ground around the Peach Orchard, farther down the Emmitsburg road. McLaws wrote to his wife five days later, "The intention was to get in rear of the enemy who were supposed to be stationed principally in rear of Gettysburg or near of it. The report being that the enemy had but two regiments of infantry and one battery at the Peach orchard."[27] So, if Lee could get Longstreet's two large divisions onto that ground, all they had to do then was follow the Emmitsburg Road to the northeast, flanking any Federal units formed along the road, and sweeping up onto Cemetery Hill, supported by artillery that could then be placed on the high ground around the Peach Orchard. And, while McLaws and Hood assaulted that key position from the southwest, Anderson's Division could hit it, or at least threaten it, from the west, Rodes' Division from the northwest, and Early's from the northeast; while Johnson could attack Culp's Hill at the same time. Thus the different parts of Lee's army, spread thinly all around the Union position, would converge on Cemetery Hill from several directions. It was a good plan – similar flank attacks had worked well for him before – except for two things: The Union line was not where Lee thought it was; and Longstreet was not yet in position to attack it.

Sometime between 7 and 9 a.m., the two reserve artillery battalions of Longstreet's corps reached the field. They halted in a grove of trees west of the seminary, and soon thereafter Longstreet sent for the commander of the larger of the two battalions, Colonel E. Porter Alexander, who possessed considerable experience as a military engineer. Alexander rode forward and found Longstreet with Lee on Seminary Ridge. There he had a good view of the Union position on Cemetery Hill and noted the batteries posted there, but that the infantry was mostly concealed behind stone fences and slight ridges. He also noted a signal flag up on Little Round Top, and, as a former signals officer himself, knew that it indicated the presence of an enemy Signal Corps detachment keeping an eye out for Confederate movements, warnings of which it could then send to Meade's headquarters. "It was explained to me," he later wrote, "that our corps was to assault the enemy's left flank, and I was directed to reconnoiter it and then to take charge of all the artillery of the corps and direct it in the attack. . . . I was particularly cautioned, in moving the artillery, to keep it out of sight of the signal-station upon Round Top."[28] In another account, Alexander said, "I do not remember seeing or hearing any thing at this time of Longstreet's infantry, nor did I get the impression that General Lee thought there was any unnecessary delay going on."[29]

At about 9 a.m. Lee evidently told Longstreet to proceed with putting his two divisions in place while Lee rode over to Ewell's headquarters. Ewell and Major Venable were out scouting, but General Trimble took Lee to the cupola of some building from which he could get a look at the positions of the two armies on that flank. (Trimble thought it was the cupola of the alms house, but that building was too far north. Lieutenant Colonel Arthur Fremantle, a British observer who had attached himself to Lee's army, said that Ewell's headquarters was "in a church with a high cupola.")[30] Trimble later claimed that Lee told him, "The enemy have the advantage of us in a shorter and inside line and we are too much extended. We did not or we could not pursue our advantage of yesterday, and now the enemy are in a good position."[31]

When Ewell returned there was some discussion, and the conference that Early remembered as taking place the night before, or parts of it, might actually have taken place there at this time. Both Longstreet (who wasn't there) and Trimble later indicated that it did. Colonel Long found General Lee at Ewell's headquarters, which he said were on the outskirts of Gettysburg, and rode with him through the town and back to Hill's position. "On arriving at the point where I left Walker a few hours before, the ridge to which his attention had been called in the morning was still unoccupied. . . ."[32] By then, that high ground on the Emmitsburg Road had been chosen for the position from which Longstreet was to launch an attack.

Long claimed that, about an hour after their return (he

thought it was 10 a.m., but it was probably at least 11), Lee remarked, in an uneasy tone, "What *can* detain Longstreet? He ought to be in position now!"[33] At one point Lee chided the commander of an artillery battalion for not hurrying his batteries to the army's right flank and had to be reminded that the battalion in question belonged to Hill's corps and not Longstreet's. Lee apologized and asked for directions to Longstreet's current location. Colonel Walker offered to guide Lee there. "As we rode together," Walker later wrote, "General Lee manifested more impatience than I ever saw him exhibit upon any other occasion; seemed very much disappointed and worried that the attack had not opened earlier, and very anxious for Longstreet to attack at the very earliest possible moment."[34]

However, Longstreet later claimed that it was not until 11 a.m., after the visit to Ewell's headquarters, that Lee ordered Longstreet's corps to move, "and put it under the conduct of his engineer officers, so as to be assured that the troops would move by the best route and encounter the least delay in reaching the position designated by him for the attack on the Federal left, at the same time concealing the movements then under orders from view of the Federals."[35] Quite possibly Longstreet – then, later or both – interpreted this visit from Lee as the occasion for that order and did not consider any previous hints, suggestions, or directions as positive orders. Lieutenant Colonel G. Moxley Sorrel of Longstreet's staff later said, "As Longstreet was not to be made willing and Lee refused to change or could not change, the former failed to conceal some anger. There was apparent apathy in his movements. They lacked the fire and point of his usual bearing on the battlefield."[36]

Captain Johnston later claimed that he joined the head of Longstreet's corps at 9 a.m., but his sense of time is already in doubt. He also claimed that he had only been ordered to join the column, not to lead it; that he did not even know where it was going; and that he was surprised to read in one of Longstreet's post-war accounts that the latter had considered

Johnston to be in charge of guiding McLaws' division, which was at the head of the column, while Longstreet himself road further back with General Hood. However, McLaws wrote that Johnston "came to me and said he was ordered to conduct me on the march."[37] But, anyway, it is doubtful that the column was to follow the same route that Johnston had taken earlier. Quite possibly Longstreet, having been ordered to make an attack he did not believe in, and having been told that Johnston would guide his column, somewhat petulantly obeyed only the letter of these instructions and determined to offer the unwelcome guide no help. As he later put it, "As I was relieved for the time from [command of] the march, I rode near the middle of the line."[38]

Be that as it may, even after Longstreet had received definite orders, whatever exact hour that might have been, the two divisions did not begin to move, for Longstreet decided to wait for Law's missing brigade of Hood's Division, which was known to be approaching. (Why McLaws' and even the rest of Hood's Division could not have proceeded to their jump-off points and let Laws join them there, Longstreet never explained.) This was said to have delayed the start some three-quarters of an hour.

All this reconnoitering and discussing on the Confederate side of the field gave the Federals time to bring up reinforcements and to get organized. At about 9 a.m. General Meade sent his son and aide, Captain George Meade, Jr., to ride about a mile south from Union army headquarters to see if the 3rd Corps was in its assigned position and whether or not General Sickles had anything to report. Captain Meade soon met Captain George E. Randolph, who was Sickles' chief of artillery, near 3rd Corps headquarters, which was in a group of tents in a grove of trees just west of the Taneytown Road. Randolph went into Sickles' tent to get the requested information and returned after a few minutes to say that the corps was not yet in position because General Sickles was not too sure about what its position was supposed to be. Actually, the two brigades of Birney's division then present had formed line west of Plum Run (and thus west of the southern part of Cemetery Ridge) between 7 and 8 a.m., with one of those brigades facing southwest, its own left flank reaching to, or almost to (but not occupying) the sizable hill then known locally as the Sugar Loaf, but now known to history as Little Round Top.

This division (as already mentioned) had skirmishers out as far as the Emmitsburg Road and beyond it (thus possibly helping to convince Lee that that road marked Meade's main battle line). Those skirmishers, like those of the 2nd Corps farther north, had been having a spirited fight with their Confederate counterparts (of A. P. Hill's corps) all morning. Sickles' other division, commanded by Brigadier General A. A. Humphreys (or the two brigades of it already on hand), was north of Birney's, but did not yet tie in with the left of Hancock's 2nd Corps, Humphreys' division being somewhat in advance of Cemetery Ridge, and Hancock's left division (Caldwell's) being on the reverse slope thereof. But Sickles was more worried about his left flank, which was also the left flank of Meade's entire army. One reason for this was that the two brigades he had left behind near Emmitsburg, along with his corps' train of supply wagons, were, of course, coming up the Emmitsburg Road, well to the left front of Cemetery Ridge.

Buford's cavalry had been on hand at first, to keep an eye in that direction, but Buford had appealed to his boss, Major General Alfred Pleasonton, Meade's chief of cavalry, to be allowed to withdraw his two brigades. (Meade treated Pleasonton more as a member of his staff than as a corps commander and kept him near army headquarters most of the time.) Buford's men were tired after the fight of the day before and lacked food, and his horses were worn down and without forage. Pleasonton, figuring that Buford's men had done their share, allowed them to withdraw to the army's new base at Westminster to rest and recuperate. The problem, so far as Sickles was concerned, was that Pleasonton did not send any other cavalry to take their place. In fact, there was still no other Union cavalry available. Merritt's detached brigade of Buford's division was still down in Maryland, Gregg's 2nd Division was far down the road toward Hanover, and Kilpatrick's 3rd Division was closing on the little village of Hunterstown, northeast of Gettysburg, with orders to make sure that the Rebels were not trying to get around the army's right flank. Buford did leave one squadron behind, which stayed until dark, and which accounts for both General Pendleton and Captain Johnston encountering a few Union cavalrymen.

Meade eventually ordered Pleasonton to send one regiment to take the place of Buford's two brigades, but he was still more concerned about his right flank than his left, and was even considering the possibility of launching an attack of his own in that sector, against Lee's left flank. At around 9:30 a.m. he asked Slocum and Warren to examine the terrain in that area with an eye to launching an attack with the 12th Corps, the 5th Corps, and the 6th Corps, although the latter was still on its way via the Baltimore Pike. Meade marked positions for each of his seven corps on Paine's map and had him make copies of it for all the corps commanders.

About then, General Sykes reported to Meade that he thought his position was too extended, and Slocum and Warren soon reported that the terrain on the army's right flank was not well suited for making an attack. This ended the necessity for the 5th Corps to be out east of the Hanover Road, so at about 10 a.m. Barnes' and Ayres' divisions (except for the 9th Massachusetts, which was left in position) began moving south beyond the Baltimore Pike and went into reserve not far behind the 2nd Corps, where they were soon joined by Crawford's Pennsylvania Reserves. Williams' division of the 12th Corps then moved into defensive positions between Rock Creek and the lower peak of Culp's Hill. There Williams was reinforced by some more of the troops that Hooker had scoured out of backwater garrisons – in this case a brigade of two large but inexperienced regiments from the Middle Department (which was responsible for Delaware and most of Maryland, especially Baltimore). They were commanded by Brigadier General Henry H. Lockwood.

The skirmishers of the 2nd Corps were still sparring with their Confederate counterparts. At around 10 a.m., the veteran 39th New York (consolidated down to four companies instead of the usual ten, because of heavy losses), sent out to the skirmish line, charged some Confederate skirmishers who were sheltered behind a fence some 200 yards west of the Emmitsburg Road, but was driven back. General Hays, that regiment's division commander and former brigade commander, rallied the New Yorkers (actually, most of them were European immigrants) and sent them back in another charge that captured the fence and pushed on beyond it. The colonel of another Union regiment remarked that it was "the first and last time I ever saw a division commander with flag and staff on the skirmish line."[39] More skirmishers were called forward from Cemetery Ridge, until much of Colonel George Willard's 3rd Brigade (Hays's former command) was involved.

Meanwhile, Young Captain Meade had returned to his father with the information that Sickles' 3rd Corps was not yet in its assigned position, and the fact that this unpleasant news was brought by his own son did not keep the general from losing a bit of his famous temper. Young George was promptly sent back to tell Sickles that his 3rd Corps was to form to the left, or south, of Hancock's 2nd Corps and extend the line down to where Geary's division of the 12th Corps had been during the night. The captain returned to the grove of trees only to find the tents struck and Sickles mounted, with his staff all around him. Sickles heard him out, replied that his corps would soon be posted but that, as far as he knew, Geary had not occupied any defensive position but had merely gone into camp; and then he rode off.

Sickles' two detached brigades, having set out at about 4 a.m., finally rejoined their corps between 9 and 10 a.m. After that, the only major Union unit still missing was the 6th Corps, which also happened to be the largest corps in Meade's army (about 13,000 men). It had started out the night before heading for Taneytown, but then Meade had decided to send it directly to Gettysburg, which had involved some backtracking, which in turn, as one of its men remembered, "caused much strong language."[40] There was a brief halt at dawn during which some of the men boiled coffee, but many were too tired for that. Then it was back on the road, with a cruel sun soon adding to their discomfort. "Toward noon the radiating heat could be observed in waves," one man said, "like colorless clouds, floating from the earth and mingling with the fine dust created by the moving column."[41] And yet it still was a long way from Gettysburg.

Even after the arrival of his two detached brigades, Sickles still didn't like the position he had been assigned. Cemetery Ridge got progressively lower as it ran south, so that his part of it, the southern end, was actually lower than the Peach Orchard ridge to his front. At Chancellorsville he had been obliged to abandon some high ground from which Confederate artillery had then bombarded his new position. What if history was about to repeat itself and the Confederates decided to occupy the Peach Orchard Ridge and place artillery there, from which place they could shoot down on his men? (Unknown to him, but as we have already seen, Confederate artillery officers had already noted this area as a good one, although they wanted it as a place from which to bombard Cemetery Hill, not the southern end of Cemetery Ridge.) Furthermore, his assigned position, along Cemetery Ridge – especially the southern end of it, assigned to Birney's division – had trees on it and in front of it, which would block the fields of fire of his own artillery. So, Sickles reasoned, why not take the higher ground himself instead of leaving it for the Rebels? At about 11 a.m. he rode over to army headquarters, at the little house beside the Taneytown Road, to ask Meade to come have a look at his area so he could see the problem for himself.

However, it did him little good. Meade apparently wrote off Sickle's concern to the tendency of all subordinate commanders to expect the enemy's attack to come in their own sector. Anyway, Meade didn't like Sickles, who was a political appointee instead of a professional soldier, like himself, and a crony of Hooker's, with a scandalous reputation for drinking and womanizing. So Meade just repeated in person his order for the 3rd Corps to extend the line southward from the 2nd Corps' left flank. Sickles then asked if he could post his corps as he saw fit. "Certainly," Meade replied, "within the limits of the general instructions I have given you; any ground within those limits you choose to occupy, I leave to you."[42] Or at least that's what Sickles later remembered him saying. But this wasn't what Sickles wanted, which was to go beyond the limits that Meade had given him and take possession of the high ground along the Emmitsburg Road. So he asked for General Warren, a topographical engineer, to be sent to examine his position. However, Warren was not available at the time, still being engaged in examining the right flank for that potential attack against Lee's left. Determined to get someone from headquarters to see his problem, Sickles then asked for General Hunt, who had just returned from an inspection of Culp's Hill.

"General Meade told me," Hunt later wrote, "that General Sickles, then with him, wished me to examine a new line, as he thought that assigned to him was not a good one, especially that he could not use his artillery there. I had been as far as Round Top that morning, and had noticed the unfavorable character of the ground, and, therefore, I accompanied Sickles direct to the Peach Orchard, where he pointed out the ridges, already described, as his proposed line. They commanded all the ground behind, as well as in front of them, and together constituted a favorable position for *the enemy* to hold. This was one good reason for our taking possession of it. It would, it is true, in our hands present a salient angle, which generally exposes both its sides to enfilade fire; but here the ridges were so high that each would serve as a 'traverse' for the other, and reduce that evil to a minimum. On the other hand it would so greatly lengthen our line – which in any case must rest on Round Top, and connect with the left of the Second Corps – as to require a larger force than the Third Corps alone to hold it, and it would be difficult to occupy and strengthen the angle if the enemy already held the wood in its front. At my instance General Sickles ordered a reconnoissance to ascertain if the wood was occupied.

"About this time a cannonade was opened on Cemetery Hill, which indicated an attack there, and as I had examined the Emmitsburg Ridge, I said I would not await the result of the reconnoissance but return to headquarters by way of Round Top, and examine that part of the proposed line. As I was leaving, General Sickles asked me if he should move forward his corps. I answered, 'Not on my authority; I will report to General Meade for his instructions.' I had not reached the wheat-field when a sharp rattle of musketry showed that the enemy held the wood in front of the Peach Orchard angle."

In retrospect, Hunt said that the choice between the position along the southern extremity of Cemetery Ridge or farther west on the Peach Orchard ridge "would depend on circumstances. The direct short line through the woods, and including the Round Tops, could be occupied, intrenched, and made impregnable to a front attack. But, like that of Culp's Hill, it would be a purely defensive one, from which, owing to the nature of the ground and the enemy's commanding position on the ridges at the angle, an advance in force would be impracticable. The salient line proposed by General Sickles, although much longer, afforded excellent positions for our artillery; its occupation would cramp the movements of the enemy, bring us nearer his lines, and afford us facilities for taking the offensive. It was in my judgment the better line of the two, provided it were strongly occupied, for it was the only one on the field from which we could have passed from the defensive to the offensive with a prospect of decisive results. But General Meade had not, until the arrival of the Sixth Corps, a sufficient number of troops at his disposal to risk such an extension of his line; it would have required both the Third and the Fifth corps, and left him without a reserve."[43]

The "rattle of musketry" that Hunt heard as he was leaving Sickles probably came from a small force of sharpshooters that Sickles had sent out. His 3rd Corps contained two units that were quite unique: the 1st and 2nd U.S. Sharpshooters. Whereas most regiments were raised and organized by individual states and then transferred to the national government, these two were composed of companies raised from several different states, and they only accepted proven marksmen. Their men were armed with Sharps breech-loading rifles, which, in addition to allowing faster reloading, were also very powerful, accurate weapons. Skirmishing was these regiments' specialty. Although officially part of Brigadier General Hobart Ward's 2nd Brigade of Major General David Birney's 1st Division of the 3rd Corps, they often operated as a small separate brigade under Colonel Hiram Berdan, commander of the 1st Sharpshooters.

"About 7.30 a.m.," Berdan later reported, "I received orders to send forward a detachment of 100 sharpshooters to discover, if possible, what the enemy was doing. I went out with the detail, and posted them on the crest of the hill beyond the Emmitsburg road, and where they kept up a constant fire nearly all day upon the enemy in the woods beyond. . . . As it was impossible with this force to proceed far enough to discover what was being done by the enemy in the rear of this woods, I reported the fact to Major-General Birney, and about 11 a.m. [Birney's report says noon] I received an order from him to send out another detachment of 100 sharpshooters farther to the left of our lines, and to take the Third Maine Volunteers as support, with directions to feel the enemy, and to discover their movements, if possible."[44] Birney sent Captain Joseph Briscoe of his staff along as an observer.

It was this second detachment that evidently caused the firing that Hunt heard. They found no Confederates south of the crossroad that ran past the soon-to-become-famous Wheatfield and Peach Orchard, nor on that road's westward extension, which ran on over Seminary Ridge to eventually join the Hagerstown or Fairfield road at Black Horse Tavern. But they soon met a local boy who warned them about the woods farther north, saying, "There are lots of Rebels in there in rows."[45] And, sure enough, about a half-mile farther north they found Confederate skirmishers and, beyond them, a large Rebel formation.

These were men of Wilcox's Brigade of Anderson's Division of Hill's corps, the same brigade that had been sent down to Black Horse Tavern the night before to guard against the Federals reported to be approaching from the south. That brigade had followed a roundabout route up to the Chambersburg Pike and then down Seminary Ridge and had just taken position on the right of Anderson's line, which at that time formed the right flank of Lee's entire army, and so Anderson had ordered it to face southeast and south, to protect against a possible Union flank attack. Wilcox was worried about his rear, as well, for the woods he was in extended on in that direction, and who knew what they concealed? So he decided to place only two of his regiments in line, facing south, and to hold his other three regiments in reserve. All these units were just moving into position when they encountered Berdan's small force moving in the opposite direction.

Berdan sent Captain Briscoe back to tell General Birney what they had found, then ordered his Sharpshooters to advance firing, a maneuver that would have been difficult with the typical muzzleloaders of that day but was easy enough with breechloaders. They drove the Rebel skirmishers back and then fired on the 11th Alabama as it was trying to change directions and sent it reeling back as well, but then they were driven back in turn by a volley from the 10th Alabama. They fell back to the line of the 3rd Maine, and the two sides exchanged fire for about fifteen or twenty minutes, but by then a third Confederate regiment had joined the fight and the sharpshooters were quickly expending their ammunition (a problem with quick-loading breechloaders), so Berdan ordered a retreat. The Federals fell back to the Peach Orchard area, and the Rebels were content to let them go and merely settled into their assigned positions. Briscoe, meanwhile, reported to Birney, and Birney to Sickles, that Confederates were moving south along Seminary Ridge, a fact that they interpreted as indicating a Rebel attempt to get around the Union left flank.

The timing of this fight is in considerable doubt. Wilcox thought it was over by 9 a.m., whereas Berdan thought it was 11 a.m. when he received the order to advance, and Birney said it was noon when he gave the order. Hunt supposedly met Sickles at Meade's headquarters at around 11 and rode with Sickles to inspect the Peach Orchard position, then heard the rattle of musketry – presumably from this fight – as he was leaving, at which time he recommended making such a reconnoissance. He also noted heavy cannonading to or from Cemetery Hill just then, which would seem to have been the artillery of the 2nd Corps opening fire in support of its skirmishers, who were still fighting over possession of the Bliss farm buildings, west of the Emmitsburg Road, which accounts place at around 10 a.m. A message from a Signal Officer to General Butterfield, timed at 11:45 a.m. in the Official Records, says, "Enemy skirmishers are advancing from the west, 1 mile from here." Another one ten minutes later says, "The rebels are in force, and our skirmishers give way. One mile west of Round Top signal station, the woods are full of them."[46] Such are the vagaries of time-telling in Civil War records and accounts.

Apparently, it was somewhere around noon (just as three companies of the 126th New York, of Willard's brigade, drove Confederate skirmishers from the Bliss barn) that Hancock, worried that Sickles had not connected with the left of his 2nd Corps, ordered General Caldwell to move his division about a half-mile farther south, where it again took position on the reverse slope of Cemetery Ridge, its infantry still in columns of battalions. But this time his accompanying battery of artillery (Battery B of the 1st New York) was unlimbered and put in position on the ridge, facing west. Hancock also took a battery just loaned to him from the Artillery Reserve, Battery C of the 4th U.S. Artillery, commanded by 19-year-old Lieutenant Evan Thomas (son of Brigadier General Lorenzo Thomas, Adjutant General of the U.S. Army), down the western slope of Cemetery Ridge to a point just south of where two farm lanes intersected, one of which connected the Emmitsburg Road with the Taneytown Road. If Sickles' 3rd Corps ever got around to occupying the position that Meade had assigned it, it would connect with this battery's position. Meanwhile, it would anchor Hancock's left flank. The lieutenant, no doubt feeling a bit isolated in this position, asked the general for some infantry support, which Hancock agreed to furnish. At around 1 p.m., Hancock found Gibbon and told him to send one regiment to support Thomas's battery, bring another one forward to strengthen the front line south of the little copse of tree, and to be prepared to send two regiments to support Humphreys' division of the 3rd Corps, if necessary. Gibbon sent the 1st Minnesota to support Thomas, and the 19th Maine to the front line.

Several miles to the west of Gettysburg a potentially important small-unit action took place at about noon that day. Captain Ulric Dahlgren, son of a Union admiral, was a cavalry officer who had been attached to army headquarters for courier and escort duty, but he was a daring and adventurous spirit who found this duty much too tame and soon convinced the Army of the Potomac's chief intelligence officer, Colonel George Henry Sharpe, to put him in charge of a detachment of scouts, at least some of whom infiltrated Confederate units disguised as Rebel soldiers or officers. One of these, Captain Milton Cline, had been riding with Jeb Stuart's cavalry until it had recently crossed into Maryland, after which Cline had managed to get away to report a conversation he had overheard at Stuart's headquarters to Dahlgren. He had heard that a packet of dispatches from Confederate President Jefferson Davis was on its way to General Lee and was to be conveyed across the Potomac River by a courier who would be escorted by a detachment of Stuart's cavalry. He even knew the precise hour the courier was supposed to cross the Potomac on the second day of July, after which they would be forwarded to Lee by way of the Greencastle Turnpike.

Dahlgren had then convinced General Pleasonton to give him and Cline ten troopers with which to go and capture that courier. They had set out on 30 June, managed to avoid all Confederate patrols, and by the morning of 2 July had reached Greencastle, some five miles north of the Maryland line, where they were greeted as saviors by the local civilians, who had been repeatedly overrun by Rebels for the previous two weeks. Dahlgren was able to curtail the celebrations, however, and had things looking normal again, with his men hidden in various spots around town, when, about noon, the Confederate courier and his escort came riding into town right on schedule.

Dahlgren's calculations were thrown off somewhat by the simultaneous appearance of a train of Rebel wagons from the opposite direction, heading for Virginia with some of the supplies the Confederates had rounded up farther north. The courier's cavalry escort already outnumbered Dahlgren's small band, and the wagons had an infantry escort that made the odds against him formidable. Nevertheless, Dahlgren gave the signal just as the two Rebel targets converged, and his men popped out of hiding with a shout and fired into both groups, stampeding some of the teams and causing their wagons to overturn. The Confederates scattered for cover, and in the confusion Cline grabbed the dispatch case from the courier. Most of the Rebels ran for their lives, not realizing how small a force had attacked them, leaving behind 3 officers and 14 men to be captured, whom Dahlgren turned over to the local authorities. The Federals rode off to the south and then split up, Dahlgren riding alone with the dispatches.

These turned out to be a letter from Confederate President Jefferson Davis to Lee, dated 28 June, and another to Lee from Confederate Adjutant and Inspector General Samuel Cooper, dated 29 June. Back on 23 June, Lee had written a long letter to Davis saying that he thought there would be no important operations by either side in the Carolinas "during the unhealthy months of the summer and autumn" and that some of the troops there should be sent to Virginia. "If an army could be organized under the command of General Beauregard, and pushed forward to Culpeper Court-House [Va.], threatening Washington from that direction, it would not only effect a diversion most favorable for this army, but would, I think, relieve us of any apprehension of an attack upon Richmond during our absence." He thought that, because of his reputation as the winner of the first battle of Bull Run and his rank as a full general, Beauregard's "presence would give magnitude to even a small demonstration, and tend greatly to perplex and confound the enemy."[47]

Davis's long letter (although it also informed Lee that his second son, Brigadier General W. H. F. "Rooney" Lee, had been captured near his home east of Richmond) was mostly an explanation of why Lee's idea could not be put into effect: mainly that all disposable forces had been sent to Mississippi because of Grant's siege of Vicksburg; that Beauregard, at Charleston, South Carolina, was still under threat from sizable Union forces; and that Major General D. H. Hill, commanding in North Carolina, had already brought forces from that state to help defend against a Federal force threatening Richmond from the east. Cooper's shorter letter said much the same thing and also responded to another letter, from Lee to Cooper, of 23 June, in which Lee had asked after Brigadier General Montgomery Corse's brigade of Pickett's Division that had been left to temporarily guard Hanover Junction, a point where two important railroads crossed each other north of Richmond. Cooper informed Lee that only two days after Corse had moved to Gordonsville, Virginia, a Union cavalry raid had hit Hanover Junction and done "some execution in breaking the railroad and burning a bridge, some buildings, public stores, &c." and that the large Federal force east of Richmond would probably continue to make such raids. He wound up by asking if Lee "might not be able to spare a portion of your force to protect your line of communication against attempted raids of the enemy."[48] Lee, of course, did not receive these letters, thanks to Captain Dahlgren.

Finally, probably somewhat after noon (McLaws thought it was about 1 p.m.), Longstreet's two divisions, of four brigades each, left their position on Herr Ridge. Lee had, meanwhile, ridden back to Seminary Ridge to investigate what the firing over there was all about but had been reassured by General Pendleton that Wilcox's Brigade had driven the Federals away and that it and the rest of Anderson's Division was now in position and ready to cooperate in Longstreet's attack. (Which indicates that Hill had also been in no great hurry to attack or had not expected it to begin any earlier than noon.)

Lee rode back to join Longstreet's column again, and Colonel Walker later claimed that Lee "for a little while, placed himself at the head of one of the brigades to hurry the column forward."[49] In one of his post-war accounts, Longstreet merely noted, laconically, that "General Lee rode with me a mile or more."[50] By then the hottest part of the day had arrived, but the column moved off at a good clip, double-timing at least part of the way. The two divisions evidently moved south a short way and then almost immediately turned, not east, toward the Union position, but west to find another road, then southwest a short way, then finally southeast, crossing the Hagerstown (or Fairfield) road at Black Horse Tavern. Following that road through a few twists and turns would eventually lead them to Seminary Ridge somewhat south of where Hill's 3rd Corps was just going into position along that ridge, and just west of where the Emmitsburg Road reached the highest part of the Peach Orchard Ridge. It was thus almost ideal for the purpose of putting the two divisions where they were wanted. There was just one problem with it, which will soon be discussed.

Colonel Alexander had, meanwhile, ridden down beyond Wilcox's position to get the lay of the land where Longstreet's troops were supposed to deploy. After that, he ridden north and conferred with the commanders of the artillery battalions attached to Hood's and McLaws' divisions before returning to his own battalion, still parked near the Chambersburg Pike. The other reserve battalion, the Washington Artillery of New Orleans (with only nine guns) was to be left in reserve there, and, after getting his own 26 guns limbered up, he set off with them. He had probably taken them along a road that ran along Marsh Creek to Black Horse Tavern and on across the Hagerstown/Fairfield road, somewhat in advance of Longstreet's marching infantry. "At one point the direct road leading to this place came in sight of the enemy's signal station," he later wrote, "but I turned out of the road before reaching the exposed part, and passing through some meadows a few hundred yards, regained the road without coming in sight. I then went about hunting up the other battalions which were attached to the infantry in order to give them all their positions for opening the attack. While thus engaged I came upon the head of an infantry column, which I think was Hood's division, standing halted in the road where it was in sight of Round Top."[51]

This was the one flaw with the route that had been chosen – by whom is not known – for Longstreet's column. The road passed over a hill that was high enough and cleared enough that the column would be easily visible to the Union signal station up on Little Round Top. It was the same hill that Alexander's artillery had bypassed. "They had been instructed to avoid being seen," Alexander later wrote, "and finding that the road on which they had been sent came at this point in full view of the signal station, they had halted, in finding themselves already exposed, and sent back to General Lee or Longstreet for orders. For some reason, which I cannot now recall, they would not turn back and follow the tracks of my guns, and I remember a long and tiresome waiting; and at length there came an order to turn back and take another road around by 'Black Horse Tavern,' and I have never forgotten that name since. My general recollection is that nearly three hours were lost in that delay and countermarch...."[52] In another post-war account, he said, "That wretched little signal-station upon Round Top that day caused one of our divisions to lose over two hours, and probably delayed our assault nearly that long."[53]

Whether the delay was of three hours or two, it was longer than it needed to have been. When McLaws and Captain Johnston, at the head of the column, had realized that they were in plain sight of the Union signal station, they had called a halt and spent quite a bit of time searching for an alternate route but somehow missed any tracks left by the wheels of Alexander's artillery or judged that route to be unsuitable for infantry. (McLaws' account says he looked for a road, so possibly he did not even consider marching across fields.) One Rebel in the ranks later remembered that McLaws returned from this reconnaissance "saying things I would not like to teach my grandson...."[54]

McLaws was soon met by Longstreet, who had ridden to the front of the column to discover why it had stopped. McLaws took him to the top of the hill and showed him the problem, and the two concluded that the only solution was to backtrack to their starting point. Meanwhile, chafing at the delay, Hood, rather than remaining behind McLaw's column, had brought his division up partially alongside it, which now complicated the problem of countermarching. Had Hood remained in place behind McLaws, Longstreet would most likely have let Hood take the lead in the new direction. But now there was no advantage to doing that, so Longstreet allowed McLaws to remain in the lead. (The two men had been classmates at West Point, in the same class with future Union generals John Reynolds, Abner Doubleday, George Sykes and others.) However, instead of letting the rear of his column become the new front, McLaws had his leading brigade, that of Brigadier General J. B. Kershaw, make a U turn, with everyone behind him doing the same as the head of the column came back past them. Then Hood's Division fell in at the rear again.

Evidently the column returned to the place where it had turned west from Herr's Ridge and went on to the east this time, filed into the Hagerstown/Fairfield road heading northeast for a while, then took a sharp turn onto a road leading southwest alongside Willoughby Run and eventually, after a march of perhaps three miles, came back to the road it had been on before, not much more than a half-mile closer to Seminary Ridge than it had been when it had turned around. The lanes the two divisions followed for a while evidently forced the regiments to narrow their fronts, which caused the column to stretch out, and delayed the units at the rear even further. As one Confederate later remembered, "The roads were the roughest and the long, sloping hills the steepest. The day was hot, and we were thirsty and had not stopped to rest or drink."[55] (The temperature in the town at 2 p.m. was recorded as 82 degrees, and that was probably in the shade.) Kershaw, whose brigade of some 2,200 South Carolinians still led McLaws' column, remembered that they were, after returning to the road they had been on, moving directly toward Little Round Top and that a battery of artillery was moving alongside his men.

Eventually the head of the column reached an intersection marked by what was known as Pitzer's Schoolhouse, and there it turned due east on what was called the Millertown Road, then angled northeast up the back side of Seminary Ridge (actually called Warfield Ridge that far south). Major John Cheves Haskell, of Hood's artillery, wrote, after the war, that he saw Longstreet and Lee arrive at the point where the road crossed Warfield Ridge ahead of the marching infantry, and that they talked for a few minutes and then parted company, Lee riding up Seminary Ridge to check on Anderson's Division, and Longstreet rejoining his column.

It must have been shortly after Lee departed that Longstreet rode up beside McLaws and, as the latter remembered it, asked, "How are you going in?" And McLaws replied, "That will be determined when I can see what is in my front." Longstreet said, "There is nothing in your front; you will be entirely on the flank of the enemy." McLaws replied, "Then I will continue my march in columns of companies, and after arriving on the flank as far as is necessary will face to the left and march on the enemy." Longstreet replied, "That suits me," and rode away. "My head of column," McLaws' account continues, "soon reached the edge of the woods, and the enemy at once opened on it with numerous artillery, and one rapid glance showed them to be in force much greater than I had, and extending considerably beyond my right."[56] Longstreet's column had not come out on the flank of the enemy, as intended, for, while Longstreet marched and countermarched, Sickles had advanced his corps to the very ground where Longstreet was supposed to form for the attack.

∽ Endnotes ∽

1 Howard Coffin, *Nine Months to Gettysburg* (Woodstock VT, 1997), 195-6.
2 Wheeler, *Witness to Gettysburg*, 170.
3 Ibid., 174-5.
4 Hunt, Henry J., "The Second Day at Gettysburg," in *B&L* III:295-6. Italics in the source. There were at least two orchards on the high ground over which the Emmitsburg Road passed. The one that became "The Peach Orchard," with capital letters, in subsequent accounts was in the southeast corner of the intersection of the Emmitsburg Road and the crossroad referred to here by Hunt, which is known to history as the Wheatfield Road after another landmark that became famous in that day's fighting.
5 "A Letter from General Meade," *B&L*, III:413.
6 David M. Jordan, *Happiness Is Not My Companion*, (Bloomington/Indianapolis, 2001), 89.
7 Hunt, "The Second Day at Gettysburg," *B&L* III:297-300.
8 Pfanz, *Gettysburg – Culp's Hill and Cemetery Hill*, 109.
9 OR, I:27:I:221-2.
10 John M. Archer, *Fury on the Bliss Farm at Gettysburg* (Gettysburg, 2012), 23.
11 Wheeler, *Witness to Gettysburg*, 169-70.
12 I. Shiebert, letter in "Leading Confederates on the Battle of Gettysburg," in *SHSP*, V:92.
13 Longstreet, *From Manassas to Appomattox*, 362. Douglas Southall Freeman, in *R. E. Lee*, Volume 3 (New York, 1935), 552-3, sorts through various conflicting statements from Longstreet and others about when he actually reached Lee's headquarters and

concludes it was probably around 5:15 a.m., some 45 minutes after sunrise. Dr. J. S. Dorsey Cullen, a surgeon in his corps, reminded Longstreet that "About three o'clock in the morning, while the stars were still shining, you left your headquarters and rode to General Lee's, where I found you sitting with him after sunrise looking at the enemy on Cemetery Hill." *SHSP* V:78. Longstreet's mention of the stars still shining when he reached Lee's headquarters probably derives from this statement.

14 *OR*, I:27:II:446.
15 Bowden and Ward, *Last Chance for Victory*, 246-7.
16 Lafayette McLaws, "Gettysburg," in *SHSP* VII:68-69. Thus, if McLaws remembered correctly, Johnston had not yet departed on his reconnaissance when McLaws arrived, even though the latter's division did not begin its march until sunrise, or around 4:30 a.m. (McLaws refers to Johnston as a major, which rank that officer achieved the following year, but at Gettysburg Johnston was still a captain.) Johnston's errors about what he saw and, possibly, even about where he went, do not instill confidence in his memory about what time it was (especially considering that he was not carrying a watch at the time). Personal prejudice against Longstreet has to be considered as an element in McLaws' statement, because, long before he wrote it, Longstreet had relieved him from command of his division and had him court-martialed for improper preparations of an attack on Fort Sanders, at Knoxville, Tenn., in the autumn of 1863. So it is conceivable that McLaws might have exaggerated the earliness of his conversation with Lee and Longstreet in order to exaggerate Longstreet's slowness in preparing his attack. Some historians have guessed that what Lee really told McLaws was that Johnston was then making his reconnaissance or even that he had already made it, and that McLaws misunderstood this, thinking that Johnston had not yet begun it. This is, of course, possible, but unprovable with the evidence available.
17 Freeman, *R. E. Lee*, III:553.
18 Ibid., III:89.
19 A. L. Long, letter reprinted in "Causes of Lee's Defeat at Gettysburg," *SHSP* IV:67.
20 Ibid.
21 Harman, *Lee's Real Plan at Gettysburg*, 22.
22 Ibid., 23.
23 *OR*, I:27:II:318-9.
24 Hunt, "The Second Day at Gettysburg," in *B&L* III:300. Italics in the source.
25 *OR*, I:27:II:358.
26 See "Mapping the Past" by Tony Horwitz, in the *Smithsonian* magazine of December 2012, for a discussion of the work of Anne Kelly Knowles with computer programs called geographic information systems, which were used to study the topography around Gettysburg and discover just what Lee could and could not see.
27 James A. Hessler, *Sickles at Gettysburg* (New York, 2009), 138.
28 E. Porter Alexander, "The Great Charge and Artillery Fighting at Gettysburg," in *B&L* III:358.
29 E. P. Alexander, "Letter from General E. P. Alexander, Late Chief of Artillery, First Corps A.N.V." *SHSP* IV:101.
30 Wheeler, *Witness to Gettysburg*, 167.
31 Trimble, "The Battle and Campaign of Gettysburg," *SHSP* XXVI:125.
32 Long, letter reprinted in "Causes of Lee's Defeat at Gettysburg," *SHSP* IV:68.
33 Pfanz, *Gettysburg – the Second Day*, 112. Italics in the source.
34 R. L. Walker, letter quoted in "A Review of the First Two Days' Operations at Gettysburg and a Reply to General Longstreet" by General Fitz. Lee, in *SHSP* V:181.
35 James Longstreet, "Lee's Right Wing at Gettysburg," in *B&L* III:340.
36 Freeman, *R. E. Lee*, III:97n.
37 McLaws, "Gettysburg," in *SHSP* VII:69.
38 Longstreet, *From Manassas to Appomattox*, 366.
39 David Shultz and David Wieck, *The Battle Between the Farm Lanes*, (Columbus OH, 2006).

40 Sears, *Gettysburg*, 247.
41 Ibid., 248.
42 Pfanz, *Gettysburg – the Second Day*, 93.
43 Hunt, "The Second Day at Gettysburg," in *B&L* III:301-2. Italics in the source.
44 *OR*, I:27:I:515.
45 Pfanz, *Gettysburg – the Second Day*, 98.
46 *OR*, I:27:III:487-8.
47 Ibid., I:27:III:924-5.
48 Ibid., I:27:I:75-6.
49 Walker's letter quoted in "A Review of the First Two Days' Operations at Gettysburg and a Reply to General Longstreet" by General Fitz. Lee, in *SHSP* V:181. Walker's account makes it sound as if Lee did this upon his first visit to Longstreet's column, but, since the column was not yet moving at that time, this incident must have occurred on Lee's second visit.
50 Longstreet, *From Manassas to Appomattox*, 366.
51 Alexander, "Letter from General E. P. Alexander, Late Chief of Artillery, First Corps A.N.V." *SHSP* IV:101.
52 Ibid., 101-2.
53 Alexander, "The Great Charge and Artillery Fighting at Gettysburg," in *B&L* III:358.
54 Pfanz, *Gettysburg – the Second Day*, 119.
55 LaFantasie, *Twilight at Little Round Top*, 53.
56 McLaws, "Gettysburg," in *SHSP* VII:69-70.

CHAPTER 7
"The Best Three Hours' Fighting Ever Done"
2 July 1863

TAKING A ROUND-ABOUT ROUTE, General Hunt had returned to army headquarters and reported to Meade that Sickles' proposed line was a good one for artillery but that it did not fit well with the rest of the army's position, that he couldn't advise taking it, and had suggested that Meade go and have a look for himself, which got him only a nod from the army commander. Hunt had then ridden on to Cemetery Hill to see what the firing was about that he had heard coming from there.

After Hunt had left him, Sickles had sent a staff officer, Major Henry E. Tremain, to army headquarters to make another try to get Meade to modify his orders. It was not Tremain's first such trip of the day, and it was no more successful than the others had been. He had found Meade alone in the kitchen of the tiny house his staff had commandeered, studying a map of Adams County (of which Gettysburg was the seat). Tremain had reported the arrival of the two brigades from Emmitsburg but had pointed out that the corps' wagon train, coming up the same road, had still not arrived, had asked if the cavalry would keep the road open, and had reported that Berdan had found Confederate units in force very near the high ground that Sickles was concerned about. When Meade had made no answer, the major had repeated the high points, and Meade had then replied that the cavalry would take care of the road and that orders had been issued about corps trains. When Tremain had returned to Sickles and reported on this interview, Sickles had evidently decided that he was not going to get any satisfaction from army headquarters.

Colonel Berdan said it was around 2 p.m. when he

reported to General Birney what he had learned on his reconnaissance into the woods to the west of the Emmitsburg Road. Birney evidently then reported to Sickles that "The skirmishers of the enemy were driven in, but three columns of their forces were found marching to our left."[1] He didn't say how big the columns were (actually regiments), but Sickles was ready to believe the worst: The Rebels were preparing to occupy the high ground he wanted, probably with the intention of attacking his corps. He decided to take matters into his own hands. "It was not through any misinterpretation of orders," Sickles later told Congress's Joint Committee on the Conduct of the War. "It was either a good line or a bad one, and, whichever it was, I took it upon my own responsibility. . . . I took up that line because it enabled me to hold commanding ground, which, if the enemy had been allowed to take – as they would have taken it if I had not occupied it in force – would have rendered our position on the left untenable; and, in my judgment, would have turned the fortunes of the day hopelessly against us."[2] He ordered Birney to advance, placing the right of his division at the intersection of the Emmitsburg and Millerstown roads. Humphreys was ordered to form on Birney's right, extending the line along the Emmitsburg road and connecting with the left of the 2nd Corps.

Birney's division was not large enough to stretch all the way back to either of the Round Tops, so its left flank was anchored on the area of large boulders called Devil's Den, which would be impassable to any sizable body of troops. The 4th New York Battery, commanded by Captain James E. Smith, was placed on the small ridge (sometimes called Houck's Ridge) that ran north from Devil's Den just west of Plum Run but east of what Hunt called Plum Branch and east of a wood lot called Rose's Woods. Four of its six 10-pounder rifled guns were placed there, just south of Rose's Woods, facing west across a field that had recently been cleared to obtain wood for lumber. The other two guns were placed behind the ridge and somewhat farther north, facing south, as protection against any enemy force that tried to swing around Devil's Den and come up the little valley of Plum Run.

At the right of Birney's line, the 3rd Maine, still detached from Ward's brigade since its foray in support of Berdan's Sharpshooters, was posted in the Peach Orchard, and Brigadier General Charles K. Graham's 1st Brigade's line ran behind it and up the Emmitsburg Road. Graham had six regiments, all from Pennsylvania. Unfortunately for Birney, the small ridges here did not run southeast back toward Devil's Den and the Round Tops but insisted on running more north-south, like most of the ridges around Gettysburg. Because of this, Birney's three brigades did not form a continuous line. But, as General Hunt said, "the ridges were so high that each would serve as a 'traverse' for the other."[3] Ward's 2nd Brigade (five regiments, not counting the 3rd Maine or the two Sharpshooter Regiments), on the left, formed a line behind Smith's 4th New York Battery, extending along Houck's Ridge for perhaps a quarter of a mile, facing west. De Trobriand's 3rd Brigade (one of the late arrivals) formed a somewhat shorter line along some wooded high ground northwest of there, called the stony hill, facing slightly north of west. There was no connection between these two units. Most of the 3rd Corps' artillery was placed in the Peach Orchard and along what is now known as the Wheatfield Road (the eastward extension of the Millerstown Road, sometimes called the Fairfield Cross Road) between Graham's left and de Trobriand's right, facing southwest.

Brigadier General Andrew A. Humphreys, commander of Sickles' other division, had been a topological engineer in the pre-war Regular Army, so one might wonder why Sickles had not asked for his opinion of the relative merits of the corps' assigned position and that along the Emmitsburg Road. One of the most likely reasons is that Humphreys was a newcomer to the 3rd Corps, having commanded a division in the 5th Corps at the battle of Chancellorsville and having been reassigned to the 3rd Corps only about five weeks back. He was a highly competent officer who would eventually rise to corps command, but evidently Sickles did not yet trust him, or perhaps did not know of, or remember, Humphreys' experience as an engineer.

All Humphreys knew was that, for reasons unknown to him, Birney's division had been advanced to the Emmitsburg Road and that now his own division was supposed to form on Birney's right. He put the 71st New York of his 2nd Brigade (Sickles' old Excelsior Brigade, now commanded by Colonel William R. Brewster) next to Graham's brigade of Birney's division, and then all of Brigadier General Joseph B. Carr's 1st Brigade running parallel to, but some 200 or 300 yards east of, the Emmitsburg Road. This left a gap of some 500 yards between his right and the left of the 2nd Corps, but he wasn't too concerned about that, as any attempt by the Confederates to enter that gap would be subject to a crossfire from his own line and that of the 2nd Corps and would be seen in time for him to send units to block the gap. Another of Brewster's regiments, the 73rd New York, was sent forward to the small home of the Daniel Klingle family, just west of the Emmitsburg Road, and told to hold that position at all hazards. The remaining four regiments of Brewster's brigade were formed in battalion columns about 200 yards behind the main line, as a reserve. Humphrey's 3rd Brigade, commanded by Colonel George C. Burling, was ordered by Sickles to be temporarily attached to Birney's division, for which it served as a reserve. This shows that Sickles was still more concerned about his left than his right or his front.

Meade was completely oblivious to Sickles' change of position, and had been misinformed about Longstreet's movements, which, despite its countermarch, had been seen by the Union signal station on Little Round Top after all. However, at the time it had been spotted it had been moving north or northeast, and the report sent to Meade said that a heavy column was moving from the Federal left toward the right, when actually its overall direction was toward Meade's left.

At 3 p.m. Meade sent off a brief report to General Halleck at Washington: "I have concentrated my army at this place today. The Sixth Corps is just coming in, very much worn out, having been marching since 9 p.m. last night. The army is fatigued. I have today, up to this hour, awaited the attack of the enemy, I having a strong position for defensive. I am not determined, as yet, on attacking him till his position is more developed. He has been moving on both my flanks, apparently, but it is difficult to tell exactly his movements. I have delayed attacking, to allow the Sixth Corps and parts of other corps to reach this place and to rest the men. Expecting a battle, I ordered all my trains to the rear. If not attacked, and I can get any positive information of the position of the enemy which will justify me in so doing, I shall attack. If I find it hazardous to do so, or am satisfied the enemy is endeavoring to move to my rear and interpose between me and Washington, I shall fall back to my supplies at Westminster. I will endeavor to advise you as often as possible. In the engagement yesterday the enemy concentrated more rapidly than we could, and toward evening, owing to the superiority of numbers, compelled the Eleventh and First Corps to fall back from the town to the heights this side, on which I am now posted. I feel fully the responsibility resting upon me, but will endeavor to act with caution."[4] After sending this off, Meade sent out a circular telling his corps commanders to come to headquarters for a conference.

Kershaw said it was 3 p.m. when his brigade, at the head of Longstreet's column, emerged from the woods and discovered that the Federals were not where they were expected be. He said that Longstreet had told him, at some point during the march, that his brigade would be attacking the enemy "at the Peach Orchard, which lay a little to the left of my line of march, some six hundred yards from us. I was directed to turn the flank of that position, extend my line along the road we were then in beyond the Emmitsburg pike, with my left resting on that road." That is, he should simply stay on the road he was on (the Millerstown/Wheatfield road) until the rear of his brigade reached the Emmitsburg Road, and then face it to the left, or northeast. This was in accordance with Lee's instructions to McLaws to form perpendicular to that road and advance along it, rolling up the Union line. But now that was clearly impossible. Kershaw sent skirmishers out to cover his front and posted his main line behind the cover of one of several stone walls in the area, facing east, directly toward the stony hill and de Trobriand's brigade. Then he took a careful look at the Federals, finding them "far beyond the point at which their left had been supposed to rest. To carry out my instructions would have been, if successful in driving the enemy from the Peach Orchard, to present my own right flank and rear to a large portion of the enemy's main line of battle."[5] (That is, to de Trobriand's and Ward's brigades.) So he kept his brigade behind the stone wall and sent a report to McLaws.

McLaws was already aware of the problem and was sending orders for Kershaw to do just what he was doing and for the next brigade, the 1,600 Mississippians of Brigadier General William Barksdale, to form on Kershaw's left. "The view presented astonished me," McLaws later remembered, "as the enemy was massed in my front, and extended to my right and left as far as I could see. The firing on my command showed to Hood in my rear that the enemy was in force in my front and right, and the head of his column was turned by General Longstreet's order to go on my right and as his troops appeared, the enemy opened on them, developing a long line to his right even, and way up to the top of Round Top. [In this, he was mistaken.] Thus was presented a state of affairs which was certainly not contemplated when the original plan or order of battle was given, and certainly was not known to General Longstreet a half hour previous."[6]

McLaws' other two brigades formed a second line about 150 yards behind Kershaw and Barksdale, with Brigadier General Paul Semmes' 1,344 Georgians behind Kershaw and Brigadier General William T. Wofford's 1,600 Georgians behind Barksdale. The artillery battalion attached to McLaws'

Division – 16 guns commanded by Colonel Henry C. Cabell – unlimbered in front of Kershaw, and Alexander's 26 guns were in front of Barksdale and between the two front-line brigades. Even before all of McLaws' men and guns were in position, Longstreet sent an officer to ask why McLaws had not attacked. McLaws sent back word that he wasn't ready yet. Longstreet sent back an order to attack, and this time McLaws explained that the enemy was in strong force in his front and he wanted to give his artillery time to soften them up. Then came a peremptory order from both Longstreet and Lee for McLaws to charge, but while he was passing this order on to his brigades another messenger dashed up with orders for him to wait until Hood was ready to join in. McLaws complained in a letter to his wife written a few days later that Longstreet had issued "contradictory orders to everyone, and was exceedingly overbearing."[7] He failed to consider that Longstreet was only the man in the middle and that it was Lee who was changing his mind, for the very good reason that circumstances had changed.

Longstreet later said that, while he was riding along his lines and examining the Union position, "General Lee . . . gave orders for the attack to be made by my right – following up the direction of the Emmitsburg road toward the Cemetery Ridge, holding Hood's left as well as could be toward the Emmitsburg road, McLaws to follow the movements of Hood, attacking at the Peach Orchard the Federal Third Corps, with a part of R. H. Anderson's division following the movements of McLaws to guard his left flank."[8] Having seen or learned that the Union line extended beyond where it had been thought to end, Lee had merely modified his original plan so that Hood would now lead the attack instead of McLaws, and as Hood's four brigades smashed into what Lee thought was the end of the Federal line McLaws would join in, and, as the line was rolled up, Anderson would also. This is called an attack *en echelon*, and was one of Lee's favorite maneuvers. Colonel Alexander later wrote that the attack should have been simultaneous instead. "Battles begun by one command and to be taken up successively by others, are always much prolonged," he said. "We had used this method on four occasions, – at Seven Pines, Gaines Mill, Frazier's Farm or Glendale, and Malvern Hill, – and always with poor success."9

Anyway, Hood's Division formed on McLaws' right, and deployed along Warfield Ridge (the southern extension of Seminary Ridge) straddling the Emmitsburg Road, which, trending southwest, crossed the ridge this far south. However, Hood was not positioned perpendicular to the road (*i.e.* facing northeast) but faced east, toward Devil's Den and the two Round Tops. Like McLaws' Division, it was formed in two lines of two brigades each, with Law's 2,000 Alabamans on the right and Robertson's 1,900 Texans and Arkansans on the left of the first line. Thomas G. Anderson's 1,900 Georgians were placed behind the Texas Brigade, and Henry Benning's 1,500 Georgians partly behind Law, partly behind Robertson. While his men were deploying, Hood sent pioneers forward to knock down fences that would, if left intact, interfere with his advance, and sent some Texas scouts to find the Federals' left flank. A battery was unlimbered to Law's right front and another one in front of the Texans. These and the guns in front of McLaws' Division, were soon engaged in an intense artillery duel with Union artillery in Sickles' disjointed line, and almost immediately Ewell's artillery, upon hearing Longstreet's guns, as pre-arranged, opened fire on the Federals on Cemetery Hill and Culp's Hill.

Hood's experience was similar to McLaws', for, as he later told McLaws, "He reported that it was unwise to attack up the Emmettsburg road as ordered, and urged that he be allowed to turn [the Union line]. General Longstreet returned answer: 'General Lee's orders are to attack up the Emmettsburg road.' That he went again, and reported that nothing was to be gained by such an attack, and the answer was: 'General Lee's orders are to attack up the Emmettsburg road.' That during these intervals of time he had continued to use the batteries against the enemy, and it seemed to his more extended reconnoissance that the position occupied by the enemy was naturally so strong, so nearly impregnable, that, independently of their flank fire, they could repel his attack by throwing stones down the mountain; and that a third time he dispatched a staff officer to explain more fully in regard to the situation, and to suggest that he (General Longstreet) come in person and see for himself, and that his Adjutant General, whom he sent the last time, returned with the same message: 'General Lee's orders are to attack up the Emmettsburg road;' and almost simultaneously Colonel Fairfax, of Longstreet's staff, rode up and repeated the order."[10]

In one post-war account, Longstreet said, "Hood's front was very rugged, with no field for artillery, and very rough for advance of infantry. As soon as he passed the Emmitsburg road, he sent to report of the great advantage of moving on by his right around to the enemy's rear. His scouting parties had reported that there was nothing between them and the enemy's trains. He was told that the move to the right had been proposed the day before and rejected; that General Lee's orders were to guide my left by the Emmitsburg road."[11]

Longstreet later complained, with some justification, that if Lee had been on hand, Hood's messages could have been referred to him, but as it was Longstreet did not feel authorized to modify the plan or to take the time to refer them to Lee and await an answer. The move that Hood evidently proposed would have taken his division clear around behind the Round Tops, which would have consumed most of what was left of the waning afternoon, required McLaws to shift over to fill the area between the Emmitsburg road and the Round Tops, and Hill's corps to extend down Seminary Ridge so as to remain connected with McLaws. Lee's army would then have been even more over-extended than it already was unless Ewell's corps was withdrawn to Seminary Ridge. But, Longstreet argued in his post-war writings, that "my right division [Hood's] was then nearer to Westminster [than the Federals were], and our scouting parties of infantry were within rifle range of the [Taneytown] road leading to that point and to Washington. So it would have been convenient, after holding our threatening attitude till night, to march across his line at dark, in time to draw other troops to close connection before the next morning."[12]

Be that as it may have been (and the Union army was also quite capable of marching after dark), Lee was still focused on a concentric attack against Cemetery Hill, and Longstreet said, in another post-war account, that, "As soon as the troops were in position, and we could find the points against which we should march and give the guiding points, the advance was ordered – at half-past 3 o'clock in the afternoon. The attack was made in splendid style by both divisions. . . ."[13] Longstreet later told McLaws that he had intended to halt the attack if the enemy position proved to be too strong for his two divisions, but that, as it turned out, the Union position was not so strong and his two divisions were in great form. "Then was fairly commenced," he wrote, "what I do not hesitate to pronounce the best three hours' fighting ever done by any troops on any battle-field."[14]

After ordering his two divisions to advance to the long-desired high ground along the Emmitsburg Road, Sickles had sent Major Tremain back to army headquarters again. If Tremain said anything to Meade about the 3rd Corps' change of position Meade failed to note it, and, after getting Meade to authorize the dispatch of some batteries of the Artillery Reserve to reinforce that corps, the major rode back and reported again to Sickles. He then rode up to the Peach Orchard, where fire from McLaws' skirmishers was forcing all the Union officers to dismount. From there General Graham took him to a point where he could see Hood's troops crossing the Emmitsburg Road south of them. He hurried to report this to Sickles, who sent him, once again, to army headquarters.

Meade did not seem alarmed at this news, and Tremain was sent back again with a request that Sickles visit headquarters. Sickles felt that he had more important things to do at the moment, and ignored the request, but one of Meade's aides soon arrived with a second invitation from Meade. Sickles asked to be excused on the grounds that he was preparing to receive a Confederate attack. In response, a positive order soon arrived for Sickles to attend a meeting of the corps commanders with Meade. Turning over command of the corps to Birney, Sickles reluctantly obeyed, taking Tremain with him, even though they could hear the sound of artillery fire on Birney's front. (Birney said that his guns opened fire on the Confederates at about 3:30 p.m.)

Meanwhile, the other corps commanders had begun to assemble at army headquarters when General Warren mentioned that the 3rd Corps was not in its assigned position. He had heard a rumor to that effect and had sent a staff officer to confirm it. Only then did Meade realize that Sickles had taken it upon himself to occupy the position he had been advocating all morning. Meade turned to General Sykes and ordered him to take his 5th Corps, then in reserve, and hold the left flank of the army at all hazards. This broke up the meeting, and just then Sickles rode up, with the sound of artillery fire behind him punctuating his arrival. "I never saw General Meade so angry if I may so call it," Captain Paine, the engineer, later recalled. "He ordered General Sickles to retire his line to the position he had been instructed to take. This was done in a few sharp words."[15] He told Sickles not to dismount but to return to his own corps, where, by the sound of the firing, he was needed, and that Meade would join him there.

Sickles immediately turned around, while Meade had to borrow a horse from General Pleasonton, as his own wasn't saddled. Warren rode with Meade at first, and as they crossed Cemetery Ridge he pointed southward and said, "Here is where the line should be."[16] Meade said that it was too late to place it there and rode on toward Sickles' new position, passing along Humphrey's line, while Warren rode on down Cemetery Ridge toward Little Round Top. Meade found

Sickles overseeing the placement of some additional batteries and regiments in or near the Peach Orchard.

Accounts of what the two generals said to each other there vary according to whether the narrator was a partisan of Sickles or of Meade in the never-ending controversy that immediately sprang up about Sickles' change of position. They differ mainly over whether Meade conceded that the new position was better than the assigned one on Cemetery Ridge or chided him for overstepping his orders. They agree however that Sickles offered to return to Cemetery Ridge if Meade thought best but that the latter said it was too late to do so. Both generals agreed that the 3rd Corps was too small to hold the position alone, but Meade said he was sending the 5th Corps to help out and that Sickles could call upon the Artillery Reserve for more guns and upon Hancock's 2nd Corps to support his right flank.

Fortunately for them, more guns were already on the way. After reaching Cemetery Hill, Hunt had soon decided that the firing there did not presage an attack (Union guns were firing on some distant Rebel infantry that were moving toward the Confederate left), and so he returned to the Peach Orchard ridge. There he met Captain Randolph, Sickles' chief of artillery, who informed him that Sickles had ordered him to place his batteries on that forward position. Not knowing that the move was not authorized by Meade, but seeing that more guns would be needed, Hunt had called on the Artillery Reserve to send some, then had ridden to join Sickles and Meade, whom he could see conversing together not far off. But this large group of mounted generals, staff officers, and orderlies soon attracted Confederate artillery fire, and one round spooked the borrowed horse Meade was riding and caused it to bolt, which pretty much broke up the meeting.

Having received the army commander's consent (however reluctant) to his change of position, and reassurance about reinforcements and supports, Sickles now sent orders for Humphreys to advance his brigades the last 200 or 300 yards up to and along the Emmitsburg Road north of the

Peach Orchard. However, before they could complete this movement an order arrived from Meade for Humphreys to go to Little Round Top, where, Warren had reported, troops were badly needed. Professional soldier that he was, Humphreys obeyed the order first, ordering the change of direction, and only then sent Meade's staff officer back with word that he thought it was a bad idea, as it would leave a huge gap between Birney's right and the 2nd Corps' left, back on Cemetery Ridge. He soon followed personally, but on the way was met by the same officer coming back with word that the order had been cancelled; the 5th Corps would take care of Little Round Top, and Humphreys should follow Sickles' order to advance to the Emmitsburg Road.

Officers and men in the nearby 2nd Corps greatly admired the spectacle, rarely seen down in heavily wooded Virginia, of two brigades of infantry wheeling and marching in precise lines across the open fields. However, General Hancock was heard to predict that "they'll come tumbling back, soon enough."[17] Carr's 1st Brigade of Humphreys' Division formed along the east side of the Emmitsburg Road and sent one regiment to replace the 73rd New York holding the Klingle place. Some of Brewster's regiments bolstered this line, and two of them served as a reserve. When Humphreys' division had settled in, the 3rd Corps' six brigades occupied a V-shaped line that was a mile and half long with fewer than 10,000 men, which meant that it was more spread out than prudence called for, and both flanks were vulnerable, especially the left one.

After a brief conference with Meade, who was on his way back to his headquarters on the Taneytown Road, Hancock ordered Caldwell's division to go help Sickles, but almost immediately countermanded the order after seeing a division of the 5th Corps cross Cemetery Ridge on its way to Sickles' support. He did, however, tell Gibbon to send the two regiments that he had earlier been told to be prepared to send to Humphreys. Gibbon sent the 19th Massachusetts and the 42nd New York (almost half of Colonel Norman Hall's 3rd

Brigade), then advanced Lieutenant Fred Brown's Battery B of the 1st Rhode Island Light Artillery some 60 yards beyond the stone wall in front of the later-famous grove of trees and brought up two regiments of Brigadier General Alexander Webb's 2nd Brigade to back them up.

It took about an hour to get Hood's and McLaws' men formed for the attack, during which they had to suffer Union artillery fire without being able to fight back. A captain in the 4th Texas later wrote that "It is very trying upon men to remain still and in ranks under a severe cannonading. One has time to reflect upon the danger, and there being no wild excitement as in a charge, he is more reminded of the utter helplessness of his present condition."[18] Federal shot and shell was tearing limbs from the trees all around the Confederates, and occasionally a lucky shot took out a man or two. One solid shot killed a captain in the 3rd Arkansas, severed an orderly sergeant's arm, took off the head of another sergeant, and mangled a corporal's leg, and still kept on bouncing along. Hood had two batteries in position to return the Union fire, but two others were kept limbered, ready to follow the infantry when it advanced.

The tactical, or detailed, plan for Longstreet's attack seems to have been for Hood's Division, still in two lines, to advance eastward at first, then wheel to the north and take Ward's and de Trobriand's brigades in flank. Then McLaws' Division would join in. Kershaw said, "I was directed to commence the attack as soon as General Hood became engaged, swinging around toward the Peach Orchard, and at the same time establishing connection with Hood on my right, and cooperating with him. It was understood that he was to sweep down the Federal lines in a direction perpendicular to our line of battle. I was informed that Barksdale would move with me and conform to my movement; that Semmes would follow me, and Wofford follow Barksdale. . . . Under my instructions I determined to move upon the stony hill, so as to strike it with my center, and thus attack the orchard on its left rear."[19]

John Bell "Sam" Hood was young for his position, about a decade younger than McLaws, and had graduated from West Point only ten years back, in 1853. He had earned a high reputation as commander of the Texas Brigade, but had not yet had much opportunity to show what he could do with a division. Now he positioned himself in front of his old Texas Brigade and, as was common in that war, made a little speech to the men. If what he said was accurately remembered by those who recorded parts of it, he stood in his stirrups and shouted, among other things, "Fix bayonets, my brave Texans; forward and take those heights!"[20] Which heights he had in mind is open to conjecture.

To the right of the Texans, the Alabamans of Law's Brigade, who had already marched some 25 miles that day, stepped off at a brisk pace without benefit of any inspirational remarks, and even briefly broke into a jog. Twenty-nine-year-old Colonel William C. Oates of the 15th Alabama, in the center of Law's line, later said that the regimental commanders had not been informed of the plan, and the same was probably true of the captains of the five companies serving as skirmishers out in front of the main line. They went up over the crest of Warfield Ridge, down a rather steep slope for some 300 yards and then up again, crossing fences, stone walls, plowed fields, rocks, brush, and trees, all of which made it difficult to maintain formation. They were heading due east, right into deadly fire coming from the 4th New York Battery near Devil's Den. (Because Devil's Den is due west of Little Round Top, between it and the Confederates, they thought the battery was on the larger hill.)

General Robertson of the Texas Brigade later reported: "The division arrived on the ground in front of the position of the enemy that we were to attack but a few minutes before we were ordered to advance. I therefore got but a glance at the field on which we had to operate before we entered upon it. I was ordered to keep my right well closed on

Brigadier-General Law's left, and to let my left rest on the Emmitsburg pike. I had advanced but a short distance when I discovered that my brigade would not fill the space between General Law's left and the pike named, and that I must leave the pike, or disconnect myself from General Law, on my right. Understanding before the action commenced that the attack on our part was to be general, and that the force of General McLaws was to advance simultaneously with us on my immediate left, and seeing at once that a mountain [Devil's Den/Little Round Top] held by the enemy in heavy force with artillery to the right of General Law's center was the key to the enemy's left, I abandoned the pike, and closed on General Law's left. This caused some separation of my regiments, which was remedied as promptly as the numerous stone and rail fences that intersected the field through which we were advancing would allow."[21]

The reason that Robertson's Texas Brigade could not fill the space between Law's Brigade and the Emmitsburg Road was that, instead of wheeling to the north, as planned, Law kept going east. He evidently considered it his job to find and turn the Federals' left flank. If he was waiting for Hood to tell him when to make his turn he would never get that order, for Law, the senior brigade commander, was himself now the division commander, although he did not yet know it, because shortly after his troops advanced Hood received a serious and extremely painful wound in the left arm from a Union shell and was carried off the field. (He never regained use of that arm and carried it in a sling for the rest of his life.)

The two regiments on the right of Law's line, the 44th and 48th Alabama, fell behind, apparently slowed by some woods, and he ordered them to turn ninety degrees to the north, behind his other three regiments, and move up the valley of Plum Run and attack the Union artillery (part of the 4th New York Battery) enfilading his left flank. Law then informed Colonel Oates that his 15th Alabama now constituted the extreme right flank of the brigade (and thus of the division, the corps, and the army). Oates later wrote that Law "directed me to hug to the foot of Round Top on its west side & pass up the valley between the two mountains until I found the federal or Union left & to turn it if possible to do all the damage I could."[22] Law also told Oates that the 47th Alabama, on his left, had been ordered to close up on the 15th and, since it had outrun its own colonel, to follow Oates's orders if it became separated from the rest of the brigade, which it soon did.

Meanwhile, in its effort to keep up with Law's Brigade, Robertson's Texas Brigade also soon broke in half; its 4th and 5th Texas followed Law, but the 1st Texas and 3rd Arkansas lost touch with them, apparently because of the rough terrain, and moved into Rose's Woods in front of Ward's Union brigade. Robertson was with this left half of his brigade, and his two regiments were probably the first Confederates to close with the Union defenders. The 1st Texas (some 450 men) assaulted the left end of Ward's brigade while the 3rd Arkansas (500 men) attacked Ward's center. Thus began a severe struggle that lasted perhaps a half hour, during which the 20th Indiana lost its colonel, its lieutenant colonel, and over half of its men.

However, de Trobriand's Union brigade, farther north, was not yet engaged, and Colonel de Trobriand sent the 17th Maine to fire into the Arkansans' left flank, causing them to fall back. Meanwhile, the two Alabama regiments that Law had moved to the north approached Ward's southern flank, and Ward moved the 4th Maine to block the Plum Run valley and protect his left and rear from the Alabamans, and moved the 99th Pennsylvania from his right to his left. Then his 124th New York (with about 230 men) charged the Texans across a triangular-shaped open field just south of Rose's Woods and drove them back as well, although it took fire from the 44th Alabama on its own flank and suffered heavy losses, including its colonel and its major. This charge gave time for Captain Smith of the 4th New York Battery to remove one of his guns, which had been disabled by Rebel artillery fire. But the 124th New York was repulsed when it ran into Georgians of Benning's Brigade.

Benning's "Rock Brigade" was supposed to follow 400 yards behind Law's Brigade, and when it emerged from the trees on Warfield Ridge Benning observed the first line about that distance to his front and followed it. He only found out later that he was following the Texas Brigade instead of Law's Brigade, which was hidden from his view by the woods at the base of Big Round Top. The 15th Georgia of his brigade became intermixed with the 1st Texas, neither regiment willing to let the other precede it, and the rest of the brigade stretched in a semicircle around the southern flank of Ward's position and connected with the 44th Alabama of Law's Brigade. Brigadier General G. T. "Tige" (for Tiger) Anderson's brigade was supposed to follow and support Robertson's Texans, but somehow Anderson got the idea that his brigade was the division's reserve, and it did not advance when Benning's Brigade did. Only when Anderson received an urgent appeal from Robertson, saying that his brigade's left was exposed, did he move his five regiments forward. He took them northeastward and formed line on Robertson's left.

Ward also asked for reinforcements, and Birney sent him the 40th New York from de Trobriand's brigade and the 6th New Jersey from Burling's brigade, and both were sent to the Plum Run valley behind Ward's main line to protect his left flank.

The two wayward Alabama regiments were pressing that area, overrunning Devil's Den and capturing about 40 Federals there, while the 20th Georgia of Benning's Brigade charged the 4th N.Y. Battery, with the 2nd Georgia keeping pace on its right. And when the colonel of the 15th Georgia, facing the 124th New York, heard the firing on their front, he advanced his regiment as well, and the 1st Texas followed suit. Those two regiments, supported by a North Carolina battery that joined the advance, drove the badly depleted 124th New York off the ridge north of Devil's Den, their respective color-bearers competing to see which could plant his flag the farthest to the front. Between them, the two regiments took about 140 prisoners, but finding themselves in a rather exposed position they fell back to the south toward Devil's Den, while General Ward ordered what was left of his brigade to retreat to the north. Parts of these two Confederate regiments also overran the three guns of the 4th N.Y. Battery that were on the ridge. Their crews had manned them as long as possible, then carried off their sights, friction primers, sponge buckets and rammer staffs to prevent the guns from being used by the Rebels.

However, the colonel of the 4th Maine (about 200 men), down in the valley of Plum Run behind the ridge, ordered his men to fix bayonets and charge obliquely to their right against the Rebels in and around Devil's Den, and the 99th Pennsylvania (300 men) soon came in on their right and swept the Confederates off the ridge. But, finding that the rest of Ward's line had fallen back, the two Union regiments, after a hard fight, eventually gave up the ridge once more. Both regiments lost over a third of their numbers there. With the 4th Maine gone, only the two remaining guns of the 4th N.Y. Battery remained in the Plum Run valley, and they held off the Rebels to the south long enough for the 40th New York (a consolidation of several units, now containing almost 600 men) to arrive and deploy about where the 4th Maine had been. It then charged down the valley into an area south of Devil's Den that would come to be known as the Slaughter Pen and slammed into the 2nd and 17th Georgia Regiments of Benning's Brigade (about 375 men each), pushing them back. Then the 6th New Jersey arrived and formed line some 200 yards behind these New Yorkers' right flank. Covered by its fire, the 40th New York fell back and rallied north of Devil's Den but was eventually driven even farther north by the 15th Georgia and 1st Texas. So the Confederates finally had undisputed possession of Devil's Den and Houck's Ridge, but doing so had required what one member of the 1st Texas called "one of the wildest, fiercest struggles of the war."[23]

While this fight was going on, Colonel Oates' two Alabama regiments, followed by the 4th and 5th Texas, continued to move east, and soon encountered two companies of

Berdan's Sharpshooters in skirmish formation behind a stone fence. The Confederates drove them back, though these Federals' accurate fire caused several casualties, including the regiment's lieutenant colonel, whose knee was shattered, and, as reported by Colonel Oates: "After crossing the fence, I received an order from Brigadier General Law to left-wheel my regiment and move in the direction of the heights upon my left [Little Round Top], which order I failed to obey, for the reason that when I received it I was rapidly advancing up the mountain [Big Round Top], and in my front I discovered a heavy force of the enemy [the Sharpshooters]. Besides this, there was great difficulty in accomplishing the maneuver at that moment, as the regiment on my left (Forty-seventh Alabama) was crowding me on the left, and running into my regiment, which had already created considerable confusion. In the event that I had obeyed the order, I should have come in contact with the regiment on my left, and also have exposed my right flank to an enfilading fire from the enemy. I therefore continued to press forward, my right passing over the top of the mountain, on the right of the line."[24]

The Sharpshooters fell back before him, keeping up a lively fire on the advancing Rebels, whose formation was completely broken by the trees and large rocks on the steep hillside. When the Alabamans were about halfway up the hill the Sharpshooters seemed to disappear, as if by magic. Fading back into the trees, one company of them withdrew to the south, and the other to the north, toward Little Round Top. Colonel Oates called a halt at the top of Big Round Top and began to think about how he could fortify his position to "hold against ten times the number of men I had."[25] But General Law's adjutant soon rode up to ask what Oates was doing up on this hill and why had he stopped advancing. Oates replied that his men needed rest and advocated holding this high ground as a defensive position, but the adjutant replied that Law, who now commanded the entire division, wanted him "to press on, turn the Union left, and capture Little Round Top, if possible, and to lose no time."[26] So Oates got his men moving again, down into the wooded saddle of land between the two Round Tops, finding the descent almost as difficult as the ascent had been.

While Meade had gone to see Sickles' new position for himself, General Warren had ridden down Cemetery Ridge, stopping to confer briefly with General Sykes of the 5th Corps and Brigadier General Stephen H. Weed, commander of the 3rd Brigade in Ayres' 2nd Division of that corps. (It was the brigade Warren had commanded before being transferred to the army commander's staff back in February.) Meanwhile, Warren's aide and brother-in-law, Lieutenant Washington Roebling (future builder of the Brooklyn Bridge) rode on to Little Round Top. He found this height occupied by nothing but the Signal Corps station, for the 3rd Corps just wasn't large enough to stretch that far from the Peach Orchard. (The signal station was at the top of a bluff of boulders at the north end of the hill's crest. The highest point on the hill was a knob about 50 yards farther south, which was some 150 feet above the flatter ground to the west. The crest then sloped to the south at a fairly gentle angle for about 150 yards, where it ended in another rocky bluff. Below that was a relatively flat shelf.)

Roebling could see Hood's advancing Confederates in the distance and hurried to report this fact to Warren, and by the time Warren arrived, or shortly thereafter, Law's Confederates were seen advancing directly toward this undefended hill. Realizing that this was a key position, he sent a staff officer to Meade to ask for a division to hold it. Meade, as described above, at first ordered Humphreys' division to go there but then changed his mind when he learned that the 5th Corps was closer. Warren also sent another officer, Lieutenant Ranald Mackenzie (who later commanded a cavalry division in the closing stages of the war) to ask Sickles for a brigade, but that general couldn't spare any troops and referred him to General Sykes of the 5th Corps. Mackenzie soon found Sykes, and he agreed to send part of General Barnes' 1st Division.

Barnes' leading brigade, the 3rd, commanded by 26-year-old Colonel Strong Vincent, had halted to await further orders near the Weikert farm, whose house and barn were serving as hospitals for men wounded the previous day. When Sykes' staff officer rode up looking for Barnes, Vincent asked him, "What are your orders? Give me your orders." The staffer replied that Sykes wanted Barnes to send a brigade to occupy "that hill yonder." Realizing that time was of the essence, Vincent said, "I will take the responsibility of taking my brigade there."[27]

Vincent, a Harvard man, then turned the brigade over to Colonel James Rice of the 44th New York, a Yale graduate, with orders to follow as quickly as possible while he rode ahead to see this hill for himself, accompanied only by his bugler, who also carried the brigade's identifying triangular pennant. They approached the hill from the northwest but judged that slope too difficult for horses to climb, so they went up the wooded eastern face nearly to the crest, then found a shelf of relatively level ground on the far side that connected with a spur of the hill that ran off to the southeast toward Big Round Top. There were few trees there, but there were numerous large rocks and boulders. At that time Ward's brigade still held Houck's Ridge and Devil's Den to the west, so Vincent figured that any Confederate attack would most likely come from the southwest, for they could approach unseen through the woods west of Big Round Top or even through the trees that covered that larger hill and the saddle of land between the two hills. He therefore decided to place the left of his brigade on the spur and run his line northwest from there along the shelf of flatter land, curving around the hill somewhat, so that his men would face south, southwest and west.

Colonel Rice brought the brigade's four regiments up the east face of the hill, and they were hit by artillery fire as soon as they came around to the south and west sides.

One Confederate shell took the head off the horse ridden by the adjutant of the 16th Michigan. Other shot and shell took the limbs off of trees, which fell and injured, or even killed, some of the men marching below them. Vincent met the column as it came up and showed the colonel of each regiment where he wanted it to form. The 16th Michigan would hold the brigade's left; then came the 20th Maine, the 83rd Pennsylvania, and Rice's 44th New York, and each regiment was to send skirmishers out to its front. Company F of the 2nd U.S. Sharpshooters, one of the two companies that Colonel Oates had encountered, passed through the 83rd Pennsylvania heading for the rear shortly before that regiment sent out its own skirmishers. The men of the brigade appreciated that they held a strong defensive position. "Each rock was a fortress," one Pennsylvanian said.[28] But evidently Vincent soon decided that his line did not stretch far enough north, for he had the 16th Michigan, minus its two companies of skirmishers, move to the right and extend the line, leaving the 20th Maine to hold the left flank. "I place you here!" Vincent told Colonel Joshua Lawrence Chamberlain, commander of that regiment. "This is the left of the Union line. You understand. You are to hold this ground at all costs."[29]

Chamberlain, a 34-year-old former college professor, maneuvered his 386 men into position on what Private Elisha Coan described as "an open level space comparatively free from rocks and bushes but in our front was a slight descent fringed by ledges of rock, and our side of the hill was covered with boulders."[30] The 20th Maine was short on officers; Chamberlain himself had only recently been promoted from lieutenant colonel (succeeding Adelbert Ames, now a general in the 11th Corps), and he had not been replaced; nor did it have a major, except that Captain Ellis Spear was filling that role unofficially. Chamberlain put Spear in charge of the left half of the regiment and Captain Atherton Clark in charge of the right half. Chamberlain's brother Tom was the regiment's adjutant. Another brother, John, a civilian member of the Christian Commission, was also present and in charge of finding a good place for the wounded men of the regiment. Company B, commanded by Captain Walter G. Morrill, was sent out as skirmishers, even though the two companies sent out by the 16th Michigan before that regiment was moved were presumably still out front.

When his men and officers had their assignments, Chamberlain walked up the line to see what was going on. He was soon joined by Colonel Rice of the 44th New York, and the two colonels walked on beyond the right of the 16th Michigan to a point where they had a view to the west. They were just in time to see the Confederates overrun Devil's Den and Houck's Ridge. Below them, other Rebels were pressing past the base of the Round Tops. The Confederate army, Chamberlain later wrote, "was rolling toward us in tumultuous waves."[31] Only Vincent's alacrity in taking his position prevented that wave from surging into the Union rear. As a private in the 16th Michigan put it, "If we had been five minutes later the enemy would have gained the ridge we were on, and turned our left flank, and it would have been very hard to drive them from it."[32]

Vincent's skirmishers advanced about 200 yards onto the saddle of land between the two Round Tops. Company B of the 44th New York spotted the 4th and 5th Texas and 4th Alabama coming their way in columns of fours, without any skirmishers of their own out front, and gave them a volley that threw them into confusion, more from surprise, probably, than from any losses. The Confederates quickly recovered, however, and answered with a volley of their own, which killed the captain of the Federal company just as he was ordering his badly outnumbered men to fall back. It was the New Yorkers' turn to fall into confusion, and several of them were captured before the rest of them reached the protection of the brigade's main line. The Rebels hastily formed line of battle, with the 4th Alabama on the right, the 5th Texas in the center, and the 4th Texas on the left, and resumed their advance with a Rebel

Yell that one Pennsylvanian said sounded "as if all pandemonium had broken loose and joined in the chorus of one grand, universal war whoop."[33] But the Confederates soon discovered that the large boulders at the base of the hill made it impossible for them to maintain coherent lines. "We could hardly have gone over them," one Texan later wrote home, "if there had been no Yankees there."[34]

But, of course, there were plenty of "Yankees" there. (To a Southerner, all Northerners are Yankees; to most Northerners, only New Englanders are Yankees. The men of the 20th Maine would, no doubt, have embraced the title; most of the 16th Michigan surely would have rejected it, and most of the New Yorkers and Pennsylvanians probably would have as well.) The Rebels had struck the front of the 44th New York and 83rd Pennsylvania, and these Federals opened a deadly fire that quickly took out the colonel and lieutenant colonel of the 4th Texas and many other Confederates. The colors of the 5th Texas went down five times, each time being picked up by another man. Few Rebels returned fire; they were too busy clambering over and around the rocks and climbing the steep hill (many of the Southerners, coming from flatter country, considered it a mountain), and the roar of the Union muskets made it impossible for orders to be heard. "Private soldiers," one Texan said, "gave commands as loud as the officers. Nobody paid any attention to either."[35] Gunsmoke soon covered the field, making it impossible to see anything clearly, but still the rain of bullets came down the hill, striking rocks, trees and men indiscriminately. Colonel Vincent climbed up on a big rock to get a better view and didn't like what he saw. He sent his adjutant off to find General Barnes and ask for reinforcements and runners back to find more ammunition.

The colonel of the 5th Texas went down with a mortal wound while urging his men forward. A private caught him as he fell and pulled him behind the cover of a boulder. The regiment's lieutenant colonel was hit in the arm and turned command over to the major. Eventually, apparently by mutual consent, the Confederates stopped trying to advance, took cover behind the rocks, and opened a return fire, but the major of the 5th Texas, seeing that the 4th Texas was falling back and that the 4th Alabama had never caught up, ordered his men to fall back about 50 yards to an open space. When his regiment had reassembled he discovered that it had lost two-thirds of its men in about an hour of fighting.

Command of the 4th Alabama had also devolved upon its major. It had started out under the command of its lieutenant colonel, but he had dropped from exhaustion soon after crossing Plum Run. His regiment was at the right end of the Confederate line (the 15th and 47th Alabama being still on their way up and over Big Round Top), and it had taken a deadly enfilade fire from the open flank as well as being hit from the front and had ground to a halt somewhat earlier than the Texans. Some of its men got to within 50 yards of the Union line, but most of them were forced to take cover farther back.

General Warren had somehow failed to notice Vincent's troops file up the back side of Little Round Top and take position on its southwest flank, but, at about the time that Vincent's men opened fire on the charging Confederates, Warren looked down from his perch on a large rock near the top of the hill and saw a company of artillerymen struggling to get their guns up its eastern slope. This was Battery B of the 5th U.S. Artillery, commanded by Lieutenant Charles E. Hazlett and accompanied by Captain Augustus P. Martin, commander of the Artillery Brigade of the 5th Corps. Warren went to help them, taking hold of one of the 10-pounder Parrott rifles and helping its crew get it over the rocks and fallen timber. (It was called a 10-pounder because it threw a 10-pound shot; the gun itself weighed about 1,800 pounds.) Some stragglers from Vincent's brigade were also rounded up and put to work, righting guns that tipped over and manhandling them over the roughest spots. At first only four of the battery's six guns could be placed on the summit of the hill, and Warren pointed out that even these would not be of much use in defending the hill, for their muzzles could not be sufficiently depressed to fire down on the Confederates attacking up the slope, but Hazlett placed them with an eye to bombarding the Rebels who had taken Devil's Den and Houck's Ridge and told Warren, "The sound of my guns will be encouraging to our troops and disheartening to the others, and my battery's no use if this hill is lost."[36]

While these artillerymen were laboring up the back side of Little Round Top, the Confederates launched another assault on Vincent's brigade, although no one could later say just who ordered it. It was, by now, around 6 p.m., and light was beginning to fade as the Rebel clambered over and around the boulders and worked their way uphill. Again the Federals opened a fire that, as Vincent's bugler and pennant-bearer put it, "laid the rebels in heaps," although they were taking casualties as well. Soon the sound of Hazlett's guns firing from the top of the hill was added to the noise of hundreds of muskets, and, as Hazlett had correctly predicted, it did affect the morale of the infantrymen fighting below. "No military music ever sounded sweeter," a member of the 44th New York said, "and no aid was ever better appreciated."[37] Many of the Federals admired the determination with which the Confederates came on in spite of their losses, but they continued to load and fire, and when ammunition ran low they scavenged more from the dead and wounded men.

Eventually the Rebels fell back again, only to take cover among the rocks and return fire as best they could. Neither side spared much time to look after the wounded among them. Soon the Confederates came on a third time, and this time they began threatening the flanks of Vincent's line. The 48th Alabama had come up and joined with the 4th and 5th Texas, and soon the 16th Michigan's colonel found his right flank was in such danger that he had to "refuse," or pull back, the right of his line. But that wasn't enough. The Rebels continued to move around the Union flank while keeping up a tremendous pressure on the regiment's center that virtually wiped out its color guard. There were even some cases of hand-to-hand combat. There was confusion in the Michigan ranks, probably caused by the order to pull the right flank back, and about a third of the small regiment ran for the rear. Vincent saw his right-flank regiment retreating and rushed to stem the tide, applying his riding crop to some of the fleeing men, but he soon went down with a bad wound that eventually proved fatal. Command of the brigade fell to Colonel Rice, who was just two years out of West Point.

Just as Hazlett's guns were going into position, General Warren had been hit in the neck by a bullet from the fight going on farther down the hill. The wound wasn't dangerous except that it bled profusely, but Warren held his handkerchief to it and, with Lieutenant Roebling, rode down the northeastern side of the hill looking for more help. Near the base of the hill he spotted Weed's brigade (the one that Warren had once commanded) marching toward the Peach Orchard. While still some 50 yards away, Warren shouted to young Colonel Patrick O'Rorke of the 140th New York, which regiment was at the tail end of the column, "Paddy, give me a regiment!" O'Rorke replied that "General Weed is ahead and expects me to follow him," but Warren said, "Never mind that! Bring your regiment up here and I will take the responsibility."[38] Warren told Roebling to lead the regiment to the top of the hill and rode on alone to the front of the brigade's column. Finding that Weed had ridden ahead to find General Sickles, Warren ordered the brigade to halt and await further instructions. He sent word to Weed to return to his command and went to report to General Sykes about the critical need for troops at Little Round Top. Sykes was irritated to learn that Weed wasn't there already, for he had intended him to go there, but Sickles had evidently ordered him elsewhere. Sykes sent word to Weed to get his men to the hill as quickly as possible. Then having done all he could do, Warren rode north to find Meade and report on all he had done.

"We went flying up the hillside," Sergeant Henry Cribben of the 140th New York later remembered, "as fast as its rocky face would permit."[39] The regiment's column was broken temporarily by Hazlett's last two guns cutting through it, but it closed up and soon reached the summit, where bullets were flying and the air was full of smoke. Just below them, the first company of New Yorkers could see Confederates bypassing the 16th Michigan and coming up a ravine right toward Hazlett's guns. Quickly, young Colonel O'Rorke, who had graduated at the top of the same West Point class that had included George Custer at the bottom, dismounted, drew his sword, and led about half his regiment down the slope, while his adjutant, Lieutenant Porter Farley, formed the other half into a defensive line along a shelf of land near the crest of the hill. O'Rorke paused only long enough to get his half into something resembling a battle line and then led it straight into the Rebels who had just pushed back the 16th Michigan. The Confederates stood up to them long enough to cause numerous casualties, including O'Rorke, who was killed by a bullet in the neck, but their advance was stopped, and soon the other half of the New Yorkers connected with Vincent's right and poured a murderous fire into the Rebels, some of whom scrambled back down the hill while about 200 surrendered. The New Yorkers and the 16th Michigan, somewhat intermingled, then formed a line that stretched diagonally up the hillside toward Hazlett's battery.

Meanwhile the 4th Alabama edged to the Confederate right, where it was soon joined by the 47th Alabama. Corporal William Livermore of the 20th Maine said that he "heard terrible musketry on our right which rolled along, coming nearer and nearer."[40] The skirmishers of the 20th Maine – its Company B – failed to find the two companies of the 16th Michigan that were supposedly still out front, but before they could deploy to cover their regiment they saw a large force of the enemy marching rapidly toward the Union left through a ravine. Captain Morrill pulled his men off through the trees to the east "so as to uncover the enemy," he later explained, "and at the same time to guard against flank movements on the left."[41] They soon encountered some of the retreating U.S. Sharpshooters, who asked to join them, and together the two groups, totaling some 75-80 men, took shelter facing west behind a stone wall that ran north-south, some 150 yards to the southeast of the 20th Maine's other nine companies.

The Rebel force that Morrill had seen was the 47th Alabama, proceeding without skirmishers of its own and missing three companies that had been left to guard the division's right rear. It had come over the western slope of Big Round Top and through the wooded saddle of land that connected the two hills, and now it ran into the left end of the 83rd Pennsylvania and the right of the 20th Maine. The Confederates evidently failed to see the Union line until it opened fire with a disciplined volley, and they returned fire only hesitantly. Nevertheless, they were heading straight for a gap between the two Federal regiments. Colonel Chamberlain had refused the right end of his line to protect his flank, leaving a gap between it and the Pennsylvanians, but now the left wing of the 83rd pulled back to connect with it. The Rebels followed and closed to with twenty feet of the new Union line but were stopped by a staggering enfilade fire from the Pennsylvanians. Caught in a crossfire in this indentation of the Union line, the Alabamans soon stopped advancing and took cover behind the numerous rocks and trees near the base of the hill, and the two sides blazed away at each other. About then the lieutenant colonel in command of the 47th received an order from General Law to charge, and he replied, "I am charging to the best of my ability."[42] He got his men moving again but soon went down with a bullet in his chest, and his men went streaming for the rear, leaving him behind. Thus another Confederate regiment fell to the command of its major, who tried, with little success, to rally his men.

While this was going on, the 15th Alabama at last came

down the northern slope of Big Round Top. As it did so, Colonel Oates could plainly see, only some 200 yards away, a train of Union ammunition wagons parked near the Taneytown Road. So, in accordance with Law's orders to do all the damage he could, he detached his Company A with orders for it to go capture those wagons. Oates failed to see the Union line on Little Round Top until his men were within sixty paces of it, when it opened a rippling volley that brought his regiment to a halt. He later said that the 20th Maine hit his regiment with "the most destructive fire I ever saw."[43] Private William Jordan, one of Oates' men, would probably have agreed with that assessment. He later wrote that he got off one shot from the cover of a tree then joined seven comrades behind the cover of a large boulder and never fired his rifle again, for every time any of them tried to move they drew fire from the Federals just up the hill. But it was only the three left companies of Oates' regiment that were pinned down. With his six remaining companies, Oates resolved to try to find and turn the Union flank.

A lieutenant commanding one of his companies soon informed Colonel Chamberlain that something strange was going on behind the Confederate line. Chamberlain mounted a rock to get a better view and spotted what he later called "a heavy force in rear of their principal line, moving rapidly but stealthily toward our left."[44] He met this threat with an unusual but, as it turned out, effective, maneuver. He had the right half of his regiment, still engaged with the 47th Alabama and part of the 15th, stretch out to cover what had been, up to now, the entire front of the regiment, so that it now had little more solidity than a skirmish line, while acting-major Spear's left half took up a new line running north, facing east, with its right flank where its left had been. The regiment's colors were placed at what had been the regiment's original left flank and was now the angle where the two halves, facing different directions, met.

No sooner had Spear's men formed their new line than Oates' Alabamans came rushing at them, only to be stopped by an unexpected volley from this previously unnoticed force. But the Rebels soon came on again, and, in hand-to-hand fighting, pushed the left wing back so far that Chamberlain later said his line had the shape of a horseshoe. The Maine men counterattacked, and Chamberlain said that "the edge of conflict swayed to and fro, with wild whirlpools and eddies."[45] Oates said that the Union fire "was so destructive that my line wavered like a man trying to walk against a strong wind."[46] He later remembered driving the Federals back five times but that each time they counterattacked and regained their lost position, twice by hand-to-hand combat. One Federal almost got his hands on the Confederates' battleflag but was bayoneted just in time.

Eventually there came a lull in the fighting after the Rebels had pulled back, and both sides got a look at all the dead and wounded men scattered down the hillside between the two forces. The 20th Maine had lost about a third of its men, while Oates later said, "My dead and wounded were then nearly as great in number as those still on duty."[47] Among the wounded was his own younger brother, a lieutenant who had just succeeded to command of a company when its captain went down. At about the same time Chamberlain was sending his own brother to find men to reinforce the color guard, which was getting shot up at the apex of his badly bent line. Spear asked Chamberlain to give him two more companies, and the colonel agreed, but, when the two companies pulled out of the line, there was such confusion that Chamberlain countermanded the order, fearing that the men would think that a retreat was intended.

Meanwhile the sound of this fight had reached other parts of the Union line, even though fighting was still going on there as well, and the adjutant of the 83rd Pennsylvanian came over to ask Chamberlain if his left flank had been turned. Chamberlain replied that his left had been almost doubled back onto his right and asked for the 83rd to send him a company as a reinforcement. The adjutant carried this word to the captain now commanding the 83rd. However, word soon came back that the Pennsylvanians could not detach a company but would sidle to their left if Chamberlain wanted to shorten his line, which he did. Although the Rebels had launched no more assaults against the rest of Vincent's – now Rice's – brigade, the Confederates there had taken cover behind rocks and trees, some apparently climbing up in the treetops, and kept up a deadly fire on the Union line. Lieutenant Farley of the 140th New York said, "Man after man fell under this murderous sharpshooting."[48] Colonel Rice sent men to find more ammunition, which, he said, arrived promptly and was distributed immediately.

The remainder of Weed's brigade soon arrived and extended the Union right flank to the north, and while it was getting itself organized for defense General Sykes arrived, perhaps to make sure that Weed was actually where he wanted him this time. Soon after his arrival Weed was hit by a Confederate bullet that paralyzed him from the shoulders down. He asked to see Lieutenant Hazlett, a close friend, and was talking to him about paying some debts he owed fellow officers when a bullet hit Hazlett in the back of the head, killing him instantly. Weed turned command of his brigade over to Colonel Kenner Garrard and told his adjutant, "By sundown I will be as dead as Julius Caesar."[49] Before long, General Crawford's two brigades of Pennsylvania Reserves arrived and took position on Garrard's right.

But the critical point was still on the Federal left. The ammunition that Colonel Rice acquired had not yet reached the 20th Maine, and its right half was running low, scavenging what it could from the cartridge boxes and pockets of the dead and wounded of both sides. Spear's left half was not yet out of ammo but was nearly exhausted. He had lost half of his men already, and he feared that if the fight went on much longer he'd lose the other half as well. Chamberlain had been slightly wounded twice (once by a bullet that struck the rock beneath his right foot, tearing his boot open and cutting his instep; and again by a bullet that struck the steel scabbard for his sword, badly bruising his left thigh), and he later said that he did not expect to get off that hill alive. But the Alabamans were not doing any better. When his adjutant suggested that he take forty or fifty men to some rocks that he could see that were beyond the Union flank, Colonel Oates approved the idea as about the only hope he had left of dislodging the Federals. The Rebels reached the rocks all right, but their fire did not seem to make any difference.

However, just then the fire of a Union detachment did take effect. Perhaps it was the movement of the adjutant's small force that did it, but for some reason Company B and the Sharpshooters behind their stone wall picked this time to open fire on the Confederate rear. With his men suddenly caught in a deadly crossfire, Oates sent his sergeant major to ask the 4th Alabama to move to its right and come to his aid, but the sergeant soon returned saying he couldn't find the 4th or any other Confederate troops to their left. The company Oates had sent to capture the Federal wagons had not returned, he had no reserves, and one of his officers reported that two Union regiments were coming up behind them. (Probably what he had seen was either Company B and the Sharpshooters, or perhaps part of the Pennsylvania Reserves on their way to reinforce the other end of the Union line.) Oates' first reaction was to hold on, but he soon decided that a retreat was mandatory, although he knew he would have to leave his dying brother behind. He sent his sergeant major to pass the word to all the clumps of men sheltered behind rocks and trees that when he gave the signal "every one should run in the direction from whence we came, and halt on the top of the Big Round Top Mountain."[50] He waited for the Federals to make another advance, knowing that their fire would slacken at that time, and when they did he gave the signal.

What he didn't know was that this Union advance was not just another surge forward to regain a lost position. His ammunition almost gone, his line melting away, Colonel Chamberlain had decided that if he could no longer defend he would have to attack. Lieutenant Holman Melcher came up and asked permission to go out in front of the line and recover some of the wounded, but Chamberlain told him, "I am about to order a right wheel forward of the whole regiment." The colonel limped along his line giving instructions, then, taking position by the colors at the apex of the line, he yelled, "Bayonet!" The responding click of steel on steel seemed to give his men renewed courage, and Chamberlain later remembered that he never got to actually order the charge, for his men didn't wait for it. He said they probably wouldn't have heard it anyway. Lieutenant Melcher leaped out front, waving his sword, the colors soon followed, and with a great shout the men rushed down the hill. The Confederates in front of the left wing – those that received the word, anyway – were already following Oates' order to retreat, and so put up no resistance. In fact, Oates later said, "When the signal was given we ran like a herd of wild cattle. . . ." He thought they ran right through a line of dismounted Union cavalry, but it must have been some of the Sharpshooters unless part of the squadron that Buford had left behind somehow got in the way. Spear's men chased the Rebels and swept down across a half-mile of hillside while the right flank held fast to the 83rd Pennsylvania. An officer in that regiment said the 20th Maine moved "like a great gate upon a post."[51]

Spear's men caught up with many of the Confederates as they were crossing a fence that ran beside a farm lane, shooting some as they clambered over, and many of them surrendered. The right half of the regiment also took many prisoners. One Federal said the Rebels "had but little time to choose between surrender and cold steel, so the most of their front line dropped their rifles and stepped to our rear for safety."[52] Billy Jordan said that six of the other seven Confederates sheltering behind a boulder with him surrendered but that he decided to take his chances of being shot in the back and ran for his life and got away. He said that those who surrendered saved those who ran because of the time the Federals took to gather them up. Chamberlain captured a Confederate officer who seemed to be of two minds; he was holding out his sword in token of surrender but also aiming a revolver at him. However, the revolver clicked on an empty chamber, and when Chamberlain put his own sword to the officer's throat he surrendered.

Colonel Oates got away, as did a soldier running next to him whose windpipe had been almost completely severed by a bullet. (The man later died in a field hospital.) Near the foot of Big Round Top, Oates found his missing Company A, which had failed to capture the Union wagons. (Why not or what else it had been up to was never reported.) That company made a stand to stave off the pursuing Federals and saved what was left of the regiment. Oates tried to rally his remnants, but decided that they were too scattered. Overcome with his trials and exertions, he collapsed and had to be carried up to the summit of Big Round Top. It was nearly dark when he turned command over to a captain with orders to lead the regiment down to a field just beyond Plum Run, near the western base of the hill, where it bivouacked for the night.

The 20th Maine's swinging door swept the saddle of land between the two Round Tops clear of all Confederates, capturing at least 84 men of the 15th Alabama and several other Rebels, including the wounded lieutenant colonel of the 47th Alabama, and even a few stragglers from the 4th and 5th Texas (these regiments retreated to the western slope of Big Round Top), and only stopped when it reached the front of the 44th New York. Then the pursuit was taken up by that regiment and the 83rd Pennsylvania. These regiments also captured many Confederates, including the wounded colonel of the 5th Texas. Little Round Top would remain in Federal hands, but things were not going so well on the rest of the field.

∾ Endnotes ∾

1   OR, I:27:I:483. Birney's report. In the post-war debate about Sickles' advance, that general maintained that Berdan had detected and delayed the head of Longstreet's column, which, of course, was not true; but Sickles might well have sincerely believed it to be.
2   Pfanz, *Gettysburg – The Second Day*, 103. Of, course, the Confederates did eventually take that position, after a severe fight, and yet that did not have the dire consequences for his own corps that Sickles here "predicts," due in part, perhaps, to Lee's continued

focus on Cemetery Hill instead of Cemetery Ridge.
3 Hunt, "The Second Day at Gettysburg," in *B&L* III:301.
4 *OR*, I:27:I:72.
5 J. B. Kershaw, "Kershaw's Brigade at Gettysburg," in *B&L* III:332.
6 McLaws, "Gettysburg," in *SHSP* VII:70.
7 LaFantasie, *Twilight at Little Round Top*, 49.
8 Longstreet, "Lee's Right Wing at Gettysburg," in *B&L* III:340-1.
9 Alexander, *Military Memoirs of a Confederate*, 393-4.
10 McLaws, "Gettysburg," in *SHSP* VII:71. However, one of Longstreet's couriers wrote, long after the war, that at about 2 p.m., while the infantry was filing into position, he saw and overheard Hood appeal directly to Lee to be allowed to send one brigade around to the south of Round Top and attack it from that direction as well as from the west; that Lee had asked Longstreet's opinion, who only said that he had great faith in Hood; but that Lee, after long thought, declined, saying, "Gentlemen, I cannot risk the loss of a brigade; our men are in fine spirits, and with great confidence will go into this battle. I believe we can win upon a direct attack." This account is somewhat suspect, however, because its author has Lee, as he turns to ride away, telling Hood, "take Round Top and the day is ours." (William Youngblood, "Unwritten History of Gettysburg Campaign" in *SHSP* XXXVIII:315.) The Confederate fixation on the Round Tops is almost certainly a postwar phenomenon; at the time, Lee was concerned with taking Cemetery Hill and most likely Round Top played no part in his plan. Also, other witnesses place Lee on Seminary Ridge at 2 p.m., greeting the long-lost Jeb Stuart.
11 Longstreet, *From Manassas to Appomattox*, 367.
12 Ibid., 369.
13 Longstreet, "Lee's Right Wing at Gettysburg," in *B&L* III:341.
14 Sears, *Gettysburg*, 346.
15 Pfanz, *Gettysburg – The Second Day*, 140.
16 Ibid., 142.
17 Shultz and Wieck, *The Battle Between the Farm Lanes*, 45.
18 Pfanz, *Gettysburg – The Second Day*, 163.
19 Kershaw, "Kershaw's Brigade at Gettysburg," in *B&L* III:333-4.
20 Pfanz, *Gettysburg – The Second Day*, 167.
21 *OR*, I:27:II:404.
22 LaFantasie, *Twilight at Little Round Top*, 93.
23 Pfanz, *Gettysburg – The Second Day*, 200.
24 *OR*, I:27:II:392.
25 LaFantasie, *Twilight at Little Round Top*, 98.
26 Ibid.
27 Pfanz, *Gettysburg – The Second Day*, 208. The words are those remembered by Private Oliver Norton, the bugler who carried the brigade's identifying pennant, who was with Vincent at the time.
28 LaFantasie, *Twilight at Little Round Top*, 111.
29 Ibid.
30 Ibid.
31 Ibid., 112.
32 Ibid., 133.
33 Ibid.
34 Ibid., 120.
35 Ibid.
36 Ibid., 144.
37 Ibid., 145; both quotes.
38 Jordan, *Happiness Is Not My Companion*, 93.
39 LaFantasie, *Twilight at Little Round Top*, 151.
40 Ibid., 161.
41 Ibid.

42 Ibid., 168.
43 Pfanz, *Gettysburg – The Second Day*, 221.
44 LaFantasie, *Twilight at Little Round Top*, 166.
45 John J. Pullen, *The Twentieth Maine* (New York, 1957), 130.
46 LaFantasie, *Twilight at Little Round Top*, 168.
47 Pullen, *The Twentieth Maine*, 132.
48 LaFantasie, *Twilight at Little Round Top*, 175.
49 Ibid., 180.
50 Ibid., 186.
51 Pullen, *The Twentieth Maine*, 134-6. All four quotes.
52 LaFantasie, *Twilight at Little Round Top*, 191.

CHAPTER 8
"The War Was Very Nearly Over"
2 July 1863

Colonel Regis de Trobriand's 3rd Brigade of Birney's 1st Division of Sickles' 3rd Corps had been placed in the middle of Birney's formation, on and near a stony hill northwest of where Ward's brigade had formed along Houck's Ridge. De Trobriand had five regiments in his brigade, but one, the 3rd Michigan, was out on the corps' skirmish line, between the Rose farm and the Emmitsburg Road, and another, the 5th Michigan, manned his brigade's own skirmish line near the Rose farm buildings. Of his remaining three regiments, one, the 40th New York, had been sent down the Plum Run valley to support Ward's brigade, and another, the 17th Maine, had been moved to the stone wall at the north edge of Rose's Woods, facing south, from which position it had supported Ward's right flank. That left only the 110th Pennsylvania, which had only six companies, and it was in line in some woods along Plum Branch, facing southwest. It was soon supported by the tiny 8th New Jersey (only 170 men), which Birney had detached from Burling's brigade (on loan from Humphrey's division), but it evidently was not placed under de Trobriand's command, although it took position between the 17th Maine and the 110th Pennsylvania.

Altogether this was a pitifully small force, facing, perhaps, in the wrong direction, but soon reinforcements arrived in the form of General Barnes' 1st Division of the 5th Corps, minus its 3rd Brigade, Vincent's, which had gone off to defend Little Round Top. Barnes was one of the oldest officers in either army, a West Point classmate of Robert E. Lee, who had left the Regular Army after seven years as a lieutenant to make his fortune in the railroad business. He was only the temporary commander of the division, whose regular commander, Brigadier General Charles Griffin, had been wounded at Chancellorsville. His 2nd Brigade, under Colonel Jacob Sweitzer, was the first to arrive and was assigned its place by General Sykes. Its three regiments, totaling only some 1,010 men, formed on de Trobriand's right, on the stony hill, with two regiments facing northwest, and one holding a refused left flank, facing southwest. (A fourth regiment, the 9th Massachusetts, had been left far behind, beyond the Hanover Road.) Barnes' other brigade, the 1st, had been his own but was now under the temporary command of Colonel William Tilton, and while it had four regiments they totaled only some 650 men. When they arrived, they extended de Trobriand's line on up Plum Branch, facing southwest, but northwest of Sweitzer's line on the stony hill, so that those two small brigades formed an L.

When General Robertson of the Texas Brigade had appealed to "Tige" Anderson to cover his left flank while he attacked Ward's brigade, Anderson's Georgians had moved eastward in line of battle at about the time that General Hood had been wounded, taking fire from Union artillery and from Federal skirmishers, whom they pushed out of the way. They stampeded some cattle, entered Rose's Woods, and connected with the left of the two regiments that Robertson had with him (the 1st Texas and 3rd Arkansas), by which time the regiment on the left of Anderson's line, the 9th Georgia, had lost all of its field officers. A staff officer brought the senior captain word that he was now in command and Anderson's order for him to refuse his left flank by turning three companies to face more to the north, but the noise of battle was already so loud that the captain's shouted orders could not be heard, so he was only able to turn his three companies by the use of gestures.

The 110th Pennsylvania of de Trobriand's brigade heard Anderson's men give a Rebel yell as they approached Plum Branch through the woods and saw cattle and hogs running to get out of their way. The 5th Michigan, serving as the brigade's skirmishers, fell back before the Confederates and formed line between the 110th Pa. and the 8th N.J., and soon another small regiment from Burling's brigade, the 115th Pennsylvania (about 150 men), came up and took position between the 8th N.J. and the 17th Maine, near a clump of small trees or bushes, known as alders. This hodge-podge of small units engaged the left half of Anderson's line, which took cover among the trees and rocks lining Plum Branch. The Federals had the help of Captain George Winslow's Battery D, 1st N.Y. Artillery, whose 12-pounder "Napoleons" were positioned on higher ground in the wheatfield, behind the 17th Maine, and were firing solid shot over the Federals' heads, but after perhaps thirty minutes of fighting the two tiny regiments from Burling's brigade (Burling was not with them) fell back to a position in the wheatfield near Winslow's guns, nor far from what is now called the Wheatfield Road. The retreat of these two regiments exposed the right flank of the 17th Maine, which was facing due south, to the Confederates who were advancing from the southwest. So this regiment refused its three right companies, placing them along what was left of a rail fence that ran north and separated the Wheatfield from some soggy ground and the alders near the base of the stony hill.

The 11th Georgia charged forward and briefly pushed the 17th Maine back from its low stone wall, but the Federals countercharged and regained their position, capturing one Georgian in the process. In the meantime, the 8th Georgia and that part of the 9th that hadn't been refused, charged into the gap between the 5th Michigan and the 17th Maine. But, when they tried to attack the former, the latter enfiladed their ranks, and when they tried to attack the latter, the former did the same. Anderson decided, after about an hour of trying, that his brigade could not, by itself, drive the Federals from their position along Plum Branch and the stone wall, so he pulled it back, with the 11th Georgia, at least, going all the way back to the west edge of Rose's Woods to rest and reform. Anderson then went over to his left flank to find and confer with the colonel of the 15th South Carolina, at the right end of Kershaw's Brigade, but as he was walking back to his own brigade he was wounded in the right thigh. Command of his brigade now devolved on Lieutenant Colonel William Lufman, who had, only minutes before, succeeded to command of the 11th Georgia when its colonel had been wounded.

In accordance with Lee's order for an attack *en echelon*, Longstreet had held McLaws' Division back until Hood's had become engaged. Colonel Alexander later wrote that it seemed to him like two hours, during which his artillery dueled with the Union guns in and near the Peach Orchard. "The range was very close," he said, "and the ground we occupied gave little shelter except a few points for the limbers and caissons. Our loses both of men and horses were the severest the batteries ever suffered in so short a time during the war."[1] On the Federal side, the infantry near the Union guns suffered heavily, not only from actual casualties but from the terror and frustration of being fired upon without being able to shoot back.

However, it was probably only about an hour before McLaws was ordered in. Kershaw later said it was about 4 p.m. when he heard the signal to advance, and his brigade (five South Carolina regiments and a smaller battalion, totaling about 1,800 men), followed by Semmes's Georgians, had started moving eastward in good order, climbing the fences bordering the Emmitsburg Road and reforming on the other side. Longstreet accompanied Kershaw on foot as far as the road, near which, Kershaw later said, "I heard Barksdale's drums beat the assembly, and knew then that I should have no immediate support on my left, about to be squarely presented to the heavy force of infantry and artillery at and in rear of the Peach Orchard."[2] For this reason, he ordered the left half of his brigade to change direction to the north and attack the batteries extending along the Wheatfield Road east of the Peach Orchard while he, with two other regiments, passed the sturdy stone house and barn of the Rose farm, heading straight for the stony hill without even bothering to return the fire of Union skirmishers falling back before him.

His 15th South Carolina, which had been separated from the rest of the brigade at first by a battery of artillery, became separated further as Semmes' Brigade moved up. Beyond the farmyard the two regiments with Kershaw began to crowd each other as they moved downhill into some marshy ground near Plum Branch, and Kershaw called to the colonel of the 7th South Carolina to move farther to the right, which solved the crowding problem but indirectly brought tragedy to the left half of his brigade.

There were some thirty Union guns spread along the Wheatfield Road facing southwest, many of them brought from the Artillery Reserve by Lieutenant Colonel Freeman McGilvery, at General Hunt's orders. These opened fire on Kershaw's and Semmes's Confederates, but they were not supported by any infantry. The Rebels took losses as they crossed a field of clover but maintained their formations and kept coming. Kershaw later claimed that the Union gunners were beginning to abandon their guns when someone, evidently hearing part of Kershaw's order for someone to move to the right, ordered the entire left wing to turn and move in that direction, which exposed the flanks of all three units to the Union artillery. "The Federals returned to their guns," Kershaw later wrote, "and opened on these doomed regiments a raking fire of grape and canister, at short distance, which proved most disastrous, and for a time destroyed their usefulness. Hundreds of the bravest and best men of Carolina fell, victims of this fatal blunder."[3] Having lost about a third of their numbers, these three units regrouped and engaged the Union batteries in a fire fight.

Meanwhile, Kershaw, with his other three regiments, caught up with the left flank of Anderson's Brigade, and it was at this time that Anderson came over to consult with Kershaw's right-flank regiment. At least part of Tilton's Federals, along Plum Branch, were lying down, with cartridges and percussion caps laid out on the ground ready for rapid loading, when these Confederates approached with a Rebel yell, driving a frightened rabbit before them. The first Union volley seemed to stagger the South Carolinians for a moment, but they soon renewed their advance. The 1st Michigan continued to fire from the prone position, although their colonel was soon wounded, but the 118th Pennsylvania stood up; its first rank would fire and then step back to reload while the second rank fired, then step to the front again for another volley.

To the right of Kershaw's Brigade, Anderson's Georgians advanced to the bank of Plum Branch again. Some of them came up against the 17th Maine, still holding a line bent at a right angle along the stone wall and rail fence, and these Federals happily shot down many Confederates as they struggled through the marshy ground near the alders, but the Rebels seemed to be gaining in strength, while the Seventeenth's ammunition supply was dwindling. By the time the Georgians attacked, Sweitzer's three small Union regiments had each changed front to face southwest in three successive lines up the slope of the stony hill. The front regiment, the 32nd Massachusetts, couldn't see much of the Confederates to their front because of all the smoke, just a Rebel battleflag sticking up and the flashes of their rifles. That regiment's commander, Colonel G. L. Prescott, soon received an order from General Barnes to the effect that when Sweitzer's brigade retired it should fall back through some woods. "I don't want to retire," Prescott replied angrily; "I am not ready to retire; I can hold this place."[4]

But Barnes was worried about the gap between his brigade and the Union troops in the Peach Orchard; half of Kershaw's Brigade was out there, faced only by the batteries strung along the Wheatfield Road, so when Kershaw's 3rd and 7th South Carolina regiments approached, Barnes ordered Tilton to change his front to the right. However, Tilton didn't just pivot his line in place, he moved north across the Wheatfield Road first and then formed a new line along the west edge of some woods belonging to the Trostle farm, facing northwest. Sweitzer was also ordered to fall back, and his brigade also retreated to the north of the Wheatfield Road, forming along the north side of that road, facing southwest, some 300 yards to the rear of its first position. This retreat eventually became the subject of much controversy both within and outside the Army of the Potomac, especially after partisans of Dan Sickles cast aspersions on Barnes' courage and the quality of his troops, but that would all come later.

At about the same time that de Trobriand saw Barnes' division withdraw from his right he learned that Ward's brigade, on his left, had also retreated, leaving him no choice but to follow suit or risk being surrounded. The Confederates followed as far as the stone wall that the 17th Maine had held but were stopped there and in the cover of Rose's Woods by the fire of Winslow's battery and of the 115th Pennsylvania, but other Rebels were pushing what must have been either some of Ward's troops or perhaps the 40th New York beyond the battery's left flank. Winslow turned two guns to face this threat and reported the situation to General Birney, who soon sent him a warning not to get cut off. With these Confederates (probably the 15th Georgia of Benning's Brigade and the 1st Texas) closing on his left and more South Carolinians advancing on his right, and his men and horses beginning to fall, Winslow finally withdrew his guns, one section at a time. The 115th Pennsylvania had already retreated, after countercharging the Rebels twice and running out of ammunition; the 8th New Jersey evidently had gone even earlier.

Anderson's Georgians then crossed the low stone wall and advanced into the Wheatfield, just as Kershaw's 3rd and 7th regiments were advancing through the trees on the stony hill. But General Birney ordered the 17th Maine, which he found standing in the Wheatfield waiting for a resupply of ammunition, to buy some time for the retreating Federals and for reinforcements to arrive. The regiment responded with a cheer and stepped forward, and the Georgians soon fell back behind the cover of the stone wall again. Birney halted the 17th on high ground in the middle of the field, about where Winslow's guns had formerly stood, then rode to the rear to find it some help. He soon sent the 5th Michigan, which took position to the right of the 17th, where it became embroiled in some close fighting with the South Carolinians on the stony hill. The 17th had been down to about 20 rounds of ammo per man when Birney had found them, and their commander now told his men they would hold their position with nothing but bayonets if necessary, but, fortunately for them, Brigadier General John Caldwell's 1st Division of the 2nd Corps soon came to their relief. "*They* did not lie down behind us," de Trobriand later wrote, thus indirectly criticizing those who had come, and gone, before.

Caldwell's division had held the left end of the 2nd Corps line on Cemetery Hill, and had been sent once, apparently on General Hancock's own initiative, to help the 3rd Corps, but had returned to its place when it had encountered troops of the 5th Corps hurrying to the front. Soon afterwards, however, an aide from army headquarters had brought Hancock an order to send a division to help General Sykes, so Hancock had sent Caldwell's troops off again, minus its attached battery, and Caldwell had sent an aide ahead to report to Sykes. Although the division consisted of four brigades, they had all been badly depleted by hard service, so that it only contained about 3,200 fighting men. The brigades moved south in numerical order, each regiment moving by its flank and all slanting down the front slope of Cemetery Ridge. An aide from the 3rd Corps soon rode up and asked Brigadier General Samuel Zook, commander of the 3rd Brigade, for help. Zook rode off with the aide to consult with Sickles, who was near the Trostle farmyard, and he soon came hurrying back to turn his brigade (some 970 men) off to the west.

The other three brigades marched on past the Trostle house and into Trostle's Woods and halted behind the fence bordering the north side of the Wheatfield Road. Then the 1st Brigade (perhaps 850 men), under Colonel Edward Cross, turned and filed to the right along the fence far enough for all four of its regiments to stretch along the road, and then faced to the left (southwest), even though, because of the way the regiments had been formed to start with, this put the front rank in the rear and the file-closers (the sergeants and lieutenants, whose job it was to keep the men in an orderly line) in the front. No sooner was this accomplished than a couple of staff officers, one from Caldwell and one from Sykes, rode up, and one of them told Cross, "The enemy is breaking in directly on your right – strike him quick."[5]

Taking only the time needed to get the file-closers into their proper positions behind the two ranks of riflemen, Cross ordered his brigade to enter the Wheatfield. This field had an irregular shape, and soon the 5th New Hampshire, on the brigade's left flank, plus part of the 148th Pennsylvania, entered a spur of Rose's Woods, but the line continued to advance until the right of it reached the high ground in the middle of the Wheatfield, capturing a few Rebel skirmishers along the way. Then it halted to return the fire of the Confederates who were along the stone wall. Only then did Cross, his staff, and the regimental field officers dismount. Cross shouted for his men to be ready to charge when he gave the order, then walked over to the woods to see how his left wing was doing, but he soon took a bullet in the abdomen and was carried off the field. Colonel H. Boyd McKeen of the 81st Pennsylvania succeeded to command of the brigade and ordered it to charge.

The 5th New Hampshire, on the Union left, ran into the 15th Georgia and the 1st Texas on some high ground within the woods, while the 81st Pennsylvania and the 61st New York, out in the Wheatfield, charged "Tige" Anderson's men behind the stone wall. The 148th Pennsylvania, the largest regiment in the brigade (about 380 men), had three companies out in the wheat, but its other seven companies, coming through the woods, worked around Anderson's right flank, which then retreated back into Rose's Woods. Cross's (now McKeen's) brigade evidently expended most of its ammunition in very short order, and General Caldwell ordered his 4th Brigade, some 850 men under 25-year-old Colonel John Rutter Brooke, to take its place.

With the support of part of Zook's brigade on its right and the 148th Pennsylvania on its left, Brooke's brigade swept across the Wheatfield and pushed Anderson's Georgians entirely out of Rose's Woods and across Plum Branch, capturing a few Rebels, including a couple of officers, in the process. This compelled the 1st Texas and 15th Georgia to also give way, and they fell back to the stone wall that ran along the north side of the triangular field west of Devil's Den, except that the colonel of the 1st Texas left one company and the regimental colors behind as a show of force to cover the withdrawal of the rest, and many of his other men refused to leave the colors. Brooke, now wounded in the ankle, soon found himself fighting both Anderson's and Semmes' brigade, each of which was much larger than his own. Both of his flanks were enfiladed, and his men were down to about five rounds of ammunition each, so he reluctantly ordered them to fall back, which they did, bringing most of their wounded with them.

Meanwhile Zook's 3rd Brigade had been told to retake the stony hill that Barnes had just abandoned, and, evidently, his men had to pass over the prostrate forms of some of Barnes' men as they advanced. Zook placed three of his four regiments in a line of battle with the large 140th Pennsylvania (which held over half the men in the brigade) on the right and his remaining regiment, the 57th New York, in a second, supporting line. Mounted, Zook led his brigade across the Wheatfield Road at an angle and was almost immediately hit by a bullet and led off the field by an aide and an orderly. The senior colonel of the brigade had already been wounded himself, and the lieutenant colonel who did assume command soon went down with three wounds, leaving the brigade virtually leaderless in the midst of exchanging fire with Kershaw's men some 100 yards ahead of them up on the stony hill.

Caldwell's 2nd Brigade, better known as the Irish Brigade (little more than 500 men), commanded by Colonel Patrick Kelly, formed line between Cross's 1st and Zook's 3rd in the

Wheatfield and joined the latter in advancing on the stony hill. The Confederates up there had been facing north, but as most of these Federals were coming at them at an angle, Kershaw pulled back part of the 7th South Carolina to face them and then rode back to consult with General Semmes (whose brigade was now only some 150 yards to his right-rear) to get him to come up on his right and close the gap between his South Carolinians and Anderson's Georgians. Semmes did as asked, although it soon cost him his life, while Kershaw rode on and found his own 15th South Carolina, which had wandered off too far to the right. Its colonel went down with a mortal wound just before Kershaw arrived, but the latter gave his instructions to the regiment's major and then returned to the 7th South Carolina just in time to see the Federals hit it with a volley at about 200 yards range and then charge.

Six companies of the 140th Pennsylvania, at the right end of Zook's brigade, went up the north slope of the stony hill at a steady pace, firing as they went, while the rest of that brigade and all of Kelly's came at it from the northeast and wheeled their lines so as to attack from the east. The two Union lines began to overlap as they converged in the smoke of battle under the trees that covered most of the hill, causing the 140th Pennsylvania to edge to its right, so that some of its companies were out in a field of oats taking fire from the 2nd and 3rd South Carolina farther to their right. The colonel of the 140th was killed, but its lieutenant colonel pulled its right back to face this incoming fire only to turn and see the left of his regiment running for the rear.

In the meantime, the little Irish Brigade, armed, by choice, with old-fashioned smoothbore muskets, each loaded with one .69 caliber ball and three .31 caliber buckshot, approached to within close range of the Rebel line, which was sheltered behind large rocks on the side of the stony hill. The Confederates, on slightly higher ground, were mostly firing too high, and, after exchanging shots for several minutes, Colonel Kelly ordered his Irishmen to charge. They moved into a gap between the 7th South Carolina and Semmes' Georgians and pushed the 7th's right wing back upon its left until Kershaw decided to order the 7th to retreat and reform behind a stone wall near the Rose farmyard. The major commanding the 116th Pennsylvania (most of whose men were only honorary Irishmen) claimed to have captured many of the South Carolinians by the simple tactic of yelling for them to lay down their arms and step to the rear. The withdrawal of the 7th left the 3rd South Carolina almost surrounded and soon it too found its right being doubled back onto its left until Kershaw ordered it to fall back and join the 7th.

Kershaw's left wing had, meanwhile, been threatening the Union batteries spread along the Wheatfield Road. One of the batteries, at the southern end of the Peach Orchard, ran out of ammunition but was immediately replaced by Battery I of the 5th U.S. Artillery, from the Artillery Reserve. This battery, however, had only four 3-inch rifles and its fire was temporarily blocked as the 3rd Maine fell back through its guns from the skirmish line. Seeing that the Confederates were advancing and that the artillerymen seemed to be preparing to pull out, the colonel of the 2nd New Hampshire (one of Burling's detached regiments) got permission from General Graham to advance. Passing through the battery and emerging from the southwest corner of the Peach Orchard, this regiment (about 350 men) opened fire on the South Carolinians. They were aided by a volley from the 141st Pennsylvania of Graham's brigade (some 200 men) which was stationed along the Wheatfield Road between some of the batteries, and then that regiment, flanked by the 3rd Maine and the 3rd Michigan, advanced to join the 2nd New Hampshire. The Rebels fell back down the slope of ground toward Plum Branch and then moved more to their right. However, the new Union battery withdrew anyway, while Confederate artillery showered the Peach Orchard with shot and shell and Colonel Alexander called up two more batteries he had been holding in reserve. Soon another line of Rebel infantry emerged from the woods behind those guns, heading for the Federal line along the

Emmitsburg Road.

This was Barksdale's Brigade, composed of four regiments from Mississippi that totaled some 1,600 men. General Barksdale was a former lawyer, newspaper editor, and congressman who had served as an enlisted man in the Mexican War, and his men had a high reputation as crack shots. Evidently they were somewhat disorganized by passing through Alexander's guns, which further slowed them, so that Kershaw had already taken the stony hill by the time Barksdale's men came on the field. They crashed through one fence and drove in some Union skirmishers, then climbed over another fence and encountered Graham's main line, which ran along the Emmitsburg Road facing northwest, supported by one battery and one section of another (eight guns in all). Graham had five regiments totaling about 1,500 men, but the 63rd Pennsylvania (240 men) had expended all of its ammunition out on the skirmish line and had been sent to the rear. The artillery had already been battered by Alexander's guns, and when Confederate skirmishers started picking off its men Captain Randolph, the 3rd Corps' chief of artillery, ordered it to withdraw. He rode back to the 114th Pennsylvania, which was behind the guns in support, and informed one of its officers, Captain Edward R. Bowen, of what he had done, saying, "If you want to save my battery, move forward."[6]

This regiment, better known as Collis's Zouaves, advanced through the battery and on across the road. (Some 250 men were present, commanded in the absence of their colonel, wounded at Chancellorsville, by Lieutenant Colonel Frederick Cavada.) The 57th (200 men) and 105th Pennsylvania (270 men) came up on its right, with some men from the 57th occupying the Sherfy house and outbuildings. Major Tremain of Sickle's staff then hurried over to General Humphreys' and asked for a regiment. Humphreys' own skirmishers were just then being driven in, and Confederate artillery fire was beginning to enfilade his line, but he reluctantly gave Tremain the 73rd New York, another zouave regiment (some 350 men), from his support line, which Tremain led to a rise of ground just behind the 114th Pennsylvania. Humphreys then sent Lieutenant Henry Christiancy to ask General Hancock for the loan of a brigade. Meanwhile, a battery just north of the Sherfy farmyard, whose line of fire was now blocked by this advance of the Union infantry, pulled out and moved to join the guns facing south along the Wheatfield Road, while one of those batteries, near the Peach Orchard, withdrew for lack of ammunition.

Barksdale's four regiments formed a line perhaps 350 yards long. On its left the 18th Mississippi headed for the Sherfy's barn and Collis's Zouaves, while on its right the 21st Mississippi made for the Peach Orchard. The latter regiment (about 300 men) came up against the 68th Pennsylvania (320 men), which was formed along the Emmitsburg Road in the edge of the Peach Orchard, south of the Wheatfield Road. The fire of these Federals caused the 21st to halt at a fence until the 17th Mississippi (440 men) came up on its left, and then the two Confederate units resumed their advance. Not far behind them another entire brigade of Rebel infantry (Wofford's) could be seen, apparently aiming straight at the 68th Pennsylvania. This sight was enough to convince that regiment's colonel that his position was untenable, and he ordered it to fall back through the Peach Orchard to take position behind the batteries lining the Wheatfield Road. Soon thereafter the 3rd Maine and 3rd Michigan changed front in the opposite direction: from facing Kershaw's Brigade to the south to facing Barksdale's to the west. The 2nd New Hampshire and the 141st Pennsylvania, which had also been facing south, found their right flanks exposed by the withdrawal of the 68th Pennsylvania and also had to fall back, the latter joining the 68th along the Wheatfield Road behind what was left of a board fence, and the former halting on some high ground in the middle of the orchard.

The large 17th Mississippi and the even larger 13th (500 men), constituting the center of Barksdale's line, then crossed the Emmitsburg Road and overran the Wentz farm, just north of the Wheatfield Road. This was the key to Sickle's entire position – the point of his shallow V. Confederates here could enfilade and outflank the Federals along both legs of the V, and that's just what they proceeded to do. The 17th and 13th, pivoting on the 18th Mississippi near the Sherfy's barn, advanced up the east side of the Emmitsburg Road and took the 114th Pennsylvania and 73rd New York in flank, driving them northeast along the road past the Sherfy house and capturing Lieutenant Colonel Cavada of the 114th in the process. Captain Bowen, now in command of that regiment, probably saved it by giving a simple, easy-to-follow order: He sent the regiment's colors some distance to the rear, across the road, and then told his men to fall back and reform on the colors. As soon as his regiment was out of its way, the 73rd New York opened fire on the Mississippians, and the two lines blazed away at each other from short range, but the New Yorkers were badly outnumbered and were saved only by an order to fall back north toward their own division, although one company was soon diverted to help one of the batteries save a couple of guns whose horses had all been shot. (The captain of the company was captured but apparently one of the guns was saved.)

The 57th Pennsylvania was the next regiment to be flanked while at the same time the 18th Mississippi was approaching its front. Its colonel ordered a withdrawal, but many of his men were inside the Sherfy house and barn. Captain Alanson Nelson was sent to retrieve these men before they were captured, but he found that the noise of battle was so great that he could only get their attention one at a time by shaking them on the shoulder. This was taking too long, and he eventually had to give it up or be captured himself. By the time he caught up with the regiment its colonel had been wounded and its major captured, and he found himself in command.

Next came Graham's last regiment, the 105th Pennsylvania. It had time to face southwest down the Emmitsburg Road toward Barksdale's oncoming line, and actually counterattacked, driving the Mississippians in its front back to the

Sherfy farmyard. But Barksdale's line extended far beyond that regiment's left, and it soon had to fall back again, heading east toward Cemetery Hill. Its colonel later calculated that his regiment rallied some eight or ten times as it fell back, and said, "The boys fought like demons."[7] His regiment lost about half of its men that day. The colonels of the 17th and 18th Mississippi urged Barksdale to pause long enough to reform their ragged lines, but he answered, "No. Crowd them – we have them on the run. Move your regiments."[8]

While three of Barksdale's regiments thus unpeeled the Union line from the Emmitsburg Road, his fourth, the 21st Mississippi, pushed into the Peach Orchard. The 2nd New Hampshire gave it a volley at close range and then fell back behind the slight crest within the orchard to reform. The 68th Pennsylvania was some 20 paces to its right rear, and the 3rd Maine to its left rear. Just about then General Graham was wounded and turned command of his brigade over to Colonel Andrew Tippin of the 68th. That regiment, which also lost almost half of its men that day, was soon driven back by the 21st Mississippi, while the 2nd New Hampshire, which also lost almost half its men, soon had to pull back to avoid being flanked by Wofford's approaching troops. The retreat of the 68th left the 141st Pennsylvania on its own somewhere north of the Wheatfield Road. Colonel Henry Madill refused to retreat without orders until what he thought was another Union regiment falling back through the battle smoke turned out to be Confederates, who hit his men with deadly volleys from close range that wiped out his color guard and cut his line to pieces. Horseless, carrying the colors himself, Madill led a remnant of about 20 men to the rear, where they encountered General Sickles. "Colonel!" Sickles cried, "for God's sake can't you hold on?" But Madill could only reply, "Where are my men?"[9] (The 141st lost 149 men in that fight.)

Sickles, himself, was forced to move on, and he made for the barn of the Trostle farm, but a solid shot from a Confederate gun soon struck him in the right knee, wounding him severely without harming or even spooking his horse. He was able to dismount, and a musician serving as a stretcher bearer made a tourniquet for his leg out of a strap from his saddle. Major Tremain caught up with the general about this time and was told to inform Birney that the latter was now in command of the 3rd Corps. However, Birney himself appeared just then (he later said it was about 6 p.m.), and Sickles turned over the command in person. Then, while waiting for an ambulance wagon to come get him, he lit a cigar (with some help from the stretcher bearer) and had himself raised on the stretcher so that his men could see that he was still alive, and he could appeal to them to stand firm. Before long the ambulance came and carted him off to the corps hospital, Tremain going with him, and the 3rd Corps surgeon promptly amputated his leg just above the knee. (The leg was sent off to the new Army Medical Museum in Washington.)

Weed's 3rd Brigade, which, as we have seen, had wound up connecting to the right of Vincent's line on Little Round Top, had led Ayres' 2nd Division of the 5th Corps onto the field. Ayres had graduated from West Point in 1847, in the same class with A. P. Hill, and had served in the artillery until back in November, when he had received a commission as brigadier general of volunteers and command of the 1st Brigade of this division. When Sykes had succeeded Meade as commander of the 5th Corps, Ayres had succeeded Sykes as division commander. The division's other two brigades were unique in being composed entirely of battalions (parts of regiments) of the regular U.S. Army. The 2nd Brigade (about 950 men commanded by Colonel Sidney Burbank) had extended Weed's line farther north, and the 1st Brigade (1,200 men under Colonel Hannibal Day) had taken position behind the 1st. But soon Ayres had received an order from Sykes to bring his two brigades of Regulars to the Wheatfield and form on the left of Caldwell's division of the 2nd Corps. They had moved to the west, Burbank still in front, crossed

Plum Run, where the mud was ankle deep, and had begun taking enfilading fire from Confederates near Devil's Den, so Burbank had placed one company of the 17th U.S. off to the left to cover that flank and had ordered the rest to increase their pace to the double-quick until they halted behind the stone wall that lined the east side of the Wheatfield. They had arrived just in time to see Caldwell's troops advance into the Wheatfield from the north. Caldwell soon rode over to confer with Ayres, and while the two were conversing Ayres' aide pointed out to the two generals that Caldwell's troops (Brooke's 4th Brigade) were retreating. Caldwell denied this, saying they were being relieved, but the aide told Ayres, "I don't care what any one says, those troops in front are running away."[10] After a closer look at the situation, Caldwell rode off.

When Kershaw had followed his 3rd South Carolina's retreat from the stony hill, he had seen another Confederate brigade coming up. This was Brigadier General William Wofford's 1,600 Georgians, who had been at the left end of the second line of McLaws Division, behind Barksdale's Mississippians. Kershaw's left-wing regiments joined the right of Wofford's line as it caught up with them. The approach of this large, fresh force threatening Caldwell's right rear, and the retreat of Brooke's brigade on their left, meant that Zook's 3rd and Kelly's 2nd brigades could not remain on the stony hill they had just recaptured. The 57th New York, Zook's reserve, was just about to wheel to its right to face Wofford's Confederates when the regiments of the front line retreated right through it, disordering its ranks. Each regiment then made for the rear, some of them stopping from time to time to show a little fight, but for all practical purposes, Caldwell's division was out of the battle.

After Caldwell rode off, Ayres decided his men were facing the wrong direction and ordered Burbank's brigade to cross the stone wall and wheel to its left, which placed most of it within the spur of Rose's Woods and part of it out in the Wheatfield, facing south. The Regulars in the woods met and relieved a Union regiment there, probably the 5th New Hampshire. Meanwhile, Caldwell went looking for help and found Sweitzer's brigade of Barnes' division, which had just settled into position in the edge of Trostle's Woods along the north edge of the Wheatfield. After some negotiating between Caldwell, Sweitzer and Barnes, the latter addressed a few patriotic remarks to the men, and the three regiments crossed the road into the Wheatfield to the east of where the Regulars were making their wheel to the left.

Sweitzer was just approaching the stone wall at the south end of the field when he noticed some of the Federals retreating from the stony hill to his right, but he assumed they had been relieved by other units. As his men took position behind the wall, where the 17th Maine had fought earlier, they began taking fire from the stony hill, but Sweitzer assumed at first that this was friendly fire. However, soon the private who carried his brigade pennant said, "Colonel, I'll be ------- if I don't think we are faced the wrong way; the rebs are up there in the woods behind us, on the right."[11] Soon the 4th Michigan, at the right end of his line, could hear Confederates passing only some 50 yards behind them, and Sweitzer had that entire regiment pivot on its center so as to face toward the stony hill. The 62nd Pennsylvania, in the center of his line, saying that the fire coming in from its right was worse than that coming from its from its front, asked and received permission to pivot that way as well. This left only the 32nd Massachusetts, which soon lost its colonel and was already taking fire from the 1st Texas on its left, to face Anderson's entire brigade, which was beginning to move north through Rose's Woods again.

Sweitzer sent an aide to ask Barnes for help. Meanwhile, Barnes sent an order for Sweitzer to withdraw, but it was never received. When his aide returned, minus his horse, to say that he couldn't find General Barnes, Sweitzer, who had lost his own horse, as well as his hat and his temper, decided it was time to go. He accused the 32nd Massachusetts of retreating without orders and made it turn and fire another volley, while the 4th Michigan had a hand-to-hand fight to avoid losing its national colors and lost its colonel in the resulting melee. The three regiments then retreated to the east and rallied behind a battery beyond the stone fence at the east edge of the Wheatfield. Here they were rejoined by the 9th Massachusetts, which had been left behind on the other side of the Hanover Road before the 5th Corps had moved into reserve.

With Sweitzer's little brigade out of the way, Ayres' Regulars were again facing the wrong way, for the Confederates were now bearing down on their right rear. The 2nd U.S. (about 200 men) faced them and exchanged fire with them for a while, but more and more Rebels were approaching (Anderson's as well as Kershaw's and Wofford's brigades), and the Federals were soon taking fire from three directions, so Ayres ordered his two small brigades to fall back to the east, back over the stone wall and back across Plum Run, which they did slowly, showing the excellent discipline of the Regular Army, and, after an absence of less than an hour, they were back at their starting place north of Little Round Top. Burbank's 2nd Brigade, which had been the front line, had lost about half of its men; Day's 1st Brigade about a third. The Confederates at last had undisputed possession of the Wheatfield and the stony hill.

During the Regulars' absence, Crawford's Pennsylvania Reserve Division, the last of the 5th Corps to reach the action, had occupied Ayres' old position. Sykes had just ordered Crawford to send one of his two brigades to reinforce Vincent's brigade on the south face of Little Round Top when the Regulars were seen to be falling back, pursued by a swarm of Confederates. Crawford sent most of Colonel Joseph Fisher's 2nd Brigade to Little Round Top, but held onto its 11th Pennsylvania Reserve and sent an aide to Sykes asking for orders. Sykes, who was off trying to rally Barnes and Ayres men, sent back word for Crawford to do whatever seemed best.

Samuel Crawford had a strange background for a general.

In the pre-war Regular Army he had been a surgeon, not a line officer. In fact, he had been the post surgeon at Fort Sumter when the Confederate attack there began the war. But he had soon been made a major in the brand-new 13th U.S. Infantry and, a year later, a brigadier general of volunteers. He had served in the 12th Corps until being wounded at Antietam, and then, after recovering, had taken over the Reserves back in May when they had been part of the garrison protecting Washington. Now he formed his remaining troops into two lines, with three regiments (825 men) in the front line and two (435 men) in the second, and then a regiment of the newly arriving 6th Corps, the 98th Pennsylvania (325 men), which had somehow become separated from its brigade, came up and took position to the left rear of the Reserves, and the other three regiments (about 860 men) of the 3rd Brigade, 3rd Division, 6th Corps, commanded by Colonel David Nevin, formed line to the right of the Reserves, just beyond a couple of batteries. The 2nd Brigade of the 1st Division of that corps was just coming up on Nevin's right, but didn't get into formation in time, and the remainder of the 6th Corps was still marching from the army's right to its left, but Barnes' division of the 5th Corps, now commanded by Colonel Sweitzer, was lying down behind a low stone wall to the right front (north) of Nevin's brigade, overlapping it somewhat.

Colonel Alexander of the Confederate artillery later wrote that, when he saw Barksdale's Brigade capture the Peach Orchard and drive the Federals in confusion before it, that he had believed, in the words of a Confederate chaplain he knew, that Providence was "taking the proper view" of things, "and that the war was very nearly over." As soon as the Confederate infantry had moved in front of his batteries he had ordered his men to limber the guns and follow along. "Now we would have our revenge," he thought, "and make them sorry they had staid so long. Everything was in a rush. The ground was generally good, and pieces and caissons went at a gallop, some cannoneers mounted, and some running by the sides – not in regular line, but a general race and scramble to get there first."[12] At last the Rebel gunners had the high ground they had been coveting all day, and Alexander soon had twenty guns in and near the Peach Orchard, including a battery of big 24-pounder howitzers, and they found no shortage of targets, but the colonel was disappointed to discover that there was another ridge (Cemetery Ridge) beyond this one that provided the Federals with a strong position to fall back upon.

∽ Endnotes ∽

1 Alexander, *Military Memoirs of a Confederate*, 398-9.
2 Kershaw, "Kershaw's Brigade at Gettysburg," *B&L* III:334-5.
3 Ibid., III:335.
4 OR I:27:I:611.
5 Pfanz, *Gettysburg – The Second Day*, 270-1.
6 Ibid., 322.
7 Ibid., 332.
8 Ibid., 349.
9 Ibid., 333.
10 Ibid., 298.
11 OR I:27:I:612.
12 Alexander, "The Great Charge and Artillery Fighting at Gettysburg," *B&L* III:360.

CHAPTER 9
"It Is All Right Now"
2 July 1863

While the rest of Barksdale's Brigade advanced northeast up the Emmitsburg Road, its 21st Mississippi followed the Wheatfield Road to the east and took the Union batteries there in flank, one by one. The first battery these Mississippians encountered had used up all of its cannister ammunition on Kershaw's men, and so, unable to defend itself, readily retreated with the help of some covering fire from the 68th Pennsylvania. Fire from Colonel Alexander's guns killed enough of its horses that it had to abandon one caisson for lack of animals to pull it. A battery that had just fallen back from the Peach Orchard had lost so many horses that it had to abandon both a caisson and a cannon. A second gun was only saved by the heroic actions of a private who cut dead and dying horses out of its traces and drove it off with only a single pair of crippled horses, for which he later received a Medal of Honor. The next battery in line was taking fire from Kershaw's skirmishers in its front even as the Mississippians bore down on its flank. It took heavy losses in horses and men but managed to pull out in time. Like the others it withdrew to the north or northeast.

The last Union battery to go was the 9th Massachusetts, commanded by Captain John Bigelow. By the time Colonel McGilvery ordered it to limber up and get out, it was under attack by some of Kershaw's men from the front and left, while the 21st Mississippi was approaching its right rear. The Rebels were too close to allow the gunners time to limber up and drive off, so Bigelow ordered them to retire by prolonge. This involved extending a rope from the trail of the gun to the limber (a 2-wheeled cart carrying an ammunition chest, to which the horses were attached), so that, as soon as the horses were made to stop, the gun would be in position to be fired. Actually Bigelow just let the guns' recoil propel them to the rear, using the prolonges (ropes) to keep them headed in the proper direction. The Mississippians were slowed by Tilton's small brigade of Barnes division, which was in Trostle's Woods to the right and rear of Bigelow's battery, but its left flank was threatened by Kershaw's and Wofford's Rebels sweeping through the Wheatfield, and it soon fell back.

When the Union guns neared the gate in a stone wall lining the Trostle farm lane (which paralleled the Wheatfield Road some 300 yards farther north), Bigelow ordered the pieces to be limbered (hooked to the limbers directly), but while his men were engaged in that Colonel McGilvery rode up and, explaining that there was no infantry on the ridge to the rear (the part of Cemetery Ridge that Caldwell's division had originally held), said that he needed Bigelow to buy him some time to bring more reserve batteries up to hold that position. Bigelow, told "to hold his position as long as possible at all hazards," deployed his six 12-pounder "Napoleon" smoothbore cannon in an arc in the corner of a stone fence just across the lane from the Trostle farm yard.[1] His battery was hidden, at first, from the Mississippians by a slight rise of ground, and vice versa, but he knew they were coming. So he had four of his guns fire solid shot in such a way as to make each round graze the top of this rise and ricochet on over the hill and into the oncoming Rebels and then to be loaded with double rounds of cannister, with which they opened a rapid fire as soon as the Confederates came over the rise.

The other two guns were used to fire occasional rounds of cannister at Kershaw's skirmishers in some trees to the south. When the Mississippians closed in, Bigelow sent this latter section off to the east. One gun was upset and temporarily blocked the gate through the stone wall, but while it was being righted the crew of the other piece removed some stones from the fence and got their gun out that way. Bigelow had them remove some more rocks so the other pieces could get away, and, seeing more batteries going into position some 300 yards to the rear, ordered the rest of his battery to withdraw. However, some of the Rebels, having circled around through the farm yard, got in among his guns. They shot down all the horses of one limber, so its cannon had to be abandoned. Another piece overturned at the gate and also had to be left behind, and the other two guns were overrun before they could get away. Bigelow was wounded, but his bugler managed to get him off the field without him being captured (for which act the bugler received a Medal of Honor thirty years later). Bigelow later reported that his six guns had fired off three tons of ammunition.

The surviving cannoneers and remaining two guns of Bigelow's battery passed through a new line of guns that McGilvery was putting together on a slight rise about halfway between the Trostle farm yard and Cemetery Ridge, on the east side of Plum Run. It was composed mostly of batteries that had retreated from the Peach Orchard area plus one fresh battery from the Artillery Reserve. The colonel of the 21st Mississippi, after driving off all the guns lining the Wheatfield Road, had intended to move north and rejoin the rest of Barksdale's Brigade, but, as he was reforming his regiment he saw the first of these Union batteries taking position to the east and knew that they would enfilade Wofford's Brigade if left alone. So he decided to charge it. This was Battery I of the 5th U.S. Artillery, commanded by Lieutenant Malbone Watson, two years out of West Point. It had come on the field with Barnes' division but had been diverted to the Peach Orchard, where its stay had been brief. It must have put up a fairly good fight against the 21st Mississippi, however, for it suffered 22 casualties, including Watson wounded in the knee, and lost half of its horses, but its remaining men eventually abandoned their guns and fled. The Confederates captured the four rifled cannon and tried to turn them against their owners but could not because the cannoneers had carried off their loading tools and friction primers.

Not far south of the 21st Mississippi, Wofford's Brigade

swept along both sides of the Wheatfield Road and crossed Plum Run, heading straight for the two batteries that separated Crawford's Pennsylvania Reserves from Nevin's 6th Corps brigade. One of these, the 3rd Massachusetts Battery, from the 5th Corps, was about a hundred yards in advance of the other, and of the infantry, posted on a slight rise that held a short farm lane running north to the J. Weikert home. Someone ordered the battery to withdraw, but the order came too late. Its commander ordered his guns to be spiked but only one was, and all six were soon overrun by the Confederates, who crossed a small tributary of Plum Run and started up the next slope for the other battery (L of the 1st Ohio), which greeted them with double loads of cannister. This brought the Rebels up short, and before they could advance again the Union infantry charged.

Apparently the 98th Pennsylvania – the 6th Corps regiment that had fallen in at the left of Crawford's line – started it, and was soon joined by the Reserves after they had fired a couple of volleys. These Federals charged down the slope to Plum Run south of Wofford's line, General Crawford out front, mounted and carrying his division flag, and met little resistance except for some fire coming in from near Devil's Den, even though Kershaw's, Semmes', and Tige Anderson's brigades were just across the run from them, apparently too spent or too disorganized to resist. The second line of Reserves shifted to the left of the first line, and four companies of the 13th Reserves (the original Bucktails) went even farther to the left to return the Confederate fire coming in from Devil's Den, but the main line drove on across Plum Run and up the opposite back, crossed bayonets with some Rebels at the stone wall on the east side of the Wheatfield, and drove the Confederates back to Rose's Woods and the stony hill. Nevin's three regiments to the north of the Reserves fired three volleys and then took up the charge, and, unknown to them, Longstreet had just ordered Wofford's Brigade to fall back. These Federals passed through the just-abandoned guns, crossed Plum Run, and finally halted near the east edge of Trostle's Woods, then fell back to the slight rise of ground where the guns were posted, where they were finally rejoined by the 98th Pennsylvania.

General Birney, thrust suddenly back into command of the 3rd Corps (he had been in temporary command until recently, while Sickles had been absent on leave), ordered General Humphreys to pull back the left of his division to face south, and Birney would try to tie it in with the troops around Little Round Top, but the Rebels didn't give either of them time to accomplish this. The Excelsior Brigade (Humphreys' 2nd), already being enfiladed by a Confederate battery of 20-pounder rifles at a range of only 600 yards, was overrun by some of Graham's men fleeing before Barksdale's advancing Mississippians, and at least two regiments on the brigade's left, the 71st and 72nd New York of the Excelsior Brigade, broke formation and retreated. However, the 120th New York (some 380 men), was stationed behind the others in reserve, lying down and probably unseen by the approaching Rebels. When the regiments to their front gave way these New Yorkers stood up and blasted the Mississippians. Meanwhile, Humphreys sent a staff officer, Captain Carswell McClellan, to get the retreating regiments back into line and to hold them there. McClellan found that part of the problem was an order from Birney for some of the regiments to fall back. He cancelled that order and told the Excelsiors to face about and charge, which they did. They didn't go far, but this show of aggression steadied them down, and they behaved well thereafter.

In accordance with Lee's plan for an attack en echelon, after Barksdale's Brigade had advanced, the attack had been taken up by the right-most brigade of R. H. Anderson's division of Hill's 3rd Corps. This was Brigadier General Cadmus Wilcox's brigade (some 1,660 Alabamans), which had earlier tangled with Berdan's Sharpshooters along Seminary Ridge, and it still had two of its five regiments facing south, despite the fact that it was no longer on the extreme southern flank of Lee's army and that Lee himself had ridden to Wilcox's position after seeing Longstreet's divisions arrive and had personally reiterated to Wilcox the order for his brigade to take up the attack as soon as McLaws advanced. Wilcox was a highly competent tactician. In fact, after graduating in the same West Point class (1846) with Stonewall Jackson and being cited for bravery during the Mexican War, he had served as an instructor in tactics at West Point. He had performed well in all his assignments so far – particularly well during the recent battle of Chancellorsville – but for some reason he was still stuck at the brigade level while most of his peers had gone on to higher commands. (Even George Pickett, who had graduated at the very bottom of the same West Point class, now commanded a division.)

Wilcox knew that if he advanced his brigade straight to its front (southeast) it would come up behind Barksdale. Therefore, as soon as it came his time to advance (evidently at about 6:20 p.m.), he had his men file some 400 or 500 yards to their left before attacking. However, his 8th Alabama (475 men), one of the regiments that had been facing south, apparently failed to get the word or misunderstood it. Since this regiment had been at the left end of the south-facing part of the brigade, its commander might have thought that the order to file to the left meant to move east, not north. At any rate, it marched to the east in a column of fours until it crossed a rise of ground near the farmyard of the Staub family, where it started taking fire from Union skirmishers, at which point it deployed into line and continued advancing toward the Sherfy buildings and the Emmitsburg Road. Consequently, there was a gap of some 200 yards between the 8th Alabama and the rest of Wilcox's Brigade, farther north, which straddled the farmyard belonging to one Henry Spangler.

The four regiments north of the farmyard received a murderous fire from the two batteries in Humphreys' line (six 12-pounder Napoleons each), as did the next Confederate brigade in line, the little Florida Brigade (700 men), commanded by Colonel David Lang (also known as Perry's Brigade after its absent general), which stepped off a few minutes after Wilcox's. These two Confederate brigades drove in the Union skirmishers (the 5th New Jersey and 1st Massachusetts and two companies of the 1st U.S. Sharpshooters) and then found respite from the Union guns as they reached some dead ground before starting up the last slope to the Emmitsburg Road. In the sudden relative silence, the Federals heard what one described as a "diabolical cheer and yells" from the advancing Rebels, followed by shouts of "here they come" from the Union soldiers.[2] The 1st Massachusetts fell back and formed line at the right end of Humphreys' line, just west of the Emmitsburg Road, next to the 26th Pennsylvania, but these two regiments were overlapped by Lang's Floridians and were gradually pushed back.

As the Federals fell back, Wilcox's Alabamans advanced, taking possession of the Emmitsburg Road, and, he later recalled, "the brigade rushed over things like a torrent when the turnpike had been crossed & the enemy made to yield."[3] After crossing the Emmitsburg Road, they were again taking fire from two widely separated Union batteries, so Wilcox sent the 9th Alabama, at the left end of his line, to attack the more northern battery and took his three center regiments toward the southern one. When Birney found that most of his own division had been driven from its positions in some confusion, making it impossible for him to form a coherent line linking Humphreys' division with the troops around Little Round Top, he knew Humphreys would soon be cut off if he stayed where he was, so he ordered him to withdraw to Cemetery Ridge. It was not an easy order to execute amid the noise and confusion of battle, with Rebels bearing down on the two brigades from two directions. One regimental commander had to shout his orders into the ears of each of his ten company commanders, one at a time, in order to make sure they were understood by all. Another Union officer wrote that the men "knew that the position could not be held, and they seemed to have simultaneously made up their minds that they were going back to a position they could hold; and back they did go, but fighting, not disorderly. They would fire at the enemy, walk to the rear, loading as they went, take deliberate aim and fire again, and so on, but slowly and deliberately, and so deliberately that the enemy kept at a respectful distance...."[4]

Humphreys ordered the consolidated companies F and K of the 3rd U.S. Artillery (from the Artillery Reserve) commanded by Lieutenant John Turnbull, to fall back from its position just south of the Rogers farm house, which it did by prolonges, often pausing to fire double cannister at the advancing Rebels. The other battery in his line, Captain Francis W. Seeley's Battery K of the 4th U.S. Artillery, which had been posted farther south, near Brewster's brigade, was nearly overrun, and Seeley was badly wounded. He was succeeded by Lieutenant Robert James, who led his guns and caissons in a mad dash to the northeast.

When Humphreys had first come under attack, he had sent Lieutenant Christiancy to ask Hancock for the loan of a brigade, but the latter, probably already feeling that his corps was becoming sadly depleted, instead gave Christiancy the two regiments that Gibbon had been told to have ready: the 42nd New York (about 100 men) and the 19th Massachusetts (about 400). The colonel of the 19th asked Christiancy what they were supposed to do, and the lieutenant said they were to support Humphreys' division. But by then Humphreys' men were falling back in increasing disorder, and the colonel replied that it was useless for such a small force as theirs to try to support a whole division that was falling apart. Christiancy rode off, possibly to get instructions, and the two regiments, which were some 300 yards to the left, or south, of the 19th Maine, had advanced only about 200 yards, then, upon coming under fire and seeing 3rd Corps units retreating in apparent confusion, had stopped and formed line on a slight rise of ground. The men lay down, and some 3rd Corps fugitives rallied and formed line on their left, but these soon melted away when the Rebels appeared through the gloom and the smoke. The two 2nd Corps regiments fired two volleys by ranks, which stalled Wilcox's Confederates momentarily, and then fell back under the cover of a line of skirmishers. After going about 200 yards they met another line going forward, but also met an officer who ordered them to rejoin their brigade.

Meanwhile, General Gibbon, whose division now held Hancock's left, had advanced another two regiments, half of Brigadier General William Harrow's 1st Brigade, to the Emmitsburg Road on Humphreys' right. Harrow had placed his 82nd New York just north of some farm buildings belonging to a Codori family, with his 15th Massachusetts extending the line northeastward along the road. Because of that road's diagonal course, these two regiments were only some 200 or 300 yards west of Gibbon's main line on Cemetery Ridge. Worried, however, about that gap, Gibbon had later sent Battery B of the 1st Rhode Island Artillery to a small rise of ground behind the 15th Massachusetts, facing northwest, so as to cover the right flank of the two infantry regiments. And then General Hancock had sent Battery C of the 5th U.S. (6 Napoleons commanded by Lieutenant Gulian Weir) to a slight swell just south of the Codori barn to cover the two regiments' left flank and the space between them and Humphreys' division of the 3rd Corps.

Gibbon had ordered Weir to open fire on the Confederates then emerging from the woods on Seminary Ridge. Hancock had also personally led the 19th Maine of Harrow's brigade to support that battery on its left. On the way there, the retreating Battery K of the 4th U.S. Artillery burst through the center of the regiment, carrying its wounded, including Captain Seeley, on its caissons. Hancock cursed Lieutenant James, now in command of this battery, telling him the infantry should have bayoneted him for breaking their line, then put the19th in place by leading the private at the left end of the regiment to where he wanted him. After he had extracted a promise from the private to stay there "until h-ll freezes over," he told the regiment to align itself on that private.[5] So these three regiments and two batteries formed a small outpost in front of the 2nd Corps' main line, just up the Emmitsburg Road from Humphreys' right flank. The only remaining regiment of Harrow's brigade, the 1st Minnesota, was farther to the southeast, in support of Lieutenant Thomas's Battery C of the 4th U.S. (6 Napoleons), which was at the right end of the position formerly occupied by Caldwell's entire division. To seal the gap between Gibbon and Humphreys, Hancock was creating another gap farther north. This was just the sort of thing that an attack in echelon was designed to cause and to exploit.

Weir's battery, south of the Codori house, fired on Lang's Floridians and Wilcox's Alabamans as those two brigades followed Humphreys' men toward Cemetery Ridge. Then it started to pull out after firing off all its cannister ammunition. Meanwhile, the 19th Maine (about 440 men) had been lying down, facing southwest just to the left of Weir's battery, waiting for Humphreys' retreating men to pass on and get out their way, when a 3rd Corps officer rode up and ordered the regiment to stand up and stop the fugitives with their bayonets. The regiment's Colonel Francis Heath refused to obey. He feared that his own men would join the retreat rather than stop it. The officer (Heath thought he was General Humphreys) rode along the regiment's line and gave the order directly to the men, but Heath followed him and countermanded it. After some arguing back and forth, Heath finally said, "I was placed here by an officer of higher rank for a purpose, and I do not intend to go to the rear. Let your troops form in the rear and we will take care of the enemy in the front."[6] The 3rd Corps officer rode off, and, when the fugitives were out of the way, Heath's men rose to their feet and exchanged eight volleys with the pursuing Rebels at a range of only 30 yards.

When the 19th Maine thus opened fire on the Rebels, Lieutenant Weir ordered his gunners to return to their position and add their own fire to that of the infantry, as did one section (2 guns) of the battery that had broken through the

19th Maine on its way forward. Meanwhile, Turnball's retreating battery had been forced to a halt not far south of the 19th Maine by rough terrain and the loss of most of its horses. Having run out of canister ammunition, it was firing at the Floridians with what was called "rotten shot" (spherical case shot from which the fuses had been removed, so that they would explode just as they emerged from the guns' barrels). "It was after Lieutenant James sped past me when I realized we could go no further," Turnbull later told General Hunt. "By then it was too late as the enemy was less than one rod off my left."[7]

Seeing these guns, not far south of them, about to be overrun, the company at the left end of the 19th Maine's line pulled back to face south, and its fire gave the battery cover long enough for it to prepare to retreat again. However, Turnbull had lost so many horses that he couldn't save all of his guns. Horses were taken from a newly arrived caisson to save 2nd Lieutenant Manning Livingston's 2-gun section, which then passed around behind the 19th Maine and went into action again about 100 yards to the right (north) of Weir's battery. But Livingston was soon killed, and the 2nd Florida captured his two guns. Attacked from three directions, Turnbull's other four guns had to be abandoned, although his men managed to spike one of them before leaving it. But the fire of his guns, and the hand-to-hand fight for their possession, delayed Wilcox's advance. Lieutenant James' battery, which had opened fire on the Floridians, were ordered by a Captain on General Hunt's staff to move south and join McGilvery's line of guns.

Meanwhile, more Confederate brigades continued to take up the attack en echelon. The next one north of the Floridians, that of Brigadier General Ambrose Ransom "Rans" Wright (some 1,600 Georgians in three regiments and a battalion) advanced toward the Codori buildings. These Rebels swept across the fields and, with supporting fire from A. P. Hill's batteries, drove the outnumbered and outflanked 82nd New York and 15th Massachusetts from the

Emmitsburg Road, both regiments losing their colonels in the brief fight. The Rhode Island battery just behind them was also forced to retreat and lost three of its guns in the process, the last one stuck in a stone wall it tried to cross just south of the little copse of trees on Cemetery Ridge. Then Wright's Georgians suddenly appeared on Weir's right. The lieutenant took a hard fall to the ground when his horse was shot out from under him, then he was hit by a spent bullet, and three of his guns were captured before he could order his battery to withdraw again. (Thirty years later, still feeling the shame of losing half his battery, Weir committed suicide.) When Rebels were seen to be passing around the 19th Maine's right, where Weir's battery had been, Colonel Heath ordered his men to fall back, but after going far enough to emerge from the battle smoke he discovered that his flanks were no longer threatened, so he ordered his men to halt, face about, and charge. However, by then much had happened.

In the meantime, General Meade had ordered Hancock to send another brigade to Birney, so Hancock had sent an aide to get one from Hays' 3rd Division. Hays gave him what, until recently, been his own command, Colonel George Willard's 3rd Brigade, containing some 1,400 men, ordering Colonel Willard to "Take your brigade over there and knock the hell out of them."[8] This unit consisted of four New York regiments that had been part of the Harper's Ferry garrison back when it had been captured by Stonewall Jackson the previous September and, since being exchanged back in December, they had been serving in the defenses of Washington until General Hooker's recent scouring of garrisons for reinforcements had rounded them up. Having been relieved of its early involvement in the fighting over the Bliss buildings, it was now in reserve near Ziegler's Grove.

Before this brigade could set off, Meade, having learned that Sickles had been wounded, asked Hancock to take command of the 3rd Corps as well as his own 2nd. So Hancock turned immediate command of the 2nd Corps over to Gibbon again and rode off at the head of Willard's Brigade. But, when he reached the part of Cemetery Ridge originally held by Caldwell's division, he encountered General Birney, who informed him that his division and its reinforcements had been driven from the Wheatfield area, toward which Hancock had been moving. Hancock sent Birney to the rear to rally his men and placed Willard's brigade in line on the ridge, to the south of the 1st Minnesota, "at the point through which General Birney's division had retired," as he later reported, and sent a staff officer to ask Meade for more reinforcements. "I directed General Humphreys," he said, "to form his command on the ground from which General Caldwell had moved to the support of the Third Corps, which was promptly done. The number of his troops collected was, however, very small, scarcely equal to an ordinary battalion, but with many colors, this small command being composed of the fragments of many shattered regiments."[9]

Unknown to Hancock, the 19th Massachusetts and 42nd New York of his own corps (Gibbon's division) were partly responsible for this rallying of Humphreys' men. They had formed line on Cemetery Ridge just east of Plum Run, south of the 1st Minnesota, and now provided a breakwater and rallying point for the retreating units, although many of the 3rd Corps men continued on down the back side of Cemetery Ridge. Colonel Brewster managed to rally about 150 men of the Excelsior Brigade farther north, east of the 19th Maine, near Thomas's battery, and eventually moved them forward to form a sketchy line in some rough ground between those two units.

Lieutenant Turnbull, meanwhile, came to Lieutenant Thomas and asked for his help in keeping the Confederates from hauling off his abandoned guns. Thomas had his guns turned in that direction and plastered the overrun battery with double canister and spherical case shot at a mere 100 yards range, mangling the abandoned guns and driving the advancing Rebels to cover.

Barksdale's, Wilcox's, and Lang's Confederate brigades pursued the retreating Federals as far as Plum Run, at the base of Cemetery Ridge, where they finally stopped to reform. Wilcox and Lang both sent requests for reinforcements to their division commander, R. H. Anderson (not to be confused with brigade commander G. T. "Tige" Anderson), but Barksdale was now out of the fight. One of his men, wounded in the arm and heading for the rear, found the general lying on the ground somewhere near Plum Run, all alone, a rifle bullet in his left leg, his left foot mangled by a cannon ball, and with a hole in his chest from a cannister round. The general asked for water and drank from the private's canteen until the water came seeping out of his wound. Then he sent the private on his way to get his own wound looked after. Colonel Thomas Griffin of the 18th Mississippi, took command of Barksdale's Brigade, most of which reached Plum Run some 300 yards or so north of where the 21st Mississippi charged a battery, and between them was McGilvery's line of Federal guns. Griffin's three regiments were tired and disordered, and the low ground around Plum Run contained a thicket of trees or bushes and numerous large rocks and boulders that further broke up their formations, and while Griffin was trying to restore order he spotted a sizable Union formation coming down the slope of Cemetery Ridge right toward him.

This was Willard's brigade. Hancock had ordered Willard to attack the Rebels in the swale below, which he proceeded to do. Although his troops were relatively inexperienced, they were well drilled (having had nothing better to do for the past several months) and were burning to remove the stigma of having been captured at Harpers Ferry; and Willard was an experienced officer, having been a sergeant in the Mexican War, a junior officer in the Regular Army until this war had begun, a major in a Regular regiment, and then colonel of the 125th New York for nearly a year now. He had four regiments in his brigade, but he sent the smallest of them, the 39th New York (265 men) off to guard his left flank, then formed his main line with the 125th and 126th New York (775 men), and left the 111th New York (390 men) on Cemetery Ridge as a reserve. The 2-regiment main line pushed steadily down the slope and across the swale, picking up a few rallying stragglers from other formations and pausing to fire now and then, and drove the Mississippians before them. Willard was killed shortly after crossing Plum Run by a shell fragment that hit him in the face and took off part of his head, but his men kept going. Hancock had meanwhile spotted a Confederate force, part of Wilcox's Brigade, that threatened Willard's right flank, so he sent the 111th New York from its supporting position to block them.

The 39th New York, on the other flank, was met by one of Birney's aides, who, in Birney's name, ordered its major to retake the battery that had been captured by the 21st Mississippi. The major replied that his regiment was part of the 2nd Corps, not the 3rd, but the aide just repeated the order in the name of General Hancock, so the four companies marched along Cemetery Ridge until opposite the battery, formed line, and, led by a lieutenant from the battery (who had started the whole thing by asking the aide to find him some help) charged straight for the guns. The 21st Mississippi, finding that it could neither fire the captured guns nor drag them away, decided to give them up without a fight and fell back before this attack.

Hancock rode north again and soon saw a line of infantry coming through the smoke and gathering darkness. Taking it for a retreating Federal unit he rode toward it, only to be fired upon at close range. The only aide still with him was wounded in two places, but Hancock was not hit, and they both escaped capture. He had run into three regiments of Wilcox's Confederate brigade, who were in the process of advancing on Thomas's battery, at the north end of Caldwell's original position. Hancock soon found the regiment of Harrow's brigade that had been placed in support of this battery as it was advancing to fill the gap between the battery and the 111th New York. It had only eight companies present (around

300 men), and Hancock exclaimed, "my God! Are these all of the men we have here? What regiment is this?" and was told by its colonel, "First Minnesota." The regiment's colonel, William Colvill, remembered that the general pointed to a Confederate battle flag in the Rebel brigade and said, "Advance, Colonel, and take those colors!"[10]

Not far north of the 111th New York, this lone regiment went down the slope of Cemetery Ridge at the double-quick, though taking care to preserve its straight line, receiving fire but not stopping to return it. Fortunately for these Federals, the Confederate line in their front, the 11th Alabama, was subjected just then to friendly fire from the wayward 8th Alabama, just coming up in its rear. Colonel Colvill ordered a charge, and the Federals surged forward. "The men were never made who will stand against leveled bayonets coming with such momentum and evident desperation," the regiment's adjutant later wrote. "The first line broke in our front as we reached it, and rushed back through the second line, stopping the whole [Confederate] advance."[11] Colvill called a halt upon reaching Plum Run and ordered a volley at a range of about four yards. After that, the charge turned into a close-range firefight, with the badly outnumbered Minnesotans taking cover behind rocks and the bank of the shallow stream while the Alabamans spread beyond both the Federals' flanks and threatened to encircle them.

Soon Colonel Colvill was wounded in the foot, and his lieutenant colonel, major, and several other officers and numerous men also fell. "The fire we encountered here was terrible," reported the captain who eventually succeeded to command of the regiment, "and, although we inflicted severe punishment upon the enemy, and stopped his advance, we there lost in killed and wounded more than two-thirds of our men and officers who were engaged."[12] Wilcox sent back a plea for help, but no help came except his own 9th Alabama, from the north end of his line, nor could he see any other Confederates to his right or left, and he was receiving fire from the 111th New York of Willard's brigade on his right front and probably from other Federal units to his left front.

His 10th Alabama, just north of the 11th, charged into a gap in the Union line, where the 111th had not quite closed up with the 126th New York, but were in turn charged by the left of the 111th, and these Confederates fell back in a near-panic, breaking into small groups. Seeing this, the colonel of the 111th ordered the rest of his regiment to charge down off the knoll where they had taken cover, leaving some 100 dead and wounded men behind, moving northwest over a dry ravine in front of the 1st Minnesota, toward Turnbull's abandoned guns and the Codori farm, taking scores of prisoners as they went. Cheered on by General Humphreys, some of the rallied 3rd Corps troops then moved up to Plum Run on the 1st Minnesota's left, and some went on farther, with the 111th New York. With no hope now of going forward or even staying where he was for long, Wilcox ordered a retreat. Colonel Colvill, having stopped the Rebels, although without capturing the flag Hancock had sent him after, ordered his senior captain to take the survivors back up Cemetery Ridge, where 47 of them were collected.

On Wilcox's right, or south, Barksdale's Mississippians fell back before the 125th and 126th New York of Willard's brigade. To the left, or north, of Wilcox's Brigade, the little Florida Brigade had paused to reform its lines on a small rise at the foot of Cemetery Ridge, where it came under a heavy fire from the 19th Maine and Brewster's remnant of the Excelsior Brigade on the crest 50 yards ahead. Colonel Lang soon learned that Wilcox's Brigade was falling back and saw that a large Union force had advanced well beyond his right flank, so he ordered his own brigade to withdraw to the Emmitsburg Road. Once there, however, he could find no protecting cover for his men, so he took them all the way back to their starting point. He was followed by the 19th Maine, which advanced deliberately, pausing to fire a well-aimed volley now and then, and shot down the color guard of the 8th Florida, whose flag was left behind. Brewster's New Yorkers and other 3rd Corps troops under General Carr followed. Brewster's men recaptured three of Turnbull's guns and picked up the 8th Florida's flag.

Beyond Lang's Floridians were Rans Wright's Georgians. After driving back the three Union regiments and two batteries near the Codori buildings, they headed up the slope of Cemetery Ridge just south of the little copse of trees, making straight for an unmanned gap in the Union line. Harrow's 1st Brigade of Gibbon's division had been parceled out and disposed of, as had two of the five regiments of Colonel Normal Hall's 2nd Brigade, but Hall's remaining three regiments fired obliquely into the Confederates' left flank, as did two batteries of 3-inch rifles. The 48th Georgia on that end of Wright's line lost all of its officers, but charged on under the command of a corporal, only to run into one of Hall's regiments and lose its battleflag as well.

Gibbon's remaining brigade, Brigadier General Alexander Webb's 3rd, had only one regiment on the front line, the 69th Pennsylvania, which confronted Wright's Rebels as they surged over the gun that the Rhode Island battery had abandoned when it had become jammed in a stone fence. The rest of Webb's brigade came up and tried, according to Colonel Hall, to form in support of his line, but Hall sent them toward the gap on his brigade's left, toward which most of the Rebels were advancing. One of Webb's regiments, the 71st Pennsylvania, moved to the left of the 69th and recaptured the abandoned Rhode Island gun. Another, the 72nd, lost its colonel and remained in a supporting line. The third, the 106th Pennsylvania, had two companies out as skirmishers farther north, but the other eight companies fired several volleys into the Confederates' flank at a range of about 60 yards and then charged with fixed bayonets, driving some of the Rebels beyond the Emmitsburg Road, capturing about 20 of them and recovering the other abandoned Rhode Island guns.

Under a white flag a Confederate officer near the Codori buildings tried to negotiate a deal with the 106th. Much of the

48th Georgia were there, including its colonel, who was badly in need of medical attention. The officer wanted to march away those who could still walk, but the Union staff officer sent to negotiate with him demanded and got their surrender, which, the Federals later claimed, amounted to over 200 men, including the wounded colonel and 20 other officers.

The remainder of Wright's Brigade continued to advance, reaching the crest of Cemetery Ridge, but it had no support on either flank. To Wright's left, or north, was – or had been before he advanced – the next brigade of R. H. Anderson's division, some 1,130 Mississippians commanded by Brigadier General Carnot Posey. Wright complained in his official report, "Just before reaching this position [the Emmitsburg Road], I had observed that Posey's brigade, on my left, had not advanced, and fearing that, if I proceeded much farther with my left flank entirely unprotected, I might become involved in serious difficulties, I dispatched my aide-de-camp, Capt. R. H. Bell, with a message to Major-General Anderson, informing him of my own advance and its extent, and that General Posey had not advanced with his brigade on my left. To this message I received a reply to press on; that Posey had been ordered in on my left, and that he (General Anderson) would reiterate the order."[13] To add further to Wright's problems, his little 2nd Georgia Battalion (175 men), which had been out in front of his line as skirmishers, had failed to move to the left of his line, as planned; instead various parts of it fell in with the other units as they caught up with it; and this caused Wright's left flank to be even further exposed.

General Posey had his own problems, one of which was that his brigade faced the buildings of the Bliss farm, about halfway between Seminary Ridge and the Emmitsburg Road. As mentioned before, these had been the scene of vicious small-unit actions all day, as skirmishers from both sides sought to make use of their cover. Consequently, Anderson had ordered Posey to use two regiments, half of his brigade, as skirmishers when he advanced, to clear the strong force of Union skirmishers from his front. The Federals soon detected this build-up of Rebels, and their senior officer, Lieutenant Colonel Edward P. Harris, commander of the 1st Delaware (240 men) from Colonel Thomas Smyth's 2nd Brigade of Brigadier General Alexander Hays' 3rd Division of the 2nd Corps, whose men were running out of ammunition, had, at about 4 p.m., ordered the Union skirmishers to fall back.

General Hancock had soon removed Harris from his command and placed him under arrest for this unauthorized retreat, but, meanwhile, Rebels skirmishers had recaptured the Bliss farm buildings. One company of Union skirmishers from the 106th Pennsylvania had tried to take them back but was simply too small for the job. However, General Hays had then ordered Colonel T. A. Smyth, commander of the 2nd Brigade of his 3rd Division of the 2nd Corps, to send 100 men to retake the buildings, and Smyth had passed the order to the 12th New Jersey, which sent four companies (actually about 150 men). These formed a small line of battle, charged forward at the double-quick, and surrounded and captured the Bliss barn and that family's house, some 75 yards farther north, plus 99 Confederates, including seven officers. The four companies lost 42 men in this brief fight and soon had to give up the buildings, as a strong line of skirmishers from Pender's Division threatened their right flank, and the advance of Wright's Brigade threatened their left flank, but they retained their prisoners, taking them back to Cemetery Ridge.

General Posey seems to have misinterpreted Anderson's order about advancing two regiments as skirmishers, as he evidently decided that it meant that this would be his entire contribution to the attack, stating in his report that he had been ordered "to advance but two of my regiments." These he had sent (not led), and they had recaptured the Bliss buildings, but then had met such stiff resistance from the Union 2nd Corps' main line that he eventually had to send a third regiment, and, when he later received word that their left flank was being threatened, he finally went to the front himself.

Posey's other problem was that there were no Confederates

advancing on his left. Brigadier General William Mahone's 1,500 Virginians, the most northerly of Anderson's five brigades, should have been, but Posey later reported that when he asked Mahone "to send me a regiment to support my left. He being at this time ordered to the right, could not comply. When I reached the barn, I found my three regiments well up in advance. They had driven the enemy's pickets into their works and the artillerists from their guns in their front. It being then nearly dark, I sent the major-general [Anderson] a message, informing him of my position. He then ordered me to fall back to my original position, in the rear of Pegram's battery."[14]

R. H. Anderson had remained in a ravine behind the lines, where one of Wilcox's aides found the general's staff officers lying on the ground, as if they didn't know that a great battle was in progress. One of Anderson's aides did go to order Mahone to advance, but that general declined, saying that Anderson had instructed him to stay where he was. After the war, Anderson claimed that his corps commander, A. P. Hill, had ordered him to keep two brigades (presumably Mahone's and Posey's) in reserve, but by then Hill was dead and could neither confirm nor deny this claim. Hill seems to have taken no part in the fight after passing on to Anderson Lee's order for that general's division to take up the attack as it rolled north, and he seems to have remained with, and as passive as, General Lee throughout the afternoon.

Colonel Fremantle, the British observer, watching the battle from up in a tree, noted that "So soon as the firing began, General Lee joined Hill just below our tree, and he remained there nearly all the time, looking through his field-glass – sometimes talking to Hill and sometimes to Colonel Long of his staff. But generally he sat quite alone on the stump of a tree. What I remarked especially was, during the whole time the firing continued he sent only one message, and only received one report. It is evidently his system to arrange the plan thoroughly with the three corps commanders, and then leave to them the duty of modifying and carrying it out to the best of their abilities."[15]

Pender's Division was supposed to take up the attack next, after Anderson's. And Pender's skirmishers had already driven their Union counterparts back beyond the Emmitsburg Road; artillery stationed to his front was busily dueling with Federal artillery, and, as soon as it came their turn, his four brigades would head straight for the west side of Cemetery Hill. But their turn didn't seem to be coming, as neither Mahone nor Posey was attacking, and finally Pender rode south toward his right flank to see what was holding things up. But he hadn't gone far before a shell fragment tore into his thigh, and he was carried from the field. By the time that his senior brigadier, Lane, had been informed that he was now in command, it was about sunset and, as Lane later reported, "At that time the firing on the right was very desultory, the heavy fighting having ended."[16]

Posey's and Mahone's misunderstandings and Anderson's passivity, coupled with Pender's wounding, left Wright's brigade out on a limb, but it was heading right for a big gap in the Union line. The battery that had been attached to Caldwell's division of the 2nd Corps had been left behind when that division had gone to help the 3rd Corps, and it had subsequently joined Colonel McGilvery's line of guns. But Hancock, remembering that it hadn't gone with Caldwell, sent his acting ordnance officer, Captain James M. Rorty, to go fetch it. Commandeering the battery (B of the 1st New York Artillery) without consulting or informing McGilvery, Rorty had brought it north to take position just south of the little copse of trees. The fire of its four 10-pounder Parrot rifles kept Lang's and Wright's Confederates from dragging Weir's guns any farther than they already had. But infantry was badly needed to meet the threat of Wright's advance.

Meanwhile, Captain John Tidball, commander of a brigade of horse artillery attached to the Cavalry Corps, had happened to be at Meade's headquarters, on the back side of Cemetery Ridge, just east of the gap in the line which Wright's Georgians were approaching, and he had mentioned to Meade that earlier he had seen troops of the 1st Corps in reserve behind Cemetery Hill. Meade had sent Tidball to ask General Newton, the new commander of the 1st Corps, to send these forces to fill the gap. Tidball had found Newton, who had passed the order on to generals Doubleday and Robinson, and he must have conveyed a real sense of urgency, for Doubleday had galloped to the nearest regiment. This was the 13th Vermont, part of the brigade of 9-months men that had arrived too late to join in the first day's battle. "Colonel, will your regiment fight?" Doubleday had asked. "I believe they will, sir," had been the reply. Colonel Francis Randall said his regiment had never been in a battle but that he had been in several, and he had great confidence in his men. He had only five of his companies with him, as the other five were posted in support of a battery on Cemetery Hill, but this half-regiment was as large as many whole ones. Doubleday had given the men a little pep talk, the Vermonters had responded with a cheer, and the general had told Randall to take his men and report to General Hancock, then went to find General Stannard and send the rest of the brigade after them.

Soon after Tidball had ridden to find Newton, Meade had headed for the point of danger himself, and for a few minutes he and his staff were all that stood between Wright's Georgians and the Union rear. "Between the left of Gibbon," Meade's son and aide later wrote, "and some troops further to their left, there seemed to be a vacant space in the lines, and apparently no organized body of troops there. Many of our men were scattered about, coming back. Directly in front of the general a line of the enemy could be seen advancing in the open between our ridge and the Emmitsburg pike . . . They seemed to be making straight for where we were. . . . Just as we were making up our minds for the worst, someone shouted, 'There they come, general.' Looking around, we saw a column of infantry come swinging down the Taneytown

Road from the direction of Cemetery Hill, a close column of divisions, at a sharp double-quick, flags flying, arms at right shoulder, officers steadying their men with sharp commands. They came on as if on review."[17] Amid wild shouting and much excitement, Meade went to lead them forward, swinging his hat and calling, "Come on gentlemen."[18]

These troops were the three Vermont regiments. Meade told them to form line along the crest of Cemetery Ridge, but Colonel Randall, who had ridden ahead of his half-regiment, had encountered Hancock, who pointed down the slope toward the Codori House. "He told me," Randall later reported, "the rebels had captured a battery he had had there, and pointed out to me the way they had gone with it, and asked me if I could retake it. I told him I thought I could, and that I was willing to try. He said it would be a hazardous job, and he would not order it, but, if I thought I could do it, I might try."[19] Randall deployed his companies into line, giving each captain his instructions as they came up, then rode to the front and ordered a charge. His men went down the slope at the double-quick but paused when a bullet hit Randall's horse, causing it to fall on him, pinning his leg to the ground. He told them to go on and that he'd catch up, but some of them came and helped him free himself, and he limped to the front.

His troops ran into some of Lang's Floridians who had not received the order to fall back. These Rebels fired on the Vermonters but didn't hurt them much, then threw themselves to the ground and were captured as the Federals went right over them. Hancock shouted for Randall to go ahead and he would take care of the prisoners. So Randall's half of his regiment charged on, angling to the southwest, while the other half, under his lieutenant colonel, came up on his right and charged more toward the west or even northwest. Randall's half recaptured Weir's guns, and didn't stop until it reached the Emmitsburg Road. There, one company rousted Confederate skirmishers out of the Peter Rogers house until, the company's captain claimed, he had more prisoners than men in his own company. Finding themselves far out in front of the rest of the army, the Vermonters reluctantly returned to their starting position, where they were cheered by other units for their exploit. As one Vermont lieutenant helped haul one of the recovered guns up Cemetery Ridge he was asked by a veteran from another unit, "What troops be you fellers?" The lieutenant told him, "Green Mountain Boys," and the veteran said, "I thought you must be green, or you'd never gone in there."[20]

"We were now in a critical condition," Wright later reported. "The enemy's converging line was rapidly closing upon our rear; a few moments more, and we would be completely surrounded; still, no support could be seen coming to our assistance, and with painful hearts we abandoned our captured guns, faced about, and prepared to cut our way through the closing lines in our rear."[21]

The momentum had now changed sides, and shortly after the 13th charged so did the other two Vermont regiments, and 19th Maine. So did the Bucktail Brigade of Doubleday's division (now down to fewer than 400 men) and two other 1st Corps regiments (totaling less that 300 men), who had also come up, as did the rallied members of Humphreys' division. They all chased the Rebels as far as the Emmitsburg Road, one member of the Excelsior Brigade picking up the abandoned flag of the 8th Florida of Lang's brigade during the chase, and Wright, who said his retreat was conducted "in tolerable order, but with immense loss," fell back to "a slight depression a few hundred yards in advance of our skirmish line of the morning."[22] He said he had lost 688 officers and men, or almost half of his brigade.

Meade was soon surrounded by many of his officers, both line and staff, and congratulations were exchanged all around. When someone said that things had looked pretty desperate for a while, Meade replied, "Yes, but it is all right now, it is all right now."[23]

"How strange the stillness seems!" Lieutenant Frank Haskell of Gibbon's staff later wrote. "The whole air roared with the conflict but a moment since – now all is silent; not a gunshot sound is heard, and the silence comes distinctly, almost painfully to the senses. And the sun purples the clouds in the West, and the sultry evening steals on as if there had been no battle, and the furious shout and the cannon's roar had never shaken the earth."[24] And yet, the day's battle was still not ended.

∼ Endnotes ∼

1 Pfanz, *Gettysburg – The Second Day*, 342.
2 Ibid., 366.
3 Ibid., 377.
4 Ibid., 370.
5 Ibid., 375.
6 Ibid., 378.
7 Shultz and Wieck, *The Battle Between the Farm Lanes*, 63.
8 Ibid., 56.
9 *OR,* I:27:I:371.
10 Pfanz, *Gettysburg – The Second Day*, 410-1. There is considerable controversy surrounding the charge of the 1st Minnesota. The traditional number of men thought to have participated, according to the regiment's adjutant, is 262, but another account (see next note) calculates the total to be 335. This regiment had 11 companies, but one was serving as the division's provost guard, another had been sent off as skirmishers to watch the regiment's left flank, and the 11th company, an attached company of sharpshooters, was supporting another battery at the other end of the 2nd Corps' position, and none of these men are included in either total.
11 John Quinn Imholte, *The First Volunteers* (Minneapolis, 1963), 118.
12 *OR,* I:27:425.
13 Ibid., I:27:II:623.
14 Ibid., I:27:II:633.
15 Wheeler, *Witness to Gettysburg*, 183.
16 *OR,* I:27:II:665.
17 Coffin, *Nine Months to Gettysburg*, 201-203.
18 Edwin B. Coddington, *The Gettysburg Campaign* (New York, 1968), 448. Both quotes.
19 *OR,* I:27:I:351-2.
20 Coffin, *Nine Months to Gettysburg*, 206.
21 *OR,* I:27:II:624.
22 Ibid.
23 Pfanz, *Gettysburg – The Second Day*, 424.
24 Frank A. Haskell, *The Battle of Gettysburg* (Boston and Cambridge MA, 1958), 52.

CHAPTER 10
"Success That Did Not Succeed"
2 July 1863

ABOUT FIVE MILES NORTHEAST of the center of Gettysburg was a little hamlet called Hunterstown. A lone squadron of Jeb Stuart's cavalry had reached there on the evening of 29 June, scouting well out from the main column, which at that time had been heading north, searching for Ewell's infantry. The squadron was still there when Stuart and his three brigades finally caught up with the infantry shortly after noon on 2 July, and its rested troopers now formed a rear guard for their exhausted comrades. By about 2 p.m. most of the column had filed through the little town and had reached Brinkerhoff's Ridge, about two miles east and one mile north of Gettysburg, while the last brigade, that of Brigadier General Wade Hampton, was only about a mile out of Hunterstown. Jeb Stuart was back with the army and so were his three best brigades, but they would be of little use to Lee until they had a long rest.

It was evidently at about this time that Stuart, riding ahead of his men, finally found Lee (and vice versa). "Well, General Stuart," Lee supposedly said, "you are here at last." As Colonel Alexander of the artillery, who was not a witness, later put it, "His manner implied rebuke, and it was so understood by Stuart.... Had he wasted no time paroling prisoners and saving wagons, his raid might have been successful, as raids go, for his whole casualties were but 89 killed, wounded and missing. But the venture was a strategic mistake, for it resulted in the battle's being one of chance collision, with the Confederates taking the offensive, whereas the plan of the campaign had been to fight a defensive battle."[1] According to another (also second-hand) account, Lee said, "General Stuart, where have you been?" which led the latter to attempt a long, involved account of his adventures that Lee cut short, saying, "I have not heard a word from you for days, and you the eyes and ears of my army!"[2]

While there was some justification for what was, for Lee, a severe rebuke of Stuart (if he really said that), he mostly had himself (a former cavalry officer in the Regular Army) to blame for any lack of information about the enemy in Stuart's absence (which he had authorized), for Stuart had left him Brigadier General W. E. "Grumble" Jones's and Brigadier General Beverly Robertson's brigades of cavalry, of which Lee seems to have made no use at all, and Ewell had Jenkins' cavalry brigade plus the 35th Virginia Cavalry Battalion and the 1st Maryland Cavalry Battalion. All in all, over 4,500 troopers had remained with Lee's main forces. As Major Henry McClellan of Stuart's staff later wrote, "It was not the want of cavalry that General Lee bewailed, for he had enough of it had it been properly used. It was the absence of Stuart himself that he felt so keenly; for on him he had learned to rely to such an extent that it seemed as if his cavalry were concentrated in his person, and from him alone could information be expected."[3]

Perhaps the real problem was that Stuart had not left one of his better subordinates, such as Hampton, to command the cavalry that had been left behind. Longstreet had evidently expected Hampton to be the one. Stuart's cavalry had only recently grown from three brigades to six, and it was still organized as a single division. With hindsight it is clear that it should have, upon this enlargement, been divided into two or three divisions, as it actually was a few months later. But Stuart relied on Hampton and Brigadier General Fitzhugh Lee, the commanding general's nephew, much as the senior Lee relied on him.

Wade Hampton was a general in a category almost by himself. Unlike most other generals on both sides, he owed his position neither to military education and experience nor to political influence.[4] He was said to be the richest man in the South, and certainly was at least one of the richest, and his wealth had enabled him, at the outbreak of war, to raise an entire South Carolina unit at his own expense. It was known as the Hampton Legion, of which he was, naturally, made the colonel. (Legions were peculiar units of roughly regimental size, consisting of infantry, cavalry and artillery, all three. Experience had quickly shown that this was a cumbersome arrangement, and their different arms had soon been separated, and, in fact, the cavalry components of three such legions made up parts of Hampton's Brigade at this time.) Hampton had proven to be a highly competent officer, however, and had soon risen to brigade command. He was a large, athletic man in his 40s, and an excellent horseman who had been known before the war for his strength and his skills as an outdoorsman, and he put that strength and skill to use on this day.

As Stuart's column had been coming in from the north, the Union cavalry division commanded by Brigadier General Hugh Judson Kilpatrick had been approaching Hunterstown from the northeast, after having ridden as far north as Berlin and Heidlersburg. Hampton was sitting his horse beside the road between Hunterstown and Gettysburg when someone began shooting at him. He rode toward the shooter and soon discovered him to be a Union cavalryman in a thicket to the north of him, who was armed with a Spencer repeating rifle. Hampton returned fire with his revolver, but neither shooter was having much luck, so Hampton charged the man, only to be stopped by a stake-and-rail fence. He yelled for his assailant to come out and fight in the open, but the trooper refused, and more shots were exchanged, one of which grazed Hampton's chest. When the Federal either emptied his rifle's magazine or it suffered a malfunction, he held up his hand as if to ask for a time out, and Hampton chivalrously complied, but when the trooper raised his weapon to fire again, Hampton got his shot off first and hit the man in the wrist, and the Federal disappeared into the thicket.

No sooner had this strange duel ended, however, than another one began, as a Union officer, Major Charles Storrs of the 6th Michigan Cavalry, came charging out of some woods behind Hampton and slashed him in the back of the head with his saber. Saved by his thick hair and felt hat, Hampton whirled about and thrust his revolver in the major's face and pulled the trigger, but it failed to fire. Storrs rode on, and Hampton pursued him, continuing to snap his empty or misfiring revolver at him, but the speeding major soon disappeared into the same cover that Hampton's first opponent had used. So Hampton rode off to find a surgeon to dress his wounds.

But at about 4 p.m., just as Longstreet's attack was getting well under way far to the south, General Stuart, who had rejoined his brigades by this time, received word that Federal cavalry had driven the rear-guard squadron out of Hunterstown. Fearing a Union attempt to get around his flank and into the rear of Ewell's infantry, Stuart ordered Hampton, whose brigade was nearest to the hamlet, to turn around and drive the Federals off. Learning from the fleeing squadron, which belonged to Cobb's (Georgia) Legion of his own brigade, that the Federals were in force, Hampton decided to stay on the defensive until he got his entire command together. He placed Cobb's Legion (375 men) across the rode leading to Gettysburg and put Phillips (Georgia) Legion (325 men) on its right and the 1st South Carolina Cavalry (400 men) on its left. His other two regiments had not arrived when a long line of Federals was seen coming down the road from Hunterstown in a column of fours, with dismounted skirmishers covering its flanks. Soon a small mounted force advanced, apparently preparing to charge, led by what was obviously a senior officer.

That officer was Brigadier General George Armstrong Custer. This was only Custer's second fight as a brigade commander, for he had just been promoted back on 29 June, prior to which he had been a mere captain on the staff of General Pleasonton. Meade had just taken over command of the Army of the Potomac the previous day, and Pleasonton had convinced Meade to promote three worthy young officers to brigadiers, of which Custer was the youngest, being only 23 years old and only two years out of West Point. One reason Pleasonton needed new brigadiers was that a division of two brigades had just been transferred to his corps from the Department of Washington, and its older, and not especially talented, commanders had been transferred out of the way so Pleasonton could pick his own men. Command of the new 3rd Division had gone to Kilpatrick, who was only four years older than Custer, had preceded him at West Point by only one year, and had worn a star for only a fortnight longer.[5] Kilpatrick's new command had collided with Jeb Stuart's three brigades at Hanover, Pennsylvania, two days before, and had acquitted itself reasonably well, holding the town but letting Stuart escape and ride on to the north. At the time, Kilpatrick had been more concerned with finding Ewell's infantry than pursuing Stuart's cavalry, but now the two were about to collide once again.

Kilpatrick's division had reached the rear of Meade's position at about the same time that Stuart had rejoined Lee, and it had been held there for a while before being sent to take position on the Army's right. Kilpatrick had sent an aide ahead with a small advance guard to reconnoiter, and they had charged into Hunterstown "hard as they could go, waving their sabers and yelling," according to a young boy who witnessed their arrival.[6] Kilpatrick soon arrived and learned from his aide that Stuart's cavalry had been found. Fearing that Stuart was trying to get around the Union right, Kilpatrick brought up his whole division.

The sun was setting as Custer's brigade, leading the way, turned down the road from Hunterstown toward Gettysburg. The road was flanked by fences, and there was a sizable body of Rebel skirmishers up ahead. Custer evidently believed that he still faced only a lone squadron, for he placed only Company A of the 6th Michigan in line across the road, though he did send three other companies of the 6th, dismounted, to a slight ridge to the right, placed an attached horse battery of six 3-inch rifles behind them, and dismounted troopers from the 7th Michigan on the left side of the road. The 1st Michigan was split, with half on each side of the road, and the 5th Michigan was held back as a mounted reserve. Kilpatrick sent his other brigade, commanded by Brigadier General Elon J. Farnsworth, another of the recently promoted young officers, to cover Custer's outer, or right, flank, going as far west as the Chambersburg Pike.

Just as the captain of Company A was about to have his bugler sound the charge, Custer, wearing an outlandish black velvet uniform with the white-starred blue collar of a sailor's blouse, a bright red cravat, and a huge black cavalier's hat, rode up and said, "I'll lead you this time, boys. Come on!"[7] The lone company charged down the road at a gallop, cheered on by the rest of the brigade, only to run into the fire of most of Hampton's Confederates and be countercharged by the whole of Cobb's Legion. The company's commander was wounded, and his first lieutenant was not only wounded, but unhorsed and captured. Custer also found himself afoot when his horse was shot out from under him, but he was saved from death or capture by a private from the 1st Michigan, who, overcome by enthusiasm, had joined the charge. The private shot down a Rebel only six feet away who had been leveling a carbine at Custer, pulled the young general up behind him on his horse, and headed for the rear, followed by those members of Company A (about half of them) who could still ride. Cobb's Legion followed them, only to run into the fire of the horse artillery, as well as the 6th and 7th regiments, the former of which was armed with repeating rifles, and the Confederates suffered about twice the casualties that Company A had.

After that, both sides were content with a standoff, Hampton borrowing a pair of rifled guns from Ewell's corps to duel intermittently with Kilpatrick's battery. Both Hampton and Kilpatrick probably believed that they had forestalled an enemy move around their respective army's flank. After dark, Hampton proceeded down the road to join Stuart's other brigades, and, at around 11 p.m., Kilpatrick received orders to take his division down the Baltimore Pike to Two Taverns. It was 3 o'clock the next morning before Custer's Michigan Brigade got there and made camp, and Farnsworth's 1st Brigade didn't arrive until dawn.

Meade's other cavalry division (besides Kilpatrick's and Buford's), the 2nd, was commanded by David McMurtrie Gregg, an 1855 graduate of West Point, a Pennsylvanian – in fact, a first cousin of the then-current governor of that state – and a highly competent, though modest, officer. This division had spent the first day of July being directed hither and yon by conflicting orders. Its 2nd Brigade and one battery of horse artillery had been sent to Manchester, Maryland, to guard the northeast approaches to the army's supply base at Westminster, and Gregg with the rest of his division had reached Hanover, Pennsylvania, in the early hours of 2 July. He had expected to find Kilpatrick's division there, and he was supposed to take command of it as well, but it was gone. A local minister had told him that both Kilpatrick's Federals and Stuart's Rebels had ridden away after their fight there on 30 June, both going off in the direction that Gregg's division was coming from. But Gregg had kept moving west, and at around 10 a.m. he had called a halt about five miles from Gettysburg. He had left Colonel John McIntosh in command of the division and had ridden ahead to find cavalry headquarters and see where his men were wanted.

While Gregg was gone, messages arrived from General Pleasonton, and in response to one of them McIntosh had sent the 4th Pennsylvania Cavalry to Cemetery Ridge, where it spent the rest of the day supporting batteries north of Little Round Top and backing up the infantry. He had also moved the main column another mile and a half closer to Gettysburg, where Pleasonton said to place it to guard the army's rear, and where most of the men had been allowed to bivouac. But some had been sent even farther west along what, from the perspective of Gettysburg, was called the Hanover Road, where they replaced the 9th Massachusetts Infantry that had been left behind by the 5th Corps. At about

3 p.m. the 10th New York Cavalry approached Brinkerhoff's Ridge. This regiment, which had spent a couple of months training around Gettysburg two years before, straddled the road; the 16th Pennsylvania Cavalry extended the line farther south, and two 3-inch rifled guns took position near the home of one Abraham Reever, near the road. (These were the only pieces of artillery that Gregg had with him, he having sent his normally attached battery off to Manchester with his 2nd Brigade. These two guns were part of Company H of the 3rd Pennsylvania Heavy Artillery, which along with a single company of cavalry, had been guarding a bridge down in Maryland until they had fallen in with Gregg's column.)

When Gregg returned late that afternoon, he found that his skirmishers were trading shots with Confederate infantry, and, at around 6 p.m., the musketry increased, indicating that the Rebels had been reinforced. So Gregg ordered Colonel J. Irvin Gregg, his cousin and commander of his 3rd Brigade, to send some dismounted men forward. The colonel sent 50 men from the 10th New York, but, before they got halfway across the intervening fields, a line of Confederate infantry advanced from the woods to their front. This was the 2nd Virginia Infantry (330 men), from the Stonewall Brigade in Johnson's Division of Ewell's 2nd Corps. Brigadier General Albert Jenkins' cavalry brigade had been ordered to screen Ewell's flank, but Jenkins had been wounded, and somehow the order did not get passed on in a timely fashion, so there was no cavalry to cover the Stonewall Brigade at the left end of Ewell's line. Upon seeing Union forces approach, that brigade had turned to face this threat, and this one regiment had been ordered to drive in the Federal skirmishers and "ascertain, if possible, what force the enemy had at that point."[8] As the infantrymen advanced, Jeb Stuart, minus his exhausted cavalry, arrived on Brinkerhoff's Ridge to evaluate the situation on this flank. He was joined there by Major Campbell Brown, Ewell's adjutant and stepson. "Stuart told me his troops were coming up on our left rear," Brown later wrote, "but were still some distance, he thought."[9]

Colonel Irvin Gregg reacted to the advance of the 2nd Virginia by sending forward the rest of the 10th New York Cavalry, its various squadrons advancing dismounted and disappearing into different clumps of woods between the two ridges. One squadron moved directly at Stuart, Brown, and other staff officers, obliging them to mount up and move off. Then Stuart, satisfied that the Stonewall Brigade adequately protected Ewell's left, rode off to see to his exhausted troopers.

Just as the 10th New York advanced, Dr. Theodore Tate, the chief surgeon of the 3rd Pennsylvania Cavalry and a native of the area, who had ridden toward town hoping to visit his family, came galloping back down the road, pursued by two small groups of Jenkins' cavalry who had (finally) been sent to find the right flank of the Federal army. The crews of the two Union guns near the road leaped to their pieces, "and, as luck would have it," the historian of Tate's regiment later wrote, "put two shells into the midst of the party. More beautiful shots were never seen, though they were the first hostile ones the gunners had ever fired." The two shots flew about six feet over the head of an old lady leaning on a crutch and a cane, who was among some civilians who had come out to see the soldiers, and sent her, as the same writer recorded, "running for dear life across the fields with as much activity as a girl in her teens, without crutch or cane, and shrieking with all her might."[10] The two groups of Rebels scattered and left Dr. Tate to return to his regiment.

The two Union guns then turned their attention to the Confederate infantry, driving it back momentarily, but it soon came on again, and drove in the dismounted troopers. Gregg then called up the rest of his division, holding his cousin's brigade in reserve and sending only Colonel John B. McIntosh's 1st Brigade (1,100 men) forward. The latter's 3rd Pennsylvania turned right off the Hannover Road just beyond the two guns and entered some woods on the northern part of Cress Ridge, about a quarter-mile east of Brinkerhoff's Ridge. Two battalions of the 1st New Jersey Cavalry plus the little Purnell Legion (the single troop of Marylanders that had been picked up along with the two guns) extended the line on the south side of the Hannover Road, while the remaining battalion of the 1st New Jersey formed a second line in the rear.

But most of the fighting fell to two squadrons of the 3rd Pennsylvania, which were sent forward dismounted to occupy a fence line that the 10th New York had just abandoned, and which was directly in the path of the oncoming Rebels. They barely managed to reach the fence ahead of the Confederates, then blasted them at the range of 20 paces with their breechloading carbines. The Virginians fell back, then rallied and came on again, but were again driven back by the rapid-firing troopers and the fire of the two Union guns. The Rebels tried several more times but could not take the fence by direct assault. However, as darkness fell the Rebels were able to get around the Federals' right flank and dislodge them, but the Pennsylvanians were soon reinforced, and, after a close-range fight in the dark, managed to drive off the Confederates, who then fell back to the woods from whence they had come, carrying their wounded with them, although neither side had suffered many casualties.

The colonel of the 2nd Virginia mistakenly reported to his brigade commander, Brigadier General James A. Walker, that he was facing two regiments of cavalry, two of infantry, and a battery of artillery. When Walker passed this information on to General Johnson, the latter told him that the division was about to attack, but that Walker should hold his whole brigade back to cover the flank if he thought it necessary, which he did. Some time after dark, probably around 8 p.m., Walker posted two companies to watch the flank and marched the rest of his brigade off to join in Johnson's attack, but it arrived too late to participate. At about 10 p.m. General Gregg pulled his men back a short distance, and at around midnight he received orders to leave only pickets there and to bring the bulk of his division to the Baltimore Turnpike, near where the Artillery Reserve was parked.

Lee's orders to Ewell had been for him to make a demonstration against the Union right simultaneous with Longstreet's attack. This was intended to prevent Meade from shifting troops from there to reinforce his left. But Ewell was to turn the feint into a real attack if prospects looked favorable; for instance, if Meade went ahead and withdrew forces from his right anyway. So Ewell's 2nd Corps had idled away the day, waiting for Longstreet's 1st Corps to start the attack at the other end of the long, concave Confederate line. When it finally came, members of Ewell's staff climbed a ladder into the cupola atop a Catholic church on High Street to watch Longstreet's attack for their one-legged commander, who remained in the street below. "Things are going splendidly!" one aide called down to the general. "We are driving them back everywhere!"[11]

Except for the Stonewall Brigade, skirmishing on the far left flank, Ed Johnson's men rested to the north of Benner's Hill, which is just northeast of Culp's Hill, wondering why the attack was being delayed for so long and listening to the Federals on the latter eminence applying axes to the trees to improve their defenses. Some of the Rebels pillaged a nearby farmhouse, a staff officer conducted religious services for some of them, and some of them wrote letters home.

West of Johnson's Division, General Early had Hays's and Hoke's (Avery's) brigades posted in the ravine of Winebrenner's Run, just east of the town, which was deep enough to cut off whatever breeze there was, and since there was no shade either, the men had been hot and miserable all day, so close to the enemy that it would have been suicide to stand up, while expecting at any time to be ordered to rise and charge the Federals on Cemetery Hill, just south of them. They too could hear chopping up on the hill they expected to assault, and knew that the Union positions were being improved with every hour that slipped by. Gordon's Brigade was farther north, by the railroad tracks northeast of town, and Smith's Brigade was still guarding the 2nd Corps' left rear, where Kilpatrick's cavalry would eventually add some substance to whatever imaginary enemy "Extra Billy" had seen the day before.

Farther west, Doles', Iverson's, and Ramseur's brigades of Rodes' Division held positions right through the heart of Gettysburg, along Middle Street from Baltimore Street to the west edge of town. O'Neal's Brigade was farther north, in the cut for the unfinished railroad that had played such a prominent part in the previous day's fighting. Daniel's Brigade was even farther west, up on Seminary Ridge, connecting, somewhat, with A. P. Hill's left and supporting three batteries of the 2nd Corps' reserve artillery. South of these 12 guns, extending down Seminary Ridge south of the Fairfield Road, were 41 guns from Hill's 3rd Corps.

All of these 53 guns faced the west side of Cemetery Hill. Ewell also put 20 guns up on Benner's Hill, facing the east side of Cemetery Hill. When Colonel Alexander's artillery had opened fire to begin Longstreet's attack, all these guns had soon joined in. "The enemy replied with at least equal fury," Colonel Fremantle, the British observer, remembered, "and in a few moments the firing along the whole line was as heavy as it is possible to conceive. A dense smoke arose for six miles. There was little wind to drive it away, and the air seemed full of shells, each of which seemed to have a different style of going and to make a different noise from the others."[12]

The cannonade shook houses and rattled windows all over Gettysburg. The residents of the town had spent the day in suspense. Many of them had tried to watch the battle, but most of it was too far away, and too covered with smoke, for them to make much sense of what was happening. But this great artillery duel was close, some of it very close, to the town. "Just before nightfall . . . I had the sensation of a lifetime," a local farm boy later remembered. "There was a thunder of guns, a shrieking, whistling, moaning . . . of shells before they burst, sometimes like rockets in the air. . . ." But still the civilians had little idea of how the battle was going. "No results of the conflicts would be noted," the boy wrote; "no shifting of scenes or movement of actors in the great struggle could be observed. It was simply noise, flash, and roar, the roar of a continuous thunderstorm and the sharp angry crashes of the thunderbolt."[13]

Benner's Hill was about a half-mile east of Gettysburg (just east of Rock Creek), about the same distance northeast of Culp's Hill, and not much farther than that west of Brinkerhoff's Ridge, with Benner's Run angling southwest between it and the latter. The open crest of the hill ran south, so that the Confederate guns placed on it naturally faced more toward Cemetery Hill than Culp's Hill. The Hannover Road split the ridge roughly in half, and a battery called the 1st Rockbridge Artillery, from the 2nd Corps' reserve, had taken position north of the road early that morning. It consisted of four 20-pounder Parrott rifles, the largest type of gun employed by either side at Gettysburg.

Just before the bombardment began, they had been joined by the 16 guns (two 20-pounders, five 10-pounder Parrotts, six 12-pounder "Napoleon" smoothbores, and three 3-inch Ordnance rifles) of the battalion that was attached to Johnson's Division, under the temporary command of 19-year-old Major Joseph W. Latimer. (Ewell's chief of artillery, Colonel J. Thompson Brown, had not been able to find any good positions for his other three battalions.) The two 20-pounders were placed north of the Hanover Road, next to those of the Rockbridge battery, and the other 14 guns extended the line south of the road. As soon as these batteries were in position, they opened fire on Cemetery Hill. "Then came a storm of shot and shell," a Northern war correspondent who was in the cemetery at the time later wrote; "marble slabs were broken, iron fences shattered, horses disemboweled. The air was filled with wild, hideous noises, the low buzz of round shot, the whizzing of elongated balls and the stunning explosion of shells overhead and all around. In three minutes the earth shook with the tremendous concussion of two hundred pieces of artillery."[14]

Over half of those were Union guns firing back at their tormentors, and Latimer's guns on Benner's Hill, being the closest, were hit the hardest, not only from Cemetery Hill but from Stevens' Knoll and even from the top of Culp's Hill, south of them. The captain of one of Latimer's batteries was among the first casualties, when a Federal shot hit his right leg, passed through his horse, and shattered his left leg; the dying horse then fell on him, breaking three of his ribs and pinning him to the ground. One Rebel described Benner's Hill as "simply a hell infernal." And shots that were fired too high fell among Johnson's infantry behind the hill, causing at least one of its brigades to hit the dirt. Some of the Confederates were also firing too high, and their shots fell among the wagons and ambulances parked behind Cemetery Hill, putting, as General Howard wrote, "a host of army followers into rapid motion farther to the rear."[15]

But some of the fire struck more important targets. A single shell took out 27 men in the 55th Ohio. Colonel Wainwright, still in charge of the Union guns on the east side of the Baltimore Pike, sat on a stone wall watching the exchange with professional detachment, and saw one 20-pound shot tear through some nearby infantrymen sheltering behind another wall, killing or wounding about a dozen of them before plowing into the ground and covering the colonel with dust. Later, a Rebel shell struck the ground near him and buried itself right under him, but the force of its explosion took the path of least resistance, back out the hole it had made upon entering the ground, leaving Wainwright unharmed. Early in the exchange, a well-aimed Federal shot exploded a Confederate ammunition chest on Benner's Hill, but soon the Rebels returned the favor by hitting a Union caisson, and a few moments later they blew up the ammo chest on a Union limber, which took out two men and two horses. Another shell broke the axle on a Federal gun, but its crew continued to use it until it finally collapsed near the end of the fight.

Latimer's battalion on Benner's Hill, dueling with about twice its number of Federal guns, was getting the worst of the exchange. The battery of 10-pounders, the same that lost its captain in the opening minutes, eventually lost so many men that it could crew only one of its four guns, and then a Union shell blew a wheel off of that one, wounding four men in the process. Latimer sent word to General Johnson that he could not hold his position, and the general told him to leave one battery to support his infantry attack and withdraw the rest. Some of the guns had to be fitted with spare wheels before they could be removed. Latimer was later mortally wounded while directing the four guns that were left on the hill.

Major Osborn, still commanding the Union guns on the west side of the Baltimore Pike, later declared the Confederate bombardment useless, saying it did little damage to the Union artillery, which seemed to be its primary target, and would have been more effective if directed against the infantry. Moreover, he felt that all such exchanges ultimately benefitted the Federals, who could more easily replenish their ammunition supply than the Rebels, who were a long way from home. When the darkness put an end to the fight, some of the Union batteries, with men and ammunition exhausted, were withdrawn and replaced by batteries from the Artillery Reserve; so that there were then more guns on Cemetery Hill than there had been before the fight.

While on the Confederate side, Lee, having devised a plan and set it in motion, played no further part once the attack began, on the Union side, Meade was actively involved in the defense, perhaps to the point of over-reacting. He already had two corps (3rd and 5th) and about half of another (2nd) – approximately a third of his army – involved in the fight against about a third of Lee's army (three large divisions) and had another corps, his largest (the 6th) coming up. (At around 5 p.m. he had even instructed General Pleasonton, his chief of cavalry, to find a good position in the army's rear and to be prepared to cover the retreat of the army, if it should become necessary.) At about 6 p.m., perhaps in response to Hancock's request for more reinforcements, Meade had ordered Slocum to send the 12th Corps, or most of it, across from the army's right flank to its left. To this extent Lee's attack en echelon, starting with Meade's left flank, was working, for it not only wrecked the Union left but weakened its reserves, center, and right by drawing off troops from those sectors before the attack ever reached those parts of the line. But neither A. P. Hill, nor Ewell exploited the opportunity fully.

Williams' division of the 12th Corps, in response to Meade's order, had headed for the far left of the Union line, cutting across the space of only about a mile that separated the two flanks. As Slocum still considered himself the commander of the right wing of the army (5th and 12th Corps), Williams still considered himself the temporary commander of the entire 12th Corps, so he had ordered his senior brigade commander, Brigadier General Thomas H. Ruger, to take the 1st Division to Cemetery Ridge, and either Williams or Slocum had sent along the newly arrived brigade of reinforcements commanded by General Lockwood. That officer was senior to Ruger but lacked experience, so to avoid having to place him in command of the division, Williams treated that brigade as an independent unit and, as corps commander, had gone along personally to command the whole, leaving instructions for Geary's 2nd Division to extend itself to take over the positions being abandoned by the 1st Division.

Lockwood's two large regiments were the first to arrive on the army's left and crossed Cemetery Ridge just south of Willard's brigade, with the 1st Regiment of the Potomac Home Brigade, Maryland Volunteers (674 men), in front, followed by the 150th New York (609 men). The Marylanders had passed through some parked batteries and survivors of Caldwell's division of the 2nd Corps and, angling somewhat south of west, passed over and around the 39th New York and kept going, taking fire from Colonel Alexander's guns, to their left front, and Barksdale's retreating Mississippians to their right front, then had driven the wayward 21st Mississippi up onto the high ground carrying the Emmitsburg Road and recaptured three of the four Napoleons of Captain Bigelow's 9th Massachusetts Battery before coming to a halt. Meade had specifically ordered Lockwood not to go as far as the Emmitsburg Road, so the Marylanders turned back, dragging the recaptured guns along, and took position just east of Plum Run.

Detaching men to help the wounded in the Plum Run ravine, the 150th New York had moved due west, coming up on the Marylanders' right, instead of following them. It had taken fire from a couple of Confederate guns posted near the Emmitsburg Road, but had encountered no Rebel infantry until it approached Barksdale's Brigade reforming behind a stone wall near that road. It, too, turned back to Plum Run and rejoined the Marylanders.

Meanwhile, Colonel McGilvery of the Artillery Reserve came to Williams and asked him to support his line of guns, which had already fallen apart, leaving him only one battery and one section of another. McGilvery later sent some artillerymen forward, who retrieved Bigelow's fourth gun. Williams deployed the two brigades of his own (now Ruger's) division to Lockwood's left in a compact formation, but soon an aide, whom Ruger had sent forward to report his division's approach, returned saying he had seen both Sykes and Sedgwick, who had told him that the Rebel attack had been repulsed and that the division would not be needed. At almost the same time, Ruger received an order from Williams to hurry back to Culp's Hill and reoccupy the line of breastworks it had built there during the day. Williams, meanwhile, rode on up to Cemetery Ridge, where he learned of the repulse of the Confederate attack there, and then stayed to participate in a meeting of corps commanders with General Meade.

There are conflicting reports as to just how much of the 12th Corps Meade had called for, but apparently he had asked for or expected all of it to make the move until Slocum had sent an aide to point out that there were Confederates in front of Culp's Hill and to ask for permission to keep one division there. The aide had returned with Meade's message that the army's left was the critical position and with permission for Slocum to retain only one brigade on the army's right. So, at about 7 p.m., General Geary received an order from one of Slocum's staff officers to leave one brigade to hold the corps' defenses and to follow the 1st Division with his other two brigades. (Geary was a huge man for that time, six feet six and 250 pounds. He had been the first mayor of gold-rush San Francisco, and then the territorial governor of Kansas during the fighting between its pro and anti-slavery factions just before the war.)

The problem was that Williams' brigades were already out of sight, it was nearly dark, and Geary didn't know where he was supposed to go or why he was supposed to go there. He left Brigadier General George S. Greene's 3rd Brigade (five New York regiments totaling about 1,200men) to hold the corps' lines and, following some men who seemed to be going in the right direction, he took his other two brigades down the Baltimore Pike beyond Rock Creek. Finding no trace of Williams' division, however, he eventually realized that something was wrong, so he called a halt and sent word of his location to corps headquarters. A half-hour later he received instructions to "hold the position down to the creek at all hazards."[16] So he formed a line with his right on the turnpike and his left on the creek, meaning that he was facing west, which would have put him in good position to cover a retreat if the army had needed to make one.

An officer on General Greene's staff later wrote that his brigade was also ordered to the left, but that, just as it was leaving its defenses, Greene had received a report that a large force of Confederates was advancing against them. Greene had called a halt, reinforced his skirmish line, and reported to Geary, but the latter had told him to follow the rest of the division. However, the officer who carried the report to Geary also encountered a member of Slocum's staff, who told him that Greene should hold his position and that he would send Geary back as well. It was extremely fortunate for the Union cause that he did so, for, had he not, the Confederates would have occupied Culp's Hill and threatened the Baltimore Pike, the lifeline of Meade's army.

Greene was one of the oldest men in either army (born in 1801), who had graduated from West Point in 1823, six years ahead of Robert E. Lee. He had been an instructor at West Point and at the artillery school at Fort Monroe, but he had left the Army while still a lieutenant to become a highly respected civil engineer. Now, he proved to be the right man in the right place that hot July evening.

The five regiments of Greene's brigade occupied the Union defenses from Culp's Hill's highest point southward for about a quarter of a mile to the saddle of land that connected its two peaks. His line had been strengthened during the day with a shallow trench that had a log barricade to the front that was covered with the earth from the trench. At the southern end of his line the defenses had originally been turned to the west to protect the brigade's right flank, but later the corps' line had been extended along the northeast face of the lower peak, and the westward-running part of the line had become a traverse, that is, a line roughly perpendicular to the front line. The new extended line had been manned by one of Geary's other brigades and by Ruger's entire division, down to and including McAllister's Woods. Now, with those troops gone, Greene extended and thinned his lone brigade enough to place one of his regiments, the 137th New York, in this northeast-facing line, beyond the traverse. He was not given time to do more.

The artillery bombardment described above had been Ewell's "demonstration," intended to pin down Federal units on Cemetery Hill and keep Meade worried about that position long enough for real attacks on both ends of the Union line to get rolling. For Ewell still wanted Culp's Hill, and he intended to finally send Johnson's Division against it. Whether Ewell knew it or not, the withdrawal of most of the 12th Corps from the Union right was giving him the "opportunity" Lee had hoped for to turn Ewell's feint into a real attack.

While the Confederate batteries on Benner's Hill had been dueling with their Union counterparts, General Johnson had sent Brigadier General John M. Jones's brigade (6 Virginia regiments with about 1,550 men) to support the artillery, and Jones had placed his 50th Virginia in close support on the south slope of the hill, just to the left of Latimer's guns, while the 25th Virginia had served as skirmishers and had fought to keep the Federal skirmishers from harassing the gunners. The rest of the brigade had formed up some 300 yards to the left rear of the artillery, then had advanced to take position extending the 50th Virginia's line.

When most of Latimer's guns were withdrawn, General Johnson rode onto the hill and told Jones to advance his brigade when the next brigade to his left, five Louisiana regiments (about 1,200 men) under Colonel Jesse Williams, came up even with his. Brigadier General George "Maryland" Steuart's brigade (1 Maryland battalion, 2 North Carolina regiments, and 3 Virginia regiments – about 1,200 men), then in the division's rear, would wheel to its right and come up and form the left of the line until Walker's Stonewall Brigade (about 1,300 men in five Virginia regiments) could fight off Gregg's cavalry and catch up. The three attacking brigades would assault Culp's Hill from the east while Walker protected their rear from the Federal troopers.

It was about 7 p.m. when Colonel Williams' brigade (technically called Nicholls' Brigade after its absent general) came up on Jones's left and the advance began, although Steuart's Brigade, making a difficult wheeling maneuver over rough terrain, had not yet caught up. Jones's Brigade took fire from the Union guns up on Culp's Hill until it was down in the valley between that eminence and Benner's Hill. The guns' barrels could not be depressed enough for their fire to reach into that low area, but Federal skirmishers began to fire on the Rebels as they crossed Rock Creek and started up the steep eastern slope of the larger hill.

Some 170 men from Greene's 60th New York constituted the Union skirmish line, but a supporting regiment had marched off with General Geary just as the Confederates began their advance, so Greene had to send his 78th New York (about 200 men) to take its place. This left Greene's main line spread to such an extent that there was about a foot of open space between each man, whereas normally regiments of that war fought shoulder to shoulder, two ranks deep. Such a dispersal of manpower meant a corresponding dilution of firepower. Soon the thin line of Union skirmishers was pushed back by the three brigades of Rebels, giving ground no faster than they had to, and becoming entangled with the Confederates enough in the dark woods to bring away a dozen prisoners when they finally ran for the cover of the defenses. The 78th New York arrived in time to exchange several volleys with the attackers before they also fell back inside the works, taking position in the center of Greene's line. Once the skirmishers were out of the way, the troops in the defenses opened fire, but between the growing darkness, the increasing smoke, and the trees on the slope, they couldn't see much of their enemies.

The Confederates couldn't see much either, including the trees, underbrush, and rocks that impeded their advance up the steep slope, so the ranks of Jones's Brigade soon became disordered. All they could see of the defenders (the 60th New York) was, as one Rebel put it, "a ditch filled with men firing down on our heads."[17] General Jones took a wound in the thigh that was bleeding badly, and he had to turn over command of his brigade to Lieutenant Colonel Robert Dungan of the 48th Virginia. His brigade fell back a few hundred yards and then charged forward again three times, but could not reach the Union works. "Now was the value of breastworks apparent," said a junior officer of Greene's brigade, "for, protected by these, few of our men were hit; and, feeling a sense of security, we worked with corresponding energy. Without breastworks our line would have been swept away in an instant by the hailstorm of bullets and the flood of men."[18]

The Louisiana Brigade, to Jones's left, was stopped about 100 yards from the defenses, from which point it returned fire and made several unsuccessful attempts to assault the works manned by the 78th and 102nd New York. The color-bearer of the 1st Louisiana got too far forward and was captured, but he successfully hid his flag under his clothes all through his captivity until he was exchanged the following winter. The 3rd North Carolina of Steuart's Brigade blundered into the angle where the Union defense line turned and was ambushed by the 149th New York to its front and the 137th New York to its left. Before long the 1st Maryland Battalion came up and attacked the 137th, relieving the North Carolinians from the flank fire, at least, but neither Confederate unit could advance farther. Most of the 1st North Carolina was brought over to support the 3rd North Carolina, and fired into the rear of the Marylanders before realizing who they were.

However, the other three regiments of Steuart's Brigade, delayed by their long wheeling maneuver, some very rough terrain, and waist-deep water in Rock Creek (they crossed it near a mill dam), came to the unmanned line so recently abandoned by the rest of the 12th Corps. The 23rd Virginia (250 men) occupied the empty works and then, followed by the other two regiments, moved to the right to come in on the flank of the 137th New York. The 23rd's commander sent a lieutenant forward to make sure that these were Federals, then arranged with a major commanding three companies of the Marylanders for a simultaneous attack from two directions. The 71st Pennsylvania, sent over by Hancock when he heard firing from the Culp's Hill area, arrived just in time to get caught in the crossfire, and its colonel soon decided that his regiment was badly needed back on Cemetery Ridge.

Leaving his two North Carolina regiments to menace the Union line from the front, the rest of Steuart's Brigade occupied the lower peak of Culp's Hill. By then full darkness had fallen and the moon had only just risen, so the Rebels couldn't see what was in front of them. They fired down on Greene's position, but had the nagging fear that they might be firing at fellow Confederates. The 10th Virginia, on Steuart's left, advanced down into the saddle of land between the two peaks and drove the 137th New York, which was also taking fire from the North Carolinians to its front, back to the south-facing traverse.

When the Rebel attack was first detected, Greene had sent requests for help to General Wadsworth, whose 1st Corps troops connected to his left and manned the line running west from the summit of Culp's Hill, and to General Howard on Cemetery Hill. Howard sent four regiments from Schimmelfennig's brigade of Schurz's division, and Wadsworth eventually sent him the 6th Wisconsin, the 14th Brooklyn and the 147th New York, after he was sure that he was not about to be attacked himself. The 11th Corps units probably arrived first, in two pairs, each guided by a different staff officer. They moved into Greene's line and helped fight off the Confederate assaults. An unknown 12th Corps officer complimented the 82nd Illinois on how well it fought and said, "If you had been here yesterday instead of that d–d 11th Corps, we would not have been driven back." The regiment's commander replied indignantly, "You are a miserable hound, sir, I and my regiment belong to that same 11th Corps your are speaking of, and we did no worse fighting yesterday."[19] At which the 12th Corps officer disappeared without further comment. At least one of the 11th Corps regiments, the 157th New York, moved to the south end of the line, where it lost one of its flags to the 37th Virginia of Steuart's Brigade.

The 147th New York, from Cutler's brigade of the 1st Corps, moved into the line near its center, but the 14th Brooklyn moved toward the right end of the line, guided by one of Greene's aides. Riding ahead, the aide and the regiment's Colonel Fowler were accosted by Rebels in the dark, who took the aide prisoner, but the colonel safely returned to his regiment. Despite this obvious sign, Fowler was concerned that there might be friendly troops ahead of him, so he sent two volunteers ahead to make sure. Eventually one of them came back to announce that the other had been wounded and that the unit to their front was the 10th Virginia. Fowler ordered his regiment to fire and then charge into the woods to their front, which brought on a confused melee in the dark that neither side was later willing to admit losing. Evidently the Brooklynites then relieved the 137th New York in the traverse line, allowing the latter to rest and prepare for another round next morning. The 6th Wisconsin was met by General Greene himself, who sent it to the right, where it ejected some Rebels from part of the traverse and held it themselves until relieved about midnight.

The relief came in the form of Brigadier General Thomas Kane's 2nd Brigade of Geary's division, which had originally, before its trip down the Baltimore Pike, held the part of the line just east of the traverse, now occupied by the Confederates. It returned between 10 p.m. and midnight, shortly after the fighting had died down for the night. It was soon followed by Geary's other brigade, his 1st, commanded by Brigadier General Charles Candy. (Yes, the two brigades really were commanded by officers named Candy and Kane, although Kane was sick with pneumonia and shared his command with Colonel George Cobham.) Kane's leading regiment (he had only three) announced its return with a loud hurrah only to have it answered with a Confederate volley. The regiment's colonel, not knowing what had transpired in his unit's absence, assumed this was friendly fire and led his men back to the Baltimore Pike, then rode back alone to announce his identity, only to receive another volley in the dark. Meanwhile the brigade moved on up the pike and turned off onto the Spangler farm lane onto the saddle between the two parts of the hill. There, one regiment tried to deploy into its old works until it too was met with a Rebel volley. Finally scouts were sent out who brought back the information that the shooting was coming from Confederates who had taken over their works while they were gone.

Skirmishers were sent up the hill, but the captain in charge was captured, along with some of his men. However, Kane and Cobham finally realized that there were a lot of Rebels up on the lower crest of the hill, so they formed their three regiments on the saddle facing south or southeast. But as the growing moonlight gave them a better look at the size of the Confederate force, and Rebel fire started coming in, they decided to withdraw northward behind the traverse and extend that line among some rocks on the lower slope of the higher peak. Thus they relieved the 6th Wisconsin and 14th Brooklyn. The lines were so close together that during the night one of Kane's pickets shot a Confederate who was carrying a lot of noisy canteens in search of water for his unit. Meanwhile, Geary held Candy's brigade in the Baltimore Pike until Kane's was settled in, then placed it, as quietly as possible, to Kane's right, overlooking Spangler's Lane, with its right in Spangler's orchard.

General Ruger was somewhat more fortunate than Geary, for when he and his (Williams') division returned from their foray to the army's left he was warned by some skirmishers that his lines might have been occupied by Confederates while he was gone. He ordered his two brigades to send out skirmishers of their own to make sure, one way or the other. The 1st Brigade, on the left, sent two companies. When the Rebels fired on them they retreated, throwing the leading regiments into some confusion, one firing into the other, but only one man was hit. The 3rd Brigade (Ruger's own) on the right, found its old works in McAllister's Woods vacant and promptly reoccupied them. Its skirmishers moved farther north and soon brought in 23 captured Rebels, including a captain, who told them that the lower peak of Culp's Hill was occupied by two brigades of Confederates. More skirmishers went even farther north and eventually confirmed that Rebels were up there in force, and Ruger was content to hold a line along the south base of the hill until daylight.

General Johnson visited Steuart's position on Culp's Hill that night and was informed that a captain, sent out for the purpose, had found the Baltimore Pike about 600 yards to the west, where, he said, he had seen wagons moving on the road and parked beside it. Johnson could hear the rumble of wheels for himself and commented that the enemy must be retreating. Major Henry Kyd Douglas, of Johnson's staff, wrote long afterwards, "Could a heavy column of our division have followed this opening and pushed on to the pike, the situation of the enemy would have been a critical one. But night came and the position of our few men in that advanced position was most perilous. The battle ended after a most unsatisfactory day's work."[20]

But not yet. When the artillery duel had ended, and Jubal Early had heard the roar of musketry over toward Culp's Hill commence, he had ridden forward to Winebrenner's Run, at the north foot of Cemetery Hill, and asked Harry Hays if he was ready to attack. Hays had already been briefed that afternoon. He would command his own and Hoke's (Avery's) brigades and assault the Union works on the hill above him, while Gordon's Brigade came up behind him in support and Rodes' Division attacked the hill from the west. In his own brigade, Hays had five Louisiana regiments (some 1,200 men, known collectively as the Louisiana Tigers), and in Hoke's Brigade there were only three regiments (down to about 900 men). The two brigades, posted in the ravine that carried Winebrenner's Run, faced to the southeast and would have to wheel 90 degrees to their right to attack Cemetery Hill from the northeast, except for the right part of Hays's own brigade, which could advance due south and hit the north side of the hill.

Directly in the path of these Confederates was the Union division now commanded by Adelbert Ames. It had taken a lot of losses the day before, and Ames later said that von Gilsa's 1st Brigade was now down to about 650 men and that his own 1st Brigade, now under Colonel Andrew Harris, was down to about 500. Hearing the heavy firing over around

Culp's Hill, to the east, Ames naturally worried about a Rebel attack coming from that direction. So he began shifting most of his small command to guard against such an eventuality. Evidently he even tried to send troops to help Greene out, for he told the commander of a nearby battery, "Captain, three times I have sent orders to that brigade to advance to the support of our men on Culp's Hill, and they will not advance one step."[21]

Nevertheless, he was able to move most of his 2nd Brigade from the crest and north slope of Cemetery Hill to a position along a wall bordering a lane that ran along the northeast face of the hill, often called Brickyard Lane because it led to a brickyard at the south edge of the town. His 107th Ohio was on the left, behind a stone wall, and faced north. The 25th Ohio was to its right, perhaps behind the same wall, turned at a right angle to begin the line along Brickyard Lane. To its right, extending down that lane, were the 75th Ohio and 17th Connecticut, then the four regiments of von Gilsa's 1st Brigade, and finally the 33rd Massachusetts (500 men), which had been sent over from von Steinwehr's division as a reinforcement. The latter regiment and the 41st New York of von Gilsa's brigade had at first been sent out into the meadow between Cemetery Hill and Culp's Hill but had soon fallen back at the approach of Hays's larger force. Colonel Harris later complained that a last-minute move of the 17th Connecticut to his brigade's right, and the attachment of it to von Gilsa's brigade, "left my line very thin and weak. All the men could get to the stone wall, used by us as a breastwork, and have all the elbow room he wanted."[22]

Hays's Confederates, preceded by a skirmish line, came up out of their ravine and hurried down into the low ground at the base of Cemetery Hill, taking fire from Union skirmishers and artillery. However, only three batteries on the hill, plus Stevens' battery on his knoll, were positioned to fire on them, and in the gathering darkness, and the clouds of smoke, the gunners were firing too high. Colonel Wainwright said he couldn't see more than 10 yards ahead, noting that "seventeen guns vomiting it as fast as they can will make a good deal of smoke."[23] There was a dead space near the Union front that the guns on the hill could not be depressed enough to hit, and the artillerymen had to be careful not to fire into their own infantry down the hill from them. Stevens' battery, however, by turning its three left-most pieces and moving the other three from the right to the left, was able to enfilade this dead space.

The Louisiana Tigers came on steadily, but the fire of Battery I of the 1st New York, commanded by Captain Michael Wiedrich, the most northerly of the batteries on the hill, seemed to force them to their left, the Union right, where they found and exploited a gap between the 75th New York and the 25th New York. There was desperate hand-to-hand combat that spread as far south as the 17th Connecticut, while Hays's Confederates were slipping through the gap and heading on up the hill. This breakthrough came to the right rear of the 107th New York, still facing north, and it was ordered to fall back before it could be surrounded and to protect Wiedrich's battery at all hazards.

Avery's brigade had to make a longer and tighter wheel than Hays's Brigade, which brought its three regiments up behind Hays's left. Sometime after ordering the wheel, Avery, one of the few mounted officers in this attack, received a mortal wound in the neck. In the darkness no one saw him fall from his horse. He was later found to have scribbled a short note in his last moments: "Tell my father that I died with my face to the enemy."[24] The left of his line's left-most regiment, the 57th North Carolina, took deadly flank fire from Stevens' guns and then from the large 33rd Massachusetts, which opened fire at a mere 50 yards, firing obliquely into the Confederate flank. The Rebels wavered, but then the survivors resumed their advance, only to be blasted again by Stevens' guns.

A slight rise in front of von Gilsa's brigade allowed the Confederates to approach that part of the Union line unseen, and von Gilsa compounded the problem by mistaking them for Federal skirmishers and ordering his men not to fire. Some of them knew better and fired anyway but failed to stop the onrushing Rebels, and the 57th and 68th New York were pushed up the hill by Avery's other two regiments and the left of Hays's line. Part of the 41st New York was swept along with them, but most of it stuck with the 33rd Massachusetts on its right and helped to hold off the 57th North Carolina. At the left end of von Gilsa's line, the 153rd New York fought the Confederates hand-to-hand, killing a Rebel color-bearer who jumped up onto the low stone wall to their front but losing the resulting tug-of-war for the fallen flag. Eventually this regiment was also pressed back up the hill toward the Union batteries. However, the 17th Connecticut and the 75th Ohio held their positions along the Brickyard Lane, holding back the center of Hays's Brigade, so that the Rebels who went up the hill did so in two separate swarms that had lost all formation.

Some Louisianans got in among Wiedrich's guns but were soon driven out again by the artillerymen and the 107th Ohio, whose adjutant captured the flag of the 8th Louisiana. Rebels also briefly captured the left gun of the next battery to the south, a Pennsylvania battery from the artillery reserve commanded by Captain R. Bruce Ricketts, even while its other guns continued to fire cannister rounds at the Confederates to their front. But evidently a moment came when all the artillery had to stop firing, probably from fear of hitting their own infantry. During this relative lull General Hays was trying to reform his regiments and waiting for help to arrive when a line of infantrymen was heard and dimly seen approaching from the cemetery. It was too dark to tell whether they were friends or foes. General Early had warned Hays that Rodes' Division would be attacking the hill from the other side, so he ordered his men to hold their fire, even when the unidentified line fired a volley their way, then a second, and a third. Finally convinced that they were Federals, Hays ordered his men to return fire, and the enemy line seemed to disappear into the darkness only to be replaced by another, with others coming up behind it, so he ordered his men to fall back to the wall at the base of the hill. He sent an officer to find Gordon's Brigade, which was supposed to support his, but the officer couldn't find it, so Hays went looking for it himself and found it posted in Winebrenner's Run, the very position his own troops had started from. It was obvious to him that it was now too late for these Georgians to be of much help, so he moved his own brigade back and placed it beside Gordon's.

The Federals involved were most likely two regiments of Krzyzanowski's brigade led over from the west side of the hill by General Schurz and/or two regiments of Coster's brigade sent from near the cemetery by von Steinwehr. General Howard had also appealed to Hancock for help, and the latter had told Gibbon to send Colonel Samuel S. Carroll's 1st Brigade of the 3rd Division of the 2nd Corps, also known as the Gibralter Brigade, though, in fact, only three of its four regiments were sent.

Carroll was a highly competent young officer, West Point class of 1856, energetic and fearless; a redhead with a temper to match. As the reinforcements from Schurz and/or von Steinwehr were pushing Hays's Louisianans back down the hill, Carroll's three regiments hurried through the cemetery and passed through a battery on the west side of the Baltimore Pike. There Carroll learned that Ricketts' battery was under attack, perhaps captured, so when he reached the pike near the cemetery's gatehouse he formed his brigade for battle. There was only room among all the guns, caissons, artillery horses, etc., for one regiment to form a line, so he placed his three regiments one behind the other, probably with the 14th Indiana in the lead, and charged straight through Ricketts' battery and down the east slope of the hill to the wall along Brickyard Lane, driving Avery's North Carolinians before him. From the wall, the Federals fired two or three volleys into the darkness beyond, but the Rebels had disappeared. Carroll then turned his 7th West Virginia to the left, and it cleared the east face of the hill of Confederates. Hoke's

Brigade, now commanded by Colonel Archibald Godwin of the 57th North Carolina, also returned to Winebrenner's Run. A captain in that brigade termed Hays's attack a "success that did not succeed."[25] Again, there had been a break-down in the Confederate plan.

Gordon had not advanced farther because Early had held him back, intending to send him forward, as he later wrote, "when the divisions on the right moved, but finding that they did not advance, it was not ordered forward, as it would have been a useless sacrifice, but was retained as a support for the other brigades to fall back upon. During the advance of my two brigades I had ascertained that Rodes was not advancing, and I rode to urge him forward. I found him getting his brigades into position so as to be ready to advance, but he informed me that there was no preparation to move on his right, and that General Lane, in command of Pender's division, on his immediate right, had sent him word that he had no orders to advance, which had delayed his own movement. He, however, expressed a readiness to go forward if I thought it proper, but by this time I had been informed that my two brigades were retiring, and I told him it was then too late. He did not advance, and the fighting for the day closed – Johnson's attack on the left having been ended by the darkness, leaving him possession of part of the enemy's works in the woods."[26]

Rodes' Division had five brigades, but three of them were strung along Middle Street in Gettysburg, one was up on Seminary Ridge, and one was up at the railroad cut. The houses of the town provided cover for the three brigades there, but the narrow streets were not suitable avenues for launching an attack on Cemetery Hill. Therefore, those three brigades had to be moved to the open fields southwest of the town and west of the hill. The problem seems to be that Rodes, who might have been ill, simply misjudged the time it would take to make this move. The three brigades from the town filed to their right and formed the first line of the division in the order Ramseur's, Iverson's, and Doles', right to left, while Daniel's and O'Neal's brigades came down to form a second, or supporting line. All five brigades were to govern their movements so as to maintain their positions relative to Ramseur's Brigade at the front right. Many of the men, including General Iverson, thought they were marching to their doom, to attack such a formidable position lined with stone walls and crowned with artillery, but, when Ramseur gave the order, the whole division stepped off, wheeling to its left, passed through the Confederate skirmishers, and pushed the Union skirmishers back toward the hill.

However, the line halted about 100 to 150 yards from the hill, and the troops laid down while Ramseur went forward cautiously to see what they were up against. He didn't like the looks of what he saw: batteries in position to hit the division from the front, the flank, and at angles; two lines of infantry behind stone walls. Perhaps most ominous was the relative quiet. He could hear Union officers shouting orders up on the hill, but the sound of battle had died away. Ramseur quickly consulted with Iverson and Doles, and they agreed that Rodes should be informed and that they should wait there for further orders. Rodes, meanwhile, had learned that Early's assault had been driven back, and it was obvious that Pender's Division, on his right, was not advancing, so he soon sent back orders for the division to fall back to a sunken road called Long Lane, which ran southwest from Gettysburg, paralleling, and about a quarter-mile from, the Emmitsburg Road. If his division had started from that position, instead of ending in it, the results of the attack, the battle, and the war, might well have been very different.

It was quite late at night by the time that all firing had ceased and quiet had returned to the hills south of Gettysburg. Then the lanterns of stretcher-bearers hauling away the countless wounded could be seen bobbing and weaving all over the field like giant fireflies. The pickets of both armies left them to their grisly work unmolested.

The fighting on Culp's Hill and on Cemetery Hill had not yet ended at 8 p.m. when General Meade sent another report to General Halleck at Washington: "The enemy attacked me about 4 p.m. this day, and, after one of the severest contests of the war, was repulsed at all points. We have suffered considerably in killed and wounded. Among the former are Brigadier-Generals Paul and Zook, and among the wounded, Generals Sickles, Barlow, Graham, and Warren, slightly. We have taken a large number of prisoners. I shall remain in my present position to-morrow, but am not prepared to say, until better advised of the condition of the army, whether my operations will be of an offensive or defensive character."[27]

Seeking that information about the condition of his army, he again called for his corps commanders to assemble at army headquarters. He also sent for Colonel George Henry Sharpe, the chief of his army's Bureau of Military Information – what today would be called Military Intelligence – whose primary function was to gather and interpret information about the enemy. Sharpe found Meade seated at a little table in the bedroom of the tiny house that served as his headquarters, with a plate of crackers and a half-pint of whiskey in front of him; General Slocum was stretched out on the bed, and Hancock was sitting on that same piece of furniture. The other generals had not yet arrived.

Meade referred to a note that had been sent to Dan Butterfield that afternoon over Sharpe's signature that indicated that even then prisoners had already been taken from nearly 100 Confederate regiments and from every brigade in Lee's army except those in Pickett's Division. Meade asked for confirmation of this note and for any further details he could provide, so Sharpe went off to consult subordinates and soon returned to modify this information only in that Lee still had some cavalry that hadn't been used and that "Pickett's Division has come up and is now in bivouac, and will be ready to go into action fresh tomorrow morning." Hancock raised a hand and said, "General, we have got them nicked!" No doubt he meant that if Lee had already thrown almost every unit he had at them, and had accomplished so little, there was not much more he could do to them. At this Slocum sat up but said nothing, and a brief silence fell while all four men eyed the crackers and whiskey on the table. (Meade had not had a meal since two days before, and the others were probably not much better off.) Finally Hancock broke the silence, saying, "General Meade, don't you think Sharpe deserves a cracker and a drink?"[28]

By 9 p.m. the corps commanders had arrived – one might say "other corps commanders," but probably Hancock and Slocum both still considered themselves wing commanders at that time. Anyway, the commanders of the seven corps, including Gibbon for the 2nd and Williams for the 12th, attended, as well as Meade, Butterfield, and Warren, although the latter slept through the whole conference. All of these men were crammed into the little room with its bed, table, and five or six straight-backed chairs. By then the whiskey and crackers were gone, replaced by a pail of water and a tin cup. They talked informally for a while on the question of what to do next; there was some concern about supplies, since there were only enough rations on hand for one more day unless they went to half rations or some such, and also some concern that Lee might still interpose his army between them and their base at Westminster.

Butterfield jotted down a few notes about what they said. Slocum wanted to stay and fight it out; Newton, the newly appointed commander of the 1st Corps, thought it was a bad position; Hancock didn't seem to think it was practical to withdraw toward their supply base and wanted to mass their forces and attack; Howard, the last to arrive, was against retiring; Birney didn't know what was best, but his 3rd Corps was not in condition to fight again; Sedgwick was in doubt. Then each corps commander estimated the fighting strength of his corps, which added up to 58,000 men (which figure was probably too high). Meade said little, just took in the information and opinions.

Eventually Butterfield, as chief of staff, decided to turn

the conference into a formal council of war and posed three questions for the corps and wing commanders to answer:

"1. Under existing circumstances, is it advisable for this army to remain in its present position, or to retire to another nearer its base of supplies?

2. It being determined to remain in present position, shall the army attack or wait the attack of the enemy?

3. If we wait attack, how long?"

As was customary in councils of war, the generals replied in reverse order of seniority; that is, the most junior spoke first, on the theory that if he heard a more senior officer's view before speaking he might fear to contradict it. Gibbon, only a one-star general, was the junior corps commander and voted, according to Butterfield's notes: "1. Correct position of the army, but would not retreat. 2. In no condition to attack, in his opinion. 3. Until he moves; until enemy moves." Williams, also only a brigadier general, was next. He said, "1. Stay. 2. Wait attack. 3. One day." Birney and Sykes, both fairly new to corps command, just agreed with what Williams had said. Newton, also new, said, "1. Correct position of the army, but would not retreat. 2. By all means not attack. 3. If we wait, we will give them a chance to cut our line [of supply]." Howard, aggressive despite the beating his corps had received, said, "1. Remain. 2. Wait attack until 4 p.m. to-morrow. 3. If don't attack, attack them." Hancock, always wanting to be active, said, "1. Rectify position without moving so as to give up field. 2. Not attack unless our communications are cut. 3. Can't wait long; can't be idle." Sedgwick said only, "Remain, and wait attack at least one day." And, finally, Slocum said, "Stay and fight it out."[29] According to Gibbon, Meade then added in a quiet but decided tone, "Such then is the decision."[30]

Newton later expounded upon his fear that Lee would cut their supply line. He wrote that he remembered "taking the ground that Lee was not fool enough to attack us in front after two days's fighting which had ended in consolidating us into a position immensely strong."[31] According to Dan

Butterfield, Newton told Meade, "I think you ought to feel much gratified with today's results." To which Meade supposedly replied, "In the name of common sense, Newton, why?" And Newton explained, with a smile, "Why, they have hammered us into a solid position they cannot whip us out of."[32] Gibbon later wrote that, "Meade said to me, 'If Lee attacks tomorrow, it will be in your front.' I asked him why he thought so and he replied, 'Because he has made attacks on both our flanks and failed and if he concludes to try it again, it will be on our centre.' I expressed a hope that he would and told Gen. Meade with confidence that if he did, we would defeat him."[33]

The meeting broke up around 11 p.m. General Williams returned to his command about midnight, and was astonished to learn that Geary had been ordered away during his absence and that Confederates had occupied part of Culp's Hill. He reported the state of affairs to Slocum, whose only reply was, "Well, drive them out at daylight."[34]

That night, General Longstreet did not follow his usual custom of visiting Lee's headquarters after a day's fight. Despite his later pride in how well his troops had fought, he had not changed his mind about the desirability of moving around the Union flank instead of assaulting Meade's lines, although his focus changed from a strategic turning movement to a grand tactical flanking move. During the night he sent scouts to circle around Round Top, to look into the possibility of cutting the Taneytown Road and turning Meade's new left flank. He proposed, as he later explained it to McLaws, to "move Ewell's corps around my rear and right so as to command this other road, and that we then place our Army in a strong position for the day and await the enemy's attack."[35] It was the very sort of thing that Meade's generals, then in conference, most feared. But it was not to be.

Major Henry Kyd Douglas of Johnson's staff, later wrote of that night, "I had occasion to go to Headquarters of

Generals Lee and Ewell, and I was not encouraged by any appearance of cheerfulness at either place. General Lee was not in good humor over the miscarriage of his plans and his orders."[36] And yet Lee was not so discouraged as to give up. He had witnessed Longstreet's attack from a distance and had received a few verbal reports on how things had gone, but he was probably not aware of the damage his own forces had sustained. Longstreet's two divisions had captured the high ground along the Emmitsburg Road, where Lee could now place artillery, and had obviously done great damage to the Union forces there; and Johnson's Division of Ewell's corps had captured part of the hill on the Federal right, Lee's left. As he later put it in an official report, "The result of this day's operations induced the belief that, with proper concert of action, and with the increased support that the positions gained on the right would enable the artillery to render the assaulting columns, we should ultimately succeed, and it was accordingly determined to continue the attack. The general plan was unchanged."[37]

By "unchanged" he undoubtedly meant that he still intended to take Cemetery Hill, which he saw as the key to the Union position, and hoped that next time, unlike this time, to achieve "proper concert of action" between his various corps and divisions. Lee's orders to renew the attack next morning, probably verbal only, reached Longstreet at about 10 p.m., but evidently did not specify an objective or an axis of advance. And Ewell was sent orders to assault the Union right at daylight in conjunction with Longstreet's attack. The Union right meant, of course, Culp's Hill, or so much of it as was still in Federal hands. Therefore, during the night, Ewell reinforced Johnson with O'Neal's and Daniel's brigades of Rodes' Division and Smith's Brigade of Early's Division.

As Colonel Sharpe had reported to General Meade, Pickett's Division had reached the vicinity of the battlefield that afternoon, after marching all day from Chambersburg. Sharpe thought it contained four brigades, but in fact it had only three, having left one back in Virginia, retained by the authorities at Richmond because of Union forces making threatening moves near that capital. Pickett had sent a staff officer to report his arrival to Lee while he had ridden ahead to confer with Longstreet. He had watched some of the fighting in company with his corps commander, who told him to put his division into bivouac until needed. This was soon confirmed by the staff officer's return with a message from Lee: "Tell General Pickett I shall not want him this evening, to let his men rest, and I will send for him when I want him."[38]

A group of Union artillerymen from the 1st Corps was sent southward from Cemetery Hill that night to find the reserve ammunition train. They went down the Taneytown Road until they came to the camp of the 6th Corps, then cut across to the Baltimore Pike and, turning up that, found the ammunition wagons parked in a field. Their route took them past the rear of the 2nd, 3rd and 5th corps, and one member of this group later wrote: "As we passed slowly along the road we could see on every side in the fields in and around such farm buildings as had escaped the flames, and fairly lining both sides of the road, innumerable groups of wounded in all stages of misery; groaning, crying, swearing, begging for water or whiskey, or for food; entreating the surgeons and attendants to come to them; some in delirium, calling for their friends at home; some even begging someone to shoot them, to escape from their present pangs; and the whole scene fitfully lighted up by the flaring lanterns of the hospital forces, or the flickering fires of rails and boards here and there; the field toward the front full of flitting lights from the lanterns of the stretcher parties busy bringing fresh additions to the wretched mass. Meantime the surgeons were at work best they could, in the darkness and confusion, dressing wounds, administering stimulants, and all that sort of thing. In the course of this mile or so of road there must have been . . . not less than 8,000 wounded men, of whom, no doubt, 1,000 died during the night."[39]

In that war, armies still included numerous marching bands; almost every regiment started out with one, and many still had them. That night the Union army's bands were instructed to place themselves between the hospitals and the front lines. "They played by detachments all night," a Federal officer wrote, "to drown out the cries of the wounded and those who were being operated upon."[40]

∼ Endnotes ∼

1 Edward Porter Alexander, *Military Memoirs of a Confederate* (New York, 1907), 376-7. Both quotes.
2 Edward G. Longacre, *The Cavalry at Gettysburg* (Lincoln NB, 1986), 202.
3 H. B. McClellan, *I Rode with Jeb Stuart* (Bloomington IN, 1958), 336-7.
4 Nathan Bedford Forrest and Turner Ashby were two other examples of men whose original claim to command had been primarily their financial ability to raise and equip a unit, although Ashby's had been only a company. All three became excellent cavalry commanders.
5 Both Custer and Kilpatrick graduated from West Point in 1861, but in separate classes. At that time the academy had briefly been on a 5-year curriculum, and Custer's class had been graduated a year early because of the sudden expansion of the Army at the start of the war. Custer had stood at the very bottom of his class.
6 Longacre, *The Cavalry at Gettysburg*, 200.
7 Gregory J. W. Urwin, *Custer Victorious* (East Brunswick NJ, 1983), 70.
8 OR I:27:II:518.
9 Eric Wittenberg, *Protecting the Flank* (Celina OH, 2002), 28.
10 Longacre, *The Cavalry at Gettysburg*, 211.
11 Bowden and Ward, *Last Chance for Victory*, 346.
12 Wheeler, *Witness to Gettysburg*, 183.
13 Ibid., 221.
14 Pfanz, *Gettysburg – Culp's Hill and Cemetery Hill*, 180.
15 Ibid; both quotes.
16 OR, I:27:I:836.
17 Pfanz, *Gettysburg – Culp's Hill and Cemetery Hill*, 216.
18 Wheeler, *Witness to Gettysburg*, 215.
19 Pfanz, *Gettysburg – Culp's Hill and Cemetery Hill*, 214.
20 Douglas, *I Rode With Stonewall*, 240.
21 Pfanz, *Gettysburg – Culp's Hill and Cemetery Hill*, 247.
22 Ibid., 249.
23 Ibid., 262.
24 Ibid., 259.
25 Ibid., 272.
26 Early, *Autobiographical Sketch*, 274-5.
27 OR, I:27:I:72.
28 Edwin C. Fishel, *The Secret War for the Union* (Boston and New York, 1996), 528.
29 OR, I:27:I:73.
30 Coddington, *The Gettysburg Campaign*, 451.
31 Sears, *Gettysburg*, 343.
32 Pfanz, *Gettysburg – The Second Day*, 438.
33 Sears, *Gettysburg*, 345.

34 Pfanz, *Gettysburg – Culp's Hill and Cemetery Hill*, 234.
35 Sears, *Gettysburg*, 347.
36 Douglas, *I Rode With Stonewall*, 240.
37 *OR*, I:27:II:320.
38 Sears, *Gettysburg*, 349.
39 Wheeler, *Witness to Gettysburg*, 225.
40 Jeffry D. Wert, *Gettysburg, Day Three* (New York, 2001), 33.

CHAPTER 11
"We Must Sacrifice Our Pride"
2–3 July 1863

News of the great battle then underway at Gettysburg had been filtering into Washington slowly and sparsely. President Lincoln, as usual when a battle was pending or in progress, spent long hours in the telegraph office of the War Department, which was near the White House, but direct telegraphic connection between the city and Gettysburg was still broken since Stuart's Confederate cavalry had cut it at numerous places. Lincoln went not only in search of news from the Army but to get away from the endless stream of visitors at the White House, almost all of whom wanted some favor from the President. He would sit at a large desk opposite the telegrapher, reading the messages as they came in and re-reading the important ones. When there were no messages waiting or coming in, he would sit at a table by the window and watch the traffic on Pennsylvania Avenue.

The news coming into this room along the telegraph wires had often been bad: First Bull Run, General George McClellan's seven days' fighting retreat from before Richmond, Second Bull Run, the indecisive bloodbath of Antietam, General Ambrose Burnside's futile frontal assault at Fredericksburg, and, perhaps worst of all, Hooker's recent retreat after indecisive fighting around Chancellorsville, ending a campaign that had begun with great promise. No matter which general Lincoln appointed, they always seemed to fail when pitted against Robert E. Lee.

Defeats and casualty lists and numerous lesser or more personal problems had worn Lincoln down in the 28 months since he had taken office. One of his sons had died of disease during that time, and on this very second day of July, 1863, his wife, Mary, was injured in a fall from her carriage as she returned to the White House from the cottage on the grounds of the Soldiers' Home, north of Washington, where the Lincolns often stayed during the hot, humid summers. Apparently the carriage had been sabotaged in an attempt to kill or injure the President. Lincoln had lost weight; his face was sallow; there were dark circles around his eyes; he always looked, and always felt, exhausted. Then had come Lee's invasion of Pennsylvania. It had caused an uproar throughout the northeast, but Lincoln looked upon it as a great opportunity for the Army of the Potomac to get at Lee and defeat him; and if he should be defeated up in Pennsylvania, how could he ever get home safely to Virginia?

Not all news was bad, of course, but what good news there had been over the past two years had mostly come from what was then still considered the West: that vast area beyond the Appalachian mountain chain. Most heartening had been a series of moves and battles that had cleared the Confederates out of most of the valley of the Mississippi River. General Halleck, then in command in the West, had received much of the credit for this, which had led to his elevation to his current position as general-in-chief the year before. Much of the real credit, however, belonged to one of Halleck's subordinates, Major General Ulysses S. Grant, who had outflanked Rebel positions on the Mississippi by opening the Tennessee and Cumberland rivers to Union gunboats and transports when he captured forts Henry and Donelson, as well as about 13,000 Rebel soldiers at the latter.

Outflanked by this Union move up the Tennessee River, the Confederate hold on the Mississippi River had soon been reduced to a relatively short stretch between Vicksburg, Mississippi, on the north, and Port Hudson, Louisiana, on the south. Both towns rested on high bluffs, from which heavy artillery could interdict all traffic on the river, and both were surrounded by earthworks on the land side to protect their garrisons, who in turn protected the big guns. Even getting at the Rebel defenses in order to attack them was not easy. In late 1862 when Halleck had been promoted, Grant had been left in command of sizable Union forces in West Tennessee (known as the Army of the Tennessee, after the river, not the state), and he had tried a two-pronged advance against Vicksburg, marching a sizable force overland through northern Mississippi, while sending his favorite subordinate, Major General William Tecumseh Sherman, down the river with four divisions on transports. This attempt had been spoiled by a pair of Confederate cavalry raids that had cut Grant's supply line and captured his forward supply base, forcing the northern prong to retreat, which, in turn, allowed the Rebels to send reinforcements to meet Sherman and turn him back as well.

After that, all through the long and wet winter of 1862-63, when the Mississippi and its tributaries had been over their banks, Grant had tried numerous schemes for getting at Vicksburg via water, but none of them had worked out. These failures had damaged Grant's reputation, which was already suffering. Although Grant had been the Union's first great hero of the war because of Fort Donelson, his popularity had dropped considerably a few months later when the Rebels had been able to surprise his camp and run up the war's first huge casualty list for both sides at the battle of Shiloh. Grant had withstood the attack and counterattacked the second day to drive the Confederates away, but many people in the North still distrusted him. There were rumors that he drank to excess, and his standing in Washington had not been helped by his failure to send frequent reports of what he was up to. However, Lincoln, who had never met him, appreciated his combative spirit – a seeming rarity among his senior generals – and was unwilling to replace him.

Back in March, Secretary of War Edwin Stanton had sent out Charles A. Dana as a civilian representative of the War Department to keep an eye on Grant. Dana had been welcomed at Grant's headquarters, partly because his own frequent reports to Stanton relieved Grant from having to send many reports himself, but mainly because Grant had nothing to hide. Dana arrived just in time to witness Grant's brilliant movement to get at Vicksburg by marching his troops down the west side of the Mississippi, running ironclad gunboats and unarmored transports past the Rebels batteries at night, and then ferrying his troops over the river south of Vicksburg. It was a complete surprise to the Confederates, who were busy at the time trying to deal with a raid by some of Grant's cavalry, who eventually rode the length of Mississippi, from West Tennessee to Baton Rouge, Louisiana, causing havoc and panic all along the way. Placed thus on the same side of the river with the Rebels and between Vicksburg and Port Hudson, Grant had the option to go against either or both.

He had originally planned to attack Port Hudson first, for he could receive assistance for that from Major General Nathaniel Banks, who commanded the Union's Department of the Gulf and the 19th Army Corps. Banks was based on New Orleans, the largest city in the South, which had been captured the year before by Admiral David Farragut of the U.S. Navy. However, coordination between Grant and Banks had been extremely difficult, what with being separated by all the Confederates around Vicksburg and Port Hudson. Banks, lacking wagons for an overland move, had taken a roundabout route up the Atchafalaya River to the Red River, driving Rebels up the latter as far as Alexandria, before turning down it, crossing the Mississippi, and approaching Port Hudson from the north with his main force and linking up with a division coming up the Mississippi from the south. The Rebels had, meanwhile, sent off much of the Port Hudson garrison to defend against Grant, and Banks had been able to surround and besiege what was left.

Grant, however, had decided not to wait for Banks. Never content to sit idle, he had struck for neither Vicksburg nor Port Hudson but had cut loose from his supply line and moved inland following the south/east bank of the Big Black River, keeping it between him and the Rebels at Vicksburg. He had captured the capital of Mississippi, Jackson, not so much for its political importance but because it was a key railroad junction, and any Confederate reinforcements would have to come through there. In fact, the first of several reinforcements had already arrived, and Grant's attack had driven them off to the north, along with General Joseph E. Johnston, commander of all Confederate forces between the Appalachians and the Mississippi, who had just arrived from Tennessee.

Only then, having cleared his rear of threats and destroyed the railroads leading east and south out of Jackson, did Grant turn west, back toward the Mississippi. He soon met and defeated Lieutenant General John Pemberton, commander of the Confederate Department of Mississippi and East Louisiana, who, in accordance with an order from General Johnston, had been moving east from Vicksburg to link up with the latter and the recently arrived, and still arriving, reinforcements. Pemberton had fallen back to the Big Black River, where Grant had defeated him again, and had then retreated into the defenses of Vicksburg. He was determined to hold that place, but his retreat allowed Grant to take in reverse the bluffs along the Yazoo River that had defied Sherman back in December and thus open for himself a riverine supply line to the North.

After two unsuccessful attempts to take Vicksburg by assault, Grant and his army had resigned themselves to taking it by siege. The garrison of around 30,000 Confederates had a fair supply of food and ammunition on hand, so it had been able to hold out for weeks, although by now it was on very short rations. Meanwhile, the Federals, despite a shortage of military engineers, had built their own earthworks to defend their camps and had dug approach trenches that had brought them, in some places, extremely close to the Rebel lines. On two occasions they had dug mines from their lines underneath a Confederate fort, placed gunpowder under it, and blown it up. But they had not been able to break into the defenses through the resulting holes.

While Grant had been thus employed, more Confederate reinforcements had arrived from Tennessee and South Carolina, joining the forces of Joseph E. Johnston, who hoped to be able to attack Grant's rear and drive him away or at least allow the garrison of Vicksburg to escape. But Grant had also received large reinforcements, both from his own garrisons in West Tennessee and from other Union departments in Missouri and Kentucky, and Grant had put Sherman in command of sizable forces that guarded his army's back, so that Johnston never felt he had a large enough force to justify an attack.

On this second day of July Johnston's forces were making reconnaissances to discover whether it was possible to attack Grant in the area north of where the railroad from Jackson crossed the Big Black River, between that stream and the Mississippi, but this was the very area where Sherman was establishing a formidable defensive line. Johnston had three of his four infantry divisions concentrated just east of the Big Black, while the fourth, commanded by Major General John Breckinridge, former vice-president of the United States, was stationed at Bolton, about halfway between the Big Black and Jackson. "This expedition was not undertaken," Johnston wrote long afterwards, "in the wild spirit that dictated the dispatches from the War Department of the 16th and 21st of June. I did not indulge in 'the sentiment' that it was better for me to waste the lives and blood of brave soldiers, 'than through prudence even,' to spare them; and therefore intended to make such close and careful examination of the enemy's lines as might enable me to estimate the probability of our being able to break them, and rescuing the army invested in Vicksburg. There was no hope of saving the place by raising the siege."[1]

Although Grant was sure that Vicksburg must surrender eventually or starve, he was growing anxious to get it over with. He wanted to deal with Johnston, but could not do so as long as he was tied up with besieging the town. He had consulted his senior officers on the last day of June, "to take judgment," as Charles Dana later put it, "on the question of trying another general assault, or leaving the result to the exhaustion of the garrison. The conclusion of the council was in favor of the latter policy, but two days later, July 2d, Grant told me that if the enemy did not give up Vicksburg by the 6th he should storm it."[2]

Dana wrote one of his frequent reports to Secretary of War Stanton that day, to be carried up the river by steamer (it would reach Memphis on the 5th, and Washington, finally, on the morning of the 8th). He began by noting, "We have no positive information concerning Joe Johnston." Then he mentioned some efforts by Union scouts to determine what that Confederate was up to, told of a force of some 200 Rebel cavalry that had crossed over to the west (Union) side of the Big Black River (a brigade of infantry was being sent to handle them), and briefly mentioned two instances of each side undermining and exploding each other's earthworks. "Orders have been given," he said, "to abandon all attempts to push forward saps [approach trenches] with a view of entering the enemy's works by that means, and to devote the labor of working parties to widening the covered ways and carrying them as near the rebel lines as practicable, in order to afford cover for storming columns. The reports of [Confederate] deserters generally agree that the town is to be surrendered on the 4th instant. They also say that mule meat is issued to the garrison, though some report that flour and bacon are both plenty. If enemy do not give up Vicksburg before 6th instant, it will be stormed on that day." He also noted that there was a force of some 7,000 Rebels on the west bank of the Mississippi, where the Federals had leased captured plantations to former slaves, "destroying plantations, burning all the buildings, and carrying off some negroes. The weather is hot; thermometer at noon above 100 degrees."[3]

More than the weather made life miserable for the Union troops. A private in the brigade that was sent out to check the Rebel cavalry that had crossed the Big Black noted: "The march was a forced one, the day was hot and sultry, the roads dusty, water scarce, the men unused to marching for nearly two months. . . . The suffering of the troops was intense." But much the same was true when they remained in their entrenchments. "As every elevation and open space was completely covered by the enemy's sharpshooters and swept by his artillery, the men were necessarily confined in close quarters, and this, with its attendant absence of sanitary provisions, together with the meagerness of the diet, the constant excitement, the intense heat and unwholesomeness of a Mississippi June, so undergone, told with sad and terrible effect upon the health of the troops. The hospitals were crowded with the victims of disease, and every day the burial parties performed their sad duties at the graves of newly departed comrades."[4]

But as bad as things were for the Federal soldiers outside Vicksburg, they were even worse for the Confederates in its defenses and for the civilians living in the town. Many of the latter had dug caves in the numerous hillsides and lived in them for defense against the artillery shells that rained down on the defenses and on the town itself. Both soldiers and civilians were living on scant rations; mules, rats, and pets providing what little meat was available; fruits and vegetables were long gone; bread made from a meal of green peas was the staple. Medicines and ammunition were also in short supply. An officer's wife wrote of seeing one soldier killed and another horribly wounded when a supposedly dud Union shell exploded while they were trying to get the gunpowder out of it.

At least one couple inside the city, Dora and Anderson Miller, were Union sympathizers. Dora was born in the West Indies and had been on an extended visit there shortly before the war began. "Surely no native-born woman loves her country better than I love America," she told her diary. "The blood of one of its revolutionary patriots flows in my veins, and it is the Union for which he pledged his 'life, fortune, and sacred honor' that I love, not any divided or special section of it."[5] On this second day of July the couple finally obtained a pass to leave the city and secured a boat with which to cross the Mississippi River. However, the boat leaked and began to sink, so they had to turn back, but just then a Rebel battery opened fire on them. It missed them, however, and, when they returned to the Confederate side the battery's commander apologized, saying he didn't know that they had a pass. Now there was nothing for them to do but return to huddling in their cellar, "shells flying as thick as ever," she wrote. "Provisions so nearly gone . . . that a few more days will bring us to starvation indeed. Martha says rats are hanging dressed in the market for sale with mule meat, – there is nothing else."[6]

On 1 July General Pemberton had addressed a letter to his division commanders, saying, "Unless the siege of Vicksburg is raised or supplies are thrown in, it will become necessary very shortly to evacuate the place. I see no prospect of the former, and there are many great, if not insuperable, obstacles in the way of the latter." Chief obstacle was, of course, Grant's army. Pemberton's men would have to cut their way out, but he was well aware that the short rations and close confinement of the siege had reduced his men's strength and stamina, so he had asked his division commanders to "inform me with as little delay as possible as to the condition of your troops, and their ability to make the marches and undergo the fatigues necessary to accomplish a successful evacuation."[7] Now, on 2 July, Pemberton received the written replies of his division commanders, some with the opinions of their brigade commanders appended. "So far as I know," Pemberton later reported, "not a solitary brigade or regimental commander favored the scheme of cutting out, and only two, whose views were presented to me, intimated the possibility of making more than one-half of their commands available for that purpose."[8]

His generals assembled that night to present their reports, and after reading them he informed them that they all indicated that most of the troops were too weak or too ill to fight, leaving them, at most, about 11,000 able men. He added that he had abandoned all hope of relief from General Johnston. As he saw it, they had only two choices, to make a forlorn attempt to cut their way out anyway, or to surrender while they still had ammunition enough to demand terms. He asked them to vote on these two propositions. Out of a dozen officers, all but two voted to surrender, and those two could offer no reasonable alternative. "I have heard your vote," Pemberton told them, "and I agree with your almost unanimous decision, though my own preference would be to put myself at the head of my troops and make a desperate effort to cut our way through the enemy. That is my only hope of saving myself from shame and disgrace. Far better would it be for me to die at the head of my army . . . than to surrender it and live and meet the obloquy which I know will be heaped upon me. But my duty is to sacrifice myself to save the army, which has so nobly done its duty to defend Vicksburg."[9]

Pemberton was a Northerner in a Southern army. He had grown up in Philadelphia and counted George Meade among his boyhood friends, but he had married a Southern girl, and when the war came he had thrown in his lot with the Confederacy. He knew that many of his officers and men already distrusted him as a "Yankee;" if he surrendered them he would be even more harshly condemned than if a "real" Southerner had done so.

He told his officers that he would write to General Grant and propose to surrender to him on Saturday, 4 July. Some of them objected to surrendering on the Union's national holiday, but Pemberton later claimed to have told them, "I am a Northern man. I know my people; I know their peculiar weaknesses and their national vanity; I know we can get better terms from them on the 4th of July than on any other day of the year. We must sacrifice our pride to these considerations."[10] General Grant later doubted that this was Pemberton's reasoning. "I have no doubt," he wrote in his memoirs, "that Pemberton commenced his correspondence on the third with a two-fold purpose: first, to avoid an assault, which he knew would be successful, and second, to prevent the capture taking place on the great national holiday, the anniversary of the Declaration of American Independence. Holding out for better terms as he did he defeated his aim in the latter particular."[11]

In far-off Richmond, Confederate President Jefferson Davis was writing on that second day of July to Lieutenant General E. Kirby Smith, who commanded all Confederate forces west of the Mississippi River: "I am convinced that the safety of Vicksburg depends on your prompt and efficient co-operation. As far as practicable, I desire you to move your forces to the Mississippi River, and command in person operations for the relief of the besieged city."[12] However, Kirby Smith was already doing about all that he could hope to do to help the defenders of both Vicksburg and Port Hudson. When the former had first seemed to be in real danger from Grant he had sent about 7,000 men under his best subordinate, Major General Richard Taylor (son of the late U.S. President Zachary Taylor) to try to interrupt Grant's supply line, which then had run down the west side of the Mississippi, but by the time they had arrived Grant had established a new supply base on the Yazoo north of Vicksburg and had abandoned his tenuous line down the west bank.

After an unsuccessful attack on Union garrisons on the west bank across from the town, Taylor had gone farther south to take charge of efforts to help relieve Port Hudson by threatening New Orleans, whose garrison had been stripped to strengthen Banks' army, and by placing batteries to interdict traffic on the river between Banks and New Orleans to cut off his supplies. Another force from Kirby Smith's department, under the overall command of Lieutenant General Theophilus Holmes, had been struggling over muddy roads and swollen streams for days trying to get into position to attack the Union garrison at Helena, Arkansas, on the west bank of the Mississippi, part of Grant's department. If they could take that town, artillery could be positioned along the river to interdict Grant's supplies coming down from Memphis.

The monotony of the siege of Port Hudson was broken on that second day of July when Confederate cavalry attacked the Union supply base at Springfield Landing, just south of the beleaguered city. At about 8:30 a.m. some 200 Rebels, divided into three groups, scattered Federal pickets stationed on the Springfield road and, at the landing, routed about 30 members of a brigade of United States Colored Troops – former slaves recruited into the Union army. Armed with matches and bottles of turpentine, the Rebels soon had the vast stores of quartermaster supplies in flames. One of their three groups then attacked the administration buildings, but the Federals inside escaped onto the armed steamer *Suffolk*, which put out into the river and began shelling the raiders. The second group of Confederates attacked a collection of huts for runaway slaves, stampeding their occupants, while the third group attacked the post commissary. The 162nd New York soon arrived and drove the Rebels off in some confusion, but as they retreated by way of a different road than they had come in on they captured more Union pickets from the rear. In addition to the damage done to the quartermaster and commissary supplies, about 100 wagons were destroyed.

Far to the west on that second day of July a small battle took place along Cabin Creek in Indian Territory, which is now the state of Oklahoma. The day before that, a Union wagon train carrying supplies from Kansas to Fort Gibson, where Union-supporting Creeks and Seminoles were virtually under siege, had found the stream, a tributary of the upper Arkansas River, too swollen for the wagons to cross and some 1,600 Confederate Cherokees, Creeks, and Texans under Colonel Stand Watie defending the south bank. During the night the commander of the Union forces escorting the wagons, Colonel J. M. Williams of the 1st Kansas Colored Volunteers, had made his plans, sent companies of Indian Home Guards up and down the stream to protect his flanks and his wagons, placed a pair of 6-pounder guns on his left flank, a 12-pounder howitzer on his right flank, and another 12-pounder howitzer and a little mountain howitzer in the center. At 8 a.m. his artillery opened fire and kept it up for

40 minutes, after which, seeing no enemy on the south side, his own regiment, followed by a battalion of the 2nd Colorado and three companies of cavalry, advanced into the now-fordable creek, led by a company of Indian Home Guards (fewer than 900 men in all).

As the Home Guards neared the south bank the Rebels rose from concealed positions in thick brush and behind fallen logs and opened fire. The major commanding the Home Guards was hit by two musket balls and his horse by five more, and when he fell his company retreated. However, Colonel Williams then deployed three companies of infantry to return the Confederate fire, along with his artillery, and brought up a company of Kansas cavalry to lead the column, which advanced through the armpit-deep water and pushed the Rebels back to the edge of the prairie, where they formed line of battle, waiting for another brigade of Confederates that was supposed to join them in capturing the wagon train. Williams placed two companies of cavalry on his right to keep from being flanked and sent a single mounted company "to charge the advance line of the enemy, penetrate it, and, if possible, ascertain his strength and position, which was gallantly executed by the lieutenant, who charged directly upon the center of the enemy's line, broke it, and put him to flight. Seeing this, I ordered forward all the cavalry in pursuit of the now fleeing enemy, who were pursued for 5 miles, killing many and dispersing them in all directions."[13]

Between the struggle for control of the Mississippi River and Lee's invasion of Pennsylvania there was one other important theater of war, roughly encompassing most of Kentucky and Tennessee. There had been no large battle there since early January, when Major General William S. Rosecrans' Union Army of the Cumberland had defeated Confederate General Braxton Bragg's Army of Tennessee along Stones River, near the town of Murfreesborough, southeast of Nashville. Bragg had then retreated a few miles farther to the southeast, along the railroad leading to Chattanooga, and Rosecrans had ensconced himself and his army around Murfreesborough, finding one reason after another for not advancing, until finally, goaded by Lincoln, Stanton, and Halleck, he had begun on the 23rd of June a brilliant movement that maneuvered Bragg out of his entrenchments and back across the Elk River. Only swollen streams and deep mud had prevented Rosecrans from getting around behind Bragg and forcing a battle, but Rosecrans had occupied Bragg's base at Tullahoma, Tennessee, on 1 July while Bragg had fallen back toward Chattanooga.

On 2 July Rosecrans wrote to General Halleck from Tullahoma: "Telegraph lines reached here a few moments since. After seven days' movements, in unexampled rains, we have dislodged the enemy from his strongly intrenched positions at Shelbyville and this place, which we occupied yesterday at 11.30 a.m. Our columns pushed on in pursuit of Bragg's retreating army, and our advance overtook their rear guard near Elk River, but too late to save the bridges. The river, swollen to unwonted height, is falling rapidly, while our columns are seeking, and will probably find, crossings, which will enable them to strike their retreating columns, already forced from the Pelham route across the mountains to the interior and more distant one by Decherd."[14]

Before this campaign had begun, Bragg had been about to send part of his cavalry on a raid into Kentucky. Raiding into his native state was the favorite pastime of Brigadier General John Hunt Morgan, commander of the small cavalry division that would make the raid. But just after he had started out he had been ordered back to chase down Union cavalry from Kentucky that was raiding into East Tennessee. Morgan never even caught sight of the Federal raiders, but when they returned to Kentucky he resumed his preparations for his raid. He had told Bragg, by way of his immediate superior, Major General Joe Wheeler, commander of Bragg's Cavalry Corps, that his objective was the huge Union supply base at Louisville, Kentucky, but in reality he had his eye on greater glory: he intended to cross the broad Ohio River into the Union states of the old Northwest Ordinance and perhaps ride all the way to Pennsylvania to join up with Lee's army.

The Federals had known Morgan was about to raid into Kentucky again since before he had turned back to chase the Union raiders. Most of Kentucky was part of the Department of the Ohio, commanded by Major General Ambrose Burnside, who had been sent there, along with the 9th Corps, which he had commanded before his brief stint as commander of the Army of the Potomac, for the purpose of at last liberating East Tennessee, where pro-Union, or at least anti-Confederate, sentiment was very strong. However, just before he had been about to begin his campaign his beloved 9th Corps had been taken from him and sent to reinforce Grant at Vicksburg. He still had the 23rd Corps, but its divisions and brigades were somewhat scattered, garrisoning various places, and had never fought together as a single unit. Burnside had warned his various subordinates that Morgan was coming and to be ready to go after him when he did.

The subordinate most likely to have first shot at Morgan was Brigadier General Henry M. Judah, commander of the 3rd Division of the 23rd Corps. Judah was a 42-year-old Marylander who had graduated from West Point in the same class (1843) as Grant, but near the bottom of the class standings (Grant was near the middle). So far in this war he had mostly held staff positions, and he had been in command of his division for less than a month when Burnside's warning reached him. He had advanced his 1st Brigade and his own headquarters from Glasgow, Kentucky, to Tompkinsville, very near the Tennessee state line and just west of the Cumberland River. Then he brought his 2nd Brigade, commanded by Brigadier General Edward H. Hobson, down to the little town of Marrowbone, near the river and northeast of Tompkinsville. The 1st Brigade of the 2nd Division of the 23rd Corps, commanded by Brigadier General J. M. Shackelford, was sent to Glasgow, from which place it could reinforce either of Judah's brigades, if needed.

On the second day of July Morgan's Division of some 2,500 mounted men and four pieces of artillery crossed the upper Cumberland River at Burkesville, Kentucky, 35 miles upriver (northeast) from Tompkinsville and 12 miles east of Marrowbone. The river was very high, and Morgan's men had to make their own boats. That afternoon General Hobson with about 300 cavalry skirmished with Morgan's advance and wounded Captain Tom Quirk, Morgan's chief of scouts, but fell back to Marrowbone, leaving the road to central Kentucky wide open to the famous raider.

In Richmond that day, in addition to writing his brief message to General Kirby Smith, Confederate President Jefferson Davis, who was ill, wrote a long letter of instructions to his Vice President, Alexander Stephens, who was being sent by Davis as a military commissioner under a flag of truce to Washington, where he was to present President Lincoln a long letter from Davis dealing with various concerns and complaints having to do with the exchange of prisoners of war. It has long been presumed that another, unwritten, purpose for Stephens' mission was to have him on hand to negotiate with Lincoln if Lee should win a decisive victory in Pennsylvania. Davis gave Stephens two versions of the letter to Lincoln: one was addressed to him as commander-in-chief of the Army and Navy of the United States, and styled Davis as the commander-in-chief of the Army and Navy of the Confederate States. If the Federals refused to receive that version because it did not address Lincoln as President of the United States, Stephens was to present the other version, which did so but which also was signed by Davis as President of the Confederate States. "To this latter," Davis told Stephens, "objection may be made on the ground that I am not recognized to be President of the Confederacy. In this event you will decline any further attempt to confer on the subject of your mission, as such conference is admissible only on the footing of perfect equality."[15]

Richmond itself was under threat in late June and early July. Union forces, known as the Department of Virginia, held Norfolk and nearby areas south of the James River, plus Fort Monroe and Yorktown on the peninsula between the James and the York, and had recently advanced up the York and its tributary the Pamunkey and seized White House Plantation, property of Robert E. Lee's second son, W. H. F. Lee, better known as "Rooney," commander of one of Jeb Stuart's cavalry brigades. The younger Lee had been home at the time, recuperating from a wound, and had been captured. This sizable Union force on the Pamunkey was only some 25 miles from Richmond, for the defense of which forces had been brought up from North Carolina and one brigade of Pickett's Division of Longstreet's corps had been held back from joining Lee's army.

On the first day of July Major General John A. Dix, commander of the Department of Virginia, had sent out two expeditions from near White House. One, a reinforced division of the 7th Corps under Brigadier General George Getty, was to march up the north-east side of the Pamunkey and attack the important bridge that carried the Richmond, Fredericksburg & Potomac Railroad over the South Anna River, a tributary of the Pamunkey. The weather was intensely hot as Getty set off on his mission. Dix's other expedition was intended as a diversion to keep the Confederates' attention away from Getty. It consisted of three brigades of infantry commanded by Major General Erasmus Keyes, commander of the much-reduced 4th Corps. Keyes was supposed to advance toward Richmond and attack Bottom's Bridge on the Chickahominy River, but he proved to be far too cautious. As Dix later complained in his official report: "Bottom's Bridge is but 13 miles from the White House, and it was expected that General Keyes would take, on the evening of the 1st, a position which should command it, and prevent the enemy from crossing." Instead, "at daybreak on the 2nd he fell back to Baltimore Store, or Talley's, though no enemy had appeared, with the exception of some skirmishers on the 1st." On the afternoon of the 2nd, the Rebels advanced, with eight pieces of artillery and an infantry force, on Baltimore Cross-Roads, causing an advanced brigade of Keyes' force to fall back for fear of being outflanked. "The enemy's field pieces were brought within a mile of Baltimore Store," Dix reported, "to which General Keyes had retired, and fired from 100 to 150 shots during the night, without doing any injury whatever."[16]

The next day, 3 July, the Confederate commander, Major General D. H. Hill, a former division commander in Lee's army and current commander of Confederate forces in North Carolina and southern Virginia, reported to the Confederate Secretary of War, James A. Seddon: "The reconnaissance yesterday has satisfied my mind that the Yankees are not in force at the White House. They were steadily driven from the Cross-Roads till 10 o'clock last night, when they were found too strongly posted for a night attack. Our men had been at work all the night before in throwing down intrenchments, and the march of upward of 20 miles had worried them very much. My brigadiers were adverse to an attack this morning, as they thought the Yankees would cross the Pamunkey and be safe, unless they felt their position to be too strong to be taken. I therefore decided to return."[17]

Down in North Carolina that day, in the absence of Hill and many of his troops, a Federal cavalry raid started out from the Union-held town of New Berne, heading toward the important Wilmington & Weldon Railroad.

Another Union raid, mostly mounted, and commanded by Brigadier General Julius White, started out from Beaver Creek Station, in southeast Kentucky, that day, heading for southwest Virginia, where there were lead mines and salt works vital to the Confederate Army, as well as the Virginia & Tennessee Railroad, which was the shortest and best connection between Richmond and the West.

Morgan's Confederate raiders advanced farther into

Kentucky that day, although they had to confiscate several oxen to pull their artillery. Morgan's men drove detachments from three Union regiments before them and entered the town of Columbia. "Our men behaved badly at Columbia," Morgan's chief of staff, Lieutenant Colonel Robert Alston, told his diary, "breaking open a store and plundering it. I ordered the men to return the goods, and made all the reparation in my power. These outrages are very disgraceful, and are usually perpetrated by men accompanying the army simply for plunder. They are not worth a ----, and are a disgrace to both armies. Passed through Columbia, and camped six miles from Green River Bridge."[18]

General Judah, commanding the division nearest to Morgan, reported to his corps commander that day, "Unless I am enabled to withdraw my force, or a portion of it, from Tompkinsville (which, with the enemy's plans undeveloped, I dare not do), I can do [no] more with the enemy [than] hold this position."[19] For now, someone else would have to deal with Morgan.

At Port Hudson on 3 July work on a Federal approach trench that had been dug to within 30 yards of an important part of the Confederate earthworks known as Fort Desperate had to be abandoned because of the fire of Rebel sharpshooters from a high platform called a cavalier, which allowed them to shoot down into the Union trench. A bit farther south the Federals had dug a covered approach trench to within 10 yards or less of another Confederate work known as the Priest Cap. There it was the Federals who had built cavaliers, two of them, as well as batteries, to cover their working parties, and they had begun digging two mines under the Rebel work, where, when completed, they would place large amounts of gunpowder and blow up the fort. However, the Confederates were aware of this activity and had dug a countermine. Shortly after midnight on the third, they set off their own explosives, causing one of the Union galleries to collapse on the men working in it. These Federals soon dug their way out, however, and none were seriously injured. Work was then concentrated on the other mine. Later that day Union soldiers began constructing a large cavalier in front of the fort known as the Citadel, at the southern end of the Confederate line, while Federal artillery destroyed a Rebel work, known as a lunette, on a commanding ridge nearby. General Banks had been planning to make another assault on the Confederates defenses on 7 July, but because of the hot weather, which was slowing work, he rescheduled it for the ninth.

Up near Vicksburg on that third day of July, Major General J. G. Walker, commander of a Confederate division on the west side of the Mississippi, was writing to Kirby Smith, commander of the Trans-Mississippi Department: "In reference to your inquiry as to the practicability of throwing re-enforcements and provisions into Vicksburg, I am reluctantly compelled to state that, with the force at my disposal or within my reach, I consider it utterly impracticable. . . . To reach a point on the Mississippi, opposite Vicksburg, it would be necessary to march for 20 or 30 miles into the narrow peninsula at the eastern extremity of which that city is situated, while on the right and left, only a few miles distant by practicable roads, overwhelming forces can without difficulty by thrown upon my rear, which could not fail to secure the destruction or capture of my command. . . . The same is true in regard to the establishment of batteries upon the Mississippi, to prevent the passage of re-enforcements to the enemy. I have examined carefully every point from Young's [Point] to Lake Providence, in order to get such a position, but between those points there is no position that my small force could occupy more than a few hours. If there was the slightest hope that my small command could relieve Vicksburg, the mere probability of its capture or destruction ought not, and should not, as far as I am concerned, weigh a feather against making the attempt, but I consider it absolutely certain, unless the enemy are blind and stupid, that no part of my command would escape capture or destruction if such and attempt should be made."[20]

On the east side of the Mississippi, General Johnston completed his reconnaissances on 3 July, which convinced him that it was impossible for him to successfully attack Grant's rear from the north, between the Big Black and Mississippi Rivers, where Sherman had forces ready and waiting for him. "I determined, therefore," he later reported, "to make the examinations necessary for the attempt south of the railroad; thinking, from what was already known, that the chance for success was much better there, although the consequences of defeat might be more disastrous. On the night of the 3d, a messenger was sent to General Pemberton with information that an attempt to create a diversion would be made to enable him to cut his way out, and that I hoped to attack the enemy about the 7th."[21] He ended his message by saying, "If Vicksburg cannot be saved, the garrison must."[22]

Getting such messages in and out of Vicksburg was not impossible but would, of course, take time. Meanwhile, not knowing what Johnston was doing, or that Lee was then fighting a major battle in Pennsylvania, but perhaps fearing that General Grant planned an assault for the Fourth of July, Pemberton addressed a note to Grant and selected Major General John Bowen, one of his division commanders who had known Grant before the war, to deliver it: "I have the honor to propose to you an armistice for several hours, with a view to arranging terms for the capitulation of Vicksburg. To this end, if agreeable to you, I will appoint three commissioners to meet a like number, to be named by yourself, at such place and hour to-day as you may find convenient. I make this proposition to save the further effusion of blood, which must otherwise be shed to a frightful extent, feeling myself fully able to maintain my position for a yet indefinite period."[23]

"On the 3d about ten o'clock a.m. white flags appeared on

a portion of the rebel works," Grant later wrote. "Soon two persons were seen coming towards our lines bearing a white flag." These proved to be General Bowen and Lieutenant Colonel L. M. Montgomery, one of Pemberton's aides, bearing that general's message. "It was a glorious sight to officers and soldiers on the line where these white flags were visible," Grant added, "and the news soon spread to all parts of the command. The troops felt that their long and wearing marches, hard fighting, ceaseless watching by night and day, in a hot climate, exposure to all sorts of weather, to diseases and, worst of all, to the gibes of many Northern papers that came to them saying all their suffering was in vain, that Vicksburg would never be taken, were at last at an end and the Union sure to be saved."[24]

A chaplain in one of Grant's regiments wrote that the first Confederate white flag was seen at 8 a.m., which, perhaps, shows how much different people's watches varied in those days, or perhaps it was just different people's memories. "Soon another appeared," he said, "and another and, directly, one in front of us. The firing ceased, and all was still, the first time since May 25th, thirty-nine days. Soon greybacks began to show themselves all along the lines. Heads first, cautiously, then bodies, and we straightened up too, in many places only a few yards from them. The works were mounted and we looked each other in the face, the line of motley and the line of blue. How eager we all were to see, and what did it all mean? Was it to bury the dead again – their dead – or the prelude to a surrender? And so the forenoon wore away. About half-past one a scare occurred. We all dropped, and a few shots were fired, but 'cease firing' rang out everywhere, and no one was especially anxious to disobey; we had all had about enough of that."[25]

"For forty-eight days we had been fighting," a Confederate colonel wrote (though, actually, this was the 47th day of the siege), "and hardly caught a glimpse of each other, save hurriedly and beneath the black smoke of a charge or the rush of a retreat. Now the two armies stood up and gazed at each other with wondering eyes. Winding around the crests of hills – in ditches and trenches hitherto undreamed of by us – one long line after another started into view, looking like huge blue snakes coiling around the ill-fated city. They were amazed at the paucity of our numbers; we were astonished at the vastness of theirs. . . . Their parallels, in many places, had been pushed to within twenty feet of us. Conversation was easy, and while the leaders were in consultation, the men engaged in the truly national occupation of 'swapping' whatever our poor boys could muster to 'dicker' for coffee, sugar and whiskey."[26]

General Bowen met with Union Brigadier General A. J. Smith and asked to see Grant, but Grant refused to see him. There would be time for old friends after the surrender. Pemberton's note was sent on to headquarters, and Grant sent the following reply: "The useless effusion of blood you propose stopping . . . can be ended at any time you may choose, by an unconditional surrender of the city and garrison. Men who have shown so much endurance and courage as those now in Vicksburg will always challenge the respect of an adversary, and I can assure you will be treated with all the respect due to prisoners of war. I do not favor the proposition of appointing commissioners to arrange terms of capitulation, because I have no terms other than those indicated above."[27] Grant had the upper hand and he knew it.

There are conflicting reports about who suggested it, Grant or Bowen, but it was agreed that if Pemberton wanted to meet with Grant personally the latter would comply, and the hour of 3 p.m. was set. Grant telegraphed the news to Sherman, some 15 miles away, and told him to be ready to go after Joe Johnston as soon as Vicksburg surrendered, for which purpose he could have all the troops in Grant's army except one corps to send to help Banks at Port Hudson. Sherman replied that as soon as Grant gave him the word he would start out and asked only for his own 15th Corps and Major General E. O. C. Ord's 13th Corps, with the 9th Corps, under Major General John Parke, in reserve: "I will order my troops at once to occupy the fords of the Big Black, and await with anxiety your further answer."[28] Charles Dana later said that, "The way in which Grant handled his army at the capitulation of Vicksburg was a splendid example of his energy. As soon as negotiations for surrender began on the 3d, he sent word to Sherman, at his camp on Bear Creek, to get ready to move against Johnston. Sherman always acted on the instant, and that very afternoon he threw bridges across the Big Black."[29]

Grant arrived at the appointed place and time with part of his staff, two of his corps commanders, and two division commanders. Pemberton and Grant had served in the same division during the Mexican War and Grant greeted him as an old acquaintance. "Pemberton came late," Charles Dana soon reported to Secretary Stanton, "attended by General Bowen and Colonel Montgomery. He was much excited, and was impatient in his answer to Grant."[30] Pemberton had come expecting to hear some modification of Grant's demand for unconditional surrender but Grant would not budge. "I soon learned that there was a mutual misunderstanding in regard to the desire for this interview," Pemberton later reported, "and therefore informed General Grant that if he had no terms to propose other than were contained in his letter, the conference could terminate and hostilities be resumed immediately."[31]

Bowen, however, then proposed that he and one of Grant's officers discuss the issue. "I had no objection to this," Grant later wrote, "as nothing could be made binding upon me that they might propose." The two army commanders sat under a stunted oak tree, Pemberton chewing a blade of grass and Grant an unlit cigar, while Bowen and his counterpart, A. J. Smith, conferred. The oak, made historical by this event, was soon dismembered by souvenir seekers. "Since then," Grant later wrote, "the same tree has furnished as many cords of wood, in the shape of trophies, as 'The True Cross.'" But Bowen overreached; he proposed that the Confederates be allowed to march out with their arms and artillery and all the honors of war. "This," Grant said, "was promptly and unceremoniously rejected. The interview here ended, I agreeing, however, to send a letter giving final terms by ten o'clock that night."[32] It was agreed that hostilities would not resume until the correspondence between the two generals ceased.

Grant then returned to his headquarters and telegraphed Sherman again, saying that Pemberton wanted conditions he could not give, but that he had ordered the 13th and 15th Corps to be ready to move with Sherman the moment Vicksburg surrendered. "I want Johnston broken up as effectually as possible, and roads destroyed. I cannot say where you will find the most effective place to strike; I would say move so as to strike Canton and Jackson, whichever might seem most desirable."[33] Then he sent for all his corps and division commanders on the front facing Vicksburg. "I informed them," he later remembered, "of the contents of Pemberton's letters, of my reply and the substance of the interview, and that I was ready to hear any suggestion; but would hold the power of deciding entirely in my own hands. This was the nearest approach to a 'council of war' I ever held."[34] What Pemberton primarily wanted was for the Confederates to be paroled instead of shipped up the Mississippi to Union prisoner-of-war camps. A parole was a soldier's written promise not to fight again until properly exchanged for a paroled soldier from the other army. Instead of being held prisoner by the other side they were held in camp by their own army. The system had worked reasonably well so far in this war, but it was obvious that if the Confederates were faced with a truly desperate situation they might be tempted to cheat on the matter of exchanges and send paroled men back into the fight.

"By the terms of the cartel then in force," Grant later explained, "prisoners captured by either army were required to be forwarded as soon as possible to either Aiken's landing below Dutch Gap on the James River [Virginia], or to Vicksburg, there to be exchanged, or paroled until they could be exchanged. There was a Confederate commissioner at Vicksburg, authorized to make the exchange. I did not propose to take him prisoner, but leave him free to perform the functions of his office. Had I insisted upon an unconditional surrender there would have been over thirty thousand men to transport to Cairo [Illinois], very much to the inconvenience of the army on the Mississippi. Thence the prisoners would have had to be transported by rail to Washington or Baltimore; thence again by steamer to Aiken's – all at very great expense. At Aiken's they would have had to be paroled, because the Confederates did not have Union prisoners to give in exchange. Then again Pemberton's army was largely composed of men whose homes were in the South-west; I knew many of them were tired of the war and would get home just as soon as they could."[35]

Grant therefore sent Pemberton the following message: "In conformity with agreement of this afternoon, I will submit the following proposition for the surrender of the city of Vicksburg, public stores, &c.: On your accepting the terms proposed, I will march in one division as a guard, and take possession at 8 a.m. to-morrow. As soon as rolls can be made out, and paroles signed by officers and men, you will be allowed to march out of our lines, the officers taking with them their side-arms and clothing, and the field, staff, and cavalry officers one horse each. The rank and file will be allowed all their clothing, but no other property. If these conditions are accepted, any amount of rations you may deem necessary can be taken from the stores you now have, and also the necessary cooking utensils for preparing them. Thirty wagons also, counting two two-horse or mule teams as one, will be allowed to transport such articles as cannot be carried along. The same conditions will be allowed to all sick and wounded officers and soldiers as fast as they become able to travel. The paroles for these latter must be signed, however, while officers are present authorized to sign the roll of prisoners."[36]

In his memoirs, written long after the war, Grant said that this message was "against the general, and almost unanimous judgment of the council," but in his report to Stanton written the very next day, Dana said that all but one general favored the plan adopted, which was, he said, proposed by Major General James McPherson, commander of the 17th Corps, and that "after long consideration, General Grant reluctantly gave way. . . ."[37] A major argument in the plan's favor, not mentioned in Grant's explanation above, was that paroling the Confederates immediately freed Grant's entire army for other fields, while transporting the Rebels north would require a large number of his men to serve as guards as well as tying up all the river boats that could otherwise be used to transport Grants forces elsewhere. A message Grant sent that day to explain the plan to Admiral David Porter, commanding the Union gunboats in the Mississippi, confirms Dana's version: "My own feelings are against this," Grant told Porter, "but all my officers think the advantage gained by having our forces and transports for immediate purposes more than counterbalance the effect of sending them north."[38]

Pemberton said he received this message at about the expected hour of 10 p.m.: "This letter was immediately submitted to a council of general officers. My own inclination was to reject these terms, but after some discussion I addressed General Grant as follows: . . . In the main, your terms are accepted; but in justice both to the honor and spirit of my troops, manifested in the defense of Vicksburg, I have to submit the following amendments, which, if acceded to by you, will perfect the agreement between us: At 10 a.m. to-morrow I purpose to evacuate the works in and around Vicksburg, and to surrender the city and garrison under my command, by marching out with my colors and arms, stacking them in front of my present lines, after which you will take possession. Officers to retain their side-arms and personal property, and the rights and property of citizens to be respected."[39] Grant did not receive this message until after midnight.

Meanwhile, Grant's chief of staff, Lieutenant Colonel John Rawlins, told the two corps commanders whose troops faced the Confederate lines: "Permit some discreet men on picket to-night to communicate to the enemy's pickets the fact that General Grant has offered, in case Pemberton surrenders, to parole all the officers and men, and to permit them to go home from here."[40] This was strictly true, but a bit disingenuous; for while the Federals would naturally have no objections to the Rebels going home, the Confederate authorities would, and sending them home would not be part of the surrender agreement. But it was good propaganda for demoralizing the Rebel troops should Pemberton decide to stay and fight a while longer.

That night, Sherman sent Rawlins a long outline of his plan for going after Johnston, and said, "If Vicksburg is ours, it is the most valuable conquest of the war, and the more valuable for the stout resistance it has made...."[41]

∼ Endnotes ∼

1 Samuel Carter III, *The Final Fortress* (New York, 1980), 288.
2 Charles A. Dana, *Recollections of the Civil War* (Collier paperback edition, New York, 1963), 99.
3 *OR*, I:24:I:113-4.
4 A. A. Hoehling and the editors, Army Times Publishing Company, *Vicksburg: 47 Days of Siege* (New York, 1969), 258-9.
5 Carter, *The Final Fortress*, 9.
6 Ibid., 292.
7 *OR*, I:24:I:281.
8 Ibid., I:24:I:283.
9 Duane Schultz, *The Most Glorious Fourth* (New York and London, 2002), 264-5.
10 Ibid., 265.
11 U. S. Grant, *Personal Memoirs of U. S. Grant* (New York, 1885), I:564.
12 *OR*, I:22:II:902.
13 Ibid., I:22:I:381.
14 Ibid., I:23:I:402-3.
15 Ibid., II:6:74.
16 Ibid., I:27:II:822-3.
17 Ibid., I:27:II:858.
18 Robert Alston, "Morgan's Cavalrymen Sweep Through Kentucky," in *The Blue and the Gray*, (Indianapolis and New York, 1950), 679.
19 *OR*, I:23:I:680.
20 Ibid., I:24:III:999-1000.
21 Ibid., I:24:I:244-5.
22 Ibid., I:24:III:987.
23 Ibid., I:24:I:283.
24 Grant, *Personal Memoirs*, I:556-7.
25 Hoehling, *Vicksburg: 47 Days of Siege*, 265-6.
26 Ibid., 269.
27 *OR*, I:24:I:60.
28 Ibid., I:24:III:461.
29 Dana, *Recollections of the Civil War*, 104.
30 *OR*, I:24:I:114-5.

31 Ibid., I:24:I:284.
32 Grant, *Personal Memoirs*, I:558-9.
33 *OR*, I:24:III:460.
34 Grant, *Personal Memoirs*, I:560.
35 Ibid., I:560-1.
36 *OR*, I:24:I:60.
37 Grant, *Personal Memoirs*, 560, and *OR*, I:24:I:115.
38 *OR*, I:24:III:460.
39 Ibid., I:24:I:284-5.
40 Ibid., I:24:III:460.
41 Ibid., I:24:III:462.

Part Three
GETTYSBURG: DAY THREE

CHAPTER 12
"I Am Going to Take Them Where They Are"
3 July 1863

GENERAL SICKLES LEFT THE Gettysburg area on the morning of 3 July, only some twelve hours after having lost his leg. He was bound for Washington, where, one suspects, he intended to impart his version of the events of 2 July before General Meade would have time to make his own report. He took with him the corps' chief surgeon to act as his attending physician, plus his three aides, a few cavalrymen to serve as scouts and couriers, and a detachment of 40 infantrymen to serve as escort. The latter took turns, four at a time, at carrying the general's stretcher, for the surgeon had ruled out riding in an ambulance wagon, probably thinking that its jolting would start his stump of a leg to bleeding again. On General Pleasonton's warning that he could not guarantee that the Baltimore Pike would be safe from Confederate cavalry, they traveled along country roads and stopped that night at a farmhouse.

During the weeks since they had crossed into Pennsylvania the Confederates had confiscated or purchased (with Confederate money) thousands of wagon-loads of food and other supplies, but General Lee wanted those for the present and future use of his own troops, not for the thousands of Federals he had captured so far. So all that day Confederate staff officers were busy collecting the names of their prisoners with a view to effecting an exchange with Meade. Union Brigadier General Charles Graham, who had been wounded and captured near the Peach Orchard the day before, informed the Rebels that an order of General-in-Chief Halleck at the beginning of this campaign forbad all Federal officers and men from giving their paroles, but the Confederates offered to accept paroles anyway. General Graham warned the men that because the paroles would not be recognized by the War Department that they would be returned to duty despite their promise, which would mean that, should they be captured again the Confederates might execute them for violating their paroles. Nevertheless almost 1,500 Federals, fearing the well-publicized horrors of Confederate prisoner-of-war facilities or perhaps just dreading the long march to Richmond, gave their paroles and were marched out the Carlisle Road on the morning of 3 July.

For the Army of the Potomac, the problem was not one of hoarding supplies for future use but of getting the supplies from where they were stored to where they were needed. Decisions by Buford, Reynolds and Hancock had drawn Meade to Gettysburg, some 25 miles from the supply depot he had just established at Westminster, Maryland (which was connected to Baltimore by the Western Maryland Railroad), and Stuart's cavalry had cut the only railroad line to Gettysburg (via Hanover Junction). Wagon trains connected Meade's army with the base at Westminster via the Baltimore Pike, but they couldn't carry enough that far to keep the army fully supplied. Horses and mules had not been fed, and the men were also hungry, as well as short of shoes. Brigadier General Herman Haupt, in charge of U.S. military railroads, telegraphed General Halleck that morning that "One of our engines proceeded to Hanover Junction yesterday afternoon; thence, over the Gettysburg Railroad, to within 7 miles of Gettysburg, where a burned bridge obstructed farther progress. . . . Nineteen bridges are destroyed between Harrisburg and Hanover Junction, on the Northern Central Railroad."[1]

At 7 a.m. on 3 July Brigadier General Rufus Ingalls, Meade's quartermaster, wrote to the Army's Quartermaster General, Brigadier General Montgomery Meigs, at Washington: "At this moment the battle is raging as fiercely as ever. The fight was renewed at 3.30 this morning. The loss has been great on both sides. All our forces have been, and still are, in action, and we shall be compelled to stand and fight it out. There is unanimous determination to resist until we drive the rebels. They began the fight, but we have repulsed them at all points, and hold our original battle-ground. This entire army has fought with terrible obstinacy, and has covered itself with glory. Pity it is not larger. We have supplies at Westminster, which must come up to-morrow if we remain here. The contest will be decided to-day, I think."[2]

The battle was indeed on again already; the fight for Culp's Hill resumed at daylight. Throughout the night both Ewell, on Lee's left, and Williams, on Meade's right, had been preparing to attack at dawn. As soon as it was light (about 4:30 a.m.), all four batteries of the Union 12th Corps, reinforced by a battery from the Artillery Reserve – 26 guns in all – opened fire on the Rebels who had occupied the lower crest, and Geary's infantry added their musketry. The major commanding the Confederates' 1st Maryland Battalion wrote that had it not been for the cover of the Union works they had occupied, and that of a stone wall and the numerous rocks and trees on the hill, not one man in Steuart's Brigade would have survived the bombardment. Three companies of Marylanders who were beyond the works and stone fence had to be hastily withdrawn. Some of the artillery rounds fell short and caused a few casualties in Colonel Archibald McDougall's 1st Brigade of Ruger's (Williams') 1st Division (which was stationed between the Baltimore Pike and McAllister's Woods), until an infantry colonel threatened to shoot a battery commander. The Rebels had no artillery in position to reply to this fire, and had to suffer it in silence until it ended after fifteen minutes.

Both General Wadsworth, to Geary's left, and Howard, on Cemetery Hill, complained to army headquarters that Geary was wasting ammunition. Howard also passed on a rumor that General P. G. T. Beauregard had a large Confederate force at Hagerstown, Maryland. Brigadier General Seth Williams, Meade's assistant adjutant-general, informed Howard that the dispatches captains Dahlgren and Cline had captured the day before showed "that the proposition to concentrate a large army under Beauregard for the support of Lee's army is regarded by President Davis as impracticable."[3]

Williams had planned to follow his bombardment with an attack by Geary's 2nd Division to retake the lost works, but the Confederates beat him to the punch. They had been ready to attack at dawn but had found it necessary to put it off until the Union artillery ceased fire. Lee had told Ewell that Longstreet would attack the Federal left again at dawn and for him to hit the Union right at the same time. So Ewell had reinforced Johnson's Division and ordered it to complete its capture of Culp's Hill. Now that the cavalry was available to protect Lee's left and rear, the Stonewall Brigade was free to rejoin Johnson's Division, and it took position on the left, behind Steuart's Brigade. Two brigades from Rodes' Division had also arrived: Daniel's Brigade took position behind and in support of Jones's Brigade, and O'Neal's Brigade evidently was placed behind Nicholls' Louisianans, who were in the center of Johnson's line. All these Confederates faced west, toward the higher crest of Culp's Hill, except for about half of Steuart's Brigade, up on the lower crest, who's line ran along the Union works and a stone wall, facing southwest, and the 2nd Virginia of the Stonewall Brigade, which extended Steuart's line eastward to Rock Creek and faced south.

However, the Confederates could not advance very far in the face of the Union fire, and the attack soon degenerated into a firefight. General Daniel later reported that "The hill in front of this position was, in my opinion, so strong that it could not have been carried by any force."[4] A half-hour after his attack began, Ewell learned that Longstreet had not been ready to attack the other end of the Union line at dawn and would not do so until 10 a.m.

While the Rebels attacked the higher part of Culp's Hill, the Federals made a smaller attack on the lower part. Very early that morning, General Williams ordered General Lockwood to attack the wooded southern end of the Confederate line with one of his two large regiments. Lockwood sent the 1st

Maryland Regiment, Potomac Home Brigade, which advanced to within 20 yards of the stone wall that sheltered the 2nd Virginia, where the 1st Maryland's colonel called a halt and ordered bayonets to be fixed, but then he received word that he was in the way of troops to his right, and, having already lost 80 men and being short on ammunition, he took his regiment back to the Baltimore Turnpike.

The Federals also made another small attack at the opposite end of the Culp's Hill line. In the pre-dawn darkness the 66th Ohio of Candy's brigade (about 300 men) had been sent to the top of the higher part of the hill, and when the Union artillery had opened fire this regiment had moved out of the defenses at the left end of the 12th Corps position and swung around to face south, connecting on its right to Greene's line and anchoring its left on a high shelf of land. This put the 66th on the right flank of Jones's Virginians, and, after a brief, hot fight, the latter, or at least their right, pulled back down the slope. After that, the 66th, and the regiment on the left of Greene's line were not seriously challenged, although they, like the rest of Geary's men, kept up a constant fire that intimidated the Rebels.

The next three regiments of Geary's line were pressed by Nicholls' Louisianans and O'Neal's Brigade, while the 137th New York, at the right end of his line, fought with the 3rd North Carolina and the 1st Maryland Battalion of Steuart's Brigade and the right of the Stonewall Brigade. Beyond the 137th, the Union line turned to follow the traverse and Spangler's lane and faced the rest of Steuart's Brigade up on the lower crest of Culp's Hill. This part of the line was manned by the three regiments of Kane's brigade and two regiments of Candy's. Three more of Candy's regiments were placed as a reserve in the cover of a ravine that ran north from Kane's position behind Greene's front line, and they took turns relieving units on the front line. A soldier in the 137th New York said, "A regiment would use up their ammunition in about two hours, when another one would relieve them and they fall back to the hollow where the balls would whistle over their heads. They would clean their guns and get some more ammunition and be ready to relieve another regiment. They would all rather be in the trenches than in the hollow. In this way we could have stood as long as the rebs chose to show themselves below, which was until 11 a.m., but few were seen after this."[5] A lieutenant in the 147th New York, still on loan from the 1st Corps, later wrote that his regiment was relieved four times to clean its guns and get more ammunition and that each man in his regiment had fired off 200 rounds by 10 a.m. Lockwood's large regiments were brought up to Geary's position and also took their turns in the trenches, including a third regiment, the 1st Maryland Eastern Shore, that had just reached the field that morning.

The Confederates also relieved front-line units at least once. At around 10 a.m. a lieutenant in Nicholls's Brigade looked back and saw another brigade, presumably O'Neal's Alabamans, coming up to relieve the Louisianans. The reinforcements arrived with a Rebel yell which, the lieutenant said, served only to cause the Federals to increase their rate of fire. Both the relieving troops as they advanced and the retiring troops as they fell back took far more casualties than they did when they were in place behind the cover of rocks and trees. The new arrivals had no more success at dislodging the Federals than the Louisianans had had. Also, two regiments of Extra Billy Smith's brigade of Early's Division arrived and replaced the 2nd Virginia at the south end of the Confederate line, after which the 2nd Virginia and part of the 1st North Carolina of Steuart's Brigade moved south on the east side of Rock Creek and deployed in a long skirmish line that guarded against any Union move to get around Johnson's southern flank, meanwhile exchanging shots with Ruger's troops around McAllister's Woods. The rest of the Stonewall Brigade went to the rear to clean its rifles and replenish its ammunition, a move that Johnson had evidently not approved, for he soon arrived and demanded, "What in the ---- are you doing here?"[6]

Around mid-morning Johnson decided to rearrange

his brigades and try a different approach. He had Steuart move his brigade farther to the left, or south, placed Daniel's Brigade in two lines where most of Steuart's Brigade had been, and sent the Stonewall Brigade, minus its 2nd Virginia, beyond Daniel to replace Nicholls' and O'Neal's brigades. Steuart sent his 10th Virginia to protect his outer, left, flank, and it pushed into some woods and faced off against the 20th Connecticut, which had been deployed as skirmishers in those woods since early morning, keeping an eye on Confederate movements and making sure they didn't try to turn Geary's right flank. When all was ready, the Stonewall Brigade and Daniel's North Carolinians attacked straight up the higher hill while Steuart's mixed brigade wheeled to its right and charged down the slope of the lower crest across an open field.

Steuart probably had about 900 men in his line, and 200 yards down the slope stood the 600 men of the 5th Ohio and the 147th Pennsylvania of Candy's brigade in the edge of some woods on the saddle between the two crests, plus, farther to their left (the Confederate right), Kane's small brigade in the cover of some boulders. Distant Union artillery soon fired on the Rebels as they entered the open field, and Candy's men opened fire at a range of 100 yards. A private in the 37th Virginia later wrote that this fire seemed to virtually wipe out the Maryland Battalion, to his right, and only himself and one other man remained standing out of his entire company. What was left of his regiment, plus the 23rd Virginia on its left, retreated to the cover of the captured breastworks. The Marylanders blamed the Virginians for starting the retreat, but most of them soon joined it, pursued by what their commander called "a merciless storm of bullets."[7]

Two companies of the Maryland Battalion plus part of the 1st North Carolina and what little was left of the 3rd North Carolina, on the Marylanders' right, had not yet passed beyond the cover of the stone wall and were not hit so badly. The 29th Pennsylvania let them approach to within about 50 yards and then opened fire, but was firing too high. The

Rebels came on until within about 40 paces, but then someone yelled for them to retreat, the captain in command of this part of the Marylanders went down with a bullet in the neck, and his men turned and fled. Finding themselves all alone and unsupported, the North Carolinians also fell back, but in good order. Beyond them the 43rd North Carolina at the left-front of Daniel's Brigade had not yet completely cleared the captured works when Steuart's Brigade, to its left, came tumbling back, and all it could do was cover the latter's retreat.

Daniel's North Carolinians and the Virginians of the Stonewall Brigade had little more success against Greene's center than the Alabamans and Louisianans had had. Some of the Confederates worked their way up the hill to within 15 yards of the Union lines, and one gallant Rebel made a dash for the colors of the 149th New York, but was shot down at the edge of the earthworks. Daniel claimed to have driven the Federals from a portion of their defenses but was unable to occupy them because of Steuart's retreat. He said one of his regiments was able to fire up a gorge into a disorganized crowd of Federals – perhaps a regiment in the process of being relieved – causing them to flee in confusion but that a fresh column came to their relief.

This attack alarmed General Geary enough to cause him to ask Slocum for more reinforcements, and Slocum sent him Brigadier General Alexander Shaler's 1st Brigade of the 3rd Division of the 6th Corps, which had reported to him at 8:45 that morning and been held in reserve along the Baltimore Pike since then. That brigade's 122nd New York moved through the hollow behind the lines and made a dash for the works, taking several casualties in the process, and went into the lines just to the right of the 149th New York. Both regiments were from Onandaga County, and there was much cheering and helloing when the two regiments recognized each other. These Federals poured out such a deadly fire that the Confederates in their front could neither advance nor retreat. One Rebel waved a white handkerchief indicating a desire to surrender, but a Confederate officer split the man's head open with his sword. However, the officer then fell with seven Union bullets in him, and other Rebels began to wave white flags. Eventually 75 Confederates surrendered to the 122nd, some of them holding back at first to see how the first few were treated. In a similar, if not the same, incident, Major B. Watkins Leigh, General Johnson's chief of staff, rode forward on his horse to attempt to stop part of the Stonewall Brigade from surrendering and was killed in the process.

Finally General Johnson ordered Daniel's Brigade to fall back about three-fourths of a mile and take position along "a run at the foot of the hill" (presumably Rock Creek).[8] Two of Daniel's aides were killed trying to get orders for the retreat to one of his regiments before a third got through. General Walker also pulled his Virginians back, "as it was a useless sacrifice of life to keep them longer under so galling a fire."[9] Steuart's Brigade rallied in the captured defenses and stayed there for an hour or so and then fell back to Rock Creek. Many Confederates were left behind, unwilling to leave the cover of the rocks and trees to make the retreat. About 130 Rebels surrendered to Greene's Brigade, in addition to the 75 that the 6th Corps men captured. In all, Geary's division captured three Confederate colors.

At around 10 a.m. General Ruger had received an order from Slocum, who thought the Rebels were shaken, to try to retake his defenses up on the lower crest of Culp's Hill. Ruger sent back a request that he first be allowed to determine the strength of the Rebels there and discretion to make the attack or not, based on what he found. Slocum consented, and Ruger sent an aide to Colonel Silas Colgrove, who had temporary command of Ruger's 3rd Brigade of the 1st Division of the 12th Corps while Ruger held temporary command of the division (Williams still considering himself the corps commander), telling him to send skirmishers north from his position in McAllister's Woods, and, if he found the enemy in not too great a force, to attack with two regiments. But Colgrove understood the order was for him to attack immediately. He chose the 2nd Massachusetts and the 27th Indiana, of which he was the colonel.

The 27th Indiana had farther to go, had to change its facing direction, and also was interrupted by a collision with the 13th New Jersey, which was trying to move into the defenses just abandoned by the 2nd Massachusetts, so it got a later start. Meanwhile, the 2nd Massachusetts, which already faced the hill it was supposed to attack, advanced into the meadow that separated its position from the hill and stopped to fire a volley that drove the Confederate skirmishers back, then followed them toward the Rebel lines. Confederates soon opened fire on these Federals from the front while others tried to get around their right flank, but this move was thwarted by the 27th Indiana coming up on that side. However, by the time these Hoosiers were halfway across the field the 2nd Massachusetts had been repulsed and had fallen back to the cover of some large rocks on its left.

The Rebels hit the 27th with a controlled volley that seemed to knock down three whole companies, and the Federals made the mistake of stopping to return fire instead of charging on ahead. This started a brief firefight, with the Confederates behind trees, boulders, and a rock wall, and the Federals standing out in the open. Colonel Colgrove ordered them to retreat, and when the 2nd Massachusetts, now commanded by its major, saw this, it too retreated, not, however, back to its starting point but by a safer route to the southwest, which took it to a stone wall some 200 yards west of its original position. Extra Billy Smith sent his 49th and 52nd Virginia in pursuit of the 27th Indiana, but they were easily driven back by Colgrove's brigade, and this part of the lines once again settled down to mere sharpshooting and skirmishing.

However, the 20th Connecticut, finding that the Rebels had left their front, soon advanced all the way to the stone wall on top of the lower crest and on to the Federal-built works beyond them. Confederate sharpshooters who had climbed up in trees to get better shots fired on them, but, as the regiment's colonel later wrote, "the last living, unwounded rebel within our [original] lines had disappeared."[10] Being low on ammunition and fearing another Confederate attack, the colonel asked his brigade commander, Colonel Archibald McDougall, for relief. McDougall not only sent the 123rd New York to replace the 20th Connecticut but advised General Ruger that the captured works had been retaken, and the general sent other regiments to occupy them as well. The Union line had now been completely restored, and the Confederates had nothing to show for all their efforts.

General Johnson reported 1,823 casualties (killed, wounded and missing), but this did not include the losses of Daniel's, O'Neal's or Smith's brigades, which were not in his division, so the total must have been nearly double that number. Among the Confederate dead was Private John Wesley Culp of the 2nd Virginia; he was a cousin of the owner of Culp's Hill and had grown up in Gettysburg, but, as a young man, he had followed his employer to Virginia, where he had joined the local militia that had later become part of the Confederate Army. The Union 12th Corps reported 1,082 losses, of which only 204 were killed. A few more would have to be added for the 1st, 6th and 11th Corps troops who participated in the fight. At 12:20 p.m. Slocum sent a message to Meade saying, "I think I have gained a decided advantage on my front, and hope to be able to spare one or two brigades to help you on some other part of the line."[11]

Although the fight for Culp's Hill was over, neither side could be sure that the other was content to leave it so, and skirmishing continued in that area throughout the day. Meanwhile, skirmishing and sharpshooting had started at dawn between the 11th Corps on Cemetery Hill and Confederates in and near Gettysburg. Part of the 5th Alabama Battalion of Archer's Brigade, Heth's Division, occupied barricades across streets, as well as outbuildings, and the second stories and attics of houses, and steeples of churches throughout the southern end of the town. They cut holes in walls to fire through or piled furniture and mattresses in windows.

The battalion's commander, Major Eugene Blackford, wrote, "My orders were to fire incessantly, without regard to ammunition."[12] His men targeted Union artillerymen on Cemetery Hill and kept up a sustained fire all morning. When their ammunition ran low Major Blackford sent a detail through the streets with a cart to collect discarded cartridges, meanwhile setting his buglers to raiding grocery stores for food and to baking bread in civilian kitchens.

Union infantry returned fire, but it was hard to hit the Confederates because of their excellent cover. Occasionally the Union artillery would be provoked into response, and it would blast some house or church; and the infantry commanders would send out volunteers to kill or drive off particularly bothersome snipers. Federals occupied Snider's Wagon Hotel, which stood at the intersection of the Baltimore Pike and the Emmitsburg Road, and exchanged fire with Rebels in John Rupp's tannery, just up the pike. Most civilians in this part of the town had abandoned their homes or had taken shelter in their cellars, but there was a brick double house about 150 yards south of the Wagon Hotel where a woman had given birth the week before, and she and her mother and her younger sister were still living in the northern half. At about 8:30 a.m., a stray bullet passed through a closed door and an open door and struck the younger sister, Mary Virginia "Jennie" Wade, in the back as she was kneading dough to make biscuits. She was the only Gettysburg civilian killed during the battle.

Around noon General Ewell, accompanied by an engineer officer, rode through the town and out toward Gordon's position along Winebrenner Run. They were warned by some of Hays's men that Union sharpshooters had the area covered, but the general scoffed at the idea that the Federals could hit anything at such a range. However, the sharpshooters had telescopic sights and special rifles, and before the two officers had ridden 20 yards the Federals opened fire on them and soon put a bullet in the engineer and another in the general. When General Gordon asked Ewell if he was hurt, the latter replied, "No, no; I'm not hurt. But suppose that ball had struck you: we would have had the trouble of carrying you off the field, sir. You see how much better fixed for a fight I am than you are. It don't hurt a bit to be shot in a wooden leg."[13]

Firing also broke out at daylight south of Cemetery Hill, between skirmishers sent out by the Federals on Cemetery Ridge and those advanced by the Confederates to the west of them. Captain Benjamin Thompson of the 111th New York, in the Harper's Ferry Brigade, said, "Line fighting is barbarous, but skirmishing is savage – nay, devilish. To juke and hide and skulk for men and deliberately aim at and murder them one by one is far too bloodthirsty business for Christian men."[14] On this part of the field it was the Confederate artillery that would occasionally join in – mostly the guns of A. P. Hill's 3rd Corps. The Union gunners were forbidden to reply. Here, too, the Federals would sometimes launch small attacks to drive the Rebels back, only to provoke Confederate counterattacks to reestablish their skirmish line. A Union 2nd Corps soldier wrote home that nearly the entire Rebel skirmish line in his regiment's front "threw down their arms and ran into our lines, the rebel batteries shelling them as they ran." He said these deserters claimed that their generals had lied to them, telling them "they would have nothing but militia to fight, who would fire one round and run, but instead of that they found the Army of the Potomac."[15]

Small artillery duels occasionally broke out along the lines. At around 8 a.m. General Hunt stopped by Battery A of the 4th U.S. Artillery, which was stationed near the center of General Gibbon's division of the Union 2nd Corps, to make sure its commander, 22-year-old 1st Lieutenant Alonzo Cushing, knew the location of the reserve artillery ammunition wagons. The discussion was joined by Cushing's first sergeant, Frederick Fuger, as well as by Brigadier General Alexander Webb, commander of the nearest infantry brigade. But the meeting was soon broken up when a pair of

Confederate guns opened fire on them. One shell struck the ammunition chest on the limber of one of Cushing's guns, and it exploded, throwing hot fragments of wood and iron into the air, some of which fell on and exploded the ammunition chests on two other limbers, throwing more fragments and even wheels all around. Some of Cushing's horses broke loose, and, although Union infantrymen stopped most of them, a few others, to the cheers of the distant Confederate gunners, ran clear across the intervening fields into the Rebel lines. Other than that, however, no one was hurt, although one cannoneer in an adjoining battery had been knocked down by the concussion of the explosions, and some of the remaining horses' tails were singed.

Not long afterwards Cushing got some revenge when he saw a group of mounted Confederates ride out into a clearing in front of Seminary Ridge about a mile across the way. He ordered one of his six 3-inch rifles to fire on this group, and the second shell burst right over the Rebels' heads, scattering them at what one artilleryman called "a lively rate." However, Captain John Hazard, commander of the 2nd Corps' artillery brigade, rode over to Cushing and yelled, "Young man, are you aware that every round you fire costs the government two dollars and sixty-seven cents?"[16]

As on the day before, the big fortress-like brick and stone barn of the Bliss farm, as well as its substantial log and frame house, again became bones of contention for the opposing skirmishers. The 12th Mississippi of Posey's Brigade had maintained possession through the night, and at dawn it began firing on the Union skirmishers along the Emmitsburg Road and the main Union line up on Cemetery Ridge. After enduring this for about three hours, Brigadier General Alexander Hays, commander of the 3rd Division of the 2nd Corps, sent five companies of the 12th New Jersey, under Captain Richard Thompson, to recapture the massive barn.

A spur of Cemetery Ridge ran southwest from Ziegler's Grove, at the southwest corner of Cemetery Hill, and formed a knoll east of the Bliss buildings that screened the New

Jersey Federals from the Mississippians, and vice versa, until they crossed the knoll. Fire from the Mississippians and from some of Pender's men in the Long Lane farther north struck them then, but the Federals broke into a double-quick, fanned out to surround the building, and broke through the stable doors on the ground level. The Rebels bolted out the back door, but a major and four enlisted men were not fast enough and were captured.

The Confederates reformed in the Bliss family's ten-acre orchard just west of the barn, from which they dueled with the Federals, who now had the cover of the sturdy walls. But Rebel batteries fired solid shot in an attempt to knock those walls to pieces, while the Mississippians and Pender's Georgians began edging forward. Captain Thompson had only been ordered to drive the Confederates out, not to hold the barn, so he ordered a retreat, which was covered by the division's skirmishers, the 8th Ohio. Behind them, the Confederates reoccupied the barn and took over the house as well.

General Hays was not ready to concede the buildings, however. He ordered Colonel Thomas Smyth, commander of his 2nd Brigade, to send a regiment to take them back again. Smyth chose his 14th Connecticut, which had only about 175 men, counting two companies that were out on the skirmish line. The 14th's commander, Major Theodore Ellis, divided his small regiment into two detachments of four companies (about 60 men) each with orders to forget about formations and each man to reach the buildings as best he could. The Mississippians opened fire on them as they passed over the knoll but couldn't stop them and again retreated to the orchard. One Federal detachment took over the barn and the other took over the house. Within minutes 30 Confederate guns up on Seminary Hill began blasting both buildings, although Colonel Alexander, Longstreet's artillerist, considered this a waste of ammunition and refused to allow his own batteries to join in.

Major Ellis soon discovered that the wooden house was

no protection against this bombardment or even from rifle fire, so he and that detachment ran a gauntlet of fire to join the other one in the barn. But even there the artillery was breaking through the brick upper story. Watching from Cemetery Hill, General Hays decided that if he couldn't have the buildings he could at least keep the Rebels from using them, and he sent a sergeant who volunteered to carry matches and paper to the defenders and tell them to burn them. As a precaution, Hays also sent a mounted courier to deliver the order. A captain on Smyth's staff volunteered for that job, and, despite having to pass through heavy fire, both he and the sergeant got through unscathed to deliver the order.

Inside the barn, Major Ellis had some of his men pile up the hay and straw while others removed the dead and wounded and a detail rushed back to the house, where they piled up the furniture and bedding. A few men then set fires in both buildings and joined the rest in the barnyard, where Ellis had them all wait until the smoke was heavy enough to cover their retreat. Some of them managed to catch some chickens that were escaping from the barn and took them along as welcome additions to their rations. Not long after they retreated to the Emmitsburg Road the roof of the barn caved in, bringing cheers from the Union lines on Cemetery Hill. With the burning of the Bliss buildings, silence fell on that part of the field. The captain later received a Medal of Honor for his daring ride, but the Bliss family never received any compensation for the loss of their house and barn.

General Meade may not have slept at all after his meeting with his corps commanders on the night of 2 July; he probably worked through the pre-dawn hours of the third in the little two-room house that served as his headquarters while staff officers caught a few winks on the floor. At 7 a.m. chief of staff Butterfield wrote a message to Major General William H. French, who commanded about 7,000 Union troops around Frederick, Maryland, that had been withdrawn from Harper's Ferry, to defend the western approaches to Washington: "General Meade directs me to say that the enemy attacked us vigorously yesterday, and was repulsed on all sides. The conflict is apparently renewed to-day, and we have retained our position. Should the result of to-day's operations cause the enemy to fall back toward the Potomac, which you would probably learn by scouts and information from Hagerstown, &c., before you would be advised from here, he desires that you will re-occupy Harper's Ferry and annoy and harass him in his retreat. It may be possible for you now to annoy and cut his communications with any cavalry or light marching infantry you have; of this you can judge. If the result of to-day's operations should be our discomfiture and withdrawal, you are to look to Washington, and throw your force there for its protection. You will be prepared for either of these contingencies should they arise."[17]

In his official report, General French said: "As soon as I heard the cannon at Gettysburg on July 3, the dispositions of the troops were changed from a passive to an active state."[18] Scouts and civilians had brought French word that Lee had a pontoon bridge over the Potomac River at Falling Waters, near Williamsport, which was guarded only by a handful of infantry and the teamsters who drove the wagons that carried the pontoons. And early on the morning of 3 July Colonel Andrew T. McReynolds, commanding a brigade of cavalry under French, suggested to French's assistant adjutant-general that a force of about 150 cavalry could make a surprise raid on that bridge, "which is the only reliance of the rebels for a retreat of their infantry, artillery and wagons in that direction."[19] French approved, and the raiders were on their way before nightfall.

Meade sent a message to General Halleck at 8 a.m., saying, "The action commenced again at early daylight upon various parts of the line. The enemy thus far have made no impression upon my position." This, of course, ignores Johnson's capture of about half of Culp's Hill the night before. He added that "All accounts agree in placing the whole

[Confederate] army here. Prisoners report Longstreet's and A. P. Hill's forces much injured yesterday and many general officers killed. General Barksdale's (Mississippi) dead body is within our lines. We have thus far sent off about 1,600 prisoners, and a small number yet to be started. I have given certain instructions to General French, which he will telegraph to you. The dispatches from you yesterday, owing to the disappearance of Caldwell, telegraph operator, are here in cipher, unintelligible."[20]

At 8:30 a.m., Meade wrote a message to Major General Darius Couch, former commander of the 2nd Corps who was now commanding the Department of the Susquehanna, created especially to protect eastern Pennsylvania from Lee's invading army. Couch had a sizable force, but it was composed almost entirely of militia units hastily called up and forwarded to him from several Northern states: "I presume you are advised of the condition of affairs here by copies of my dispatches to the General-in-Chief. The result of my operations may be the withdrawal of the rebel army. The sound of my guns for these three days, it is taken for granted, is all the additional notice you need to come on. Should the enemy withdraw, by prompt co-operation we might destroy him. Should he overpower me, your return and defense of Harrisburg and the Susquehanna is not at all endangered."[21] At 9 a.m. Couch was writing to Meade: "My scouts inform me that Lee is hurrying everything forward. Troops passed through Greencastle yesterday on the way to Chambersburg. Even his raw troops were pushed forward. Lee has a depot of stolen horses and baggage at Cashtown. [Union] General [W. F.] Smith [at Carlyle] is hoping to look after it. Is moving this morning."[22]

At the same hour, Couch wrote a message to Colonel Lewis B. Pierce at Bloody Run, Pennsylvania, who commanded a couple of thousand Union troops who had managed to escape from the Shenandoah Valley when Lee's army had swept through there on its way to Pennsylvania. They had originally been led by their division commander, Major

General Robert Milroy, but General-in-Chief Halleck had ordered Milroy's arrest for getting most of his division captured by Ewell at Winchester. Couch told Pierce: "Lee has been fighting Meade. Can't you put forward your cavalry toward Chambersburg, and harass his rear, keeping a sharp lookout? No time is to be lost. So far, our people have the advantage. Put your whole column, infantry and cavalry, in motion toward McConnellsburg. In case of reverse, you can retire to the mountains – Mount Union or Perry County."[23]

At Gettysburg, as the day progressed, early morning clouds slowly gave way to bright sunshine. Lieutenant Frank Haskell said that on Cemetery Ridge the men of the Union 2nd Corps "were roused early, in order that the morning meal might be out of the way in time for whatever should occur. . . . It is the opinion of many of our Generals that the Rebel will not give us battle to-day – that he had enough yesterday – that he will be heading towards the Potomac at the earliest practicable moment, if he has not already done so; but the better, and controlling judgment is, that he will make another grand effort to pierce or turn our lines – that he will either mass and attack the left again, as yesterday, or direct his operations against the left of our center, the position of the Second Corps, and try to sever our line." Haskell saw General Meade that morning, riding along the line and examining the opposite ridge through his field glasses. "His manner was calm and serious, but earnest. . . . He was well pleased with the left of the line to-day, it was so strong with good troops. He had no apprehension for the right where the fight now was going on, on account of the admirable position of our forces there. He was not of the opinion that the enemy would attack the center, our artillery had such a sweep there, and this was not the favorite point of attack with the Rebel. Besides, should he attack the center, the General thought he could reinforce it in good season. I heard Gen. Meade speak of these matters to Hancock and some others, at about nine o'clock in the morning, while they were up by the line, near the Second Corps."[24]

But, as Lee stated in his report, quoted near the end of Chapter 10, "The general plan was unchanged." He still wanted to take Cemetery Hill. Ewell had failed to take it on the evening of 1 July; Early and Rodes had failed to take it on the evening of 2 July (perhaps mainly because Pender and then Rodes never attacked); Lee would try again. After two or three hours of sleep, he had been up and about since before dawn, and the sun was still not up when he reached Longstreet's headquarters, accompanied, or soon joined, by A. P. Hill and Harry Heth. "I was disappointed," Longstreet later wrote, "when he came to me on the morning of the 3d and directed that I should renew the attack against Cemetery Hill, probably the strongest point of the Federal line. . . . I stated to General Lee that I had been examining the ground over to the right, and was much inclined to think the best thing was to move to the Federal left. [In fact, Longstreet had already issued orders to start such a move.] 'No,' he said; 'I am going to take them where they are on Cemetery Hill.'"[25]

Colonel Long, who was also part of the discussion, wrote later that: "Cemetery Ridge, from Round Top to Culp's Hill, was at every point strongly occupied by Federal infantry and artillery, and was evidently a very formidable position. There was, however, a weak point upon which an attack could be made with a reasonable prospect of success. This was where the ridge, sloping westward, formed the depression through which the Emmitsburg road passes. Perceiving that forcing the Federal lines at that point and turning toward Cemetery Hill the [Union] right would be taken in flank and the remainder would be neutralized, as its fire would be as destructive to friend as to foe, and considering that the losses of the Federal army in the two preceding days must weaken its cohesion and consequently diminish its power of resistance, General Lee determined to attack that point. . . ."[26]

Lee's target is confirmed by Colonel Alexander of the artillery, who said, "Early in the morning General Lee came around, and I was then told that we were to assault Cemetery Hill, which lay rather to our [Longstreet's] left."[27] Long after the war, Alexander wrote, "As long as Gettysburg stands and the contour of its hills remains unchanged, students of the battle-field must decide that Lee's most promising attack from first to last was upon Cemetery Hill. . . ."[28] Even more than Sickles' position the day before, Cemetery Hill was a salient that could be enfiladed and assaulted from several directions. Alexander thought, with the advantage of hindsight, that the best jump-off points for such an attack were Winebrenner Run, from which Early had attacked the northeast side the night before, and the Long Lane, into which Rodes had settled his division after failing to attack from the west.

Lee, however, still wanted Longstreet to attack from the southwest, up the Emmitsburg Road, using his entire corps, including the three fresh brigades of Pickett's Division, supported by his artillery firing from the newly captured Peach Orchard area. Longstreet rightly pointed out that should he do so the Federals, known to be around the two Round Tops, could enfilade or even counterattack his right and rear. Just how well Lee and Longstreet understood the Federal position is hard to tell, but probably not very well. Many Union units were out of sight behind the crest of Cemetery Ridge when the two generals examined the position that morning. Nor was the ridge line entirely straight. They knew, of course, that the Federals held Little Round Top, but the Union position along the southern part of Cemetery Ridge – just about everything south of Gibbon's division, including a line of batteries collected by Lieutenant Colonel McGilvery – would not have been apparent. Nor was the Confederate definition of "Cemetery Hill" at that time necessarily the same as that now used by historians, but might well have included the northern part of Cemetery Ridge, where two divisions of Hancock's 2nd Corps occupied high, open ground, easily visible to the Confederates.

The two generals rode along Longstreet's lines, and Lee stopped to talk to General Wofford, whose brigade was in

McLaws' Division, and asked him about the Union position. "I told him," Wofford wrote after the war, "that the afternoon before, I nearly reached the crest. He asked if I could not go there now. I replied, 'No, General, I think not.' He said quickly, 'Why not?' 'Because,' I said, 'General, the enemy have had all night to intrench and reinforce. I had been pursuing a broken enemy and the situation was very different.'"[29] Lee and Longstreet then rode out to the fields north of the Peach Orchard to get a better view of the Union position, but could probably still see few Federals south of Gibbon's division. However, Lee eventually agreed to let Longstreet leave Hood's and McLaws' depleted and exhausted divisions where they were to guard his flank while Pickett made the attack reinforced by about half of A. P. Hill's corps.

It might have been this decision that caused the two generals to be joined by Hill and Heth, the latter still suffering the effects of being hit in the head, or it might have been one of them that suggested the change. Either way, it was decided that Heth's Division, under the temporary command of his senior brigadier, Johnston Pettigrew, plus two brigades of Pender's Division, would join Pickett's fresh division in making the assault. Apparently Lee estimated that there would thus be some 15,000 men in the attack. "I think I can safely say," Longstreet later claimed to have replied, "there never was a body of fifteen thousand men who could make that attack successfully. The general seemed a little impatient at my remarks, so I said nothing more. As he showed no indication of changing his plan, I went to work at once to arrange my troops for the attack."[30]

Hill must still have been less than well; otherwise, with two thirds of the brigades making the assault being from his corps, one might well expect that Lee would have put him in charge of it. Or, as Longstreet later said of Lee, "He knew that I did not believe that success was possible; that care and time should be taken to give the troops the benefit of positions and the grounds; and he should have put an officer in charge who had more confidence in his plan."[31] Colonel C. S.

Venable of Lee's staff later said, "They were terribly mistaken about Heth's Division in the planning. It had not recovered, having suffered more than was reported on the first day."[32] Why all of Pender's Division, now under Lane, was not used, instead of only half of it, has never been explained.

It would be quite some time before the attack could begin, not so much because Pickett's Division had camped the night before some three miles northwest of Gettysburg, back along the Chambersburg Pike, and had only started moving forward from there about dawn, or at about the time that Lee and Longstreet started conferring, but because the brigades from Hill's 3rd Corps had to be brought into position as well. Some time between 7 and 8 a.m. Pickett's three brigades, all of them composed entirely of regiments from Virginia, reached the fields west of Seminary Ridge. There each man was issued an extra twenty rounds of ammunition, and they had their weapons inspected by their officers. Longstreet took Pickett up to the crest of Seminary Ridge, where they could get a panoramic view of the area, and explained the plan of attack. The two were old friends, having served together in the same regiment during the Mexican War. Pickett, four years younger than Longstreet, had graduated at the very bottom of his West Point class, and Longstreet, though fond of him, always took special care to make sure his friend understood his orders.

"He seemed to appreciate the severity of the contest upon which he was about to enter," Longstreet later wrote, "but was quite hopeful of success. Upon receipt of notice, he was to march over the crest of the hill down the gentle slope and up the rise opposite the Federal stronghold. The distance was about fourteen hundred yards, and for most of the way the Federal batteries would have a raking fire from Round Top, while the sharp-shooters, artillery, and infantry would subject the assaulting column to a terrible and destructive fire. With my knowledge of the situation, I could see the desperate and hopeless nature of the charge and the cruel slaughter it would cause. My heart was heavy when I left Pickett. I rode once or twice along the ground between Pickett and the Federals, examining the positions and studying the matter over in all its phases so far as we could anticipate."[33]

As Longstreet later wrote, "Orders were given to Major-General Pickett to form his line under the best cover that he could get from the enemy's batteries, and so that the center of the assaulting column would arrive at the salient of the enemy's position, General Pickett's line to be the guide and to attack the line of the enemy's defenses, and General Pettigrew, in command of Heth's division, moving on the same line as General Pickett, was to assault the salient at the same moment. Pickett's division was arranged, two brigades in the front line, supported by his third brigade, and Wilcox's brigade [of Anderson's Division, 3rd Corps] was ordered to move in rear of his right flank, to protect it from any force that the enemy might attempt to move against it. Heth's division, under the command of Brigadier-General Pettigrew, was arranged in two lines, and these supported by part of Major-General Pender's division, under Major-General Trimble. All of the batteries of the First and Third Corps, and some of those of the Second, were put into the best positions for effective fire upon the point of attack and the hill occupied by the enemy's left."[34]

Actually, in addition to Wilcox's brigade, Lang's little Florida Brigade was also assigned to guard Pickett's right flank, and Lang, who ordered his men to dig in, was told by Anderson to conform to Wilcox's movements. Both Lang and Wilcox were convinced that the attack could not succeed and discussed what to do if they received orders to advance after it became evident that it had failed. Wilcox told Lang "that he would not again lead his men into such a deathtrap" as he had done the day before.[35] The remaining three brigades of Anderson's Division were also placed under Longstreet's authority, to serve as supports for the assaulting brigades and either exploit their success or cover their retreat. The two remaining brigades of Pender's Division and the three brigades of Rodes' Division that were still in the Long Lane were to cover the assaulting force's left and join in the attack if things looked favorable.

Pickett brought his two front-line brigades over Seminary Ridge, through Spangler's Woods, along a dirt path, and deployed them in a shallow area between two rises of ground less than a quarter-mile west of the Emmitsburg Road, lined up parallel with that road, facing southeast. As they advanced they passed a burial detail disposing of bodies from the second day's fight. A captain in the 1st Virginia recalled that "they have only the ghastly and mangled remnants of their gallant friends to deposit in these hastily dug pits."[36] About a quarter-mile behind them, the third brigade formed behind the second rise, near the east edge of Spangler's Woods, facing the same direction. All of this movement and deployment was hidden from the Federals by the woods on the ridge and the low rises in front of them.

General Pettigrew reported to Longstreet by midmorning, and began moving his four brigades forward at about 10 a.m. After being severely handled by the Union 1st Corps on 1 July, they had sat out the fighting on the second in the fields west of Seminary Ridge. Now Pettigrew halted them in a line of battle, and had them lie down just behind the crest of the ridge, about 200 yards to the left-rear of Pickett's front line. There was little shade where the men lay, and they suffered from the heat and humidity. A Union signal station far to the south, near Emmitsburg, spotted Pettigrew's advance and sent a warning to Meade's headquarters.

Colonel Birkett Fry, the new commander of Archer's Brigade, which was at the right end of Pettigrew's line, had just been watching generals Lee, Longstreet and Hill sitting on a nearby log, consulting a map, when Pettigrew rode up and informed him that they were going to assault the Union line and sent him to consult with Pickett. Fry found the latter in excellent spirits, and, after some reminiscing about their common service in the Mexican War, they were joined by Brigadier General Richard Garnett, who commanded the brigade on the left of Pickett's front line. Fry later claimed that the three officers agreed that Fry's brigade would be the center of the Confederate formation and that all the other brigades in the attack would align themselves with it as they advanced, Pettigrew's men dressing to their right to stay on the same line with Fry's, and Pickett's men guiding to their left to converge with Fry's line. (This is contrary to Longstreet's statement or intention: "General Pickett's line to be the guide." Either Pickett, Garnett and Fry, perhaps unknowingly, changed the plan, or Fry might have exaggerated his brigade's importance in his post-war account.)

It was late morning by the time Brigadier General James Lane, who had succeeded to the command of Pender's Division, received orders to report to Longstreet with two of his brigades. Lane took the two brigades from his second line, his own and that of Brigadier General Alfred Scales; but Scales had been wounded on 1 July, and his brigade was now commanded by Colonel W. Lee Lowrance, who had never previously commanded a brigade and had only been a colonel for less than five months. Longstreet told Lane to place his two brigades, both composed of North Carolina regiments, behind Pettigrew's four brigades, which he was to follow and support when they advanced.

Just as Lane completed this deployment General Trimble rode up with orders from Lee himself to take command of the two brigades. Trimble, at 61, was one of the oldest men on the field, but he was a fiery, aggressive officer, known to Lee, who was refusing to serve any longer under Ewell after the latter had failed to heed his advice to attack Cemetery Hill on the evening of 1 July. Giving Trimble command of this demi-division served to separate him from Ewell and offered a way to make use of his experience and aggressiveness. Trimble used his stentorian voice to introduce himself to the men in the ranks, telling them not to fire their weapons until the enemy line had been broken and promised to stay with them as far as they would go.

Meade wrote to General Halleck again at 12:30: "At the present moment all is quiet. Considerable firing, both infantry and artillery, has taken place in various parts of our line, but no development of the enemy's intentions. My cavalry are pushing the enemy on both my flanks, and keeping me advised of any effort to outflank us. We have taken several hundred prisoners since morning."[37]

Lee had turned down Longstreet's plan to swing around south of the Round Tops and attack Meade from the south, but the Federals also had ideas about turning the enemy flank in this area. Brigadier General Wesley Merritt's Reserve Brigade – the part of Buford's cavalry division that had missed the first two day's fight – being replaced in guarding the Union rear by Buford's two tired brigades, had been ordered to come up the Emmitsburg Road and threaten Longstreet's right rear. But it was still on the way when, around 11 a.m., Farnsworth's brigade of Kilpatrick's division was approaching the right flank of Hood's (now Law's) Division. The only Rebels protecting this flank were the 9th Georgia of "Tige" Anderson's brigade, posted near a house on the west side of the Emmitsburg Road, and a thin picket line of the 1st Texas. When he detected the Union cavalry approaching, Law sent skirmishers from the 1st Texas to fill the gap between that regiment and the 9th Georgia, sent two more of Anderson's regiments to join the 9th Georgia, and turned two batteries to face south.

Extending his thin line west of the Emmitsburg Road were a few cavalrymen under Colonel John Logan Black of Wade Hampton's brigade. Black had just returned to the army from leave, along with about 100 men of his regiment, the 1st South Carolina Cavalry, not all of them mounted, and had not yet rejoined Hampton. Black also had command of a battery of three Blakely rifles from the horse artillery, and about 100 walking wounded and their medical attendants. To escape shells from that battery, Farnsworth's brigade moved into some woods southwest of Big Round Top, and from there, just about 1 p.m., Kilpatrick sent two squadrons of the 1st Vermont Cavalry to test the strength of the Rebel line. These Federals went up a narrow country lane and drove a picket outpost away from a stone house not far from the Emmitsburg Road, which Kilpatrick told them to hang onto. Meanwhile, he sent other units to probe the Confederate lines just west of Round Top, but they reported that the terrain there was too full of boulders and fences to allow for a mounted charge.

Kilpatrick's other brigade, Custer's, had been supposed to follow Farnsworth's, but before his column had moved more than a few hundred yards from its bivouac at Two Taverns it had been intercepted by an aide sent by General Gregg, commander of the 2nd Cavalry Division. Gregg had been ordered by Pleasonton, early that morning, to take position on a ridge near where Rock Creek crossed the Baltimore Pike to guard the army's immediate right flank, but Gregg had considered his position of the day before, farther east, on the Hanover Road about three miles north of Two Taverns, to be too important to abandon. He sent Pleasonton's aide back to say "that I was familiar with the character of the country east of Brinkerhoff's Ridge, that it was open, and that there were two roads leading toward the Hanover Road to the Baltimore Turnpike, that if these were not covered by a sufficient force of cavalry it would be to invite an attack upon our rear with possibly disastrous results."[38] Pleasonton had sent back word for Gregg to go on to the new position but had authorized him to take one of Kilpatrick's brigades to hold his old position, so an aide brought his order to Custer for his four Michigan regiments to join Gregg's two brigades on the Union right. Custer's "Wolverines" moved north along a lane known as the Low Dutch Road and took position near the Hanover Road and the scene of Gregg's previous day's fight with the Stonewall Brigade.

Even after placing Custer's brigade in his own old position, however, Gregg still had his problems, especially when Meade's headquarters detached his cousin Colonel Irvin Gregg's brigade from him for the idiotic idea someone had dreamed up of having it move up the Taneytown Road to probe the Confederate positions in Gettysburg. Fortunately for the colonel and his men, Meade found out about this suicide mission in time to squash it, but once the brigade had rejoined its division orders arrived from cavalry headquarters that sent one of its regiments, the 16th Pennsylvania Cavalry, across the fields south of the Hanover Road to connect with the infantry's flank. It encountered some opposition from Ewell's Confederates, and Gregg sent it a section of artillery for support. For most of the afternoon this regiment held an extended line from the Hanover Road to Wolf' Hill, where there was an infantry regiment belonging to the 6th Corps. The 4th Pennsylvania Cavalry was detached to Cavalry Corps headquarters, and the rest of this brigade was in reserve.

Meanwhile, David Gregg ordered his other brigade, under Colonel John McIntosh, to support Custer, and it took position about halfway between the Baltimore Pike and the Hanover Road. Soon thereafter, Gregg received from General Pleasonton a copy of a message that General Howard had sent to Meade notifying the latter "that large columns of the enemy's cavalry were moving toward the right of our line."[39] Despite this warning, however, Pleasonton ordered Gregg to send Custer to rejoin Kilpatrick on the army's left. While this order was being passed to Custer, about noon, one of the latter's scouting parties reported that there were thousands of Rebel cavalrymen, with artillery, filtering into the trees on Cress Ridge, about a mile to the west.

In fact, Jeb Stuart was moving with the brigade commanded by Colonel John R. Chambliss (in lieu of its normal commander, Brigadier General W. H. F. "Rooney" Lee, R. E. Lee's second son, who had just been captured down in southern Virginia), plus part of Jenkins' Brigade, now under Colonel Milton J. Ferguson, that had accompanied Ewell's corps (the rest of it was guarding prisoners) and three batteries of horse artillery to get around the Union right flank and attack the rear of the Federals on Culp's Hill.[40] Sending orders for Hampton's and Fitz Lee's brigades to meet him,

Stuart went northeast on the York Pike and then turned to the southeast, and by late morning Jenkins' troopers, leading the column, had reached the area where Stuart had witnessed the Stonewall Brigade fight Gregg the previous evening, but they saw no sign of the Federals now. Continuing to the southeast along a country road, the Rebels passed beyond Brinkerhoff's Ridge and reached another, fairly steep and much longer, elevation called Cress Ridge, which ran northeast-southwest between the York Pike and the Hanover Road some two miles east of the left flank of Ewell's infantry near Culp's Hill. The ridge's northern half was heavily wooded and thus screened the road along which Stuart's brigades were traveling.

"A glance satisfied Stuart that he had gained the position he wanted," Major Henry McClellan of his staff later remembered. "The roads leading from the rear of the Federal line of battle were under his eye and could be reached by the prolongation of the road by which he had approached. Moreover, the open fields, although intersected by many fences, admitted of movement in any direction. When Stuart reached this place the scene was as peaceful as if no war existed. The extension of the ridge [Brinkerhoff's] on his right hid from view the lines of the contending armies, and not a living creature was visible on the plain below."[41] While waiting for Hampton's and Fitz Lee's brigades to join him, Stuart moved Ferguson's and Chambliss's men into the trees on Cress Ridge. But then he did a strange thing.

According to Major McClellan, "While carefully concealing Jenkins' and Chambliss' brigades from view, Stuart pushed one of Griffin's guns to the edge of the woods and fired a number of random shots in different directions, himself giving order to the gun." Why conceal the men and then announce his presence by firing a cannon in various directions? "I have been somewhat perplexed to account for Stuart's conduct in firing these shots," McClellan wrote; "but I suppose that they may have been a prearranged signal by which he was to notify General Lee that he had gained a favorable position; or, finding that none of the enemy were within sight, he may have desired to satisfy himself whether the Federal cavalry was in his immediate vicinity before leaving the strong position he then held; and receiving no immediate reply to this fire, he sent for Hampton and Fitz Lee, to arrange with them for an advance and an attack upon the enemy's rear."[42]

In his official report, Stuart wrote, "I moved [Ferguson's] command and W. H. F. Lee's [Chambliss's] secretly through the woods to a position, and hoped to effect a surprise upon the enemy's rear, but Hampton's and Fitz. Lee's brigades, which had been ordered to follow me, unfortunately debouched into the open ground, disclosing the movement, and causing a corresponding movement of a large force of the enemy's cavalry."[43]

However, it wasn't the appearance of the two Confederate brigades that caused the Federal movement, it was David Gregg's refusal to abandon the area. Colonel McIntosh ordered his 1st New Jersey Cavalry to replace Custer's skirmishers as the latter prepared to finally go rejoin Kilpatrick. This regiment moved north of the Hanover Road along the Low Dutch Road and took position in the trees on both sides of the lane, a half-mile southeast of Stuart's position, while McIntosh made his headquarters in the nearby farmhouse of the Jacob Lott family. The rest of his brigade was placed in column of squadrons below the woods, and a section of guns took position south of the Hanover Road, supported by Gregg's reserve, about half of Irvin Gregg's brigade.

Meanwhile, Stuart placed Hampton's Brigade to the left (north) of Chambliss's, and placed Fitz Lee's to the left of Hampton's, with most of these men hidden by the woods on Cress Ridge. The portion of Jenkins' Brigade on hand was commanded by Lieutenant Colonel Vincent Witcher of the 34th Virginia Cavalry Battalion. He had only about 600 men with him: his own battalion plus eight companies drawn from two regiments. They were armed with British Enfield muzzle-loading rifles and were thus accustomed to fighting dismounted. So Stuart sent Witcher's battalion south, dismounted, to a line of fence and the barn of a farm belonging to John and Sarah Rummel. John Rummel was taken prisoner and sent to the Confederate rear on one of his own horses, while Sarah was allowed to flee to a neighbor's house.

Custer's attached horse artillery, the six 3-inch rifles of Battery M, 2nd U.S. Artillery, commanded by Lieutenant Alexander Pennington, took position on a slight rise north of the Hanover Road, near the home of Joseph Spangler, and opened fire on the Confederates. Just a few rounds caused Stuart to withdraw his section of guns and sent some of Witcher's men who had been foraging around the Rummel's buildings scurrying for cover. Custer also sent his 5th Michigan Cavalry, armed with 7-shot Spenser repeaters, north of the Hanover Road as dismounted skirmishers.

Soon after these dispositions were made, everyone's attention was drawn to the west, for, somewhere beyond Cemetery Ridge, the fire of scores and scores of cannon suddenly erupted. "The very ground shook and trembled," a Pennsylvania trooper later recorded, "and the smoke of the guns rolled out of the valley as tho there were thousands of acres of timber on fire."[44]

Endnotes

1 *OR*, I:27:III:511.
2 Ibid., I:27:III:502-3.
3 Ibid., I:27:III:498.
4 Ibid., I:27:II:568.
5 Pfanz, *Gettysburg – Culp's Hill and Cemetery Hill*, 299.
6 Ibid., 314.
7 Ibid., 317.
8 *OR*, I:27:II:569.
9 Ibid., I:27:II:519.
10 Pfanz, *Gettysburg – Culp's Hill and Cemetery Hill*, 351.
11 *OR*, I:27:III:500.
12 Wert, *Gettysburg, Day Three*, 157.
13 Pfanz, *Gettysburg – Culp's Hill and Cemetery Hill*, 357.
14 Wert, *Gettysburg, Day Three*, 155.
15 Ibid., 156-7.
16 Kent Masterson Brown, *Cushing of Gettysburg* (Lexington KY, 1993), 225-6. Both quotes.
17 *OR*, I:27:III:501.

18 Ibid., I:27:I:489.
19 Kent Masterson Brown, *Retreat from Gettysburg* (Chapel Hill NC, 2005), 89.
20 *OR*, I:27:I:74.
21 Ibid., I:27:III:499.
22 Ibid., I:27:III:501.
23 Ibid., I:27:III:506.
24 Haskell, *The Battle of Gettysburg*, 69-70 and 74-5.
25 Longstreet, "Lee's Right Wing at Gettysburg," *B&L* III:342.
26 Richard Rollins, ed., *Pickett's Charge* (Mechanicsburg PA, 1994), 42-3.
27 Alexander, "The Great Charge and Artillery Fighting at Gettysburg," *B&L* III, 361.
28 Alexander, *Military Memoirs of a Confederate*, 417.
29 Doubleday, *Chancellorsville and Gettysburg*, 188.
30 Longstreet, "Lee's Right Wing at Gettysburg," *B&L* III:343.
31 Longstreet, *From Manassas to Appomattox*, 388.
32 Freeman, *Lee's Lieutenants*, III:181.
33 Longstreet, "Lee's Right Wing at Gettysburg," *B&L* III:343.
34 *OR*, I:27:II:359.
35 Wert, *Gettysburg, Day Three*, 119.
36 Ibid., 113.
37 *OR*, I:27:I:74.
38 Wittenberg, *Protecting the Flank*, 48.
39 *OR*, I:27:I:956.
40 McClellan, *I Rode with Jeb Stuart*, 341. "The Result of this battle shows that there was no probability that Stuart could successfully have carried out *his intention of attacking the rear of the Federal right flank*, for it was sufficiently protected by Gregg's command." Emphasis added.
41 Ibid., 338. However, Tom Carhart, contends, in his *Lost Triumph*, p. 200, that only the Hanover Road could have been seen from Cress Ridge, not the Baltimore Pike, and that Custer's cavalry was only about a mile south of Stuart when McClellan claimed that "not a living creature was visible on the plain below." Carhart also points out that this statement contradicts McClellan's claim that Stuart at Cress Ridge was in a position to observe the Union rear.
42 Ibid.
43 *OR*, I:27:II:697.
44 Longacre, *The Cavalry at Gettysburg*, 225.

CHAPTER 13
"The Air Seemed Filled With Shells"
3 July 1863

ALL MORNING, WHILE THE fighting had raged around Culp's Hill, the Confederates had been putting together a tremendous collection of artillery. Colonel Alexander later wrote: "I was directed by Longstreet to post all of his artillery for a preliminary cannonade, and then to take a position whence I could best observe the effect of our fire, and determine the proper moment to give the signal to Pickett to advance. The signal for the opening of the cannonade would be given by Longstreet himself after the infantry brigades were all in position.

"A clump of trees in the enemy's line was pointed out to me as the proposed point of our attack, which I was incorrectly told was the cemetery of the town, and about 9 a.m. I began to revise our line and post it for the cannonade. The enemy very strangely interfered with only an occasional cannon-shot, to none of which did we now reply, for it was easily in their power to drive us to cover or to exhaust our ammunition before our infantry column could be formed. I can only account for their allowing our visible preparations to be completed by supposing that they appreciated in what a trap we would find ourselves. Of Longstreet's 83 guns, 8 were left on our extreme right to cover our flank, and the remaining 75 were posted in an irregular line about 1300 yards long, beginning in the Peach Orchard and ending near the northeast corner of the Spangler wood.

"While so engaged, Gen. Pendleton offered me the use of nine 12-Pr. howitzers of Hill's corps, saying that that corps could not use guns of such short range. I gladly accepted and went to receive the guns under command of Maj. Richardson. I placed them under cover close in rear of the forming column with orders to remain until sent for, intending to take them with the column when it advanced.

"A few hundred yards to left and rear of my line began the artillery of the 3d corps under Col. Walker. It comprised 60 guns, extending on Seminary Ridge as far as the Hagerstown road, and two [very long-range] Whitworth rifles located nearly a mile farther north on the same ridge. In this interval were located 20 rifle guns of the 2d corps under Col. Carter. Four more rifles of the same corps under Capt. Graham were located about one and a half miles northeast of Cemetery Hill. These 24 guns of the 2d corps were ordered to fire only solid shot as their fuses were unreliable.

"There remained unemployed of the 2d corps 25 rifles and 16 Napoleons, and of the 3d corps, fifteen 12-Pr. howitzers. It is notable that of the 84 guns of the 2d and 3d corps to be engaged, 80 were in the same line *parallel to the position of the enemy and 56 guns stood idle*. It was a phenomenal oversight not to place these guns, and many beside, in and near the town to enfilade the 'shank of the fish-hook' and cross fire with the guns from the west."[1]

General Pendleton, Lee's chief of artillery, should have seen to such things, but he was something of a joke in Lee's army. He was then 53 years old but had served only three years in the old Regular Army after graduating from West Point in 1830, one year after Lee. At first he had gone into teaching, and then had been ordained an Episcopal priest. He was, in Alexander's estimation, "too old & had been too long out of army life to be thoroughly up to all the opportunities of his position."[2] Artillery had changed a lot while Pendleton's thoughts had been on religious matters instead of military things. Lee liked him, and, as usual, didn't want to hurt his feelings, but he had recently broken up his artillery reserve, which had been directly under Pendleton, and placed all the guns under the corps commanders, leaving Pendleton as only an advisor. One of Longstreet's staff officers said that Pendleton, despite his title, was little more than an ordnance officer. And, indeed, at this time he seemed more concerned about the location of the ammunition wagons than the positions of the army's batteries. Certainly, he was not the artilleryman his Union counterpart, Henry Hunt, was.

By 10 a.m. Alexander had his guns in position, "so disposed as to fire on Cemetery Hill and the batteries south of it, which would have a fire on our advancing infantry. Pickett's division had arrived, and his men were resting and eating." About an hour later the fight for the Bliss farm buildings broke out on Hill's front, drawing in the guns of the 3rd Corps and some Union batteries, "until over a hundred guns were engaged, and a tremendous roar was kept up for quite a time. But it gradually died out, and the whole field became as silent as a churchyard until 1 o'clock. The enemy, aware of the strength of his position, simply sat still and waited for us.

"It had been arranged that when the infantry column was ready, General Longstreet should order two guns fired by the Washington Artillery. On that signal all our guns were to open on Cemetery Hill and the ridge extending toward Round Top, which was covered with batteries. I was to observe the fire and give Pickett the order to charge. I accordingly took position, about 12, at the most favorable point, just on the left of the line of guns and with one of Pickett's couriers with me. Soon after I received the following note from Longstreet:

"'Colonel: If the artillery fire does not have the effect to drive off the enemy or greatly demoralize him, so as to make our efforts pretty certain, I would prefer that you should not advise General Pickett to make the charge. I shall rely a great deal on your good judgment to determine the matter, and shall expect you to let General Pickett know when the moment offers.'

"This note rather startled me. If that assault was to be made on General Lee's judgment it was all right, but I did not want it made on mine. I wrote back to General Longstreet to the following effect:

"'General: I will only be able to judge of the effect of our fire on the enemy by his return fire, for his infantry is but little exposed to view and the smoke will obscure the whole field. If, as I infer from your note, there is any alternative to this attack, it should be carefully considered before opening fire, for it will take all the artillery ammunition we have left to test this one thoroughly, and, if the result is unfavorable, we will have none left for another effort. And even if this is entirely successful, it can only be so at a very bloody cost.'

"To this presently came the following reply: 'Colonel: The intention is to advance the infantry if the artillery has the desired effect of driving the enemy off, or having other effect such as to warrant us in making the attack. When the moment arrives advice General Pickett, and of course advance such artillery as you can use in aiding the attack.'

"I hardly knew whether this left me discretion or not, but at any rate it seemed decided that the artillery must open. I felt that if we went that far we could not draw back, but the infantry must go too. General A. R. Wright of Hill's corps was with me looking at the position when these notes were received, and we discussed them together. Wright said, 'It is not so hard to *go* there as it looks; I was nearly there with my brigade yesterday. The trouble is to *stay* there. The whole Yankee army is there in a bunch.'

"I was influenced by this, and somewhat by a sort of camp rumor which I had heard that morning, that General Lee had said that he was going to send every man he had upon that hill. At any rate, I assumed that the question of supports had been well considered, and that whatever was possible would be done. But before replying I rode to see Pickett, who was with his division a short distance to the rear. I did not tell him my object, but only tried to guess how he felt about the charge. He seemed very sanguine, and thought himself in luck to have the chance. Then I felt that I could not make any delay or let the attack suffer by any indecision on my part. And, that General Longstreet might know my intention, I wrote him only this: 'General: When our artillery fire is at its best, I shall order Pickett to charge.'

"Then, getting a little more anxious, I decided to send for

the nine howitzers and take them ahead of Pickett up nearly to musket range, instead of following close behind him as at first intended; so I sent a courier to bring them up in front of the infantry, but under cover of the wood. The courier could not find them. He was sent again, and only returned after our fire was opened, saying they were gone. I afterward learned that General Pendleton had sent for a part of them, and the others had moved to a neighboring hollow to get out of the line of the enemy's fire at one of Hill's batteries during the artillery duel they had had an hour before [during the fight for the Bliss buildings].

"At exactly 1 o'clock by my watch the two signal-guns were heard in quick succession. In another minute every gun was at work. The enemy were not slow in coming back at us, and the grand roar of nearly the whole artillery of both armies burst in on the silence, almost as suddenly as the full notes of an organ would fill a church."[3] The professor at the college who was keeping track of the weather said it was 1:07 on his watch when the artillery opened fire. The temperature was 87 degrees, the air still and humid. Civilians in the town, many huddled in the cellars for safety, were startled by the sudden outburst. Sally Broadhead told her diary it sounded "as if the heavens and earth were crashing together," and said of the noise, "More terrible never greeted human ears. We knew that with every explosion, and the scream of each shell, human beings were hurried through excruciating pain, into another world, and that many more were torn and mangled and lying in torment worse than death, and no one able to extend relief."[4]

On the Union side, General Hunt had been watching the fight for Culp's Hill, but between 10 and 11 a.m., satisfied that everything looked favorable there, he had crossed over to Cemetery Ridge. "Here a magnificent display greeted my eyes," he later wrote. "Our whole front for two miles was covered by [Confederate] batteries already in line or going into position. They stretched – apparently in one unbroken mass – from opposite the town to the Peach Orchard, which bounded the view to the left, the ridges of which were planted thick with cannon. Never before had such a sight been witnessed on this continent, and rarely, if ever, abroad. What did it mean? It might possibly be to hold that line while its infantry was sent to aid Ewell, or to guard against a counter-stroke from us, but it most probably meant an assault on our center, to be preceded by a cannonade in order to crush our batteries and shake our infantry; at least to cause us to exhaust our ammunition in reply, so that the assaulting troops might pass in good condition over the half mile of open ground which was beyond our effective musketry fire."[5]

With this in mind, Hunt rode along the lines instructing battery commanders and corps chiefs of artillery "to withhold their fire for fifteen or twenty minutes after the cannonade commenced, then to concentrate their fire with all possible accuracy on those batteries which were most destructive to us – but slowly, so that when the enemy's ammunition was exhausted, we should have sufficient left to meet the assault. I had just given these orders to the last battery on Little Round Top, when the signal-gun was fired, and the enemy opened with all his guns. From that point the scene was indescribably grand. All their batteries were soon covered with smoke, through which the flashes were incessant, whilst the air seemed filled with shells, whose sharp explosions, with the hurtling of their fragments, formed a running accompaniment to the deep roar of the guns."[6]

The sound of the massed guns at Gettysburg was heard 140 miles away, but to the Union soldiers on Cemetery Hill and Cemetery Ridge, it wasn't so much the bass of the guns firing as the higher notes of the shells that mattered. "Streams of screaming projectiles poured through the hot air falling and bursting everywhere," said Major St. Clair Mulholland, commander of the 116th Pennsylvania in the Irish Brigade. "Men and horses were torn limb from limb; caissons [of ammunition] exploded one after another in rapid succession, blowing the gunners to pieces. No spot within our lines was free from this frightful iron rain. . . . It was literally a storm of shot and shell that the oldest soldiers there – those who had taken part in almost every battle of the war – had not yet witnessed. That awful rushing sound of the flying missiles which causes the firmest hearts to quail was everywhere."[7] Lieutenant Haskell had just finished a satisfying lunch of stewed chicken and potatoes, shared with numerous other staff officers and Generals Meade, Hancock, Gibbon, Pleasonton, and Newton, and the group was breaking up when the Rebel artillery opened fire. Major Mulholland said that the meal was still in progress, however, and that one of the first Confederate shots struck an orderly who was passing the butter to some officers, and cut him in two.

"The wildest confusion for a few moments obtained sway among us," Haskell wrote, though he didn't mention the severed orderly. "The shells came bursting all about. The [generals'] servants ran terror-stricken for dear life and disappeared. The horses, hitched to trees or held by the slack hands of the orderlies, neighed out in fright and broke away and plunged riderless through the fields." He went with Gibbon to the crest of the ridge. "We thought that at the second Bull Run, at the Antietam and at Fredericksburg on the 11th of December, we had heard heavy cannonading; they were but holiday salutes compared with this. Besides the great ceaseless roar of the guns, which was but the background of the others, a million various minor sounds engaged the ear. The projectiles shriek long and sharp. They hiss, they scream, they growl, they sputter; all sounds of life and rage; and each has its different note, and all are discordant. . . . We watched the shells bursting in the air, as they came hissing in all directions. Their flash was a bright gleam of lightning radiating from a point, giving place in the thousandth part of a second to a small, white puffy cloud, like a fleece of the lightest, whitest wool. These clouds were very numerous. We could not often see the shell before it burst; but sometimes, as we faced toward the enemy, and looked above our heads, the approach would be heralded by a prolonged hiss, which always seemed to me to be a line of something tangible, terminating in a black globe, distinct to the eye, as the sound had been to the ear. The shell would seem to stop, and hang suspended in the air an instant, and then vanish in fire and smoke and noise."[8]

A news correspondent on Cemetery Hill said, "The storm broke upon us so suddenly that soldiers and officers – who leaped as it began from their tents, and from lazy siestas on the grass – were stricken in their rising with mortal wounds, and died, some with cigars between their teeth, some with pieces of food in their fingers, and one at least – a pale young German from Pennsylvania – with a miniature of his sister in his hands."[9] Once the surprise and chaos of the first few minutes had passed, however, the Union infantry was not much harmed. Lieutenant Haskell said, "The men of the infantry have seized their arms, and behind their works, behind every rock, in every ditch, wherever there is any shelter, they hug the ground, silent, quiet, unterrified, little harmed."[10]

The Union artillerymen could not take cover, however, since they had to man their guns. Captain Samuel Fiske was impressed by the sight of "our gallant artillerists, serving their guns with the utmost precision and coolness . . . knowing they were the mark aimed at by an equally brave and skillful enemy, and clinging to their beloved pieces to the bitter end."[11] "We see the solid shot strike axle, or pole, or wheel, and the tough iron and heart of oak snap and fly like straws," Haskell wrote. "The great oaks there by Woodruff's guns [Ziegler's Grove] heave down their massy branches with a crash, as if the lightning smote them. The shells swoop down among the battery horses standing there apart. A half a dozen horses start, they tumble, theirs legs stiffen, their vitals and blood smear the ground. And these shot and shells have no respect for men either. We see the poor fellows hobbling back from the crest, or unable to do so, pale and weak, lying on the ground with the mangled stump of an arm or leg, dripping their life-blood away; or with a cheek torn open or a shoulder smashed."[12]

But casualties among both the infantry and the artillery were not as bad as they might have been, for the Confederate gunners were firing too high. "Most of the enemy's projectiles passed overhead," General Hunt said, "the effect being to sweep all the open ground in our rear, which was of little benefit to the Confederates – a mere waste of ammunition, for everything here could seek shelter."[13] Well, not everything. "Ambulances, passing down the Taneytown road, with wounded men, were struck," Lieutenant Haskell wrote. "The hospitals near this road were riddled. The house which was General Meade's headquarters was shot through several times, and a great many horses of officers and orderlies were lying dead around it. . . . Mules with ammunition, pigs wallowing about, cows in the pastures, whatever was animate or inanimate, in all this broad range, were no exception to their blind havoc."[14] Captain Fiske said, "It was touching to see the little birds, all out of their wits with fright, flying wildly about amidst the tornado of terrible missiles and uttering strange notes of distress. It was touching to see the innocent cows and calves, feeding in the fields, torn in pieces by the shells. . . ."[15]

Major Mulholland remembered seeing General Hancock and his staff riding along his lines, with his corps flag flying, while shot and shell roared and crashed around them. "It was a gallant deed, and withal not a reckless exposure of life, for the presence and calm demeanor of the commander, as he passed through the lines of his men, set them an example which . . . bore good fruit and nerved their stout hearts."[16] When a staff officer suggested that Hancock should not take such risks, the general replied, "There are times when a corps commander's life does not count."[17] Frank Haskell said that the bombardment had been going on for an hour, without signs of abatement, when he and General Gibbon also moved along the lines, although they, at least, had the good sense to go on foot. "We went along the lines of the infantry as they lay there flat upon the earth, a little to the front of the batteries. They were suffering little, and were quite cool. How glad we were that the enemy were no better gunners, and that they cut their fuses too long. To the question asked the men, 'What do you think of this?' the replies would be, 'O, this is bully,' 'We are getting to like it,' 'O, we don't mind this.' And so they lay under the heaviest cannonade that ever shook the continent, and among them a thousand times more jokes than heads were cracked."[18]

Meanwhile, the Union gunners were giving the Confederates a taste of their own medicine. "The enemy's position seemed to have broken out with guns everywhere," Colonel Alexander remembered, "and from Round Top to Cemetery Hill was blazing like a volcano. The air seemed full of missiles from every direction." His own battalion of six batteries, including infantrymen who had volunteered to help serve the guns, lost 144 men and 116 horses, worse even than its losses at Antietam, which it remembered as "artillery hell."[19]

As McIntosh's brigade of Gregg's cavalry division was replacing Custer's brigade, so that the latter could finally go and rejoin Kilpatrick on the Union left, the mild-mannered 30-year-old Gregg met the flamboyant 23-year-old Custer. The latter said, "General Gregg, you are going to have a big fight on your hands today. The woods beyond are full of the enemy." "Well, in that case," Gregg replied, "I shall have to keep you to help me out."[20] And again he ordered Custer, who was more than willing, to stay with him.

Nine Confederate guns of various types were now visible on Cress Ridge, so Gregg brought up Captain Alanson Randol's consolidated batteries E and G, 1st U.S. Artillery, placing one section about 250 yards to the right front of Pennington's battery, and the other section farther to the front, near an orchard of the Anthony Howard farm. At about 2 p.m., Stuart's horse artillery opened fire, but the Union gunners quickly replied and soon gained the upper hand. "As a rule," Captain Randol later asserted, "their [Confederate] Horse Art'y was so badly handled in battle we Art'y officers paid but little attention to it."[21] The Federal horse artillery, on the other hand, contained some of the best batteries in the Union Army. Within minutes the Union gunners disabled one of Stuart's guns and killed about two dozen of his artillerymen, as well as a similar number of horses. Stuart brought up three more guns, farther south, on the Trostle farm, but they had to fire slowly because they had a limited supply of ammunition, and within ten minutes the Federals had wounded four of their gunners and killed half their horses. Those three guns and two on the ridge were soon withdrawn by their crews. Pennington's gunners also bombarded John Rummel's barn, which was full of Witcher's men.

While the big guns dueled, Colonel McIntosh sent his 1st New Jersey forward dismounted, and it halted behind a rail fence on a rise overlooking Little Run. The 34th Virginia Battalion was stationed behind a stone wall on the other side of the stream and opened what one Federal called a murderous fire, and the Jerseymen returned the favor. Stuart responded by sending the rest of Witcher's men forward and part of Chambliss's brigade; some of Fitz Lee's men were also on the skirmish line. The 1st New Jersey soon fired off all of its carbine ammunition, and McIntosh ordered it to withdraw, but its men refused to budge, holding their position with their revolvers until they could borrow ammunition from the 3rd Pennsylvania, which McIntosh had sent to support them. Witcher's Rebels soon had their own ammunition problem, however, because, through some oversight, they had only been supplied with ten rounds apiece. Stuart ordered them to hold their ground anyway.

Custer sent four companies of the 6th Michigan, dismounted, to extend the Union line to the left, or south, while another battalion of the 6th Michigan, mounted, supported Pennington's guns. The 1st and 7th Michigan were in reserve near the junction of the Hanover and Low Dutch roads; the lone company of the Purnell Legion, from Irvin Gregg's brigade, was next to part of the 3rd Pennsylvania; and the 1st Maine Cavalry, of the same brigade, supported Randol's battery. And when he heard that the 1st New Jersey and 3rd Pennsylvania were running low on ammunition, Custer sent the 5th Michigan forward, dismounted, with its 7-shot repeating rifles.

Chambliss's Rebels were advancing on the Union front and flank when the 5th Michigan joined the line. A Union lieutenant helping with the horses of these dismounted men watched from near Pennington's battery as the Confederates approached his regiment. "Our boys held their fire until the rebs got within less than twenty rods [110 yards]," he said, "then they opened on them. After the first volley, the rebel officers called out, 'Now for them before they can reload!' But our boys did not have to stop to reload their Spencers, but gave them a second, third, and a fourth volley. Many a reb fell, either dead or wounded; the rest were unable to stand the rain of lead and the most of them got back faster than they came. Our boys called out to those nearest to them to come in or we will shoot; about one hundred did come in."[22] The lieutenant added that "One tall, lean lank Johnny, after he came in, asked to see our guns, saying: 'You'ns load in the morning and fire all day.'"[23]

The 5th Michigan had arrived just in time to prevent Chambliss's men from dislodging the 1st New Jersey and 3rd Pennsylvania, and it drove the Confederates back to a fence a few hundred yards in front of Stuart's main force, the Federals halting along another fence on the edge of a wheatfield. Colonel Witcher, having found more ammunition for his men, then ordered them to counterattack, and by then the 5th Michigan was also low on ammunition (one problem with repeaters was that it didn't take long to shoot off all of their ammo) and it gave ground. Major Noah Ferry, commanding its right battalion, was killed while rallying his men. But, meanwhile, the colonel of the 5th Michigan had managed to mount one squadron of his regiment and send it to counterattack two of Chambliss's regiments. Again low on ammunition and being pounded by the Union artillery, Witcher's and Chambliss's men fell back before this charge all the way to the woods on top of Cress Ridge, and the Federals advanced to the Rummel farm buildings, a move that threatened to split

Stuart's forces in two.

Evidently it was at this time, while Hampton was off conferring with Stuart, that Fitz Lee ordered some or all of Hampton's men to charge the Federals' flank, but Hampton returned in time to countermand the order, "as I did not think it a judicious one, and the brigade resumed its former position; not, however, without loss, as the movement had disclosed its position to the enemy."[24] Colonel George Gray, the 6th Michigan's commander, sent his bugler to inform Custer that his right flank was vulnerable and any force of mounted Confederates could charge right around it.

Stuart later claimed that he had been planning to hold the Federals with his dismounted men and attack their flank with his mounted elements. (He said their "left flank," but their right, his left, seems more logical.)[25] But this Union advance threatened to cut off and capture part of his dismounted men, so he ordered a couple of newly arrived batteries to bolster his line and then ordered one of Chambliss's regiments to counterattack. At the same time the 1st Virginia Cavalry of Fitz Lee's brigade made a mounted charge on the Union right flank. The battalion of the 3rd Pennsylvania near the Lott farm house fired into the flank of the advancing 1st Virginia, but when Colonel McIntosh galloped over to the Lott farm to get his 1st Maryland, he discovered that General Gregg had moved it elsewhere. However, Gregg made up for this by quickly ordering the 7th Michigan, which he had just ordered to replace the 1st Maryland, to charge the oncoming Confederates. Custer fell in at the head of this regiment, and as it passed through the Union guns he drew his saber and shouted: "Come on you Wolverines!"[26]

"The ground over which we had to pass was very unfavorable for the maneuvering of cavalry," Custer later reported, "but despite all obstacles this regiment advanced boldly to the assault, which was executed in splendid style, the enemy being driven from field to field, until our advance reached a high and unbroken fence, behind which the enemy was strongly posted. Nothing daunted, Colonel [William] Mann, followed by the main body of his regiment, bravely rode up to the fence and discharged their revolvers in the very face of the foe."[27]

It was a sturdy post-and-rail fence built over a low stone wall, and it proved to be an impassable barrier between the Federals and Confederates. As Captain J. H. Kidd of the 6th Michigan, watching from near the Union guns, later wrote: "The squadrons coming up successively at a charge, rushed pell mell on each other and were thrown into a state of indescribable confusion, though the rear troops, without order or orders, formed left and right into line along the fence, and pluckily began firing across it into the faces of the Confederates, who, when they saw the impetuous onset of the Seventh thus abruptly checked, rallied and began to collect in swarms upon the opposite side. Some of the [Union] officers leaped from their saddles and called upon the men to assist in making an opening. . . . The task was a difficult and hazardous one, the posts and rails being so firmly united that it could be accomplished only by lifting the posts, which were deeply set, and removing several lengths at once. This was finally done, however, though the regiment was exposed not only to a fire from the force in front, but to a flanking fire from a strong skirmish line along a fence to the right and running nearly at right angles with the one through which it was trying to pass."[28]

With a section of the fence finally torn down, the 7th Michigan passed through the gap and resumed its charge, and the Confederates again fell back before it. "The charge was continued," Kidd recalled, "across a plowed field to the front and right, up to and past Rummel's, to a point within 200 or 300 yards of the Confederate battery. There another fence was encountered, the last one in the way of reaching the battery, the guns of which were pouring canister into the charging column as fast as they could fire."[29]

Colonel Chambliss, meanwhile, had sent a staff officer looking for help, and General Hampton responded by sending his veteran 1st North Carolina and Jeff Davis Legion in a mounted charge against the relatively inexperienced 7th Michigan. Disorganized by their fight by the first fence and subsequent advance, taking heavy fire from the Rebel guns, and now charged by two fresh units, the Wolverines retreated. "No troops could have maintained this position," Custer claimed; "the Seventh was, therefore, compelled to retire, followed by twice the number of the enemy."[30] However, fire from the Union horse artillery and the dismounted men of the 5th and 6th Michigan, 3rd Pennsylvania, and 1st New Jersey, covered their retreat and allowed them to get away.

Hampton later reported that his two regiments "drove back the enemy; but in their eagerness they followed him too far, and encountered his reserve in heavy force. Seeing the state of affairs at this juncture, I rode rapidly to the front, to take charge of these two regiments, and, while doing this, to my surprise I saw the rest of my brigade (excepting the Cobb Legion) and Fitz. Lee's brigade charging."[31] It was evidently about 4 p.m. when these two brigades (eight regiments) emerged from the woods in close column of squadrons with sabers drawn, and a Pennsylvania captain later said, "A grander spectacle than their advance has rarely been beheld. They marched with well-aligned fronts and steady reins. Their polished saber blades dazzled in the sun. All eyes turned upon them."[32] Stuart's cavalry often preferred to use their revolvers for mounted fighting instead of their swords, but on this occasion Federals heard Confederate officers yelling, "Keep to your sabers, men, keep to your sabers!"[33] "Their line was almost perfect," one Wolverine noted, "until they reached the fence that our boys had held so long."[34]

The Union horse artillery targeted this massed formation, as did the various dismounted Federal units. "On and on, nearer and nearer, came the assaulting column, charging straight for Randol's guns," Captain J. H. Kidd remembered. "The storm of cannister caused them to waver a little, but that was all."[35] David Gregg turned to the veteran 1st Michigan Cavalry and ordered it to charge the head of the Confederate column. As it advanced, Custer, unaware of Gregg's order, rode up and also ordered it to charge and took position next to its colonel. As the 1st Michigan rode right at the front of the oncoming Rebel column, the 5th Michigan charged its right flank, three of McIntosh's squadrons charged its left, as did McIntosh himself and his staff, and one troop of the 7th Michigan also joined in. "Then," J. H. Kidd wrote, "it was steel to steel."[36]

One Virginian said, "The field is soon alive with moving squadrons – here a group retiring in disorder – there a mass mixed up in hand to hand conflict; horses rearing, swords uplifted, smoke and dust."[37] Captain William Miller of the 3rd Pennsylvania said the two forces collided "Like the falling of timber, so sudden and violent that many of the horses were turned end over end and crushed their riders beneath them."[38] He and his squadron charged into the flank of the Confederate column, cut off part of it, and drove that portion back toward Cress Ridge. These Rebels, part of Fitz Lee's brigade, thought they had been attacked by a lot more than a single squadron. After going as far as the Rummels' wagon shed, Miller and his men turned around and cut their way back through the Rebels, returning to the safety of the woods on the Lott farm.

"For minutes – and for minutes that seemed like years – the gray column stood and staggered before the blow; then yielded and fled," Kidd said. The 5th Michigan and McIntosh's men had pierced the column's flanks, and the 1st Michigan "went through it like a wedge, splitting it in twain, and scattering the Confederate horsemen in disorderly rout back to the woods whence they came."[39] Major McClellan, watching from the Confederate rear alongside General Stuart, saw it somewhat differently. "For many minutes," he said, "the fight with sabre and pistol raged most furiously. Neither party seemed willing to give way. The impetuous attack of the Federal cavalry was, however, finally broken; and both parties withdrew to the lines held at the opening of the fight."[40] Despite McClellan's spin, it was the Confederates whose charge was broken. They retreated to the woods on Cress

Ridge, with Stuart himself rallying the 1st Virginia, his old regiment, and making a countercharge that ended the Union pursuit.

Custer's horse went down early in the fight when it was shot in a foreleg, but the young general was thrown clear and soon grabbed a riderless horse and got back in the fight. Several troopers of the 1st New Jersey attacked Wade Hampton and had him hemmed against a fence, but the huge Confederate took out one man with his saber and shot another with his revolver. Two Mississippians of the Jeff Davis Legion tried to save him but were both cut down by Federal sabers. Hampton got another enemy trooper with his pistol, but the head wound he had received the day before opened again when he was hit by a saber, and another Union trooper shot him in the side. When the general, now soaked in blood from his reopened scalp wound, tried to help another Confederate, he received another cut to the head but brought his own saber down on his latest attacker with such force that it cleaved through the man's skull from crown to chin. Finally, two of his men opened up a lane of escape for the general, who spurred his horse over a fence and got away. Nevertheless, he would be out of action for months while he recuperated from his wounds.

The two forces continued to skirmish with each other until dark, but the real fighting was now over on this part of the field. After dark, Stuart left the 1st Virginia on picket duty and withdrew the rest of his command to the York turnpike. Custer finally led his brigade to rejoin Kilpatrick on the army's left, and Gregg's two brigades held the ground over which the cavalry had fought. Custer was very proud of his men after this fight, challenging the "annals of warfare" to produce a more brilliant or successful charge of cavalry. But his men were proud of him as well. They boasted that he did not send them to charge, he led them. And soon his officers and men were starting to sport red cravats in imitation of their young leader. But, as J. H. Kidd later stated, the major credit for the Union success lay with David Gregg, who recognized the importance of the Hannover Road-Low Dutch Road intersection and its surrounding fields and refused to be removed from it.

Stuart never explained exactly what his intentions had been that day, though the available evidence indicates that he wanted to ambush the Union cavalry, separate it from its infantry, and get into the rear of the Federal army – whether to attack it from that direction or merely to intercept a retreat is unclear. However, Gregg and his men, as he later put it, "did not propose to be entertained by a line of sharpshooters," but engaged the Confederates to the point where Stuart had to employ his entire force, only to see it driven off the field.[41]

While the cavalry fought for control of the Union rear, Longstreet finally launched the infantry attack on Cemetery Hill. "Before the cannonade opened," Colonel Alexander later wrote, "I had made up my mind to give Pickett the order to advance within fifteen or twenty minutes after it began. But when I looked at the full development of the enemy's batteries, and knew that his infantry was generally protected from our fire by stone walls and swell of the ground, I could not bring myself to give the word. It seemed madness to launch infantry into that fire, with nearly three-quarters of a mile to go at midday under a July sun. I let the 15 minutes pass, and 20, and 25, hoping vainly for something to turn up. Then I wrote to Pickett: 'If you are coming at all you must come at once, or I cannot give you proper support; but the enemy's fire has not slackened at all; at least eighteen guns are still firing from the cemetery itself.' [He also sent a similar note to Johnston Pettigrew, commanding Heth's Division.] Five minutes after sending that message, the enemy's fire suddenly began to slacken, and the guns in the cemetery limbered up and vacated the position."[42]

Just which guns Alexander might have seen withdraw is not known, especially given that he was mistaken about the actual location of the cemetery. Some Union guns were knocked out, and a few were withdrawn, but these were partially replaced between the end of the artillery duel and the arrival of the Confederate infantry. And many guns that were neither hit nor withdrawn merely ceased firing in order to save their ammunition for use against the infantry attack that was surely going to follow the bombardment. Several Union officers claimed credit for ordering the guns to cease firing, including Meade and Major Osborn, both of whom later claimed that they did so for the purpose of luring the Rebels to their destruction, but most of the credit probably belongs to Hunt. Hancock, however, ordered the guns of his corps to continue firing, in order to keep up the courage of his infantrymen. As a result, they expended most of their long-range ammunition in counter-battery fire.

When the Confederate guns had opened fire Hunt had ridden to the Artillery Reserve, parked behind Cemetery Ridge, "to order fresh batteries and ammunition to be sent up to the ridge as soon as the cannonade ceased; but both the reserve and the [ammunition] train had gone to a safer place. Messengers, however, had been left to receive and convey orders, which I sent by them; then I returned to the ridge. . . . Our fire was deliberate, but on inspecting the chests I found that the ammunition was running low, and hastened to General Meade to advise its immediate cessation and preparation for the assault which would certainly follow. The headquarters building, immediately behind the ridge, had been abandoned, and many of the horses of the staff lay dead. Being told that the general had gone to the cemetery, I proceeded thither. He was not there, [but] on telling General Howard my object, he concurred in its propriety, and I rode back along the ridge, ordering the fire to cease."[43]

"We Confederates often did such things as that," Alexander said, "to save our ammunition for use against infantry, but I had never before seen the Federals withdraw their guns simply to save them up for the infantry fight. So I said, 'If he does not run fresh batteries in there in five minutes, this is our fight.' I looked anxiously with my glass, and the five minutes passed without a sign of life on the deserted portion, still swept by our fire, and littered with dead men and horses and fragments of disabled [gun] carriages. Then I wrote to Pickett, urgently: 'For God's sake, come quick. The eighteen guns are gone; come quick, or my ammunition won't let me support you properly.'"[44]

Pickett was with Longstreet when this note reached him. He read it and then handed it to the latter, saying, "General, shall I advance?" "The effort to speak the order failed," Longstreet later wrote, "and I could only indicate it by an affirmative bow. He accepted the duty with seeming confidence of success, leaped on his horse, and rode gayly to his command."[45] After riding only a few paces Pickett remembered a note he had been writing to his young sweetheart, and he turned back to ask Longstreet to mail it if he didn't come back. He noticed that there were tears on Longstreet's cheeks and in his beard.

After Pickett left, Longstreet rode alone to join Colonel Alexander. "I had grown very impatient to see Pickett," Alexander later wrote, "fearing ammunition would run short, when Longstreet joined me. I explained the situation. He spoke sharply, – 'Go and stop Pickett where he is and replenish your ammunition.' I answered: 'We can't do that, sir. The train has but little. It would take an hour to distribute it, and meanwhile the enemy would improve the time.' Longstreet seemed to stand irresolute (we were both dismounted) and then spoke slowly and with great emotion: 'I do not want to make this charge. I do not see how it can succeed. I would not make it now but that Gen. Lee has ordered it and is expecting it.'"[46] (Alexander's I Corps guns had indeed expended most of their long-range ammunition, but the II Corps and III Corps guns had not. General Pendleton had, meanwhile, and without informing anyone, moved the ammunition train farther to the rear, where it was both out of danger and next to useless.)

"I listened, but did not dare offer a word," Alexander said later. "The battle was lost if we stopped. Ammunition was far too low to try anything else, for we had been fighting three days. There was a chance, and it was not my part to interfere. While Longstreet was speaking, Pickett's division swept out of the wood and showed the full length of its gray ranks and shining bayonets, as grand a sight as ever a man looked on. Joining it on the left, Pettigrew stretched farther than I could see. General Dick Garnett, just out of the sick ambulance, and buttoned up in an old blue overcoat, riding at the head of his brigade passed us and saluted Longstreet. Garnett was a warm personal friend, and we had not met before for months. We had served on the plains together before the war. I rode with him a short distance, and then we wished each other luck and a good-bye, which was our last."[47]

Like their Union counterparts, the Confederate infantrymen had suffered some losses during the artillery duel, but admired the courage of their artillerymen. Also like them, their morale was enhanced by the appearance of various senior officers braving the bombardment. A captain later remembered seeing Longstreet ride by several times, and Pickett, and General Lee once. "His appearance at a place of such eminent danger both thrilled and horrified the line," he said, "and men shouted to him to go away to shelter. . . . he took off his hat in acknowledgment of their affectionate solicitude, and then rode on. . . ." "We could see nothing whatever of the opposing lines," a lieutenant in Pickett's Division later remembered, "but knew from the fire that they must have a strong position and many guns. Our loss was considerable under this storm of shot and shell; still there was no demoralization of our men in line. They waited almost impatiently for the order to advance, as almost anything would be a relief from the strain upon them."[48] At last the order came, and, for a few moments, the guns fell silent.

They had been firing for a lot longer than Alexander had originally intended – at least an hour, maybe two. Lieutenant Haskell said, "At three o'clock almost precisely the last shot hummed, and bounded and fell, and the cannonade was over. . . . [M]en began to breathe more freely, and to ask,

What next, I wonder? The battery men were among their guns, some leaning to rest and wipe the sweat from their sooty faces, some were handling ammunition boxes and replenishing those that were empty. Some batteries from the artillery reserve were moving up to take the places of the disabled ones; the smoke was clearing from the crests. There was a pause between the acts, with the curtain down...."[49] One soldier noted that "The heat can be seen quivering along the line."[50]

After telling Garnett to "make the best kind of time in crossing the valley; it's a hell of an ugly looking place over yonder," Pickett rode out in front of his first line and shouted, "Up, men, and to your posts! Don't forget today that you are from Old Virginia!" Armistead told his men, in the second line, "Men, remember what you are fighting for! Your homes, your firesides, and your sweethearts! Follow me!"[51] Such speeches, often much longer, were traditional in that war and often inspiring, but not always. Lieutenant John Dooley in the 1st Virginia said, "When you rise to your feet as we did today, I tell you the enthusiasm of ardent breasts in many cases *ain't there*, and instead of burning to avenge the insults of our country, families and altars and firesides, the thought is most frequently, *Oh, if I could just come out of this charge safely how thankful would I be!*"[52] A few of the Confederates did not rise to take their places in line; some had been killed or wounded by the artillery; some were suffering from heat stroke; others just didn't have the courage. But most did.

Soon the long Confederate lines advanced into the open. Major Edmund Rice, in Gibbon's division, watching from atop a boulder on Cemetery Ridge, said, "A line of [Confederate] skirmishers sprang lightly forward out of the woods, and, with intervals well kept, moved rapidly down into open fields, closely followed by a line of battle, then by another, and by yet a third. Both sides watched this never-to-be-forgotten scene.... [We] looked with admiration on the different lines of Confederates, marching forward with easy swinging step, and the men were heard to exclaim: 'Here they come!' 'Here they come!' 'Here comes the infantry!'"[53]

∼ Endnotes ∼

1   Alexander, *Military Memoirs of a Confederate*, 418-9. Italics in the source. The clump of trees mentioned here was almost certainly Ziegler's Grove, at the southwest end of Cemetery Hill, not the tiny "copse of trees" later made famous by John Bachelder. When viewed from the Peach Orchard area, the copse would have been right in front of Ziegler's Grove, anyway, and would have been indistinguishable from it.
2   Wert, *Gettysburg: Day Three*, 126.
3   Alexander, "The Great Charge and Artillery Fighting at Gettysburg," *B&L* III, 362-3.
4   Wheeler, *Witness to Gettysburg*, 251.
5   Henry J. Hunt, "The Third Day at Gettysburg," in *B&L* III, 371-2.
6   Ibid., 372-3.
7   Wheeler, *Witness to Gettysburg*, 231.
8   Haskell, *The Battle of Gettysburg*, 85 and 88.
9   Wheeler, *Witness to Gettysburg*, 231-2.
10 Haskell, *The Battle of Gettysburg*, 83.
11 Wheeler, *Witness to Gettysburg*, 232.
12 Ibid., 86.
13 Hunt, "The Third Day at Gettysburg," *B&L* III, 373.
14 Haskell, *The Battle of Gettysburg*, 88.
15 Wheeler, *Witness to Gettysburg*, 232.
16 Ibid., 233.
17 Sears, *Gettysburg*, 400.
18 Haskell, *The Battle of Gettysburg*, 89-90.
19 Alexander, "The Great Charge and Artillery Fighting at Gettysburg," *B&L* III, 364.
20 Wert, *Gettysburg: Day Three*, 263.
21 Ibid., 264.
22 Wittenberg, *Protecting the Flank*, 79-80.
23 Urwin, *Custer Victorious*, 76.
24 *OR*, I:27:II:724.
25 Ibid., I:27:II:698.
26 J. H. Kidd, *A Cavalryman with Custer* (New York, 1991), 83-4.
27 Wittenberg, *Protecting the Flank*, 86.
28 Kidd, *A Cavalryman with Custer*, 84-5.
29 Ibid., 85
30 Wittenberg, *Protecting the Flank*, 88.
31 *OR*, I:27:II:725.
32 Wittenberg, *Protecting the Flank*, 95-6.
33 Ibid., 98.
34 Ibid., 96.
35 Kidd, *A Cavalryman with Custer*, 88.
36 Ibid. 89.
37 Ibid., 103.
38 Wittenberg, *Protecting the Flank*, 102.
39 Kidd, *A Cavalryman with Custer*, 89.
40 McClellan, *I Rode With Jeb Stuart*, 340-1.
41 Wittenberg, *Protecting the Flank*, 126.
42 Alexander, "The Great Charge and Artillery Fighting at Gettysburg," *B&L* III, 364. Note the concern for Cemetery Hill, not Cemetery Ridge. In an August 1863 letter to Colonel Moxley Sorrel of Longstreet's staff, Alexander specifically spoke of the 18 guns as firing from "the point (the cemetery) he was to charge." Also, in a letter to

John Bachelder written in 1876, he said he was "ordered to prepare for an assault on Cemetery Hill." Both quotes from Harman, *Lee's Real Plan at Gettysburg*, 80.

43 Hunt, "The Third Day at Gettysburg," in *B&L* III, 373-4.
44 Alexander, "The Great Charge and Artillery Fighting at Gettysburg," *B&L* III, 364.
45 Longstreet, *From Manassas to Appomattox*, 392.
46 Alexander, *Military Memoirs of a Confederate*, 424.
47 Alexander, "The Great Charge and Artillery Fighting at Gettysburg," *B&L* III, 365.
48 Wheeler, *Witness to Gettysburg*, 233-5. Both quotes.
49 Haskell, *The Battle of Gettysburg*, 94-5.
50 Wert, *Gettysburg: Day Three*, 192.
51 Sears, *Gettysburg*, 415.
52 Ibid., 420.
53 Edmund Rice, "Repelling Lee's Last Blow at Gettysburg," in *B&L* III:387. Three lines would indicate that he was seeing Pettigrew's and Trimble's formations, as Pickett's Division was arranged in only two lines.

CHAPTER 14
"Fredericksburg on the Other Leg"
3 July 1863

PICKETT'S THREE BRIGADES, in two lines (Armistead's Brigade trailing the other two), had been placed in positions paralleling the low ridge to their front, which in turn roughly paralleled the Emmitsburg Road, so they began by advancing to the southeast, through Alexander's line of guns. A band began to play as they stepped off. At first Kemper's Brigade marched by the left flank the length of one regiment in order to close toward Garnett's right, then had to pass through Wilcox's Brigade as it advanced. A member of the 7th Virginia, at the left-center of Kemper's line, later remembered one of Wilcox's Alabamans telling the Virginians, "Boys that's a hot place, we were there yesterday."[1]

Kemper and Garnett were mounted; Armistead led his brigade on foot, with his black felt hat held aloft on the tip of his sword to make him easy for his men to see (at least until the point penetrated the felt and the hat slid down the blade.) General Pickett, accompanied by four aides, rode about twenty yards behind his first line, so that he could keep an eye on the whole formation. Colonel Lewis Williams of the 1st Virginia, in the middle of Kemper's Brigade, was one of the few other mounted officers in Pickett's Division. He was soon hit by a Union shell that severed his spine, and when he slipped from the saddle he fell on his own naked sword.

After saying goodbye to his friend Garnett, Colonel Alexander rode down his line of batteries, selecting guns that had enough ammunition left to follow Pickett's advance and support it. "I got, I think, fifteen or eighteen, in a little while, and went with them," he later remembered. "Meanwhile, the infantry had no sooner debouched on the plain than all the enemy's line, which had been nearly silent, broke out again with all its batteries. The eighteen guns were back in the cemetery, and a storm of shell began bursting over and among our infantry. All of our guns – silent as the infantry passed between them – reopened over their heads when the lines had got a couple of hundred yards away, but the enemy's artillery let us alone and fired only at the infantry. No one could have looked at that advance without feeling proud of it."[2]

Federal skirmishers lined the fences bordering the road near the Codori house. Lieutenant G. W. Finley, in the 56th Virginia of Garnett's Brigade at the left end of the first line, later remembered that, "As we came in sight, there seemed to be a restlessness and excitement along the enemy's lines, which encouraged us to hope they would not make a stubborn resistance. Their skirmishers began to run in, and the artillery opened upon us all along our front. I soon noticed that shells were also coming from our right. . . . I discovered that they came from . . . the Round Tops. This fire soon became strictly enfilading as we changed the point of direction . . . to the left while on the march, and whenever it struck our ranks was fearfully destructive."[3]

The change in direction was an oblique or wheel to the left to bring Pickett's two lines almost perpendicular to the Emmitsburg Road, making Pickett's attack, in effect, a resumption of Longstreet's attack of the day before, up the Emmitsburg Road, but beginning from a point farther north. It was apparently designed to straddle the road and strike the Union line along Cemetery Ridge at an angle, so that, as it broke through, it would carry straight on to Cemetery Hill.

Some of the artillery fire Lieutenant Finley mentioned was, indeed, coming from Little Round Top (there was still one battery up there), but by the time the Confederates had crossed half of the valley only two of its guns could bear on them. Most of the flanking fire probably came from Colonel McGilvery's line of guns on the southern part of Cemetery Ridge. And its fire was indeed destructive. "One company, a little to my right," Lieutenant Finley continued, "numbering thirty-five or forty men, was almost completely swept, to a man, from the line by a single shell."[4] His regiment had barely passed Alexander's guns when its colonel fell mortally wounded and command of it passed to its senior captain.

McGilvery later reported, "At about 3 p.m. a line of battle about 3,000 or 4,000 men appeared, advancing directly upon our front, which was completely broken up and scattered by our fire before coming within musket range of our lines. Immediately after, appeared three extended lines of battle, of at least 35,000 men, advancing upon our center. These three lines of battle presented an oblique front to the guns under my command, and by training the whole line of guns obliquely to the right, we had a raking fire through all three of these lines."[5] Obviously he vastly overrated the Confederate force, since Pickett's, Pettigrew's and Trimble's nine brigades numbered no more than 13,000 and perhaps as few as 10,500 men, not 35,000. So the "line of battle about 3,000 or 4,000 men" strong might well have been mere skirmishers. Or perhaps the confusion is due to the fact that Kemper's and Garnett's brigades did not form one continuous line, nor did either advance in a straight line. Both needed to edge to the north (their left) as well as move to the east, but they did so in different ways. Garnett's brigade obliqued to the left, while Kemper's, on the outer flank, made a series of facing changes, marching "alternately by the front & by the left flank."[6] Kemper's 11th Virginia, the second regiment from the right of his line, had to split in two as it passed around both sides of the Rogers' house near the Emmitsburg Road.

Most accounts and maps of the battle have Pickett's Division advancing directly against the Union 2nd Corps on Cemetery Ridge, perhaps after sidling to its left for a while, but this is not an accurate picture. General Doubleday, whose division of the 1st Corps was positioned just south of Gibbon's division of the 2nd Corps, later wrote, "At first the direction of their march appeared to be directly toward my division. When within five hundred yards of us, however, Pickett halted and changed direction obliquely about forty-five degrees, so that the attack passed me and struck Gibbon's division on my right."[7]

For, after advancing a few hundred yards, Pickett's Division reached the shelter of a slight swale of ground that straddled the Emmitsburg Road and hid most of it from most of the Federals. Garnett's Brigade arrived first and waited for the other two to catch up. Armistead's Brigade closed the gap between it and the two front-line brigades, and the division dressed ranks, facing roughly east-northeast, straddling the Emmitsburg Road. Pickett sent back word to Longstreet that his division was in position and ready to make the assault, and he told Captain Robert Bright, who would carry the message, that he "would take the Hill, but could not hold it, without reinforcements."[8] When the division stepped off again Kemper's Brigade, and part of Garnett's right-most regiment, the 8th Virginia, passed to the southeast of the Codori house, while the rest of Garnett's line passed it on the northwest side. Pickett evidently remained near the Codori house during the rest of the attack.

Following the same plan as the day before, that is for an attack en echelon, Pettigrew's brigades were supposed to start their advance when they saw Pickett's Division align almost perpendicular with the Emmitsburg Road and resume its advance, or, as Longstreet later put it, "The divisions of the Third Corps were arranged along his left with orders to take up the line of march, as Pickett passed before them, in short echelon."[9] Pettigrew's regiments were each formed in double lines, that is with half their companies in a second line (of two ranks) some 100 yards behind their first line (of two ranks). Archer's Brigade, now commanded by Colonel Fry, was at the right end of Pettigrew's line; to his left was Pettigrew's own brigade, under the temporary command of Colonel James K. Marshall; to Marshall's left was Davis's Brigade; and on the far left was Colonel Brockenbrough's small brigade of Virginians. It is not clear, from the records, whether Brockenbrough was still in command of his brigade, but it probably was commanded that day by Colonel Robert M. Mayo.

Isaac Trimble's two brigades constituted a third line. At its right end, some 150 yards behind Fry's second line, was Scales' Brigade, now reduced to about 500 men and commanded by Colonel W. Lee Lowrance. On its left, behind Marshall's and part of Davis's lines, was Lane's Brigade, relatively fresh. Because Trimble's line was shorter, it did not stretch far enough to support Brockenbrough's brigade.

Why Trimble's two brigades were not placed behind this more critical left end of Pettigrew's line, rather than its right, or, even better, behind and to its left, *en echelon*, to protect it from being flanked, cannot be known for sure, but was possibly due to confusion caused by the ad hoc command arrangements: Trimble replacing Lane, who had replaced Pender, as well as the uncertain relationship of Trimble to Pettigrew, whom he outranked, and to Hill and Longstreet. Trimble belonged to the 2nd Corps, his troops belonged to Hill's 3rd Corps, but Longstreet, the 1st Corps commander, was in tactical control of the attack. A more confused chain of command would be difficult to construct. In fact, it's hard to see why Trimble could not have been placed in command of Pender's entire division, which could have merely advanced from where it began the day, just to the right of Rodes' Division, at the end of the Long Lane, from which place it could have fallen in on the left of Pettigrew's division as it marched past. Instead, half of Pender's division was left in place with, apparently, no role planned for them whatsoever.

Like Pickett's men, many of Pettigrew's were so glad to have the artillery bombardment over with that, as Colonel Fry later recalled, "it seemed a relief to go forward to the desperate assault. At the command the men sprang up with cheerful alacrity."[10] But a man in Davis's Brigade remembered that his comrades had ashen faces when the order came to fall in. A Captain in Rodes' Division, in the long lane just to the northeast of Pettigrew's starting position, later wrote, "As far as the eye can reach on the right long rows of infantry clear the woods and enter the field and move down towards the line occupied by us [and] to the right of us. It was a grand sight, never did men move in better lines – never did a flag wave over a braver set of men."[11]

"Beautiful," one Federal soldier wrote home, "gloriously beautiful, did that vast array appear in the lovely little valley."[12] Union General Schurz, watching from Cemetery Hill, wrote, "The alignment was perfect. The battle flags fluttered gaily over the bayonets glittering in the sunlight.... Through our fieldglasses we could distinctly see the gaps torn in their ranks and the ground dotted with dark spots – their dead and wounded. Now and then a cheer went up from our lines when our men observed some of our shells striking right among the advancing enemy and scattering death and destruction around. But the brave rebels promptly filled the gaps from behind or by closing up on their colors; and unshaken and unhesitating they continued their onward march...."[13]

However, the Rebel ranks were not so well ordered as they appeared. Joe Davis's brigade got a late start, compared with Marshall's brigade to its right. Brockenbrough's brigade, of course, did not advance until Davis's did, and its commander was not to be found when that brigade finally did step off, so it stood fast while the regimental commanders conferred on whether to start without him; then their troops had to run to catch up. Pettigrew started to send an aide to fetch Davis's Brigade, only to see it at last emerge from the trees behind him. The aide asked if he should go find Brockenbrough's brigade, but Pettigrew said it didn't much matter whether that brigade advanced or not. It was both tiny (now about 600 men) and demoralized after its fight of 1 July, its commander's ability was suspect, and apparently Pettigrew considered it virtually worthless.

General Davis, who wound up in command of Pettigrew's (Heth's) division before the campaign was over, later reported that "The order had been given that, when the artillery in our front ceased firing, the division would attack the enemy's batteries, keeping dressed to the right, and moving in line with Major-General Pickett's division, which was on our right, and march obliquely to the left."[14] Like Pickett's division,

Pettigrew's and Trimble's line originally faced southeast, and if they had advanced directly to their front Fry's brigade, at the right of the front line, would have marched straight past the buildings of the Codori farm and hit the left end of Gibbon's division of the Union 2nd Corps. Instead, Fry's brigade just followed along the north side of a post-and-rail fence that ran almost due east from the northwest corner of Spangler's Woods, well south of what was left of the Bliss house and barn, and reached the Emmitsburg Road some 300 yards north of the Codori buildings, almost directly in front of Lieutenant Cushing's battery. The rest of Pettigrew's and Trimble's brigades, as pre-arranged, aligned on Fry's. Apparently this is what Davis meant by "obliquely to the left."

So the converging Confederate divisions of Pettigrew, Trimble, and Pickett wound up assaulting Hancock's 2nd Corps on the northern part of Cemetery Ridge. Hancock's 1st Division, Caldwell's, was still detached, and Doubleday's 3rd Division of the 1st Corps, reinforced by Stannard's 9-months Vermonters, had been inserted in the line between Caldwell and the rest of the 2nd Corps. However, Pettigrew's attack was coming straight at Hancock's two remaining divisions, Gibbon's 2nd, and Brigadier General Alexander Hays's 3rd, the latter on the Union right, extending to the buildings of a farm belonging to one Abraham Bryan and, just north of that, Ziegler's Grove. Hays had only two of his three brigades on hand, as Carroll's 1st Brigade had not returned from reinforcing the 11th Corps the night before, except that the 8th Ohio of that brigade was still out on the skirmish line.

Together these two Union divisions contained fewer than 6,000 men, perhaps as few as 4,000, and covered a front of about 1,000 yards. Most of the front line, near the crest of Cemetery Ridge, followed a low stone wall, which the men had improved and patched with dirt and with rails from the neighboring fences, making at least parts of it an effective breastwork, but so low that the men would have to kneel or lie down to be covered. They could, of course, fire from such positions, but it was very difficult to load a muzzle-loader without standing up. Near where the two divisions came together, and the now-famous copse of trees [Lieutenant Haskell said they were sassafras and oak], this stone fence made a right angle turn to the west for about 68 yards, then turned to the south again.[15] This second turn is known to history as "the angle" (the former is "the inner angle"). "I could not help wishing all the morning," Lieutenant Haskell later wrote, "that this line of the two divisions of the Second Corps was stronger; it was, so far as numbers constitute strength, the weakest part of our whole line of battle. What if, I thought, the enemy should make an assault here to-day, with two or three heavy lines – a great overwhelming mass; would he not sweep through that thin six thousand?"[16]

At the far right, or north, end of Hays's 3rd Division, when the bombardment ended the 126th New York of his 3rd (Harper's Ferry) Brigade and the 108th New York of Colonel Thomas Smyth's 2nd Brigade advanced from Ziegler's Grove, where they had probably been out the Confederates' sight, and aligned themselves with the division's main line. Six 12-pounder Napoleons of Battery I, 1st U.S. Artillery, commanded by 5-foot-tall Lieutenant George "Little Dad" Woodruff, had been positioned in the west edge of Ziegler's Grove, but they had fired off all their ammunition except close-range cannister and, during the bombardment, with the help of infantrymen from the 108th, had withdrawn into the woods. However, due to the Confederate artillery's tendency to overshoot, one of the battery's caissons had been hit there and exploded, and many of its horses had been killed or wounded. When the bombardment ended, Woodruff got the infantry to help his men push four of the guns back into position near the edge of the woods, and the other two guns on to the front line between the 126th and 108th.

South of the 108th, and behind the northern end of the stone wall that began at Bryan's barn, was the 111th New York of the Harper's Ferry Brigade, the left of which was behind the next regiment, the 12th New Jersey of Smyth's brigade. Then came Smyth's 1st Delaware and 14th Connecticut and the five 3-inch rifles of Captain William Arnold's Battery A of the 1st Rhode Island Artillery, which were now rolled forward to join the infantry line. General Hays sent officers to round up stragglers, and he moved the 39th and 125th New York of the Harper's Ferry Brigade (now commanded by Colonel Eliakim Sherrill) from the Bryan orchard, just south of Ziegler's Grove, to a position behind these three regiments of Smyth's 2nd Brigade. Just south of Arnold's battery the stone wall was unmanned for about 50 feet, down to the inner angle, as was the stretch of wall that ran west.

Lieutenant Cushing's battery was stationed between that east-west stretch of wall and the now-famous copse of trees, well back from the again-southward-running stone wall. There had been bushes and small trees in this area until they had been cut down the day before by some of Gibbon's infantry, but there wasn't enough of a downward slope here to make it safe to station infantry in front of Cushing's guns. This battery had taken a real beating by the Confederate bombardment. Only three of its six guns were still in working order and there were not enough men left to man all of those. Cushing himself, the only officer left in his battery, had taken a terrible wound in the groin and both thighs as well as another in the shoulder, but, bleeding profusely, his pain and nausea perhaps numbed by shock, he refused to go to the rear. "No," he had told Sergeant Fuger, now his second in command, "I stay right here and fight it out or die in the attempt."[17] (Cushing had been in the same West Point class as Lieutenant Woodruff and General Custer, which illustrates how much better Regular Army artillery officers could fare by transferring to the volunteer infantry or cavalry. His oldest brother was a paymaster in the Navy; another older brother, Howard Cushing, without benefit of a military education, was then a private in an Illinois battery in Grant's army but would eventually take Alonzo's place in this Regular battery; and his younger brother, William, a graduate of Annapolis, was already making a name for himself as a junior naval officer, and would, the following year, almost single-handedly sink a Confederate ironclad.)

The 71st Pennsylvania of Brigadier General Alexander Webb's 2nd Brigade of Gibbon's 2nd Division was lying down well to the rear of Cushing's battery as its support. Webb's brigade had originally been known as the California Brigade, because that state, too far away to send its own men, had helped to sponsor the raising of these four regiments, and, in fact, the 71st, which had been the 1st California, was still sometimes called the California Regiment; but the brigade was more commonly known by this time as the Philadelphia Brigade, because all but a few of its companies hailed from that city. General Webb had only recently taken command of this brigade, and he had found it necessary to clamp down hard on it, threatening stragglers with execution and ordering officers to wear all the insignia of their ranks. (Officers of the 71st had evidently been trying to avoid being picked off by sharpshooters by looking as much like privates as possible. The 71st had originally been a zouave regiment, but had by this time replaced its showy uniforms for more ordinary apparel.) The 71st had been sent over to Culp's Hill the previous evening, blundered into a Confederate crossfire, and returned to the 2nd Corps without having done the Rebels any harm or the 12th Corps any good, but the brigade had fought well enough before that to repel Wright's attack, from which Webb claimed about 270 prisoners.

South of Cushing's battery, behind the stone wall and just in front of the copse of trees, was Webb's 69th Pennsylvania. It was composed mostly of Irishmen, and sported a green flag. To their rear, behind the little copse of trees, was the 72nd Pennsylvania, known as the Fire Zouaves because it had been recruited largely from firemen. It's men still stuck with their flashy uniforms, including their white leggings. Webb's fourth regiment, the 106th Pennsylvania, had been sent, like Carroll's brigade, to Cemetery Hill the night before, but some of its men who had been left behind had attached themselves to the 72nd. All together, Webb had only about 940 men on hand.

To the left of the 72nd were the four 12-pounder Napoleons of Lieutenant T. Frederick Brown's Battery B of the 1st Rhode Island Artillery, posted about 200 feet back from the stone wall, which had been torn down at this point the previous day to allow guns to pass through. This battery had also taken a beating. Lieutenant Brown was seriously wounded; one of his guns had been disabled by multiple hits and had one of its own shells stuck in its dented barrel; and it had also lost 30 horses, two limbers, and several cannoneers.

The line then continued southward without benefit of a stone wall, but a slight breastwork had been thrown up, and there was rough ground just in front of part of that. This portion of the line, due east of the Codori house, was held by three regiments of Colonel Normal Hall's 3rd Brigade of Gibbon's division, with his other two regiments forming a second line a hundred yards to their rear. South of Hall's brigade were the four regiments of Brigadier General William Harrow's 1st Brigade, all on the front line, including what little was left of its 1st Minnesota (which had been revived somewhat by the return of two detached companies).

Behind Harrow's right and Hall's left were the four 10-pounder rifles of Captain James Rorty's Battery B of the 1st New York Artillery. South of Harrow's brigade the line was extended by two 1st Corps regiments, the 80th and 151st Pennsylvania, who had become separated from Rowley's (Biddle's) brigade of Doubleday's division. There had been a battery from the Artillery Reserve stationed behind these two regiments, but it had been wrecked by the Confederate bombardment and had withdrawn.

Next came Stannard's 9-months men of the 2nd Vermont Brigade, now the 3rd Brigade of Doubleday's division. Two of its three large regiments were, as Lieutenant Haskell noted, "behind a small bush-crowned crest that ran in a direction oblique to the general line. These were well covered by the crest, and wholly concealed by the bushes, so that an advancing enemy would be close upon them before they could be seen."[18] The 13th Vermont came first, angling off to the southwest from the line farther north. Then the 14th Vermont was on its left, advanced even farther. The 16th Vermont had been out on the corps' skirmish line, but when the Confederates advanced it fell back and took position behind the 13th. The rest of Doubleday's division was farther back, in reserve and did not get into this fight. Two other regiments of the Vermont brigade were detached to the rear, guarding wagons, and would go home without ever seeing a major battle.

When the Confederate bombardment ended, Brown's Napoleons, which had expended all of their cannister ammunition the day before, were withdrawn, and General Webb sent a staff officer to find batteries to replace them and possibly Cushing's rifles, and he soon found, down near Doubleday's portion of the line, Captain Andrew Cowan's 1st New York Independent Battery, a 6th Corps unit that had been transferred from the Culp's Hill area to Cemetery Ridge that morning. Cowan's six 3-inch rifles took Brown's place, though their caissons were left behind. One of his guns went on to the north of the clump of trees and took position to the left of, and in advance of, Cushing's battery.

Cushing and Sergeant Fuger went to Webb and asked for some infantrymen to help them man their guns, and Webb ordered the 71st Pennsylvania to detail some men for that job, and these helped the cannoneers advance two pieces to the wall in their front, alongside Cowan's one gun. Cushing had all his cannister ammunition stacked near the guns and all the battery's hand-spikes, which made good weapons for hand-to-hand fighting, collected as well. The infantrymen manned one gun and the remaining artillerymen the other. General Webb then had the 71st Pennsylvania advance, eight of its companies moving up on the right of Cushing's two guns – between them and the "angle" – and the other two forming farther back along the fifty yards of open wall between Smyth's brigade and the inner angle.

Meanwhile, General Hays rode along his line and exhorted his men to hold their fire until the Rebels reached the Emmitsburg Road, after which they should "give them hell!"[19] He told his men to grab any extra rifles they could find and clean and load them, so they could get off multiple volleys before having to reload. "Some of the men were so energetic as to have four loaded muskets," one of Hays's aides remembered; "it was very common for men to have two."[20] Gibbon also rode down his line and told his men, in a calm voice, to not hurry and fire too fast, but to let the Confederates come close and then aim low. Many of the Federals in the 2nd Corps were glad to see the Rebel infantry advance. (They probably didn't see Pickett's Division at first, only Pettigrew's, followed by Trimble's.) They felt they had a strong defensive position and remembered how they had been cut up trying to take a similar one from the Confederates back in December at Fredericksburg, where the Rebels had stood behind a stone wall on a hill and mowed them down. "The moment I saw them," a captain in Hall's brigade remembered, "I knew we should give them Fredericksburg. So did every body."[21]

Gibbon sent Haskell galloping to inform General Meade that the enemy was advancing. Meade had left his headquarters, but Haskell had the Signal Corps pass the word to him, then he returned to the ridge to watch the Confederates come on, noting that they weren't raising the Rebel yell this time, but advancing in silence as the Union artillery pummeled them. Meade had been driven out of his headquarters by the Confederate artillery bombardment. One shot or shell just barely missed him before he left. He had insisted that he needed to stay where his subordinates could find him, and at first he and his staff had merely adjourned to the house's back yard, then to a barn, but that too was being hit by Rebel shells that overshot the Union lines. Butterfield, the chief of staff, was slightly wounded, and eventually Meade had been persuaded by his staff to move to Slocum's headquarters, where there would be signalmen who could keep him in contact with other signalmen back at his own original location. But when he arrived at Slocum's, he discovered that the Signal Corps had also abandoned the Leister house shortly after Haskell had shown up. So he had returned to his headquarters, but he had soon set off again, this time heading for the front lines.

There the Union infantry was finally getting into the act. As Pickett's men emerged from their swale Kemper's Brigade unknowingly presented its right flank to Stannard's 90-days men, hidden behind the bushes of the little oblique ridge Lieutenant Haskell mentioned. "The enemy's right flank sweeps near Stannard's bushy crest," Haskell wrote, "and his concealed Vermonters rake it with a well-delivered fire of musketry. The gray lines do not halt or reply, but withdrawing a little from that extreme, they still move on."[22] Colonel Francis Randall of the 13th Vermont said: "The heavy rebel column, which I need not describe, bore down steadily upon us until about half way from the Emmitsburg road to our position. Our men were directed to withhold their fire up to this time, when the two regiments [13th and 14th] rose up and poured in a volley that seemed to level their front rank and all mounted officers. We continued to pour in our fire as best we could, and very soon the charging column seemed to slacken and nearly halt. In this way they staggered for a moment, and commenced to move by their left flank toward a position more nearly in front of the cemetery."[23]

From Haskell's viewpoint, the infantry fight began there on the Union left – where, he said, the two opposing forces were now only a hundred yards apart – and then rolled north. "First, Harrow's breastworks flame; then Hall's; then Webb's," he said; and the Confederates paused to return fire. "All along each hostile front, a thousand yards [wide], with narrowest space between, the volleys blaze and roll; as thick the sound as when a summer hail-storm pelts the city roofs; as thick the fire as when the incessant lightning fringes a summer cloud. When the Rebel infantry had opened fire our batteries soon became silent, and this without their fault, for they were foul by long previous use. They were the targets of the concentrated Rebel bullets, and some of them had expended all their cannister. But they were not silent before Rorty was killed, Woodruff had fallen mortally wounded, and Cushing, firing almost his last cannister, had dropped dead among his guns shot through the head by a bullet."[24]

While Pickett's Division had stopped to realign itself, Pettigrew's division had passed the still-smoking ruins of the Bliss buildings and halted about half-way to the Emmitsburg Road in a similar swale, or continuation of the same one, along a small stream called Stevens Run. Here these units also dressed ranks, the right of Pettigrew's line contacted the left of Pickett's, Brockenbrough's errant brigade caught up with Davis's, despite having received much of the attention of the Union guns on Cemetery Hill, and apparently Pettigrew's two lines now merged. Lieutenant Colonel Franklin Sawyer of the 8th Ohio, on the Union skirmish line, said the Confederates "advanced at the first in three long lines of battle, but ployed into close column by division as they advanced, excepting, perhaps, a regiment on each flank." Apparently Sawyer saw Brockenbrough's brigade as the "regiment" in line on the left flank of the Confederate column, and it was coming straight at his position.

The little 8th Ohio (about 160 men), had been sent forward to the picket line the day before by its brigade commander, Colonel Carroll, who also told Sawyer, according to Sawyer's report, "to throw forward four companies as an advanced line, and to support them with the balance of the regiment, and to hold my line to the last man."[25] The regiment had been stuck out there for 24 hours, even though Carroll and the rest of the brigade had been sent the evening before to reinforce Cemetery Hill and had not returned. During the Confederate cannonade these Federals had taken cover in a ditch bordering the Emmitsburg Road; then after the bombardment ended they had advanced to a fence line west of the road and north of the Bliss farm buildings. Now they rose up, seemingly from nowhere, and blasted Brockenbrough's brigade at a range of about 100 yards.

Not many of the Virginians were actually hit, but the fire was so sudden and unexpected that panic swept their ranks. A few of them stood their ground and exchanged fire with the Ohioans, but at least a couple of them surrendered and most of them turned and ran back the way they had come. Colonel Sawyer reported that "we poured in a well-directed fire, which broke the rebel line, and it soon fled in the wildest confusion."[26] At least half the brigade didn't stop until it had put Seminary Ridge between themselves and the Federals. One regimental commander in Lane's Brigade of Trimble's line, just coming up, ordered his North Carolinians to fix bayonets to prevent the retreating Virginians from disrupting his own line, and they flowed past his flank. Colonel Lowrance, commanding Scale's Brigade, complained that "ere we had advanced over two-thirds of the way, troops from the front came tearing through our ranks, which caused many of our men to break. . . ."[27] Not all of these were from Brockenbrough's brigade, however.

When Davis's and Marshall's brigades reached the Emmitsburg Road their advance was blocked by two stout post-and-rail fences, five rails high, one lining each side of the road. Farther south the fence on the west side had been knocked down by Reynolds' men on the way to the battle two days before, but here it was still intact. As the Confederates climbed the first fence, the Union infantry of Hays's division opened fire with their multiple muskets. One Federal soldier said the front rank of Confederates "dropped from the fence as if swept by a gigantic sickle swung by some powerful force of nature."[28] One Rebel said that the men had to "climb up to the top of the fence, tumble over it, and fall flat into the bed of the road. All the while the bullets continued to bury themselves into the bodies of the victims and the sturdy chestnut rails."[29]

Fry's brigade, on the column's right, encountered board – not rail – fences where it crossed the road. One of his men said, "We reached the first slab or plank fence and the men clambered over with the speed of a stampeded retreat. The time it took to climb to the top of the fence seemed to me an age. It was not a leaping over; it was rather a tumbling to the ground." He said the bullets hitting the boards "rattled with the distinctness of large raindrops pattering on a roof."[30] After a few minutes, some of these men rose and climbed the second fence; others took cover behind one fence or the other and returned fire. A lieutenant in Fry's brigade said, "I know when I reached the top of the second fence there seemed to remain a line of battle in the road."[31] Fry himself went down only a few paces beyond the road when a bullet fractured his thigh bone.

In addition to the murderous fire coming in from their front, Pettigrew's men were under attack on their outer (or northern) flank by the little 8th Ohio, which had now been joined by about 75 skirmishers belonging to the 125th New York, who had been farther north but now extended the flanking line eastward to the Emmitsburg Road. And, seeing that the right of his line was no longer under direct threat, General Hays sent the 126th New York, part of the 108th, and a company of Massachusetts sharpshooters to extend this line along a farm lane from the Emmitsburg Road on back to the main line on the ridge. Colonel Sawyer didn't mention this help but said that, after seeing off Brockenbrough's brigade, "I changed front forward on the left company, thus presenting our front to the left flank of the advancing rebel column. Our fire was poured into their flank with terrible effect for a few minutes before the Second Brigade at the battery opened, but almost instantly on the fire from the front, together with the concentrated fire from our batteries, the whole mass gave way, some fleeing to the front, some to the rear, and some through our lines, until the whole plain was covered with unarmed rebels, waving coats, hats, and handkerchiefs in token of a wish to surrender."[32]

These Federals were able to attack the flank of Pettigrew's and Trimble's forces for the simple reason that the

Confederates north of Pettigrew's line failed to advance. It was the same story as the day before. The next troops north of Pettigrew's and Trimble's were the two remaining brigades of Pender's Division: Thomas's and Perrin's, lying in the Long Lane to the right of Rodes' Division of the 2nd Corps. However, Pender's successor, Lane, was off with his own brigade in Trimble's force, and the two remaining brigades seem to have been left with no orders and no overall commander. Thomas's Georgians did advance as far as the ridge above Stevens Run, but when they were hit by Union artillery fire they retired to the protection of the lane. If Rodes was waiting for them to advance before he took up the charge he was going to have a long wait.

In his report, Rodes claimed that the detachment of two of his five brigades to reinforce Johnson's morning attack on Culp's Hill had "left me powerless to do more than hold my position, unless the enemy should be very much weakened in my front, for I had now remaining but a single thin line, composed of two small brigades, about the third of another, and one regiment (the Fifth Alabama) of O'Neal's brigade (in all, not over 1,800 men), facing what I believed then and now to be the most impregnable portion of the enemy's line of intrenchments." He added that "On the 3d, my orders were general, and the same as those of the day before, and accordingly, when the heavy cannonade indicated that another attack was made from the right wing of our army, we were on the lookout for another favorable opportunity to co-operate. When the sound of musketry was heard, it became apparent that the enemy in our front was much excited. The favorable opportunity seemed to me close at hand. I sent word to Lieutenant-General Ewell by Major [H. A.] Whiting, of my staff, that in a few moments I should attack, and immediately had my handful of men, under Doles, Iverson, and Ramseur, prepared for the onset; but in less than five minutes after Major Whiting's departure, before the troops on my immediate right had made any advance or showed any preparation therefor, and just as the order forward was about to be given to my line, it was announced, and was apparent to me, that the attack had already failed."[33]

Watching from Seminary Ridge, General Ewell sent a note to General Early: "Longstreet & A. P. Hill are advancing in splendid style. If you see an opportunity, strike."[34] But Early, like Rodes, saw no opportunity. Thus once again, as the day before, Lee's attack *en echelon* broke down when someone failed to take up the advance. If Pender's Division was going to be broken up, the static half should have been placed under Rodes, and, in any event, the latter should have been flat ordered to advance as soon as Pettigrew's line swept by, "favorable opportunity" or not, in order to protect Pettigrew's left from just the sort flanking maneuver that resulted from Rodes' inactivity.

The rifle fire coming in on Pettigrew's left flank plus oblique artillery fire from Cemetery Hill caused his men to crowd toward their right, and the same thing happened to Trimble's two brigades as they reached the same area. The Federals spread along the farm lane had a rail fence to rest their rifles on and were eager for more targets. "Come on, come on," one yelled; "come to death."[35] The lieutenant commanding the Massachusetts sharpshooters later said, "This fresh division would probably have forced our line back and gained the shelter of Ziegler's Grove had it not been subjected to our flank fire, which destroyed its formation and sent its shattered and disordered masses along the other side of the lane and in front of the Third Division of the Second Corps."[36] Only about 1,000 of the bravest of Pettigrew's men actually crossed the Emmitsburg Road and headed on up the hill. Lieutenant Finley, still near the left end of Pickett's front line, said when he looked to his left "there was but a fragment" of Pettigrew's force continuing to advance.[37] The Federals marveled at the bravery of those few when they stopped to dress ranks on the east side of the road.

Arnold's battery had been withdrawn, but it had been promptly replaced by Lieutenant Gulian Wier's Battery C of the 5th U.S. Artillery, from the Artillery Reserve. His six

12-pounder Napoleons opened fire with double rounds of cannister, and the men of Smyth's brigade blasted the Rebels with musketry. Some of the Confederates advanced as far as the remnants of a low stone wall and rail fence that ran north from the Angle, which they mistook for an abandoned Union line. "By the time we had reached this work," reported Lieutenant Colonel S. G. Shepard, who had succeed the wounded Fry, "our lines all along, as far as I could see, had become very much weakened; indeed, the line both right and left, as far as I could observe, seemed to melt away until there was but little of it left. Those who remained at the works saw that it was a hopeless case, and fell back."[38] One Federal called it "Fredericksburg on the other leg."[39]

Colonel Marshall's brigade suffered the same fate, and Marshall himself went down with two bullets in his head within 50 yards of the Union line. Davis's Brigade fared only slightly better. So many of its officers were killed or wounded that, as one of Davis's Mississippians put it, "No one seemed to be in command."[40] The 11th Mississippi, at the left of Davis's line, lost both of its field officers and all of its captains; a lieutenant led the remnant of the regiment until he fell just north of Bryan's barn. The sixth man to carry that regiment's colors placed it on the defender's stone wall, only to be knocked down by a Union soldier. The few men left in the regiment took cover around the barn under the command of another lieutenant. Even Pettigrew was down, his horse shot out from under him and his left hand crushed by a cannister ball.

While the Federals were busy with Pettigrew's attack, Trimble's men knocked down the first fence along the Emmitsburg Road, but only about half of them dared to climb over the second fence. Trimble himself was hit in the leg. (He would soon lose it.) A gap developed in the middle of Lane's Brigade, and only about 500 of Trimble's men actually went on up the slope to join Pettigrew's remnants in front of Hays's line. General Hancock said in his report, "Those of the enemy's troops who did not fall into disorder in front of the Third Division were moved to the right, and re-enforced the line attacking Gibbon's division."[41]

There were no fences lining the Emmitsburg Road to slow the advance where Pickett's Division crossed it, and most of the men of all three brigades charged on up the gentle slope of Cemetery Ridge. Colonel Hall, whose brigade held the center of Gibbon's line, wrote in his report of the battle, "The conformation of the ground enabled the enemy, after advancing near the lines, to obtain cover. Arrived at this point, one battalion [regiment] continued to move toward the point . . . occupied by the Second and Third Brigades of the Second Division [Webb's and his own]. The other battalions moved by the flank until completely masked by the preceding one, when they moved by the flank again, thus forming a column of regiments. The few pieces of [Union] artillery still in position were directed upon this column, while the rebel cannon again opened with shell, firing over their own troops. . . .

"There was a disposition in the men to reserve their fire for close quarters, but when I observed the movement the enemy was endeavoring to execute, I caused the Seventh Michigan and Twentieth Massachusetts Volunteers to open fire at about 200 yards. The deadly aim of the former regiment was attested by the line of slain within its range. This had a great effect upon the result, for it caused the enemy to move rapidly at one point and consequently to crowd in front – being occasioned at the point where his column was forming, he did not recover from this disorder."[42] Hall even included a diagram (reproduced in the map section at the beginning of this work) with his report to show how the Confederates were sidling left and forming a column aimed at Webb's brigade, to his right.

Major Rice, watching from Hall's second line, also claimed that the Rebels formed a column, or tried to, before making their final push. "I had an excellent view of the advancing lines," he wrote years later, "and could see the entire formation of the attacking column. Pickett's separate brigade lines lost their formation as they swept across the Emmitsburg road, carrying with them their chain of skirmishers. They pushed on toward the crest, and merged into one crowding, rushing line, many ranks deep. As they crossed the road, Webb's infantry, on the right of the [copse of] trees, commenced an irregular, hesitating fire, gradually increasing to a rapid file firing, while the shrapnel and canister from the batteries tore gaps through those splendid Virginia battalions."[43] These Confederates no longer marched in silence. Some Federals said they were screeching the familiar Rebel yell, but General Gibbon described it as "a kind of savage roar."[44] Gibbon was soon wounded and carried off the field.

This dense mass of perhaps 3,000 Confederates, which evidently included some of Fry's men, was heading right for the eight companies of the 71st Pennsylvania that were manning the low stone wall from the outer angle to Cushing's guns, just north of the copse of trees. In the face of such overwhelming odds, these Pennsylvanians broke ranks and ran back toward the crest. "When we were about seventy-five or one hundred yards from that stone wall," remembered Lieutenant Finley, in Garnett's Brigade near the front of this column, "some of the men holding it began to break for the rear, when, without orders, save from captains and lieutenants, our line poured a volley or two into them, and then rushed upon the fence. . . . The Federal gunners stood manfully to their guns. I never saw more gallant bearing in any men. They fired their last shots full in our faces and so close that I thought I felt distinctly the flame of the explosion."[45]

Lieutenant Haskell, just returning from Meade's headquarters and unable to find Gibbon, saw the 71st break, and, being the only mounted officer on that part of the field, rode forward to try to rally it. He said that he then drew his sword for the first time in any battle and used it both as a symbol of command and for whacking retreating soldiers with its flat side. General Hancock gave him special mention in his report. The 71st rallied behind the 72nd Pennsylvania and two companies of the 106th, which stood just beyond the crest of the ridge. General Webb tried to get the 72nd to counterattack, but it would not move from its reserve position. Webb tried to seize the regiment's colors in order to lead it forward, but the color-bearer wrestled him to the ground, refusing to yield it, and he finally gave up and went to join the 69th Pennsylvania.

Lieutenant Finley said that some force of Federals did exchange a few rounds with the Confederates at the stone wall but then fell back behind the crest of the ridge. He said that it was this burst of fire that killed General Garnett. "Almost instantaneously with these movements," he said, "General Armistead, on foot, strode over the stone fence, leading his brigade most gallantly, with his hat on his sword, and calling upon his men to charge. A few of us followed him until, just as he put his hand upon one of the abandoned guns, he was shot down."[46]

Colonel Dennis O'Kane of the 69th Pennsylvania, to the 71st's left, in front of the copse of trees, had meanwhile ordered the right end of his line to pull back through the trees to face the right flank of this mass of Confederates. But his Company F failed to get the order because its captain was killed about then, and every man in that company was either killed, wounded, or captured by the Rebel tide. To the left of the 69th was another gap, faced by Cowan's battery. Some of Kemper's men entered this gap, threatening the 69th's left flank, which also pulled back into the trees. General Webb went down with a bullet in the groin, Colonel O'Kane was mortally wounded, his lieutenant colonel was killed, and his major was seriously wounded; command devolved on a captain. Dozens of their men turned and fled, others stood and used their muskets as clubs.

The retreating Federals fled past the five guns of Cowan's battery that were south of the trees. An artillery corporal, evidently disgusted with this behavior, crowned one retreating infantryman with a coffee pot, but the man kept right on going, pot and all. A Confederate major shouted, "Take the guns!" And a sizable contingent of Rebels followed him. The gunners loaded double rounds of cannister and waited until the Confederates came within 20 yards. The resulting blasts,

Cowan said, "literally swept the enemy from my front."[47] Cowan later found the major among the fallen and took his sword, though 25 years later he gave it to some of Pickett's surviving veterans.

Farther south, about 300 Rebels of Kemper's Brigade charged Rorty's guns. There it was Kemper himself who yelled, "There are the guns, boys, go for them." Colonel Joseph Mayo of the 11th Virginia later said that "it was an injudicious order." Again the gunners let the Rebels get close and then blasted them with cannister. A Confederate captain managed to lay a hand on one of the guns, but an artillery sergeant killed him with a handspike. The sergeant was, in turn, riddled with bullets, but the surviving Confederates ran back down the slope. "Few of them lived to get back," a Union gunner said.[48]

Haskell said that the Rebels who crossed the stone wall north of the 69th were soon shot down, but that part of the wall was lost, and the Confederates were using it for cover while they poured out a storm of fire. "At this point little could be seen of the enemy," he said, "by reason of his cover and the smoke, except the flash of his muskets and his waving flags."[49] He added that more red flags were accumulating there by the moment.

Haskell rode in search of reinforcements. "I galloped to the left in the execution of my purpose," he wrote, "and as I attained the rear of Hall's line, from the nature of the ground and the position of the enemy it was easy to discover the reason and the manner of this gathering of Rebel flags in front of Webb. The enemy, emboldened by his success in gaining our line by the group of trees and the angle of the wall, was concentrating all his right against and further pressing that point. There was the stress of his assault; there would he drive his fiery wedge to split our line. In front of Harrow's and Hall's Brigades he had been able to advance no nearer than when he first halted to deliver fire, and these commands had not yielded an inch. To effect the concentration before Webb, the enemy would march the regiment on his extreme right of each of his lines by the left flank to the rear of the troops, still halted and facing to the front, and so continuing to drawn in his right, when they were all massed in the position desired, he would again face them to the front, and advance to the storming. This was the way he made the wall before Webb's line blaze red with his battle flags, and such was the purpose there of his thick-crowding battalions."[50]

General Hancock's report agrees: "The right of the attacking line having been repulsed by Hall's and Harrow's brigades, . . . assisted by the fire of the Vermont regiments . . . , doubled to its left and also re-enforced the center, and thus the attack was in its fullest strength opposite the brigade of General Webb."[51]

Colonel Hall had a somewhat different view of things. "There was but a moment of doubtful contest in front of the position of this brigade," he wrote. "The enemy halted to deliver his fire, wavered, and fled, while the line of the fallen perfectly marked the limit of his advance. The troops were pouring into the ranks of the fleeing enemy that rapid and accurate fire, the delivery of which victorious lines always so much enjoy, when I saw that a portion of the line of General Webb on my right had given way, and many men were making to the rear as fast as possible, while the enemy was pouring over the rails that had been slight cover for the troops. Having gained this apparent advantage, the enemy seemed to turn again and re-engage my whole line. Going to the left, I found two regiments that could be spared from some command there [probably the two 1st Corps regiments to the right of the Vermonters], and endeavored to move them by the right flank to the break, but, coming under a warm fire, they crowded to the slight cover of the rail fence, mixing with the troops already there. Finding it impossible to draw them out and reform, and seeing no unengaged troops within reach, I was forced to order my own brigade back from the line, and move it by the flank under a heavy fire."[52]

Hall had to call on the two 1st Corps regiments for help because General Hancock, riding down the length of his line from north to south, had already ordered the two regiments in Hall's second line to move toward the copse of trees. Major Rice said, "With a cheer the two regiments left their position in rear of Hall's right, and made an impetuous dash, racing diagonally forward for the clump of trees. Many of Webb's men were still lying down in their places in ranks, and firing at those who followed Pickett's advance, which, in the meantime, had passed over them.... One battle-flag after another, supported by Pickett's infantry, appeared along the edge of the trees, until the whole copse seemed literally crammed with men. As the 19th and 42nd passed along the brigade line, on our left, we could see the men prone in their places, unshaken, and firing steadily to their front, beating back the enemy. I saw one leader try several times to jump his horse over our line. He was shot by some of the men near me."[53]

These two regiments, joined by a company of the 1st Minnesota, drove out the Rebels who had penetrated the Union line south of the 69th Pennsylvania. Rice said those Confederates then moved farther north and joined those who had broken through north of the 69th. Major Rice had his cap knocked off his head by one bullet, his sword knocked from his hand by another, and took a third in the abdomen. He was said to have gotten closer to the Rebels on that part of the field than any other Federal and later received a Medal of Honor for his bravery.

Lieutenant Haskell went farther south and got the four regiments of Harrow's brigade moving north; they were all mixed up together, every man wanting to be first.

Meanwhile, Hancock had ridden on down to the 90-days Vermonters. "I thought him the most splendid looking man I ever saw on horseback," a lieutenant on Stannard's staff later wrote, "and magnificent in the flush and excitement of battle."[54] Hancock spoke with Stannard and then turned his horse to ride north again when a bullet struck his saddle, dislodging a nail and driving it into his thigh. Colonel Randall helped him to dismount, as he was bleeding profusely, but the lieutenant tied a handkerchief around the wounded leg as a tourniquet, and the general refused to leave the field until the attack was repulsed.

Hancock had arrived just as the Vermonters were making another important contribution to the Union defense. "As our front became uncovered," Colonel Randall's report continues, "I moved my regiment a little by the flank, so as to extricate my left from some shrubbery that partially surrounded and hid them, when I changed front forward on my right company, throwing my left flank toward the rebel main line of battle. . . . General Doubleday at this time rode up to me, and assured me that my movement would be a success, and he ordered the regiments to my right to cease firing and allow me to pass in front of their line, which we did, following the rebel column so close that when they faced to charge up Cemetery Hill we were within 15 rods [c. 80 yards] of them, and they passed directly in review before us, my men at the same time pouring one of the most withering fires I had ever beheld into their exposed flank."[55]

A member of the 1st Minnesota, which had demonstrated its own qualities the day before, said these 90-days Vermonters marched "with as much apparent coolness, as much steadiness and with as perfect a line as I ever saw a regiment of veterans pass in review on a gala day." A Confederate captain later told a friend, "There off on our right was the grandest sight I have ever seen. A body of Yankees . . . coming at double quick 'right shoulder shift,' uniforms looking black in the distance muskets glittering in the sunlight and battle flags fluttering in the breeze created by their quickened motion."[56]

General Kemper turned the regiment at the right end of his line and part of the next one to face this threat. But, Colonel Randall said, "We had fired about 10 rounds per man when they seemed to be in utter confusion, and large numbers came in in rear of my regiment for shelter. I do not know how many prisoners my regiment captured, but I had apparently more than there were men in my regiment."[57] General Stannard added that the 16th Vermont "formed on the left of the Thirteenth, at right angles to the main line of our army, bringing them in line of battle upon the flank of the charging division of the enemy, and opened a destructive fire at short range, which the enemy sustained but a very few moments before the larger portion of them surrendered and marched in – not as conquerors, but as captives."[58]

∽ Endnotes ∽

1. Wert, *Gettysburg: Day Three*, 198.
2. Alexander, "The Great Charge and Artillery Fighting at Gettysburg," *B&L* III, 365.
3. Wheeler, *Witness to Gettysburg*, 239.
4. Ibid.
5. *OR*, 27:I:884.
6. Wert, *Gettysburg: Day Three*, 199.
7. Doubleday, *Chancellorsville and Gettysburg*, 192.
8. Ibid., 206.
9. Longstreet, "Lee's Right Wing at Gettysburg," *B&L* III: 343.
10. Wert, *Gettysburg: Day Three*, 191.
11. Ibid., 193.
12. George R. Stewart, *Pickett's Charge* (New York, 1959), 167.
13. 13. Wheeler, *Witness to Gettysburg*, 240.
14. *OR*, 27:II:650-1.
15. Harman, *Lee's Real Plan at Gettysburg*, 98. Stewart, in *Pickett's Charge*, said the distance has been established in Pennsylvania courts as 239 feet (almost 80 yards); Lieutenant Haskell estimated it as 20 or 30 yards. But Harman, a park ranger at Gettysburg, says 68, and he ought to know.
16. Haskell, *The Battle of Gettysburg*, 72-4.
17. Brown, *Cushing of Gettysburg*, 238.
18. Haskell, *The Battle of Gettysburg*, 73.
19. Wert, *Gettysburg: Day Three*, 196.
20. Sears, *Gettysburg*, 399.
21. Ibid., 409.
22. Haskell, *The Battle of Gettysburg*, 101.
23. *OR*, I:27:I:353.
24. Haskell, *The Battle of Gettysburg*, 101-2.
25. *OR*, I:27:I:461.
26. Ibid., I:27:I:462.
27. Ibid., I:27:II:671.
28. Wert, *Gettysburg: Day Three*, 204.
29. Bradley M. Gottfried, *The Maps of Gettysburg* (New York, 2007), 256.
30. Wert, *Gettysburg: Day Three*, 205.
31. Ibid.
32. *OR*, I:27:I:462.
33. Ibid., I:27:II:556-7. Just who made this announcement? Rodes seems to be hiding someone, or himself, behind the passive voice of this statement.
34. Wert, *Gettysburg: Day Three*, 239-40.
35. Ibid., 234.
36. L. E. Bicknell, "Repelling Lee's Last Blow at Gettysburg, IV," *B&L* III, 392.
37. Wert, *Gettysburg: Day Three*, 213.
38. *OR*, I:27:II:647.

39 Wert, *Gettysburg: Day Three*, 216.
40 Ibid., 217.
41 *OR*, I:27:I:373-4.
42 Ibid., I:27:I:437-9.
43 Rice, "Repelling Lee's Last Blow at Gettysburg, I," in *B&L* III, 387-8.
44 Wert, *Gettysburg: Day Three*, 207.
45 Wheeler, *Witness to Gettysburg*, 241-2.
46 Ibid., 243.
47 Wert, *Gettysburg: Day Three*, 225. Both quotes.
48 Ibid., 225-6. All three quotes.
49 Haskell, *The Battle of Gettysburg*, 105.
50 Ibid., 107.
51 *OR*, I:27:I:374.
52 Ibid., I:27:I:439.
53 Rice, "Repelling Lee's Last Blow at Gettysburg, I" in *B&L* III, 388.
54 Wert, *Gettysburg: Day Three*, 219.
55 *OR*, I:27:I:353.
56 Wert, *Gettysburg: Day Three*, 227. Both quotes.
57 *OR*, I:27:I:353.
58 Ibid., I:27:I:350.

CHAPTER 15
"We Can't Expect Always to Gain Victories"
3-4 July 1863

As with the Union attack on the charging Confederates' northern flank, this attack on their southern flank was only possible because no Rebel supporting units advanced far enough to protect it. Captain Bright had delivered Pickett's message to Longstreet, saying that he could take the hill but not hold it without reinforcements, but before Longstreet could reply Colonel Fremantle, the British observer had come up and said, "General Longstreet, General Lee sent me here, and said you would put me in a position to see this charge. I would not have missed it for the world." Longstreet was not amused. "I would," he replied; "the charge is over Colonel Fremantle; Captain Bright ride back and tell General Pickett what you heard me tell Colonel Fremantle." But as the captain had turned to ride away, Longstreet had added, "Captain, you can tell Pickett that he can order Wilcox's brigade."[1]

When Bright took this reply to Pickett the latter sent him and two lieutenants to General Wilcox; the extra messengers being to insure that the order arrived. All three got through, and Bright, the last to return, got there just in time to see the division being flanked. Pickett sent his own brother, Major Charles Pickett, to again ask Longstreet for help, and sent Bright to obtain artillery support. Major Pickett could not find Longstreet. Captain Bright went to Major James Dearing's artillery battalion, but was told by an artillery captain that they had fired off almost all of their ammunition and could not find the reserve ordnance train.

Longstreet had already ordered three brigades of Richard Anderson's division of Hill's 3rd Corps (Mahone's, Posey's, and Wright's) to advance in support of Pettigrew, but they took too long to get moving. Some of the men refused to go; others formed ranks, but without enthusiasm. By the time they actually advanced from Seminary Ridge Pettigrew's and Pickett's men were already in trouble. When Anderson's brigades reached the line of Confederate artillery they were met by a courier from Longstreet with orders to halt. In his report, Anderson said, "I was about to move forward Wright's and Posey's brigades, when Lieutenant-General Longstreet directed me to stop the movement, adding that it was useless, and would only involve unnecessary loss, the assault having failed."[2]

The Confederates who held the wall at the outer angle near Cushing's guns were about the only ones still fighting, and they were in danger of being surrounded. "Bullets seemed to come from front and both flanks," a lieutenant in Garnett's Brigade remembered, "and I saw we could not hold the fence any longer." Some of the Confederates were looking back for any sign of supports or reinforcements. "Why don't they come!" some were heard to ask. But none were seen. At last the gathering Union units seemed to reach some critical mass, and a counterattack was launched. "Whether the command 'Charge!' was given by any general officer I do not know," a Union lieutenant said later. "It seemed to me to come in a spontaneous yell from the men, and instantly our line precipitated itself on the enemy."[3]

Federals from all three of Gibbon's brigades and some from other units that had just arrived all charged forward, with Corporal Henry O'Brien carrying the flag of the 1st Minnesota in the lead. O'Brien soon took a bullet in the hand, but later received a Medal of Honor for his bravery. The color-bearer of the 71st Pennsylvania led his regiment back toward its old position and was killed within about ten feet of the wall. Those Confederates who stayed to fight were rapidly cut down. The rest either surrendered or ran for their lives. "They're broke, boys! They're running!" yelled a Massachusetts sergeant. "There they go! See 'em run!" A Confederate private said that "It was almost as bad going back as it was coming forward. They continued to shoot at us."[4] Many Rebel battle flags were captured. Some were found lying among the dead and wounded, others were extracted forcibly from the hands of their bearers, many of whom fought to the death to defend their charges. Some Federals received Medals of Honor for the flags they captured; others did not.

General Kemper was one of the last to fall. Somehow he had managed to remain both whole and mounted until this retreat began, then he went down with a bullet in the groin. Lying there in excruciating pain, his legs temporarily paralyzed, he was found by some Federals, who lifted him onto a blanket, preparing to carry him away, but then some of Kemper's own men came to his rescue, killing or scattering his captors, and carried him to the Confederate rear. Hundreds of men from Pickett's, Pettigrew's and Trimble's divisions also escaped. Hundreds of others surrendered. Hundreds more lay dead or dying. General Armistead was found, badly wounded, lying beside Cushing's guns. He was an old friend of Hancock, the two having served together on the West Coast until the war came. "'Tell General Hancock,' he said to Lieutenant Mitchell, Hancock's aide-de-camp, to whom he handed his watch, 'that I know I did my country a great wrong when I took up arms against her, for which I am sorry, but for which I cannot live to atone.'" Or so Lieutenant Haskell wrote. And he estimated the unwounded Rebels who surrendered at 4,000 men. "More in number of the captured than the captors," he said.[5]

General Meade, accompanied only by two aides (one of them his son and the other Lieutenant Ranald McKenzie, who later would command a division of cavalry in the Appomattox campaign and become one of the Regular Army's best Indian fighters), reached the crest of Cemetery Ridge behind Hays' 3rd Division just minutes after the Confederates had been repulsed. He asked an artillery lieutenant if the Rebels had been defeated there, and the lieutenant replied that they had been and that General Hays had one of their flags. Meade, who tended to be cross with subordinates when he was stressed, replied, "I don't care for their flags. Have they turned?" The lieutenant assured him that they had, and Meade rode on to the south, encountering a party of surrendering Confederates along the way, who asked where they should go. With a laugh Meade pointed them in the right direction, though the Rebels were soon scattered by the resumption of Confederate artillery fire, which was still overshooting the ridge.

Meade continued south and came upon Gibbon's division from the rear. "As he arrived near me," Lieutenant Haskell remembered, "he asked, in a sharp, eager voice: 'How is it going here?' 'I believe, General, the enemy's attack is repulsed,' I answered. Still approaching, and a new light began to come in his face, of gratified surprise, with a touch of incredulity, of which his voice was also the medium, he further asked: 'What! Is the assault already repulsed?' His voice quicker and more eager than before. 'It is, sir,' I replied. By that time he was on the crest, and when his eye had for an instant swept over the field, taking just a glance of the whole – the masses of prisoners, the numerous captured flags which the men were derisively flaunting about, the fugitives of the routed enemy, disappearing with the speed of terror in the woods – partly at what I had told him, partly at what he saw, he said, impressively, and his face lighted: 'Thank God.' And then his right hand moved as if it would have caught off his hat and waved it; but this gesture he suppressed, and instead he waved his hand, and said 'Hurrah!' The son, with more youth in his blood and less rank upon his shoulders, snatched off his cap, and roared out his three 'hurrahs' right heartily."[6] Learning that Hancock and Gibbon had both been put out of action, Meade gave Haskell some orders to be passed to their successors (Caldwell and Harrow, respectively) about reforming the troops in case the Rebels were crazy enough to attack again, and then rode north to check with General Howard.

Colonel Alexander, watching from his artillery line, said, "The conflict [at the wall] seemed to last five minutes before they were melted away, and only disorganized stragglers pursued by a moderate fire were coming back. Just then, Wilcox's brigade passed by us, moving to Pickett's support. There was no longer anything to support, and with the keenest pity at the useless waste of life, I saw them advance. The men, as they passed us, looked bewildered, as if they wondered what they were expected to do, or why they were there."[7]

Wilcox's and Lang's (Perry's) brigades belonged to Anderson's Division, but they had been separated from it and placed on the opposite side of Pickett's Division, to cover its right flank. Wilcox said, in his report, that Pickett's "advance had not been made more than twenty or thirty minutes, before three staff officers in quick succession . . . gave me orders to advance to the support of Pickett's division. My brigade, about 1,200 in number, then moved forward. . . . [He didn't mention that Lang's Floridians went with him.] As they advanced, they changed direction slightly to the left, so as to cover in part the ground over which Pickett's division had moved. As they came in view on the turnpike, all of the enemy's terrible artillery that could bear on them was concentrated upon them from both flanks and directly in front, and more than on the evening previous. Not a man of the division that I was ordered to support could I see; but as my orders were to go to their support, on my men went down the slope until they came near the hill upon which were the enemy's batteries and intrenchments.

"Here they were exposed to a close and terrible fire of artillery. Two lines of the enemy's infantry were seen moving by the flank toward the rear of my left. I ordered my men to hold their ground until I could get artillery to fire upon them. I then rode back rapidly to our artillery, but could find none near that had ammunition. After some little delay, not getting any artillery to fire upon the enemy's infantry that were on my left flank, and seeing none of the troops that I was ordered to support, and knowing that my small force could do nothing save to make a useless sacrifice of themselves, I ordered them back."[8]

The two lines of Union infantry that Wilcox saw were two regiments of Stannard's brigade. The first one encountered was the 14th Vermont, which guarded the rear of the other two regiments as they attacked Pickett's flank. General Stannard had just ordered his 13th and 16th regiments to return to their original position "when I saw another rebel column charging immediately upon our left. Colonel [W. G.] Veazey, of the Sixteenth, was at once ordered to attack it in its turn upon the flank. This was done as successfully as before."[9] Colonel Veazey reported, "I moved about 15 rods by marching by the left flank and filing to the left, so as to gain upon the enemy and bring my front facing obliquely to his left flank. When this position was gained I received permission to charge."[10]

Lieutenant Colonel Hilary Herbert, commanding Wilcox's 8th Alabama, claimed that Wilcox was still with the artillery when the retreat began. Wilcox sent a courier with an order to withdraw, but the courier was killed before he could deliver the message. Lang's Floridians were already scattered among the bushes to avoid the Union artillery fire when four companies of the 14th Vermont advanced against their front and the large 16th Vermont charged their left flank, and amid the noise and confusion they could not be turned to meet the threat. ". . . therefore, I ordered a retreat," Lang reported, "which, however, was not in time to save a large number of the Second Florida Infantry, together with their colors, from being cut off and captured by the flanking force on the left. . . . I am afraid that many of the men, while firing from behind rocks and trees, did not hear the order, and remained there until captured."[11] The commanders of Wilcox's regiments conferred and agreed that "nothing could save us but a retreat."[12]

The Confederate artillery found enough ammunition left in their chests to cover this retreat, and the two Rebel brigades returned to their starting place, as did the two Union regiments. Colonel Veazey later received a Medal of Honor for his part in repulsing what was seen by the Federals as a second attack upon their line. Years later Lang blamed Wilcox for not obeying the order to advance as promptly as it should have been. But the real problem was that these two brigades had not been ordered to advance almost simultaneously with Pickett's three, while the Union artillery and Stannard's Vermonters had been otherwise occupied. The same would apply to Anderson's other three brigades, Pender's (Lane's) other two, and Rodes' three. To throw all these brigades into the attack was to risk half of Lee's army on the result, but Lee was nothing if not a risk taker, and he had stayed to fight here at Gettysburg in hopes of gaining a decisive victory that would effectively end the war on Confederate terms. But, as Porter Alexander later opined, "once the leading Confederate units had advanced 400 yards and the supports had not yet moved, "the battle failed of being fought as Gen. Lee expected & wished."[13]

Lee had watched the assault while sitting on a tree stump that was covered with an oil cloth, up on Seminary Ridge. As the charge neared the crest of Cemetery Ridge he mounted his famous gray horse, Traveller, and rode out to the Confederate artillery line, where he found Colonel Alexander. By the time he reached there, Wilcox and Lang were making their futile advance. Lee was quite alone, but Alexander had a lieutenant with him. When loud cheering was heard coming from within the Union lines Lee sent the lieutenant to discover its cause. The lieutenant's horse balked, and he took a stick to it, but Lee admonished him for it, saying, "Oh, don't do that. I once had a foolish horse and I found gentle measures so much the best." Evidently he was right, for the lieutenant was soon able to ride off, and eventually he came back to report that the Federals had been merely cheering some senior officer riding along their lines.[14] "Lee remarked," Alexander remembered, "that he had thought it possible that Johnson's division in the Federal rear might have gained some success. Evidently he was not yet informed that Johnson, about noon, had withdrawn to a defensive position.

"Kemper was brought by on a litter. Lee rode up and said, 'General, I hope you are not badly hurt.' Kemper replied, 'Yes, I'm afraid they have got me this time.' Lee pressed his hand, saying: 'I trust not! I trust not!' Col. Fremantle, of her Majesty's Coldstream Guards, had also joined the party. We sat on horseback on the slope behind the guns where we could see over the crest, but the group of horses was not visible to the enemy."[15]

Fremantle said that when he joined Lee, "He was engaged in rallying and in encouraging the broken troops, and was riding about a little in front of the wood, quite alone – the whole of his staff being engaged in a similar manner further to the rear. His face, which is always placid and cheerful, did not show signs of the slightest disappointment, care, or annoyance; and he was addressing to every soldier he met a few words of encouragement. . . . He spoke to all the wounded men that passed him. . . . I saw many badly wounded men take off their hats and cheer him. He said to me, 'This has been a sad day for us, Colonel – a sad day; but we can't expect always to gain victories.'" General Wilcox approached Lee, almost crying, and lamenting the fate of his brigade. According to Fremantle, "General Lee immediately shook hands with him and said cheerfully, 'Never mind, general; all this has been *my* fault; it is *I* that have lost this fight, and you must help me out of it in the best way you can.'"[16]

And still the battle was not over. When Stuart had left Virginia with his three favorite brigades of cavalry to ride around the Union army and try to find Ewell's corps up in Pennsylvania, he had left two other brigades behind to guard the passes of the Blue Ridge Mountains and screen Lee's marching infantry from the Federals. One of these brigades was composed of Virginians who had served in and around the Shenandoah Valley for most of the war so far. This brigade had grown out of the collection of units that had originally been commanded by the late Brigadier General Turner Ashby; it was now under Brigadier General William E. "Grumble" Jones. This officer came by his nickname honestly, being inclined to grouse and complain about almost everything. He and the ever-ebullient Stuart did not get along at all, which is at least one reason why Stuart selected his brigade to be one of those left behind.

The other brigade consisted of two large North Carolina regiments recently sent up from that state under Brigadier General Beverly Robertson. Neither Stuart nor Lee had much confidence in Robertson, which should have been a good reason not to leave him behind, because he was senior to Jones and thus was in charge of both brigades. But it was also, evidently, a reason Stuart didn't want his brigade to come with him. And the job he was assigned was not, as it turned out, very difficult. Stuart's orders to Robertson, before he rode off, had been to screen the Confederate infantry until it was all across the Potomac, guarding its flank and rear; and once the Federals moved north the two brigades were to move in the army's wake, after leaving a few troops to protect the Valley and watch the Federals around Harper's Ferry, and then to rejoin Stuart in Pennsylvania. The two brigades were not, however, to use the paved roads, which would be hard on the horses' hooves.

Robertson had managed to botch even this easy assignment by waiting three days after the Federals marched north before beginning his own move in that direction. Early on the last day of June the two brigades (minus one regiment of Jones's Brigade, left to keep an eye on Harper's Ferry) had crossed the Potomac, and they had reached Greencastle, Pennsylvania, late on 1 July. Early on Friday the third, they reached Chambersburg where they met up with an independent Rebel brigade, consisting of one regiment of cavalry, one regiment of mounted infantry, one company of mounted "partisan rangers," and a battery of horse artillery, all commanded by Brigadier General John D. Imboden. This brigade had been raiding farther west in Maryland and Pennsylvania and had come to Chambersburg, on Lee's orders, to replace Pickett's Division in guarding the army's rear. As Imboden took up this duty Robertson took his own two regiments toward Gettysburg, and Jones led his three regiments toward Fairfield in accordance with orders from Lee to guard some supply wagons parked there.

It was a fortuitous move, because as Merritt's Reserve Brigade of Buford's Union cavalry division moved north from Emmitsburg that day Merritt had been advised by a farmer of the presence of these Confederate wagons, loaded with plunder, and the fact that, at the time, they didn't have much protection. Merritt, one of the three young cavalry officers recently promoted to brigadier general on Pleasonton's recommendation, had therefore sent the 6th U.S. Cavalry to capture them and to hold the town of Fairfield and prevent any units coming up from Virginia from joining Lee.

This regiment had been raised at the outbreak of the war, primarily from western Pennsylvania, while the old 1st and 2nd Dragoons, the Regiment of Mounted Rifles, and the original 1st and 2nd Cavalry had been redesignated 1st, 2nd, 3rd, 4th, and 5th Cavalry respectively. (The 7th Cavalry, of Little Big Horn fame, and higher numbered units, were not raised until after the war.) The 6th was commanded by Major Samuel "Paddy" Starr, a crusty old Regular who was Merritt's senior by 23 years, and who had briefly commanded the entire brigade before Merritt's promotion over him. Quite possibly Merritt sent this particular regiment for this detached duty to get his old former boss out of his hair.

So the 6th U.S. rode ahead of Merritt's main column, which was slowed by accompanying supply wagons of its own, and at Millerstown Starr sent one squadron (two companies) under Captain George Cram along the cut of an unfinished railroad that led north along the foot of the South Mountain ridge, in order to outflank the wagons and their guards. (The regiment was already short one squadron, which served as escort for General Pleasonton, and evidently another squadron remained with Merritt.) The men of the regiment didn't care much for Major Starr, who was something of a martinet, but Cram was even less popular with the men and disliked by Starr as well. And at least some of the men didn't trust the farmer who had brought Merritt word of the Confederate wagons at Fairfield, thinking he might be a Rebel spy sent to lure them into a trap.

Starr's main column, thus reduced to three squadrons (half the regiment) rode on to Fairfield and was told by women there that a train of eight wagons had just left town, heading north, loaded with loot. The leading squadron, under Lieutenant Christian Balder, spotted the wagons not far north of the town and chased them for more than a mile until it ran into the head of Grumble Jones's column, coming down from Cashtown, behind which the wagons escaped. Seeing that he was badly outnumbered, Balder retreated, with Jones's Confederates in pursuit. The Rebels chased the lone squadron for two miles before it rejoined the other two. Starr then dismounted one of his squadrons in an orchard west of the road and another behind a fence to the right, and when they opened fire with their carbines the pursuing Virginians, hemmed in by sturdy fences lining both sides of the road, were thrown into confusion.

"Shattered and broken the head of the charging column faltered," the brigade's historian wrote, "the men behind it halted, and soon the whole regiment returned in spite of the strenuous efforts of its officers to force it forward."[17] Badly outnumbered and having no guns with which to reply to the Confederate battery that Jones ordered to deploy in a nearby wheat field, Starr should have retreated; instead, he ordered a countercharge, but first his men had to mount up. Meanwhile, the 7th Virginia retreated 3 or 400 yards to where Jones's other two regiments were just coming up. One retreating Rebel called out to them, "Boys, you are going to catch it; we have been badly beaten."[18] Jones turned to his next regiment and shouted, "Shall one damned regiment of Yankees whip my whole brigade?"[19] The 6th Virginia replied in the negative and, with Jones at their head, charged toward the Federals, joined by some men from the 7th and a few from the 11th.

Starr had, meanwhile, led his single mounted squadron up the road in a countercharge, without waiting for his dismounted men to mount up and follow, and the Confederates quickly overcame that lone squadron, driving it back. The other Federals were caught in the act of mounting and were soon scattered, mostly on foot. Captain Cram's squadron arrived and tried to cover the retreat of the others, but it was also soon overwhelmed, Cram himself being wounded and captured. Lieutenant Balder almost cut his way out but was shot in the streets of Fairfield and mortally wounded. Starr's arm was badly mangled by a pistol bullet, and he was captured. Only two officers, a pair of lieutenants, each leading a small group of men, managed to escape. They met up at Mechanicstown and circled around to rejoin Merritt.

That night Jones's Brigade bivouacked near a peak of the South Mountain ridge known as Jack's Mountain and picketed the passes on either side of it: Monterey Pass on the south, and Fairfield Gap on the north.

Throughout the afternoon, General Kilpatrick had probed Longstreet's southern flank. At about 3 p.m. Merritt's brigade, coming up the Emmitsburg Road, made contact with Kilpatrick, who ordered it to take position about 300 yards to the west of that road and of Farnsworth's brigade of his own division. At around 4 p.m. the two battalions of the 1st Vermont Cavalry that he had ordered to hold onto a house a few hundred yards east of the Emmitsburg Road finally gave it up after exchanging shots with Rebel skirmishers for some hours. Meanwhile, Kilpatrick had been disappointed to learn that the ground between that house and Big Round Top was not suitable for mounted operations.

About 4:30 Merritt sent his 6th Pennsylvania Cavalry up the Emmitsburg Road, supported by his battery of horse artillery and his Regulars. (This regiment had once been known as Rush's Lancers, and had, in fact, carried lances until a few weeks back. They had given them up because they were hard to use or even carry in the heavily wooded terrain of Virginia. Ironically, just as they gave them up the war had carried them into the more open country of southeastern Pennsylvania.) This advance caused the 9th Georgia to give up its hold on a house near the road and fall back, and then the 5th U.S. Cavalry made a mounted charge that broke through Colonel Black's thin line west of the road, inflicting quite a few casualties in the process. But the rest of "Tige" Anderson's brigade came rushing up to block any further Union advance. Merritt had his Pennsylvanians dismount and continue the attack, but the fire of the Georgians, and of two batteries stationed just east of the road, brought this to a halt.

At about 5 p.m. a messenger brought Kilpatrick word that Lee's infantry attack had been repulsed with, as the courier put it, "nine acres of prisoners!"[20] Evidently Kilpatrick didn't want the battle to end before he had made his own mark upon it, for he now made a rash and totally unjustified decision. Merritt was trying to at least hold onto what he had gained, but General Law personally led two of Anderson's regiments against Merritt's left flank, and the cavalrymen fell back several hundred yards. But, seeing this concentration against Merritt near the Emmitsburg Road, Kilpatrick decided to make a breakthrough farther east while Law was busy elsewhere. Even though he knew it was rough and broken ground, he ordered a mounted charge.

Kilpatrick ordered the 1st West Virginia Cavalry of Farnsworth's brigade to attack the center of the 1st Texas's skirmish line, but he neglected to give it artillery support from his horse battery, and the West Virginians encountered a fence that should have been spotted before. The Federals tried to knock down the fence or hack it apart with their sabers, but a volley from the Texans drove them back. They rallied and tried again, but with the same result, and finally gave up.

Kilpatrick then ordered the 1st Vermont to make a charge farther east. Farnsworth protested but was overridden in a heated exchange, possibly with a sneer concerning his personal courage. So, at about 5:30 p.m., Farnsworth (the other of the three new brigadiers, besides Merritt and Custer) led one battalion (two squadrons, about 150 men) of the 1st Vermont Cavalry on a charge straight at the skirmish line of the 1st Texas, while a second battalion of the same regiment, under Captain Henry Parsons, charged the line farther east. Farther west, the 18th Pennsylvania Cavalry made a limited attack, and the other battalion of the 1st Vermont and the horse battery provided covering fire.

The charge of the 18th Pennsylvania was quickly broken up by the Rebel artillery, but Parsons' battalion, passing the 1st West Virginia as it fell back, broke through the Confederate skirmish line riding in a column of fours, and turned north, passing the Rebel guns so closely that the gunners couldn't get a shot at them, then followed a lane that brought them abreast of the 4th Alabama of Law's Brigade, coming down from Big Round Top. The Alabamans' first volley was too high, but their second drove the Federals back to the south, where they jumped a stone wall into a grove; then they circled back to the north, looped to the south again, and jumped another wall into an open field. From there Parsons could see Farnsworth's battalion moving northward beyond yet another fence. His battalion jumped this one as well, but found it impossible to connect with Farnsworth. He moved south and broke back through the Rebel line about where he had broken in, his men bringing with them about enough prisoners to match their losses.

Farnsworth had, meanwhile, turned east to take Law's original line in the rear; he smashed through Colonel Oates' 15th Alabama, which was also coming down from Big Round Top, before it could form to meet him, and then turned north, moving along behind Law's main line. These Rebels turned around and blasted his troopers with musketry, so he curved to the west and then south, only to encounter the

Rebel batteries and the 9th Georgia, which was just coming up after helping to repulse Merritt's attack. Farnsworth's horse was shot out from under him, but he found another mount. However, while he was down most of his men had broken through the Confederate line again to rejoin Kilpatrick. Farnsworth, perhaps disoriented, turned back the way he had come with about ten followers and ran smack into the 15th Alabama again. He swerved to the east and then to the south, almost surrounded now by Rebels, who called on him to surrender, but he rode on until shot out of the saddle by Oates' men. Wounded in several places, he yelled a refusal to surrender, and died.

The two-and-a-half Confederate infantry divisions in Pickett's Charge had lost about 5,400 men that day, or something approaching 50% of their strength, although "only" 800-1100 were killed. They had inflicted anywhere from 1,500 to 2,300 casualties on the Federals. Add in the fighting over Culp's Hill plus the cavalry battles, and the Rebels lost some 7,500 men, killed, wounded, and missing or captured (over 10% of Lee's total strength), on 3 July alone; the Federals, a bit over 4,000. As usual in that war, many key officers were lost, disrupting or diminishing the units' ability to function until they got reorganized. On both sides, men of various units had become intermixed and jumbled together, another reason for a pause to reorganize.

Of Lee's nine infantry divisions, all had seen some combat over the past three days; most were fought out, for now; only parts of Rodes', Pender's and Anderson's divisions were still relatively fresh. In three days of fighting Lee had lost about a third of his army; Meade about a quarter of his. The Union 1st, 2nd, 3rd, and 11th Corps had all now been severely battered; the 5th Corps had done some severe fighting on the second day and now held the army's left, and the 12th Corps, after a hard fight, was still needed to hold its key position on the right. Hancock, a bold and aggressive fighter in command of the Union center, was soon carried off the field, Gibbon was also wounded, and Meade's only relatively fresh corps, the 6th, was down on the Union left, somewhat scattered in defensive and reserve positions. For these good and sufficient reasons, the Federals did not immediately counterattack, as both Lee and other Confederates expected or feared at first.

"When all the fugitives had passed and there was still no sign of counter-stroke, Lee rode off," Colonel Alexander later wrote. "I continued to hold my line of guns with few changes until after dark. There were some advances by Federal skirmish lines, which we kept in check with our guns, sometimes having to use canister sharply. But the Federal guns did not interfere, for which we were duly grateful. During the afternoon I quietly withdrew guns, one at a time, sending them to be refitted, and by 10 o'clock our whole line had been retired about to the position from which the attack began on the 2d."[21]

Meade, after checking on Cemetery Hill, had ridden south to Little Round Top, and there he had conferred with General Sykes, of the 5th Corps, and ordered the latter to conduct a reconnaissance in force by clearing Rose's Woods, east of the Wheat Field. Sykes had passed the order to General Crawford, who sent one brigade of his Pennsylvania Reserves, reinforced with an extra regiment, while asking a brigade of the 6th Corps to take its place on Big Round Top. Crawford's Pennsylvanians, entering the woods from the north, encountered the 15th Georgia, as Crawford reported, "behind a stone wall running through the woods, and which they had made stronger by rails and logs. We fell upon their flank, completely routing them, taking over 200 prisoners, one stand of colors belonging to the Fifteenth Georgia, and many arms." The Federals continued to advance, finding that the Rebels were falling back before them, and "the whole of the ground lost the previous day was retaken, together with all of our wounded, who, mingled with those of the rebels, were lying uncared for."[22]

The Confederates fell back before this relatively small

force because, at around 5 p.m., near the time that Kilpatrick had ordered his pointless attack, Longstreet had sent a staff officer to Hood's (now Law's) and McLaws' divisions with orders for them to return to the positions from which they had launched their attacks the day before. McLaws objected that if Lee wanted to renew the fight his men held good ground from which to launch an attack, but the staff officer told him Longstreet's orders were firm, and the two divisions pulled back that evening.

Lt. Haskell exchanged his badly wounded horse for another and rode in search of generals Gibbon and Hancock and the 2nd Corps hospital. Passing many skulkers he happily lied to them that General Meade had ordered the Provost Guard to arrest and shoot them all. "The whole neighborhood in rear of the field became one vast hospital of miles in extent," he wrote. Every house, barn and shed, he said, was filled with wounded men. "Every conceivable wound that iron and lead can make, blunt or sharp, bullet, ball and shell, piercing, bruising, tearing, was there. . . ." Most of the wounded men were cheerfully discussing their victory, he said, except for those who were near death. Others were impatiently waiting for their turn to have an arm or leg cut off. "The surgeons, with coats off and sleeves rolled up, and the hospital attendants with green bands upon their caps, are about their work," he wrote; "and their faces and clothes are spattered with blood; and though they look weary and tired, their work goes systematically and steadily on. How much and how long they have worked, the piles of legs, arms, feet, hands, and fingers about partially tell. . . . Near by appear a row of small fresh mounds, placed side by side. They were not there yesterday. They will become more numerous every day."[23]

What was left of Pickett's Division returned to the ground behind the low ridges from which it had advanced this day, and Pettigrew's and Trimble's men gathered on the western slope of Seminary Ridge. The sun set at about 7:30, and, at last, another day of terrible battle had ended at Gettysburg.

But, as Colonel Wainwright, chief of the 1st Corps artillery, wrote, night did not bring "a certainty that the fight was done, or even that Lee might not try it again tonight or tomorrow, but a feeling that he had done his worst and failed."[24]

Out in front of the Union 2nd Corps, windrows of dead and wounded men "lay thicker than wheat sheaves," as one Federal soldier wrote.[25] Indeed, the entire valley south of Gettysburg was something of a wreck, and the stench of death was so strong that at least one Federal said he could not eat, drink or sleep. "Thousands of men were lying unattended," one Federal wrote, "scattered over the field, mingled with broken gun carriages, exploded caissons, hundreds of dead and dying horses, and other ghastly debris of the battlefield. . . . The field was covered with the slain; the full moon looked down with serene, unclouded, and softened luster on the field of Gettysburg, trodden down for miles by the two great armies; surgeons were cutting off limbs, administering whiskey, chloroform, and morphine to deaden pain; hundreds of men were going back and forth from the fields where the actual fighting had occurred, to the rear, with the mangled bodies of the wounded. . . . The survivors were waiting to see what would come on the morrow, when suddenly a band of music began to play in the rear of the Union line of battle, down somewhere on the Taneytown Road."[26] The little band expressed the longings of the men of both sides as it played the gentle melody of "Home Sweet Home."

"When we were permitted at length to lie down under the caissons, or in the fence corners," one Confederate artilleryman remembered, "and realized that we had escaped the death that had snatched away so many others, we felt too well satisfied at our good fortune – in spite of the enemy still near us – not to sleep the soundest sleep it is permitted on earth for mortals to enjoy."[27]

Alonzo Cushing's younger brother, William, a lieutenant in the Navy, whose ship was in the Potomac, helping to protect Washington, arrived on the battlefield that evening. Born only two years apart, the two brothers had been very close. He told Captain John Hazard, commander of the 2nd Corps' artillery brigade, that he wanted to take command of his brother's battery, but there wasn't much left of it, and it had been consolidated with Woodruff's battery. In that case, he wanted to take his brother's body home, but it had already been shipped to West Point for burial. There was nothing for him to do but return to his ship. "There is suffering greater than the dying know," he wrote their mother, "the prolonged anguish of those left behind to mourn them."[28]

The men slept, but there was little rest for the commanders. Sometime that night Meade's headquarters issued special orders assigning General Hays to the command of the 2nd Corps but putting General Newton, recently appointed commander of the 1st Corps, in overall charge of "the portion of the line commencing at the left of Howard's line and terminating at the right of Sykes."[29]

At 8:35 p.m. Meade wrote to General Halleck again giving a brief account of the artillery bombardment and the infantry attack (he called it two attacks). He claimed nearly 3,000 prisoners, including General Armistead plus "a large number of wounded in our hands." He said his own loss had been "considerable," including generals Hancock and Gibbon, and said, "After the repelling of the assault, indications leading to the belief that the enemy might be withdrawing, an armed reconnaissance was pushed forward from the left, and the enemy found to be in force. At the present hour all is quiet." He mentioned that his cavalry had been engaged on both flanks and concluded with, "The army is in fine spirits."[30]

At 9:57 p.m. Meade wrote to General Couch, at Harrisburg: "I do not think Lee will attack me again, but am as yet uncertain whether he will assume an offensive attitude, and await an attack from me or whether he will withdraw down the Cumberland Valley, holding strongly the mountain passes, which, I understand, he has fortified. Should the former be the case, I will apprise you of the fact so soon as I am certain of it, and I then desire you either to form a junction with me, or, if in your judgment the same can be done without jeopardizing the safety of your command, attack him. Should I be satisfied that he is retreating, I shall then move down on this side of the mountain, and wish you to pursue him as rapidly as possible down the Valley."[31]

Almost simultaneously, Couch was writing to Meade: "I will move 9,000 men from Carlisle after 12 o'clock tonight. We hope to strike near Cashtown. I have also ordered my men in Bedford County forward, to harass near Chambersburg and Greencastle. My cavalry have been at Fayetteville." Apparently in reply to this, Meade wrote to Couch: "Telegraph dispatches reach me through Baltimore and Frederick. My cavalry have been at Berlin. The country between this and you is probably clear of all but stragglers – your easy prey. Your officers could communicate with me now via Hanover and Taneytown."[32] With his former headquarters now being used as a hospital, Meade moved down the Taneytown Road about a quarter of a mile and slept that night among the rocks.

Lee was going to retreat, but not, as Meade expected, down the Cumberland Valley (the Maryland-Pennsylvania extension of the Shenandoah Valley of Virginia). He met after sunset with his senior officers at A. P. Hill's headquarters on the Cashtown Road and informed them that, unless Meade should attack them the next day, they would return to Virginia. Ewell's 2nd Corps was ordered to give up its position east of the town after all, and the town as well, and take position on Seminary Ridge at the left end of Lee's now-straightened and shortened line, which it did between 10 p.m. and 2 a.m. These Confederates found themselves camped in the middle of the first day's battlefield, still strewn with the dead from both sides who had been lying there some 30-36 hours. "Corpses so monstrously swollen," Major Campbell Brown, Ewell's son-in-law, remembered, "that the buttons were broken from the loose blouses & shirts, & the baggy pantaloons fitted like skin – so blackened that the head looked like an immense cannon ball, the features being nearly obliterated. . . ." An artilleryman said that the odor of decaying flesh was too much to take. "In a short time we all sickened and were lying with our mouths close to the ground, most of us vomiting profusely." The Rebels were battered and sickened, but still ready to fight. "It would be ridiculous to say that I did not feel whipped," Brown added, "– or that there was a man in that Army who didn't appreciate the position just as plainly. But the 'fight' wasn't out of the troops by any means – they felt that the position & not the enemy had out done us. . . ."[33] There was some grumbling against their generals, however, and a feeling that if Stonewall Jackson had still been leading them things would have turned out differently.

The courier sent to deliver orders to Stuart's cavalry never arrived, but when Stuart saw Ewell's infantry begin to pull out he rode to find Lee, and between them it was decided to send the brigades of Hampton (now commanded by Colonel Lawrence Baker) and Fitzhugh Lee to Cashtown, commanded by Fitz Lee. They would provide protection for the army's rear as it marched southwest, and for the trains of Longstreet's and Hill's corps. Robertson's and Jones's brigades, still under Robertson, were to cover two roads that led around Jack's Mountain to Monterey Pass: the Jack's Mountain Road on the east and the Maria Furnace Road on the west. These roads connected with the turnpike that led westward from Emmitsburg to Waynesborough. Stuart himself was to protect the army's left flank as it moved south by taking his other two brigades, Chambliss's and Jenkins', to Emmitsburg, at which place he would turn west and cross the South Mountain range at Monterey Pass.

Even after the meeting broke up, Lee stayed on and conferred with Hill on just how to conduct the retreat. General Imboden, having just arrived from Chambersburg, found them there in Hill's tent, "seated on camp-stools with a map spread upon their knees." But Lee told Imboden to wait for him at Lee's headquarters, about a mile away.

Lee suspected that the Federals would attack him at

daylight or soon thereafter, so at about 1 a.m. orders went to all three corps directing them to have their artillery in place along Seminary Ridge and Oak Ridge and ready to resist an attack. But the artillery battalions were to send all their wagons not needed with the guns, loaded with as many sick and wounded men as they could carry, to report to Lee's chief quartermaster, Lieutenant Colonel James L. Corley. It was also about 1 a.m. on Saturday, 4 July, when Lee returned to his own headquarters to find Imboden and one of the latter's aides waiting for him.

Lee's own staff officers were asleep, and there was not even a sentinel on duty at his tent, and Lee seemed to be so exhausted as to need assistance in dismounting from his equally weary horse, so Imboden went to help him, but Lee managed to alight by himself, then stood looking down, with one arm across the saddle, leaning on his mount. "Awed by his appearance," Imboden later wrote, "I waited for him to speak until the silence became embarrassing, when, to break it and change the silent current of his thoughts, I ventured to remark, in a sympathetic tone, and in allusion to his great fatigue:

"'General, this has been a hard day on you.'

"He looked up, and replied mournfully: 'Yes, it has been a sad, sad day to us,' and immediately relapsed into his thoughtful mood and attitude. Being unwilling again to intrude upon his reflections, I said no more. After perhaps a minute or two, he suddenly straightened up to his full height, and turning to me with more animation and excitement of manner than I had ever seen in him before, for he was a man of wonderful equanimity, he said in a voice tremulous with emotion:

"'I never saw troops behave more magnificently than Pickett's division of Virginians did to-day in that grand charge upon the enemy. And if they had been supported as they were to have been, – but, for some reason not yet fully explained to me, were not, – we would have held the position and the day would have been ours.' After a moment's pause he added in a loud voice, in a tone almost of agony, 'Too bad!

Too bad! Oh! Too Bad!'"

But Lee soon mastered his emotions, and, after speaking feelingly of some his fallen officers, he invited Imboden into his tent. "We must now return to Virginia," Lee told him. "As many of our poor wounded as possible must be taken home. I have sent for you, because your men and horses are fresh and in good condition, to guard and conduct our train back to Virginia. The duty will be arduous, responsible, and dangerous, for I am afraid you will be harassed by the enemy's cavalry." Lee then asked how many men Imboden had and was told about 2,100 effectives, all well mounted, including a 6-gun battery of horse artillery.

"I can spare you as much artillery as you require," Lee told him, "but no other troops, as I shall need all I have to return safely by a different and shorter route than yours. The batteries are generally short of ammunition, but you will probably meet a supply I have ordered from Winchester to Williamsport. Nearly all the transportation and the care of all the wounded will be intrusted to you. You will recross the mountain by the Chambersburg road, and then proceed to Williamsport by any route you deem best, and without a halt till you reach the river. Rest there long enough to feed your animals; then ford the river, and do not halt again till you reach Winchester, where I will again communicate with you."

"After a good deal of conversation about roads," Imboden later wrote, "and the best disposition of my forces to cover and protect the vast train, he directed that the chiefs of his staff departments should be waked up to receive, in my presence, his orders to collect as early next day as possible all the wagons and ambulances which I was to convoy, and have them in readiness for me to take command of them. His medical director [Dr. Lafayette Guild], was charged to see that all the wounded who could bear the rough journey should be placed in the empty wagons and ambulances. He then remarked to me that his general instructions would be sent to me in writing the following morning.

"As I was about leaving to return to my camp, as late, I

think, as 2 a.m., he came out of his tent to where I was about to mount, and said in an undertone: 'I will place in your hands by a staff-officer, to-morrow morning, a sealed package for President Davis, which you will retain in your possession till you are across the Potomac, when you will detail a reliable commissioned officer to take it to Richmond with all possible dispatch and deliver it into the President's own hands. And I impress it on you that, whatever happens, this package must not fall into the hands of the enemy. If unfortunately you should be captured, destroy it at the first opportunity."[34]

Meanwhile all empty quartermaster's, subsistence and ordnance wagons were being sent to the various hospitals to be loaded with wounded men who could not walk. But it was soon found that there were not enough wagons. Men who could walk were told to do so. Their objective was the General and Receiving Hospital at Staunton, Virginia. From there they could be forwarded to Richmond by railroad if necessary. Many of the wounded were in no condition to be moved, and surgeons, nurses, cooks and stewards were detailed to stay behind with them even though it meant becoming prisoners of war. Some 446 wounded men had to be left behind in the hospitals of Johnson's Division, northeast of Gettysburg; Early's Division left 259 wounded men in the town; Rodes' Division left 760 men behind. General Trimble, whose leg had to be amputated, was not considered fit to be moved and was also left behind to become a prisoner.

However, moving as many of his wounded men as possible was only one of Lee's problems as he contemplated a return to Virginia. One of the principal reasons for his invasion of Pennsylvania had been the opportunity to live off of Northern resources for a while, both to improve his own supply situation and to relieve Virginia, much of which had been ravaged by the armies that had been campaigning on its soil for two years. Abundant supplies of food, clothing, and much else had been collected all over southeastern Pennsylvania over the past weeks, but they filled thousands of wagons, which Lee now needed to move safely to Virginia.

Supplies being hoarded for long-term needs filled the reserve quartermaster and subsistence train of wagons commanded by Major John Alexander Harman, chief quartermaster of Ewell's 2nd Corps. This train was situated some eight miles west of Gettysburg, parked along the north-south road that connected Cashtown with Fairfield.

At 3 a.m. Major Harman ordered these wagons to take to the road, heading south for Monterey Pass, a more direct route than that which Imboden would take. Herds of cattle and sheep led the way, and others moved alongside the wagons at intervals. Hogs rode in wagons or were tied behind them. Once stretched out on the road, his train probably extended for at least fifteen miles, maybe twenty. For protection, this train depended on one battery of four 12-pounder Napoleons and the 1st Maryland Cavalry Battalion, which had joined Ewell's corps as it had swept down the Shenandoah and had marched with it ever since.

All wagons from Ewell's three divisions that would not be needed with the troops were ordered to join Harman's reserve train. It was midmorning by the time that the leading wagons of Johnson's Division, coming down the Herr Ridge Road, reached the Fairfield (or Hagerstown) Road, and the reserve train was still passing, so they pulled over and waited. The last wagon of Rodes' Division was still probably some twenty miles back. Temporary hospitals were soon set up in nearby houses to care for some of the wounded traveling with this train. Some of them did not live to travel any farther.

Many of these wagons, ranging in size from those needing only two mules or horses to pull to those needing four- and six-mule teams, had, like their contents, and the animals pulling them, been plundered from Pennsylvania and Maryland; though some of them had been captured from the Union Army when Ewell had driven the Federals out of the Shenandoah Valley on the way north. The teamsters driving the vast majority of these wagons were slaves, leased or seized by the Confederate Army. A Northern newspaper reporter described it as "a mongrel train – all stolen, or what is still worse – paid for in Confederate notes, made payable six months after the recognition of the southern Confederacy by the United States Government – or in other words – never."[35]

~ Endnotes ~

1. Wert, *Gettysburg: Day Three*, 237-8.
2. *OR*, I:27:II:615.
3. Wert, *Gettysburg: Day Three*, 230. All three quotes.
4. Ibid., 231. Both quotes.
5. Haskell, *The Battle of Gettysburg*, 115. Armistead had been hit in both an arm and a leg, but no bones were broken, and Union surgeons at first thought he would recover, but his immune system had been weakened by recent over-exertion and lack of sleep, and he died two days later.
6. Ibid., 118-9.
7. Alexander, "The Great Charge and Artillery Fighting at Gettysburg," *B&L* III:366.
8. *OR*, I:27:II:620.
9. Ibid., I:27:I:350.
10. Ibid., I:27:I:1042.
11. Ibid., I:27:II:632.
12. Wert, *Gettysburg: Day Three*, 241.
13. Ibid., 243.
14. Alexander, *Military Memoirs of a Confederate*, 426.
15. Ibid.
16. Wheeler, *Witness to Gettysburg*, 245-6. Emphasis in the source.
17. Eric J. Wittenberg, *Gettysburg's Forgotten Cavalry Actions* (revised edition, New York and El Dorado Hills CA, 2011), 120.
18. Ibid., 122.
19. Longacre, *The Cavalry at Gettysburg*, 236.
20. Ibid., 233.
21. Alexander, *Military Memoirs of a Confederate*, 426.
22. *OR*, I:27:I:654.
23. Haskell, *The Battle of Gettysburg*, 143-4.
24. Sears, *Gettysburg*, 465.
25. Wert, *Gettysburg, Day Three*, 248.
26. Wheeler, *Witness to Gettysburg*, 247.
27. Ibid., 249.
28. Ralph J. Roske and Charles Van Doren, *Lincoln's Commando* (New York, 1957), 182.
29. *OR*, I:27:III:503.
30. Ibid., I:27:I:75.
31. Ibid., I:27:III:499.
32. Ibid., I:27:III:502.
33. Sears, *Gettysburg*, 472-3. All three quotes.
34. John D. Imboden, "The Confederate Retreat from Gettysburg," in *B&L* III:421-2.
35. Brown, *Retreat from Gettysburg*, 106.

Part Four
RETREAT AND PURSUIT

CHAPTER 16
"Lee Must Fight His Way Through Alone"
4 July 1863

AT 4:10 A.M., SATURDAY, 4 July, General Halleck, or someone at his office in Washington, received a message from Meade's chief of staff, Dan Butterfield, written the day before, that enclosed the letters to Lee that Captain Dahlgren had captured two days before.

The implications of these letters were not lost on the general-in-chief. At 8 a.m., he wired Major General William S. Rosecrans, commander of the Union Army of the Cumberland, out in Tennessee: "A letter from Jefferson Davis to General Lee, dated at Richmond on the 28th instant [ultimo], was captured yesterday. It recapitulates reasons why re-enforcements cannot be sent from Richmond to Lee, one of which is that 'General Bragg has been weakened by withdrawing his troops and sending them to Joe Johnston; that he is threatened with attack; has fallen back to his entrenched position at Tullahoma, and called on Buckner for aid.' A three day's battle has been going on near Gettysburg between General Meade and General Lee; thus far successful on our side, with promise of a brilliant victory."[1]

General Braxton Bragg was the commander of the Confederate Army of Tennessee, who had just been maneuvered out of the central part of that state by Rosecrans. Major General Simon Bolivar Buckner was the Confederate commander in East Tennessee, who, as Halleck had gleaned from Davis's letter, had been called on to reinforce Bragg. Halleck's point was that Bragg's Army of Tennessee had been weakened by sending troops to join General J. E. Johnston in Mississippi.

Rosecrans, probably feeling an implied criticism of his own efforts against his weakened foe, replied before the day was out: "Your dispatch of this morning is received. Our movement commenced on 24th of June. Have driven Bragg from his intrenched positions at Shelbyville and Tullahoma. Either of them is stronger than Corinth [Mississippi – which Halleck had captured, after a cautious advance, the year before]. Have pursued him through the mountains. Incessant rains and the impassable state of the roads alone prevented us from forcing him to a general battle. [Major General Philip] Sheridan's division occupied Cowan yesterday at 3 p.m. The enemy has retreated toward Bridgeport [Alabama] and Chattanooga. Every effort is being made to bring forward supplies and threaten the enemy sufficiently to hold him. As I have already advised you, Tullahoma was evacuated Tuesday night. Our troops pursued him, and overtook his [wagon] train at Elk River. He burned the bridge. In that operation our losses in killed and wounded will not exceed 500. The loss of the enemy may be safely put at 1,000 killed and wounded, 1,000 prisoners, 7 pieces of artillery, 500 or 600 tents. The country is filled with deserters from the Tennessee troops, and it is generally thought a very large portion of these troops will never leave their native State. Nothing but most stringent coercion can detain them. It is impossible to convey to you an idea of the continuous rains we have had since commencement of these operations or the state of the roads. I pray God that every available soldier may be sent to me, and that our arms may be successful against Lee. He should be destroyed."[2]

On that same fourth day of July, Bragg fell back to Chattanooga, a key railroad junction on the upper Tennessee River just north of the Georgia state line, and began crossing his army to the south side of the river. He had written to Joe Johnston, his nominal superior, the day before, explaining that he had been forced to retreat out of Middle Tennessee by threats to his flanks and line of communications, saying "it was perfectly practicable for the enemy to destroy our means of crossing the Tennessee, and thus secure our ultimate destruction without a battle. Having failed to bring him to that issue, so much desired by myself and troops, I reluctantly yielded to the necessity imposed by my position and inferior strength, and put the army in motion for the Tennessee River. Should we succeed in crossing it successfully (and I hear of no formidable pursuit up to this morning), the Tennessee will be taken as our line."[3] It would take Rosecrans a few weeks to repair the railroad and various bridges now in his rear and bring forward enough supplies to allow him to push forward again.

At the same hour of 8 a.m. Secretary of War Stanton wired Major General Ambrose Burnside at Cincinnati, Ohio, that "A letter from Jeff. Davis to General Lee, captured from a courier yesterday, states among other things that Bragg, being threatened with attack, and weakened by withdrawing his troops and sending them to Johnston, 'has called on Buckner for aid.'" Burnside, who had commanded the Army of the Potomac in its ill-fated attack on Fredericksburg back in December, now commanded the Department of the Ohio and was responsible for protecting Kentucky, but he was also supposed to be working on liberating East Tennessee, an area with strong pro-Union sentiment. "From the letter of Davis," Stanton told Burnside, "you will understand in how tight a place Bragg and Buckner are, and will know whether and how to strike Buckner to prevent him aiding Bragg." He added that "Meade, after three days' battle near Gettysburg, has the prospect of complete victory."[4]

At 10:50 a.m. General Halleck added his own prompting of Burnside, spelling out the obvious in case Burnside didn't see it: "Buckner's forces have been called from East Tennessee to re-enforce Bragg, and there can be no considerable force now to prevent your advance. A rapid movement, living as far as possible on the country, may produce important results. It is not possible for Bragg to make any considerable detachment to oppose you."[5]

Burnside forwarded Stanton's message to Major General

George L. Hartsuff, at Lexington, Kentucky, commander of the 23rd Corps, but before the day was out Burnside replied to Stanton: "All our troops are well down to the front. One party is threatening Abingdon, and another party has gone to destroy Loudon Bridge. Strawberry Plains Bridge and two other important ones are already destroyed, and I hope to throw a considerable force of men into East Tennessee. You know my line is long, and my disposable force small after taking out railroad guards, &c. Morgan broke through our lines at Burkesville yesterday with 4,000 or 5,000 cavalry and started for the interior of the State. Our forces are concentrating, and we hope to catch him."[6]

Morgan's advanced guard had reached the south bank of Green River at Tebb's Bend on the night of 3 July and could hear Federals on the other side felling trees. Two hundred infantrymen under Colonel Orlando Moore of the 25th Michigan had been building defenses on a knoll in a loop of the steep-banked river, thus providing themselves with a ready-made moat on three sides. And woods along the river-bank would make it difficult for Rebel artillery to shell them. On the morning of the 4th, Morgan demanded the fort's complete and unconditional surrender. Moore replied that "the Fourth of July was no day for me to entertain such a proposition." Morgan ordered two regiments to make a dismounted charge while the rest of his division crossed Green River at another ford, but his men became entangled in an abatis of felled trees and were met by deadly fire from the Federals. "The conflict was fierce and bloody," Moore later reported. "At times the enemy occupied one side of the fallen timber, while my men held the other, in almost a hand-to-hand fight."[7]

Morgan called off the attack after three and a half hours of this. Lieutenant Colonel Robert Alston, Morgan's chief of staff, said Colonel Moore "is a gallant man, and the entire arrangement of his defence entitles him to the highest credit for military skill. We would mark such a man in our army for promotion.... The place was judiciously chosen and skilfully defended, and the result was that we were repulsed with severe loss. . . ." He added that "Our march thus far has been very fatiguing – bad roads, little rest or sleep, little to eat, and a fight every day. Yet our men are cheerful, even buoyant. . . ." As they rode north that afternoon, he heard a pistol shot behind him and turned to find that one Confederate officer had shot another. "He was killed by Captain Murphy," he noted in his diary, "because Magennis, by the direction of General Morgan, had ordered Murphy to restore a watch taken from a prisoner."[8]

At 1 p.m. on that fourth day of July Secretary of War Stanton received a telegram from Brigadier General Lorenzo Thomas, the Adjutant General of the U.S. Army, who was visiting General Couch's headquarters at Harrisburg, Pennsylvania. Thomas passed on information from a judge who had arrived there the day before from Chambersburg to the effect that Lee's army totaled not over 75,000 men, including 12,000 cavalry, and had 200 pieces of artillery and 3,000 wagons. "There is a belief in the rebel army," he added, "that Beauregard, with 40,000 men, is in the vicinity of Manassas."[9]

Stanton replied at 4:40 p.m.: "We have sure information, by intercepted dispatches from Jeff. Davis and General Cooper, that on last Saturday Lee made an urgent appeal to Davis for re-enforcements from Beauregard, Bragg, and from Richmond, and they were refused, because Beauregard had sent all he dared part with to Joe Johnston, and so had Bragg; that the force in North Carolina and at Richmond was too small to defend Richmond and protect Lee's communications, and that they could not spare a man. The story about Beauregard coming, no doubt, has been told by Lee to keep up the spirits of his men. Davis' dispatch is the best view we have ever had of the rebels' condition, and it is desperate. They feel the pressure at all points, and have nothing to spare in any quarter, so that Lee must fight his way through alone, if he can."[10]

Outside Gettysburg at first light on 4 July a Union sergeant commanding a picket detail belonging to the 74th Pennsylvania in Schimmelfennig's brigade of the 11th Corps could see civilians out in the middle of Baltimore Street "waving their handkerchiefs for us to come on."[11] Cautiously he led his men into the town and found that the Confederates were gone, except for the wounded and a few sleepy stragglers. Much of the town was damaged. Many houses and other buildings had been struck by shot, shell and bullets; windows had been broken, gardens trampled, stores ransacked. Many streets were littered with debris, dead animals, even dead men.

Federals who had been hiding in the town for three days emerged, among them General Schimmelfennig himself. General Schurz found him waving his hat from the door of a house and was invited in for a breakfast of eggs fried by the lady of the house. General Barlow was found in another house, recuperating from his wound. At 6 a.m. Dan Butterfield wrote a note to General Newton: "General Barlow, in town, sends word that he believes the movement of the enemy a mere feint. General Barlow was wounded and left in town on the first day's fight. The general [Meade] thinks that Barlow's opportunities for judging are good. The general only desires to know where the enemy are, and not by any means to bring on an action."[12]

South of the town, skirmishers from Posey's Brigade in and around the remains of the much-contested Bliss farm buildings again dueled with Federals of the 1st and 2nd Corps near Zeigler's Grove. Some members of the Harpers Ferry Brigade thought that this fight was some of the most dangerous work they did in their entire terms of service. Farther south, a detachment of Berdan's Sharpshooters went as far west as the Peach Orchard, where a few of them were shot by Confederates hidden behind breastworks of stone. On the Union right, the Federals on Culp's Hill could see no Rebels in their front, so General Slocum ordered a reconnaissance, and General Ruger took most of his (Williams') division on a roundabout march, about two miles down the Baltimore Pike, then up to the Hanover Road, and west along that to Gettysburg. Only a few Confederate stragglers were found.

Some of the defenders of Culp's Hill went down to examine the former Confederate position and found some Rebels, after all. "The dead lay all about," one Federal remembered, "some with a smile upon their faces, and others horribly contorted as if the death agony had there been photographed or modeled in clay." Another found bodies "massed in large numbers, the sight was truly awful and appalling. The shells from our Batteries had told with fearful and terrible effect upon them and the dead in some places were piled upon each other and the groans and moans of the wounded were truly saddening to hear. Some were just alive and gasping but unconscious."[13]

At 7 a.m. Meade wrote to General Halleck: "This morning the enemy has withdrawn his pickets from the positions of yesterday. My own pickets are moving out to ascertain the nature and extent of the enemy's movement. My information is not sufficient for me to decide its character yet – whether a retreat or maneuver for other purposes."[14] Sometime that morning his headquarters sent a circular to all corps commanders telling them to report the position and condition of their commands, and added, "The intention of the major-general commanding is not to make any present move, but to refit and rest for to-day. The opportunity must be made use of to get the commands well in hand, and ready for such duties as the general may direct."[15] Another circular directed corps commanders to detail parties to bury the Confederate dead in their vicinity, keeping track of the numbers and to collect all arms and equipment found on the field and turn them in to the ordnance officers. The 29th Ohio gathered up about 5,000 Confederate weapons on Culp's Hill. But not all such arms were turned in. The 155th Pennsylvania, in the 5th Corps, picked up enough abandoned Springfield rifles to completely replace all their old smoothbore muskets, and the 15th New Jersey of the 6th Corps even abandoned their British Enfields to replace them with similar American-made Springfields, which were considered slightly superior.

Signal Corps personnel soon occupied the Adams County courthouse in Gettysburg and used its cupola as an observation post, but about all they saw were wagons and cavalry units moving about. Smoke, presumably from the Confederates' numerous campfires, hung low in the humid air and obscured distant objects. Showers had fallen during the night and continued intermittently during the morning for up to twenty minutes at a time, some of them pretty heavy and evidently building toward something even heavier, and these further blocked the observers' view.

At 6:35 a.m. Union Signal Corps officers on Little Round Top sent a message up the line saying, "The wagon trains of the enemy are moving toward Millerstown, on the road leading from Gettysburg to the Fairfield road."[16] But for some reason this wasn't received at Meade's headquarters until 9 a.m. At 6:45 a.m. Lee signed a note to Meade proposing an exchange of prisoners, but at 8:25 a.m. Meade replied that "it is not in my power to accede to the proposed arrangement."[17] This note reached Lee at about 9 a.m. He had not slept all night and was not in a good mood. His chief of ordnance, Lieutenant Colonel Briscoe Baldwin, told Ewell's ordnance chief that Lee was "in the worst possible humor and everybody fears to approach him."[18]

Some time that morning Lee's written instructions and the envelope addressed to President Davis were handed to General Imboden by a staff officer. "In pursuance of verbal directions given you last night," the instructions said, "I desire you to take charge of the train belonging to this army, which I have directed to be assembled in the vicinity of Cashtown this afternoon.

"I advise that you start the train at least by 5 p.m. to-day, and endeavor to push it through to Greencastle by to-morrow morning by the road turning off at Greenwood. Thence you can follow the direct road to Williamsport, where the train must be put across the Potomac at once, and advance beyond Falling Waters, whence it can proceed more leisurely to Winchester. It will be necessary to escort it beyond Martinsburg, at least as far as Bunker Hill. I have directed two batteries to report to you this afternoon, to accompany the train, so that you may have sufficient artillery to guard the front and rear, and distribute along at intervals, in order to repel any attack that may be made along the line by parties of the enemy. I advise that in turning off at Greenwood you have your scouts out on the Chambersburg road until the rear of your train has passed it, and that you also keep scouts out on your left toward Waynesborough. From Greencastle you had better send a scouting party through Hagerstown, and hold that place until the train shall have crossed the river. At the river you can post your artillery to hold the ford, keeping out your scouts toward Hagerstown, Boonsborough, &c., until further orders. After the train has reached a place of safety, you can return to the Maryland side, taking position in front of Hagerstown, so as to keep open communications. I need not caution you as to preserving quiet and order in your train, secrecy of your movements, promptness and energy, and increasing vigilance on the part of yourself and officers. I inclose a letter to the commanding officer at Winchester, which I wish you would forward to him immediately upon crossing the river, unless you can find opportunity to send it securely before." In a postscript, Lee added, "I desire you to turn back everybody you may meet on the road coming to join this army, to Falling Waters."[19]

In his letter to President Davis that Imboden was to carry, Lee gave a very brief account of the battle, claiming to have taken 4,000 prisoners on the 1st of July alone (or so the wording implied). Of the 2nd of July he said only that, with two of Longstreet's divisions, "we attempted to dislodge the enemy, and, though we gained some ground, we were unable to get possession of his position. The next day, the third division of General Longstreet having come up, a more extensive attack was made. The works on the enemy's extreme right and left were taken, but his numbers were so great and his position so commanding, that our troops were compelled to relinquish their advantage and retire. It is believed that the enemy suffered severely in these operations, but our own loss has not been light."[20] He then named the generals who had been killed or wounded, but made no mention of any intention to retreat to Virginia.

In the letter to the unnamed commander at Winchester, Lee said: "I wish you to convey to the commanding officers of the [3] regiments of Ewell's corps [that had been left in the Shenandoah Valley], instructions, from me to proceed to Falling Waters, where they will take position, and guard the pontoon bridge at that place, and also the ford at Williamsport, holding there all persons belonging to this army, and collecting all stragglers from it. Any sick, of course, will be forwarded to Winchester. The senior officer present will take command. Should it be necessary that a part of that force remain at Winchester, you have my authority for retaining it there. Upon the arrival of the sick and wounded at Winchester, they will be forwarded to Staunton as rapidly as possible, as also any surplus articles not needed for the army in the field."[21]

Lee's concern for the crossings of the Potomac were wise, but a bit late. His pontoon train had been used, back in mid-June, to construct a floating bridge across the Potomac River a few miles south of Williamsport, Maryland, at Falling Waters, West Virginia, which was named for a cascading stream that entered the river there. But when Lee's troops had crossed the Potomac heading north they had simply forded the shallow stream at Williamsport and farther south at Shepherdstown, West Virginia. Between these two points, the Potomac flows due south from Williamsport for about a mile and a half and then turns sharply to the west for another mile and a half, and Falling Waters is at the westernmost point just before the river turns back to the east. So Falling Waters is just east of the macadamized Valley Turnpike, which runs southwest-northeast to Williamsport. There were a few houses and a tavern at Falling Waters, on the West Virginia side, and a good road connecting to the turnpike, and before the war there had been a ferry there. Because the Chesapeake & Ohio Canal paralleled the Maryland bank of the Potomac, there were also wharves along the river on that side and a warehouse in the strip of land between the river and the canal.

When Lee's army had crossed the river, the bridge, although never used, was left in place, guarded only by the small detachment of infantrymen, teamsters, and engineer officers that had brought it there and put it in place. Three regiments from Ewell's 2nd Corps had been left behind to garrison Winchester and Martinsburg, but they do not seem to have received any instructions to protect the bridge prior to this letter that Lee gave to Imboden. The bridging detachment protected their charge by periodically dismantling it and moving its boats and trestlework to the West Virginia bank, where they had their own camp.

As mentioned in Chapter 12, General French, commanding Union forces at Frederick, Maryland, had received notice of the presence of this bridge and its scant protection, and had authorized Colonel Andrew McReynolds, commander of a cavalry brigade, to send a force to break it up. McReynolds (who had previously commanded the Union garrison at Martinsburg before Ewell's corps had driven the Federals out of the Valley) had given the job to Major Shadrack Foley, commander of a detachment of the 14th Pennsylvania Cavalry. To his own force, Foley had added detachments from the 13th Pennsylvania, 1st West Virginia, and 1st New York (Lincoln) cavalry regiments, adding up to about 300 men. They were accompanied by Cadet George Greenough, a member of the West Point class of 1865 who was serving temporarily as an aide on French's staff. Preceded by scouts, these Federals had left Frederick before nightfall on 3 July. Heavy, fast-moving clouds interfered with the moonlight as this force rode through Middletown and Boonsborough and then turned southward to the river and followed the towpath of the C&O Canal. Scouts soon reported that they had not found any Confederate guards or pickets on the Maryland side, nor could they see any on the other side, but the disassembled bridge was over on the West Virginia side.

Foley halted his force far enough downstream to prevent the sounds made by his horses from reaching the Rebel detachment, and Cadet Greenough and two troopers volunteered to swim the river, which was too deep to ford at that point, and bring back pontoon boats with which a force could be ferried over for an attack on the Confederate camp. So, while Foley led a larger mounted force upstream to attack the Rebels guarding the ford at Williamsport and keep them from interfering, the three volunteers, covered by the sound of the nearby cascading stream, swam over, carefully cut three pontoons loose from their moorings, and quietly returned with them to the Maryland side. Greenough and about forty troopers then poled the boats back across without being detected by the Rebels, whose first inkling that there were Federals in the area was a volley from the Union carbines that sent most of them scurrying into the nearby woods. One officer and thirteen men were captured, along with all the pontoons and trestlework, plus four wagons used to transport the pontoons, as well as various equipment, ammunition and supplies. The prisoners were hurried away so they wouldn't delay the Federals' return, and the pontoons and trestlework were ferried to the Maryland side and burned. With daylight coming on, Foley then had his force, which had not sustained a single loss, mount up and head back to Frederick. Although a few pontoons were not completely destroyed, for all practical purposes Lee's only bridge had been eliminated.

Sometime that fourth morning of July, Dan Butterfield wrote to General French: "The major-general commanding directs that you proceed immediately, and seize and hold the South Mountain passes with such force as in your judgment is proper and sufficient to prevent the enemy's seizing them, to cover his retreat. With the balance of your force, reoccupy Maryland Heights, and operate upon the contingency expressed yesterday in regard to the retreat of the enemy. General Buford will probably pass through South Mountain to-morrow p.m. from this side." However, Butterfield wrote again at 10:20 a.m., saying: "More recent developments indicate that the enemy may have retired to take a new position and await an attack from us. The general countermands his dispatch requiring you to reoccupy Maryland Heights and seize the South Mountain passes, resuming the instructions contained in the dispatch of July 3, making your movements contingent upon those of the enemy."[22] But French had already sent a large brigade of infantry, a battery of artillery, and a detachment of cavalry (about 4,000 men all together) to occupy the two southernmost passes in the South Mountain ridge (Crampton's and Turner's), west of his position at Frederick. He also posted one regiment of infantry on the road between Frederick and Emmitsburg, with a detachment of cavalry at the latter town.

―――――

General Sickles and party reached Littlestown, southeast of Gettysburg, that fourth day of July. It was the terminus of a branch railroad that led to Hanover Junction, and a captain had ridden ahead and secured a railroad car for the general. Sickles (still on his stretcher) his surgeon, the aide, and probably a few orderlies or hospital stewards, then took the train for Washington by way of Baltimore, while the soldiers who had accompanied him returned to Gettysburg.

Fireworks had started going off at Washington the evening before, in celebration of Independence Day, and continued during the morning of Saturday, the fourth, and the celebration turned ecstatic when at 10 a.m. President Lincoln issued a press release through the War Department "that news from the Army of the Potomac, up to 10 p.m. on the 3rd, is such as to cover that Army with the highest honor, to promise a great success to the cause of the Union, and to claim the condolence of all for the many gallant fallen," and the *Star*, a local newspaper, put out a bulletin announcing that Lee's army had been badly defeated at Gettysburg.[23] Infantry, cavalry and artillery marched along the Mall, and a crowd gathered south of the White House, with the mayor and the city council, to hear a reading of the Declaration of Independence, patriotic speeches, and the Marine Corps band play the "Star-Spangled Banner." The traditional Independence Day open house at the White House began at noon, even though Mary Lincoln was still bedridden because of her fall from her carriage two days before. Thousands of people attended, milling about, excited and celebrating the victory over Lee.

At Gettysburg sight-seers and other visitors were already converging on the battlefield. Confederate Colonel R. M. Powell, of the 5th Texas, who had been wounded on 2 July, was lying in a field hospital behind Little Round Top on 4 July, and later remembered that whole families, babies and all, came to witness the results of the battle, "The typical farmer, the German costumed in clothes of the last century, the village belle and the country housewife, all moving in pursuit of the same object and animated only by idle curiosity, seeming without thought or care for the hundreds of suffering men lying so near them." He said, "A torn and bloody garment would attract a crowd, which would disperse only to concentrate again to look at a hat perforated by bullets."[24]

A newspaper reporter noted that "The roads were lined with ambulances with the last of the wounded; soldiers exchanging greetings after the battle with their comrades, and comparing notes of the day; officers looking after their wounded men, or hunting supplies for their regiments. Detachments of rebel prisoners every few minutes, passed back under guard. . . . Everybody was in the most exuberant spirits. For once the army had won a real victory – the soldiers felt it and the sensation was so novel, they could not but be ecstatic."[25]

At noon General Meade wrote another message to Halleck, saying, "The enemy apparently has thrown back his left, and placed guns and troops in position in rear of Gettysburg, which we now hold. The enemy has abandoned large numbers of his killed and wounded on the field. I shall require some time to get up supplies, ammunition, &c., rest the army, worn out by long marches and three days' hard fighting." And some time that day Dan Butterfield wrote to Major Thomas Eckert at Washington, who was in charge of the Military Telegraph, asking who had authority over telegraph operators who had the cipher for decoding military messages. "The operator, Mr. Caldwell, at these headquarters presumes to act in an independent manner, and has left headquarters for Westminster, selecting his own location, without authority or permission. The commanding general is unable to send dispatches from these headquarters in cipher in consequence thereof, or to understand those he receives."[26]

"Shortly after noon of the 4th the very windows of heaven seemed to have opened," General Imboden later recalled. "The rain fell in blinding sheets; the meadows were soon overflowed, and fences gave way before the raging streams. During the storm, wagons, ambulances, and artillery carriages by the hundreds – nay, by the thousands – were assembling in the fields along the road from Gettysburg to Cashtown, in one confused and apparently inextricable mass. As the afternoon wore on there was no abatement in the storm. Canvas was no protection against its fury, and the wounded men lying upon the naked boards of the wagon-bodies were drenched. Horses and mules were blinded and maddened by the wind and water, and became almost unmanageable. The deafening roar of the mingled sounds of heaven and earth all around us made it almost impossible to communicate orders, and equally difficult to execute them."[27]

Major Kidd of Custer's cavalry, which at the time was on its way to Emmitsburg, said, "It seemed as if the firmament were an immense tank, the contents of which were spilled all at once. Such a drenching as we had! Even heavy gum coats and horsehide boots were hardly proof against it. It poured and poured, the water running in streams off the horses' backs, making of every rivulet a river and of every river and mountain stream a raging flood."[28] For the Federals, there was a consolation in all this rain, for as Major Luther Trowbridge of the 5th Michigan Cavalry put it, "it was evident that before night the Potomac would be bank full with no possibility of fording for some day to come."[29] Meaning that Lee's army would find it difficult to get back to Virginia.

At about 1 p.m. the last of Major Harman's wagons cleared Fairfield. The wagons of Rodes's Division were then ordered to pass those of Early and Johnson, but it was around 2 p.m. by the time they started moving. They were followed by Early's wagons, and Johnson's now brought up the rear until some ambulances from Anderson's Division of the 3rd Corps fell in behind them. By 2 p.m. wagons carrying the baggage of Lee's headquarters were on the road, moving out the Chambersburg Pike to the Herr Ridge Road and down that toward Fairfield. They were escorted by a company of the 39th Virginia Cavalry Battalion, newly issued with infantry rifles.

At 4 p.m. Imboden's wagons carrying the wounded began to move west toward the Cashtown Gap in South Mountain. The 18th Virginia Cavalry of his brigade, commanded by his brother, Colonel George W. Imboden, took the lead, accompanied by a 2-gun section of artillery and followed by an ambulance wagon bearing generals Pender and Scales, "both badly wounded," Imboden said, "but resolved to bear the tortures of the journey rather than become prisoners.... The trip cost poor Pender his life."[30] (Generals Hampton and Hood, both badly wounded, were placed together in an ambulance wagon, along with Hood's chief surgeon, and would travel with Hood's troops.)

Imboden's own brigade wagons came next, then the long line of wagons of all descriptions bearing the wounded. The quartermaster's train of Hill's 3rd Corps fell in behind these, followed by the wagons of Pender's Division. The wagons of Heth's Division followed them. Most of the wagons from Anderson's Division came next, followed by the wagons of Longstreet's quartermaster and of his three divisions, then most of the wagons belonging to Stuart's cavalry, including many that had been captured from a Federal supply train west of Washington on 28 June, most now filled with sick and wounded men. Detachments of Imboden's cavalry and 2-gun sections of artillery were interspersed among Imboden's wagons every half-mile or so, and the two cavalry brigades commanded by Fitzhugh Lee brought up the rear.

"My orders had been peremptory that there should be no halt for any cause whatever," Imboden said. "If an accident should happen to any vehicle, it was immediately to be put out of the road and abandoned. The column moved rapidly, considering the rough roads and the darkness, and from almost every wagon for many miles issued heart-rending wails of agony.... Scarcely one in a hundred had received adequate surgical aid, owing to the demands on the hard-working surgeons from still worse cases that had to be left behind. Many of the wounded in the wagons had been without food for thirty-six hours. Their torn and bloody clothing, matted and hardened, was rasping the tender, inflamed, and still oozing wounds. Very few of the wagons had even a layer of straw in them, and all were without springs.... The jolting was enough to have killed strong men, if long exposed to it."[31] And long exposure was in the works, for the long column would keep moving all night. Darkness had fallen by the time that Imboden was satisfied that everything was properly organized. It took him four hours of riding to reach the head of his column.

At 4:15 p.m. Meade's headquarters issued General Orders No. 68, congratulating his army "for the glorious result of the recent operations." After briefly enumerating its accomplishments, it added, "Our task is not yet accomplished, and the commanding general looks to the army for greater efforts to drive from our soil every vestige of the presence of the invader."[32]

It was only some 45 minutes later that the Confederates began to abandon Union soil: At about 5 p.m. Lee's infantry began to withdraw from their positions. Hill's 3rd Corps hit the road behind the wagons of Anderson's Division that were following the wagons of Ewell's 2nd Corps. The men marched along the edges of the fields, leaving the Fairfield Road itself clear for wagons and mounted messengers. Wright's Brigade led the way, and a private in that brigade noted that the roads and fields were already "powerful wet and muddy."[33]

About an hour later a colonel on Ewell's staff rode up to General Iverson, whose brigade of Rodes' Division was holding the line of defenses near the Seminary, and ordered him to march his badly battered command some fourteen miles down the Fairfield Road to help protect Ewell's wagons at Monterey Pass. His brigade was in bad condition, having lost about half of its men on 1 July and so many senior officers that three of its four regiments were now commanded by mere captains; further, the wagons had a four-hour head start on them; but the men moved off at the double-quick on what Iverson called "the most fatiguing march ever witnessed."[34]

At about the same time that Iverson started out, Lee's headquarters wagons stopped near Blackhorse Tavern. Topographical engineers of the 2nd Corps were working nearby, copying maps for various commanders, showing the roads the army would use to retreat. The artillery battalions of the 3rd Corps were parked in nearby fields, waiting for their turns to take to the road.

Meade met with his corps commanders that evening to consider what to do next. He reviewed for them his instructions from Halleck to cover Washington and Baltimore and said he had no concrete information about any reinforcements, then asked for their views. Slocum, speaking first, advocated moving most of the army to Emmitsburg while sending forces to keep Lee from crossing the Potomac back to Virginia. Sedgwick, however, advocated keeping the army where it was until it was certain what Lee was up to. Howard suggested a compromise of keeping most of the army where it was while sending one corps to Emmitsburg. Meade then put four questions to all assembled: 1. Shall we remain here? 2. If we do, shall we assume the offensive? 3. Do you deem it expedient to move towards Williamsport through Emmitsburg? And 4. Shall we pursue the enemy as he is retiring on the direct line of retreat?

Newton, of the 1st Corps, Slocum, and Pleasonton of the cavalry all answered no to the first question, for reasons unrecorded, while all the rest said yes to staying but voted no to the second question, as they undoubtedly considered Lee's position on Seminary Ridge at least as strong as their own line on Cemetery Ridge, and they had just seen the results of attacking it. Most preferred moving south by way of Emmitsburg over a direct pursuit of Lee through the mountains, but only Birney, of the battered 3rd Corps, opposed a direct pursuit by even some fraction of the army. In short, as General Warren, who was present, later told a Congressional committee: "There was a tone among most of the prominent officers that we had quite saved the country for the time, and that we had done enough; that we might jeopard all that we had done by trying to do too much."[35]

Another stumbling block was an absence of good information about Lee's intentions. Warren expressed dissatisfaction with the day's reconnaissance and asked Meade for the use of a division, with which he promised he would find out whether Lee was retreating or not. Meade took him up on this proposal and placed Brigadier General H. G. Wright's 1st Division of the 6th Corps at his disposal with which to make a better reconnaissance the next day.

Meanwhile, various Union peripheral forces were under orders to do what they could to attack Lee's communications. Brigadier General Benjamin F. Kelley, commander of the newly created Department of West Virginia (split off from the Middle Department when Lee had taken over the

Shenandoah Valley), under orders from the War Department to advance against Williamsport and Falling Waters, was preparing to concentrate a force at Hancock, Maryland, for that mission. And a mixture of cavalry and infantry under Colonel Lewis B. Pierce that had escaped from Ewell's capture of Winchester on his way north back in June, was in the mountains west of the Cumberland Valley and was under orders from General Couch to move toward Chambersburg by way of McConnellsburg to harass Lee's rear. Also, a few hundred cavalry commanded by Captain William Boyd were also heading toward Chambersburg from Shippensburg, to the north.

Farther north, Brigadier General W. F. "Baldy" Smith had led a force of some 6,000 New York and Pennsylvania militia south from Carlisle, Pennsylvania, early that morning. Smith was a capable but contentious officer. He had been a major general for a while and had briefly commanded the 6th Corps in the Army of the Potomac, but after the battle of Fredericksburg he had complained so vigorously against General Burnside, then that army's commander, that the Senate had refused to confirm his appointment as a major general. His men (also part of General Couch's Department of the Susquehanna) who had only been called to active service when Lee invaded Pennsylvania, were not used to hard marching; they were further slowed this day by supply problems, but by late that afternoon they were approaching Cashtown and the rear of Imboden's wagon train.

Seth Williams of Meade's staff wrote to Smith some time that day, saying, "Major-General Meade directs me to say that he remains here with this army to-morrow, burying his dead and the enemy's, as well as determining by a reconnaissance the nature and movements and intentions of the enemy." After very briefly describing the fight of the last three days, he added, "The general is of the opinion that the enemy is retreating via Fairfield and Cashtown, but is not certain on his present information. Should the enemy be retreating, he will pursue by the way of Emmitsburg and Middletown, on his flank. This army has been very much reduced by the casualties of service, and the general would be glad to have you join him."[36]

Down in southeast Virginia, the expedition under General Getty was moving to attack the railroad bridge over the North Anna River, which would severe communication between Lee and Richmond. However, General Halleck had written to Getty's boss, General Dix, the day before, "As soon as the expedition now out terminates, you will draw in all your forces to Yorktown, Fort Monroe, and the defenses of Norfolk, and send to this place [Washington] all the troops not absolutely required for the defense of those three places."[37]

―――∞∞∞―――

That evening Secretary of the Navy Gideon Welles informed President Lincoln that a flag-of-truce boat had brought Confederate Vice President Alexander Stephens down the James River from Richmond to Fort Monroe, on Hampton Roads. Stephens, whom Lincoln had known and respected when they were both Whig Congressmen many years before, had told Admiral Samuel P. Lee, Union commander of the North Atlantic Blockading Squadron, that he wished to go to Washington as a military commissioner, along with Judge Robert Ould, Confederate agent for the exchange of prisoners, serving as his secretary, to deliver a letter to Lincoln from Jefferson Davis. Stephens had asked the admiral for permission to pass the blockade on his Confederate steamer "For the purpose of delivering the communication in person and conferring upon the subjects to which it relates...."

Secretary Welles told his dairy that he showed the admiral's dispatch to Postmaster General Montgomery Blair, who made no comment, and to Secretary of War Stanton, "who swore and growled indignantly. The President was at the Soldier's Home and not expected for an hour or two. Consulted [Secretary of State William] Seward, who was emphatic against having anything to do with Stephens or Davis.

Did not see the President till late. In the mean time Stanton and others had seen him, and made known their feelings and views. The President treats the subject as not very serious nor very important, and proposes to take it up to-morrow."[38]

At 8:10 p.m. Meade's quartermaster, General Ingalls, wrote to General Meigs, in Washington, "The enemy has been defeated and has retreated to the mountain passes, and will probably flee rapidly across the Potomac. We have about 12,000 wounded, I think, though not known yet. The enemy's wounded lie on the field still. The battle was a long and most desperate one. I trust now that the Army of the Potomac may be regarded as capable of fighting. Our supplies are coming up. We marched and fought this battle without baggage or wagons."[39]

Getting supplies to Gettysburg was very much on the mind of Brigadier General Herman Haupt that day. Before dawn he had reported to Secretary of War Stanton that he had arranged for fifteen trains a day each way on the Western Maryland Railroad, despite the fact that "Trains cannot pass at any point on this road, from want of sidings, and there is no telegraph line; still, if cars are promptly loaded and unloaded, and no accident occurs, I hope to pass one hundred and fifty cars per day each way, capable of carrying from 2,000 to 4,000 wounded." At 12:35 p.m. General Halleck received a message from Haupt, who by then was at Hanover Junction, saying that "All the supplies offered for transportation on Westminster branch have been sent forward, and sidings at Relay are clear. Our arrangements work well. Transportation of the wounded should be sent via Westminster, to fill return cars. I have so requested. Our men rebuilt entirely the bridge at this Junction, three spans of about 40 feet, this morning." Another message reached Halleck at 4:20 p.m. By then Haupt was at Hanover. "A bridge is broken between this place and Littlestown," he said. "I will proceed at once to repair it, and commence to send off wounded; then return and take the

Gettysburg Railroad, and commence repairing it. It will be well to make a good hospital in York, with which place I expect in two days to be in communication by rail. Until then, temporary arrangements can be made for the wounded. I learn that the [telegraph] wire is intact for 9 miles toward Gettysburg. I will have it repaired and communicate any information of importance I can obtain."[40]

Sometime during that fourth day of July Stanton received a message from the superintendent of the Adams Express Company, offering to "get up a hospital corps of their own – they sending men, food, suitable comforts, &c., to the front, with a number of spring wagons, to bring in the wounded."[41] All they asked was the secretary's authority to go within the lines of the army and railroad transportation as far as Westminster. Stanton agreed and had General Meigs send instructions to General Haupt to provide such transportation for them that did not interfere with forwarding any supplies that the army might need for pursuing the enemy, but advised the express company that "probably the best and speediest route will be, with their spring wagons, over the turnpike roads from Baltimore to Westminster. . . ." He told Haupt, "Let nothing interfere with the supply of rations to the men and grain for the horses."[42]

Horses were another subject of messages flashing between generals Ingalls and Meigs that day. Ingalls wrote to Meigs that "The loss of horses in these severe battles have been great in killed, wounded, and worn down by excessive work. . . . I think we shall require 2,000 cavalry and 1,500 artillery horses as soon as possible, to recruit the army. Both these arms have done glorious service. I hope you have enough to make up deficiencies." Meigs wrote to Ingalls to "Stand on no ceremony, but, by purchase or impressment of all serviceable horses within range of your foraging parties, refit the artillery and cavalry in the best possible manner."[43] He added that orders had been sent to officers at Philadelphia, Baltimore, Boston, Detroit, and Indianapolis to send horses to the Army of the Potomac immediately.

The horses would be badly needed. Meade wrote to Halleck again at 10 p.m.: "No change of affairs since dispatch of 12 noon. I make a reconnaissance to-morrow, to ascertain what the intention of the enemy is. My cavalry are now moving toward the South Mountain Pass, and, should the enemy retreat, I shall pursue him on his flanks."[44]

The cavalry was indeed in motion. David Gregg's 2nd Division had been dispersed, while he remained at Gettysburg, evidently having fallen ill. J. Irvin Gregg's brigade of that division was ordered north to Hunterstown, from which it was to move westward toward Cashtown; McIntosh's brigade was ordered south to Emmitsburg to protect the army's left and hold that town; and Colonel Pennock Huey's brigade, which had been at Manchester, was also ordered to Emmitsburg, where it would join Kilpatrick's 3rd Division. Thus reinforced, Kilpatrick was to march southwestward through Emmitsburg to Frederick, Maryland, and on toward the South Mountain passes. Buford, with his two brigades at Westminster, was also ordered to Frederick, where he would be rejoined by Merritt's Reserve Brigade. Pleasonton and Cavalry Corps headquarters would remain at Gettysburg.

Far out in advance was Captain Ulric Dahlgren and about a hundred Regulars from Merritt's brigade. They had left Emmitsburg the day before and bivouacked at Waynesborough. This day, the fourth, they rode back into Greencastle, where they had captured the Confederate courier two days before. There they had a brief skirmish with a squad of Rebel cavalry that then retreated to Williamsport on the Potomac.

With his cavalry thus detached, Meade used his infantry to secure his supply line. The 2nd and 12th Corps and Artillery Reserve were sent down the Baltimore Pike to Two Taverns and Littlestown, and to guard the army's southern flank, in the absence of Kilpatrick's cavalry, he moved the 5th Corps to Marsh Creek.

By 9 p.m. the head of Major Harmon's reserve train of Confederate wagons, after eighteen hours on the road, was approaching Hagerstown, but the tail of the column was still passing through Monterey Pass, some 25 miles back. Still to come were the wagons of Rodes' Division. "Our column," one Confederate recalled, "consisted of ambulances loaded with wounded men, wounded men on foot, cows, bulls, quartermasters, portable forges, surgeons, cooks, and camp-followers in general, all plodding gloomily along through the falling rain." In another Confederate's memory, "The road was muddy and slippery, the night dark, rainy, dreary and dismal. The train moved very slowly, with halts and starts all night. Every time an ambulance struck a rock I heard the pitiful groans of the wounded."[45]

Iverson's brigade of infantry was still marching to catch up, so, for the time being, only 21-year-old Captain George M. Emack's Company B of the First Maryland Cavalry Battalion and one piece of artillery held the steep eastern approaches to the pass, near a four-story resort hotel known as the Monterey House. The gun, a 12-pounder Napoleon for which there was less than a dozen rounds of ammunition, was in the middle of the side road that came up from Emmitsburg, supported on both sides by a detachment of Emack's troopers under a couple of sergeants. The rest of the company was in reserve about a quarter of a mile west of the hotel, while Captain Warner Welsh's Company D was guarding the western slope and the road leading up from Waynesborough through the village of Waterloo. Alerted by his scouts, far down the road toward Emmitsburg, of the approach of Union cavalry, Captain Emack halted the train of wagons about midway up the mountain on the Maria Furnace Road. General "Grumble" Jones was also worried about a Union attack from the direction of Emmitsburg, and he was moving with two regiments and four guns to reach the threatened point. However, they were slowed by the mud and the now-halted wagons, so the general rode on ahead with his staff officers and couriers. He overruled Emack's halt order and urged the teamsters to get their wagons moving again.

The Confederate worries about an attack were well-founded. At about 3 p.m., Kilpatrick's two brigades of Union cavalry had been joined at Emmitsburg – ten miles east of Monterey Pass – by Colonel Huey's brigade of Gregg's division and its accompanying battery of horse artillery. What had been Farnsworth's brigade, now led by Colonel Nathaniel Richmond, had been fed before leaving Gettysburg, and Custer's men and horses had found food at Littlestown, but Huey's brigade had not been so fortunate; his horses and men were hungry and exhausted, but they fell in at the rear of the column.

Custer's Wolverines led the way westward on the Emmitsburg-Waynesborough Turnpike, followed by Pennington's battery. They had already been on the move for twelve hours, and many of them were asleep in the saddle. Although the downpour had subsided somewhat toward evening, Major Kidd said that "the swollen and muddy streams that ran along and across our pathway fretted and frothed like impatient coursers under curb and rein. Their banks could hardly hold them."[46]

Kilpatrick called a halt when the head of his column reached an intersection, and he sent most of his leading regiment, the 1st Michigan Cavalry, down the Jack's Mountain Road to the north, to protect his flank. These Federals soon ran into two regiments of Jones's and Robertson's Confederate brigades and a battery of horse artillery, holding a line near Fairfield. A Union squadron charged, followed by dismounted troopers, and the Rebels counterattacked several times, but were driven back each time. Finally the Federals erected barricades across the road and, while a few companies were left to man them, the remainder rejoined the main column.

In the meantime the advanced squad of the 1st Michigan had continued on up the road leading to Monterey Pass, and it soon encountered a local farm boy named C. H. Buhrman, who had ridden out into the rainy night to inform any Union soldiers he could find about all the Confederate wagons retreating along the Maria Furnace Road. The squad sent him on to General Custer, who, in turn, passed him on to Kilpatrick. After hearing what the boy had to say, Kilpatrick ordered his column to pick up the pace.

About two miles from the eastern slope of the pass, the advanced squad encountered another civilian, Hetty Zeilinger, a girl of twelve years or less who lived near the hotel at the summit. She warned the Federals that the Confederates had artillery covering the road through the pass, but when Kilpatrick determined to proceed anyway she agreed to serve as a guide and was taken up behind one of the troopers of the advanced squad.

When the column reached the gate of young Buhrman's farm he wanted to go home, but Kilpatrick, perhaps not trusting the boy completely, ordered him to stay with the column. "Up this narrow, unknown way," one Federal remembered, "in a drizzling rain, and enveloped in darkness so deep that the riders, though jostling together, could not see each other, the exhausted, sleepy soldiers on their weary animals slowly toiled, the heavy tread of the horses and the jingling of steel scabbards, the only sound that broke the silence."[47]

∼ Endnotes ∼

1 *OR*, I:23:II:512.
2 Ibid., I:23:I:403.
3 Ibid., I:23:I:584.
4 Ibid., I:23:II:514.
5 Ibid.
6 Ibid.
7 *OR*, I:23:I:646. Both quotes.
8 Alston, "Morgan's Cavalrymen Sweep Through Kentucky," in *B&G*, 678.
9 *OR*, I:27:III:525.
10 Ibid., I:27:III:526.
11 Sears, *Gettysburg*, 469.
12 *OR*, I:27:III:513.
13 Coco, *A Strange and Blighted Land*, 22-23. Both quotes.
14 *OR*, I:27:I:78.
15 Ibid., I:27:III:520.
16 Ibid., I:27:III:514.
17 Ibid..
18 Brown, *Retreat from Gettysburg*, 107.

19. *OR*, I:27:III:966-7.
20. Ibid., I:27:II:298.
21. Ibid., I:27:III:967.
22. Ibid., I:27:III:517-8; both messages.
23. Roy P. Basler, editor, *The Collected Works of Abraham Lincoln* (New Brunswick NJ, 1953),VI:314.
24. Coco, *A Strange and Blighted Land*, 26.
25. Henry W. Pfanz, "The Gettysburg Campaign After Pickett's Charge," *The Morningside Notes* (no issue number given), Dayton OH, 1981, 1-2.
26. *OR*, I:27:I:78. Both messages.
27. Imboden, "The Confederate Retreat from Gettysburg," *B&L* III:423.
28. Kidd, *A Cavalryman with Custer*, 95-6.
29. Eric J. Wittenberg, J. David Petruzzi, and Michael F. Nugent, *One Continuous Fight* (New York and El Dorado CA, 2008), 54.
30. Imboden, "The Confederate Retreat from Gettysburg," *B&L* III:424.
31. Ibid.
32. *OR*, I:27:III:519.
33. Brown, *Retreat from Gettysburg*, 122.
34. *OR*, I:27:II:581.
35. Pfanz, "The Gettysburg Campaign After Pickett's Charge," *The Morningside Notes*, 5.
36. *OR*, I:27:III:517.
37. Ibid., I:27:II:818.
38. Basler, editor, *The Collected Works of Abraham Lincoln*, VI:315, n.1.
39. *OR*, I:27:III:520.
40. Ibid., I:27:III:522. All three messages.
41. Ibid., I:27:III:521.
42. Ibid., I:27:III:523.
43. Ibid., I:27:III:524. Both messages.
44. Ibid., I:27:I:78.
45. Brown, *Retreat from Gettysburg*, 127. Both quotes.
46. Kidd, *A Cavalryman with Custer*, 97.
47. Brown, *Retreat from Gettysburg*, 131.

CHAPTER 17
"Vicksburg Has Surrendered"
4 July 1863

OFF THE COAST OF SOUTH Carolina, the U.S. Navy's South Atlantic Blockading Squadron kept watch on ports to cut off all Confederate trade with the outside world. But it was also under orders to cooperate with the Army in its attempt to capture Charleston, where the war had begun. That city was not only a major Southern port, but an important symbol of rebellion. On Saturday, the Fourth of July, Rear Admiral John A. Dahlgren (father of the Union cavalry officer who had captured the messages to Lee from Richmond) arrived to take command of the squadron. Unlike most of the Navy's senior officers, Dahlgren was not an experienced deep-water sailor; he had spend much of his career as an ordnance officer and had invented the Dahlgren shell guns that now armed many of the Navy's ships. As commander of the Washington Navy Yard he had come to the notice of President Lincoln, and he had served as chief of the Ordnance Bureau before receiving this new assignment to the blockade.

The admiral was a tall, thin, energetic man who immediately met with his Army counterpart, Brigadier General Quincy Adams Gillmore, commander of the Department of the South. The two officers shared an interest in cannon, for Gillmore, then a captain of engineers, had, in April 1862, demonstrated the power of rifled guns by using them to pulverize Fort Pulasky, at Savannah, Georgia. On the basis of that achievement he had been promoted to general, and, after serving in Kentucky for a while, had been sent to South Carolina this April to apply his methods to the capture of Fort Sumter, which was not only the key to the Confederate defenses of Charleston, but a very important political symbol – for the war had begun with the Rebel bombardment and capture of that fort. Recapturing it would be very good for Union morale.

On 7 April 1863, shortly before Gillmore had arrived, the Navy had tried to subdue Fort Sumter, but, even though it had used nine ironclads in its assault, it had been turned back by overwhelming fire from Confederate forts all around the harbor. Now it was the Army's turn. But first it had to solve the problem of how to even get at Fort Sumter, which sat on a small artificial island in the middle of the harbor. The coast of South Carolina was made up of islands, though most of them were only separated from the mainland, or from each other, by narrow twisting channels. Gillmore's predecessor, Major General David Hunter, had landed troops on one of these, Folly Island, while the Navy's assault had distracted the Confederates, but Folly Island did not touch on the harbor. However, the north end of Folly Island was separated from the south end of Morris Island only by one of those narrow strips of water, known as Lighthouse Inlet; and the other end of Morris Island did touch the harbor. In fact, there was a Confederate earthwork there, facing the harbor, known as Battery Gregg. But even getting at Battery Gregg would not be easy, because there was another Rebel earthwork stretching across Morris Island at its narrowest point facing south to guard Gregg's rear; it was known as Battery Wagner. There were also Confederate guns placed at the south end of Morris Island: eleven detached batteries, plus a line of rifle pits for infantry.

At his first meeting with Admiral Dahlgren, General Gillmore outlined the plan he had been working on since his arrival back in April. Just five days hence, on 9 July, he would make his move. A full division of Union infantry, commanded by Brigadier General Truman Seymour, would be landed on Morris Island under the cover of fire from hidden batteries at the northern tip of Folly Island, just completed the day before, and from the Navy's ironclads. Meanwhile, two other Union forces would attempt to divert Confederate attention: Another division of infantry would move up the Stono River, at the south end of Folly Island, and land on James Island, a larger island closer to the mainland, and act as if it intended to attack strong Rebel positions there; and a single regiment, the 1st South Carolina, made up of escaped slaves, would ride armed transports up the South Edisto River, farther south, and try to cut the Charleston & Savannah Railroad. Although he had not even formally assumed command of his squadron yet, Dahlgren agreed to the Navy's part in Gillmore's plan.

Down in Louisiana that fourth day of July, Confederate Major General Richard Taylor, commander of the District of Western Louisiana, was writing to his boss, Lieutenant General E. Kirby Smith, commander of all Confederate forces west of the Mississippi. Taylor proudly detailed his accomplishments in reclaiming most of southwest Louisiana for the Confederacy while Union General Nathaniel Banks was busy besieging Port Hudson, on the east bank of the Mississippi. He was placing heavy guns in old forts on Berwick Bay and had pushed to within 20 miles of New Orleans, Banks' base of supply, which had been in Union hands since April of 1862. He also had some cavalry on the west bank of the Mississippi between New Orleans and Port Hudson with six rifled guns, and expected, he said, "to prevent transports, at least, from passing," which would, of course, cut Banks's line of supply. "One of my scouts has returned from the city with journals up to the 1st," he said. "The city is greatly excited. Enemy have worked night and day to remove negroes and stores from Algiers to the other side. A steamer for New York was stopped, all her passengers put ashore, and she was sent to Pensacola to bring the garrison to New Orleans. She returned with about 600 men. . . . A [Confederate] party has been sent over the river to cut the telegraph from Baton Rouge and gather intelligence. Another party for the same purpose has been sent to Plaquemine, on this side. Banks' army is undoubtedly much reduced by casualties and sickness, and, I have no doubt, disheartened. . . . If any opportunity, however slight, offers, I will throw myself into New Orleans, and make every effort to hold it, leaving my communications to take care of themselves."[1]

He then referred to a recent letter from General Johnston, in Mississippi, to Kirby Smith, of which he had just received a copy. In it Johnston had seemed to complain that not enough was being done by the Confederate forces west of the Mississippi to rescue Vicksburg. Taylor pointed out that in previous messages Johnston had indicated that he, Johnston, would relieve Vicksburg, but that, as he had no forces to spare for the aid of Port Hudson, he wished the Trans-Mississippi troops to go to its rescue, which was what Taylor was doing, to the best of his ability. He concluded by stating that, "I beg leave to add, with great respect, that if all the forces in Arkansas were thrown upon Helena, and firmly established there, with adequate artillery, more could be done to relieve Vicksburg than by any other move on this side of the river."[2]

That same day Kirby Smith wrote to Johnston making the same points about Johnston's request for help for Port Hudson. "The relief of Vicksburg from this side, which General Taylor, with his force, found impossible, with the means at my command is now absolutely impracticable," he said. He added that "Any escape of the garrison by the river is, I believe, impracticable. It, with the character of the peninsula opposite, is an insurmountable obstacle to success. Finding nothing is to be done opposite Vicksburg, I have ordered General [John G.] Walker to occupy a point above Lake Providence, which, whilst his flanks are protected, and his retreat secured, offers advantages for intercepting communications on the river."[3]

The Federals at New Orleans were indeed alarmed about General Taylor's activities in southwest Louisiana. On that same fourth day of July Brigadier General William Emory, commander of the Union defenses of New Orleans, wrote to General Halleck, in Washington: "I have information, which I think reliable, that the enemy, from 10,000 to 15,000 strong, are marching on this city, by the line of the La Fourche. I have notified General Banks, but he is not in a condition to detach any re-enforcements to me. My force here is wholly inadequate, but with the check I gave them at La Fourche Crossing, and the decided repulse I gave them at Donaldsonville, aided by the gunboats, I may be able to hold them in check till re-enforcements come from some quarter. I think the circumstances justify me in asking you to send me re-enforcements here with all possible dispatch."[4]

Meanwhile, Taylor was not the only Confederate general to realize that the capture of Helena, Arkansas, would serve to relieve the siege of Vicksburg by cutting Grant's Mississippi River supply line. (At Helena there was high ground, known as Crowley's Ridge, overlooking the river, from which Rebel guns could fire upon the unarmored steamers that carried supplies down the river to Grant's army.) Lieutenant General Theophilus Holmes, commander of the Confederate District of Arkansas, had telegraphed Kirby Smith back on 14 June that he thought he could take the place, which had been in Union hands for a year. The garrison there had been a thorn in his side all that time, a constant threat of further encroachment by the Federals into his district. As mentioned in Chapter 11, Holmes's forces had been struggling over rain-swollen streams and extremely muddy roads for several days now, trying to get in position to attack Helena. Four days behind schedule, they had arrived within five miles of Helena on 3 July.

"Having received full, accurate, and reliable information of the forces and fortifications of the enemy in Helena," Holmes later reported, "and the topography of the surrounding country, I here made the final dispositions for the attack. That information disclosed that the place was very much more difficult of access, and the fortifications very much stronger, than I had supposed before undertaking the expedition, the features of the country being peculiarly adapted to defense, and all that the art of engineering could do having been brought to bear to strengthen it. The fortifications consisted of one regular work heavily armed with siege guns, and four strong redoubts mounted with field pieces and protected by rifle-pits on suburban hills." Nevertheless, Holmes ordered an attack to begin at daylight on 4 July.

Holmes, who was nearly deaf, was a North Carolinian who had graduated from West Point in the same class as Robert E. Lee. His early service in this war, in Virginia, had not been exemplary, but he had been promoted and sent to command all Confederate forces west of the Mississippi. But again he had failed to accomplish anything notable and had eventually been superceded by Kirby Smith and relegated to command of just the forces in Arkansas, where his chief accomplishment had been to resist all calls upon him to send forces across the river to Mississippi. Now, his army of about 8,000 men just outside of Helena consisted of a division of two infantry brigades under Major General Sterling Price, former governor of Missouri, a division of two brigades of cavalry under Brigadier General John Marmaduke, a separate brigade of infantry under Brigadier General James Fagan, and a small separate brigade of cavalry under Brigadier General Lucius "Marsh" Walker. The latter unit had been screening Helena during the approach of the other forces, and was the source of most of Holmes's information about the defenses.

The senior Union officer at Helena was Major General Benjamin Prentiss, commander of the Union's Military District of East Arkansas, which, because it was crucial to guarding his supply line, was part of Grant's Department of the Tennessee. Prentiss had commanded a division under Grant at the Battle of Shiloh, where he had stubbornly held the position the Confederates called the Hornet's Nest. But, perhaps due to an earlier argument that he and Grant had had over who ranked who as brigadiers, Grant was not fond of him, and had shunted him off to this side-show command. Prentiss had about 4,000 men fit for duty, including the two infantry brigades of Brigadier General Frederick Salomon's 13th Division of the 13th Corps (retaining its high division number from the days before Grant's army had been divided into four corps), a brigade of two cavalry regiments, under Colonel Powell Clayton, and two batteries of artillery.

Prentiss's defenses were just as strong as Holmes had been informed. He had constructed the four redoubts (detached earthworks) that Holmes mentioned, each on a separate hill and named batteries A, B, C and D, from north to south. They commanded all roads leading into the town, and an attack on any one of them would be exposed to flank fire from at least one of the others. He had also caused all the trees in front of these positions to be cut down, giving the guns clear fields of fire, but he had the felled trees left on the ground as obstacles to any attack. As a back-up, there was a five-sided closed earthwork on the west edge of the town, known as Fort Curtis, from which heavy siege guns not only covered the western approaches but could cover the nearby hilltops and their redoubts, should any of them fall to an attack. There were, of course, rifle pits for the infantry, and all the roads coming into town had been obstructed in numerous places, to make it difficult for the enemy to bring up artillery. Colonel William McLean's 1st Brigade (three regiments) of Salomon's division held the left or southern end of the Union position; Colonel Samuel Rice's larger 2nd Brigade held the right, while Rice's 33rd Missouri manned the guns at Fort Curtis and in the four redoubts. Cavalry and light artillery guarded the approaches along the river on each flank.

Having survived the Confederate surprise attack at Shiloh, Prentiss knew the importance of being prepared and alert. When 's cavalry had sealed off all the roads leading out of town, he had known that the Rebels were up to something. He also knew of the Confederates' penchant for attacking at dawn, so for the past week he had been having his men awakened at 2:30 a.m. and in their defenses by first light. So when his scouts had brought him word on 1 July that Confederates were indeed approaching, he was about as ready for them as he could be, and on that same day he had received a welcome reinforcement in the form of the wooden gunboat *Tyler*, whose presence was unknown to Holmes.

Holmes planned a concentric attack on the Union defenses. Price's two brigades of infantry would attack the center from due west, making their target Battery C on Graveyard Hill. On the Confederate right, Fagan would attack Battery D on Hindman's Hill with three of his infantry regiments while his fourth regiment, supported by some cavalry and artillery, would make a feint attack up the Lower Little Rock Road from the south. On the left, Marmaduke's cavalry was to make a dismounted attack on Battery A on Rightor Hill, while Walker's two regiments were to block the Sterling Road, leading north, protect Marmaduke's flank, and be prepared to enter the town when Marmaduke took his objective. The various columns began to move into position during the night, but ran into Prentiss's roadblocks a full mile out of the town, causing them to have to leave their artillery behind. And Confederate timing soon broke down over a matter of semantics.

Holmes had ordered the attack to begin at "daylight." Fagan and Marmaduke took this to mean at first light; Price evidently took it to mean actual sunrise, over an hour later. Perhaps thinking that he was running ahead of schedule, Price halted his division a mile and a half out. While waiting there he was joined by Holmes, who made no attempt to hurry him forward. Perhaps the confusion was simply over what constituted the beginning of the attack, for at 4 a.m., first light, Price did resume his advance, with the Missouri Brigade, under Brigadier General Mosby Parsons, on his right, and the Arkansas Brigade, under Brigadier General Dandridge McRae, on his left. But they still had a long way to go to even make contact with the Federals.

Meanwhile, Fagan's three regiments in his main force encountered Union pickets at about 3 a.m. but drove them in, and reached their assigned position at 4 a.m. Marmaduke's cavalry dismounted three miles out and moved forward in the darkness on foot, but by the time they had reached the first of Prentiss's obstructions their guides were lost. Slowly probing their way forward they too encountered Union pickets at about 3 a.m. These were driven in, but it was 4:30 by the time Marmaduke's men were in position to make their attack. The Union pickets soon warned Prentiss that the long-expected attack was developing at last. His men were in their defenses, ready and waiting, when the actual attack began.

The eastern sky started to grow light at about 4 a.m., so, despite the fact that his men were already worn down by their approach march in the hot muggy darkness, Fagan sent his three regiments forward at that hour toward Hindman's Hill. Prentiss promptly detached the 33rd Iowa from Rice's 2nd Brigade and sent part of it to reinforce McLean's 1st Brigade in front of Battery D and the rest of it to take position near a Catholic convent just west of the town, to cover a deep cut that separated batteries D and C, through which ran the Upper Little Rock Road. Fagan's men drove the Federals out of their first line of rifle pits, but there were four more behind those, all protecting Battery D.

Fagan's other regiment, the 34th Arkansas, supported by three companies of cavalry and a pair of guns, drove in Federal pickets at daybreak and moved north along the Lower Little Rock Road until within artillery range of some Union rifle pits manned by the 35th Missouri. Since he was only ordered to make a feint, the regiment's commander contented himself with conducting a long range artillery duel with the rifled guns of Battery K of the 1st Missouri Light Artillery.

Marmaduke's dismounted cavalry attacked at 4:30 a.m., but Prentiss sent the 29th Iowa and 36th Iowa to protect Battery A. These two regiments advanced and drove Marmaduke's skirmishers back several hundred yards. And Clayton's two Union cavalry regiments, plus part of the 3rd Iowa Battery, fired on Marmaduke's left flank from behind the levee running along the Mississippi north of the town. The Confederates hit the ground and stayed there to avoid this fire.

By 5 a.m. Price's advance had finally encountered Union pickets, and soon thereafter Parsons' three guides disappeared. The line stopped while McRae sent one of his two guides to help Parsons, but then his remaining guide deserted to the Federals. By then Fagan's men had been fighting for an hour, driving the Federals from one line of rifle pits after another. They were not only taking fire from their front but also from Battery C to their left, which Price had not yet attacked. However, at about 5 a.m. a fog began to rise in the low ground between Hindman's Hill and Graveyard Hill, which served to hide the Confederates from the Federals in and near Battery C, and Fagan's men kept advancing.

At 5:50 a.m. the gunboat *Tyler* weighed anchor, steamed south, and opened fire on the 34th Arkansas and its accompanying artillery. The Rebel gunners returned fire, but their little 6-pounder smoothbores were no match for the 8-inch guns and 30-pounder Parrott rifles of the Tyler. The Confederates soon retired behind a hill and stayed there for the rest of the morning, occasionally running a gun up to fire a shot or two at the Union line.

By 7 a.m. Fagan's main attack had taken the first four lines of rifle pits protecting Battery D, and Price's Division had finally reached the position from which it was to attack Battery C. His men were already exhausted, however, from toiling up and down the hills, so Price allowed them to stop and rest. However, Holmes soon appeared again and this time demanded to know why this division was not advancing. Price replied that the attack would begin any minute now; Parson's brigade, still on the right, would attack as soon as McRae's brigade was in position to support its left. Several minutes went by without anything happening, so Price sent a staff officer to ask Parsons why he had not yet attacked. Parsons said he was still waiting for McRae to cover his left. A messenger sent to McRae found that brigade in position and waiting for Parsons to advance. It was finally realized that a ridge separated the two brigades so that neither could see that the other was in position and ready to go. So finally Price got both brigades moving, but by then it was 8 a.m. and the ground fog was lifting, and Battery C was set well back from some infantry positions to its right and left, Fagan's attack had temporarily stalled, and both Battery D and Battery B turned their guns on this new threat to the center, so that Price's attack was subjected to fire from both flanks as well as from straight ahead. Moreover, Prentiss had had plenty of time to learn of Price's advance and had sent a request for the *Tyler* to fire its big guns in support of Battery C.

Price's men faltered twice, but on their third try they broke through the Union rifle pits and into Battery C itself, although the defenders had spiked one of its guns and carried off the primers for both of them, so that the Confederates could not use them. Seeing Price's success, Fagan ordered his exhausted men to make one more charge, and they scrambled up the side of a steep ravine and overran the fifth and last line of rifle pits protecting Battery D and took cover in the Union defenses to hold what they had gained. But the redoubt itself was still in Union hands.

Prentiss ordered up reinforcements from his northern and southern flanks to strengthen his center, where Fort Curtis still barred the way into town. Union guns from there, from Battery B, and from the *Tyler* pounded the two hills now occupied by the Rebels. Holmes rode to the top of Graveyard Hill and found everything in confusion, which he only added to by issuing imprecise, sometimes conflicting, orders. He ordered the colonel of the 10th Missouri, in Parsons' brigade, to charge "the fort," then sent a message to Price saying that he was ordering Parsons to attack Battery D, which was evidently the "fort" he had in mind. The colonel, however, assumed that Fort Curtis was his objective and advanced his regiment accordingly, and other parts of Parson's brigade joined in. Seeing these men set off in the wrong direction, Holmes then ordered McRae to gather his men and attack Battery D.

However, Price, unaware that Holmes had jumped the chain of command, sent orders for Parsons to assault Hindman's Hill (Battery D) and McRae to hold Graveyard Hill (Battery C). Parsons replied that his troops were scattered and recommended that he hold the captured hill and that McRae be sent against Battery D. No sooner had Parsons sent that message off, however, than he received Holmes's order for just the opposite – Parsons to attack and McRae to defend. But when Price received Parsons' message he agreed with it and ordered Parsons to defend and McRae to attack. Holmes then encountered McRae and gave him a peremptory order to attack. McRae had so far assembled 200 of his men, and with these he set out to attack Battery D from the north, and Parsons stayed to defend the captured hill after all.

The 10th Missouri and the other troops who had joined its advance were soon pinned down at the foot of Graveyard Hill by fire from Fort Curtis and from the Union troops near the Convent. Soon they began waving white handkerchiefs and surrendered. McRae's assault on Hindman's Hill also soon bogged down in the low ground between the two hills under flank fire from these same Federals. Then Battery K of the 1st Missouri moved into a position from which it could rake McRae's men in the ravine between the hills.

At about 9 a.m. Fagan ordered his men forward one more time, to attack Battery D from the front while McRae threatened its flank, but only a few men actually arose and charged, and the battery blasted them with point-blank canister fire. The Federal infantry then counterattacked, capturing many of Fagan's men who were too tired to get away, while those who could still move fell back down the hill.

On the northern flank all this while, Marmaduke refused to advance his two brigades of dismounted cavalry until Walker drove off the Union cavalry and artillery that was threatening his left flank. Walker, however, was more concerned about his own left flank, which could easily be turned by Federals sidling northward along the levee, leading him to break his small command up by companies to guard various positions.

At about 9:30 a.m. the 1st Indiana Cavalry withdrew from the north flank, in front of Walker (he prided himself on driving them away) and moved at Prentiss's order to Fort Curtis, dismounted. Their commander, Lt. Col. Thomas Pace, formed them in a line along a small ridge that faced Graveyard Hill, and sight of this fresh line of formed troops caused most of the Confederates on the forward slope of that hill to fall back, leaving behind only some sharpshooters who occupied a ravine running down the hillside. At General Salomon's order, Pace sent his troopers up both sides of the ravine, with some infantry support on each flank. With a yell, the cavalrymen stormed up the slope and quickly surrounded and captured about 100 of the sharpshooters, upon which Salomon ordered a general assault on the crest of Graveyard Hill, and the disorganized, exhausted Confederates fled down the other side.

At 10:30 a.m. Holmes ordered a general withdrawal. Prentiss followed only cautiously, fully aware that he was still severely outnumbered, and by 2 p.m. the two sides' skirmishers had lost contact with each other. Prentiss reported a loss of 57 killed, 146 wounded, and 36 men missing. Holmes reported losing 173 killed, 687 wounded, and 776 missing, but Prentiss claimed to have buried 427 Rebels and to have captured 1,101. The 10th Missouri of Parson's brigade and the 37th Arkansas of Fagan's each lost over half of their men that day. Prentiss sent Admiral Porter an unsolicited commendation of Lieutenant Commander W. H. Brooks, captain of the *Tyler*, and recommended him for promotion. Marmaduke soon accused Walker of cowardice, which prompted the latter to challenge him to a duel, in which Marmaduke wounded Walker fatally. Holmes tried to blame his defeat on McRae, but Price defended his subordinate, and Kirby Smith cleared him of the charge. Prentiss received little credit for his victory, which was overshadowed by events in Pennsylvania and Mississippi, and when he was not chosen to lead a later invasion of Arkansas he resigned his commission and returned to Illinois to practice law.

At Vicksburg, in the early hours of 4 July, General Grant received the message General Pemberton had written at 10 p.m. (see Chapter 11). Grant's oldest son, 12-year-old Fred, who had been with his father's army since it had crossed the Mississippi back at the end of April, was sitting on his cot in Grant's tent while his father was at his writing table. "Presently a messenger handed father a note," Fred later remembered. "He opened it, gave a sigh of relief, and said calmly, 'Vicksburg has surrendered.' I was thus the first to hear the news officially, announcing the fall of the Gibralter of America, and, filled with enthusiasm, I ran out to spread the glad tidings. Officers rapidly assembled and there was a general rejoicing."[5]

Grant replied to Pemberton's note: "The amendment proposed by you cannot be acceded to in full. It will be necessary to furnish every officer and man with a parole signed by himself, which, with the completion of the rolls of prisoners, will necessarily take some time.

"Again, I can make no stipulations with regard to the treatment of citizens and their private property. While I do not propose to cause them any undue annoyance or loss, I cannot consent to leave myself under any restraint by stipulations. The property which officers will be allowed to take with them will be as stated in my proposition of last evening; that is, officers will be allowed their private baggage and side-arms, and mounted officers one horse each.

"If you mean by your proposition for each brigade to march to the front of the lines now occupied by it, and stack arms at 10 a.m., and then return to the inside, and there remain as prisoners until properly paroled, I will make no objection to it.

"Should no notification be received of your acceptance of my terms by 9 a.m., I shall regard them as having been rejected, and shall act accordingly. Should these terms be accepted, white flags should be displayed along your lines to prevent such of my troops as may not have been notified from firing upon your men."

Pemberton soon replied, "I have the honor to acknowledge the receipt of your communication of this day, and in reply to say that the terms proposed by you are accepted."[6] Soon white flags began to appear along the Confederate lines.

The chaplain of the 45th Illinois, in the 17th Corps, said it had felt strange that night and morning, while the truce was in force, to "stand up straight whenever we chose." But they didn't know the final outcome of the generals' negotiations. There was even a rumor that Grant's terms had been rejected. However, there eventually came an order to blacken their boots and otherwise improve their appearance, and "What the battle and sickness had left of us looked well. Just before 10 o'clock, 'Fall in!' was the word, and in a moment we were in our places, shoulder to shoulder, as we had often been, but never with such a feeling, never so proud of each other before.

"A moment later our brigade band, one of the best in the service, startled the leaden air and us together, by bursting out with 'Hail Columbia,' hidden from us in the white house on our left. We had not thought of music; it had been so long since we had heard any, that its place had dropped out, or been filled with shot and shell. Since Utica Cross Roads, May 10th, but few of us had heard a note, save a bugle call one evening in the direction of Pleasant Dale, some miles away. And now as these strains welled out so exultantly, and the chords of our hearts were swept, we went down before them, and strong men wept like babes. This was followed by 'The Star-Spangled Banner,' during the playing of which we received a mail. While the Johnnies marched out in front of us, and at many other places along the line, stacked arms, and marched back again. 'See the rebs,' we cried, under our breath, lest we should lose a note of the music, then 'Forward, march!' rang out, and the gallant 1st brigade, General M. D. Leggett commanding, of Logan's fighting 3d Division, took up its line of march into Vicksburg.

"Past the rebel gun stacks, over the works, with our field bands playing, through the gazing Johnnies, right down the

Jackson Road we went, the 45th leading. Not a dog barked at us, not a cat shied round a corner. Poor things, they had all been eaten in the straitness of the siege.

"The roads were dusty and the day was hot, but this was our celebration, and our steps did not falter. On we went through the scorching road cuts, sweltering. It was farther than we thought. When should we reach the retreating city? But at last the houses grew thicker, the hospital was passed, and cheer upon cheer was heard. 'Ah! That is the courthouse, and, see? The Stars and Stripes are floating down from the cupola where the 45th have placed them. Now boys, hip, hip, hurrah!' And we shouted lustily. Our wild huzzas rent the air. We shall never, we can never shout so again. The long beleaguered, stoutly defended, and sadly punished city was ours at last, and it has ever since seemed to us, who shared in the glories of that day, that we had two Fourths to celebrate. One for our national birth, and one for Vicksburg."[7]

"While the army was entering the city from the rear," a young girl inside the town later wrote, "the river-front presented a scene of unsurpassed grandeur. To say that the scene looking from the upper porch of our residence, where we commanded a fine view, was superb in its magnificence is to say little. The inspiring grandeur of gunboat after gunboat, transport after transport, with flags flying to the breeze, broadside after broadside belching forth in honor of a victory dearly won, bands playing, made a picture that can never fade from memory."[8]

There was some bitterness among the Rebel soldiers, aimed mostly at General Pendleton, but the Federals treated them respectfully. Late that afternoon a Confederate chaplain saw Union soldiers moving about the town and entering stores. "Sugar, whiskey, fresh fruit and air-tight cans are enjoyed in great abundance. They invite our men to share in the abundance and they feel no reluctance in participating. Now the steamers come pouring down the river as if by magic. Ten or 12 can be seen landing at the same time. In a short time these line the levee up and down the river for nearly a mile in distance. They are loaded down with provisions of every kind."⁹

There was some looting of stores and homes by Union soldiers, but Grant soon issued stern orders against it. A young boy of the town later remembered, "In their knapsacks the [Confederate] men of the rank and file, now waifs of war, carried for the first time in many months ample rations, pressed upon them by a hospitable and admiring foe. . . . This spirit of brotherly appreciation for a brave though fallen foe was reflected in the men from the qualities of their heroic leader, General Grant, who, paradoxical as it may seem, was even then a popular conquering general. He suppressed with an iron hand looting, violence and vandalism. He collected and listed all stolen goods which could be found among his men, and placarded the city and surrounding country with a proclamation calling upon all citizens who had been despoiled to call at headquarters and identify and reclaim their property."¹⁰

"At eleven o'clock Grant entered the city," Charles Dana later wrote. "He was received by Pemberton with more marked impertinence than at their former interview. Grant bore it like a philosopher, and in reply treated Pemberton with even gentler courtesy and dignity than before."¹¹

"I rode into Vicksburg with the troops," Grant later wrote, "and went to the river to exchange congratulations with the navy upon our joint victory. . . . I returned to my old headquarters outside in the afternoon, and did not move into the town until the sixth. On the afternoon of the fourth I sent Captain Wm. M. Dunn of my staff to Cairo [Illinois], the nearest point where the telegraph could be reached, with a dispatch to the general-in-chief. It was as follows:

"'The enemy surrendered this morning. The only terms allowed is their parole as prisoners of war. This I regard as a great advantage to us at this moment. It saves, probably, several days in the capture, and leaves troops and transports ready for immediate service. Sherman, with a large force, moves immediately on Johnston, to drive him from the State.

I will send troops to the relief of Banks, and return the 9th army corps to Burnside.'

". . . I at the same time wrote to General Banks informing him of the fall and sending him a copy of the terms; also saying I would send him all the troops he wanted to insure the capture of the only foothold the enemy now had on the Mississippi River."[12]

General John A. Logan, whose division marched into the town, was made commander of the city. His corps commander, Major General James B. McPherson, had overall charge of defending what had been captured. A division of reinforcements that had come down from Missouri was also sent inside the Confederate lines to keep the Rebels from escaping, but was soon alerted to be ready to go down the river to reinforce General Banks at Port Hudson, should it be necessary. Most of the rest of Grant's army was placed under Sherman, and started out that very day. "The Thirteenth Corps (General Ord) was ordered to march rapidly, and cross the Big Black at the railroad-bridge," Sherman later wrote; "the Fifteenth by Messinger's, and the Ninth (General Parke's) by Birdsong's Ferry – all to converge on Bolton."[13]

"I rode into Vicksburg at the side of the conqueror," Charles Dana later wrote, "and afterward perambulated among the conquered. The Confederate soldiers were generally more contented even than we were. Now they were going home, they said. They had had enough of the war. The cause of the Confederacy was lost. They wanted to take the oath of allegiance, many of them. I was not surprised to learn a month later that of the twenty-odd thousand well men who were paroled at Vicksburg the greater part had since dispersed, and I felt sure that they could never be got to serve again. The officers, on the other hand, all declared their determination never to give in. They had mostly on that day the look of men who had been crying all night. One major, who commanded a regiment from Missouri, burst into tears as he followed his disarmed men back into their lines after they had surrendered their colors and the guns in front of them.

"I found the buildings of Vicksburg much less damaged than I had expected. Still, there were a good many people living in caves dug in the banks. Naturally, the shells did less damage to these vaults than to dwellings. There was a considerable supply of railroad cars in the town, with one or two railroad locomotives in working condition. There was also an unexpected quantity of military supplies. At the end of the first week after our entrance sixty-six thousand stand of small arms had been collected, mainly in good condition, and more were constantly being discovered. They were concealed in caves, as well as in all sorts of buildings. The siege and seacoast guns found exceeded sixty, and the whole captured artillery was above two hundred pieces. The stores of rebel ammunition also proved to be surprisingly heavy. As Grant expressed it, there was enough to have kept up the defense for six years at the rate they were using it. The stock of army clothing was officially invoiced at five million dollars – Confederate prices. Of sugar, molasses, and salt there was a large quantity, and sixty thousand pounds of bacon were found in one place. . . .

"The paroling of the Confederate troops began as soon as the occupation was complete, and was pushed with all possible rapidity. At the same time those parts of the fortifications which we were now to defend were selected, and the men began to obliterate the siege approaches at which they had worked so hard and so long."[14]

The ever-eloquent Sherman wrote to his friend Grant as soon as the telegraph brought him word of Pemberton's surrender, saying, "I hardly can contain myself." After warning his friend against the flattery of the press that he was sure to receive for his victory, he said, "This is a day of jubilee, a day of rejoicing to the faithful, and I would like to hear the shout of my old and patient troops; but I must be a Gladgrind – I must have facts, knocks, and must go on. Already are my orders out to give one big huzza and sling the knapsack for new fields."[15]

Grant, meanwhile, in a note to Sherman, told him, "I

have no suggestions or orders to give. I want you to drive Johnston out in your own way, and inflict on the enemy all the punishment you can. I will support you to the last man that can be spared."[16]

In southeast Virginia on 4 July, the Union expedition under Brigadier General George W. Getty had been advancing to the northwest along the northeast bank of the Pamunkey River since 1 July, destroying all bridges and boats on the river as it went. Its objective was to destroy the bridge carrying the Richmond, Fredericksburg & Potomac Railroad over the North Anna River, a tributary of the Pamunkey, some 25 miles due north of Richmond. Getty was the commander of the 2nd Division of the 7th Corps, in the Department of Virginia, but he had with him, in addition to the three brigades of his own division, a provisional brigade of two regiments under Colonel David W. Wardrop, a brigade of five regiments under Brigadier General Robert S. Foster, three batteries of artillery, and a regiment and a half of cavalry under Colonel Samuel Spear.

On the march the day before "the heat and dust were intolerable," Getty later reported, "and the troops suffered exceedingly. There were numerous cases of sunstroke, and many men fell out from exhaustion. In addition to these, there were great numbers of stragglers. . . ."[17] The latter came mostly from two regiments of Pennsylvania militia. Now, on the fourth, Getty left the 2nd Brigade of his division, two batteries, and a company of cavalry, plus all the sick, exhausted and footsore, at Taylorsville and advanced with the rest of his force to Littlepage's Bridge, where it crossed the Pamunkey. He left his 3d Brigade at the bridge to secure the crossing and marched on to Hanover Court House, where he left his 1st Brigade to guard his rear.

Then he sent all that was left, his attached troops – the brigades of Wardrop and Foster, one battery, and most of the cavalry, all under Foster's command – to destroy the bridge and tear up railroad track.

Colonel Spear's cavalry and battery had led the way all day and reached the vicinity of the bridge at about 6 p.m., finding it well guarded. He said the railroad bridge "was of wooden trestle-work, about 100 yards long, and in the center about 70 feet high." There was also a wooden wagon bridge about 400 yards upstream. He and the battery commander advanced to within 100 yards of the defenses when they were fired upon by musketry and a 12-pounder howitzer. "I immediately halted," Spears reported, "placed my cavalry in position, and got Davis' battery together, and was in the act of placing it in position in an adjoining field when General Foster rode up, took command, and changed the position selected by me for the battery."[18] By then it was 7:30 p.m.

Foster placed his units where they could defend themselves or attack, while he scouted the area. Meanwhile, the Confederates opened fire with artillery, "and for hours shelled the country for some distance to my right and left," Foster later reported. "I deemed it imprudent to reply, not wishing to expose my position, and considering that the enemy were endeavoring to find out my position, and the probable strength of command." A civilian whose house overlooked the railroad told him that for the last three days trains had been bringing reinforcements to the earthworks that defended the bridge. "He told me that the trains, two to four a day, had come loaded with soldiers, and that one train contained artillery exclusively, viz, eight pieces, and also that his son was over the river that morning, and saw six pieces of artillery mounted and in position." (Spear reported that, judging by the sound and the ammunition used, that there were only three Confederate guns used against them, a 12-pounder howitzer, an 18-pounder howitzer, and a 10-pounder Parrott rifle.) Foster considered himself to be in a "very precarious" position, fearing attack from all sides. He sent out cavalry and infantry pickets to warn of any approaching enemy, three companies of infantry as skirmishers, who, with some difficulty, drove in the Rebel pickets, and one company of infantry to destroy railroad track in the direction of Richmond. Some time around midnight the skirmishers, from Wardrop's little brigade, captured ten Confederates, who confirmed what civilians had told Foster "and also stated that the enemy's garrison had received three regiments from Fredericksburg, in addition to those from Richmond. They said it was the intention of the commanding general to surround my force, and capture it."[19]

The regiments from Fredericksburg were from Brigadier General John R. Cooke's brigade, recently brought up from North Carolina. Cooke was the son of a Union general (Philip St. George Cooke) and the brother-in-law of Jeb Stuart, Lee's cavalry commander. His report of this affair makes no mention of any intention of attacking or surrounding the Federals.

Taking counsel of his fears, Foster made no real attack on the defenses of the bridge. "I resolved to leave the place before daylight," he reported, "with the satisfactory knowledge that it would be dangerous to remain longer, unless I received orders from the general commanding to the contrary. I, however, received orders from the general commanding to return at once, which I presume was forwarded on the report I made, and which I had forwarded to him.... I left as soon as practicable for Hanover Court-House, and, without any interruption, arrived there at 4 a.m."[20] In his report, Getty said that Foster, "in abstaining from entering into a general engagement at the bridge over the South Anna, displayed commendable prudence, and his course on that occasion was in accordance with my orders, and meets with my full approval."[21]

In his report to the Confederate War Department the next day, Cooke said, "They tore up a portion of the track toward Ashland, and from the light seen just before day would not be surprised had they burned that place."[22] In this surmise he was correct. Spear had detached Major Franklin Stratton with two companies of his 11th Pennsylvania Cavalry to attack Ashland, which was roughly halfway between the railroad bridge and Richmond. Stratton reached it at about

1:30 a.m. without opposition and divided his squadron into four parties: one to tear up track at the northern end of town, another to do the same about a mile and half farther south, a third another mile and a half south to destroy a 50-foot bridge, and the fourth to destroy the railroad buildings in the town, plus a warehouse, three freight cars, the water tank, some bridge timber, 100 bags of salt, etc., and capture the telegraph instruments. They also tore down the telegraph wire for a quarter of a mile and cut it into small pieces. Getty called this exploit "the most brilliant that occurred during the expedition."[23]

In his report of the campaign, General Dix said, "It is my opinion that if a prompt and vigorous attack had been made on the 1st July on Bottom's Bridge, it would have been regarded as a real movement and not a mere demonstration; that the enemy's troops would have been retained in Richmond, and that General Getty would have succeeded in destroying the railroad bridge over the South Anna. But when General Keyes fell back on the morning of the 2d without being attacked, and it became manifest that the movement was a mere feint, a large portion of the force in Richmond was sent against General Getty."[24]

In Richmond, Union officers in Libby Prison celebrated Independence Day by hanging a homemade U.S. flag from the rafters and began an elaborate ceremony of prayers, the reading of the Declaration of Independence, and a speech by Colonel Abel Streight, who had been captured while leading a daring mounted raid through northern Alabama and Georgia. A Confederate guard eventually tore down the flag and forbade the continuation of the ceremony, so Streight and other officers staged a long "debate" about whether or not they should defy this order. "Really we were having our celebration," a Union captain noted, "and about every speech that had been prepared for the occasion was delivered, if not in full, yet in synopsis."[25] Having thus succeeded in violating the spirit of the Confederate order while obeying its letter, the assembled Federals proceeded to sing patriotic songs, such as "Rally 'Round the Flag," and "The Star-Spangled Banner," and "We'll Hang Jeff Davis From a Sour Apple Tree."

∼ Endnotes ∼

1. OR, I:26:I:213-4.
2. Ibid., I:26:I:214.
3. Ibid., I:22:II:904.
4. Ibid., I:26:I:616-7.
5. Hoehling, *Vicksburg: 47 Days of Siege*, 272.
6. OR, I:24:I:61, both messages.
7. Hoehling, *Vicksburg, 47 Days of Siege*, 278-9.
8. Ibid., 276-7.
9. Ibid., 282.
10. Ibid., 287-8.
11. Dana, *Recollections of the Civil War*, 103.
12. Grant, *Memoirs*, I:566-8.
13. Sherman, William T., *Memoirs of General William T. Sherman*, New York, 1875; one-volume Da Capo Press paperback edition, 1984, 331.
14. Dana, *Recollections of the Civil War*, 103-5.
15. OR, I:24:III:472.
16. Ibid., I:24:III:473.
17. Ibid., I:27:II:838.
18. Ibid., I:27:II:852.
19. Ibid., I:27:II:841.
20. Ibid., I:27:II:842.
21. Ibid., I:27:II:839.
22. Ibid., I:27:II:858.
23. Ibid., I:27:II:839.
24. Ibid., I:27:II:823.
25. Joseph Wheelan, *Libby Prison Breakout* (New York, 2010), 36.

CHAPTER 18
"My Army Is All in Motion"
5 July 1863

As Kilpatrick's Union cavalry wearily climbed up toward Monterey Pass on the night of 4-5 July, they were taken completely by surprise when Captain Emack's lone cannon opened fire on them, and some of the riders, startled suddenly awake, fell off their mounts. The gun fired three rounds, all of which passed over the Federals' heads, then eight Rebel cavalrymen charged the front of the Union column, driving it back in disorder, while Emack sent for his reserve. At young Buhrman's suggestion, Kilpatrick sent part of the 18th Pennsylvania Cavalry, dismounted, through the woods to the left of the road to outflank the gun, which caused the artillerymen to retreat about 200 yards up the road, although they left their empty caisson behind, to be captured by the Pennsylvanians.

Kilpatrick asked Buhrman what he thought was the destination of the Confederate wagons and was told that they were either heading toward Boonsborough by way of Smithsburg and on to Sharpsburg and Shepherdstown or to Williamsport via Leitersburg and Hagerstown. The general then asked how he could head the Rebels off, and Buhrman said he knew a road that would either catch them at Leitersburg or at the western end of the mountain. So Kilpatrick detached the 1st Vermont Cavalry of Richmond's (formerly Farnsworth's) brigade for this task, with Buhrman as its guide. That regiment, commanded by Lt. Col. Addison Preston, rode southward through darkness and rain, following what one trooper called "a mere wood road over and amongst the rocks."[1] Many of the horses lost their shoes on the rough surface and soon were lamed. The Vermonters came to Smithsburg, Maryland, without finding any Rebels, but Buhrman said they'd find plenty if they rode west to Leitersburg. Not far down that road the Federals captured several Confederate stragglers, some wounded, some not. Preston took their paroles (not to fight until exchanged) rather than be slowed by taking them along.

Just before sunrise the regiment approached Leitersburg, and there it found a small part of Major Harman's Reserve Train that had become separated from the rest. There was a brief firefight in the dark, and then the Federals broke through the few defenders and were in among the wagons. "The mules attached to the wagons were running away down the hill," Bugler Joe Allen remembered; "but we had to go by them, which we did, yelling and firing pistols. The train we were after was two miles long, and I saw many wagons go over the bank into the gulch below. Most of the wagons had wounded in them, and as we tore along we could hear the cries of these unfortunate men. Some of them were looking out, and some of them jumped. Many of the drivers were shot by our men; others deserted their teams, and the scene was frightful."[2]

Once they reached the head of this portion of the train, the Federals brought it all to a halt. After fighting off a Confederate counterattack, Preston had the wounded Rebels removed from the wagons and placed by the side of the road, while his men chopped the spokes of the wagons' wheels and set some on fire. Preston later reported the capture of about 100 prisoners and a drove of cattle. Having learned that more wagons had passed this way two hours before, he pressed on as far as Hagerstown, six miles to the southwest. "Not succeeding in overtaking them," he later reported, "and having marched our horses thirty-six hours with scarcely any food or rest, I went into camp near Hagerstown, throwing out strong pickets."[3]

Meanwhile, after an hour of reorganizing, Custer's brigade resumed its advance. The 1st Michigan, most of which had returned to the main column by then, took the lead on foot, with one man in four holding the others' horses. In the rainy darkness they approached to within a dozen paces of Emack's Confederates before the Rebels opened fire. This brought the column to a halt again, the Federals unable to see how small was the force opposing them, and the lone cannon making "the night hideous with [its] bellowings," as one Federal remembered, "the echoes of which reverberated [through] the mountain gorges in a most frightful manner."[4]

The road was narrow, with a deep ravine on the left and a rugged mountain on the right, and the rain was coming down in torrents again. But Union return fire and a third advance by Custer's men eventually drove the Confederates on up to the eastern summit of Monterey Pass and almost to the junction of their road with the Maria Furnace Road. Just behind them cattle and sheep and the subsistence wagons of Rodes' Division were passing.

Captain Emack found General Jones, who had just arrived on the scene, and pleaded with him to keep both roads clear, to prevent the Federals from getting in among the wagons and animals, but Jones refused; the trains must keep moving, he insisted, but he encouraged Emack with word that two regiments of cavalry and a battery of artillery were on their way to reinforce him. Jones ordered his couriers and staff officers to join Emack's men and positioned the lone Napoleon in the middle of the road, though it only had a couple of rounds of ammunition left.

The 5th and 6th Michigan dismounted and advanced through deep brush and thickets on the north side of the road, but in the darkness a Federal stepped on one of Emack's men, who immediately shot him, triggering another burst of fire from the Confederates that brought Custer's men to a halt again. In response, Kilpatrick called up two guns from Lieutenant Pennington's battery. They unlimbered in a clearing just west of the Monterey House with Kilpatrick's escort company for support and threw their shots just over the heads of the Federals to explode amid the Confederate wagons. On the other side of the road the 6th Michigan advanced as skirmishers, stumbling in the dark. Major Kidd said, "One had to be guided by sound and not by sight."[5]

By that time about 100 of Jones's men had arrived, though the remainder, and the battery, were still stuck in traffic, and Iverson's infantry was still six miles back, having just reached Fairfield. Subsistence wagons belonging to Iverson's, Ramseur's and O'Neal's brigades and to some artillery battalions were passing now, but the animals that had been following Rodes' wagons had gotten loose and were wandering in the woods or blocking the road, bellowing in fright.

The Federals soon came to a bridge over a very deep gorge that carried a branch, swollen by the rain. The colonel of the 5th Michigan sent skirmishers to see if the bridge was intact, and they reported that it was, so he took his leading companies across in a rush and spread them in a line of battle just 60 yards from the wagons and their defenders. Kilpatrick ordered Custer to make a charge, but most of his men were dismounted, and just then the one Confederate gun opened fire again, though it didn't do much damage. Kilpatrick sent Custer the 1st West Virginia Cavalry, and he ordered its commander to charge the wagons.

About 100 men of this mounted regiment, supported by Kilpatrick's escort company, galloped headlong toward the Rebels, whooping and yelling. The Confederate gun was now out of ammunition, and the men almost were, so, in spite of already having three or four wounds, Emack led a countercharge, and the two forces collided in a hand-to-hand melee. Emack was soon hit three or four times by saber blows to his already wounded arms, and his horse was shot out from under him, so some of his men carried him off the field. Custer, leading his men forward behind the West Virginians, was also unhorsed and nearly captured, and Grumble Jones also narrowly avoided becoming a prisoner. He told his men to stop addressing him as "General," or the Federals, overhearing, would make a special effort to get him.

Lieutenant Pennington sent one of his guns to fire down the Maria Furnace Road, and it soon smashed enough wagons to completely block the way. Meanwhile, down near

Waterloo, a broken-down wagon was blocking the road there and stalling the entire column. Then the mounted Federals were suddenly in among the wagons, spreading panic among the wounded Confederates.

A Rebel artillerymen, who had been helping his battery's surgeon with some wounded, had been riding a stolen horse back in the column when the firing had broken out up ahead. He couldn't see where he was going and wasn't too sure that the horse could either. Not long after he saw three riderless cavalry horses pass by, his own mount suddenly dashed forward. He saw the flash of guns beside the road, heard a cannon go off behind him and sensed the canister balls flying all around him. He wasn't hit but thought his horse had been, but it kept moving, and he soon discovered that it could still run, for, he said, an "approaching clatter, with sharp reports of pistols, brought on another rush, and away we went – wagons, wounded men, negroes, forges, ambulances, cavalry – everything."[6]

Rushing along the stalled column, Kilpatrick's men captured all the quartermasters' wagons of three artillery battalions and the last ten wagons of O'Neal's Brigade, including the brigade headquarters' wagon, which had been captured from Federals down in the Shenandoah Valley only two weeks before. In addition there were numerous ambulance wagons carrying wounded men and their medical attendants, including all those from Iverson's and Daniel's brigades. The Federals forced many of the wagons off the road and down into some ravines on the west side of the mountain.

At the foot of the mountain, just before Waterloo, Captain Welsh's company of the 1st Maryland Cavalry (Confederate), joined by a handful of quartermasters and walking wounded, finally stopped the Union onslaught and even recovered two ambulances. But the Federals soon came on again, capturing 32 of Welsh's men, and by 3 a.m. every wagon and ambulance from the summit of Monterey Pass to Waterloo – about 290 of them – had been taken, along with about 1,300 Confederates, whole and wounded, including many slaves who served as teamsters, cooks, or servants. Grumble Jones escaped to the west, toward Waynesborough, and wandered for hours in the dark and rain. Kilpatrick reported losing five men killed, ten wounded, and 28 missing.

Looking over what they had captured, the Federals soon found that there was more than wounded men in the wagons. A newspaper correspondent, riding with Kilpatrick's column, said there were wagons "filled with barrels of molasses, others with flour, hams, meal, clothing, ladies and children's shoes and underclothing mainly obtained from the frightened inhabitants of York County and vicinity.... Our men filled their canteens with molasses and replenished their stock of clothing, sugar, salt, and bacon. Some very expensive Confederate uniforms were captured; several gold watches and articles of jewelry were found."[7]

At 5:30 a.m. on 5 July, General Butterfield wrote from Meade's headquarters near Gettysburg to General W. F. "Baldy" Smith, who was bringing a division of militia down from Carlyle, saying, "The general directs me to say that he is holding on here in a state of uncertainty as to the enemy's movements and intentions. His reconnaissance and scouts will to-day, he trusts, furnish it. Meanwhile, he considers that your position is precarious in the direction in which you are coming, as you are out of reach of his support. Your re-enforcement of this army would be a valuable one and appreciated. Should the enemy be retreating, the general will move rapidly through the Valley toward Frederick."[8] Smith's men, unused to marching even in the best of weather, moved south that day as best they could. "Mud more than ankle deep, up hill and down hill, through deep meandering streams, on, on toward Pine Grove," one militiaman complained. "Hundreds gave out and lay in the wayside in the woods."[9]

At 5:40 a.m. a Signal Corps officer reported to Meade from the courthouse in Gettysburg: "The enemy have evacuated the position they held yesterday. No indications of the enemy anywhere, only on the Chambersburg road, and in small force. Their batteries have all disappeared from the hills near the seminary. Prisoners report that the enemy have gone to Hagerstown." And sometime that morning the signal officers up on Round Top reported to General Sykes: "Though the atmosphere is smoky, yet many of the points which yesterday composed the enemy's front and reserve lines can be distinctly seen. At these points not a single object can be seen moving on either line, which leads to the belief that the enemy have left our front."[10]

The reconnaissance that Butterfield mentioned to Baldy Smith was that of Wright's division of the 6th Corps, which had formed up in the Plum Run valley, just south of the Wheatfield Road in the early hours, and had then been led westward by General Warren. The rest of the 6th Corps followed, supported by what was left of the 3rd Corps. They moved forward cautiously, half-expecting at any moment to be challenged by a Confederate battle line. But the only Rebels they found were dead or dying or severely wounded. They also found dead horses, a dismounted cannon, an exploded caisson, and, as one Federal put it, "everything belonging to soldiers afoot or on horseback, such as caps, hats, shoes, coats, guns, cartridge and cap boxes, belts, canteens, haversacks, blankets, tin cups, horses, saddles, and swords."[11] Just beyond Seminary Ridge, the Federals received a report that Lee's army was dug in along the next ridge to the west, so the 6th Corps halted and began building breastworks.

In fact, Ewell's 2nd Corps of Lee's army was arrayed in line of battle in front of the ridge overlooking Willoughby Run, east of Blackhorse Tavern and three miles west of Gettysburg. But Butterfield had cautioned Sedgwick that, "The orders for a reconnaissance were with a view to ascertaining the position and movement of the enemy, not for a battle. The general expects, after the desired information has been obtained, you will return to your original position, ready for the general movement which he proposes to order, should the reconnaissance confirm his belief that the enemy has withdrawn across the mountains."[12]

Meanwhile, pursuant to that belief, Meade's headquarters had sent a circular to all corps commanders. It placed General Sedgwick in temporary charge of the battered 1st and 3rd Corps, as well as his own relatively fresh 6th; General Slocum in command of the 2nd Corps and his own 12th; and General Howard in charge of the 5th Corps as well as his own 11th. And it spelled out the routes the various corps were to follow south, all of which would converge at Middletown, Maryland, west of Frederick. Soon thereafter, Butterfield sent a note to General Sykes, telling him that if his 5th Corps was well in hand he could begin moving it south down the Taneytown Road, but he was to turn to the west before crossing Rock Creek and move toward Emmitsburg. After going four or five miles he was to halt, mass his troops off the road, and wait for orders from General Howard. And, sometime that day, Butterfield wired Brigadier General Henry Benham, commanding the pontoon depot at Washington, D.C., to put his bridge train and troops in motion for Harper's Ferry at once, which would give Meade the means to cross the Potomac River into the Shenandoah Valley.

Also, sometime that day, Meade's headquarters published an order relieving General Doubleday from duty with the Army of the Potomac and directing him to report to the adjutant-general of the Army at Washington. Doubleday was very unhappy at being superceded by Newton, whom he ranked, challenged Meade's right to place Newton over him (appointing corps commanders was a job reserved to the President), and had asked to be relieved if he could not retain command of the 1st Corps. Meade, who had been a division commander in the 1st Corps alongside Doubleday in the Fredericksburg campaign, did not trust him to command a corps and thus granted his request to be relieved. He never received another field command. The same order directed that batteries that had been swapped between the various corps and the Artillery Reserve be returned to their proper commands.

Meade received a message from Halleck that morning that said, "You will assume the general command of such of General Couch's forces as are operating in the field, and direct their movements as you may deem best. It seems to me that they should connect with your right flank. I think that the troops sent here from Harper's Ferry and a part of the forces now in Baltimore could join General French, and be available for your operations. Four small regiments from North Carolina have reached Baltimore. I am awaiting an answer from my dispatch, sent through General French this morning, in regard to re-enforcing him as above indicated. So long as your movements cover Baltimore and Washington from Lee's main army, they are in no danger from any force the enemy may detach for a raid. We have heard nothing from you since yesterday morning, and are anxious to learn more of the results of your brilliant fighting."[13]

At 8:30 a.m. Meade replied: "The enemy retired, under cover of the night and heavy rain, in the direction of Fairfield and Cashtown. All my available cavalry are in pursuit, on the enemy's left and rear. My movement will be made at once on his flank, via Middletown and South Mountain Pass." He added that he didn't have time to count prisoners or other captures nor to pick up all that might be useful on the battlefield. "My wounded, with those of the enemy in our hands, will be left at Gettysburg," he added. "After burying our own, I am compelled to employ citizens to bury the enemy's dead." He added that, not counting cavalry, wagon guards, etc., he was down to about 55,000 men. "Every available re-enforcement is required, and should be sent to Frederick without delay."[14] Halleck replied: "Your movements are perfectly satisfactory. Your call for re-enforcements to Frederick has been anticipated. Call to you all of Couch's force."[15]

However, all soon changed, for when Meade learned that Sedgwick had found a large Confederate force in line of battle to the west, he suspended the movement ordered in his circular until further notice. General Pleasonton, of the cavalry, wrote to General French, down in Maryland, that morning: "Major-General Meade desires me to say that, in consequence of a large body of the enemy being concentrated in the road toward Hagerstown, beyond Fairfield, he has suspended his operations for the present. Indications go to show that he intends evacuating the Cumberland Valley, but it is not yet positively ascertained. Until so ascertained, the general does not feel justified in leaving here and moving down toward you."[16]

General Haupt and his construction crews reopened the railroad through Hanover Junction to Gettysburg that day, and that general came to Gettysburg and conferred with Meade and Pleasonton in the tiny house that Meade used for his headquarters. Haupt was a former resident of Gettysburg, his wife was from there, and he had been a professor of mathematics and engineering at the college there, but before that he had been Meade's roommate at West Point. Meade and Pleasonton gave him an account of the battle, and then Haupt asked about the army's future movements, so that he would know what was required of the railroads, and he was shocked, he later wrote, that Meade said he could not begin moving his army yet. As Haupt later remembered it, Meade's reason was a need to rest the men. Haupt said he argued with his old friend that the men had been fighting on the defensive and had been fairly well supplied and should be better rested than the Confederates, and that it was little more than a day's march from Gettysburg to the Potomac River. But Meade countered, Haupt said, by saying that the Potomac was swollen and unfordable and that Lee had no bridge, so there was plenty of time to catch him. "Do not place confidence in that," Haupt said he told Meade. "I have men in my Construction Corps who could construct bridges in forty-eight hours sufficient to pass that army, if they have no other material than such as they could gather from old buildings or from the woods, and it is not safe to assume that the enemy cannot do what we can."[17] But he failed to convince his old roommate that haste was necessary.

At 10 a.m. Butterfield wrote to Sedgwick: "A scout just reports enemy's cavalry column four hours in passing – from 1 to 5 o'clock this morning. Passed from the Fairfield road on to the Emmitsburg road, via Moritz tavern, turning toward Emmitsburg. There were two guns. This may be a raid, or may be a movement to cover their flank."[18]

The Rebel cavalry in question consisted of two brigades (Ferguson's, and Chambliss's) and two batteries (not just two guns) of horse artillery, with Jeb Stuart himself in command. Having left Fitz Lee with two brigades (his own and Hampton's, now under Col. L. S. Baker) to guard the army's rear in the Cashtown area, and Robertson's and Jones's brigades to guard (supposedly) the Fairfield-Monterey area, Stuart was proceeding to Emmitsburg to protect Lee's eastern flank. The night had been so dark that he had decided to halt for several hours, for, as he later reported, "We were in danger of losing the command as well as the road."[19] Eventually he procured a guide, and as soon as there was a bit of light the march was resumed.

Just at dawn, the Confederates entered Emmitsburg, where they captured 60 or 70 Union soldiers, including some Signal Corps men, and some valuable hospital supplies en route to Meade's army from Frederick, plus a civilian photographer who was on his way to Gettysburg from Washington to take pictures of the battlefield. Here Stuart learned that a large force of Union cavalry (Kilpatrick's), and possibly infantry (the Signal Corps men tried to give him that impression) had passed through the town during the night, heading west. Stuart called another halt to procure some rations for his men while he had his breakfast and studied his map of the area. He assumed that the Federals would have been foiled in any attempt to penetrate Monterey Pass, which Robertson and Jones had been ordered to hold, or the gap at Fairfield, where it would have run into Confederate infantry. But he worried that if the Federals had turned left and gone through the next pass to the south, Eyler's Gap, they could then move due west to Hagerstown, "and thus seriously threaten that portion of our trains which, under Imboden, would be passing down the Greencastle pike the next day, and interpose itself between the main body and its baggage. . . . I therefore determined to adhere to my instructions, and proceed by way of Cavetown, by which I might intercept the enemy should he pass through Eyler's Gap."[20]

Accordingly, the Rebels resumed their march, going south until they came to what Stuart called Cooperstown (actually Creagerstown), where they stopped again to feed their horses. An hour later they took the road again, heading west now, over Catoctin Mountain and across the narrow northern end of the valley that separates that range from the South Mountain range. Coming to a fork in the road beneath an imminence called Raven Rock, Stuart sent Ferguson's brigade to the left toward Smithsburg (Stuart called it Smithtown), just north of Cavetown, and took Chambliss's brigade to the right, toward Leitersburg. Ferguson soon found his way blocked by Union cavalry.

After riding all day and fighting all night, Kilpatrick's men and horses had been exhausted, so he had called a halt about 10 miles south of Monterey Pass. Worried that the captured wagons would slow him down, Kilpatrick had ordered most of them turned out into a large field and burned. He kept 30 wagons full of wounded and 8 traveling forges, plus all serviceable horses, and any rations and fodder. A few ambulance wagons with wounded Rebel officers were retained as prisoners. Several hundred other Confederate wounded were left on the field.

Aware that Lee's entire army was now bearing down on him, Kilpatrick planned to proceed south through Smithsburg and Cavetown to Boonsborough, near which he knew he would find part of General French's division, holding Turner's Gap through South Mountain. Once there he could get food and fodder and rid himself of his prisoners and captured wagons. He sent the 5th New York Cavalry ahead to Smithsburg to clear it of any Confederate pickets, and at around 9 a.m., with the rain having ceased and the sun shining brightly, the division arrived to an enthusiastic welcome by the local civilians – young ladies singing patriotic songs and their mothers offering the troopers plates piled high with bread, butter and jelly.

While at Smithsburg, Kilpatrick received a report from Lt. Col. Preston of the 1st Vermont, which was resting near Hagerstown after its own foray through Smithsburg and Leitersburg, that Imboden (he thought it was Jenkins) was coming south from Greencastle. Kilpatrick replied with orders for the 1st Vermont to rejoin the division at Boonsborough, which it promptly set out to do. Meanwhile, Kilpatrick sent his prisoners ahead to Frederick, and sent scouts into the passes to the east to see if any Rebels were approaching from that direction. About six miles out, the scouts ran into Stuart's vedettes, who ordered them to surrender. Instead, they turned and dashed back down the mountain road, and the Confederates chased them for nearly four miles. Thus learning of Stuart's approach, Kilpatrick formed his division facing east. Huey's brigade and a battery of horse artillery took position along a hill overlooking the pass; to Huey's right-rear, Richmond's brigade and another battery were formed along another hill; while Custer's brigade and Pennington's battery formed a third line on yet another hill to the left rear, overlooking another road that came over the mountain to Cavetown.

At about 5 p.m., Ferguson's brigade found its way blocked by Huey's and Richmond's brigades. His skirmishers pushed their way down the slope to an open clearing, where they were met by artillery fire. Confederate horse artillery unlimbered on higher ground to add its weight to the battle. Meanwhile, Stuart, with Chambliss's brigade, moved on up the other road, then hooked around to the south to hit the Federals' flank with a dismounted attack at about 5:30 that soon had Huey's troopers in trouble. The 5th New York Cavalry hurried over from Richmond's brigade but was unable to stop the Rebels.

Stuart then sent a courier to tell Ferguson to break contact with the enemy and move to join him on the other road.

Thus released, the Federals retreated to the south – or in Kilpatrick's version, resumed their march toward Boonsborough – which they reached at about 10 p.m. Stuart did not pursue. "It was nearly night," he later reported, "and I felt it of the first importance to open communication with the main army, particularly as I was led to believe that a portion of this force [presumably, the 1st Vermont Cavalry] might still be hovering on its flanks. I sent a trusty and intelligent soldier (Private Robert W. Goode, First Virginia Cavalry) to reach the commanding general by a route across the country, and relate to him what I knew, as well as what he might discover *en route*, and moved toward Leitersburg as soon as Colonel Ferguson came up, who, although his advance had forced the passage of the gap, upon receipt of my dispatch turned back and came by the same route I had taken, thus making an unnecessary circuit of several miles, and not reaching me till after dark."[21]

A civilian informed Stuart that the force he had been fighting was that of Kilpatrick, "who had claimed to have captured several thousand prisoners and 400 or 500 wagons from our forces near Monterey; but I was further informed that not more than 40 wagons accompanied them, and other facts I heard led me to believe the success was far overrated. About this time, Captain Emack, Maryland cavalry, with his arm in a sling, came to us, and reported that he had been in the fight of the night before, and partially confirmed the statement of the citizen, and informed me, to my surprise, that a large portion of Ewell's corps trains had preceded the army through the mountains."[22] This interesting statement reveals that Stuart, charged with protecting the army's flanks, did not know, or fully understand, the movements of its supply trains. Possibly either Lee or someone at his tiny headquarters had failed to fully inform the cavalry commander of what it was doing, or Ewell had failed to inform army headquarters of what his quartermaster was doing.

At nightfall, Stuart was joined at Leitersburg by Jones's and Robertson's brigades and their two batteries, although Jones himself was missing. His whereabouts were unknown to his brigade. In fact, Jones, separated from his command by the fight at Monterey Pass, had made his way across the fields and by-ways of two counties, crossed the Mason-Dixon line, and wound up at Williamsport, Maryland, early on the morning of the fifth. There he had found that the rains had swollen the Potomac to the point that it could not be forded. Many wagons had arrived and more were coming in, but the single ferry boat, or flat, propelled by men pushing poles into the river bottom, could carry not more than two wagons at a time, and could not make more than about 70 trips over the river in 24 hours. The result was mass confusion as every driver tried to make sure that his wagon was one of the few to get across.

Jones decided that the only way to bring order out of the chaos was to stop the ferry completely, "to deprive all of the hope of what but a small fraction could attain.... I assumed command, and put 15 or 20 infantry (the only organized men I could see) to guard the boat and stop the crossing. Officers and men, appealed to, cheerfully took up arms, posting themselves in buildings to resist cavalry attacks. Soon a respectable defense could have been made, and a rash attack would doubtless have been severely punished. Order being restored, the wounded and wagons with important papers were allowed to recommence crossing the river."[23] But more and more wagons were still coming; the Reserve Train still stretched all the way back to Leitersburg; behind it came twenty miles more of wagons belonging to Ewell's three divisions and to Anderson's Division of the 3rd Corps; and the head of Imboden's immense train was still several miles to the north on the Valley Turnpike, having just reached Greencastle, Pennsylvania, at about the time that Jones had reached Williamsport.

Imboden's train, carrying most of the Confederate wounded on a more westerly route, had stretched out, covering more than 30 miles of road as the head of the column pressed on and others could not keep up. The tail of it finally cleared Cashtown at dawn on 5 July. Dead and dying men were being left all along its route, unable to go any farther. Wagons became mired in the mud and abandoned if they could not be dislodged. Some teamsters fell asleep and failed to keep their horses moving. One Pennsylvania farmer claimed that it took 56 hours for the entire column to pass his place.

General Fitzhugh Lee's two brigades of Rebel cavalry protected the rear of the train itself, but stragglers were left to their own devises. Colonel J. Irvin Gregg's 3rd Brigade of his cousin David Gregg's division of Union cavalry followed in the train's wake and captured many of the stragglers, some wounded, some whole. A member of the 10th New York Cavalry, in Gregg's brigade, recorded his impression of these captured Rebels, whom he saw plodding dejectedly along the road, on their way back to Gettysburg: "Some were under guard, others marched without. They were, generally speaking, a surly, uncommunicative lot. Every building that would afford shelter from the storm or protection from the burning rays of the sun was filled with Confederate wounded and stragglers."[24] Before the day was out, almost that entire Union regiment had been sent back to Gettysburg, guarding captured Rebels.

Imboden's train had traveled all night, unmolested so far, with the lead wagons pressing relentlessly on, despite the pleas of the wounded passengers. "No help could be rendered to any of the sufferers," Imboden later wrote. "No heed could be given to any of their appeals. Mercy and duty to the many forbade the loss of a moment in the vain effort then and there to comply with the prayers of the few. On! On! we *must* move on. The storm continued, and the darkness was appalling. There was no time even to fill a canteen with water for a dying man; for, except the drivers and the guards, all were wounded and utterly helpless in that vast procession of misery. During this one night I realized more of the horrors of war than I had in all the two preceding years.

"And yet in the darkness was our safety," he continued, "for no enemy would dare attack where he could not distinguish friend from foe. We knew that when day broke upon us we should be harassed by bands of cavalry hanging on our flanks. Therefore our aim was to go as far as possible under cover of the night. Instead of going through Chambersburg, I decided to leave the main road near Fairfield after crossing the mountains, and take 'a near cut' across the country to Greencastle, where daybreak on the morning of the 5th of July found the head of our column. We were now twelve or fifteen miles from the Potomac at Williamsport, our point of crossing into Virginia.

"Here our apprehended troubles began. After the advance – the 18th Virginia Cavalry – had passed perhaps a mile beyond the town, the citizens to the number of thirty or forty attacked the train with axes, cutting the spokes out of ten or a dozen wheels and dropping the wagons in the streets. The moment I heard of it I sent back a detachment of cavalry to capture every citizen who had been engaged in this work, and treat them as prisoners of war. This stopped the trouble there, but the Union cavalry began to swarm down upon us from the fields and cross-roads, making their attacks in small bodies, and striking the column where there were few or no guards, and thus creating great confusion."[25]

The Union cavalry that attacked the column at Greencastle was the small force led by Captain Dahlgren. He and his 100 troopers of the 6th Pennsylvania Cavalry had crossed Monterey Pass the night before, ahead of the Confederates, and had spent the night near Waynesborough. At 2 a.m. they had mounted up and headed west, returning to Greencastle, where they had captured the letters to Lee from Richmond three days before. Scouts and civilians brought Dahlgren word of the immense train of wagons making its way along the Pine Stump Road (Imboden's "near cut") and onto the

Cumberland Valley Turnpike at Marion.

Keeping his men out of sight, Dahlgren waited until about 300 wagons had passed, then made his move. He sent two forces, under lieutenants, to cut the column at two places. They captured two artillery pieces and double their number of Confederates, most of them from among the wounded, but including a major of the 18th Virginia Cavalry, and tried to turn the column eastward, toward Waynesborough. However, two companies of the 18th, one from the front and one from the rear, counterattacked and recaptured the guns and many of the Rebels, as well as a wounded Union lieutenant and 10 troopers. But between Dahlgren's troopers and the civilians wielding axes, about 130 wagons had been destroyed, and many of their teams had been captured. Civilians also ran off some of the Confederate cattle and riding horses, and the train had been delayed by more than an hour. Imboden himself came close to being captured at one point. Dahlgren's men scattered through the woods to avoid pursuit.

Other Confederates in the column were captured as the result of a simple ruse. Daniel Mull, a resident of Marion, where Imboden's "near cut" along the Pine Stump Road ended, was roused from his bed in the middle of the night by a Rebel pounding on his door and asking if they were on the right road to Hagerstown. Mull told him he was, but that when he soon came to a crossroad to turn to the right. The trusting Confederate and a handful of wagons followed his directions, which took them north to Chambersburg, where they were promptly captured, and local doctors took charge of the badly wounded men. A resident of that city said the Rebels were "filthy, bloody, with wounds undressed and swarming with vermin, and almost famished for food and water, they presented such a sight as I hope I may never see again."[26]

The head of Imboden's train finally reached Williamsport near dark. The town was already jammed with the wagons of the Reserve Train, and the wagons of Ewell's three divisions were just arriving from the direction of Hagerstown. The tail of Imboden's column was way back at New Franklin, Pennsylvania, almost 25 miles to the north. The Potomac was now ten feet above fording stage.

Grumble Jones turned over command of the vicinity to Imboden and rode off to rejoin his brigade, which he eventually found at Leitersburg, where it had joined Stuart. Imboden, meanwhile, sent one company of his 18th Virginia Cavalry, commanded by his brother Frank, back up the turnpike to guard that road's intersection with the National Turnpike, which connected Cumberland, Maryland, on the Potomac to the west, with Hagerstown and went on to Baltimore. Imboden ordered the civilians of the town to cook meals for the wounded men, threatening to send soldiers into their kitchens to do it if they failed to. Meanwhile, the surgeons who had accompanied the wounded finally were able to get to work on their charges. Some men who had died along the way were buried in the city cemetery.

Imboden's worries for the safety of his charges was partially relieved when he received word that two regiments of infantry, the 54th North Carolina and 58th Virginia, were approaching the south side of the river, escorting an ordnance train carrying ammunition for Lee's army. They reached the river at about 2 p.m., and Imboden had most of the two regiments ferried over to Williamsport, leaving a few Carolinians on the south side to guard the ordnance train, which was left on that side. (The last thing he needed just then was more wagons.) Also on the Virginia side was Company F of the 21st Virginia, which was bringing a group of stragglers back to the army. The 58th Virginia was sent to join Company H of Imboden's cavalry at the National Turnpike intersection. The 54th North Carolina was placed on a ridge about a mile east of town, between the roads coming in from Hagerstown and Boonsborough. A battery of three guns, almost out of ammunition, was placed just south of the Hagerstown-Williamsport Turnpike. Company F of the 21st Virginia, and its assorted stragglers, crossed to the north side of the river after the Carolinians, and were kept in the town as train guards.

However, Imboden's troubles were not yet at an end. The infantry he had met had been placed to provide security for Williamsport itself, at least from any small attack from the east, but the long line of wagons stretching to the north was still vulnerable. Colonel Lewis B. Pierce, who had inherited command of various Union troops who had escaped into the mountains of Pennsylvania west of the Cumberland Valley when Lee's army had swept through the Shenandoah on its way north, was under orders from General Couch to move toward Chambersburg by way of McConnellsburg to harass the rear echelons of Lee's army. Pierce, who was colonel of the 12th Pennsylvania Cavalry, considered the infantry he had with him virtually useless; their morale was low and their stock of ammunition even lower. But he had set out on 3 July with parts of two cavalry regiments (his own plus the 1st New York (Lincoln) Cavalry, other parts of which were with French). They had reached McConnelsburg, on the west side of the Cove Mountains, at about nightfall on the fourth. Pierce had no definite information about the location of Lee's army, or Meade's either, although he had heard uncertain rumors about a big battle at Gettysburg. So, that night he decided to send a picked force of 200 men over the mountain and into the Cumberland Valley in search of more definite information. Captain Abram Jones of the 1st New York would lead.

Jones divided his force into three commands, under lieutenants Franz Passegger and Charles Woodruff, both of the 1st New York, and David Irwin of the 12th Pennsylvania, and they had set out from McConnelsburg on the morning of 5 July, heading southeast in a driving rain. About noon they reached Mercersburg, on the east side of the mountains, where they stopped to feed and water their horses, while the men were treated to pies, cakes and other refreshments by the local civilians, who had been looted by Confederates more than once lately. There the Federals learned that a vast train of Confederate wagons was moving down the Valley Turnpike several miles to the east. It sounded like a tempting target.

Jones found a local citizen to serve as a guide and got his men back in the saddle, heading southeast on the road to Hagerstown. This road would intersect the Cumberland Valley Turnpike about ten miles on, just beyond Conococheague Creek and about midway between Greencastle and Williamsport, at a place called Cunningham's Crossroads. His scouts soon reported that there was a long ridge on the west side of the turnpike, where Jones could conceal his force while he got a look at what they were up against.

When the Federals reached the ridge, Jones studied the passing column, noting that squads of mounted men rode beside the wagons and that a section of artillery came along at intervals of about a mile. Beyond the ridge, the land was level, offering little cover for the Confederates except a few woods and an occasional house. Figuring that the guns would be the biggest problem, he decided to attack them first and not give the gunners time to unlimber their pieces, so Lieutenant Passegger's command was given the job of attacking the Rebel escorts and capturing or driving off the artillery. Meanwhile, Lieutenant Woodruff's command would spread out along the train and force the drivers to turn their wagons onto the road to Mercersburg. There Lieutenant Irwin's detachment, held in reserve behind the ridge, would take charge of them. Jones told his men, "If you get into close quarters, use your sabres. Don't strike, but thrust!"[27]

It went off just as planned. Passegger's troopers broke concealment late that afternoon and rushed the train just as the ambulances of Davis's Brigade of Heth's Division were passing. Behind them were the ambulances of Pettigrew's Brigade, and just approaching the crossroads were three rifled guns of a Louisiana battery. The artillery horses were in pitiful condition, but upon the sudden and unexpected attack one of the guns managed to get away; the other two had to be spiked and abandoned. Many of the mounted escort, men of Imboden's 62nd Virginia Mounted Infantry, fell off their horses, they were so startled, and they all scattered at the sudden onslaught. Woodruff's detachment raced along the train, turning wagons onto the road to Mercersburg, and the walking wounded were ordered to climb into the captured wagons and ambulances. One Union trooper who lost his horse captured 13 wounded Confederates and brought them along as he rejoined his command.

More of the Confederate escorts were arriving each minute, and the chief quartermaster of Heth's Division was organizing them for a coordinated counterattack, while the chief quartermaster of Pender's Division was riding north with part of Company H of the 18th Virginia Cavalry to the sound of conflict, but Passegger and Woodruff formed their commands into a protecting line while Irwin's detachment hurried the prisoners and captured wagons up the road toward Mercersburg. Captain Jones spotted one large wagon full of Confederate wounded sitting beside the road without a driver. Nearby was a young African-American, so Jones asked him if he could drive that wagon, and the man said he could. Evidently he was one of many freemen or escaped slaves who had been rounded up in Pennsylvania by the Rebels to be taken or returned to Virginia and slavery, for when he bounded onto the wagon's seat he called to his passengers, "By golly, you toted me off, now I tote you off."[28]

Darkness soon put an end to the fight. Jones's little command and their captured wagons began to reach Mercersburg shortly after dark, but the tail of the column didn't arrive until late that night. The whole town turned out to see the sight, and a seminary, a church, a house, and a barn were all soon turned into hospitals for the wounded. The small band of cavalrymen had captured 100 wagons and ambulances, 300 horses and mules, two 3-inch rifled guns and their caissons, and 653 Rebels, of whom 308 were badly wounded.

During all this moving and fighting by the wagons and

the cavalry, Lee's infantry and artillery were also on the march. A. P. Hill's 3rd Corps had the lead, headed by three companies of the 35th Virginia Cavalry Battalion, and then Anderson's Division. "We were up to our knees in mud and water all night," one of Hill's men later remembered.[29] It took six hours for the head of Hill's column to march the eight miles to Fairfield. Wright's Brigade was ordered to double quick another six miles from there to the summit of Monterey Pass, which took another six hours. Meanwhile, Iverson's weary men finally reached Monterey Pass on the morning of 5 July, only to find that they were far too late to protect the wagons from Union cavalry. Wright's Georgians arrived at about 9 a.m. and immediately dropped to the wet ground and fell asleep. But, after a brief halt to rest, General Wright sent both brigades hurrying on, anxious to clear the mountain pass for the rest of the column. Some of Anderson's brigades went along the east side of Jack's Mountain and took the Emmitsburg-Waynesborough road, leaving the Maria Furnace Road to Pender's and Heth's divisions, who had reached Fairfield at around 8 a.m., just as Iverson's and Wright's men were reaching Monterey Pass.

Longstreet's 1st Corps had been ordered to be ready to march by sundown 4 July, but this had proven to be far too optimistic, as rain, mud and congestion slowed the retreat. Then the time for their move had been changed to 10 p.m., but this also proved to be unrealistic. It was 2 a.m. on 5 July before the 1st Corps began to march up the Willoughby Run Road, heading for the juncture with the Fairfield Road just east of Blackhorse Tavern. When they got there, the Fairfield Road was still full of passing troops. In fact, it took twelve hours for Hill's 3rd Corps to clear the intersection, and the sun was coming up by the time Hood's Division, at the head of the 1st Corps, was able to turn into the Fairfield Road. It was followed by McLaws' Division.

Pickett's Division, greatly reduced by its losses on the third, was placed in charge of some 4,000 Union prisoners. Many of these had not eaten since being captured, until early that morning they were able to cook and eat some raw flour they'd been given the night before and small amounts of beef or liver that some of them had received. The prisoners were forced to march all day without any more food, marching in a column on the road while Pickett's men formed files on either side of them. They finally halted about midnight at Monterey Springs.

Ewell's corps was to bring up the rear of the column, and at about 2 a.m. on 5 July, just as the 1st Corps began to move, the 2nd Corps left the defenses along Seminary and Oak ridges, leaving the other three companies of the 35th Virginia Cavalry Battalion to hold what had been the entire corps' line. According to men who saw him that day, Lee was hoping for another fight, preferably at Fairfield Gap, which was only about 100 yards wide. Ewell, too, was eager for a fight, wanting to revenge the loss, during the night, of so many wagons. A private in the 5th Alabama said his regiment didn't go more than two and a half miles before finding the road ahead was blocked. They stopped and made fires despite the drenching rain. "Several hours after day light we continued the march through mud & water ankle deep in places. The wagon trains kept the road & a column of troops marched thro' the fields & woods on each side."[30] At the rear of Ewell's column was Early's Division, and its rear guard was Gordon's Brigade, with one battery of artillery. Behind them came the three companies of cavalry. Behind them came Sedgwick's Union 6th Corps, also slowed by the mud.

The Confederate traffic jam was eased temporarily when Lee split his column. Instead of following Hill's 3rd Corps along the Maria Furnace Road, taken by the Reserve Train and division trains, late that afternoon Lee had Longstreet's 1st Corps turn south on the Jack's Mountain Road, then take the Emmitsburg-Waynesborough road that Kilpatrick had used the night before. Ewell's corps could then follow Hill's corps along a road obstructed only by the mud churned up by the passing of thousands of wheels, hooves and feet. That proved to be enough, however, for the head of Early's Division had to stop as it reached Fairfield, at the eastern base of South Mountain, because the wagons up ahead had bogged down in the mud beyond the town. The Rebels were stalled, but Sedgwick kept on coming. At half past noon Meade had written to Sedgwick: "All the information I can obtain proves withdrawal of enemy through Cashtown and Fairfield road. Push forward your column in a westerly direction. Fire on his force. If rear guard, it will be compelled to return; if not, you will find out. Time is of great importance, as I cannot give order for a movement without explicit information from you. General Sykes will cover your withdrawal, if necessary, and General Warren, who carries this, will read it to General Sykes."[31]

That afternoon, when he received word from his cavalry that a Union force was advancing on his rear guard, Early ordered some artillery into position and had it open fire as the Federals came into view along a distant ridge, then ordered General Gordon to send out a single regiment while he formed the remainder of his division in a line of battle a couple of miles short of Fairfield. Gordon sent the 26th Georgia, which formed line straddling the road in front of a large woods, and when the Union skirmishers approached to within 100 yards, it charged and drove them back through the woods. The Federals unlimbered two batteries of artillery, which began to shell the Georgians, but the Rebels stood their ground, thus giving time for the rest of Early's Division to slip away through the town when the wagons up ahead finally began moving again. Sedgwick was under orders not to bring on a battle, and after about an hour the Georgians fell back through the woods and the town, and rejoined the Confederate column. The Federals did not pursue, and darkness soon covered the Rebels' retreat. The 6th Corps bivouacked for the night there outside of Fairfield.

At 5:15 p.m., General Pleasonton telegraphed to Secretary Stanton: "My cavalry horses are fast being used up. Please send me, to Frederick City, by to-morrow night the 2,000 cavalry which are at Washington, and most of them belonging to my regiments here. I really need them. The Quartermaster's Department has nearly 1,000 horses that can come up under their escort."[32] That evening General Couch wired Meade's quartermaster that he was sending him 500 horses by way of York and Hanover Junction.

At 6 p.m. Meade, still at Gettysburg, wrote to Halleck again: "I send copies of all my dispatches since yesterday morning. My army is all in motion. I shall be at Frederick to-morrow night. I desire the forces mentioned in your dispatch to Major-General French to be thrown to Harper's Ferry by rail as soon as possible. I shall so instruct Major-General French. It is of importance to get possession of South Mountain passes and Maryland Heights."[33] The latter is high ground at the south end of South Mountain that overlooks and dominates Harper's Ferry from the north.

French had already been thinking about Harper's Ferry, but in terms of the Confederates using it as a place to cross the Potomac. Before receiving the above-mentioned instructions, he had sent a small expedition there on this fifth day of July, which found that the enemy "had floored the railroad bridge, and was crossing the river in small detachments. Under the direction of Major [H.A.] Cole, the trestle-work on each side of the bridge was destroyed; also the bridge over the [Chesapeake & Ohio] canal."[34] Had French's men captured, rather than destroyed, the bridge, either he or Meade could have used it to put forces south of the river to prevent Lee from crossing it there or anywhere.

At that same hour of 6 p.m., General Slocum was writing to Meade from Two Taverns: "The Twelfth Corps and Reserve Artillery will encamp tonight at Littlestown. If the Second Corps has started, I shall direct it to encamp to-night at this point. Unless otherwise ordered, the entire command will move at 5 a.m., and encamp to-morrow night near Frederick, and will reach Middletown at an early hour on Tuesday."[35]

At 7:30 p.m., Meade wrote to Sedgwick again, saying that

he had authorized Sykes to move his 5th Corps, but that the 1st Corps had been ordered to support him and that he could call on the 3rd Corps also, if necessary. "I am awaiting some definite intelligence of your position and movements. Believing the enemy were in full retreat, and for the Potomac, I authorized the issue of the order of march, and several corps have moved, but, as they cannot get very far to-day, they can be recalled if the information obtained through your operations should justify same."[36]

While the Confederates, at least, began to move out of the Gettysburg area, civilians from near and far began to arrive. Some came in search of wounded or dead relatives, but many came just to get a look at a battlefield – most previous battles having been fought in places difficult for Northern civilians to reach. Late that morning a team of photographers, led by Alexander Gardner, had arrived from Washington and had begun taking pictures of the field. It was one of his men, on the way up from Washington, who had been captured by Jeb Stuart's cavalry near Emmitsburg, but released. The three photographers evidently first set up their cameras and wagon-mounted darkrooms in the Rose farm area, near the Emmitsburg Road, scene of part of the second day's fight, where there were many bodies not yet buried. In fact, their favorite subject was dead soldiers. Gardner had done the same on the Antietam battlefield, near Sharpsburg, the previous September, and that series of photos had proven to be very popular when reproduced in newspapers and magazines. The pictures brought home to the public the pathos and human cost of the war.

In Washington, Lincoln had, as usual, been keeping an eye on the military telegrams flying between the various commands. At 9 a.m. on the fifth he telegraphed General French, at Frederick: "I see your despatch about destruction of pontoons. Cannot the enemy ford the river?"[37] And at 10:30 a.m. Halleck wired French: "The forces from Harper's Ferry, with two batteries of artillery and some troops from Baltimore, can be sent to you at Frederick, should General Meade desire that disposition of them. Should he deem it preferable, they can be sent back, by Poolesville, to Point of Rocks. Please communicate immediately with General Meade, and get his instructions. I have had no communication from his since yesterday morning."[38]

French replied at 3 p.m., saying, "Meade's instructions to me require the force sent back from Harper's Ferry. No time is to be lost. Buford is passing through to-day. I have destroyed the bridge at Williamsport, and am fortifying the South Mountain passes. Lee, it is reported, has massed at Chambersburg, and will rest his right on the river at Williamsport. Should he find his passage there impracticable, as the river is rising, he will endeavor to seize the passes. I have one good brigade holding them. I also hold the Monocacy bridges, and have only a few unreliable infantry in reserve. Should you send me re-enforcements, they should come direct by rail. The cavalry is broken down. I have issued a proclamation for horses, and will remount as fast as they are brought in. It was reported to me that artillery was being placed on the heights at Sheperdstown Ford, and a bridge in readiness to swing across. Buford will visit that place to-night. To reoccupy Maryland Heights will require time, and probably the holding for awhile of the opposite side of the river. The enemy can get nothing by having them, and a small force without depot would be in a *cul-de-sac*."

He then quoted to Halleck the two messages Butterfield had sent him, the first saying that Lee had not retreated far and countermanding previous orders for French to reoccupy Maryland Heights, and the second saying Lee was in full retreat and to go ahead with the original order. "I will, therefore," he added, "require the re-enforcements."[39]

Halleck then sent orders to Major General Samuel Heintzelman, commander of the Department of Washington, to send the detachment from Harper's Ferry and two batteries by rail to French at Frederick, and orders to Major General

Robert Schenck, commander of the Middle Department, to send French "all the troops in Baltimore not absolutely necessary to man the fortifications."[40] And at 7:31 he notified French that these were on the way. Schenck replied that he already didn't have enough men to man the fortifications at Baltimore, but that he would put together a brigade "of the best that I have," about 3,000 strong.[41] Halleck assured him that Lee was in retreat and that Baltimore was in no possible danger.

At 9:15 p.m. Halleck received another message from French, saying: "Five hundred wagons (rebel), guarded by about 150 infantry, 150 cavalry, three pieces of inferior-looking artillery, and from 3,000 to 5,000 head of cattle passed through Hagerstown last night after 11 o'clock to about 4 o'clock. Could not cross the ford at Williamsport, the river being too high. Supposed to have gone to Falling Waters, having started from Williamsport in that direction this morning. The wagons were loaded with sick, wounded, and stores."[42]

As French's 3 p.m. message says, Brigadier General John Buford's 1st Division of the Cavalry Corps was expected at Frederick that day. Merritt's Reserve Brigade of that division had started moving south from near Gettysburg early on the fourth, but the rain that had begun drenching the area about noon that day had turned its march into a terrible ordeal for men and horses. It had not seen its supply wagons for days; the men were hungry, and the horses were literally starving. Hundreds of horses collapsed along the road, which further slowed the column to the pace of the men who were thus left on foot. But after a brief halt at Mechanicstown, the column had set out again and didn't stop for the night until 3 a.m. on the fifth. After four hours of rest on the wet ground, they started off again and reached Frederick about noon. Some supplies for men and horses were obtained there from General French.

Buford's other two brigades, that had started the battle of Gettysburg on 1 July, had spent most of the fourth at Westminster, Maryland, re-shoeing their horses, replenishing their ammunition and supplies, and watching Confederate prisoners of war march through. They did not begin to leave Westminster until around 4 p.m. on the fourth. On their march, they came to a large, brick mill that belonged to a "Pennsylvania Dutchman" (German), who was a Union man through and through. When Buford informed him that "The Rebel army is whipped and in full retreat. We are trying to get to the Potomac ahead of him," and that his men could use some flour and his horses hay and corn, the man said he had about thirty tons of hay, several thousand bushels of unshelled corn, and plenty of corn meal, wheat flour and buckwheat flour, all of which he offered the tired and hungry cavalrymen. He tried to refuse a receipt that he could present to a Union quartermaster for compensation, but Buford made him take it. "I wonder if mortal man ever made six thousand men more happy and grateful than that Dutchman did," a Union captain wrote.[43]

The two brigades reached Frederick at about 7 p.m. on 5 July, where they hooked up with Merritt, and the division made camp about a mile west of town in fields beside the National Road. That night several civilians sought passage through Buford's camp or lingered just outside of it. Buford sent several of them to French's headquarters in Frederick as possible spies, but feared that nothing would be done with them, so finally he announced that the next one caught would not get off so lucky. And, later that night, a man was detained by the camp's pickets who said his name was Richardson and claimed to be returning to his home in Baltimore after trying to locate his sons, who were in Lee's army. Notes were allegedly found in his boot from General Ewell and other Confederates vouching for him. Buford ordered him hanged, saying, "If I send him to Washington they'll send him back promoted."[44]

General Kelley reported to the War Department that night that his forces in West Virginia would be delayed in taking part in cutting off Lee's retreat. Most of his cavalry, under Brigadier General W. W. Averell, was off pursuing Confederate raiders. "It will be impossible for me to concentrate my force at Hancock as promptly as I could wish, as it will require Averell some days to get back. Shall I move what force I have at New Creek and Cumberland to Hancock (about 4,500 effective men), or shall I wait for Averell's command?" Halleck replied at 9:30 p.m., Send forward your forces in hand, and order the others to follow as rapidly as possible." A half-hour later he added: "Do everything in your power to capture or destroy Lee's trains, which will endeavor to cross at Williamsport or Falling Waters. His army is in full retreat." A half-hour after than came a message from Secretary of War Stanton: "I have seen your dispatch to the Adjutant-General, and regret to hear you talk about 'some days' to concentrate, when minutes are precious. The instructions and information given by the General-in-Chief this evening will show what an opportunity you have, by rapid and vigorous motion, to inflict a heavy blow upon the enemy. It will be a matter of deep regret if, by tardy movement, you let the chance escape. There should be no rest, night or day. Why are you still at Clarksburg?"[45]

In Washington, the President met with his cabinet at 11 a.m. on 5 July to discuss the presence of Confederate Vice President Alexander Stephens at Fort Monroe and the message he wanted to deliver to Lincoln. According to Secretary of the Navy Welles, "The President said he was at first disposed to put this matter aside without many words, or much thought, but a night's reflection and some remarks yesterday had modified his views. While he was opposed to having Stephens and his vessel come here, he thought it would be well to send some one – perhaps go himself – to Fortress Monroe."[46] Both Secretary of State Seward and Secretary of War Stanton were startled by this remark. Seward did not think that Lincoln or anybody else should go to meet Stephens and would only let Stephens submit his message through General Dix, whose command included Fort Monroe. Stanton was emphatically against having anything to do with Stephens or his message, and Secretary of the Treasury Salmon Chase agreed. Nothing definite was decided.

Dan Sickles reached Washington that day and was taken to a house on F Street. But his surgeon would still not allow the general to be removed from his stretcher, even to place him on a bed. Word of his arrival soon spread across the city, and visitors began to arrive. One of the first was the quartermaster of Sickles' 3rd Corps, Lieutenant Colonel James Rushling, who was on sick leave himself. And he was soon followed by none other than President Lincoln, who had his young son Tad in tow. Lincoln, of course, wanted to know all about the battle.

"Sickles, recumbent on his stretcher, with a cigar between his fingers, puffing it leisurely, answered Mr. Lincoln in detail," Rushling later remembered, "but warily, as became so astute a man and soldier; and discussed the great battle and its probable consequences with a lucidity and ability remarkable in his condition then – enfeebled and exhausted as he was by the shock and danger of such a wound and amputation. . . . He certainly got his side of the story of Gettysburg well into the President's mind and heart that Sunday afternoon. . . ."[47] In Sickles version, of course, his unauthorized advance of the 3rd Corps to the Emmitsburg Road on 2 July had disrupted the Confederate plan – which it obviously had, but at the cost of the smashing of his 3rd Corps (which, of course, Sickles had not witnessed – at least not in full). But he also claimed that it prevented Meade from carrying through with a planned retreat – for which there is no real evidence. But this is the story Sickles told and retold until his death in 1914.

∼ Endnotes ∼

1   Wittenberg, Petruzzi and Nugent, *One Continuous Fight*, 70.
2   Ibid., 71.
3   *OR*, I:27:I:1014.

4   Brown, *Retreat from Gettysburg*, 132.
5   Kidd, *A Cavalryman with Custer*, 98.
6   Brown, *Retreat from Gettysburg*, 138.
7   Wittenberg, Petruzzi and Nugent, *One Continuous Fight*, 69.
8   OR, I:27:III:531.
9   Wittenberg, Petruzzi and Nugent, *One Continuous Fight*, 256.
10 OR, I:27:III:532. Both messages.
11 Wittenberg, Petruzzi and Nugent, *One Continuous Fight*, 81.
12 OR., I:27:III:531.
13 Ibid., I:27:I:79-80.
14 Ibid., I:27:I:79.
15 Ibid.
16 Ibid., I:27:III:534.
17 Wittenberg, Petruzzi and Nugent, *One Continuous Fight*, 77.
18 OR, I:27:III:533.
19 Ibid., I:27:II:700.
20 Ibid.
21 Ibid., I:27:II:701.
22 Ibid., I:27:II:700-1.
23 Ibid., I:27:II:753.
24 Brown, *Retreat from Gettysburg*, 161.
25 Imboden, "The Confederate Retreat from Gettysburg," *B&L* III:424-5.
26 Wittenberg, Petruzzi and Nugent, *One Continuous Fight*, 13-14.
27 Brown, *Retreat from Gettysburg*, 202.
28 Ibid., 205.
29 Wittenberg, Petruzzi and Nugent, *One Continuous Fight*, 40.
30 Ibid. 41.
31 OR, I:27:III:535.
32 Ibid., I:27:III:543.
33 Ibid., I:27:I:79.
34 Ibid., I:27:I:489.
35 Ibid., I:27:III:537.
36 Ibid.
37 Ibid., I:27:III:544.
38 Ibid.
39 Ibid, I:27:III:544-5.
40 Ibid., I:27:III:545.
41 Ibid., I:27:III:546.
42 Ibid.
43 Wittenberg, Petruzzi and Nugent, *One Continuous Fight*, 96-7. Both quotes.
44 Brown, *Retreat From Gettysburg*, 217. The man was evidently William Richardson, a Rebel spy, who might have even been the "farmer" who caused Merritt to send the 6th U.S. Cavalry to its doom at Fairfield. See Wittenberg, *Gettysburg's Forgotten Cavalry Actions*, 114n.
45 OR, I:27:III:550. Both messages.
46 Basler, ed., *The Collected Works of Abraham Lincoln*, VI:315 n. 1.
47 Pfanz, *Gettysburg the Second Day*, 437.

CHAPTER 19
"A Dreadful Reminiscence of McClellan"
5 – 6 July 1863

Down in Mississippi, General McPherson and his 17th Corps began paroling the Confederate garrison of Vicksburg that fifth day of July. All Confederates would remain there as prisoners until all of their paroles were signed. As General Grant later explained, "The paroles were in duplicate, by organization (one copy for each, Federals and Confederates), and signed by the commanding officers of the companies or regiments. Duplicates were also made for each soldier and signed by each individually, one to be retained by the soldier signing and one to be retained by us. Several hundred refused to sign their paroles, preferring to be sent to the North as prisoners to being sent back to fight again. Others again kept out of the way, hoping to escape either alternative."[1] Pemberton wrote to McPherson that day to ask for clarification of the terms regarding officers' servants (slaves) and generals' mounted couriers. Grant told McPherson that no servants should be forced to go with the Confederates, but if any desired to go, not to prevent them.

Charles Dana, the emissary of the War Department who had been with Grant's headquarters since before his army had crossed to the east side of the Mississippi, wrote a message that day to be taken up the river and telegraphed to Secretary Stanton: "General Grant, being himself intensely occupied, desires me to say that he would like to receive from General Halleck as soon as practicable either general or specific instructions as to the future conduct of the war in his department. He has no idea of going into summer quarters, nor does he doubt his ability to employ his army so as to make its blows tell toward the great result; but he would like to be informed whether the Government wishes him to follow his own judgment or to co-operate in some particular scheme of operations."[2]

Sherman's move against Johnston had been delayed somewhat, as he explained in a message to Grant that day: "Troops all in position, but somewhat disordered by Vicksburg, Fourth of July, and the terrible heat and dust. My new bridges interrupted somewhat by a rise of 4 feet in Big Black River, making ford impassable, but I expect to cross this afternoon and move out almost to Edwards Station, tomorrow noon at Bolton, and next day Clinton, by which time I will know the purposes of the enemy, and act accordingly."[3] Johnston, meanwhile, learned this day that Vicksburg had surrendered the day before, and he began to fall back to the east, toward Jackson.

At Delhi, Louisiana, some 25 miles west of Vicksburg, that day, Lieutenant General Kirby Smith ordered Major General J. G. Walker to take his division to Ashton, on the west bank of the Mississippi, to try to blockade the river with his artillery, to prevent supplies and troops from getting to or from Banks' army at Port Hudson. Meanwhile, Brigadier General Thomas Green, commander of a cavalry brigade under General Taylor, sent a young aide-de-camp across the river with a note addressed "To any Confederate Officer commanding on the east of the Mississippi: We have a sufficient force on this side, of cavalry, infantry, and artillery, to hold it against any force the Yankees can bring against us. If a force on the east, below Donaldsonville, could hold their own on the river, we can stop the supplies to Banks' army, and force him to raise the siege of Port Hudson. We will, I am confident, be able to whip his army in the open field should he move on this side."[4] These Confederates did not, of course, yet know about the surrender of Vicksburg. But the Federals were aware of their efforts to blockade the lower Mississippi. Admiral Farragut was writing that day to reassure Brigadier General William H. Emory, Union commander at New Orleans: "I understand the play of the rebels, and think we can foil them. I have ample force on the river to keep them in check."[5]

Out in far off Indian Territory (now Oklahoma), the Union wagon train that had fought through an ambush at Cabin Creek three days before, pulled into Fort Gibson on 5 July, breaking up a Confederate siege of that place.

In Kentucky, Morgan's Confederate cavalry division arrived that morning before the town of Lebanon, site of a Union supply depot at the end of a spur railroad. They found it defended by 380 Federals of the 20th Kentucky Infantry and small detachments from three other regiments, strung out in a skirmish line behind fences and overturned wagons.[6] The Union commander, Lieutenant Colonel Charles S. Hanson, was well known to several members of Morgan's band; his brother had been a Confederate brigadier general, killed at the battle of Stones River six months before. In his diary, Colonel Alston, Morgan's chief of staff, called it "Another day of gloom, fatigue, and death." After his guns had fired a few rounds to make their presence known, Morgan sent Alston to demand an unconditional surrender. Alston said he was fired on five times as he went in with a flag of truce, but that Hanson apologized, saying they thought he was a man in a white coat. "Very dangerous mistake," Alston wrote, "at least for me." Hanson refused to surrender, so Alston "ordered him to send out the non-combatants, as we would be compelled to shell the town. He posted his regiment in the depot and in various houses, by which he was enabled to make a desperate resistance."[7]

Slowly, Morgan's men drove the defenders from several buildings and captured their only piece of artillery, a 24-pounder, before it ever fired a shot. At noon, Morgan again demanded their surrender or he would burn the town, but Hanson refused to acknowledge the message because the Rebels abused the white flag by advancing their skirmishers and a cannon while the demand was being presented. The cannon that had been advanced, a 10-pounder Parrott rifle, then opened fire from a range of only 300 yards, but its shells merely burst in the upper story of the depot without harming the men on the lower floor. After about an hour of this, Morgan learned that Union reinforcements were only three miles away on the road from Danville. He ordered some of his men to burn the business buildings near the depot, and, as the flames spread, he had his 2nd Kentucky Cavalry make a dismounted charge up Main Street, during which one of his brothers, 19-year-old Lieutenant Tom Morgan, was killed. By then the depot itself was on fire, and Hanson, after holding out for more than six hours, finally surrendered. "By this surrender," Colonel Alston wrote, "we obtained a sufficient quantity of guns to arm all our men who were without them; also a quantity of ammunition, of which we stood sorely in need."[8]

Morgan and his other brothers, however, were enraged by the death of Tom. Captain Charlton Morgan threatened to shoot two Union captains, and, when Hanson tried to intervene, Charlton grabbed him by his beard and told him, "I will blow your brains out, you damned rascal."[9] However, other Confederates pulled him away, and he apologized. But Morgan's men took Tom's death as an excuse to go on a rampage, and they burned much of the town, destroying about twenty buildings, including private homes and the Marion County court house, with its archive of deeds, wills and other important records. "It required the utmost energy and promptitude on the part of the officers to prevent a scene of slaughter," Colonel Alston told his journal, "which all would deeply have lamented. Our men behaved badly here, breaking open stores and plundering indiscriminately. All that officers could do was done to prevent, but in vain. . . ."

Hanson blamed the loss of the battle on Colonel James L. David for taking too long to come to his rescue with the 8th and 9th Michigan Cavalry regiments and a battery, who took over four hours to cover the last three miles from Danville.

General Burnside at first blamed Hanson, whom he had warned of Morgan's approach, and had him arrested, but latter admitted that this was a mistake. The casualties were again disproportionate in favor of the defenders, except, of course, that all the surviving Federals became prisoners. Among the Confederates severely wounded was Morgan's latest chief of scouts.

"While I was paroling the prisoners," Alston said, "a courier arrived, informing me that the enemy were approaching with two regiments of cavalry and a battery of artillery, and that skirmishing was then going on with our pickets. I was therefore obliged to order the prisoners to Springfield on the double-quick. Soon after we left Lebanon, the hardest rain I ever experienced commenced to fall, and continued till nine o'clock." It was nine miles from Lebanon to Springfield, with Morgan's mounted men spurring the weary prisoners along. At least one Federal died of exhaustion. Two others who collapsed in the road were run over by artillery wheels; one of them survived, the other died a few hours later. Once arrived at Springfield, about dark, it took Alston two hours to parole all the prisoners who had not been paroled at Lebanon, meanwhile Morgan's column had moved on, and Alston set out to overtake it. From Springfield, Morgan had turned to the west, heading for Bardstown. "Wet and chilly, worn out, horse tired and hungry," Alston wrote. "Stopped to feed her. Falling asleep, was aroused by one of the men. Started on to the command. When I reached the point on the Bardstown road where I expected the Second brigade to encamp, was halted by a party of cavalry. Supposing them to be our own pickets, I rode up promptly to correct them for standing in full view of any one approaching, when lo! To my mortification, I found myself a prisoner."[10]

General Judah, the Federal commander who had allowed Morgan to slip past him, belatedly dispatched General Hobson with cavalry from two of his brigades that day, to follow Morgan, while Judah himself took the rest of his cavalry, about 1,200 men, directly north, hoping to head him off at

Elizabethtown, on the Louisville & Nashville Railroad.

Morgan's Confederates entered Bardstown at 4 a.m. on 6 July after riding all night. There they found that an advanced detachment was besieging a brick livery stable and 25 troopers of the 4th U.S. Cavalry, who had already refused one demand for surrender. Morgan repeated the demand and threatened to blow the building to Hell with his artillery. Again the Federals refused, but after four artillery pieces were brought up to within 100 yards of the building they accepted. Morgan's brother Dick refused to accept their surrender after they had rejected two chances, but he soon recanted.

At 10 a.m. the Rebels departed and rode westward all day. At dusk they came to the main line of the Louisville & Nashville Railroad at the Rolling Fork River, 25 miles south of Louisville, where they captured a stockade and burned the trestle. A northbound passenger train soon arrived and was methodically robbed by the Confederates, who took not only the U.S. mail and the money from the express company's safe, but hats, boots, money, watches and jewelry from the passengers. The train was then allowed to back its way to Elizabethtown, and Morgan's men returned to their saddles, still moving west. Few knew it, other than Morgan himself, but they were heading for the Ohio River. (Far north of that formidable stream, Confederate-sympathizing Copperheads forced their way into the depot at Huntington, Indiana, near Fort Wayne, that day and seized guns and ammunition.)

Behind Morgan, Union pursuit was beginning to get more organized. General Burnside telegraphed to Lebanon that day telling General Hobson to take command of all the cavalry that had converged there, find out where Morgan was, or was going, and overtake him or cut him off. "You are authorized to subsist your commands upon the country and impress the necessary horses to replace the broken-down ones," Burnside said. "This should be done in a regular way. Morgan ought to be broken to pieces before he gets out of the State."[11]

Hobson had arrived at Lebanon with two regiments of

cavalry from his own 2nd Brigade of Judah's 3rd Division of the 23rd Corps, accompanied by Brigadier General James M. Shackelford with a regiment and a battalion of cavalry and a section of artillery from his 1st Brigade of the 2nd Division. (The infantry units of these brigades had, necessarily, been left behind.) And Colonel Frank Wolford, with four regiments of cavalry and mounted infantry and a battery of mountain howitzers, had come up from Somerset, to the southeast. When Colonel August V. Kautz arrived, Hobson organized everything into a provisional cavalry division of three brigades, under Shackelford, Wolford, and Kautz, with two batteries of two and four guns respectively. This new division departed Lebanon at 5 p.m., heading for Bardstown, which Morgan had left seven hours before.

Down in Mississippi on 6 July, General Grant sent north his long official report of his campaign against Vicksburg. Also that day, Charles Dana, feeling that his mission with Grant was accomplished, headed north by steamboat, intending to stop at Helena, Arkansas, to get news of the recent battle there, and then to return to Washington by way of Cairo, Illinois.

That same day Pemberton had another question for McPherson, in command of the Union garrison of the city. He wanted to know if his generals could take mounted couriers with them, and, if so, how many. In reply to this question and to the previous day's question about the Confederates taking servants (slaves) with them, McPherson said that officers wishing to take servants along should send the servant in to his provost-marshal (future-general James H. Wilson), who would make sure the servant really wanted to go and understood that he did not have to go. As for mounted couriers, General Grant forbade it. He would, however, allow them to take a limited number of wagons and horse or mule teams for carrying their supplies.

Sherman's move against Joe Johnston got rolling that day,

and he published orders for Ord's 13th Corps, with one division of the 16th Corps attached, to cross the Big Black River at the railroad bridge and head for Clinton on the direct road east, which would take it past the battlefield of Champion's Hill; his own 15th Corps, under the temporary command of its senior division commander, Major General Frederick Steele, would take a more northerly route to Clinton, while the 9th Corps, with another division of the 16th Corps attached, would head for the same place by way of Brownsville, farther south. The move was to begin at 4 p.m., with each corps aiming to arrive at Bolton Station at 10 a.m. the next day and at Clinton by the same time the day after. The final paragraph of the order admonished that "Private pillage and plunder must cease; our supplies are now ample, and there is no use or sense in wanton damage. Brigade quartermasters and commissaries may collect by regular foraging parties such forage and provisions as are needed by the troops, but the people of the country should be protected as far as possible against the cruel and wanton acts of irresponsible parties. Stragglers and camp-followers found out of place should be dealt with summarily."[12]

In Washington, Lincoln's Cabinet met again on 6 July, and again considered what to do about Confederate Vice-President Stephens, waiting at Fortress Monroe. The result was a short message from Secretary of the Navy Welles to Rear Admiral S. P. Lee at Hampton Roads: "The request of Alexander H. Stephens is inadmissable. The customary agents and channels are adequate for all needful military communication and conference between the U.S. forces and the insurgents."[13]

General Halleck sent a longer message that day to Lieutenant Colonel W. H. Ludlow, who was the assistant adjutant general of the 7th Corps and the U.S. agent for the exchange of prisoners in the East, and with it went a copy of War Department General Orders No. 207, dated 3 July, regarding the parole of prisoners. Ludlow was instructed to communicate the contents of that order to Mr. Robert Ould, his Confederate counterpart. "You will also notify Mr. Ould that it is understood that officers of the United States and Confederate officers have at various times and places paroled and released prisoners of war not in conformity with the cartel, and that the Government of the United States will not recognize and will not expect the Confederate authorities to recognize such unauthorized paroles. Prisoners released on parole not authorized by the cartel after your notice of May 22 will not be regarded as prisoners of war and will not be exchanged . . . such release will be regarded as unconditional and the party released as subject to the orders of his Government without exchange the same as if he had never been captured."[14]

In Richmond that day, news of the victory at Gettysburg reached the Union officers in Libby Prison. Inspired by this news, Chaplain Charles McCabe taught his fellow prisoners the new words to the song "John Brown's Body," which he had seen in the *Atlantic Monthly* magazine, which converted the old marching song into "The Battle Hymn of the Republic." It became the prisoners' favorite song, and the one the Confederates hated most of all.

In another part of the same prison that same day all the captured Federals of the rank of captain were assembled around a table, and another Union chaplain drew two slips of paper from a box. The name of each captain had been written on such a slip and placed in the box, and the two now drawn at random were to be executed in retaliation for two Rebel captains from Kentucky (a Union state) who had been captured there while recruiting for the Confederate army and shot as traitors and spies. The two Federal captains whose names were drawn were taken to the prison's dungeon and allowed only bread and water pending their executions, which were delayed for two weeks to give them time to write home and inform their families of their fate.

Near Gettysburg early in the morning of the sixth, Lee's infantry was on the march again. The head of the column started near Waynesborough that morning, while the tail, some twenty miles back, had not gone more than two miles beyond Fairfield. Longstreet's 1st Corps had bivouacked for the night in Monterey Pass, which it had reached by way of the Emmitsburg-Waynesborough Turnpike. But its further progress was blocked by the wagons passing along the Maria Furnace Road. Hood's Division held the summit, and McLaws' Division held the eastern base, deployed across the road.

Elements of Johnson's and Anderson's wagons were just ahead of Hill's infantry column, north of Hagerstown, which Early's wagons were just approaching, while Rodes' trains were nearing Williamsport. To protect all these wagons, Jeb Stuart sent Chambliss's and Robertson's cavalry brigades to Hagerstown ahead of them, and personally took Ferguson's and Jones's brigades eastward to Chewsville.

Lee had intended to have Ewell's 2nd Corps lead this day, but his men were too far behind and so were stuck in the rear again. Instead, McLaws' and Hood's divisions of Longstreet's 1st Corps took the lead, followed by Hill's 3rd Corps, Lee's small headquarters, and Pickett's Division with the Union prisoners. At the base of the mountain, the infantry took to the fields beside the road, which was left to the wagons, and pioneer teams with axes took the lead to cut through any fences that might block the way. Ewell rotated his three divisions' places in the column, having Early's Division, which had been at the rear the day before, take the lead this day, followed by Johnson's Division, with Rodes' bringing up the rear. His rear guard was Daniel's Brigade of North Carolinians. But it took nine hours for the other two corps to clear the road so that Ewell's corps could take up the march again.

Meanwhile, a dense mist covered the area, threatening more rain and limiting visibility. A few of the Federal prisoners escaped in the morning fog; others gave their paroles until Lee ordered that more paroles should not be accepted because the Union government would not recognize them. The Confederates continued to forage all along the road, taking animals, grain, hay, and whatever they could find.

Meade was still uncertain whether Lee was in full retreat for Virginia, or holed up in the mountain passes, ready to pop out again. At 2 a.m. he wrote to General Sedgwick, saying, "I think under existing circumstances you had better push your reconnaissance, so as to ascertain, if practicable, how far the enemy has retreated, and also the character of the gap and practicability of carrying the same, in case I should determine to advance on that line. You must be careful to watch your right and rear, as roads from Cashtown are open to the enemy to advance against you. My cavalry sent to Cashtown have not reported, but I have reason to believe that the enemy is there in force. I beg you will keep me fully advised of what occurs, and I desire you will report at least every two or three hours. Both the First and Third Corps are under your orders, and can be called to your support, if you require them. I shall not move the army from its present position until I am better satisfied the enemy are evacuating the Cumberland Valley."[15]

At the same hour, Seth Williams, of Meade's headquarters, wrote to General Newton, commanding the 1st Corps that "The commanding general does not wish to have your command move, unless you receive orders to do so from General Sedgwick. It is not improbable that General Sedgwick may remain where he is to-day." But at 3 a.m. Newton replied to Williams that "My messenger to General Sedgwick has just returned. He desires that the First and Third Corps proceed to Emmitsburg to-day. If there is no objection, I will start at 5 a.m., and in accordance with instructions from General Sedgwick, have directed General Birney to follow immediately after."[16]

At 4:15 a.m., General Howard, in charge of both the 5th

and 11th Corps, wrote to Dan Butterfield that he had received reports that indicated "the enemy moving from Fairfield, through Jack's Mountain. He might pass through Jack's Mountain to Mechanicstown, moving on to Frederick, or through the mountain toward Hagerstown. In either case, ought I not to move on Emmitsburg as quickly as possible?" At 4:30 a.m., Williams replied to Newton that Meade approved of the movement of the 1st and 3rd Corps to Emmitsburg.

An officer later wrote home about his impressions of the battlefield near the Emmitsburg Road as the 1st Corps began this march away from Gettysburg: "The ground was still marked with newly made graves, with the bloated and disgusting bodies of horses with their mouths open and eyeballs protruding. Many human bodies were still unburied and the faces were black and the teeth grinning horribly. The trees were shattered by shot and shell. Wheat fields were trodden down. War had done its work; and the air was terribly offensive with the odor of thousands of rotting bodies. It was a relief to reach the outside of the terrible scene, to come again among beautiful farms, and through fields of ripe grain...."[17]

Early that morning Sedgwick sent forward a staff officer (then lieutenant, later brigadier general, Ranald Mackenzie) with a squadron of cavalry, through the fog, supported by Brigadier General Thomas Neill's brigade of infantry, to see if the Rebels were still in place. Sedgwick replied to Meade that he had ordered Neill's brigade "to move cautiously forward toward the gap. I am afraid to move my whole command, on account of the character of the country and density of the fog. I cannot learn definitely whether they have taken the Hagerstown road or the Emmitsburg road, or both. The people here say they moved on both roads, but no one seems to know. I had determined, if General Neill found them as strong as I believe they are, to cross over from near my present camp to Emmitsburg, and I would advise that move.... I believe, from the immense number of camp-fires seen last evening, that the enemy have a very strong rear guard, and will hold the gaps strongly. I will remain with my principal command in this position until further orders. A recaptured prisoner (a civilian) reports that while at Gettysburg one division was sent out by the enemy on the Cashtown road, to meet and hold in check a force of ours, supposed to be 40,000 strong, reported advancing from the direction of Carlisle. I have sent no orders to the First or Third Corps."[18]

The last sentence of this message threw a wrench in the works, and Williams wrote to Newton again at 7:40 a.m., saying, "I am directed by the commanding general to say that you will immediately, on receipt of this communication, halt your command, and report by a staff officer to Major-General Sedgwick for further orders. It appears from a dispatch just received from General Sedgwick that he had given no orders for the movement of your command...."[19] At 8:30 a.m., Meade himself wrote to Howard, telling him to take one of his corps to Emmitsburg and to place the other one "in position on a road leading to Fairfield, from whence it could be thrown either to Fairfield or Emmitsburg."[20]

At 9 a.m., Meade wrote to Sedgwick, saying that he could not approve of the latter moving to Emmitsburg, that he had stopped the 1st and 3rd Corps, and that he had ordered Howard to send a corps to Emmitsburg and another part way there, giving Sedgwick three corps under his direct orders and two more within supporting distance, and, further, that he had just received word that cavalry had passed through Cashtown without opposition and were then at the Caledonia Iron Works, some 11 miles northwest of Fairfield, so his right and rear were secure. "All evidence seems to show a movement to Hagerstown and the Potomac. No doubt the principal force is between Fairfield and Hagerstown; but I apprehend they will be likely to let you alone, if you let them alone. Let me know the result of Neill's operations – whether they retire before him, or threaten to push him and you. Send out pickets well on your left flank; reconnoiter in all directions, and let me know the result. This is all the instruction I can now give you. Whenever I am satisfied that the main body is retiring from the mountains, I shall continue my flank movement. I am going to direct Couch to move down the Cumberland Valley to threaten their rear."[21]

At that same hour of 9 a.m., some of Neill's infantry ran into one of Daniel's regiments, which charged them with fixed bayonets, while Rodes sent Doles' Georgians to extend Daniel's line. An officer from Neill's brigade, sent to inform Sedgwick, recorded that "By the time I returned to our line, it had ceased firing and was resting, the enemy had retired in confusion, and our object was gained." Another Union officer said, "We scarcely pressed them at all, as far as I could judge, but merely followed and occupied the ground as they evacuated. Thus we slowly advanced all day[,] and night found us six miles from Gettysburg!"[22] "I wonder," another Federal officer wrote, if Napoleon or even Robt. Lee were our commander this evening would *they* pursue a defeated army in this cautious, courteous way?"[23]

At 9:50 a.m. Meade wrote to General Couch: "I cannot get very reliable intelligence of the enemy's movements. My belief is they are in retreat for the Potomac. A captured dispatch to a rebel cavalry officer, dated July 5, says Longstreet is moving through Jack's Mountain, and orders him to picket roads to Emmitsburg, and to report to Longstreet, at Jack's Mountain, and Ewell, at Fairfield. Sedgwick, with his corps, is pushing them at Fairfield; other corps are in support. I have delayed my flanking movement until I am positively satisfied they are retreating to the Potomac. I hope some time to-day to determine this."[24]

At 10:40 a.m., General Pleasonton wrote to Sedgwick that he was ordering McIntosh's brigade of cavalry "to communicate with you from Emmitsburg, and also to send forward toward Waynesborough to feel for the enemy."[25] But it was not until 3:45 p.m. that McIntosh received the order. At that hour he wrote to Pleasonton that he had advanced on the Waynesborough road, from Emmitsburg, and included the sort of intelligence that Meade was hoping for: "I engaged the enemy for two hours, until they moved out a strong infantry force against me. I was in sight of their train. It is moving off in the direction of Waynesborough. The enemy had formed two lines of infantry, and were busy forming a third whilst I engaged their rear guard. The bulk of Lee's army passed on to the Waynesborough pike yesterday from Fairfield. They passed through Fountain Dale and Monterey, and, I think, were moving to Hagerstown. I will at once attempt to carry out your order just received, to communicate with General Sedgwick, in front of Fairfield. The Eleventh Corps has arrived at Emmitsburg."[26]

Sometime during that sixth day of July, Halleck wired to Meade and to French: "Fifteen hundred cavalry left here this forenoon on Rockville and Frederick turnpike. They are detachments from the Army of the Potomac, remounted. You can send orders to them on the road to move as you deem best. Elliott's command, with two new batteries, left by railroad this morning." And at 12:30 p.m. he wired the same two generals: "It is just reported here that the bridge at Harper's Ferry was left intact when General French's command abandoned that place. If so, it gives Lee a good crossing, unless it be occupied by us in strong force. No time should be lost in throwing troops on to Maryland Heights."[27]

At 2 p.m., Meade, still at Gettysburg, wrote a long message to Halleck: "Yesterday I sent General Sedgwick with the Sixth Corps in pursuit of the enemy toward Fairfield, and a brigade of cavalry toward Cashtown. General Sedgwick's report indicating a large force of the enemy in the mountains, I deemed it prudent to suspend the movement to Middletown until I could be certain the enemy were evacuating the Cumberland Valley. I find great difficulty in getting reliable information, but from all I can learn I have reason to believe the enemy is retreating, very much crippled, and hampered with his trains.

"General Sedgwick reported that the gap at Fairfield was very formidable, and would enable a small force to hold my column in check for a long time. I have accordingly resumed the movement to Middletown, and I expect by to-morrow night to assemble the army in that vicinity. Supplies will be then provided, and as soon as possible I will cross South Mountain, and proceed in search of the enemy.

"Your dispatch requiring me to assume the general command of the forces in the field under General Couch has been received. I know nothing of the position or strength of his command, excepting the advance under General Smith, which I have ordered here, and which I desire should furnish a necessary force to guard this place while the enemy is in this vicinity. A brigade of infantry and one of cavalry, with two batteries, will be left to watch the enemy at Fairfield, and follow them whenever they evacuate the gap. I shall send general instructions to General Couch to move down the Cumberland Valley as far as the enemy evacuates it, and keep up communications with me; but from all the information I can obtain, I do not rely on any active co-operation in battle with this force. If I can get the Army of the Potomac in hand in the Valley, and the enemy have not crossed the river, I shall give him battle, trusting, should misfortune overtake me, that a sufficient number of my force, in connection with what you have in Washington, would reach that place so as to render it secure.

"General Trimble, of the Confederate army, was to-day found wounded just outside of Gettysburg. General Kemper was found mortally wounded on the road to Fairfield, and a large number of wounded, estimated as several thousand. Generals Heth, Wade Hampton, Jenkins, and Pender are reported wounded. The losses of the enemy were no doubt very great, and he must be proportionately crippled.

"My headquarters will be here to-night, and to-morrow I expect to be at Frederick. My cavalry have been attacking the enemy on both flanks, inflicting as much injury as possible."[28]

At 2:30 p.m., Lieutenant Mackenzie forwarded to Sedgwick a message from General Warren (who was now acting as Meade's chief of staff in addition to his duties as chief engineer, because Butterfield's wound needed attention – Warren was sharing these duties with Pleasonton, who also continued to be chief of cavalry): "You will take every precaution to maintain the position you now hold till dark. You will then withdraw all the Sixth Corps, excepting General Neill's brigade and a rifled battery, and proceed with your command (the First and Third Corps included) to execute the order of march of July 5. General Neill will follow the enemy cautiously as he (the enemy) retires, keeping the commanding general constantly informed. The commander of the rifled battery will report to him. Colonel McIntosh, with his brigade of cavalry, will be directed to report also to General Neill. General Newton has been halted near Emmitsburg. General Birney has not moved from this place."[29]

So, finally convinced that Lee was retreating for the Potomac, Meade re-activated his orders for a flanking march. Howard's 11th and 5th Corps, at and north of Emmitsburg, would proceed via Highknob Pass over Catoctin Mountain to Middletown, some ten miles west of Frederick. Sedgwick's three corps would march via Emmitsburg to Middletown by way of Lewistown and Hamburg. Slocum, with the 12th Corps and Reserve Artillery at Littlestown and the 2nd Corps at Two Taverns, was to follow a more easterly route, southeast to Taneytown, then southwest to Frederick and west to Middletown. Meade's supply base would be moved from Westminster to Frederick, on a spur of the Baltimore & Ohio Railroad, and orders were issued late that afternoon for the supply wagons of the various corps to leave the old base and march for the new one.

Although Meade's route was considerably longer than Lee's, once his army reached Middletown and Frederick, it would be on the macadamized National Road that led directly to Williamsport. But to follow Lee into the mountains would have been risky and would have moved Meade away from his supply base. As Meade later testified before Congress, "From information which I had previously received of the character of the passes at Fairfield and Cashtown, having been informed that they had been fortified by the enemy, and that a small force could hold a large body in check for a considerable time, I made up my mind that a more rapid movement of my army could be made by the flank through the Boonsboro Pass, than to attempt to follow the enemy on the road which he himself had taken."[30]

The real problem was the head start that Lee had gained while Meade had hesitated in uncertainty about his opponent's intentions. As one soldier of the 1st Corps laments, after marching only six miles, to Emmitsburg, "I fear that the efforts to bag Lee will prove a failure for he is already a day and a half the start of us, and unless we have a sufficient force at Williamsport the rebel army will effect an escape."[31]

Baldy Smith's division of militia from Couch's department was under orders from Meade to move to Gettysburg to protect the wounded that had not yet been evacuated and the rear of Meade's columns. Couch had written to Meade at 8 a.m. that day, saying, "I regret that you gave such an order, for he and myself think that he could do more good in our [Cumberland] valley," and also reported Captain Jones's captures near Mercersburg.[32] At 4:40 p.m., Meade wrote to Couch: "The General-in-Chief has directed me to assume the general command of all the troops you have in the field. This, in view of my ignorance of the number, organization, and position of your troops, is a very difficult matter. Lee, from all I can learn, is withdrawing toward Hagerstown and Williamsport. I propose to move via Middletown and South Mountain. If the condition of the roads and the impediments in his way should delay him, I may have an opportunity of attacking him. In this you can co-operate either by directly re-enforcing, by moving down the Valley and establishing communication with my army, or the movement may be confined, as I previously desired it to be, to a simple demonstration.

"In these points I do not wish to hamper you with instructions, but leave to your knowledge of your troops and the necessity of the defense of the Susquehanna. I think I have inflicted such injury on Lee that he will hardly contemplate another demonstration against Harrisburg. Still, if I have to meet with disaster, such a contingency should be held in view. I would like your opinion, with the remark that all the assistance I can get will be not only needed, but most gratefully received. General Smith being very near me, I have ordered him to this place, where a force should be left to cover our withdrawal and protect the hospitals and public property.

"If you can spare Smith, I should like to have him, so soon as the movements of the enemy indicate a force to be no longer necessary at this point. My headquarters to-night will be here; to-morrow night at Frederick. The army is in motion."[33]

That evening Couch wrote a reply: "General Smith, on the 4th and 5th, received your order to join him. At 1 a.m. to-day I directed him to obey your orders, unless he found the enemy in retreat and could operate effectually where he had been ordered to strike – at Cashtown and Chambersburg. He should have nearly 10,000 men, but one-half are very worthless, and 2,000 cavalry, with a battery, can capture the whole party in an open country. This is why I put them in or near the mountains; there they could do service.

"I have 2,000 men here; 500 that ran so rapidly from Gettysburg, much demoralized, and one regiment New York troops that won't march; 3,000 men nearly equipped, and probably 5,000 at Reading are being equipped. Between Bedford and Milroy's [Pierce's] men (Mercersburg) there may be 4,000, 1,500 of when [sic] are reported by the commander as utterly worthless. I have about 1,000 men that I did not march, having been demoralized at York. Have six guns and six mountain howitzers in the field. In a day or two will have ten.

"I shall strictly carry out any order you may give, having been notified by the War Department to that effect days ago, and do it with pleasure. My dispositions have been made in reference to the character of my troops, topography of the country, and to assist your heroic army."[34]

At 7 p.m., Smith wrote to Couch from Newman's Gap, in South Mountain, on a road leading to Gettysburg: "I encamp here to-night, having made 14 miles through the mountains. If nothing happens, I shall move to-morrow toward the next gap south, and so on up the Cumberland Valley, holding the gaps and keeping well in the mountains, where I can make a good fight. Will you send me some provisions to Fayetteville, and all the haversacks you can raise? The rebels, some of them, passed through here, but left Chambersburg to the right. I imagine it was principally a cavalry force, with infantry enough to escort the trains. The main body is still on the eastern slope, working through the other passes. If you send an order for this command to report to Meade, will you at the same time order me to return to you, leaving [Brigadier General Joseph] Knipe in command? You can appreciate how unpleasant it would be for me to serve under existing circumstances with the Army of the Potomac. I learn the river is impassable."[35] Smith had once been senior to Meade before his second star and corps command had been rejected by the Senate, so he did not relish the idea of serving under Meade now.

One of Smith's men wrote that "On the 6th day of July, we marched till late at night, expecting to cut off the rebel wagon-train. On reaching Newman's Gap, we found that Lee's rear-guard had passed through, about eight hours before we got there. We were compensated by obtaining something to eat; and in addition had the pleasure of having pointed out to us, no less than six houses, in all of which Longstreet had died the previous night, and two others, where he was yet lying mortally wounded."[36]

Irwin Gregg's cavalry was at Fayetteville on the sixth, about halfway between Smith's location and Chambersburg, charged with following Imboden's train of wagons. Gregg ordered Colonel William Doster and his 4th Pennsylvania Cavalry to gallop all the way to Greencastle this day, and sent his adjutant along to make sure they kept up the pace. Doster picked up about 100 Confederate stragglers along the road, and at Marion a local civilian informed him that Fitzhugh Lee's entire brigade of Rebel cavalry was grazing its horses about a mile off the road. Doster later lamented that there was nothing he could do about it. He said that the rigors of this campaign, climaxed by this long gallop, had reduced his fine regiment to about 25 mounted men still with him. "The rest are, heaven only knows where, dismounted, killed, wounded, scattered, and not at hand."[37] He told his diary that if he had had even 200 men he would have attacked Fitz Lee, but didn't think 25 were enough. After sending scouts to confirm what the civilian had told him, he sent word to Gregg, asking for reinforcements. Instead, Gregg ordered him back to Fayetteville.

Down along the South Carolina coast, Admiral Dahlgren took official command of the South Atlantic Blockading Squadron on 6 July, leaving him only three days to plan his squadron's part in General Gillmore's upcoming attack on Morris Island.

Early that same day, his son, with eighty members of his cavalry force, linked up with Kilpatrick's division near Hagerstown, bringing with them thirty Confederates captured at Greencastle. During the night, Kilpatrick had learned that Rebel cavalry was at Hagerstown and that Confederate wagons were near there and at Williamsport. So, after a brief rest just west of Boonsborough, he had put his men back in the saddle, heading for Hagerstown, but stopped at Funkstown. Huey's attached brigade, which was at the tail of the column, started at 1 a.m., although by now it had only about 200 mounted men, and its accompanying battery could only provide enough ammunition and serviceable horses to take two guns along. Meanwhile, Buford's division left its camp near Frederick at about 4 a.m., heading west.

"While on the march," Kilpatrick later reported, "I was informed that Brigadier-General Buford was at Boonsborough, and about to march on Williamsport. I rode back, and informed General Buford of my intentions, at the same time placing my command at his disposal. It was then decided that my division should attack Stuart, while General Buford's command attacked Williamsport."[38] Buford's division didn't reach Boonsborough until about noon, so Kilpatrick must have rested his men at Funkstown for most of the morning. Rain was falling again when the Federals approached Hagerstown from the southeast along the National Road at about 1:30 p.m. Colonel Richmond sent three squadrons a couple of blocks west, to then move north and uphill along the town's main business street.

The town was defended by the 9th and 10 Virginia Cavalry regiments of Chambliss's brigade of Stuart's cavalry. Chambliss sent riders to Chewsville to inform Stuart of the Federals' approach, and quickly barricaded the streets while placing some troopers in buildings and in the steeples of churches. The wagons of Early's Division, which had already entered the town, had to be turned back up the road toward Leitersburg, and the wagons of Johnson's and Anderson's divisions were halted north of town, guarded by Robertson's Brigade. When Stuart received Chambliss's message, he started Ferguson's brigade toward Hagerstown and sent Jones's Brigade south toward Funkstown to get behind the Federals.

Stuart, with Ferguson's troopers, appeared from the east just as Richmond's brigade came up against Chambliss's barricades. Richmond sent his attached battery of six 10-pounder rifles to block Stuart from some high ground east of town near the Hagerstown Female Seminary, supported it with the 5th New York Cavalry, and ordered a battalion of the 1st Vermont Cavalry out in front of the guns as skirmishers. In response, Stuart deployed a pair of guns that had come over from Robertson's Brigade, and the rival artillerymen dueled with each other for about fifteen minutes. The Federals had the upper hand, though (one of their shots exploded an ammunition chest on a Confederate limber), and held off Ferguson's brigade for most of the afternoon.

At about 2:30 p.m., Richmond ordered three mounted squadrons, led by Captain Dahlgren, to charge up South Potomac Street toward the town square, and they drove the

9th Virginia back onto the 10th Virginia. The colonel of the 10th was captured after being pinned under his dying horse, as the two Confederate regiments retreated in confusion. But a small company of the 1st Maryland Cavalry charged out of a side street and broke the momentum of the now-disorganized Union attack, and Robertson's Brigade advanced to block its further progress. Dahlgren rode back in search of reinforcements, found a company of the 18th Pennsylvania Cavalry, and led it forward dismounted. As they advanced, they were joined by a local civilian, carrying his own musket.

The Confederates retreated before this small force until they reached a church on a corner, where the Rebels dismounted to fight behind a fence and the tombstones of the church's cemetery. There the civilian was killed, as was another who was firing from an upper window of a store, and Dahlgren was wounded in the right foot and would soon lose the leg as a result. Richmond sent two more companies of the 18th Pennsylvania forward, mounted, followed by two from the 1st Vermont, and Robertson's 5th North Carolina Cavalry countercharged, bringing on an intense hand-to-hand mounted melee, with sabers and revolvers. One of the captains leading the Union charge killed three Rebels before being simultaneously shot and sabered; another was shot in one leg just before his horse fell on his other one; and the third captain was wounded and captured, along with his lieutenant. Eventually both sides dismounted and continued the battle as a fire fight for about an hour, until Iverson's Brigade of Confederate infantry arrived.

Several volleys from this source soon caused the Federals to fall back. A sergeant in the 1st Vermont Cavalry said, "We found ourselves being gradually forced back, but we went very slow. In fact we had sat down right before Lee's Army and they had to remove us before he could proceed."[39] As he fell back, another Union sergeant, who was from nearby Waynesborough, was wounded by a shot from a second-story window fired by a Confederate-sympathizing young girl. A local man, who had joined the fight on the Union side after a trooper had given him a musket taken from a captured Rebel, helped the wounded sergeant into a nearby house. As the Federals withdrew, Stuart, with Ferguson's brigade, joined the pursuit. A group of fourteen men from the 1st Vermont Cavalry found themselves cut off, and hid in the town for a week, with the help of a loyal civilian. At first the Federals tried to withdraw towards Williamsport, but soon found that way blocked.

Rain was falling from dark clouds again as Buford's column rode west, crossing Antietam Creek not far north of the previous year's battlefield. Merritt's Reserve Brigade led, followed by a battery, then Gamble's 1st Brigade, another battery, and finally Devin's 2nd Brigade. Contact was made with Rebel pickets near St. James College, and skirmishing fire broke out as they were driven west.

At about 5 p.m., General Imboden, at Williamsport, was informed that a strong force of Union cavalry and artillery was approaching along the road from Boonsborough. That general's position was perilous, for his back was to an unfordable river, and he had hundreds of wagons full of wounded men and badly needed supplies to defend with a very small force. Other than his own two mounted regiments, Imboden had only the two infantry regiments who had been escorting Lee's ammunition train north, plus a few separate companies, to back up his 26 pieces of artillery. The terrain, however, favored his defense, as it included a range of hills just east of the town that were well suited for the placement of artillery.

Colonel John Logan Black of Hampton's Brigade, who had just reached Williamsport in an ambulance, was suffering from typhoid fever, but he volunteered to help, and Imboden sent him up the turnpike to the north to organize teamsters and lightly wounded soldiers from the wagon train still backed up along the road, plus men of the commissary and quartermasters corps, and arm them with weapons and ammunition from the quartermasters' wagons. A wounded member of Hood's Division dryly remarked that, "Just as a mouse will fight when cornered, so will commissaries, quartermasters and their immediate subordinates."[40] Black led his men out the road towards Hagerstown, from which direction firing had been heard all afternoon, and deployed them in some fields to the left of a line of guns. More wagon drivers, dismounted cavalrymen, and walking wounded, culled from the trains that had already reached Williamsport and led by a wounded colonel and two majors from Davis's Brigade of Heth's Division, soon joined them, bringing the total to nearly 400 men. Meanwhile, Colonel William Aylett of the 53rd Virginia, Pickett's Division, though suffering from a chest wound, recruited nearly 300 men from the wagons parked near the river and took them out the road towards Boonsborough, where they joined a small company of the 23rd Virginia.

Imboden's own 62nd Virginia Mounted Infantry and his company of Partisan Rangers were moved from north of the town to the east side of town and placed in reserve behind the 58th Virginia, while his 18th Virginia Cavalry remained in position north of town, between the Cumberland Valley Turnpike and the Hagerstown pike. Part of the 54th North Carolina was stationed between the Downsville Road and the Boonsborough Road. One 2-gun section of a Virginia battery was placed to guard the far left flank near Conococheague Creek, another was placed to guard the right flank near the road leading south to Downsville, near Falling Waters, and the third section was placed in the middle of the east-facing line, between two full batteries.

Long-range fire from some of these guns eventually caused Buford to halt his column and deploy his forces. He sent Merritt's brigade and the first battery of horse artillery to his right, to occupy a slight ridge between the Boonsborough road and the one leading to Hagerstown, and soon the battery's six 3-inch rifles were returning the Rebels' fire. Gamble's brigade and the other battery peeled off to the left, and Devin's brigade massed in some woods behind Gamble as a reserve.

The Confederates seemed to have more than the handful of train guards that Buford had expected, but he ordered Merritt's brigade to advance dismounted, with, as usual, every fourth man holding the horses of the other three. Merritt sent the 6th Pennsylvania Cavalry ahead as skirmishers, and they drove the Rebel skirmishers back. The full formidable line of Confederate artillery now opened fire, but was rapidly depleting its small supply of ammunition. Urgent appeals were sent into town for more, and two Napoleons were moved over from the Hagerstown road to the Boonsborough road.

Meanwhile, Imboden ordered his 18th Virginia Cavalry to join his 62nd Virginia Mounted infantry and his company of Partisan Rangers. He formed them as a second line behind his guns, and ordered his first line, the two infantry regiments, Colonel Black's ad hoc battalion, and another one, about 200 strong, that Colonel William Delony had put together, to advance between the Hagerstown and Boonsborough roads, going some 50 to 100 yards beyond the artillery before slowly falling back again. This unusual maneuver served to convince Merritt that Imboden's line was deeper and stronger than it really was, causing Merritt to hesitate. Eventually some artillery ammunition was ferried over the Potomac from the ordnance train parked on the other side, and renewed fire from the Confederate guns held Merritt at bay.

On the Confederate right, Union left, Gamble spotted a train of Confederate wagons coming north on the Downsville road and sent his 3rd Indiana Cavalry to capture it. These wagons were mostly filled with hay that had been gathered from the area south and southeast of Williamsport to feed all the horses and mules of the wagons parked there. The Federals swooped down on them and captured some 27 wagons and 100 horses and mules, and took 46 prisoners. Then Gamble ordered a dismounted attack, supported by his attached battery, on a gap in Imboden's line near the Downsville road. Some of the Union artillery fire was aimed at the wagons that the Federals could see parked in and near the town. Many of the slaves used as teamsters took cover by plunging into the river up to their necks.

The gap in the Confederate line was soon partially filled by a company of the 21st Virginia and a 4-gun battery of artillery. The captain of the company was killed, but his men and the guns held up Gamble's brigade for about an hour. Eventually, however, the odds told, and Imboden had to send both of his own regiments, dismounted, and two more guns to block Gamble's attack. Colonel Black sent a company of about 114 wounded men from Hood's Division to join them and a part of the 54th North Carolina and two other guns that were already nearby. This combined force served to hold off Gamble, and at about 7 p.m. Imboden ordered a counterattack by his 62nd Mounted Infantry and Colonel Aylett's ad hoc battalion, but this failed to drive the Federals back.

On the other end of the line, a Confederate battery, joined by the section that had been guarding the northern flank, galloped out the Hagerstown pike, unlimbered, and opened fire on Merritt's right flank, and they were soon joined by troopers of Fitzhugh Lee's cavalry brigade, part of the force that had been guarding the rear of Imboden's column. Meanwhile, Fitz Lee sent Hampton's Brigade, now under Colonel L. S. Baker, through the northern edge of Williamsport and out the Clear Spring road to guard against any attack from the northwest, and other elements of his own brigade plus his attached horse artillery, farther up the Hagerstown road to threaten Kilpatrick's rear.

This sudden attack on his flank just as darkness was falling caused Merritt to fall back. This, in turn, caused Buford to order Gamble to fall back, which his men did grudgingly, and Buford ordered Devin to deploy his brigade to cover a retreat. But at the same time some of Kilpatrick's men were retreating down the Hagerstown-Sharpsburg road, not far to Buford's rear, blocking their way. "Had the daylight lasted another hour we would have suffered the most disastrous defeat," one of Merritt's men said later.[41]

Kilpatrick had sent Custer's Michigan Brigade down the

Hagerstown-Williamsport Turnpike to guard his own left and to connect with Buford, and Custer was about to lead a mounted charge when Kilpatrick rode up and countermanded the order. "I have always thought that if the order to charge had been executed as first intended, we would broken through Imboden's lines and burned up the wagons," one of Custer's buglers later opined.[42] And Imboden agreed. "A bold charge at any time before sunset would have broken our feeble lines, and then we should all have fallen easy prey to the Federals," he later wrote.[43] Instead, Kilpatrick had Custer's men advance dismounted, but Custer's left flank came under a destructive fire of Confederate artillery, and his other flank was threatened by Fitz Lee's cavalry, so he eventually withdrew toward Hagerstown just as Richmond's brigade was being driven out of that town by Chambliss's, Ferguson's, and Robertson's brigades.

Then the 11th Virginia Cavalry of Jones's Brigade, coming from Funkstown, hit Richmond's right flank, but was held off by the 1st West Virginia Cavalry, Richmond's rear guard. The rest of Jones' Brigade and his attached battery moved to get behind these Federals, and the battery did manage to get off one volley in the gathering darkness, in what one artilleryman called "a splendid display of dangerous fireworks," but the recoil of the guns drove them so deep into the muddy field that the gunners had to use fence rails to pry them out.[44] The Federals got away, and the Rebels finally gave up the chase at about 10 p.m. By 10:30 Confederate wagons were rolling through Hagerstown, heading for Williamsport.

Longstreet's two divisions led Lee's infantry column into Hagerstown at about 5 p.m., just after the cavalry fight there had ended, marched on through, and bivouacked for the night just west of Funkstown. Hill's corps reached Hagerstown about midnight and camped just west of that town. Ewell's corps, after marching past the ruins of their own wagons that Kilpatrick had destroyed two nights before, reached Waynesborough about dark and bivouacked just east of that town, some twelve miles behind Longstreet's divisions at the head of the column. Hagerstown was mostly pro-Union, and a Confederate artilleryman noted that, "the people seem jubilant over what they suppose to be our defeat. Now it is true we did not gain a victory, but we are far from being defeated."[45]

Late that afternoon, Lee had received word from Imboden that he had repulsed a Union attack on the wagons at Williamsport, but that Lee's train of ammunition wagons had reached only the opposite bank, and that the pontoon bridge at Falling Waters had been destroyed and the river was unfordable. But an officer of Ewell's 2nd Corps, sent ahead to find army headquarters, who saw Lee shortly thereafter, later remembered that "with all these misfortunes weighing upon him he was as calm as on a peaceful summers day."[46]

President Lincoln saw, that day, a copy of Meade's congratulatory order to his army. Colonel James B. Fry, the Army's provost marshal, was present at the time. "When he came to the sentence about 'driving the invaders from our soil,'" Fry later remembered, "an expression of disappointment settled upon his face, his hands dropped upon his knees, and in tones of anguish he exclaimed, 'Drive the *invaders* from our soil. My God! Is that all?'"[47] Lincoln's secretary, John Hay, later noted in his diary why that phrase so bothered the President: "This is a dreadful reminiscence of McClellan. The same spirit that moved McClellan to claim a great victory because Pennsylvania and Maryland were safe [after the battle of Antietam]. The hearts of ten million people sunk within them when McClellan raised that shout last fall. Will our Generals never get that idea out of their heads? The whole country is our soil."[48] From the beginning, Lincoln had seen Lee's invasion of Pennsylvania as an opportunity to cut him off from his base and destroy his army. Unfortunately for him, this conviction, when filtered through Stanton's and Halleck's caution, had not been adequately communicated to Meade.

Lincoln had recently talked with General Haupt, the

railroad man, who had come to Washington to warn Halleck that Meade was being too cautious, so the President had been watching the military telegraph closely for signs of such. At 7 p.m. on 6 July, he wrote to Halleck from the Soldiers Home, just north of Washington, where he and his family lived during the summer to escape the heat and humidity of the city: "I left the telegraph office a good deal dissatisfied. You know I did not like the phrase, in Orders, No. 68, I believe, 'Drive the invaders from our soil.' Since that, I see a dispatch from General French, saying the enemy is crossing his wounded over the river in flats, without saying why he does not stop it, or even intimating a thought that it ought to be stopped. Still later, another dispatch from General Pleasonton, by direction of General Meade, to General French, stating that the main army is halted because it is believed the rebels are concentrating 'on the road toward Hagerstown, beyond Fairfield,' and is not to move until it is ascertained that the rebels intend to evacuate Cumberland Valley.

"These things all appear to me to be connected with a purpose to cover Baltimore and Washington, and to get the enemy across the river again without a further collision, and they do not appear connected with a purpose to prevent his crossing and to destroy him. I do fear the former purpose is acted upon and the latter is rejected.

"If you are satisfied the latter purpose is entertained and is judiciously pursued, I am content. If you are not satisfied, please look to it."[49]

∽ Endnotes ∽

1 Grant, *Personal Memoirs of U. S. Grant*, I:568-9.
2 Dana, *Recollections of the Civil War*, 105.
3 *OR*, I:27:II:520-1.
4 Ibid., I:26:I:183.
5 Ibid., I:26:I:617.
6 One of the author's great-grandfathers, William Jasper Small, was a private in the 20th Kentucky, later a lieutenant in the 48th Kentucky Mounted Infantry.
7 Alston, "Morgan's Cavalrymen Sweep Through Kentucky," in *B&G*,

680.
8. Ibid., 681.
9. James A. Ramage, *Rebel Raider: The Life of General John Hunt Morgan*, Lexington KY, 1986, 164.
10. Alston, "Morgan's Cavalrymen Sweep Through Kentucky," in *B&G*, 681.
11. *OR*, I:23:I:694.
12. Ibid., I:24:III:482.
13. Ibid., II:6:84.
14. Ibid., II:6:85.
15. Ibid., I:27:III:554.
16. Ibid., I:27:III:555. Both messages.
17. Coco, *A Strange and Blighted Land*, 39.
18. *OR*, I:27:III:555.
19. Ibid., I:27:III:557.
20. Ibid., I:27:III:557-8.
21. Ibid., I:27:III:558.
22. Wittenberg, Petruzzi and Nugent, *One Continuous Fight*, 87. Both quotes.
23. Ibid., 89. Emphasis in the source.
24. *OR*, I:27:III:559.
25. Ibid.
26. Ibid., I:27:III:560-1.
27. Ibid., I:27:I:81. Both messages.
28. Ibid., I:27:I:80-1.
29. Ibid., I:27:III:561-2.
30. Wittenberg, Petruzzi and Nugent, *One Continuous Fight*, 149.
31. Ibid., 145.
32. *OR*, I:27:III:577.
33. Ibid., I:27:III:578-9..
34. Ibid., I:27:III:577-8.
35. Ibid., I:27:III:579-80.
36. Barnett Schecter, *The Devil's Own Work*, 27.
37. Wittenberg, Petruzzi and Nugent, *One Continuous Fight*, 156.
38. *OR*, I:27:I:995.
39. Wittenberg, Petruzzi and Nugent, *One Continuous Fight*, 115.
40. Ibid., 132.
41. Ibid., 137.
42. Ibid., 135.
43. Imboden, "The Confederate Retreat from Gettysburg, *B&L* III:428.
44. Brown, *Retreat from Gettysburg*, 253.
45. Wittenberg, Petruzzi and Nugent, *One Continuous Fight*, 141.
46. Brown, *Retreat from Gettysburg*, 271.
47. Carl Sandburg, *Abraham Lincoln: The War Years, 1861-1864*, 356.
48. Kenneth P. Williams, *Lincoln Finds a General*, II:732-3.
49. Basler, ed., *Collected Works of Abraham Lincoln*, VI:318.

CHAPTER 20
"If General Meade Can Complete His Work"
7 – 9 July 1863

GENERAL LEE WROTE TO President Davis from Hagerstown the next day, Tuesday, 7 July, and tried to put the best possible face on his defeat and retreat: "Finding the [Union] position too strong to be carried, and being much hindered in collecting necessary supplies for the army by the numerous bodies of local and other troops which watched the passes, I determined to withdraw to the west side of the mountains. This has been safely accomplished with great labor, and the army is now in the vicinity of this place. One of my reasons for moving in this direction after crossing the mountains, was to protect our trains with the sick and wounded, which had been sent back to Williamsport, and which were threatened by the enemy's cavalry. Our advance reached here yesterday afternoon in time to support our cavalry in repulsing an attempt of the enemy to reach our trains.

"Before leaving Gettysburg, such of the sick and wounded as could be removed were sent back to Williamsport, but the rains that have interfered so much with our general movements have so swollen the Potomac as to render it unfordable, and they are still on the north side. Arrangements are being made to ferry them over today. We captured at Gettysburg about six thousand prisoners, besides the wounded that remained in our hands after the engagements of the 1st & 2d. Fifteen hundred of these prisoners and the wounded were paroled, but I suppose that under the late arrangements these paroles will not be regarded. The rest have been sent to Williamsport where they will cross. We were obliged to leave a large number of our wounded who were unable to travel, and many arms that had been collected on the field at Gettysburg."[1]

He went on to name a few more generals who had been killed or wounded who had not been mentioned in his letter of 4 July, and mentioned that Union cavalry had captured about 40 wagons of Ewell's train – but did not mention the ones that were destroyed – and that Stuart had driven back an attack by Union cavalry the day before, there at Hagerstown. Conspicuous by its absence is any mention of where he would go or what he would do next, but Lee had his engineers out examining the countryside for the best defensive positions. He made his own headquarters about two and a half miles down the road toward Williamsport.

Lee's Union prisoners, still guarded by what was left of Pickett's Division, were finally halted south of Leitersburg at about 2 a.m. on the seventh. They had been allowed only two brief halts on the sixth, during which they had been given small amounts of flour as their rations. They were roused again at dawn on the seventh, but had to wait for some of Ewell's corps to pass before taking to the road again. They reached Hagerstown at about 10 a.m., where they were cheered by the loyal residents as they marched through, and finally halted about a mile north of Williamsport, where they received another meager ration of flour and meat. "It may appear grand and delightful to talk of soldiering," one of Pickett's men wrote home, "but the reality, sleeping in a mud hole the rain wetting to the skin, with but a filthy saddle blanket to keep out the cold, is exactly the reverse."[2]

Ewell's 2nd Corps set out at dawn on the seventh and marched through a pouring rain through Leitersburg to Hagerstown, where it made camp just northwest of the town. The famished soldiers ransacked the stores and houses of Hagerstown for anything they could eat or drink. Lee ordered guards posted, but they were not very effective. A couple of Mississippi regiments found a large supply of whiskey and got very drunk. An officer of one of the regiments who tried to stop this was shot by a man from the other regiment.

At Williamsport that day, 700 cattle and more than 1,000 sheep, being driven across the ford, were swept downstream by the swift current and drowned. Their carcasses could be seen lining the river as far downstream as Harper's Ferry and Sandy Hook. Others were able to swim across to the West Virginia side.

At 2:30 a.m., Baldy Smith wrote to Seth Williams of Meade's staff from Newman's Gap, three miles west of Cashtown, saying that he had received the order to move to Gettysburg: "Two [paroled] officers of the First Corps, who left the enemy last night near Waynesborough, have reached me, and report the enemy in rapid retreat, and nearly out of artillery ammunition. They also report that the rebels said D. H. Hill and Beauregard were both on the other side of the Potomac, with heavy reinforcements. I had thought of going on to the next gap to-morrow, if I got no orders, but shall begin the march to Gettysburg in the morning. Yesterday my command was re-enforced by about 2,500 men."[3] However, at 5 a.m., Pleasonton, in his capacity as acting chief of staff, wrote to Smith: "Major-General Meade desires me to say you can continue the pursuit of the enemy; that he only needs one regiment to guard the property and wounded at Gettysburg, for which he has sent to General Couch, supposing you were on the way to Chambersburg. The army is concentrating at Middletown. You can join it there, after pushing the enemy to the best advantage."[4] So Smith's militia moved south that day, again staying close to the mountain passes.

At 4 a.m., Irvin Gregg, who had been following in Imboden's wake, reported to Cavalry Corps headquarters from the Caledonia Iron Works, near the western outlet of Cashtown Gap, just north of where Smith had spent the night: "My advance came up with the enemy's rear at 7 p.m. last night. My horses were too much broken down to push him. I think his train is stuck in the mud between this and Greencastle. Will follow him up this morning, and engage him."[5]

While Gregg's brigade cautiously followed Imboden and Fitz Lee down the Cumberland Valley Turnpike, Neill's combined-arms force followed Lee's infantry through the mountains, at a safe distance, and the various corps of the Army of the Potomac finally took up the march that Meade had originally planned for two days earlier. Pontoons that Meade had requested were on their way to Harper's Ferry, some via the B&O Railroad, others via the C&O canal. Union supply wagons began to reach Frederick on the afternoon of the seventh, and until meeting up with them there, or nearby, the soldiers marched through more rain and more mud, most of them without rations, and many of them losing or wearing out their shoes. The 12th Corps marched 32 miles that day. But a Union chaplain claimed that "every man is enthusiastic at the hope of overtaking Lee before he crosses the Potomac, and at once and forever finishing up the rebellion."[6] When Meade reached Frederick that day, he was greeted enthusiastically by the local citizens, and the ladies of the town presented him with bouquets of flowers. At Bealsville a group of school girls, all dressed in stars and stripes and waving a flag, sang "The Battle Cry of Freedom" as the men of the 1st Corps marched past.

Meanwhile, Buford and Kilpatrick gave up their hopes of taking Williamsport and decided to break contact with the Rebels, but, at dawn, Colonel Devin sent a squadron of the 6th New York Cavalry to probe back up the road toward Williamsport. It drove in the Confederate pickets, only to soon be pushed back to Devin's main body, near St. James College. Devin fell back to the east about two and a half miles, where he formed a line to protect the rest of Buford's and Kilpatrick's cavalry while they crossed to the east side of Antietam Creek. It was about 11 a.m. by the time Confederate infantry and artillery approached Devin's position, and by then most of the Union horsemen were across the stream. Most of Devin's brigade soon followed, with the 9th New York Cavalry fighting a lively rear-guard action. Once across the creek, Devin posted two dismounted squadrons on a hill overlooking the bridge, the Rebels gave up their pursuit, and the Federals made camp near the old Antietam battlefield, except for the 6th U.S. Cavalry, or what was left of it, which was sent to reconnoiter back up the National Road toward Funkstown. Near there, these Regulars ran into Grumble Jones's 7th Virginia Cavalry, the same regiment they had fought at Fairfield four days before.

Two companies of the Virginians charged the leading Federals and drove them back, wounding their commander, a captain. His second in command, a mere lieutenant, took over, and began an orderly retreat back down the National Road, but this eventually broke down as the Confederates pressed them, and when they came to a narrow bridge high over a swollen stream all order was lost, and many men and horses were pushed over the side into the water by the press of too many bodies trying to cross the bridge at the same time. The Rebels pursued them right up to Buford's camp, where they fired one volley and then fell back the way they had come.

Soon, however, they were galloping to get away, with the 6th Pennsylvania Cavalry in hot pursuit, and the Confederates' horses were so tired from chasing the Regulars that the Pennsylvanians soon caught up with them. Then followed a running mounted saber fight that was ended only when the Virginians were reinforced by more of Jones's men, and the Pennsylvanians, in turn, gave up the chase. Jones felt that the 7th Virginia had thus made up for its poor showing at Fairfield, and claimed 66 prisoners taken. It rained again that night, but because a Confederate night attack was feared, the troopers of the 6th Pennsylvania stayed awake all night, standing in knee-deep mud at their horses' heads, ready to mount at an instant's notice, soaked to the skin. One Federal noted in his diary that a Baltimore newspaper called "Lee's retreat a rout and the capture of his army a certainty," but added, "I don't see it."[7]

At 1:20 p.m., Baldy Smith reported to General Couch that Meade no longer wanted him to go to Gettysburg and said that he was now moving toward Waynesborough. At 1:30 p.m. Captain William Boyd of the 1st New York Cavalry reported to Couch that he had just reached Chambersburg from Waynesborough and had 44 prisoners. Boyd's company, augmented by other detachments, had been acting independently, and doing very good service, since Lee had swept through the Shenandoah, first in delaying the Confederate advance into Pennsylvania, and now in pursuing the retreat. "Have captured, since I left Harrisburg," he reported, "7 wagons, 29 mules, 52 horses, and 165 prisoners." Couch replied, "It is said that there are a great many [Confederate] stragglers in the mountains northeast of Chambersburg. See that they don't get to the front."[8]

Sometime during that day, Couch sent orders to Colonel Pierce, at Loudon, at the western edge of the Cumberland Valley, due west of Chambersburg, for him to communicate with Boyd and told Pierce, "The enemy are in full retreat, but probably a large cavalry force will cover their rear. Have your infantry in such position along the mountain roads as to support your cavalry, and whip any force of horse sent against you." Pierce replied at midnight that a scout sent to Clear Spring, only 6 miles from Williamsport, had contacted a friendly civilian, known to Pierce, who reported that Imboden was at Williamsport with 5,000 wagons guarded by 7,000 men and 16 pieces of artillery, and had beaten off one attack (he thought by French). "The Potomac is still rising," he said, "the rains being heavy in all the region clear to Hancock [Maryland]." He suggested sending some of his infantry down to the mountains overlooking Clear Spring, which he thought would be "sufficient to check the enemy in any attempt to take their trains in the direction of Hancock. I will send my cavalry as near Hagerstown, or in that direction, as prudent regard for safety of the command will permit. I think an advance by General Kelley's force, via Hancock, upon Clear Spring would be of infinite service in the capture of Lee's forces."[9]

Halleck was also thinking about Kelley's forces in West Virginia that day. He telegraphed General W. T. H. Brooks, commander of forces in western Pennsylvania: "All available troops in your department should be sent by Grafton

[W. Va.], to co-operate with General Kelley on the enemy's flank. Report how many you can send, and when they leave." Brooks replied that night: "There are 650 six-months' volunteers in camp here, all armed and equipped. Also 2,500 three-months' militia that can be ready to move to-morrow night."[10] Some 5,000 of Kelley's men reached Hancock, on the evening of 7 July, ready to dispute any attempt by the Confederates to retreat in that direction. But they were still some twenty miles west of Williamsport, thus not yet in position to attack Lee's supply line, as ordered by Halleck two days before.

At 3 p.m., General Halleck informed Meade: "It gives me great pleasure to inform you that you have been appointed a brigadier-general in the Regular Army, to rank from July 3, the date of your brilliant victory at Gettysburg."[11] He was already a major general of volunteers, but in the Regular Army until this promotion he had been only a major of Topographical Engineers. (Lee often referred to him as "Major Meade.") While the war lasted, the promotion would not mean much, but it would mean a great deal when the war ended and the volunteer forces were disbanded. Halleck did not mention the fact that he had recommended the promotion to Secretary of War Stanton, nor that he had also recommended Grant for promotion to major general in the Regular Army, one grade higher than Meade, which recommendation had also been approved.

At 3:10 p.m. Meade wired Halleck from Frederick: "General Buford reports that he attacked Williamsport yesterday, but found it guarded by a large force of infantry and artillery. Heavy forces were coming into Williamsport all night. French having destroyed their bridges, and the river being unfordable, they are crossing in country flat-boats – a slow operation. My army will be assembling to-day and to-morrow at Middletown. I will immediately move on Williamsport. Should the enemy succeed in crossing the river before I can reach him, I should like to have your views on subsequent operations – whether to follow up the army in the Valley, or cross below and nearer Washington." He added a postscript at 4 p.m., saying, "An officer of the cavalry from the front reports the enemy's army as occupying Hagerstown and Williamsport, and guarding their artillery and trains, which they cannot cross. So soon as my command is supplied and their trains up, I shall move."[12]

Sometime during the seventh, Halleck sent a message to Frederick, to be delivered to either Meade or French, asking, "What force has been sent to Maryland Heights, and how many have reached there? It seems to me, at the present, to be a most important point, and should be held with force sufficient to prevent its occupation by the enemy. Should his crossing above be impossible, he will probably attempt to take and hold that position until he can make the passage."[13]

Also at 4 p.m., Meade acknowledged his promotion and informed Halleck: "Maryland Heights are at present occupied by [Brigadier General John R.] Kenly's brigade, 1,700 men. Three thousand additional men and two batteries of artillery left here this morning for that place. No indications of the enemy this side of Williamsport and Hagerstown. The bridge at Harper's Ferry was rendered impassable at both sides by General French."[14] Kenly's Maryland Brigade (four regiments of Maryland infantry) was part of French's division of the 8th Corps (Middle Department) and had been guarding bridges over the Monocacy river and ferries on the Potomac. It had reoccupied Maryland Heights at around 11 that morning, after a sharp skirmish with a few Rebels.

Also sometime that day, with the Army of the Potomac then moving into French's area around Frederick, Meade's headquarters issued orders transferring French's troops (including Brigadier General W. L. Elliott's command just arrived from Washington, but not including Kenly's brigade) to the 3rd Corps and appointing French to command that corps, replacing the wounded General Sickles. Meade's headquarters also issued a circular that day, saying: "The commanding general has received information, deemed reliable, that the enemy has not yet recrossed the river in any considerable force. He therefore desires that corps commanders keep the troops well in hand, and prepared to move to the South Mountain Pass at a moment's notice."[15]

Warren, as acting chief of staff, wrote to General Couch at 4:40 p.m., saying: "An order was sent this morning to General Smith to continue the pursuit of the enemy to the best advantage, and not to go to Gettysburg. The Potomac River is now bank full at Williamsport, and there is no bridge. General Buford attempted to take Williamsport yesterday. The enemy's infantry compelled him to retire. There are a good many wagons at Williamsport. Troops and wagons are being ferried over very slowly in two flat-boats. The main army of the enemy has not crossed, and must fight us before he can cross."[16] Halleck later wired Meade, "I have seen your dispatch to General Couch of 4.40 p.m. You are perfectly right. Push forward, and fight Lee before he can cross the Potomac."[17]

Imboden did, in fact, now have a second flat, or ferry boat, which his men had constructed. It was attached to a cable run across the river upstream from the mouth of Conococheague Creek. But, of course, this was still not nearly enough to make more than a dent in the number of wagons and ambulances collecting around Williamsport. Some of the wounded men never made it across the Potomac, having died while waiting. On the other hand, more wounded were added to the column by the fighting of the sixth. Meanwhile, the large number of horses, cattle, sheep, and pigs accumulated in the relatively small area caused an awful stench, and attracted thousands of flies.

At 8:45 p.m., Halleck wired Meade: "You have given the enemy a stunning blow at Gettysburg. Follow it up, and give him another before he can reach the Potomac. When he crosses, circumstances will determine whether it will be best to pursue him by the Shenandoah Valley or this side of the Blue Ridge. There is strong evidence that he is short of artillery ammunition, and, if vigorously pressed, he must suffer."[18]

Late that night, General Neil, commanding the all-arms

force left to follow Lee's army, reported to Warren: "I marched my command from Fairfield to Waynesborough to-day, and just missed capturing the rear guard of Lee's army, which left at 10 a.m. this morning. The whole of the rebel army is by this time at least as far as Hagerstown. I cannot overhaul them to-night, but will push them toward Hagerstown to-morrow. The whole of the rebel army have taken the pike toward Hagerstown, and I believe they are making rapidly, but in tolerably good order, toward Williamsport. Captain [George C.] Cram, now prisoner of war at Monterey, states that the discipline of the enemy seems to be very much relaxed. In the last two days I have taken a great many prisoners, or, rather, deserters, from the rebels."[19] The citizens of Waynesborough lined the sidewalks to present Neill's weary men with meat, buttered bread, pies and such, and then sent to Chambersburg for flour to bake more bread.

The various corps of the Army of the Potomac made hard marches on the seventh, through clinging mud and off-and-on rain. One division of the 11th Corps reached the point that Meade had chosen for concentrating his army, Middletown, after a day's march of 25 miles, "Which is pretty good," a member of Howard's cavalry escort opined, "considering half the men were bare footed and had marched every day for a Month."[20] The other two divisions were back up the road, stuck in the mud. The 1st Corps covered 35 miles in 17 hours of marching, finally calling a halt at 9 p.m. in the dark and rain up on the side of South Mountain near the hamlet of Hamburg. The 6th Corps was nearby, and the 5th not far to the northeast. The 2nd Corps marched from Two Taverns to Taneytown, and the 12th from Littlestown to Walkersville. The 3rd Corps marched through Emmitsburg to Mechanicstown, leaving Gettysburg to the dead, the wounded, the surgeons, and the burial parties.

The first news of Vicksburg's surrender reached Washington at about noon on 7 July by way of a dispatch from Admiral Porter, commander of the gunboats on the upper Mississippi, to the Navy Department. Navy Secretary Welles immediately headed for the White House, where he found Lincoln, Secretary of the Treasury Salmon Chase, and others tracing Grant's movements on a map. Lincoln immediately rose and said he would go and personally telegraph the news to General Meade. He took his hat, but then looked down at Welles and said, "What can we do for the Secretary of the Navy for this glorious intelligence? He is always giving us good news. I cannot, in words, tell you my joy over this result. It is great, Mr. Welles, it is great!" As the two men walked over to the War Department to send the telegram, Lincoln remarked that the surrender of Vicksburg would relieve General Banks, then besieging Port Hudson while trying to hang onto New Orleans, and added, "It will inspire me."[21]

So, sometime during that day, Meade receive a telegram for Halleck that said: "I have received from the President the following note, which I respectfully communicate: 'Major-General Halleck: We have certain information that Vicksburg has surrendered to General Grant on the 4th of July. Now, if General Meade can complete his work, so gloriously prosecuted thus far, by the literal or substantial destruction of Lee's army, the rebellion will be over. Yours truly, A. Lincoln."[22]

Halleck also wired General Rosecrans, at Tullahoma, Tennessee: "We have just received official information that Vicksburg surrendered to General Grant on the 4th of July. Lee's army is overthrown; Grant victorious. You and your noble army now have the chance to give the finishing blow to the rebellion. Will you neglect the chance?" Rosecrans took umbrage at this, and replied: "You do not appear to observe the fact that this noble army has driven the rebels from Middle Tennessee, of which my dispatches advised you. I beg in behalf of this army that the War Department may not overlook so great an event because it is not written in blood."[23] In a message written to Rosecrans that same day, General Thomas, Rosecrans' senior corps commander, noted:

"But for the rains our success would have been as complete as Meade's or Grant's, but we have been eminently successful in driving the enemy from his two strongholds by a maneuver which cost us but a few men, while his loss is as great in number as if he had fought a grand battle, in addition to which his army is in a completely demoralized condition."[24]

That evening celebrants gathered outside the White House to serenade the President, and Lincoln made a few remarks that show that his future Gettysburg Address was already beginning to take shape in his mind: "How long ago is it?" he asked, rhetorically, "– eighty odd years – since on the Fourth of July for the first time in the history of the world a nation by its representatives, assembled and declared as a self-evident truth that 'all men are created equal.' That was the birthday of the United States of America." He went on to list a number of other events that had occurred on a fourth day of a July, then added, "and now, on this last Fourth of July just passed, when we have a gigantic Rebellion, at the bottom of which is an effort to overthrow the principle that all men were created equal, we have a surrender of a most powerful position and army on that very day, and not only so, but in a succession of battles in Pennsylvania . . . on the 4th the cohorts of those who opposed the declaration that all men are created equal, 'turned tail' and run." This was followed by long and continued cheers. Then he added, "Gentlemen, this is a glorious theme, and the occasion for a speech, but I am not prepared to make one worthy of the occasion."[25] It would take several months of thought, but when the speech finally came it too would make history.

General Banks, down at Port Hudson, only learned the good news about Vicksburg at 10:45 that same morning, when the *General Price*, a wooden gunboat the Federals had captured from the Rebels some months back, brought Colonel T. Kilby Smith of Grant's staff down the river. Cheers soon filled the air as the news was passed down the Union lines, and a

Federal colonel wrapped his copy of the announcing dispatch around a stick and threw it into the Confederate trenches. Other Federals shouted the news across to the Rebels, who shouted back that it was "another damned Yankee lie."[26] Union musicians soon filled the air with patriotic tunes, and Banks ordered a salute of 100 shotted guns to be fired. He also wrote an immediate reply to Grant, congratulating him. "It is the most important event of the war," he said, "and will contribute most to the re-establishment of the Government. The freedom of the Mississippi puts an end to the rebellion, so far as an independent Confederacy in concerned. There is no room for an independent government between the Mississippi and the Atlantic. Port Hudson will be in our possession before the close of this week."[27]

Eventually an official copy of Grant's dispatch, sent by Banks, reached the Confederate commander, Major General Franklin Gardner, and he immediately called for his senior officers to meet him at his headquarters. That night they held a council of war and decided that they should ask Banks what terms he would offer for their surrender. Meanwhile, Banks' adjutant sent a copy of Grant's dispatch down the Mississippi to General Emory at New Orleans, reassuring him that he didn't think that city was in immediate danger and that Banks' army would soon be finished with Port Hudson.

In Washington, General Halleck was also writing to Emory that day, in response to an appeal for reinforcements that Emory had sent north on 5 July: "General Grant has been urged to send all possible assistance to General Banks. General Gillmore, commanding Department of the South, was ordered, on the 5th instant, to send all his available forces to New Orleans. All drafted men in the Eastern States have been ordered to New Orleans as fast as they can be collected. The law of the draft is so complicated and defective, and the machinery of enrollment so cumbersome, that it works slowly."[28]

Word of Vicksburg's surrender also reached Confederate General J. G. Walker that day. Walker commanded a division stationed at Delhi, Louisiana, a few miles west of the Mississippi, not far from Vicksburg. He had started his forces that morning toward Ashton, on the river, where he hoped to place artillery so that it could interdict Union transports and supply boats, when he was met by a staff officer who brought him the information, "derived from sources that I did not wholly credit. . . ," he later reported. "Not considering this entirely certain, I continued my movements, but the same day I received the intelligence unfortunately too well authenticated to admit of a doubt. At the same time I received instructions from Lieutenant-General [Kirby] Smith to return to [Delhi], and if forced to abandon the Washita Valley by superior numbers, to fall back to Red River or Natchitoches."[29]

At Vicksburg that day (7 July), the Confederates were still in the process of being paroled. General McPherson wrote to General Pemberton that day: "I am constrained, in consequence of the abuse of the privilege which was granted to [Confederate] officers to take out one private servant (colored) each, to withdraw it altogether, except in cases of families and sick and disabled officers. The abuses which I speak of are:

1. Officers coming here with their servants, and intimidating them, instead of sending them by themselves to be questioned.

2. Citizens have been seen and heard in the streets urging negroes who were evidently not servants to go with the officers.

3. Negroes have been brought here who have been at work on the fortifications."

In a separate message, McPherson told Pemberton: "With regard to any portion of your command who refuse to be paroled, they will have to be placed under guard and sent north as prisoners of war, to be confined in such places as the General Government may direct. Major-General Grant directs me to state that not one of them will be sent north as prisoners of war until the whole of your command who accept paroles have marched out."[30] In his memoirs, Grant wrote: "Several hundred refused to sign their paroles, preferring to be sent to the North as prisoners to being sent back to fight again. Others again kept out of the way, hoping to escape either alternative. Pemberton appealed to me in person to compel these men to sign their paroles, but I declined. It also leaked out that many of the men who had signed their paroles, intended to desert and go to their homes as soon as they got out of our lines. Pemberton hearing this, again appealed to me to assist him. He wanted arms for a battalion, to act as guards in keeping his men together while being marched to a camp of instruction, where he expected to keep them until exchanged. This request was also declined. It was precisely what I expected and hoped that they would do. I told him, however, that I would see that they marched beyond our lines in good order."[31]

Major General Stephen A. Hurlbut, commander of the 16th Corps in Grant's Department of the Tennessee and of the garrisons in West Tennessee and northern Mississippi, forwarded a message to Grant's headquarters that day from a Union colonel with the information that one of Pemberton's division commanders, Major General John S. Bowen, had broken a previous parole, given to the late Brigadier General Nathaniel Lyon after having been captured near St. Louis two years before. Bowen, however, had contracted an illness during the siege and was not detained. He died six days later at Raymond, Mississippi. Hurlbut also claimed that Confederate General Price, having been repulsed at Helena, Arkansas, was now trying to cross the Mississippi River and link up with Confederates in northern Mississippi. He asked for the return of one of his divisions from Vicksburg to oppose this, if it could be spared. Brigadier General Grenville Dodge (later the chief construction engineer of the Union Pacific Railroad) was appointed by Hurlbut that day to command what was known as the Left Wing of the 16th Corps, with headquarters at Corinth, Mississippi. He replaced Major General Richard Oglesby, who was suffering from old wounds.

Meanwhile, Sherman was experiencing problems getting his pursuit of Joe Johnston going. He was near Bolton, Mississippi, that day, but had to issue orders cancelling his planned movement on to Clinton the next day because the 9th Corps had not yet arrived at Bolton. Instead, the 13th and 15th Corps were to go into camp while his small cavalry force probed toward Clinton, then north toward Brownsville, and thence back to camp.

In New York City on that seventh day of July, Horace Greeley's *Tribune*, a Republican newspaper, reprinted an anti-administration broadside that had appeared in many places throughout that city on the fourth. It was a manifesto denouncing the Federal government as despotic, and proclaiming that, "Should the Confederate army capture Washington and exterminate the herd of thieves, Pharisees, and cutthroats which pasture there, defiling the temple of our liberty, we should regard it as a special interposition of Divine Providence." It was signed "Spirit of '76." Greeley cited this as evidence that Copperheads "have for months conspired and plotted to bring about a revolution in the North," which was to coincide with Lee's invasion of Pennsylvania, timed for the Fourth of July, and which he believed had been prevented by Meade's victory at Gettysburg.[32]

In Kentucky, Morgan's raiders rode all night and all day on 7 July, except for brief halts to water and feed their horses, while Morgan detached a few companies here and there to confuse the Federals about his true route. A company sent to Danville had the two regiments of Michigan cavalry marching back and forth between that town and Lebanon and accomplishing nothing but wearing out their horses. Other Federals were puzzled that Morgan was not doing more damage to the L&N Railroad. Meanwhile, an advanced detachment of about 100 of Morgan's men rode into Brandenburg, on the Ohio River, that day and concealed themselves between buildings and trees by the wharf. At about 2 p.m., the steamboat *John T. McCombs* began to take on passengers, and the Rebels rushed on board and captured it. After robbing the passengers, they moved the boat to where it would appear to be aground and sent out distress signals when another steamboat, the *Alice Dean*, came along. When she stopped to help, they captured her as well, again robbing the passengers.

When Morgan's main column reached Brandenburg early on 8 July they found waiting for them not only the two officers who had been sent ahead to capture a boat, but also Captain Tom Hines, who was just returning from a small raid into Indiana himself, with only a dozen of the 80 men he had set off with. Colonel Basil Duke, Morgan's brother-in-law and commander of his 1st Brigade, found Hines at the wharf, "apparently the most listless, inoffensive youth that was ever imposed upon."[33] Unknown to Duke, Hines had been in Indiana primarily for the purpose of conferring with the Copperheads there. Innocent as he looked, Hines was one of the most daring officers in the Confederacy. Morgan promptly appointed Hines as the latest officer to command his scouts, the fourth to hold the position in less than a week.

Meanwhile, Hobson's pursuing Union cavalry, of about the same strength as Morgan's division, departed Bardstown at 7 a.m. and followed the Rebels' tracks, reaching Bardstown Junction on the L&N at about 5 p.m. and stopping there so that a train could bring them supplies from Louisville that night. Hobson sent word to Brigadier General Jeremiah Boyle, commander of the District of Kentucky, that Morgan was heading for Brandenburg, and asked that a gunboat be sent there to keep the Rebels from crossing the river to Indiana.

Morgan's crossing of the river, which began around midmorning, was immediately interrupted. The evening before, some civilians had gone downriver to Mauckport, Indiana, and reported Morgan's presence at Brandenburg to Colonel

William J. Irvin, of the Indiana militia. Irvin had immediately dispatched a messenger to inform Colonel Lewis Jordan, at Corydon, Indiana. He had also commandeered a steamboat to pick up a detachment of 30 home guards and a cannon and bring them to Mauckport, from which they marched to Morvin's Landing, directly opposite Brandenburg. There they were joined by Colonel John Timberlake and three militia companies (about 130 men) of the 6th Indiana Legion. Before Morgan could get a single man across the broad Ohio, these Hoosiers' lone gun put a crimp in his plans.

Colonel Irvin had ordered the gun's commander to direct his fire at the boilers and machinery of the two captured steamboats, which, had he done so, might have foiled Morgan right there, but Irvin was not on hand, and Colonel Timberlake had the gun fire on Morgan's men instead. The first shot took out several members of Dick Morgan's 14th Kentucky Cavalry, but the rest took cover in a ravine behind the town. Timberlake yelled across a demand for the Rebels to surrender, but the Rebels ignored it except to invite him to come over for a drink. He also had his infantry open fire, but the river was wide and the range much too long. Morgan's battery then deployed on the hill that held the court house on the Kentucky side, and when the fog on the river lifted the fire of its four guns soon drove the militiamen to cover, leaving their lone gun behind. Then the two captured steamers ferried two of Morgan's regiments across, minus their horses, and these troopers soon drove the militiamen out of the canyon they had taken cover in, and they retreated north toward Corydon.

But before any more of the raiders could be ferried across, the U.S.S. *Springfield,* one of a class of gunboats known as tinclads – armored well enough to stop small-arms fire, but not cannon fire – came steaming down the river. Armed with six 24-pounder boat howitzers, she was commanded by Acting Ensign Joseph Watson, and, for a while, Colonel Duke noted, Morgan was looking pretty nervous – the river and the gunboat separating him from the two regiments that had already crossed (and who were without horses), while every hour brought Hobson's pursuing cavalry that much closer. However, like the militia before him, Watson made the mistake of firing on Morgan's troops instead of on the captured steamboats. When Morgan's battery returned fire, it drove the *Springfield* back to where its howitzers could just barely reach the town, which, of course, minimized their accuracy. And, after exchanging fire with the battery for almost an hour and a half, it withdrew upstream around a bend.

However, about 5 p.m., with the ferrying well under way, the *Springfield* returned, accompanied by two transports bringing 500 Union infantrymen down from Louisville. When Morgan's battery opened fire again, the two transports lagged behind while the gunboat engaged the Rebel artillery. Meanwhile the two captured steamers continued their ferrying, and again Watson made the mistake of ignoring them while dueling with the battery. When the transports informed him that they could not find a suitable place to disembark their men, Watson gave up and steamed with them back to Louisville.

Meanwhile, Hobson was moving closer. "As soon as rations were issued, the pursuit was continued," Hobson later reported. His men rode all day on 8 July, and at about 7 p.m., he said, "I received information that Morgan had captured two boats, and was crossing his command into Indiana; also that a gunboat and transports with troops were at Rock Haven." He halted his column three miles from that place and twelve from Brandenburg and rode into Rock Haven to see if he could get the gunboat and the troops there to cooperate with him in a night attack on the Rebels at Brandenburg, but when he got there he found that the boats were gone. "The night being very dark, and my troops very much fatigued, I did not deem it prudent to attack the enemy with my force alone, as this point is capable of defense by a small force against vastly superior numbers."[34] Had he attacked, he would probably have captured the tail end of Morgan's forces, which finished crossing the river at about midnight.

From his headquarters near Hagerstown, Maryland, Lee wrote another report to President Davis on 8 July: "My letter of yesterday will have informed you of the position of this army. Though reduced in numbers by the hardships & battles through which it has passed since leaving the Rappahannock, its condition is good and its confidence unimpaired. Upon crossing the Potomac into Maryland, I had calculated upon the river remaining fordable during the summer, so as to enable me to recross at my pleasure, but a series of storms commencing the day after our entrance into Maryland has placed the river beyond fording stage, and the present storm will keep it so for at least a week. I shall therefore have to accept battle if the enemy offers it, whether I wish to or not, and as the result is in the hands of the Sovereign Ruler of the Universe, and known to Him only, I deem it prudent to make every arrangement in our power to meet any emergency that may arise. From information gathered from the papers, I believe that the troops from North Carolina and the coast of Virginia under Genls Foster & Dix have been ordered to the Potomac and that recently additional reinforcements have been sent from the coast of South Carolina to Genl Banks. If I am correct in my opinion this will liberate most of the troops in those regions, & should Your Excellency have not already done so, I earnestly recommend that all that can be spared be concentrated on the upper Rappahannock under Genl Beauregard, with directions to cross that river and make a demonstration upon Washington. This command will answer the double purpose of affording protection to the capital at Richmond & relieving the pressure upon this army.

"I hope Your Excellency will understand that I am not in the least discouraged, or that my faith in the protection of an all merciful Providence, or in the fortitude of this army, is at all shaken. But, though conscious that the enemy has been much shattered in the recent battle, I am aware that he can be easily reinforced, while no addition can be made to our numbers. The measure therefore that I have recommended is altogether one of a prudent nature."

He added, in a postscript: "I see it stated in a letter from a special correspondence of the *New York Times* that a bearer of despatches from Your Excellency to myself was captured at Hagerstown on the 2d July, & the despatches are said to be of the greatest importance, & to have a great bearing on 'coming events.' I have thought proper to mention this, that you many know whether it is so."[35]

Lee also wrote to General Pickett that day, whose division, with the prisoners, he wanted sent across the Potomac. "The present storm will place the Potomac beyond fording stage," he said, "and I fear you will have to rely upon the boats to pass over the wounded and prisoners. In sending forward the officers, send with them such a guard as will secure their safety, and Garnett's brigade might not be too large to take them to Winchester, but from that point to Staunton I should think a smaller guard would be sufficient. You can use the rest of your division in guarding the remaining prisoners to Winchester with one of the batteries, unless you think both necessary. But I do not wish the division to go further than Winchester. You must halt there, collect all your stragglers, convalescents, &c., and use every exertion to resuscitate the command. You will assume command at Winchester. I wish you to make every exertion to aid this army, by protecting its trains and coming to its assistance, if necessary. I do not think Corse can be spared at this time from his present position, and for the present you must rely for recruits upon your convalescents and absentees, which I hope you will gather in. After reaching Winchester with the prisoners you can arrange a guard to take them to Staunton, and to Richmond if necessary. Establish your headquarters at Winchester for the present, and get together your men as soon as practicable."[36] However, when Pickett's troops started to ferry the Union prisoners across the swollen river, the rope guiding the flat broke. Only the Union officers were taken across, on the other flat, and the enlisted men were marched back to their camp.

Lee and his officers of engineers conferred with his corps commanders and their engineers at his headquarters that eighth day of July, and then they all reconnoitered the area around Hagerstown and Williamsport, selecting a line of defense. Meanwhile, Lee sent Jeb Stuart with five brigades of his cavalry and five batteries of horse artillery, towards Boonsborough, to delay the Federals while he constructed his defenses, and to gather up more food and forage for Lee's men and animals. Robertson's Brigade stayed behind to guard the road leading east to Smithsburg, while the Maryland Cavalry Battalion patrolled the Cumberland Valley Turnpike, leading north, and Imboden's Brigade patrolled the road leading west, going as far as Clear Spring.

A Union Signal Corps station, atop the ruins of a monument in Turner's Gap, spotted Stuart's cavalry and sent word to General Buford, who had to hold Boonsborough so that Meade's infantry could cross South Mountain unmolested. Buford placed Gamble's 1st Brigade and a battery of horse artillery to the right of the National Road (which came down from Funkstown) just south of Beaver Creek, about a mile and a half out of Boonsboro; Devin's 2nd Brigade and another battery blocked the road from Williamsport; and Merritt's Reserve Brigade was placed between those two. Kilpatrick's division was held in reserve east of Boonsboro, meanwhile gathering food and fodder from the local area. "For five days we had been without forage for our horses, and in almost constant motion," a member of Merritt's brigade later complained.[37] A heavy rain had fallen all night but stopped near daybreak, allowing the men to dry their soaked clothes and blankets.

Grumble Jones's Confederates, leading Stuart's column, came down the National Road and spotted Gamble's Federals. Jones sent his men forward dismounted, supported by one battery of horse artillery, which opened fire at about 10 a.m. Three more brigades and three more batteries remained mounted behind Jones, waiting to see what developed, while foraging teams from all four brigades fanned out to gather up all the grain and hay they could find and take some of the grain to mills along Antietam Creek to be ground into flour. Stuart then moved up his other brigades, also dismounted, "the ground being entirely too soft from recent rains to operate successfully with cavalry," as he later reported, and slowly drove Gamble's and Merritt's men back towards Boonsboro.[38]

Meanwhile, Ferguson's brigade, coming along the Williamsport road, found its way blocked by Devin's Union troopers two miles west of Boonsboro. Ferguson posted his men behind a stone fence, and placed a battery on some high ground that dominated the area. Devin sent the 6th New York Cavalry (his own regiment) to take a hill on the left of the road, but the Rebel battery drove it back. At around 2 p.m. the Confederates attacked, and Devin dismounted two regiments to hold them, with, as he later reported "varying success, sometimes being forced back and again regaining their lost ground. I was obliged to relieve those engaged with others as their ammunition became expended, so that by 5.30 p.m. my whole command had been engaged, and I had not a dozen cartridges left. I was, therefore, obliged to retire the brigade, after notifying General Kilpatrick of my action."[39]

Kilpatrick's division had already come up to support Buford's. He had notified General Pleasonton, mistakenly, that Buford was about to withdraw to the mountain pass and that "I shall hold the town as long as possible, and then retire, fighting, on Buford."[40] This caused Meade's headquarters to order the 1st and 11th Corps to the top of the pass and the 6th Corps to their support. But in the meantime, Richmond's 1st Brigade of Kilpatrick's division reinforced the Union center and found the Rebels there in the cover of trees and large rocks. Richmond deployed one regiment as dismounted skirmishers, and ordered three pieces of horse artillery to shell the woods. When the Confederates pulled back, Richmond ordered the 1st Vermont Cavalry to charge down the pike while he took two other regiments and one gun on the left of the pike "in pursuit of the fleeing enemy, who made such excellent time that it was impossible for me again to engage him," he later reported.[41]

On the Union right, the 5th Michigan Cavalry of Custer's brigade, fighting dismounted over the muddy fields, had driven Jones's men back for a while, but then they were stopped by a Confederate battery. Buford called for one of Gamble's regiments, but Gamble insisted on using his entire brigade. His dismounted skirmishers, yelling like Indians and followed closely by Buford himself, were enough, however, to drive the Rebels back, probably due to the Confederate center giving way. Stuart withdrew his brigades behind Beaver Creek and, after dark, fell back another two miles towards Funkstown, while Ferguson's brigade withdrew to its former position near Williamsport. Both sides felt they had accomplished their objectives: Stuart to keep the Union cavalry too busy to interfere with the entrenching of Lee's infantry and artillery; Buford and Kilpatrick to keep the pass over South Mountain open and protect the arriving columns of Union infantry. "I have had a very rough day of it," Buford admitted to Cavalry Corps headquarters in a message written that night and forwarded to Meade's headquarters the next day. After briefly describing his fight and complaining that the 11th Corps had interfered with his supply wagons, he added, "The river is 5 feet higher than before, and rising," noted that plenty of "rebs" could be found between Hagerstown and Williamsport, and closed with "Hurrah for Vicksburg."[42]

Part of the 11th Corps crossed the mountain during the day, which is what interfered with Buford's wagons. Howard reported to Meade's headquarters: "My column left camp at 3.30 p.m., and arrived at the top of the mountain at 5.20. General Buford applying for support, I sent General Schurz's division, and one battery, now posted on the first ridge beyond Boonsborough. The enemy were retiring before General Buford at sunset."[43] He closed his message with a request for 3,000 pairs of shoes.

The rest of the 11th Corps and all of the 1st moved into Turner's Gap up on South Mountain that evening of the eighth. At the top of Catoctin Mountain, General Robinson had gathered his division of the 1st Corps around him and read them the dispatches announcing the fall of Vicksburg. "I propose three cheers for Grant and his army," he told them, "feeling assured that while we shout their victories from this mountain top, they are shouting our victory along the Mississippi Valley."[44] Their energy thus refreshed, the men resumed their march.

Meade moved his headquarters to Middletown that day, and the 5th and 6th Corps reached there as well, where they received new clothing and the first decent meal they had had in days. Then, after a short rest, the 6th Corps marched another five miles that afternoon. The roads were still extremely bad, so the men marched through the fields. The 6th Corps' batteries were stuck in the mud up on the mountain between Frederick and Middletown, their horses broken down and unable to haul the guns. The supply wagons didn't even try to cross the mountain that day. The 2nd and 3rd Corps were back near Frederick, while the 12th Corps swung farther south and camped that night near Jefferson, several miles south of Middletown. An officer in Gregg's 2nd Division of the Cavalry Corps, then on its way to Middletown, noted that it was near there that the army, then under General McClellan, had fought and won the battle of South Mountain the previous year, on its way to the larger battle of Antietam. "Meade's army is moving rapidly and I hope will compel Lee to fight again in Maryland. He is not moving at the rate of six miles a day as the young Napoleon [meaning McClellan] did, but twenty, and that, too, after fighting one of the hardest contested battles of the war."[45]

At 10:30 a.m. on the 8th, while the cavalry was fighting, Meade wired Halleck: "I have ordered General Naglee, with the eight regiments of his command, to Harper's Ferry, to re-enforce General Kenly and to assume command. This will make a force of between 6,000 and 7,000 men. He is directed to hold his command in readiness to move forward to my support, if required. I have also sent a bridge train there, with an engineer party, the bridge to be thrown over only when any command, cavalry or other, should arrive there to cross. I leave the Seventh New York Regiment and a battery of six pieces to defend this depot against raids."[46] The same order that sent Brigadier General Henry M. Naglee to Harper's Ferry appointed Major General A. A. Humphreys, formerly the commander of the 2nd Division of the 3rd Corps, as Meade's new chief of staff, but he would not be able to reach headquarters and take up his new responsibilities until late that night.

At 2 p.m. Meade wrote to Halleck again: "General Couch learns from scouts that the train at Williamsport is crossing very slowly. So long as the river is unfordable, the enemy cannot cross. My cavalry report that they had a fight near Funkstown, through which they drove the enemy to Hagerstown, where a large infantry force was seen. From all I can gather, the enemy extends from Hagerstown to Williamsport, covering the march of their train. Their cavalry and infantry pickets are advanced to the Hagerstown and Sharpsburg pike, on the general line of the Antietam. We hold Boonsborough, and our pickets, 4 miles in front, toward Hagerstown, are in contact with the enemy's pickets. My army is assembling slowly. The rains of yesterday and last night have made all roads but pikes almost impassable. Artillery and wagons are stalled; it will take time to collect them together. A large portion of the men are barefooted. Shoes will arrive at Frederick to-day, and will be issued as soon as possible. The spirit of the army is high; the men are ready and willing to make every exertion to push forward. Be assured I most earnestly desire to try the fortunes of war with the enemy on this side of the river, hoping through Providence and the bravery of my men to settle the question, but I should do wrong not to frankly tell you of the difficulties encountered. I expect to find the enemy in a strong position, well covered with artillery, and I do not desire to imitate his example at Gettysburg, and assault a position where the chances were so greatly against success. I wish in advance to moderate the expectations of those who, in ignorance of the difficulties to be encountered, may expect too much. All that I can do under the circumstances I pledge this army to do."[47]

Meade, like the rest of his army, was being worn down. He wrote in a letter to his wife that night: "From the time I took command till to-day, now over ten days, I have not changed my clothes, have not had a regular night's rest, and many nights not a wink of sleep, and for several days did not even wash my face and hands, no regular food, and all the time in a great state of mental anxiety."[48]

To add to that anxiety, Halleck wrote to Meade that day, "There is reliable information that the enemy is crossing at Williamsport. The opportunity to attack his divided forces should not be lost. The President is urgent and anxious that your army should move against him by forced marches."[49] Meade replied at 3 p.m.: "My information as to the crossing of the enemy does not agree with that just received in your dispatch. His whole force is in position between Funkstown and Williamsport. I have just received information that he has driven my cavalry force in front of Boonsborough. My army is and has been making forced marches, short of rations, and barefooted. One corps marched yesterday and last night over 30 miles. I take occasion to repeat that I will use my utmost efforts to push forward this army."[50]

To this Halleck replied: "Do not understand me as expressing any dissatisfaction; on the contrary, your army has done most nobly. I only wish to give you opinions formed from information received here. It is telegraphed from near Harper's Ferry that the enemy have been crossing for the last two days. It is also reported that they have a bridge across. If Lee's army is so divided by the river, the importance of attacking the part on this side is incalculable. Such an opportunity may never occur again. If, on the contrary, he has massed his whole force on the Antietam, time must be taken to also concentrate your forces. Your opportunities for information are better than mine. General Kelley was ordered some days ago to concentrate at Hancock and attack the enemy's right.

General Brooks is also moving from Pittsburgh to re-enforce Kelley. All troops arriving from New York and Fort Monroe are sent directly to Harper's Ferry, unless you order differently. You will have forces sufficient to render your victory certain. My only fear now is that the enemy may escape by crossing the river."[51]

Brigadier General Lorenzo Thomas, Adjutant General of the U.S. Army, who had been at Couch's headquarters at Harrisburg for some time, helping to organize militia regiments, had wired Secretary Stanton that morning that a general, three regiments of infantry, and a battery of little 4-pounder guns was now south of Carlisle and would soon be joined by two more regiments from Harrisburg. "This force can make a junction with Pierce, and move down the Cumberland Valley on the enemy's rear. Four regiments are nearly ready at Reading. These will also be pushed forward." President Lincoln, still haunting the telegraph office at the War Department and anxious lest Lee should escape, wired Thomas early that afternoon: "The forces you speak of will be of no imaginable service if they cannot go forward with a little more expedition. Lee is now passing the Potomac faster than the forces you mention are passing Carlisle." He said they would be as likely to capture the man in the moon "as any part of Lee's army." Thomas replied to Stanton: "I am afraid the President supposed the troops in advance were to delay until those behind came up, but not so, as the orders are to press forward." He added that a regiment just in from Philadelphia on a train was being sent on to Shippensburg, just north of Chambersburg, without changing cars.[52]

Baldy Smith's militia division from Couch's department reached Waynesborough that day, where he found Neill's force that had been pursuing Lee. At 4 p.m., Smith so notified Meade's headquarters: "I have camped so as to render him all possible assistance till definite instructions are sent to me. My command is an incoherent mass, and, if it is to join the Army of the Potomac, I would suggest that the brigades, five in number, be attached to old divisions, and thus disperse the greenness. They cannot be maneuvered, and as a command it is quite helpless, excepting in the kind of duty I have kept them on in the mountains. I have here about 4,000 men, and I suppose 2,000 have straggled away since I left Carlisle. General Knipe is the only one I have with me who is at all serviceable, and he is anxious to get back to his own brigade in the Twelfth Corps. I am utterly powerless, without aid and in the short time allotted, to infuse any discipline into these troops, and for the reasons given above make the suggestion as being for the best interests of the service."[53] He was, no doubt, correct, but breaking up his command would also put him out of a job and save him the embarrassment of having to serve again in the Army of the Potomac in a lesser capacity than he had held in it before.

Couch wired Halleck that afternoon that "Everything is being thrown down that can be to join Meade, excepting my forces at Loudon [Pierce's], which have been ordered into Clear Spring country, to keep the rebels from seizing stock, flour, &c., to feed themselves. In my judgment they cannot be better employed. That force has taken 700 prisoners, two pieces of artillery, and 100 wagons up to this time, as well as help drive in their trains, that have now been six days without forage." At 11 p.m. he wired Meade: "My headquarters will probably be at Chambersburg to-morrow. I am putting troops in the Valley as fast as railroad can do it, having had some ten regiments organized and equipped in last ten days. I will endeavor to effect a junction with Smith and your army."[54] He also wired Major General John E. Wool, commander of the Department of the East, at New York, that he was returning the 11th New York Heavy Artillery Regiment to him because it refused to march to the front as infantry.

There were no fighting troops left at Gettysburg by then, and Rufus Ingalls, Meade's quartermaster, reported to General Meigs, at Washington that day: "I saw citizens carrying off arms, and doubt not it will require coercive steps to recover them. A large quantity, though, was already delivered at the depot, which had been gathered from the field. The people there are doubtless loyal, but they seemed to be very simple and parsimonious, and evinced but little enthusiasm."[55]

That same morning, Meigs' son, Lieutenant John R. Meigs, who had just recently graduated from West Point at the top of his class, wired Meade himself that he had, at Harper's Ferry, five ironclad railroad cars (which he had designed himself), armed with a 6-pounder gun and four little mountain howitzers, and he wanted permission to rebuild the railroad bridge over the Potomac at Harper's Ferry and press on, perhaps as far as Martinsburg, in the Shenandoah Valley. He added that the river was still rising. At noon he wired General Schenck at Baltimore, commander of the Middle Department, with the same request. Schenck replied with advice to be "cautious as well as active," and to consult with General French. "Remember that the duty assigned to you is not to seek a fight, but to help keep open and protect the railroad."[56]

General Haupt, the railroad man, also wrote to General Meigs that day, saying he had straightened out a traffic problem on the rails, evidently caused by French hanging onto 20 trains at Frederick. Next, he said, he would go to Harrisburg and push the repair of the railroad from there to Hagerstown as soon as they got possession of that place. "We should be able to capture many prisoners and take wagons and ambulances, and perhaps artillery, before the enemy can cross the river. The late rains and bad roads will help us, but I do not believe we can prevent Lee's army from crossing. I could build trestle-bridges of round sticks, and floor with fence rails. It is too much to assume that the rebels cannot do the same." Like Meigs' son, Haupt thought that Union forces should be operating south of the Potomac. "It seems to me that every effort must be made by the rebels to save Lee by sending him supplies via the Shenandoah Valley. If we could find force enough to occupy the passes of the Blue Ridge, we could capture supply trains, and reduce the rebels to such a state of destitution as would compel a surrender. Our course seems to me to be a clear one, and, if you concur in this opinion, I hope you will talk it over with General Halleck."[57]

In addition to giving advice to Meade about how to deal with Lee, Halleck was writing to Grant that day: "I fear your paroling the garrison at Vicksburg without actual delivery to a proper agent, as required by the fourteenth article of the cartel, may be construed into an absolute release, and that the men will be immediately placed in the ranks of the enemy. Such has been the case elsewhere. If these prisoners have not been allowed to depart, you will retain them till further orders."[58]

It would, of course, be a few days before Grant received that message down in Mississippi. In the meantime, General Pemberton continued to make nagging complaints to McPherson, including that some of his men had been crossing the Mississippi. And Major N. G. Watts, the Confederate commissioner for the exchange of prisoners at Vicksburg, was claiming that the paroles would not be binding unless he should receipt all rolls of the men paroled. Grant wrote to McPherson: "The only object in issuing rolls made out is that the Government may have something in a compact form, which will be recognized, to enable them to negotiate for the exchange of prisoners hereafter." In a separate message, Grant told McPherson: "General Pemberton's acceptance of the terms proposed to him bind the Confederate Government not to accept the services of any man who formed a part of the garrison on the morning of the 4th instant until properly exchanged. The object of the [individual] parole is to make each individual feel the same obligation."[59]

Meanwhile, that day Sherman's forces were following Joe Johnston eastward across the state. "On the 8th all our troops reached the neighborhood of Clinton," he later related, "the weather fearfully hot, and water scarce. Johnston had marched rapidly, and in retreating had caused cattle, hogs, and sheep, to be driven into the ponds of water, and there shot down; so that we had to haul their dead and stinking carcasses out to use the water."[60]

Down at Port Hudson, General Gardner suggested that the two commanders appoint officers to discuss the terms of Port Hudson's surrender. Banks agreed to this, and the officers met and began negotiating at 9 a.m. on 8 July, with the Confederates stalling in hopes of allowing time for some of them to escape before surrender. Eventually the Rebels agreed to surrender everything, while the Federals agreed to respect private property. It was after 2 p.m. before the two commanders finally signed the articles of surrender, and, due to the late hour, it was arranged that the actual surrender ceremony would take place, as the Confederates hoped, the following day.

Banks wrote a message to Grant to be taken up the river by the same Colonel Smith who had brought Banks the news of Vicksburg's surrender: "It gives me great pleasure to inform you that Port Hudson surrendered this day. We are unable to determine the number of prisoners or the extent of the armament. The commissioners ask for 6,000 rations. The surrender is in effect unconditional. I declined to stipulate for the parole of officers or men, but necessity will compel me to parole at once a considerable portion of the prisoners, selecting those representing States mainly in our control, as Louisiana, Arkansas, &c. About 12,000 or 15,000 of the enemy have been threatening my communications, and have occupied the La Fourche districts. I shall move against them forthwith. My disposable force is about equal to their number if I detain General Grierson's cavalry [borrowed from Grant]. This I hope to do for a term of not more than two weeks, when I will return him in good condition to your camp. He has been of infinite service, and I know not in what way we could have supplied his place. . . . The enemy in my rear disposed of, I earnestly desire to move into Texas, which is now denuded of troops. The enemy here is largely composed of Texans. We hope to capture them. Will it be possible for you to spare me for this expedition, which should be closed in two months from this date, a division of 10,000 or 12,000 men?"[61]

At about 3 p.m. the Federals sent in a wagon train of food and medicine for the garrison. That night many Confederates slipped through the lines around Port Hudson or floated down the river, though some were captured in the attempt. On the morning of 9 July, the Confederates lined up to officially surrender, and the Union occupying force marched in at 7 a.m. General Gardner offered his sword to Brigadier General George L. Andrews, Banks' chief of staff who was now to be the post commander, who returned the sword "as a proper compliment to the gallant commander of such gallant troops – conduct that would be heroic in another cause." Gardner replied that "This is neither the time nor the place to discuss the cause."[62] By 9:30 the Rebels had grounded their arms, though with a considerable lack of enthusiasm.

Banks paroled 5,935 enlisted men and civilian employees, and held 405 officers as prisoners of war, some of whom were shipped down river to New Orleans and some north to Memphis and eventually to Johnson's Island, Ohio. In his report, Banks said that he paroled the enlisted men because "It was impossible to drive the enemy from the river below, and leave troops enough at Port Hudson to maintain the position and guard between 6,000 and 7,000 prisoners."[63] He claimed that, in his entire campaign, which began on 25 March, his forces had captured 10,584 men, 73 cannon, 6,000 small arms, 4,500 pounds of gunpowder, 150,000 rounds of ammunition, 20,000 head of horses, mules and cattle, 10,000 bales of cotton, and 4 steamboats. It had also destroyed 3 gunboats and 8 other steamboats. His parole of the enlisted men was not in accordance with the cartel on the exchange of prisoners and was later held to be invalid. Before the day was out, seven transports loaded with troops headed downriver with three of Banks' brigades and three batteries, bound for Donaldsonville to protect his army's line of communications with New Orleans.

Up in Mississippi on 9 July, Sherman continued to move towards Jackson, the state capital, as Joe Johnston fell back before him, and his headquarters issued detailed orders on how his three corps were to approach the city. At Vicksburg the paroling process was nearing completion, and Grant issued orders for Major General F. J. Herron's division, which had been sent down to him from Missouri and did not belong to any corps, to prepare to go downriver in a day or two to reinforce Banks temporarily, leaving its artillery and convalescents in camp, as it was expected to return as soon as Port Hudson fell.

At Brandenburg, Kentucky, that ninth day of July, only Morgan's rear guard, a half a regiment, remained, the rest having crossed the Ohio River during the night. It was skirmishing with Hobson's advancing Federals when a sudden fog enveloped them, and they too made it safely across the river to Indiana. An officer of that regiment, Major James B. McCreary (a future governor of Kentucky), told his diary, "We are now fairly into Yankee land. What the result will be God only knows."[64]

At 7 a.m. Hobson's Union troopers rode into Brandenburg, but found only the steamer *John T. McCombs* and the smoldering hull of the *Alice Dean*. The *McCombs* had been spared because its captain was a friend of Colonel Duke. Hobson sent it upriver to Louisville with a request for transports for his command. It was evening by the time the requested transports arrived and Hobson's men and horses began crossing the river. General Boyle, at Louisville, was concerned for the safety of the suburbs on the Indiana side near there, while Governor Oliver P. Morton of Indiana was worried about the safety of Indianapolis. Both were firing telegrams off to General Burnside in Cincinnati. General Judah, at Litchfield, Kentucky, was refusing to obey orders from Boyle, even when issued in Burnside's name, insisting that orders to him had to come from or through General Hartsuff, commander of the 23rd Corps.

Morgan, meanwhile, conferred with Colonel Adam R. Johnson, commander of his 2nd Brigade. Earlier, Morgan had promised Johnson that the latter could take one regiment, two guns, and whatever boats they captured, and move downstream toward Evansville, Indiana, while Morgan took the rest of the division upstream. But now, Morgan decided to keep his command together. He probably realized that there was too much local opposition, both on the river and north of it, for a lone regiment to operate safely. At any rate, he headed north from the river, and a few miles up the road, just south of the town of Corydon (about 15 miles due west of Louisville, Kentucky), the head of his column ran into about 450 militiamen and home guards, including those who had opposed his crossing, deployed behind a mile-long barricade of logs and fence rails.

This forced Johnson, who had the lead, to take the time to dismount and deploy his men. Then, with the support of long-range fire from his other regiments, he ordered the 7th Kentucky to charge the Federals' right flank. Unfortunately for these Rebels, that flank was held by a company armed with 15-shot Henry repeating rifles, the predecessor of the famous Winchester, and the very latest thing in American small arms at that time. The Rebels were repulsed by a storm of lead. The Confederate artillery was then brought into action while Johnson put together simultaneous attacks on both Union flanks. Having no artillery of their own, and their barricade offering insufficient protection from cannon fire, the home guards and militia soon began to fall back, and their retreat soon became a rout. When part of Dick Morgan's 14th Kentucky cut across the road leading to Louisville and a cannon was advanced to a hill overlooking Corydon's fairgrounds, Colonel Jordan surrendered his infantry, 345 men, but most of his mounted men got away.

While lunching at a hotel, Morgan learned from the owner that Lee had been defeated at Gettysburg and that Vicksburg had surrendered to Grant. Meanwhile, his men plundered the town, and, as a Corydon newspaper later reported, "They entered private houses with impunity, ate all the victual the ladies had cooked for the Home Guards, and compelled them to cook more."[65] Morgan asked three flour mills to pay $1,000 each or he'd burn them down; however, he settled for a total of $2,100 in greenbacks. He paroled his prisoners, spreading the rumor that he intended to continue going north all the way to Indianapolis, some 120 miles away, and did proceed a few more miles in that direction, bivouacking for a few hours at Palmyra.

Without waiting for orders from Burnside, Hobson and his officers unanimously decided to cross the Ohio and continue their pursuit, and throughout the day steamboats ferried their men and horses over to the Indiana side.

∽ Endnotes ∽

1 Clifford Dowdey, editor, *The Wartime Papers of R. E. Lee* (New York, 1961), 540-1.
2 Brown, *Retreat from Gettysburg*, 270.
3 *OR*, I:27:III:584.
4 Ibid., I:27:III:585.
5 Ibid., I:27:III:584.
6 Wittenberg, Petruzzi and Nugent, *One Continuous Fight*, 170.
7 Ibid., 171.
8 *OR*, I:27:III:594. Both messages.
9 Ibid., I:27:III:595. Both messages.
10 Ibid., I:27:III:599. Both messages.
11 Ibid., I:27:I:82.
12 Ibid., I:27:I:81-2.
13 Ibid., I:27:I:83.
14 Ibid., I:27:I:82.
15 Ibid., I:27:III:584.
16 Ibid., I:27:III:585.
17 Ibid., I:27:I:83.
18 Ibid., I:27:I:82-3.
19 Ibid., I:27:III:595-6.
20 Wittenberg, Petruzzi and Nugent, *One Continuous Fight*, 152.
21 Sandburg, *Abraham Lincoln*, II:359.
22 *OR*, I:27:I:83.
23 Ibid., I:23:II:518. Both messages.
24 Ibid., I:23:II:52.
25 Basler, ed., *The Collected Works of Abraham Lincoln*, VI:319-20.
26 Edward Cunningham, *The Port Hudson Campaign 1862-1863* (Baton Rouge, 1963), 117.
27 *OR*, I:26:I:619.
28 Ibid.
29 Ibid., I:24:II:466.

30 Ibid., I:24:III:484. Both messages.
31 Grant, *Memoirs*, I:560.
32 Schecter, *The Devil's Own Work*, 29-30.
33 James D. Horan, *Confederate Agent* (New York, 1954), 28,
34 *OR*, I:23:I:659.
35 Dowdey, ed. *The Wartime Papers of R. E. Lee*, 543-4.
36 Ibid., 542-3.
37 Wittenberg, Petruzzi and Nugent, *One Continuous Fight*, 175-6.
38 *OR*, I:27:II:703.
39 Ibid., I:27:I:941.
40 Ibid., I:27:III:602.
41 Ibid. I:27:I:1007.
42 Ibid., I:2;7:I:925.
43 Ibid., I:27:III:604.
44 Wittenberg, Petruzzi and Nugent, *One Continuous Fight*, 190.
45 Ibid., 192. "The young Napoleon" was a nickname conferred upon McClellan by the press.
46 *OR*, I:27:I:83-4.
47 Ibid. I:27:I:84.
48 Wittenberg, Peruzzi and Nugent, *One Continuous Fight*, 196.
49 *OR,* I:27:I:84.
50 Ibid., I:27:I:85.
51 Ibid.
52 Ibid., I:27:III:612-3. All 3 messages.
53 Ibid., I:27:III:611.
54 Ibid. Both messages.
55 Ibid., I:27:III:607.
56 Ibid., I:27:III:608.
57 Ibid., I:27:III:609.
58 Ibid., I:24:I:62.
59 Ibid., I:24:III:488-9.
60 Sherman, *Memoirs*, I:330.
61 *OR*, I:26:I:624-5. The following spring, T. Kilby Smith, by then a brigadier general, commanded a small provisional division of the 17th Corps in Banks' ill-fated expedition up the Red River.
62 Cunningham, *The Port Hudson Campaign*, 119.
63 *OR*, I:26:15.
64 James B. McCreary, "Morgan's Raid Comes to an Inglorious End," in *B&G*, 682.
65 David L. Mowery, *Morgan's Great Raid* (Charleston SC, 2013), 76.

Part Five
ESCAPE

CHAPTER 21
"I Should Like to See a Clear Day"
9 – 11 July 1863

FROM KNOXVILLE, TENNESSEE, on that ninth day of July, Major General Simon Bolivar Buckner, commander of the Confederate Department of East Tennessee, telegraphed the Confederate War Department in Richmond: "I have returned from Tullahoma with the re-enforcements I took to General Bragg."[1] Bragg's Army of Tennessee, now minus Buckner's troops, had retreated from Tullahoma to the southeast bank of the Tennessee River at and on both sides of Chattanooga, and that same day orders were issued sending one of Bragg's brigades, under Brigadier General Bushrod Johnson, up to Loudon, on the East Tennessee & Virginia Railroad about two-thirds of the way to Knoxville, to protect the bridges between there and Chattanooga. Bragg's opponent, Rosecrans, had halted his Army of the Cumberland not far northwest of the Tennessee River, to rest and get resupplied, while his engineers worked to repair the railroad from Nashville to his camps. It would be a few weeks before he began his next move.

In Maryland that day, Lee and his corps commanders continued to define their best defensive line until, satisfied at last, Lee ordered his engineers to begin to lay it out. Primarily, it used what was known as Salisbury Ridge, a somewhat broken line of hills that began just west of Hagerstown and ran south to Downsville before turning southwest almost to the banks of the Potomac. It thus covered both Williamsport and Falling Waters from any Union attack from the east. In some places it rose some 150 feet higher than the boggy lands, where, about a mile east of it, ran aptly named Marsh Creek from just north of the Williamsport-Boonsborough road to the Potomac. Lee himself oversaw much of the work of laying out breastworks and gun emplacements.

Even as his wounded from Gettysburg were being ferried over the river and temporary hospitals in Hagerstown were being cleared of patients, Lee ordered new division and brigade hospitals to be established in Williamsport, which was about three miles west of the new defense line, so as to be ready to receive the wounded from the new battle he expected to have to fight soon. Thousands of wagons were still parked in that town and along the river nearby, and thousands of horses, cattle, sheep and hogs were corralled among them, in a sea of mud and standing water. One Confederate wrote that the "whole flat on which the wagons are parked was almost like a pond."[2] Another Rebel noted that "The houses are riddled and almost all deserted and the country for a mile around is feted with beef offal and dead horses."[3]

By then the broken ferry rope had been repaired or replaced, and additional ropes had been strung for use by a couple of boats taken from the C&O Canal, which had been hauled to fords upstream. That afternoon most of the Union prisoners and their guards were ferried across, 25 men per boatload. A Confederate, who went across on the first boat, said, "The river is very full, muddy and swift, making the passage a not entirely safe or pleasant undertaking."[4] Although he would not admit to feeling "whipped," he found the contrast with his enthusiastic passage of the same stream in the opposite direction 16 days before to be a sad one.

Lee had changed his mind about having Pickett's Division escort the Union prisoners farther south. General Imboden was ordered to take charge of them as far as Staunton and guard them with only one of his regiments, the 62nd Virginia Mounted Infantry. He was also to take charge of some new companies being organized in the Valley. "When the general assigned me to this duty he expressed an apprehension that before I could reach Winchester the Federal cavalry would cross at Harper's Ferry, intercept and capture my guard and release the prisoners. Before we had left the river I had an interview with him at his headquarters near Hagerstown, in which he expressed great impatience at the tardiness in building rude pontoons at the river, and calling in Colonel James L. Corley, his chief quartermaster, told him to put Major John A Harman in charge of the work; remarking that without Harman's extraordinary energy to conduct the work, the pontoons would not be done for several days. Harman took charge that day, and by tearing down warehouses on the canal got joists to build boats with, and in twenty-four hours had enough of them ready to float down to Falling Waters and construct a bridge."

While Lee and Imboden were talking, Longstreet entered the tent, and Imboden noted that the two were getting on quite cordially. Imboden went off to follow his new orders, but "Before I had gone two miles on my anxious march toward Winchester a courier overtook me with a note from General Lee directing me to return immediately to his headquarters." Imboden hurried back but found that Lee and his staff had ridden toward Hagerstown to investigate some artillery firing. "When I overtook him he said that he understood I was familiar with the fords of the Potomac from Williamsport to Cumberland, and with the roads to them. I replied that I was. He then called up one of his staff . . . and directed him to write down my answers to his questions, and required me to name and describe ford after ford all the way up to Cumberland, and to describe minutely their character, and the roads and surrounding country on both sides of the river, and directed me, after I had given him all the information I could, to send to him my brother and his regiment, the 18th Virginia Cavalry, to act as an advance and guide if he should require it. He did not say so, but I felt that his situation was precarious in the extreme. When about to dismiss me, referring to the freshet in the river he laughingly said: 'You know this country well enough to tell me whether it ever quits raining about here? If so, I should like to see a clear day soon.'"[5]
The 18th Virginia Cavalry was sent westward, up the river, to

watch for and guard against General Kelley's Federals gathering at Hancock.

From Richmond, President Davis wrote to Lee that day: "Intelligence of the presence of the enemy near Williamsport has induced me, with a view to cover your communication[s], to order General Sam. Jones, with 3,000 infantry and two batteries of artillery [from southwest Virginia], to proceed to Winchester, where he will receive your orders."[6]

Meade's army mostly rested in place or made shorter marches on the ninth, in order to bring up and distribute supplies and recover batteries that had been stuck in the mud, as well as stragglers from all the recent hard marching. The 6th Corps moved forward to replace Schurz's division of the 11th Corps beyond Boonsborough, arriving about noon. The 1st Corps remained in the pass, up on South Mountain. The 5th Corps went into camp at about 9 a.m. near the intersection of roads leading to Sharpsburg and Rohrersville and reported to headquarters that there were no Confederates at Sharpsburg and that Antietam Creek was very high and swift. The 12th Corps reached Rohrersville by noon and reported that the 2nd Corps was still some eight or ten miles back.

For most of the day, Buford's and Kilpatrick's cavalry divisions remained in camp near Boonsborough, and Gregg's 2nd Division of cavalry reassembled and bivouacked near Middletown. Kilpatrick was suffering from a kidney ailment, which motivated him to stay out of the saddle. Colonel Othneil de Forest returned from leave that day to take command of the 1st Brigade of Kilpatrick's division, which had been under Colonel Richmond since the fall of General Farnsworth at Gettysburg.

A 40-man detachment of the 20th Pennsylvania Cavalry, a new regiment raised due to the threat of Lee's invasion of the state, and now part of Baldy Smith's force, captured 50 Confederates and 3 wagons between Greencastle and Hagerstown that day. Seth Williams of Meade's staff wrote to Smith at 9 a.m. (with a copy to Couch): "The army will occupy the line from Boonsborough to Rohrersville to-day. The army (both men and animals) is very much exhausted, and cannot advance as rapidly as desired. Although the information respecting the position of the enemy is not very definite, yet he is believed not to have crossed any large part of it over the Potomac, but to be concentrating it between Hagerstown and Williamsport. Under these circumstances; definite instructions cannot be sent to you. You will look to the security of your command; join this army when you can do so with security, unless the operations of General Couch require you to unite with him. Definite instructions will be sent you as soon as practicable. Although highly desirable that General Neill should rejoin his corps, yet he must be governed by your instructions."[7]

Meanwhile, Meade's headquarters (now near the signal station up on South Mountain) published a circular to all corps detailing how they should move the next day. General French assumed command of the 3rd Corps, and the troops of his prior command officially became the 3rd Division of that corps. Many of the men of the older two divisions were not happy with French's appointment, favoring Major General David Birney, commander of its 1st Division, who had been in that position since even before Sickles had taken over the corps, and who had been in command of the corps since Sickles was wounded. Birney was a capable commander, but possessed a rather cold personality that won him few friends, and Meade, especially, was no friend of his. The two had quarreled at Fredericksburg when Birney had been slow to come to the aid of the division then commanded by Meade. Also, the veterans of the first two divisions did not take to French's troops, who had, until now, been guarding railroads and garrisoning rear areas while they had been fighting the big battles. Colonel Phillippe Regis de Trobriand, a brigade commander in Birney's division, said, "What the Third Corps gained in numbers it lost in homogeneity."[8]

Brigadier General Henry W. Benham of the engineers reported to Meade's headquarters that day that he had pontoons and materials for two bridges in the C&O Canal, ready to be towed anywhere they might be needed up the river, but that he doubted that they would be needed at Harper's Ferry, as the railroad bridge there could easily be repaired. He had ordered his men to clear the wreckage and make it ready. Meanwhile, Lieutenant Meigs reported to General Schenck, at Baltimore, that he had climbed out on what was left of the railroad bridge without drawing any enemy fire. "I do not believe there is an armed rebel nearer than Bolivar Heights, a mile and a half beyond Harper's Ferry, where there seems to be a picket. I have ordered the timbers that can be collected brought to the end of the bridge so as to be ready the moment General Meade orders its construction."[9]

But Meade was not thinking about crossing the Potomac at Harper's Ferry or anywhere else to get south of Lee. Instead he was thinking of drawing most of the troops from near there to reinforce him for a battle north of the river. General Naglee, now in command near Harper's Ferry, was told that day by Meade's headquarters that reinforcements for the Army of the Potomac from Washington would be sent first to him, that he was to see that they were properly supplied and equipped, and that he was to have his force ready to join Meade at a moment's notice, leaving at Maryland Heights "such force as may be necessary to hold the position against a *coup de main*."[10] Naglee replied at 5 p.m. that he had 1,633 men in 3-years regiments, 4,150 men in units whose enlistments were nearly expired, plus 280 cavalrymen, 70 heavy artillerymen, and three batteries of light artillery; three regiments from Washington were included in the total. "Will you please specify the force to be left, if I am ordered to join the Army of the Potomac?"[11]

Evidently General Halleck was no longer thinking about putting any forces south of the Potomac either, for at 3:20 that afternoon he wired General Kelley, at Hancock, Maryland: "If Lee gives battle, do not be absent, but come in and help General Meade gain a victory. A battle is not far off."[12] Kelley interpreted this order as replacing Halleck's order of 5 July to attack Lee's supply line, and thus he kept most of his force north of the Potomac.

General Haupt reported to General Meigs at 1:20 p.m. from Hanover, Pennsylvania: "I am on my way to Gettysburg again. Find things in great confusion. Road blocked; cars not unloaded; stores ordered to Gettysburg, where they stand for a long time, completely preventing all movement there; ordered back without unloading; wounded lying for hours, without ability to carry them off; all because the simple rule of promptly unloading and returning cars is violated."[13]

About 4 p.m., General Buford ordered Devin's brigade up the road toward Funkstown to see what the Rebels had on the other side of Beaver Creek. Eventually these Federals came upon some Confederate cavalry and artillery on some high ground. Devin sent dismounted skirmishers forward and brought up a battery of horse artillery. Meanwhile, Ferguson's, Jones's and Chambliss's brigades of Stuart's cavalry, plus one battery, deployed along a ridge, with skirmishers out front. The Rebel skirmishers won a footrace for a rail fence between the two forces, but the Union guns soon forced Chambliss's men to retire. Their retreat exposed Ferguson's flank, while Devin's troopers attacked his front. Ferguson's men also gave way, and the Federals overran one of Stuart's camps. Gamble's Union brigade joined the advance, and the Federals pushed the Confederates up the road about two miles, then bivouacked on the field.

Down along the South Carolina coast, the time had arrived to put General Gillmore's elaborate plan into effect for taking Morris Island and opening the way into Charleston Harbor. Early on the morning of 9 July, 13 transports led by two gunboats and a monitor steamed up the Stono River, and while the armed vessels provided covering fire, two regiments landed on Battery Island. These troops then waded through waist-deep mud to Sol Legare Island, where they drove off a few Confederate pickets and seized a causeway leading to the much larger James Island. Brigadier General Alfred Terry kept the rest of his men on their transports, however, as Gillmore had ordered him not to bring on a battle. He was merely making a feint. But General Beauregard, commander of the Confederate Department of South Carolina, Georgia and Florida, telegraphed Major General W. H. C. Whiting, commanding at Wilmington, North Carolina, correctly predicting that "Gillmore will attack Sumter along Folly and Morris Islands probably. Can you send me one or more regiments?"[14] He also ordered troops from his own department to Morris Island.

As he predicted, Gillmore's real attack was to be made from Folly Island across Lighthouse Inlet to the south end of Morris Island, whose north end overlooked the entrance to Charleston Harbor. At the north end of Folly Island masked batteries had been constructed to cover the crossing. But near dawn the attack was called off and the men of the assault force returned to their camps. The naval launches, which were to carry them across the inlet, had been delayed by a heavy squall, but the real problem was that Gillmore's engineers had not cut a large enough passage through Confederate obstructions in the Folly River. Gillmore ordered his engineers to clear those obstructions while he and his officers, fearful that the Rebels now knew something was up, set to work to revise and simplify their plan. The two-pronged night attack was given up in favor of a direct attack that would depend on the superior firepower of his batteries and the Navy's ships.

At 9 p.m., men under the command of Brigadier General George Strong started filling boats in Folly Island Creek. Everything was now ready, and the obstructions had been removed. The men were not experienced at rowing but managed to propel their boats quietly, if awkwardly, until, in the early hours of 10 July nearly 2,500 of them were in their proper places in Lighthouse Inlet, waiting for daylight, along with four Naval launches armed with boat howitzers, who would give close fire support for the landing. A second wave of another 1,350 infantrymen and a battery of light artillery was held near the batteries on Folly Island, and another 1,450 men were in reserve. At 4:15 on a hot, still, humid morning, Brigadier General Truman Seymour, commander of the assault, ordered the batteries on Folly Island to be unmasked. This took almost an hour, and as Seymour had calculated, by then there was enough light to see the Confederate works on the south end of Morris Island.

The Confederates had just begun eating their breakfast of rice, bread and watermelon, when fifteen Union mortars and 32 rifled guns opened fire on them. The Rebel gunners ran to their pieces while two regiments of infantry rushed to their rifle pits. However, the infantry of both sides had nothing to do for the first hour but huddle in their trenches and in their boats while their respective artillery dueled across Lighthouse Inlet. Neither side gained any real advantage until Admiral Dahlgren led four ironclad monitors into positions to enfilade the Confederate works. As shrapnel and grapeshot from the Navy's heavy guns plowed through their lines, the Rebels' fire soon slackened, which brought forth a loud cheer from the Union infantry, watching from their boats. This drew the attention, and fire, of the Confederates onto the boat-bound infantry, which in turn caused Lieutenant Commander Francis Bunce to move his howitzer-armed cutters into position and join the bombardment, which was now so loud that it could be heard fifty miles away at the Union base at Port Royal.

And slowly the boats, filled with infantrymen, worked their way toward shore. One Federal, wedged into a boat full of men so tightly that he could "neither pray, fight nor swear," said that he was willing to be killed, or drowned, but not both.[15] Just as the boats reached an area that was safe from the Confederate artillery, because the muzzles of the big guns could not be depressed enough to bear on them, the Rebel infantry opened fire. General Strong ordered his men to land, coming in near the right, or north, end of the Confederate works, where they had to scramble ashore through knee-deep mud. Strong disembarked a bit too early, and all but his hat disappeared under the water, but he soon reached land and stripped off his water-filled boots to lead the attack.

Skirmishers armed with Spencer repeating rifles fanned out ahead while the regiments formed their ranks. Then the leading regiment, the 7th Connecticut, headed straight for the Rebels in the rifle pits, while the 6th Connecticut, which had landed farther downstream, threatened their flank and rear. After some heavy hand-to-hand fighting, the Confederate infantry retreated. The artillerymen held out a little longer, but soon they too had to let go, and the Rebels fled northeastward up the island toward the next line of defense, Battery Wagner, sweeping along with them the first two companies of reinforcements that were being rushed to their aid. The Union ironclads followed along, just offshore, as Admiral Dahlgren allowed his men to open hatches and come out on deck for some fresh air.

General Strong, now mounted on a captured mule, sent his men in pursuit. An officer of the 3rd New Hampshire ran among them carrying a newspaper he had found in the Confederate camp, crying, "Vicksburg captured; Great victory at Gettysburg!" It was the first news the men of this department had heard of either event. They cheered and rushed on, but the heat, humidity and exertion were taking their toll. As they approached Battery Wagner, Confederate artillery fire soon forced a halt (and wounded the officer with the newspaper). Around 9 a.m., the exhausted Federals hit the sand for rest and cover. As bad as the heat and humidity were on the beach, they were much worse inside the monitors, but the sailors returned to their posts and began a steady bombardment of Wagner that continued until dark, while the soldiers consolidated their position.

During the pursuit, the second wave and reserves were ferried across the inlet, but they were not used to push on against Battery Wagner. Three fourths of Morris Island was now in Federal hands, and Gillmore was confident that the remaining fourth could be taken the next day. The attack had certainly gone well so far. When assaulting a prepared position, the attackers could usually figure on taking two or three times the number of casualties as the defenders, but in this instance the ratio was reversed, for the Federals had lost a little over 100 men, and the Confederates almost 300, including many valuable artillery officers, as well as 11 big guns. But in failing to push on, Gillmore had lost his momentum and had given the Confederates time to recover. Beauregard sent off more requests for help. Instead of a regiment, Whiting was sending a full brigade from Wilmington under Brigadier General Thomas Clingman, to be followed by two regiments under Brigadier General Alfred Colquitt. A brigade from the Richmond area was being sent to Whiting to replace them. Most of Brigadier General William Taliaferro's brigade was being sent from Savannah, Georgia, and the governor of South Carolina was calling out his militia.

The brigade from Savannah would have been delayed had another part of Gillmore's plan succeeded. Colonel Thomas Higginson steamed up the South Edisto River on the morning of the tenth with 250 men of his 1st South Carolina Infantry Regiment (composed of escaped slaves) plus a section of light artillery. Despite opposition from a pair of Rebel guns, he cut through some obstructions in the river and landed some of his men to destroy a rice mill and to help about 200 slaves to escape, but he failed to reach his primary target, a bridge on the railroad that connected Charleston with Savannah. He was defeated in reaching his objective not by the Confederates but by the receding tide. His transport ran aground. Fortunately, he had a tug boat along, and it rescued the transport, but then the tug ran aground. Higginson gave up and returned to his base at Beaufort, South Carolina, after abandoning the tug and the two field pieces it carried.

About midnight, a mixed force of Georgia infantry and artillery companies, under Colonel Charles Olmstead, was transported across the harbor to Morris Island, where it joined the garrison of Battery Wagner. During the night, more land mines, known as Rains torpedoes, were implanted just south of the fort's defenses. And the first of Taliaferro's troops from Savannah arrived near Charleston before noon on the tenth.

In Indiana, Morgan's raiders continued riding north on 10 July until they reached the town of Salem, where they had another skirmish with some 200 home guards, many of whom surrendered. The Confederates burned the large brick depot, along with all the railroad cars on the track and the railroad bridges on each side of town, and demanded contributions from area flour and grist mills. After looting stores and taking about $500, they departed that afternoon. "Then we captured Canton," Major McCreary recorded, "tore up the railroad, and tore down the telegraph, and then rapidly moved on, like an irresistible storm, to the vicinity of Vienna, where, for a brief period, we bivouacked. The citizens seemed frightened almost to death, for Federal papers have published the wildest tales about us."[16] Along the way, a detachment was sent to Seymour to destroy track and bridges on the Ohio & Mississippi Railroad.

Meanwhile, General Hobson had his Union cavalry across the Ohio River by 2 a.m. on the tenth, and at daylight they headed north toward Corydon, where Morgan had fought militia the day before. "On the way," he later reported, "I passed the ruins of a farm-house and flouring-mill, which were burned by the rebels."[17] He reached Salem that evening, seven hours after the Confederates had ridden out.

Indiana Governor Oliver Morton sent out an order for all able-bodied men south of the National Road to organize themselves into companies and asked Major General Lew Wallace, then home on leave, to take charge of defending Indianapolis, not that there was much to defend it with. Wallace suggested that instead of standing on the defensive they should push Morgan out of the state and loaded what troops he could find – about 1100 raw recruits – onto a train and headed for Columbus, Indiana, which they reached at about 10 p.m.

The state legislature was dominated by Peace Democrats and Copperheads, and Morton worried that they might get control of the weapons in the state arsenal. So Colonel Henry Carrington, as he later wrote, "made a requisition upon him for return to the United States of all arms which the state had received from the Government and then wrote out a transfer which he signed so that he was able to notify the legislature that the state had no arms."[18]

There was a camp just outside Indianapolis that held some 6,000 Confederate prisoners of war. Had Morgan liberated them and added them to his force, armed with the weapons from the arsenal, he could really have raised havoc throughout the Old Northwest. However, instead of continuing toward Indianapolis, from Salem Morgan had turned eastward to Vienna, as Major McCreary said, where his men burned a railroad bridge and the depot and listened in on the telegraph to see what the Federals were up to. Then they rode farther eastward to Lexington, Indiana, almost due north of Louisville, Kentucky, where they spent the night. The Copperheads did not rise up to join the Confederates, but a few did offer their services as guides. Most of them did not want to fight for the Confederacy any more than they wanted to fight for the Union. They just wanted the war to end.

In New York City that day the *Daily News* published antidraft speeches that had been made at a peace rally. The prospect of being forced into the army was unpopular enough, and being required to risk one's life for the emancipation of slaves made it even worse in some men's eyes, and the fact that the well-to-do could buy themselves an exemption for $300 was unfair discrimination against the poor, who could not come up with such a sum. "This act is very simple," said New Jersey congressman Chauncey Burr, who readily accepted the Copperhead label, "– it is merely a highwayman's call on every American citizen for '$300 or your life.'" He advised his listeners, if drafted, to obtain a writ of habeas corpus and to appeal all the way to the Supreme Court if necessary, although these do not seem like remedies that would be readily available to the poor.

The *Herald*, which claimed to be nonpartisan, asserted that his speech went too far, saying, "If Mr. Burr is not careful he will raise a storm that will terminate in insurrection and bloody scenes in this city. When this mob spirit is once started no person can tell where it will end or who will be sacrificed by its vengeance."[19]

Down in Mississippi, Sherman continued to follow Joe Johnston. "On the 10th of July," he later wrote, "we had driven the rebel army into Jackson, where it turned at bay behind the intrenchments, which had been enlarged and strengthened since our former visit in May. We closed up our lines about Jackson; my corps (Fifteenth) held the centre, extending from the Clinton to the Raymond road; Ord's (Thirteenth) on the right, reaching Pearl River below the town; and Parke's (Ninth) the left, above the town."[20] Sherman's headquarters issued detailed instructions to the corps commanders to construct defenses for batteries and rifle pits for the infantry, and to dig wells near their encampments. Ord was ordered to send his cavalry to the south "to tear up and effectually destroy at least 1 mile of the track, and as many bridges as possible for a distance of at least 15 miles from Jackson." And Colonel Cyrus Bussey, commanding Sherman's main cavalry force, was to "proceed to the north, and destroy the railroad at Canton and the railroad bridge at Black River, above Canton, and as many other bridges along his route as possible. . . ."[21] Ord was officially confirmed that day as the commander of the 13th Corps.

Grant wrote a long letter that day to Banks, informing him that he was sending him the infantry of Herron's division. "I feel confident that Port Hudson will be in your possession before the troops reach you, but learning of the position of

General Taylor's forces, I did not know but you might want to make a prompt movement to capture him, which could not be done without other forces to take the place of yours where they now are." He said Sherman was still out after Joe Johnston with most of Grant's army. "With the exception of cleaning out Kirby Smith's forces, on the west side of the Mississippi River, I have but little idea of what is next to be done with our western forces. Hope to have instructions from Washington, however." He added that Prentiss had successfully beaten off an attack at Helena, Arkansas, on the fourth, and that he had received word that "Meade has whipped Lee badly, and that the latter was retreating and Meade in full pursuit." Finally, he said that the troops under Herron were leaving their baggage, hospitals and artillery behind near Vicksburg. "I hope you will send them back as soon as their services can be dispensed with. I will also ask that General Grierson be sent here as soon as possible. I am very much in want of cavalry and of Grierson to command them."[22]

In far off Washington, Halleck was writing to Grant again that day: "On a full examination of the question, it is decided that you, as the commander of an army, were authorized to agree upon the parole and release of the garrison of Vicksburg with the general commanding the place."[23]

General Pemberton wrote to Confederate President Jefferson Davis that day from Vicksburg: "The great and apparently intentional delay in paroling the garrison made it necessary to leave General Smith behind to complete the rolls. These have been sent for, but cannot be sent to you earlier than five days. An approximate statement can now surely be given: 1 lieutenant-general, 4 major-generals, 8 brigadier-generals, and 1 State brigadier, with their staffs; the regimental and other officers, and rank and file and men amount to some 29,000 of which not less than 10,000 are ineffective from sickness and wounds. Most of the Mississippi and Missouri troops have already deserted. Very few will remain. I have no arms, and cannot prevent it. Whatever your orders are, I will use every exertion to carry out."[24]

In Maryland on 10 July a light rain fell on the two armies all day, which among other things added high humidity to the heat. Lee's headquarters issued orders that day temporarily merging Iverson's Brigade of Rodes' Division, 2nd Corps, into Ramseur's Brigade of the same division. Iverson would continue to be the provost-marshal at Williamsport, but without his brigade. The same order also temporarily merged Archer's Brigade of Heth's Division, 3rd Corps, into Pettigrew's Brigade of the same division. Both Iverson's and Archer's brigades had taken heavy losses at Gettysburg, and the latter's commander had been captured.

Having selected and marked out his line of defense, Lee set his engineers to building a floating bridge to reconnect him with Virginia. Each division in his army detailed a few men to do the work. They found suitable lumber in a couple of sawmills at Williamsport and told one of the lumbermen to "Charge it to Jeff Davis and Company."[25] They were able to salvage ten of the sixteen pontoons of the bridge that had been destroyed by French's cavalry at Falling Waters, while the engineers drew up plans for the construction of sixteen new ones, as well as for the spans to hold them all together. They would be held in place by several anchors composed of wooden boxes filled with rocks plus heavy cables that would tie them to both shores. Kettles were "borrowed" from the ladies of the town, in which to boil tar for caulking the boats. Pioneers were also put to work preparing the ferry site at Falling Waters, where the bridge would be placed. The road had to be improved on both sides of the river, and the bridge over the C&O Canal had to be strengthened so that it could handle the weight of all the men, guns and wagons that would have to cross it.

That afternoon and night Lee's three infantry corps moved into their new defensive line, although work on it continued around the clock for the next three days. Longstreet's 1st Corps, minus Pickett's Division and three brigades left near

Funkstown to back up the cavalry, moved to hold the right, near Downsville. Lee himself supervised this move, as he felt that Meade was most likely to attack his right and try to cut him off from the river. At this end of the line was a very heavy concentration of artillery behind parapets six feet thick to foil just such a move. Guns were also heavily concentrated at Longstreet's other flank where there was a gap in Salisbury Ridge through which the headwaters of Marsh Creek flowed and through which passed the Boonsborough-Williamsburg road – another possible Union target. Beyond that gap was Hill's 3rd Corps, holding the center, while Ewell's 2nd Corps held the left, which ended north of the National Road, just west of Hagerstown. "The troops were put to work, and, in twenty-four hours, our line was comfortably intrenched," Longstreet later reported.[26]

The defenses were more than nine miles long, and actually consisted of two lines, one for skirmishers along the forward slope of the ridge, and a main line just below the crest, both having a trench or rifle pits for the infantrymen, fronted by thick earthen walls, with a moat-like ditch in front of that to slow any attackers. The road from Hagerstown to Downsville, running along the western slope of the ridge, would enable easy sheltered movement along the line, while the roads fanning out from Williamsport would provide convenient lines of supply and retreat. And the recent rains had turned Marsh Creek into a real swamp that would greatly slow and hinder any attacking force.

It was an extremely strong line versus any attack from the east. But only Stuart's cavalry guarded against any attack from the north, most of it being in the vicinity of Funkstown; Robertson's Brigade was keeping an eye on Smith's and Neill's forces, while Jones's Brigade watched the approaches to Hagerstown from the Smithsburg-Cavetown area to the northeast, and Ferguson's brigade watched the direct approach to Williamsburg from Boonsborough, to slow any direct Union advance. "We must prepare for a vigorous battle," Lee wrote to Stuart that morning, "and trust in the mercy of

God and the valor of our troops. Get your men in hand, and have everything ready."[27]

Lee wrote to Jefferson Davis again that day, saying: "The Potomac continues to be past fording, and owing to the rapidity of the stream and the limited facilities we have for crossing, the prisoners and wounded are not yet over. I hope they will be across today.

"I have not received any definite intelligence of the movements or designs of the enemy. A scout reports that a column which followed us across the mountains has reached Waynesboro in Pennsylvania and other bodies are reported as moving by way of Frederick from Emmitsburg, as if approaching in this direction.

"If these reports be correct, it would appear to be the intention of the enemy to deliver battle, and we have no alternative but to accept it if offered. The army is in good condition, and we have a good supply of ammunition.

"The chief difficulty is to procure subsistence. The supply of flour is affected by the high waters, which interfere with the working of the mills."[28] Each infantry brigade in his army sent out one company that day, accompanied by supply wagons, to gather up any food that they could find.

Later in the day he followed up with a brief telegram, in which he acknowledged receipt of Davis's wire of the day before and thanked him for sending Sam Jones's men his way. He said, "The enemy is gradually making appearance against us. I have sent all the prisoners and most of the wounded across the river."[29]

The Federals were, indeed, gradually closing in on Lee's position. Kenly's brigade marched away from Maryland Heights, opposite Harper's Ferry, that morning to join the Army of the Potomac. Also, some 1,500 Union troopers, collected from the cavalry remount camp at Giesborough Point, near Washington, rejoined the army that day, and Quartermaster General Meigs informed General Ingalls that three brigades were on their way from Fort Monroe, and, for the sake of speed, would be sent forward without baggage wagons.

Kelley's Union forces from West Virginia, 6,000 strong, were still gathering at Hancock, Maryland, twenty miles to the west, but Baldy Smith's militia had reached Waynesborough, only twelve miles north of Lee's left flank. Smith's men, in addition to being soaked by the rain and covered with mud, were shoeless and hungry. Their supply wagons were bogged down far behind them, and the Rebels had already stripped the area of everything edible. Neill's brigade, which, as Lee said, had followed him over the mountains, was also at Waynesborough. McIntosh's cavalry brigade, which had accompanied it, probed south that day toward Smithsburg and Cavetown. It found no Rebels in that area but collided with part of Stuart's cavalry near Leitersburg late in the day before returning to Waynesborough. Seth Williams, of Meade's headquarters, informed both Neill and Smith that there was an abundance of rations at Gettysburg that they could draw on. "No further instructions can be sent to you than to occupy the enemy to the best advantage in your front, and be prepared to join us or General Couch, as the movements of the enemy will permit or may require." Smith replied, "I had proposed to move the command to join the Army of the Potomac to-morrow morning, but, in consequence of your dispatch, shall await orders, do my best here."[30]

Adjutant General Lorenzo Thomas, still at Harrisburg, asked General Haupt that evening to inform Meade that Smith's division totaled 7,662 men, and that Major General N. J. T. Dana had another division, of 11,007 men, at Chambersburg, where General Couch was, that there were 900 cavalrymen near the two divisions, and that Colonel Pierce had 2,700 men at Loudon, about to be joined by 1,300 more from Mount Union. That night Couch wrote to Smith, "I cannot give you an order to join Meade, not knowing about your position in reference to the Army of the Potomac. With my present force, if you go forward, I must remain here for a time. If it is in accordance with Meade's wishes, go by all means."[31]

Meade's army was catching up with Lee at last, groping forward cautiously to discover his exact position. In accordance with a circular sent out by Meade's headquarters the day before, on the left, the 12th Corps, followed by the 2nd, marched to Bakersville, north of Sharpsburg; in the center, the 5th Corps, followed by the 3rd, moved up the road toward Williamsport as far as the bridge over the Antietam; on the right, the 6th followed by the 1st, was ordered up the National Road beyond Beaver Creek; and the 11th Corps and Artillery Reserve were held near Boonsborough. Army headquarters would be near the 3rd Corps that night.

Halleck wrote to Meade at 9 a.m.: "I think it will be best for you to postpone a general battle till you can concentrate all your forces and get up your reserves and re-enforcements. I will push on the troops as fast as they arrive. . . . Beware of partial combats. Bring up and hurl upon the enemy all your forces, good and bad." In a 1 p.m. dispatch, Meade informed Halleck that Lee was entrenching a line between Hagerstown and Falling Waters and that he was advancing to a line running from north of Beaver Creek to Bakersville, near the Potomac. "I shall advance cautiously on the same line tomorrow until I can develop more fully the enemy's force and position, upon which my future operations will depend."[32]

Meanwhile, the Union cavalry probed ahead. Huey's brigade led the way for the 12th Corps on the Federal left, crossed Antietam Creek at about 10 a.m. and ran into some of Ferguson's Rebel cavalry near Jones's Crossroads, some three miles east of Williamsport. In some pretty heavy fighting, for cavalry, his troopers drove the Confederates from three successive positions and allowed Slocum's infantry to secure that crossing of the Antietam. Kilpatrick's cavalry was covering the left flank, down along the Antietam.

On the northern flank, Buford's cavalry division preceded the 6th Corps up the National Road. Jeb Stuart had withdrawn most of his cavalry behind Antietam Creek to cover Lee's open left flank, leaving Lieutenant Colonel Vincent Witcher's 34th Virginia Cavalry Battalion of Ferguson's brigade, backed by one battery of horse artillery, to cover the National Road about two miles south of Funkstown, and one company of the 4th Virginia Cavalry of Fitz Lee's brigade to watch the Beaver Creek Turnpike, farther east. Both units were in dismounted skirmish lines behind stout stone fences. Around mid-morning a battery from Longstreet's 1st Corps arrived to back up the company on the Beaver Creek pike.

It took all morning for Buford's dismounted cavalry to push Stuart's skirmishers back to a series of ridges just southeast of Funkstown as Stuart fed in more of his cavalry. "Fight commenced very early and lasted through the entire day," noted a trooper in Hampton's Brigade.[33] Witcher's battalion beat off several attacks by dismounted Union cavalry long enough for it to be reinforced by most of the rest of Ferguson's brigade. A 6th Corps infantryman, back down the road, said that he could hear the carbines cracking and see shells exploding in the air two miles ahead. "We understood perfectly that it meant our cavalry were indulging their meddlesome curiosity to the utmost in finding the position of things. They succeeded admirably in stirring up a regular hornet's nest."[34]

Devin's brigade held the left of Buford's line, extending almost to Antietam Creek; Gamble's brigade held the center, its left just west of the National road; and Merritt's brigade had the right, moving onto a high ridge and extending across the Beaver Creek Turnpike, supported by two batteries, one in the road, the other in the middle of his line. Some of Merritt's men occupied a large barn near the Beaver Creek road, from which they were sniping at Fitz Lee's skirmishers and the battery from Longstreet's corps, and the battle was heating up as the Confederates were running out of room to back up. Buford, who didn't particularly want to drive the Rebels into Funkstown and get involved in street fighting, went up onto the ridge to have a look for himself, and within seconds bullets cut five holes in his coat, and he heard the Rebels cheering the arrival of what appeared to be Confederate infantry.

Stuart had indeed sent for help from Longstreet's infantry. He found it in the form of G. T. Anderson's Brigade of

Hood's Division. Both Hood and Anderson had been wounded at Gettysburg, so the division was now commanded by Brigadier General Evander Law, and the brigade was under the temporary command of Colonel William W. White of the 7th Georgia, even though that regiment had been detached to back up Ferguson's cavalry on the Williamsport road. The bulk of White's brigade had been guarding a stone bridge over Antietam Creek at Funkstown since the eighth and foraging in that vicinity.

At around 1 p.m. a cavalry courier told Colonel White to take his brigade and report to Stuart east of Funkstown. White refused to move his brigade on the grounds that it had been posted at this bridge by General Law, but he went without it to see Stuart, who said he didn't know this General Law, but gave White peremptory orders to advance his brigade at once. When a colonel receives a direct order from a major general he obeys, or else. So White went back and got his brigade moving, and one of Stuart's aides conducted him to Fitz Lee, who had him halt for about ten minutes while the artillery fired a few rounds, then ordered him "to move forward by the flank through a narrow lane, *a la cavalry*, to within 150 yards of the enemy, before deploying in line of battle."

White protested this order, "wishing to deploy my line before getting under fire of the enemy, but was not allowed to do so. I was subjected to a raking fire from the enemy, and it was with great difficulty that my line was formed, there being several fences and small houses in the way. Once formed, we pushed forward to the crest of the hill, driving the enemy's sharpshooters from the barn behind and in which they advanced in heavy force." But then Stuart's horse artillery exploded a few shells in the ranks of White's right-most regiment, killing and wounding several men, and Fitz Lee ordered the brigade to fall back, even though White felt that his other three regiments "were advancing in splendid order."[35]

Behind White's brigade came another brigade of Georgians – Semmes' Brigade of McLaws' Division, under the temporary command of Colonel Goode Bryan – which had also been foraging in the Funkstown area for a couple of days. Also, Kershaw's Brigade of McLaws' Division and one battery were held in reserve west of Funkstown, near the stone bridge. Bryan's brigade came up to the right of White's and exchanged fire with Gamble's and Devin's troopers as the battery of horse artillery that had supported Witcher's cavalry was withdrawn for lack of ammunition, but neither side tried to advance. Buford's men were also running out of ammunition, so he sent a note back to Brigadier General Albion Howe, commander of the 2nd Division of the 6th Corps, the nearest Union infantry formation. Howe's division, in the van of the corps, had crossed Beaver Creek and approached to within about two miles of where the cavalry was fighting, but was ordered by Sedgwick to wait for the rest of the corps to catch up.

Gamble complained in his official report that his pleas for the infantry already going into bivouac behind his line to come and take over his position were ignored . "When our ammunition was expended, we were ordered by General Buford to fall back. The rebels then occupied our position, and our infantry afterward had to retake it, with the unnecessary loss of several killed and wounded."[36] There was evidently more to it than that. General Howe wanted to help, but he was under orders from Sedgwick not to bring on a general battle. Buford, on the other hand, had received orders from General Pleasonton, head of the Cavalry Corps, to move farther to his right, but Buford held an excellent position, and didn't want to give it up. He rode back and told Howe, "I ought to go to the right. Suppose you move up there, or send up a brigade or even a part of one, and hold that position." Howe sent an aide back to Sedgwick for permission, but he returned with only the same admonition not to bring on a general engagement. Buford reiterated, "They expect me to go further to the right. That position is a strong one and we ought not to let it go." So Howe sent to Sedgwick again, and this time was told he could occupy the position if Buford abandoned it. Howe winked and said, "If you go away from there, I will have to hold it." To which Buford said, "That's all right. I will go away."[37]

Howe sent forward Colonel Lewis A. Grant's Vermont Brigade, one of the best in Meade's army, to take over Buford's position, two miles long, while the cavalry moved to its right, beyond the road to Smithsburg. The Vermonters were weary from all their recent marching – one of them calculated that day that they had marched 266 miles in two weeks – but they easily repulsed three attacks and drove the Rebels back to Funkstown. In fact, the two Georgia brigades failed to even drive in the Vermonters' skirmish line. "Yet," Howe later complained, "there was no permission to move on and follow up the enemy."[38]

Nightfall soon put an end to the fighting and an increase in the fall of rain. But Meade's army was now within rifle range of Lee's left at Hagerstown and about two miles from his right at Downsville. "I don't care about going farther just now," Buford reported that night. "I will cease firing and try to watch their movements."[39] As for the Confederates, Stuart later reported, "Owing to the great ease with which the position at Funkstown could be flanked on the right, and, by a secret movement at night, the troops there cut off, it was deemed prudent to withdraw at night to the west side of the Antietam, which was accordingly done."[40] That night most of his men unsaddled their horses for the first time in ten days.

The next morning, 11 July, Devin's and Gamble's brigades were moved back through Boonsborough to Bakersville, on the southern flank. There they picketed between Meade's infantry and the river. Meanwhile, Kilpatrick's division moved around to the east and approached to within a mile of Hagerstown along the road to Chewsville and Cavetown without meeting any opposition. Huey's brigade again skirmished along the road to Williamsport, pushing Rebels out of an advanced position and holding it until nightfall, when they returned to their camp near Jones' Crossroads. And the rest of Gregg's 2nd Cavalry Division finally reassembled that day, near Boonsborough, but remained in camp.

At noon, General Slocum of the 12th Corps, on Meade's left, extending along the Sharpsburg pike, reported to headquarters that his right was at Jones' Crossroads but that "I regard the position utterly untenable. There are two ranges of hills in my front, the first of which commands my position, and the second commands the first. Both ranges are occupied by the enemy. I have been informed that the enemy have been constructing works on the second range." He was also worried that "there is nothing to prevent the enemy from passing around my left, and cutting off my trains."[41] Chief of Staff Humphreys replied, with perhaps a touch of sarcasm, to ask if there was any position in his front or rear that he considered tenable that would connect with Jones' Crossroads, and advised him that Buford's cavalry had been ordered that morning to probe toward Downsville, which would cover his left.

At 2:45 p.m. Humphreys sent an order for the 3rd Corps to advance and mass in the rear of the 5th Corps, and fifteen minutes later he told the 5th Corps to move its line of battle up to where its skirmishers were and to connect its skirmishers with those of the 6th Corps, along Antietam Creek. "Then push forward to reconnoiter between the creek and Sharpsburg pike, and drive the enemy toward Funkstown, till he is found in superior force. . . . Similar reconnaissances will be made by the Sixth Corps on the opposite side of the Antietam, and by the Second Corps on the Sharpsburg pike."[42]

These probes, plus a report from a Signal Corps officer and a message received from Couch saying that he had information that the Confederates had abandoned Hagerstown, satisfied Meade that the Confederates had moved farther west, and at 11:45 that night Humphreys told Sedgwick to "send a division and a brigade to advance upon Funkstown. Take possession of that town, and effect a lodgement upon the high grounds beyond, over looking it. Should the enemy endeavor to prevent this by a very large force, you will bring forward as much of your command as may be necessary to support your troops." At the same hour he told General Howard, of the 11th Corps, to "send a brigade (1,500 men) to make a reconnaissance in conjunction with Kilpatrick's cavalry, of Hagerstown and the vicinity. This command should march at the earliest practicable hour to-morrow, the 12th instant."[43]

General Schurz, commander of the 3rd Division of the 11th Corps, complained to Howard that day that his entire division was now down to about 1,500 men, which seemed too small a command for a major general, and asked to receive some of the new reinforcements. He also complained that generals junior to him were commanding entire corps. "I want to be understood, however, that in any case, even if neither of these requests be complied with, I mean to do my duty faithfully in this army as long as I have a platoon to command." Probably prompted by this, Howard wrote to Seth Williams that day, complaining that he thought his was now the only command that had not received reinforcements. "If I could have only one regiment to a division, it would do me much good.... I have one regiment whose time is out on the 14th instant."[44]

One thing that might have set off this request for reinforcements was that Kenly's brigade, just arrived from Maryland Heights, was assigned to the 1st Corps that day, replacing the brigade of Vermont nine-months men, who had played an important part in repulsing Pickett's Charge at Gettysburg but were now on their way home to be discharged. The 13th Vermont reached Baltimore that day, and General Schenk complained to Secretary Stanton about having to send its 663 men home because their enlistments had expired on the ninth. "Can nothing be done to stop this?"[45]

More Union forces continued to converge on Lee's army that day. The value of some, however, was questionable. General Dix of the Department of Virginia notified Halleck that day: "Ten thousand men have been sent you since yesterday morning. I shall send from 4,000 to 5,000 more; enough, with [Brigadier General Francis] Spinola's brigade, to make 17,000. I am waiting for transportation. Expect transports to-night."[46] However, in a long letter to Halleck reporting his situation that afternoon, Meade said: "From the representations of General Spinola that the nine months' men of his command could not be relied upon, as their time had nearly expired, I have directed the regiments of his brigade to be posted in the rear. Troops of this character can be of little service unless they are pledged to serve beyond their terms of enlistment; and the supplies they consume and the space they occupy on the lines of communication can be illy spared; besides, their presence may have an injurious effect upon other troops. I do not, therefore, desire to be re-enforced by such troops unless they have pledged themselves to remain beyond their terms of service and until I can dispense with their services." Halleck replied at 9 p.m., "The nine months' men told me that they were willing to serve through this crisis under any one but General Spinola, but would not serve under him, as they regarded his as worthless. You are authorized to relieve him and send him away."[47]

General Seth Williams of Meade's headquarters wrote at 9 a.m. to General Neill, at Waynesborough, to bring his brigade to rejoin the 6th Corps "by the shortest line that you may think it safe to move upon."[48] And to bring McIntosh's cavalry with him. Baldy Smith's militia, however, remained behind, and at 11:45 Williams replied to a dispatch from him, saying, "I am directed to say that the major-general commanding has no active orders or instructions to give you at present other than those which you have already been furnished."[49] Smith decided to move south as well. Couch wrote to Smith that day from Chambersburg, saying that he was thinking of sending Dana's division south from there, and that he might go with it. But he said, "I dread the effect on the Army of the Potomac, if our men should conclude not to fight in Maryland or break on the field; I think, however, that a good many of the Pennsylvania troops would do well."[50]

General Kelley, of the Department of West Virginia,

wrote to the War Department that day from Indian Springs, Maryland, a few miles west of Clear Spring: "I moved to this place last night. It is at the west base of North Mountain. Will cross the mountain to-night, and camp on the east base. My force is small, but I cannot be well driven out of the mountain. I am blockading with fallen timber all the roads between the turnpike and the river, so as to prevent any detachments making their escape to fords above. My cavalry scouts had a spirited skirmish with the enemy's cavalry near Clear Spring yesterday; several wounded on both sides. River falling slowly. . . . Weather cloudy and strong indications of rain." He complained that Brigadier General W. W. Averell had not yet arrived with the bulk of his cavalry. "His movement is exceedingly slow. I could now use his cavalry to a good purpose."[51]

President Lincoln wired a friend back in Illinois that day to answer his question about how things were going against Lee. After a quick summary of the situation, he said, "I am more than satisfied with what has happened North of the Potomac so far, and am anxious and hopeful for what is to come."[52]

Major General Sam Jones, commander of the Confederate Department of Southwest Virginia, telegraphed Secretary of War Seddon that day that he was cancelling the movement of 2,000 of his men to the Shenandoah Valley. He followed up with a long letter later in the day, explaining that he had received word that the Federals in the Kanawha Valley had concentrated and were preparing to attack one of his brigades with superior force. So he needed those men to reinforce the threatened commander. "The position he holds I regard as very important, and if my force there were driven away and overwhelmed, the way to the Virginia and Tennessee Railroad would be entirely open to the enemy, and this section of country would have to be temporarily abandoned."[53] He said another 1,100 of his men were already on their way to the Shenandoah and he would let them proceed.

Lee's men continued to work on their entrenchments

and his pontoon bridge on the eleventh, and by the end of the day they had completed one boat and most of a second. Mail for some of the men arrived, and word of the surrender of Vicksburg made its way through the Confederate camps. Nevertheless, Lee's men seemed confident that they could hold their position against any attack. Meanwhile, Lee issued an order to his troops, calling on them for another major effort. A Virginia cavalryman said, "All eyes saw in this order unmistakable evidence that we were in a critical situation and that fighting was a matter of necessity, not of choice."[54]

∽ Endnotes ∽

1 OR, I:23:II:905.
2 Brown, *Retreat from Gettysburg*, 295.
3 Ibid., 297.
4 Ibid., 296.
5 Imboden, "The Confederate Retreat from Gettysburg," *B&L* III:428-9.
6 OR, I:27:III986.
7 Ibid., I:27:III:621-2.
8 Wittenberg, Petruzzi and Nugent, *One Continuous Fight*, 195.
9 Ibid.
10 OR, I:27:III:616.
11 Ibid., I:27:III:618.
12 Ibid., I:27:III:625.
13 Ibid., I:27:III:619.
14 Ibid., I:28:II:183.
15 Wise, *Gate of Hell*, 69.
16 McCreary, "Morgan's Raid Comes to an Inglorious End," *B&G*, 682.
17 OR, I:23:I:659.
18 Horan, *Confederate Agent*, 30.
19 Schecter, *The Devil's Own Work*, 115.
20 Sherman, *Memoirs*, I:331.
21 OR, I:24:III:496.
22 Ibid., I:24:III:492-3.
23 Ibid., I:24:I:62.
24 Ibid., I:24:III:1000.
25 Brown, *Retreat From Gettysburg*, 321.
26 OR, I:27:II:361.
27 Ibid., I:27:III:991.
28 Dowdey, ed., *Wartime Papers of R. E. Lee*, 545.
29 Ibid., 546.
30 OR, I:27:III:633. Both messages.
31 Ibid., I:27:III:635.
32 Ibid., I:27:I:80. Both messages.
33 Wittenberg, Petruzzi and Nugent, *One Continuous Fight*, 212.
34 Ibid., 213.
35 OR, I:27:II:398.
36 Ibid. I:27:I:936.

37 Wittenberg, Petruzzi and Nugent, *One Continuous Fight*, 215-6. Their own end notes seem to be muddled, and their source for this conversation is not discernable.
38 Ibid., 216.
39 *OR*, I:27:I:926.
40 Ibid., I:27:II:704.
41 Ibid., I:27:III:646-7. Both messages.
42 Ibid., I:27:III:648.
43 Ibid., I:27:III:649-50. Both messages.
44 Ibid., I:27:III:650. Both messages.
45 Ibid., I:27:III:649.
46 Ibid., I:27:III:655.
47 Ibid., I:27:I:91. Both messages.
48 Ibid., I:27:III:654.
49 Ibid.
50 Ibid., I:27:III:651.
51 Ibid., I:27:III:652.
52 Basler, ed., *Collected Works of Abraham Lincoln*, VI:323.
53 *OR*, I:27:III:995.
54 Wittenberg, Petruzzi and Nugent, *One Continuous Fight*, 228 and 241. These authors repeat this quote in two different chapters, and have Lee's order published on the 10th in one chapter and the 11th in another. The latter date is correct.

CHAPTER 22
"Broadway Looked Like a Field of Battle"
11 – 13 July 1863

From Knoxville, Tennessee, on 11 July, General Buckner telegraphed to General Bragg's chief of staff, at Chattanooga: "I have received instructions to move into Kentucky for the purpose of a demonstration. To do this, concert with General Bragg is essential. Can he spare me two or three brigades?"[1] And the same day one of Buckner's subordinates, Brigadier General William Preston, commander of a district in southwest Virginia, wrote a long letter to the Confederate War Department saying that he had heard that Buckner's Department of East Tennessee might soon be combined with Bragg's army, and he thought, if that was true, that his district should not be included in the new combined command. "The main vulnerable point here is Saltville," he said, "which produces 10,000 bushels of salt per diem, and which is of vital consequence to the Confederacy. The approaches are through Pound Gap and Louisa Gap, in Northeastern Kentucky. The enemy have already along the Sandy 4,000 to 5,000 men, menacing a raid on Abingdon and Saltville." He pointed out that almost half the men of the district, and those the best disciplined and trained, had been withdrawn. "The remainder are wretchedly armed, and have a large territory to guard. To atone, as far as possible, for these deficiencies, the only remedy will be prompt and energetic action on my part, without waiting for orders from a remote point. Chattanooga is farther from me than Richmond. I fear that this portion of the department, if annexed to that of General Bragg, will be neglected." Finally, he said, "I think it would be better that I should report directly to the [War] Department . . . or to be attached to the department of Major-General [Sam] Jones."[2]

From Tullahoma, Rosecrans reported to Halleck that

Donald S. Lowry   *Page 631*

day: "Our troops as far south of Elk [River] as they can be and get supplies. Railroad open to Elk, where we are working at bridge 450 feet long; open to McMinnville, where have a division; our advance at Pelham. A division of cavalry has gone to Huntsville, Decatur, and Florence, and thence up the Central Alabama Railroad, and will endeavor to connect with Hurlbut at Tuscumbia. It is important to know if it will be practicable for Burnside to come in on our left flank, and hold the line of the Cumberland; if not, a line in advance of it and east of us. The operations now before us involve a great deal of care, labor, watchfulness, and combined effort, to insure the successful advance through the mountains on Chattanooga."[3]

General Halleck wrote two long messages to General Grant on that eleventh day of July, which, of course would take several days to reach him. In one he said, "I am anxiously waiting for more definite information of the capture of Vicksburg than that contained in your brief telegram of July 4. I am also exceedingly anxious about General Banks' command, having heard nothing from him since June 29. I hope you have re-enforced him sufficiently to secure the capture of Port Hudson and to enable him to reopen his communications with New Orleans. I also hope you will send north the Ninth Corps as early as possible, for if Johnston should now send re-enforcements to Bragg, I must add that corps to Rosecrans' command. Unfortunately, Burnside's army is employed in repelling petty raids, instead of advancing into East Tennessee to co-operate with Rosecrans. Your idea of immediately driving Johnston out of Mississippi is a good one, but it will not be safe to pursue him into Alabama, nor will it be best at present to hold the line of the Tombigbee, even after he has been driven east of that river.

"The Mississippi should be the base of future operations east and west. When Port Hudson falls, the fortifications of that place, as well as of Vicksburg, should be so arranged as to be held by the smallest possible garrisons, thus leaving the mass of the troops for operations in the field.

"I suggest that colored troops be used as far as possible in the garrisons. If this meets your approval, raise and arm as many as you can, and send on the names of suitable persons for their officers, and I will submit them to the War Department for appointments. Name none but those known to be competent and reliable, and of good moral character."

He then went on to speculate on what should be done next, again saying that the 9th Corps might have to be sent to Rosecrans. He said that some reinforcements were on their way to Banks from the North, but that Grant would still need to give him some troops so he could drive the Confederates out of Louisiana.

"Large forces are comparatively neutralized in Missouri by the forces of Price and Marmaduke threatening the southern frontier of that State. If Little Rock and the line of the Arkansas River were held by us, all of Arkansas north of that river would soon be cleared of the enemy, and all the troops in Missouri, except the militia, could join your army in its operations at the South. . . .

"If the organized rebel forces could be driven from Arkansas and Louisiana, these States would immediately be restored to the Union. Texas would follow, almost of its own accord.

"I present these general views for your consideration. Circumstances may compel you to pursue a course entirely different from the one suggested; for example, Johnston may be so re-enforced as to require all your means to oppose him. In that case Rosecrans should be able to occupy East Tennessee without any additional forces, and East Tennessee being once occupied, Burnside's forces in Kentucky can be sent to your or to Rosecrans. In other words, wherever the enemy concentrates, we must concentrate to oppose him."

Halleck's other message was more personal than official. In it he informed Grant that Meade had been appointed a brigadier general in the Regular Army at the same time that

Grant had been made a major general. And he said there was a vacancy for one more brigadier and that he hoped three more would soon be opened up by retirements. He said the most prominent candidates for the opening(s) were Sherman, McPherson, George Thomas of Rosecrans' army, Sedgwick and Hancock, and wanted Grant to write an official letter recommending Sherman and McPherson, which Grant soon did.

"We are anxiously waiting to hear of the fall of Port Hudson and the entire opening of the Mississippi River," he said. "The President will then issue a general order congratulating the armies of the East and West on their recent victories. . . .

"Meade has thus far proved an excellent general, the only one, in fact, who has ever fought the Army of the Potomac well. He seems the right man in the right place. Hooker was more than a failure. Had he remained in command, he would have lost the army and the capital.

"Give my kindest regards to my old friends among your officers. I sincerely wish I was with you again in the West. I am utterly sick of this political hell."[4]

Grant wrote to Sherman that day: "Dispatches just received from General Banks announces the good news of the surrender of Port Hudson, with 5,000 prisoners and all the armament of the place. News came from the East of the defeat of Lee and his precipitate retreat, with Meade in full pursuit. I have nothing definite from you since the morning of the 9th, but, not hearing, suppose all is right. Is there any probability that Johnston may be receiving re-enforcements and intends standing? I have just learned from Yazoo City that all the steamers from above have just come down there, and that Johnston sent orders to press all the negroes that can be got, to prosecute the work of fortifying [Yazoo City] with all vigor. More than 1,000 negroes are said to be at work now. I immediately ordered a division from here to break them up. The well prisoners have been paroled and about out of town. The number reached 25,000. There are still those in hospital, near 6,000, yet to parole, besides many escaped without paroling...."[5]

So Pemberton's captured Confederates finally left Vicksburg. "By the eleventh, just one week after the surrender, the paroles were completed and the Confederate garrison marched out," Grant later wrote. He added that "When they passed out of the works they had so long and so gallantly defended, between the lines of their late antagonists, not a cheer went up, not a remark was made that would give pain. Really, I believe there was a feeling of sadness just then in the breasts of most of the Union soldiers at seeing the dejection of their late antagonists."[6] Confederate Major General Martin Luther Smith was left behind to effect the paroling of the sick and wounded Rebels not able to march.

Grant also wrote a reply to Banks: "It is with pleasure I congratulate you upon your removal of the last obstacle to the free navigation of the Mississippi. This will prove a death to Copperheadism in the Northwest, besides serving to demoralize the enemy. Like arming the negroes, it will act as a two-edged sword, cutting both ways.

"Immediately on receipt of your dispatches I forwarded them by Colonel Riggin, of my staff, who will take them as far as Cairo. I ordered the boats and other articles you required at once, and as many of the boats as can be got ready will go down at the same time with this. I also ordered, on the strength of Colonel Smith's report, about 1,000 men to Natchez, to hold that place for a few days, and to collect the cattle that have been crossing there for the rebel army. I am also sending a force to Yazoo City, to gather the heavy guns the rebels have there, and to capture, if possible, the steamers the enemy have in Yazoo River.

"Sherman is still out with a very large force after Joe Johnston, and cannot well be back under six or seven days. It will be impossible, therefore, for me to send you the forces asked for in your letter until the expiration of that time. I telegraphed to Washington, however, the substance of your request and the reason for it. So far as anything I know of being expected from my force, I can spare you an army corps of as good troops as ever trod American soil. No better are found on any other. It will afford me pleasure to send them if I am not required to do some duty requiring them. When the news of success reached me, I had General Herron's division on board transports, ready to start for Port Hudson. That news induced me to change their direction to Yazoo City."[7] In addition to sending Herron's division up to Yazoo City, he also ordered McPherson to send part of A. J. Smith's division.

Grant's lack of concern for Sherman's forces at Jackson was well founded, but significant. Many generals would have been worried sick that some disaster had or would befall any force with which he was out of contact. But Grant was always the optimist, and he had complete confidence in Sherman's abilities.

"On the 11th we pressed close in," Sherman later wrote, "and shelled the town from every direction. One of Ord's brigades (Lauman's) got too close, and was very roughly handled and driven back in disorder. General Ord accused the commander (General Lauman) of having disregarded his orders, and attributed to him personally the disaster and heavy loss of men. He requested his relief, which I granted, and General Lauman went to the rear, and never regained his division. . . . The weather was fearfully hot, but we continued to press the siege day and night, using our artillery pretty freely. . . ."[8]

General Johnston telegraphed Confederate President Davis that day: "If the position and works were not bad, want of stores (which could not be collected) would make it impossible to stand a siege. If the enemy will not attack, we must, or at the last moment withdraw. We cannot attack seriously without risking the army."[9]

On Morris Island, South Carolina, General Strong conferred with Lieutenant Colonel Daniel Rodman of the 7th Connecticut during the early hours of the eleventh, and they agreed that Rodman's regiment would lead a pre-dawn attack on Battery Wagner. After the easy success of the day before, the Federals thought that a bold bayonet charge would drive the Confederates from this second line of works.

Under the cover of darkness and a thick fog, Strong led Rodman's 185 men along the firm sand exposed by low tide to within 500 yards of Wagner. They were followed by the 76th Pennsylvania and the 9th Maine. Altogether, the three regiments totaled about 1200 men. Unknown to them, there were about 1800 Rebels in Wagner, counting about 150 men who manned shallow rifle pits on a sand ridge south of the main earthworks. There were also ten heavy guns (32-pounders and up) in the fort, not counting a seacoast mortar.

Wagner was built to defend against an enemy coming at it from the south, as the Federals would be, so as to protect the rear of Battery Gregg, at the north end of the island, bearing on Charleston Harbor. The island was narrow, and Wagner's earthworks, revetted with palmetto logs, extended all the way across it, from Vincent's Creek on the west to the Atlantic Ocean's high tide mark on the east. Near that east end, a salient jutted out to the south. Two heavy guns on the salient's eastern flank could fire at ships offshore, while two others could get a crossfire on anyone attacking the main line. Just south of the thick parapets was a deep moat, designed to fill with ocean water at high tide.

General Strong sent Rodman's men forward at a rush, but quietly, with orders not to stop to fire until they reached the fort. They were only some 25 yards short of the rifle pits when the Confederates there hit them with a volley and fell back, pausing to fire twice more before running down to the beach and along the fort's sea wall. Instead of following them, the Federals made straight for the fort. The defenders waited until the men from the rifle pits were out of the way, then the big guns opened fire with cannister, followed by a controlled volley of musketry.

Most of this fire went right over the heads of Rodman's men, who by then had reached the moat, but the two following Union regiments had lagged behind, and they were staggered and stopped by it. Several of Rodman's men tried to clamber up the parapet into the fort, but they were thrown back. A few others managed to work their way around to the sea face of the salient and into the works, but most of the Federals were trapped in the moat under a deadly enfilade fire from the salient plus the rifles and hand grenades of the Confederate infantry in front of them. Rodman ordered a retreat but then cancelled the order when he saw the other two regiments trying to move forward again. However, the Rebel fire soon stopped this second advance, with only a few individuals joining the 7th in the moat. Again Rodman, now wounded himself, ordered a retreat, adding "every man for himself."[10] Going back was more dangerous than the advance had been, and some of his men chose to stay and surrender. Those who managed to get away, including the other two regiments, fell back behind two reserve regiments.

The 7th Connecticut lost over half of its men. Total Union casualties were well above 300. The Confederates lost six men killed, six wounded. Strong ordered his reserve regiments to build a defensive line of their own across the island, to protect against any counterattack. That same day, Beauregard ordered his chief engineer to construct a zigzag covered way between Wagner and Battery Gregg and to place obstructions in Vincent's Creek to prevent surprise attacks by boat from that direction. Getting into Charleston Harbor by way of Morris Island was not going to be as easy as it had looked.

The draft began peacefully that day in Boston, Providence, New Haven, Pittsburgh and other northern cities. The Providence *Journal* pointed out that only those who could not raise $300 would actually have to serve, and that a soldier's pay would "little more than pay the rent of a small tenement." Therefore, "The families of such should be provided for at public expense, and the sooner steps are taken to do this the more cheerfully will men of this class take their places in the ranks, knowing that their wives and little ones will be cared for during their absence."[11]

In New York, rumors were circulating that groups within the city were organizing to resist the draft. Metropolitan Police Superintendent John Kennedy, with a large force of policemen, was on hand at the Ninth District draft office at 9 a.m. when a blindfolded clerk began drawing names on slips of paper from a cylindrical drum that the *Daily News* called "the wheel of misfortune." A crowd of about 150 people were on hand to witness the procedure, but it all went off peacefully. By 4 p.m. about half of the district's quota of 2,500 men had been selected, and the office closed, intending to reopen on Monday, the thirteenth. However, the New York *Herald* later reported that by that evening "there was intense excitement in the neighborhood."[12]

Kennedy had sent fifteen men to guard an arsenal that morning because of a rumor that the Knights of the Golden Circle were plotting to seize it and its weapons, but no attack came – maybe there was no such plot, or maybe the presence of the police prevented it. The Knights of the Golden Circle, also known as the Sons of Liberty, was a secret fraternal organization, complete with passwords and secret handshakes, founded in Cincinnati in 1854 by George Bickley, a Virginian with a long list of forged medical degrees, who had traveled the country establishing "castles" and initiating members. Originally the organization had espoused the spread of slavery, then it had backed secession, and now it opposed the Union war effort. By 1863 its membership had grown to some 300,000 men, including several prominent Democrats, such as Congressman Fernando Wood, former mayor of New York, whose brother, also a congressman, was the publisher of the *Daily News*. Only those who took the two highest degrees were told that the organization espoused armed rebellion.

In Indiana on 11 July, Lew Wallace's Union forces reached North Vernon by rail at 7 a.m. and marched on foot to camp near Holton. When Morgan's raiders approached Vernon at about 4 p.m. they found over a thousand Federal troops and Indiana militia, complete with artillery, deployed on the bluffs overlooking the Muscatatuck River south of the town. Morgan sent two demands for surrender, both of which were refused, after which one of the Union officers sent over a demand for Morgan to surrender. The Confederates could not afford to fight such a large force, well placed, giving time for Hobson to come up in their rear, so Morgan turned about and led his men southeast to Dupont, where the head of his column went into camp at about 11 p.m.

The Rebels would average over 20 hours a day in the saddle, a pace that was killing their horses. They took every horse they could find, of course, to replace those lost, but the Indiana horses were bred for farm work, not for carrying riders on long marches, and they broke down even faster than their Kentucky and Tennessee steeds. The men, too, were gradually being ground down. Major McCreary said his Confederate regiment, the 11th Kentucky, "Marched without any hindrance through Vienna, New Philadelphia, Lexington, and Paris, and came to Vernon, where we found the enemy in great force. The enemy consisted of Volunteers and Militia. We made a flank movement, tore up all the railroads around Vernon, and then traveled all night to Dupont, where we rested and fed our horses.... Man never knows his powers of endurance 'till he tries himself."[13]

While crossing Blue River near New Pekin, Confederate Captain William J. Davis and some of his men were captured by members of the 73rd Indiana and a detachment of the 5th U.S. Infantry. They were taken to New Albany and held in the county jail. Even without fighting a battle, Morgan's move to Vernon and then back to Dupont helped Hobson to gain ground and time on him. His pursuing provisional division reached Lexington that same evening, seventeen miles from Dupont. The Federals, however, were having an even more difficult time finding replacements for their worn-out mounts, the Confederates already having scoured the country they passed through for every horse they could find.

The next day, 12 July, Morgan's men raided a packing plant near Dupont, which provided them a nice supply of hams. The head of his column set out at 3 a.m., and along their way they destroyed tracks, bridges and warehouses of the Madison & Indianapolis Railroad. They moved northeast through Bryantsburg to Versailles, where 300 home guards surrendered without firing a shot. At Versailles, $5,000 of public funds were taken, and some of the men invaded the local Masonic Lodge and lifted its silver-coin jewelry, but Morgan, himself a Mason, ordered it returned. The column moved on through Pierceville, Milan, and Clinton, and halted for a couple of hours rest that night two miles south of Sunman. "We move rapidly through six or seven towns without any resistance, and tonight lie down for a little while with our bridles in our hands," Major McCreary recorded.[14]

Hobson's Federals were still pursuing. "On Sunday," he later reported, "I moved to within a mile of Versailles, and halted to feed."[15] From his headquarters in Cincinnati, General Burnside called upon the governor of Ohio to send militia to defend that city. The governor then called out the militia and consented for Burnside to declare martial law there.

At 9 a.m. on Sunday, 12 July, the first pontoon for Lee's bridge was placed in the Potomac River at Williamsport, loaded with lumber, and floated down to Falling Waters, which it reached at about 11:30. More soon followed, and the engineers and pioneers began assembling the bridge from the West Virginia side, strapping the pontoons together with trestlework. Other pioneers were improving the approaches to the bridge on both sides of the river and strengthening the bridge over the C&O Canal. Meanwhile, Lee's infantry and artillery continued to improve their entrenchments along Salisbury Ridge, while engineers constructed a shorter fallback line along a high ridge about a mile and a half from

Falling Waters for use by the rear guard when it came time to cross the river.

Lee wrote another letter to Jefferson Davis that day, although, he said, he had little of importance to add to his previous letters. "So far," he said, "everything goes well. The army is in good condition, and occupies a strong position, covering the Potomac from Williamsport to Falling Waters. The enemy seems to be collecting his forces in the Valley of the Antietam, his main body stretching from Boonsborough to Sharpsburg. But for the power he possesses of accumulating troops, I should be willing to await his attack, excepting that in our restricted limits the means of obtaining subsistence are becoming precarious. The river has now fallen to 4 feet, and a bridge, which is being constructed, I hope will be passable by to-morrow. . . ."[16]

Colonel Walter Taylor of Lee's staff wrote to General Sam Jones that day saying that Lee wanted him to assume command when he reached Winchester with his reinforcements and to organize stragglers and convalescents from Lee's army and send them on to Williamsport. However, Jones wrote to Secretary Seddon that day saying that, since he had found it necessary to withhold two thirds of his troops intended for that move, he did not intend to go there himself, pending further instructions.

At 5:30 p.m., Lee wrote to Jeb Stuart: "Colonel [A. L.] Long has returned from a survey of our position occupied by the corps of Longstreet and Hill. He has discovered the enemy massing their troops in their front, and thinks their principal attack on our lines will be between the Williamsport and Boonsborough road and the Frederick road, embracing both said roads. He has not been in Ewell's front (has just gone), but from your reports and those of General Ewell, there seems to be no enemy in that quarter. He thinks the attack will be made early to-morrow morning. Should it be, and there be nothing to occupy you, I wish you to bear down on the enemy's right, endeavoring to select good positions with your horse artillery, to harass and retard him. You will have, however, to keep a good lookout on the Chambersburg and Greencastle road, and not leave our left uncovered."[17]

But there were Federals facing Lee's left. That morning, Kilpatrick's cavalry and part of Howard's 11th Corps had advanced up the National Road from Funkstown to Hagerstown, driving Confederate cavalrymen and skirmishers before them. Kilpatrick's escort company charged and captured an entire company of dismounted Confederate cavalrymen. Custer's brigade then stormed into the town, where they rescued a trooper who had been captured in the fight on 6 July. The 1st Vermont Cavalry and Howard's leading regiment, most of its men barefoot, pushed on through Hagerstown and found the main Confederate line on the high ground to the west.

General Howard climbed a church steeple to have a look around, and the Signal Corps soon established a station on top of another church in the town, but fog and smoke from campfires obscured much of the view. However, Howard soon gleaned enough information from Union-loyal civilians to send Meade a pretty good description of Lee's line, although he mistakenly reported that the Confederates were short on ammunition but had plenty of provisions, when just the opposite was the case.

Other Union units pushed out to the west, and Meade's line soon ran south along high ground from just northwest of Funkstown, passing between Antietam Creek, to the east, and the Hagerstown-Sharpsburg Turnpike to the west, except that the pike passed through and to the east side of Meade's line near its center before continuing to the south. To Howard's left was part of Newton's 1st Corps, with the remainder in reserve, and to his left was Sedgwick's 6th Corps. Sedgwick also had control of the 1st and 11th Corps, and his headquarters was established in Funkstown, with a field telegraph line running to Meade's headquarters. Sykes' 5th Corps straddled the turnpike where it crossed through the lines. The 2nd Corps (under Hays since the wounding of Hancock and Gibbon at Gettysburg) extended the line to the

Williamsport-Boonsborough road, and Slocum's 12th Corps held the left, not quite reaching Tilghmantown, just north of the old Antietam battlefield. French's 3rd Corps was in reserve around Jones's Crossroads, near Meade's headquarters. The men began to construct light earthworks all along the line, while French and Sykes got into something of a spat about whether or not any troops of the 3rd Corps were in the front line instead of in reserve. French also criticized the placement of the 2nd Corps' line and lectured Meade on how to obtain information about the enemy.

As best the fog and smoke would allow, Buford's cavalry kept an eye on the rough country beyond Slocum's left flank, probing Longstreet's defenses. Buford reported that the terrain in this area was unsuitable for an advance. Captain L. B. Kurtz swam his horse across the river near Falling Waters, and back, to report to Devin that the Confederates were building a pontoon bridge while using a flatboat to ferry wagons and artillery across the river. Huey's brigade again tried to push up the Williamsport-Boonsborough Road, but met stiff resistance near the College of St. James, just beyond Marsh Creek, and could go no farther. At 10:20 a.m., Meade's headquarters issued a circular to all commands saying that General Warren, as chief engineer, would examine the position of the army, and that corps commanders should conform their lines to any changes that Warren deemed necessary.

At 12:30 p.m., General Couch wrote to Warren, thinking he was still Meade's chief of staff: "It is reported that the rebels crossed a good many horses yesterday at Williamsport, swimming the river, and that fourteen flats were nearly completed yesterday. . . . My Second Division will move down so soon as my provisions are up."[18] Meade wrote to Couch at 2 p.m.: "My troops occupied Hagerstown this morning, the enemy retiring before them toward Williamsport. The enemy are intrenched on a line one mile and a half from Hagerstown, in the direction of Dam No. 4, on the river. The road is open for you to Hagerstown."[19] Baldy Smith's 1st Division of Couch's command finally connected with Meade's army that day, and

Smith again suggested that his men be parceled out among the veteran units, but Meade declined to do that.

Other reinforcements were also arriving. A new regiment was assigned to the 11th Corps that day, and Colonel George Thom, an aide to General Halleck, reported to that general from Frederick at 10:15 a.m. that a brigade of three regiments had reached that place the day before and had proceeded to Boonsborough, and that two regiments of three-years' men had arrived that morning and were preparing to leave for the front. These latter two regiments were assigned to the 1st Corps that day. And General Naglee wrote to Meade's headquarters that day from near Harper's Ferry that he was sending a brigade of 1,648 men to Boonsborough, to report to the army's headquarters.

However, at noon, Ranald Mackenzie, a lieutenant of engineers and a future general of cavalry, wired General Warren some alarming news from Sandy Hook, near Harper's Ferry: "The river has fallen here 18 inches in the past twenty-four hours, and is still falling. A citizen states that he is acquainted with the river above here, and that he judges from its appearance at this place that the fords near Shepherdstown and Williamsport are now practicable for infantry."[20]

Meade did not mention this when he wrote to Halleck at 4:30 p.m. After briefly describing his own advance and what he knew of Lee's position, he added: "It is my intention to attack them to-morrow, unless something intervenes to prevent it, for the reason that delay will strengthen the enemy and will not increase my force."[21]

But something did intervene shortly thereafter. That evening he brought his senior officers together for a council of war. Present, besides Meade, were Humphreys, his new chief of staff, Warren, chief engineer, Pleasonton, chief of cavalry, Baldy Smith, whose militia had just reached the army, and all of his corps commanders, except Newton, who was ill – division commander Brigadier General James Wadsworth represented his 1st Corps. Meade read his officers Lee's recent order to his troops, which had somehow made it through the lines. General Howard later wrote that "All regarded that proclamation as something to keep up Confederate courage and allowed to come to us for 'strategic' effect."

Meade then called for a vote on whether or not they should attack. "Pleasonton, Wadsworth and I voted to attack," Howard remembered, but the others "voted to leave well enough alone." Pleasonton, Howard said, "was very anxious to attack . . . I was in favor of throwing out a strong skirmish line, and then with the main body, attack Lee's left flank." Meade discounted Pleasonton's vote because he considered the cavalryman a staff officer, not a corps commander. He also discounted Warren's vote for the same reason, and Wadsworth's because he was only a division commander. That left only one corps commander, Howard, favoring an attack, and his corps was the weakest in the army, and, anyway, Meade said, Howard always voted to fight. French told Meade, "If you give the order to attack, we will fight just as well under it as if our opinions were not against it."[22] But Meade would not go against the judgment of almost all of his corps commanders.

At 11 p.m., Lee directed that all of the ambulances carrying his wounded, and all of his ordnance, subsistence and quartermaster wagons take the towpath of the C&O Canal from Williamsport down to Falling Waters and start crossing the river. There were so many of them that he allowed 26 hours for their crossing. After that, his troops would follow.

Down along the Mississippi River on 12 July, General Banks was writing to General Grant from Port Hudson, saying, among other things: "As soon as possible after the surrender, I sent the First and Fourth Divisions down the river, to land at Donaldsonville. I have no official reports, but the steamer brings news that the enemy has spiked his heavy guns and fallen back from the river. It is certain that the steamers were unmolested. Before the movement, I requested Admiral Farragut to send all his light-draught gunboats around, by way of the Gulf, into Berwick Bay, to intercept the enemy's retreat by way of Brashear City, while my troops occupy and push him in front. My chief embarrassment is the great want of water transportation. The movement of the two divisions, without their baggage, 80 miles, has occupied nearly three days. . . . I have the honor to request that, if you can possibly spare them, you will send me as quickly as practicable a full division of infantry, embarked on two classes of transports; one with strong decks, for the transportation of artillery and cavalry, the other of very light draught, suitable for the navigation of bayous and shallow lakes. I shall be very glad if you send down with this division a small force of cavalry, as I made arrangements which will enable you to expect the return of Brigadier-General Grierson with his command to your headquarters within a week from this time. I have plenty of artillery. Barges are also much needed. . . ."[23]

Grant, however, was still concerned with Joe Johnston's army, now semi-besieged by Sherman at Jackson, Mississippi. That same day he ordered Brigadier General John McArthur, commanding a division of McPherson's 17th Corps stationed near the bridge over the Big Black River east of Vicksburg, to be ready to move to reinforce Sherman as soon as troops arrived to replace his. Those replacements consisted of one brigade from Vicksburg and one from Snyder's Bluff.

That same morning Sherman, not yet aware of this move, wrote to McArthur to thank him for sending news of Port Hudson's fall. "I have met no accident or reverse," he said. "Nothing troubles me but water. Johnston has taken refuge in Jackson with all his army, variously estimated at figures similar to what we had before crossing the Black. The place has been completely fortified and strengthened, and the lines extended so as to rest on Pearl River. I have the place closely invested, and have this morning given them an hour's shelling. The full effect is not reported. All my trains are up, and I have ten days' rations in camp, and am within 35 miles of your depot, to which I hear cars are regularly moving. Please telegraph to have sent to you about 4,000 rounds of ammunition for 20-pounder Parrotts and 10,000 rounds of 6-pounder case shot, also 1,000,000 rounds of assorted musket ammunition, to be sent forward to me on call, or when you have reason to believe me in want. You could make me more easy as to the enemy's cavalry threatening my communications if you would occasionally send an expedition to Raymond and Brownsville. . . . If General Grant sends out a new division, I want it posted on Baker's Creek, near Champion's Hill, to picket out well to the right and left, and forward to Bolton, the officer to send forward to me a report of his position. We are all in good health and spirits, in possession of all avenues out of Jackson this side of Pearl River, and now threatening the rear."[24]

General Pemberton wrote to Johnston from Raymond that day: "The most of my troops, paroled prisoners, will be in Raymond to-day. Stevenson's division to-morrow. Many of the men are leaving for their homes without authority. Unless you send me orders to the contrary, I shall move via Bovina to Brandon."[25]

Major General Benjamin Butler, at home in Lowell, Massachusetts, wired Secretary Stanton that day, Sunday, 12 July: "Much mischief is done by the publication of the names of drafted men in the newspapers in advance of the official notification. Drafts [draftees] are evading without any liability to the penalties. Would suggest that no publication be permitted." And Captain George Shaw, the provost marshal for the Third District of Massachusetts, wired Provost-Marshal-General Fry: "Drafted men are leaving the State in large numbers before there is time to serve notice on them. Can authority be given to prevent this by an order forbidding all persons liable to the draft to leave without pass from provost-marshal?" Fry replied to Shaw that same day, saying: "I am happy to say the evil you complain of does not seem to be general, and for the mere purpose of meeting it I cannot recommend to the Government that any of the law-abiding people shall be controlled or incommoded in their movements. All men who absent themselves in the manner stated are forever to be deserters, and it is the duty of all officers of the Army and of all good citizens, but especially of the officers and employes of this department, to arrest and turn them over for trial and punishment whenever and wherever they may be found. I have no doubt this duty will be faithfully performed, and with a view to it the names of the deserters must be published and posted throughout the country. If, however, they should escape arrest, the burden of military duty may fall a little heavier upon the loyal and brave, but this voluntary exile of cowards or traitors will relieve the country of a class of men it can well spare."[26]

Flags still adorned New York City that day, in celebration of the victories at Gettysburg and Vicksburg, when the first names for the Union draft in that city appeared in the newspapers. Many people stayed home from church to scan the list for their own names or the names of friends or relatives. "Throngs of excited men began to crowd the hotels and barrooms," according to James Gilmore, who was on the editorial staff of the *Tribune*. "Gathering in little knots, they denounced conscription, and openly talked of attacking the draft offices. Mingling among them were men in common, and in some instances shabby, clothing, but whose speech indicated cultivation, and whose hands showed them unused to labor. They advised concert of action, and the gathering of clubs, fence-rails, stones, rusty guns, and every variety of offensive weapon, to be secreted in convenient places, in readiness for a grand outbreak on the morrow."[27] An undercover detective notified police headquarters that day that he was tailing a Copperhead agitator, one John Andrews, a Virginia lawyer, but he lost him later that night.

It certainly had been a mistake to start the lottery on a Saturday and have the results published on a Sunday, when few people were at work. As journalist Joel Tyler Headley said, "To have the list of twelve hundred names that had been drawn read over and commented on all day by men who enlivened their discussion with copious draughts of bad whiskey, especially when most of those drawn were laboring-men or poor mechanics, who were unable to hire a substitute, was like applying fire to gunpowder."[28] Members of a notorious volunteer fire-fighting company, known as the Black Joke, who had a habit of rioting with members of rival companies, noted that Sunday that one of their members was among those drafted, even though firemen had previously been exempt from militia service. They met that day and vowed to destroy the draft office and its records.

Working men, in those days, usually began their 12 hours of labor at 6 a.m., but by that hour on Monday, 13 July, workers had gathered at several points in southwest Manhattan and had begun to move north, and about fifty rough-looking men were prowling the wharfs on the East River side, picking up recruits. Men and women from squatters' shacks and the slums the police called "Mackerelville" soon fell in, and the mob began entering factories, foundries, etc., and forcing a work stoppage at each, demanding a one-day strike. The workers, willingly or not, joined the growing mob as it moved north up the island. Among the leaders was John Andrews, the Virginia lawyer the detective had lost track of the night before, and Francis Cusick, an Irish-born stagecoach driver and former policeman. They were not all Irish, as a sizable German contingent was also present, led, in part, by an escaped convict.

After listening to speeches by some of these leaders, many men who wanted only a strike and not a crime spree fell away, but at about 8 a.m. the others started moving again, carrying placards that simply said, "No Draft." Small detachments of police were swept aside. Journalist Headley estimated that the mob now consisted of about 10,000 people, since it filled the street from curb to curb and, although moving rapidly, took 20 to 25 minutes to pass a single point. It was making for the Ninth District draft office at Third Avenue and 46th Street, though some men took time to cut down telegraph poles with axes stolen from a hardware store, and some women used crowbars to pry up the tracks of a railroad running up Fourth Avenue.

These two acts threatened to disrupt communications between the Central Office of the police and its precincts, and to cut off the city from the outside world. James Crowley, the superintendent of the police telegraph system, was riding on a street car on Third Avenue when the mob stopped it, forced the passengers off, and pushed the car off the track. He noticed the downed telegraph wires in the gutter and began to coil them around a lamppost and ground them, which caused several of the rioters to threaten his life. But he told them he was only getting the wires out of their way, then slipped off to a station house, where he was able to telegraph the Central Office.

Thus alerted, Superintendent Kennedy dispatched about 60 policemen to join the dozen that were already on hand at the Ninth District draft office, and sent almost 70 more to another draft office on Broadway, at 29th Street, where another mob was gathering. He also managed, before his lines went dead, to get messages to all of his police stations, including those in Brooklyn, across the East River, to call in their reserves. The police managed to disperse the mob at the Broadway draft office, so Kennedy sent them and other detachments toward the Ninth District office, and then went there himself after quickly checking the arsenal.

Francis Cusick, the former policeman, was just exhorting the mob to storm the draft office when Kennedy arrived. Cusick recognized him and knocked him down with a club, then turned on the officer who had driven Kennedy up in a buggy, beat him up, robbed him, and took his pistol. And a third policeman, a clerk from headquarters, was also attacked. The 60-year-old, unarmed, Kennedy was thrown over an embankment and into some muddy water in a vacant lot. He started to rise, but was knocked down again and beaten, until an acquaintance of his, a Democratic politician named John Eagan, convinced the mob that Kennedy was dead or soon would be. The other two policemen managed to flag down a wagon and get Kennedy into it and take him to the Central Office. Meanwhile the mob began to celebrate as the rumor spread that the superintendent of the Metropolitan Police was dead.

Inside the Ninth District draft office, the lottery had resumed peacefully at about 10 a.m., and the blindfolded clerk had drawn about 75 names, which were read aloud by Provost Marshal Charles Jenkins, when the Black Joke Engine Company arrived outside with its steam-powered fire engine, its men all wearing their firemen's gear. There was a single pistol shot, as of a starting gun, a hail of rocks came crashing through the windows, and then the mob, led by the firemen, stormed the office, shouting "Down with the rich men!"[29] Several of the officers in the building were injured by blows from clubs, and the building was set on fire, but the police were able to fight off the rioters without having to use their pistols, and a federal marshal was able to stash the enrollment records in a safe that the mob could neither open nor carry off. The police and other officials managed to escape out the back, but the fire soon spread to nearby buildings.

As Acting Assistant Provost-Marshal-General of the Southern Division of New York, Irish-born Colonel Robert Nugent, former commander of the famous 69th New York Regiment in the Irish Brigade of the Army of the Potomac, was in charge of the draft in the city, but he had only 70 soldiers, all of whom were members of the Invalid Corps, which was composed of soldiers too disabled by wounds or disease to stand the rigors of camp life any longer. When he had received word that morning that the draft would be resisted by a mob, he had sent 25 of his men to the Ninth District and 25 more to the state arsenal at Seventh Avenue and 35th Street, which left him only 20 men in their barracks as a reserve. He had conferred with other Army and militia commanders, but most of the troops and militia in the entire state had been sent off to Pennsylvania to help protect that state from Lee's army, and were now part of General Couch's department.

What few were available, it had been decided, should protect the state arsenal to keep the weapons stored there out of the hands of rioters.

The invalid soldiers sent to the Ninth District draft office arrived just after it had been stormed and set on fire, and they were pelted by the rioters with rocks and paving stones. The soldiers fired a volley of blanks, but this failed to frighten the mob, so some of the men loaded real cartridges, and the next volley killed or wounded several rioters. This enraged the mob, which disarmed the soldiers before they could reload, clubbed two of them to death with their own muskets, and threw a third to his death off a ledge near the East River. Most of the other soldiers got away, some with, some without injuries. One, with a fractured skull and a broken arm, was carried into a store by its Irish-American owner, who hid him in the basement and brought a doctor in to dress his wounds.

The mayor of New York had no control over the Metropolitan Police, which answered only to a 5-man commission that had been set up by the state legislature (due to corruption in the old Municipal Police). So, at 10 a.m., Mayor George Opdyke, a Republican, sent a note to Thomas Acton, head of the commission, also a Republican, and he also contacted Major General John Wool, commander of the U.S. Army's Department of the East, headquartered in the city, and Major General Charles Sandford of the state militia. But Opdyke described the mob as a demonstration, and only asked that forces be held in readiness in case it got out of hand. Fifteen minutes later, however, Sandford came to the mayor's office with a report that the police uptown were being overwhelmed by a large mob and informed him that the State Militia Act empowered the mayor to order out the military in the event of a riot. Opdyke immediately declared that a riot did exist and ordered Sandford to suppress it without delay. However, Sandford had few men to work with, and Opdyke was not certain that some of them would not join the rioters.

And rioters they were, as some of them began looting

several large homes on Lexington Avenue after throwing cobblestones through the front windows to gain entrance. Many of them moved down Third Avenue, which prevented the various detachments of Metropolitan Police from reaching the Ninth District draft office. The police coming up from the Broadway draft office only got to within two blocks of it before being forced back, and two other detachments were also forced to retreat. When two more detachments arrived, the combined force, minus those who had already been injured, managed to push to within a block of the draft office before encountering the real heart of the mob. Now badly outnumbered, the policemen were scattered and driven south again. Sergeant Robert "Fighting Mac" McCredie was chased into a building where a German woman hid him on the second floor and told his pursuers that he had escaped out a window. However, the mob set fire to the building, so the woman carried the badly injured sergeant to Lexington Avenue and put him in a cab that took him to a police station. The mob also prevented the fire department's chief engineer and his men from getting to the draft office, even though poor families lived in the upper stories of that building and in others nearby.

Some of the rioters threatened to burn St. Luke's Hospital, at Fifth and 55th, which held about a hundred sick and wounded men from the Army. But just then a wounded rioter was admitted, and the hospital's founder and director, Rev. Dr. William Muhlenberg, explained to the mob that his hospital was open to anyone and asked if they still wanted to burn it. The crowd promptly changed its tune and even left a vigilance committee to protect the place. However, most of the mob was still on Third Avenue. Joel Headley said people filled that street for about thirty blocks, but of the estimated 50,000 people only about 10,000 were active rioters, the others being only spectators.

"Captain [Benjamin] Manierre, in the eighth district, had proceeded with the drawing in his district, and had drawn about 216 names from the wheel," Colonel Nugent later reported, "when he received information of the proceedings in the ninth district. He immediately suspended the drawing, and, hastily getting his records and books together, they were safely deposited in the police station nearby. He had hardly succeeded in doing so before the mob was upon them, and the same scenes were enacted as in the ninth district, ending by firing the building, and the destruction of an entire block of eight or ten stores. The mob here was so great that it was deemed useless to order up the guard, only to share the same fate as their companions in the ninth district."[30]

By 11:30 a.m. all six draft offices in the city had received orders from Colonel Nugent to close and to send all their records to Governors Island for safekeeping. Meanwhile, the wagon carrying the badly beaten Kennedy reached the Central Office, which was at Mulberry and Bleeker, a few blocks southeast of Washington Square. A surgeon determined that no bones were broken, so he was sent to a friend's house to recover, and Thomas Acton, president of the police commission, took charge.

Of the five members of the commission, three were Republicans, including Acton, but one had gone to the army as a brigadier general of volunteers. Acton, a firm supporter of the war effort, put the other Republican in charge of Brooklyn and Staten Island and took personal charge in Manhattan. Journalist Headley recorded that Acton was "quick and prompt, yet cool and decided, and relentless as death in the discharge of his duty. Holding the views of the first Napoleon respecting mobs, he did not believe in speechmaking to them. His addresses were to be locust clubs and grape-shot."[31] He called for all available officers, except a few left to guard each station house, to assemble at the Central Office. He also sent detectives to mingle with the mob and report its movements, requested the mobilization of the state militia, and called for Federal troops to be sent from the forts in the harbor.

Around noon, John Andrews, the Virginia lawyer, harangued the rioters, telling them, "You must organize and keep together, and appoint leaders, and crush this damned abolition draft into the dust." This was followed by tremendous cheering, after which Andrews modestly volunteered, saying, "If you don't find any one to lead you, by Heaven! I will do it myself."[32] Many in the cheering crowd thought he was Congressman Benjamin Wood.

About a half-hour later, John Decker, the chief engineer of the fire department, addressed the crowd. He said he sympathized with their objections to the draft but asked them to let his men through to save lives and property that had nothing to do with that. The foreman of the Black Joke fire company supported this appeal, and the crowd started to let the firemen through, but then a more militant element blocked their way again. Soon the fire engines were put to use in an attempt to save a block of stores and homes that were being plundered, but most of the block was burned out.

Downtown, a mob of about 500 people, armed with clubs and rocks, gathered in front of the *Tribune* building, near City Hall. James Whitten, a barber at the Astor House, who frequently spouted anti-war sentiments to his customers and associates, spent his lunch break stirring up this crowd and making loud calls for Horace Greeley to show himself. When his lunch hour was up, he went back to work, but tried to enlist the hotel's waiters in an attack on the *Tribune* offices that evening, telling them, as the headwaiter later recalled, that if they "did not turn out and help they would get their own heads broke, as the mob would be the strongest party."[33]

Meanwhile the larger mob, uptown, now moved south along Third Avenue, growing larger as it went, and smaller groups broke off to loot the side streets. At 43rd, near Lexington, one group with axes chopped their way into a hotel where the American Telegraph Company had an office, doused the place with turpentine, and set it on fire. Others tore up more railroad track on Fourth Avenue. But the leaders' main objective was a state armory that filled the top three stories of a warehouse at the corner of Second Avenue and 21st Street, which happened to be owned by Mayor Opdyke and his son-in-law. One block north of that was the Union Steam Works, which manufactured carbines for the Union army. Thirty-two policemen of the "Broadway Squad," an elite formation of men picked for their size and strength, were sent to defend that armory, armed, in addition to their revolvers and clubs, with carbines from the nearby factory.

Just after 1 p.m. several thousand rioters assaulted the armory after failing to set the brick building on fire. They fired guns and threw rocks at the doors and windows and then charged. When they started breaking down the doors, the policemen fired on them and kept them out. But the officers were now besieged. They managed to send out a request for reinforcements, but none came, so finally they escaped through a hole in the back wall, dropped eighteen feet to the ground, fled across back yards, and fought their way to the nearest police station. However, they were soon attacked again, and so they made their way to the Central Office.

Those rioters who were not chasing the Broadway Squad or making other mischief then broke down the arsenal doors and began seizing weapons, most of which were on the third floor. But while they were doing so about a hundred policemen retreating down Second Avenue from the fight near the Ninth District draft office came on the scene. They quickly dispersed the onlookers outside the armory and then formed lines on either side of the door, and as rioters emerged with their stolen weapons and other loot the policemen clubbed them down. The rioters on the third floor then barricaded themselves in, but those on the lower floors set the building on fire. Flames shot up the stairwells, as those on the lower floor made for the doors and windows. At least ten rioters died when the third floor collapsed and dumped them into the flames below.

General Wool had deployed his few troops on hand to protect Federal offices, such as the Post Office and the Customs House. General Sandford had sent militiamen to guard armories in Central Park, at Seventh and 35th, and at White and Elm Streets downtown. Mayor Opdyke tried to call a meeting of the Board of Aldermen, but could not get a quorum together. He sent off telegrams to Governor Horatio Seymour and Secretary of War Stanton but did not at first ask either for help from beyond the city and surrounding areas. Only at 2 p.m. did his requests begin to sound urgent.

General Wool responded by sending Marines from the Brooklyn Navy Yard and troops (a lieutenant and 80 men) and some artillery from the forts, all of which fit on a single gunboat that carried them from Governors Island. Being himself in poor health, Wool, aged 79, declared Sandford in charge of all the state and federal forces, but Wool's deputy, Brigadier General Harvey Brown, only a few years younger than Wool, refused to serve under the militiaman. He gave orders for all of the some 300 men in the harbor forts to be ready to move at a moments notice, defied Sandford's order to report to the arsenal at Seventh and 35th, and instead took the small force under his immediate command to the police's Central Office and put himself under the orders of Commissioner Acton, whom he saw as the only legitimate authority for the conservation of law and order in the city. Acton was still in the process of gathering and organizing a force large enough to confront the mob. General Sandford held his militia in reserve all day while sending retired officers and veterans out to recruit volunteers, who were to assemble at the Seventh Avenue arsenal that evening. He also held Federal troops out of action and complained to General Wool that General Brown was not following his orders.

"Before night fell," wrote Anna Dickinson, a writer and lecturer on abolition, temperance and women's rights, "it was no longer one vast crowd collected in a single section, but great numbers of gatherings, scattered over the whole length and breadth of the city, some of them engaged in actual work of demolition and ruin, others, with clubs and weapons in their hands, prowling round apparently with no definite atrocity to perpetrate, but ready for any iniquity that might offer, and, by way of pastime, chasing every stray police officer or solitary soldier or inoffensive Negro who crossed the line of their vision...."[34]

Many rioters saw the war as being fought to free slaves in the South who would then move north and compete with them for jobs. A British visitor to the city said he "inquired of a bystander what the Negroes had done that they should want to kill them? He replied civilly enough – 'Oh, sir, they hate them here; they are the innocent cause of all these troubles.'"[35] At around 2 p.m. two homes for black seamen, downtown, about halfway between City Hall and the East River docks, were attacked, and some of the residents escaped onto the roofs. One group of African-American women heated pans of soapy water and ashes with which to scald anyone who attacked them.

However, Acton's attention was focused in a different direction. Mayor Opdyke lived on Fifth Avenue at 14th Street, and his home had been attacked already. The first mob to show up there had been dissuaded from attacking by a neighbor, a judge and Tammany Hall Democrat, who denounced the draft but urged them to obey the law and trust to the courts to protect their rights. A second mob had been driven off by a police squad, and a third, of 5-10,000 rioters, had been deterred by the 88-man artillery unit from Governors Island and instead made their way down Broadway toward police headquarters. However, unaware of this, at about 4 p.m. Acton dispatched 200 policemen under Inspector Daniel Carpenter, to the mayor's home.

Carpenter told his men, "We are to meet and put down a mob. We are to take no prisoners. We must strike quick and hard."[36] They moved down Bleeker Street, and when they turned into Broadway they could see the mob only a block away, filling the street as far as the eye could see, while the sky was black with the smoke of burning buildings. Carpenter sent detachments of 50 men each up side streets to the left and right, and as soon as they were in place he gave the order for the remaining 100 men to charge. The nearest rioters tried to turn and flee, but they were blocked by the mob behind them. When some tried to escape via side streets they were blocked by the two detachments. The rioters were armed with everything from sticks to firearms and vastly outnumbered Carpenter's men, but the disciplined ranks of policemen closed in on the mob from three directions, cracking heads with clubs as fast as they could reach them. The rioters fled in the one direction left open to them, and when it was over, Joel Headley said, "Broadway looked like a field of battle, for the pavement was strewn thick with bleeding, prostrate forms."[37]

Another group of about 200 rioters was streaming down Fifth Avenue, headed for the *Tribune* offices, singing "We'll hang old Greeley to a sour apple tree!" to the tune of the "Battle Hymn of the Republic" (then better known as "John Brown's Body"). One of Greeley's friends, James Parton, who saw them, said they were not dressed like laborers or mechanics, and guessed that they were, "dock-thieves, plunderers of shipyards, and stealers of old iron and copper." This mob turned onto 10th Street and then into Broadway, where it ran right into Carpenter's 200 policemen, still on their way to the mayor's house. The rioters scattered, leaving only one man behind, who, Parton noted, "staggered into a drug store as I got into an omnibus. He was evidently in a damaged condition about the head, and his face was covered with blood."[38] Finding no mob at the mayor's home, Carpenter and his men returned to the Central Office.

While the police were thus engaged downtown, at about 4 p.m. some 500 rioters chopped down the front door of the Colored Orphan Asylum, on Fifth Avenue at 42nd Street, one of them shouting, "Burn the niggers' nest!" Fires were set in numerous places in the building while teachers led the frightened children out onto 44th Street, which was filled with rioters and onlookers. Anna Shotwell, founder and director of the orphanage, saw and heard an Irishman shout, "If there's a man among you, with a heart within him, come and help these poor children." But the mob, she said, "laid hold of him, and appeared ready to tear him to pieces." Meanwhile, the children got away, heading for a police precinct house several blocks off. About twenty children who became separated from the main group were rescued by a young Irishman, four stagecoach drivers, and a company of firemen, and taken to the same police station. A couple of kids were rescued by individuals, who carried them to safety. John Decker, chief engineer of the fire department, soon arrived at the orphanage, but with only a dozen men and two fire hoses. They fought the fires and defied death threats from the mob, but they had no means of reaching a fire in the garret. Within twenty minutes the building was destroyed.[39]

John Andrews had meanwhile taken charge of the mob outside the *Tribune* and was giving it a rousing speech when managing editor Sidney Gay urged editor Horace Greeley to arm his employees and/or sneak out the back door, but Greeley refused to do either. He and a friend were going out to eat. "If I can't eat my dinner when I'm hungry," he said, "my life isn't worth anything to me."[40] He and his friend went right out the front door and walked to a nearby restaurant, and nobody laid a hand on them. After eating, Greeley went home.

Just after 5 p.m. Gay went in search of Mayor Opdyke in hopes of obtaining police protection for the *Tribune*. Meanwhile, James Parton arrived to find the five-story building almost empty. All the reporters and editors were out covering the riots. The windows were open, the doors unlocked. James Gilmore, a free-lance writer, also arrived, and the two men went to the publisher, Samuel Sinclair, who told them of Greeley's order against bringing firearms into the building. Gilmore and Parton decided to do it anyway. They went to police headquarters, where they were promised 100 policemen to protect the *Tribune*. Then they went to General Wool's headquarters, in the St. Nicholas Hotel on Broadway at Spring, where they found not only the general but the mayor, and they obtained an order for 100 muskets, with ammunition. The problem was, they had to take the order to Governors Island to get it filled. Gilmore took an omnibus down to the Battery, arriving after 7 p.m., and found that all the boatmen were gone, probably having joined the mob. He finally found an old fellow whom he paid to row him to Governors Island.

A little after 6 p.m. a black cartman named William Jones went out to buy a loaf of bread, but found himself in the middle of a chase. Three rioters had been chasing three black men. Two of these had escaped, but the rioters, joined by a growing mob, caught the other man more than once, beating and kicking him. However, each time he managed to get up and run off again, and he made his final escape by shooting the man who had started the chase in the first place. So the enraged mob vented its anger on William Jones, who was just then heading home with his loaf of bread. They beat him until he was senseless, hanged him from a tree that shaded the sidewalk beside St. John's Cemetery, and then set his clothes on fire, "burning him," *Harper's Weekly* later reported, "almost to a cinder."[41] It took two attempts and 100 policemen to recover what was left of the body.

James Parton returned to the *Tribune* building at about 7 p.m. and found that the doors were now closed and the windows shuttered. More than 2,000 people were milling around outside, although most of them seemed to be harmless spectators. But there was not a single policeman in sight. Parton said that "one good-natured-looking bull of a man was declaiming a little, 'What's the use of killing the niggers? The niggers haven't done nothing. They didn't bring themselves here, did they! They are peaceable enough! They don't interfere with nobody!' Then, pointing to the editorial rooms of the *Tribune*, he exclaimed, '*Them* are the niggers up there.'"[42]

The mob, however, remained quiet until a gang of men like those Parton had seen earlier on Fifth Avenue arrived. Soon someone threw a paving stone that banged against one of the shutters, and the crowd applauded and yelled its approval. Parton hurried over to the police station in nearby City Hall and told the six policemen there that the mob was beginning to throw stones, but that "Five men can stop the mischief now; in ten minutes, a hundred cannot." Five policemen followed him back to the *Tribune*, where they found that the mob was breaking windows. Brandishing their billy clubs they placed themselves between the crowd and the entrance, and the rioters fell back – until they realized how few policemen there were and that they were armed only with clubs. Then they rushed forward, brushed the policemen aside, and broke into the building.

Inside, they began smashing desks and chairs and setting fire to loose papers. The *Tribune*'s foreman and engineer were preparing to puncture a boiler and scald the rioters with steam when the promised 100 policemen (110 actually), led by Inspector Carpenter, came marching up Nassau Street in what Parton called, "a rushing torrent of dark blue cloth and brass buttons."[43] Some rioters were killed, but most escaped via City Hall Park. Sidney Gay, who had also gone out earlier looking for help, returned about 8 p.m. to find the lower floor of the building a mess, and only seven employees on hand, but he found about a dozen more out in the street, and others soon began to filter in, and they all went to work to turn out the next edition of the paper. However, by 9 p.m. a mob had gathered outside the building again, even larger than before. A reporter who mingled with the mob discovered that they planned to attack the building at 11 p.m.

Abolitionist William Powell, who owned and ran the Colored Sailors' Home on Dover Street, had defended the place all day, until a mob broke in at about 8:30 p.m., at which time he joined his family and boarders on the roof of an adjacent building. But about an hour later, fearing that the mob was going to set fire to the place, he decided they needed to escape but was at a loss as to how to go about it. Fortunately, a Jewish neighbor loaned him a long rope, "and though pitchy dark," he later wrote, "I took soundings with the rope, to see if it would touch the next roof, after which I took a clove hitch around the clothesline which was fastened to the wall by pulleys, and which led from one roof to the other over a space of about one hundred feet. In this manner I managed to lower my family down to the next roof, and from one roof to another, until I landed them in a neighbor's yard."[44]

Many African-Americans were being sheltered inside police stations, which were, therefore, becoming targets themselves. Most of the policemen were out fighting the rioters, leaving only token forces to hold their precinct houses, often doing so by brandishing revolvers and muskets. The 18th Precinct's station was abandoned at about 9 p.m. and later burned down.

General Brown came to General Wool at about 9 p.m. to denounce General Sandford for not using his troops against the rioters and to demand command of all Federal troops in the city. Instead, Wool replaced Brown with Colonel Nugent and reiterated that Sandford was in command of all troops, militia and Federal. A lieutenant just coming into the city reported to Wool's headquarters and asked the general's adjutant what was going on, only to be told, "this is the one spot in New York where the least is known of what is taking place!"[45] Wool sent the lieutenant to General Sandford, who merely assigned him and his men quarters inside the Seventh Avenue arsenal.

Members of the Union League Club, staunch Republicans, arrived at Wool's headquarters calling for martial law to be declared. General Wool said that only Mayor Opdyke could do that, but Opdyke claimed that only Wool could do it. George Templeton Strong, a member of the League, suggested that Opdyke call on all law-abiding citizens to be enrolled in a volunteer force, but the mayor said that would start a real civil war. Tammany Hall Democrats also showed up, and they adamantly opposed imposing martial law, which they said would further enrage the mob. Opdyke agreed, saying that declaring martial law without sufficient troops to back it up would only make things worse. Anyway, he believed that the worst of the rioting was over, but he promised to keep the military option open if the situation did not improve over the next few days.

A little before 10 p.m. a steamer landed at the Battery carrying James Gilmore with the 100 muskets he had obtained from Governors Island. The old longshoreman who had rowed him over there met him and told him the *Tribune* had been burned to the ground and that a mob of 10,000 was emptying the banks on Wall Street, but, although the sky was aglow with distant fires, Gilmore could see no signs of any fire near the *Tribune*. He offered to pay the old man to find him a wagon to carry the muskets, but the fellow said he'd already been paid enough and was at his orders for the rest of the night. They soon found a drayman who agreed to transport the heavy boxes of muskets and ammunition. Gilmore went on ahead and found that the *Tribune* building still stood, although it was surrounded by a huge mob. Going to a side door, he obtained 30 policemen who escorted the cart the last few blocks, and the boxes of muskets and ammunition were hoisted through second-story windows.

By this time there were more than enough employees on hand to use all 100 muskets, but the mob was so large that Gilmore doubted that they would have much effect if the rioters decided to attack. Further, it was soon discovered that the ammunition he brought did not fit the muskets. Their only hope was to bluff. He sent the old longshoreman over to the City Hall police station with the information that the rioters intended to attack at 11 p.m. and to request that plainclothes men mingle with the mob and spread the word that the newspapermen were well armed. This seemed to work, as the mob soon seemed to sway back and forth while its leaders were seen to be conferring. However, just before 11 p.m. there was a long shout from the streets, and the newspaper men stopped working, seized their weapons, and moved to the windows. Down below, Gilmore saw that, "Streaming from Broadway into the Park was a gang of about three hundred ruffians, mostly in red shirts, shouting and yelling like fiends." He could see that they were armed and moving with precision. "They were the fiery nucleus of the entire riot. It was for them that the mob below had waited, and the long yell they had sent up was a shout of welcome."[46]

However, Inspector Carpenter and his 110 policemen

arose from the shadows of the iron fence along City Hall Park and fell upon these 300 rioters, cracking heads with their locust-wood clubs. Those who were not killed or knocked out scattered in all directions. Carpenter than formed his men some five or six deep, and this phalanx drove into the remaining mob, which also began to scatter. Then a heavy rainstorm suddenly struck the city, completing the rout of the mob and helping to put out most of the fires that had been set all over town.

Under cover of this storm, Acton sent out two telegraphers to make repairs on the telegraph lines. They were dressed as workmen and mingled with the mob at first, then, over the next two days, began to recover and reconnect the wires, running them down alleys and over rooftops. Sometimes they posed as hack drivers in order to move about the city, occasionally having to give rides to rioters in order to maintain their cover. One was almost killed by policemen who thought he was looting a damaged building. Fifteen police detectives were also blending in with the rioters, in order to keep Acton appraised of the mob's intentions. One of these was recognized by a rioter, and he was badly beaten by the crowd before escaping into a nearby house. The Black Joke fire company, which had started the riots, eventually changed sides and went back to putting out fires and saving lives and property. At around midnight, General Sandford, wearing civilian clothes, went home to bed, leaving a couple of staff officers in charge at the 35th Street arsenal. Not long after that, General Wool retired to his room at the St. Nicholas Hotel.

Edward S. Sanford, a civilian in the U.S. Military Telegraph Service, had sent Secretary of War Stanton a couple of brief reports during the day, and he followed those up at 9:30 p.m. with a longer message: "The situation is not improved since dark. The programme is diversified by small mobs chasing isolated negroes as hounds would chase a fox. I mention this to indicate to you that the spirit of mob is loose, and all parts of the city pervaded. The Tribune office has been attacked by a reconnoitering party, and partially sacked. A strong body of police repulsed the assailants, but another attack in force is threatened. The telegraph is especially sought for destruction. One office has been burned by the rioters, and several others compelled to close. The main office is shut, and the business transferred to Jersey City.

"In brief, the city of New York is to-night at the mercy of a mob, whether organized or improvised, I am unable to say. As far as I can learn, the firemen and military companies sympathize too closely with the draft resistance movement to be relied upon for the extinguishment of fires or the restoration of order. It is to be hoped that to-morrow will open upon a brighter prospect than is promised to-night."[47]

∾ Endnotes ∾

1. *OR*, I:23:II:906.
2. Ibid.
3. Ibid., I:23:II:529. I suspect that the punctuation is wrong in the next-to-last sentence quoted and that it should read, "It is important to know if it will be practicable for Burnside to come in on our left flank and hold the line of the Cumberland, if not a line in advance of it and east of us."
4. Ibid., I:24:III:497-8. Both messages.
5. Ibid., I:24:III:501.
6. Grant, *Memoirs*, I:569-70.
7. *OR*, I:24:III:499-500.
8. Sherman, *Memoirs*, I:331.
9. *OR*, I:24:I:245.
10. Wise, *Gate of Hell*, 78.
11. Schecter, *The Devil's Own Work*, 120.
12. *Ibid.*, 121.
13. McCreary, "Morgan's Raid Comes to an Inglorious End," *B&G*, 682.
14. Ibid.
15. *OR*, I:23:I:659.
16. Ibid., I:27:II:301-2.
17. Ibid., I:27:III:998.
18. Ibid., I:27:III:663.
19. Ibid. I:27:III:664-5.
20. Ibid., I:27:III:669.
21. Ibid., I:27:I:91.
22. Wittenberg, Petruzzi and Nugent, *One Continuous Fight*, 259-60.
23. *OR*, I:24:III:504-5.
24. Ibid., I:24:III:506.
25. Ibid., I:24:III:1001.
26. Ibid., III:3:485, both quotes.
27. Schecter, *The Devil's Own Work*, 121.
28. Ibid.
29. Ibid., 131.
30. *OR*, I:27:II:900.

31 Schecter, *The Devils Own Work*, 133.
32 Ibid., 135.
33 Ibid., 136.
34 Anna Dickinson, "Anna Dickinson Sees the Draft Riots in New York City," in *B&G*, 716.
35 Schecter, *The Devil's Own Work*, 142.
36 Ibid., 152.
37 Ibid., 153.
38 Ibid., 153-4.
39 Ibid., 147.
40 Lois M. Starr, *Bohemian Brigade* (New York, 1954), 222.
41 Schecter, *The Devil's Own Work*, 156.
42 Ibid., 158.
43 Ibid., 159.
44 Ibid., 161.
45 Ibid., 163.
46 Ibid., 167.
47 *OR*, I:27:II:886-7.

CHAPTER 23
"The War Will Be Prolonged Indefinitely"
13 – 14 July 1863

IN INDIANA, SOME 2,500 militiamen had sat all night on a train on a side track at Sunman, unaware that Morgan's men were camped only a couple of miles south of them. Early on the morning of Monday, the 13th, the train moved on to Lawrenceburg, clearing Morgan's path only moments before his advanced guard reached the tracks. The head of Morgan's column reached the Whitewater River about noon that day, but the column was now strung out for miles. After a four-hour halt to let the column close up, the Confederates pushed on, passing from Indiana into Ohio, while Morgan sent captains Tom Hines and Sam Taylor to reconnoiter the defenses of Cincinnati. By now, straggling and casualties had reduced the division to about 2,000 men.

Major McCreary declared Harrison, on the border between the two states, to be "the most beautiful town I have yet seen in the North – a place, seemingly, where love and beauty, peace and prosperity, sanctified by true religion, might hold high carnival. Here we destroyed a magnificent bridge and saw many beautiful women."[1]

By noon of that day, nearly 10,000 Federal soldiers, Ohio militiamen, and home guards had gathered at Cincinnati and nearby Hamilton. And Hobson's Union cavalry was now only about five hours behind the Rebels and gaining, but the burnt bridge would soon delay them. "From Versailles," Hobson later reported, "I marched to Harrison, on the State line between Indiana and Ohio, my advance arriving about dark. The enemy crossed the Whitewater River at this place, burning the bridge, about an hour before my advance arrived. The rear of my command did not arrive until nearly morning, being detained in getting the artillery over the hills and fording the river."[2]

After conferring with his brigade commanders, Duke and Johnson, Morgan determined on a night march around Cincinnati, for to camp anywhere near it was to invite an attack from the large forces presumed to be gathering. From Harrison, detachments were sent towards both Hamilton and Cincinnati, to feign attacks on both of those places and keep their defenders in place, while the main force passed between those two cities. Thus began a grueling 32-hour, 95-mile ride around Cincinnati. About a fourth of Morgan's force, including Major McCreary's regiment, rode to Miami Town, where they brushed aside some home guards and destroyed a bridge over the Miami River. The other 1,500 men, the artillery, and the wagons, all went by way of New Haven.

Colonel Johnson also sent two officers into Cincinnati to see what its defenders were up to. They rejoined the column at Bevis to report that, although the city was filled with Union troops, they seemed to be completely disorganized. No attack could be expected from that direction that night. Burnside could get no timely information about Morgan's location. Reports concerning the detachments he had sent to threaten Cincinnati and Harrison didn't help, nor did fake messages that Morgan's own telegrapher sent in. To add to his distractions, he received a message from General Halleck that day, saying, "I must again urge upon you the importance of moving forward into East Tennessee, to cover Rosecrans' left. Telegraph what you are doing toward that object, so that we can have definite information to act upon." Halleck wired Rosecrans that same day: "General Burnside has been frequently urged to move forward and cover your left, by entering East Tennessee. I do not know what he is doing. He seems tied fast to Cincinnati."[3]

Down in Louisiana on the thirteenth, two brigades of Banks' 19th Corps advanced from near Donaldsonville along Bayou La Fourche, one on each side of the stream, against

Confederates under Brigadier General Thomas Green, who had retreated from the banks of the Mississippi upon the Federals' arrival, and who also had one brigade on each side of the bayou. The Rebels fell back for a while until Green felt he had a good idea of the Federals' numbers and dispositions, then he launched a counterattack, threatening both their flanks and forcing them back with heavy casualties. "The enemy frequently rallied in the ditches across the fields," Green reported, "but one of the flanks or the other was invariably turned by us at every stand they made, and a fire poured down the ditches, while Colonel [P. T.] Hebert, with his command, moved upon them in front, and thus we drove them for about 4 miles and almost to the walls of the fort."[4]

Brigadier General Cuvier Grover, in overall command of the Union forces, put the blame on one of his brigade commanders, Colonel Joseph S. Morgan, and had him court-martialed for retreating against orders and thus exposing the flank of the brigade on the other side of the bayou. The court found him guilty, but Banks disapproved the findings and eventually returned him to duty. "This victory," Green wrote, "completely paralyzed the enemy in our rear, and enabled us to move from the La Fourche after the fall of Vicksburg and Port Hudson without molestation."[5]

A small brigade from Grant's army, under Brigadier General T. E. G. Ransom, occupied Natchez, Mississippi, that day, seizing Texas cattle there that had been ferried over the Mississippi for the Confederate army. And a telegraph operator reported to Brigadier General James Chalmers, Confederate commander in northern Mississippi: "The operator at Yazoo City reports that Colonel [W. B.] Creasman has abandoned his position at Yazoo City, leaving guns, ammunition, and everything in perfect order. Enemy not yet entered city. He destroyed no guns, no ammunition; burned all the steamers. . . ."[6] Herron's Union division occupied the town without a fight, but the ironclad gunboat *Baron DeKalb* (originally known as the *St. Louis*) was sunk by a "torpedo" below the city. Interestingly, Herron's force at Yazoo City was seen by Joe Johnston as a threat to his own flank, and he telegraphed President Davis that day that a large force had lately left Vicksburg ". . . to turn us on the north. This will compel us to abandon Jackson. The troops before us have been intrenching and constructing batteries since their arrival."[7]

Meanwhile, Grant was writing a long letter to Sherman: "The object of the expedition you are commanding being to break up Johnston's army and divert it from our rear, and, if possible, to destroy the rolling stock and everything valuable for carrying on war, or placing it beyond the reach of the rebel army, you may return to Vicksburg as soon as this object is accomplished. . . .

"Do you think Johnston is receiving re-enforcements, or is he simply holding Jackson until the road east of him is completed, so that he can get off all the rolling stock on this side? Can you make a safe retreat to the Big Black, if it is found Johnston is receiving re-enforcements from the east?

"I would not advise your infantry going any farther east than they are, except you should find it advantageous to hasten the retreat of the enemy. Should you find it impossible to drive Johnston from his position, and your remaining endangers either it or this place, you can then return.

"I have sent Mower's brigade and one brigade from Kimball's division to relieve McArthur, and ordered the latter forward. The remainder of Kimball's division is still disposable, but there is no other force here to spare well. . . .

"An intercepted letter from Jeff. Davis to Lee was sent me from Washington. From that it would seem that Lee has been asking for Beauregard to be sent to Culpeper Court-House with an army of 30,000. Davis speaks of the impossibility of doing so, and says Johnston is still calling for more re-enforcements, though his first requisition had been more than filled. He does not say whether he will still send more troops west, but from alarm expressed in the letter for the safety of Richmond, I judge Johnston can expect nothing more."[8]

Sherman, in turn, wrote to McArthur that day: "I want

to give Johnston a good shelling as soon as I can afford the ammunition, and have sent down a [wagon] train to bring up all they can get. I have plenty for an open field fight, but not enough to shell a town. I have my troops well disposed, and design you for a reserve. Please be sure to order the bridge at Messinger's to be carefully guarded. A regiment will be plenty. The depot and bridges at the railroad crossing should be perfected. You can leave a brigade anywhere at Champion's Hill to escort up the train, and come on to Clinton and Jackson. I cannot do much till the ammunition is up, by which time I can make the time pretty lively. Halt the head of your column about 1 mile back of my headquarters, and report in person."[9]

Not all of President Lincoln's attention was on Lee and Meade, for he wrote a personal letter to General Grant that day: "I do not remember that you and I ever met personally. I write this now as a grateful acknowledgment for the almost inestimable service you have done the country. I wish to say a word further. When you first reached the vicinity of Vicksburg, I thought you should do, what you finally did – march the troops across the neck, run the batteries with the transports, and thus go below; and I never had any faith, except a general hope that you knew better than I, that the Yazoo Pass expedition, and the like, could succeed. When you got below, and took Port-Gibson, Grand Gulf, and vicinity, I thought you should go down the river and join Gen. Banks; and when you turned Northward East of the Big Black, I feared it was a mistake. I now wish to make the personal acknowledgment that you were right, and I was wrong."[10]

From Richmond, the Confederate agent for the exchange of prisoners of war, Judge Robert Ould, wrote to his Union counterpart that day, saying that he had "declared exchanged" several Confederate officers just captured and paroled at Vicksburg, including Pemberton and all his division and brigade commanders. "You can take the equivalents out of the officers captured and paroled by us at Chancellorsville, or from privates, as you prefer."[11]

Also, the Confederate War Department issued orders on the thirteenth for D. H. Hill, then commanding the Department of North Carolina and the troops in the vicinity of Richmond, to "forthwith repair to Jackson, Miss., and report to General Joseph E. Johnston for duty with the army in Mississippi."[12] The order named Hill as being a lieutenant general, whereas he had been, up to this time, only a major general.

At 9 a.m. on 13 July General Couch wrote to General Meade from Chambersburg: "The part of General Milroy's troops serving with me, infantry and cavalry, were last evening ordered to join the Army of the Potomac, via Greencastle. I trust they will be with you to-morrow. Dana's division, 12,000 strong, including fourteen [12-pounder] Napoleons, Pennsylvania militia, I hope will get to Greencastle to-morrow night. If it is your wish for them to march into Hagerstown, I think they can be suppled from this point. My transportation is increasing. The roads south of this point are not in condition to haul any great amount of supplies."[13] However, later in the day Couch wrote that Dana's division had only 9,000 men (although returns show that it had 12,644 men) and 8 guns, and reported himself "Wholly unable to move it upon Leitersburg, on account of want of transportation for supplies. It may be twenty-four or forty-eight hours before it can go forward. The railroad cannot be repaired to this place in at least five days. The pike to Greencastle is badly cut up. Information that the enemy have a pontoon bridge at Williamsport is not wholly reliable." Halleck, having received a copy of this, wired Couch at 9 p.m.: "Your telegram to General Meade, that you cannot move for want of transportation, is received. Take it wherever you can find it, and, if you can find none, go without it, and live on the country. Do not stop at trifles at this crisis, but prove yourself equal to the emergency."[14]

The report that Lee had a pontoon bridge at Williamsport

had come from General Kelley, who had telegraphed it to the War Department from Fairview, Maryland, at 4:30 p.m. At 9 p.m., Halleck wired General Kelley: "Move up upon the enemy's flank and rear, and attack and harass him wherever you can. If you can reach his crossing, annoy him as much as possible."[15]

Kelley's report was erroneous, in that the bridge was at Falling Waters, not Williamsport, but the important point was that such a bridge existed, and Lee's immense trains of wagons began crossing it that day. Grumble Jones's brigade of cavalry swam across the Potomac to scout ahead, while one of his regiments, which had been left in the Valley when the brigade had moved north to join Lee's army, moved eastward toward Harper's Ferry, and Imboden gave close protection to the ambulances and wagons on the West Virginia side, as they moved up the Valley Turnpike. The weather that day alternated between periods of steaming heat and cooling rains, while all during the day the wagons continued to cross the floating bridge, and huge herds of horses, mules, cattle, and sheep were driven across the river near Williamsport.

Skirmishing broke out between Lee's and Meade's troops that day, many of whom expected the other army to launch an attack upon them. But many of the Federals were also expecting to make an attack themselves and wondering why none had yet been ordered. However, after the vote of his corps commanders against launching such an attack, Meade was reluctant to order one until he knew more about Lee's position and defenses. At 5 p.m. he wrote to Halleck: "In my dispatch of yesterday I stated that it was my intention to attack the enemy to-day, unless something intervened to prevent it. Upon calling my corps commanders together and submitting the question to them, five out of six were unqualifiedly opposed to it. Under these circumstances, in view of the momentous consequences attendant upon a failure to succeed, I did not feel myself authorized to attack until after I had made more careful examination of the enemy's position, strength, and defensive works. These examinations are now being made. So far as completed, they show the enemy to be strongly intrenched on a ridge running from the rear of Hagerstown past Downsville to the Potomac. I shall continue these reconnaissances with the expectation of finding some weak point, upon which, if I succeed, I shall hazard an attack. General W. F. Smith, of the advanced division of General Couch's forces, has arrived here to-day, but from the organization and condition of these troops, and the short time they have to serve, I cannot place much reliance upon them."[16]

Kilpatrick, whose cavalry now covered the Union right, or northern, flank, tried to get Smith's militia to help him drive in Confederate pickets that day, so he could get a better look at Ewell's lines, but the militiamen were reluctant to leave the shelter of Hagerstown, doing so only when the cavalry actually launched a charge. This, in turn, drew a note from Meade complaining that the cavalry's attack was interfering with his own plans for making an assault the next day. Kilpatrick replied that his attack was necessary in order for him to hold on to Hagerstown, then told his staff, "I know that is not quite true, but I did not want the cowardly militia to return home without meeting the enemy."[17]

Buford's troopers pushed stubborn Confederate cavalry back past the College of St. James and closed to within a half-mile of Longstreet's lines. And skirmishers of the 1st Division of the 6th Corps drove their Rebel counterparts from some high ground to their front just before dark and held it. Jeb Stuart later reported that most of his cavalry spent the thirteenth reconnoitering on Lee's left. "Cavalry pickets were extended beyond the railroad leading to Chambersburg," he said, "and everything put in readiness to resist the enemy's attack. . . . but it appeared that the enemy, instead of attacking, was intrenching himself in our front, and the commanding general determined to cross the Potomac."[18]

Meade himself rode out in the rain trying to get a look at Lee's defenses. A newspaper correspondent visiting headquarters saw him return, his uniform wet but his spirits undampened. "We shall have a great battle tomorrow," he told the newspaperman. "The reinforcements are coming up, and as soon as they come we shall pitch in." The correspondent later rode along the army's lines with General Howard, who was not so confident. "I fear that Lee is getting away," Howard said.[19]

Halleck replied to Meade's message at 9:30 p.m.: "You are strong enough to attack and defeat the enemy before he can effect a crossing. Act upon your own judgment and make your generals execute your orders. Call no council of war. It is proverbial that councils of war never fight. Re-enforcements are pushed up as rapidly as possible. Do not let the enemy escape."[20] Individual regiments were being assigned to the 1st, 11th, and 12th Corps that day as they arrived from southern Virginia via Washington and Baltimore.

However, Meade, frustrated at his inability to get a good grasp of Lee's position, was not yet ready to launch a real attack. A half-hour earlier, Meade's headquarters had sent out a circular, ordering the 2nd, 5th, 6th, and 12th Corps to each make a division-sized reconnaissance in force the following morning, to begin at 7 a.m. "The enemy's pickets, supports, and guards will be driven in until a distinct view of his position, defensive works, force, and its arrangements can be had. If it should be necessary [in order] to obtain this information, and should be practicable, the enemy should even be made to display his line of battle. The character of the ground passed over, the facilities it affords, and the obstacles it opposes to the movement of artillery and infantry, will be carefully noted, as well as the advantages it affords for offensive and defensive operations. . . . The commanders of corps will hold their troops under arms in readiness for a general engagement, should the enemy offer one in front of his line of supposed intrenchments."[21] The cavalry on each flank was told to cooperate, and, in separate orders, at 9:30, General French of the 3rd Corps was told to send a division each to the 2nd and 12th Corps to support their defensive lines while those corps participated in the reconnaissance in force. The 1st and 11th Corps, both badly battered at Gettysburg, were not included in the reconnaissance.

Evidently it finally occurred to Meade that day to put some forces south of the Potomac, but he sent too little and too late. At 9 p.m. General Pleasonton told General Gregg of the 2nd Division of cavalry: "Report is confirmed that a part of the enemy's cavalry swam the river at Williamsport last night. You will, therefore, proceed early to-morrow morning, with the two brigades of your division at Boonsborough, to Harper's Ferry, where a bridge will be prepared for you to cross the river at that point. You will cross to the opposite side, and move in the direction of the enemy's line of communication from Williamsport and Winchester, to annoy their trains and communication. . . . Huey's brigade will remain for the present where it is."[22] Why Meade didn't think to do this before Confederate cavalry was in position to oppose his own is unknowable. Or, for that matter, why not send a corps or more of infantry? A sizable Union force on the southwest bank of the Potomac at Falling Waters and Williamsport could have prevented Lee from crossing; his army would have been surrounded and starving.

As it was, when darkness fell that evening Lee's troops began to evacuate their defenses. Ewell's 2nd Corps, on the left, was to wade the river at Williamsport, while Hill's 3rd Corps, in the center, and Longstreet's 1st Corps, on the right, would follow the wagons over the floating bridge at Falling Waters. Rodes' Division, on the left end of Ewell's line, was the first to take to the Hagerstown-Williamsport Turnpike, followed by Johnson's Division from the corps' right, then Early's Division brought up the rear. Regimental bands played patriotic and sentimental songs to drown the noise of moving columns, and Union bands across the way unwittingly helped out by replying with their own tunes. Burning campfires, logs painted to look like cannon, and pieces of cloth painted to look like flags were left behind, while each brigade left one regiment, and each artillery battalion a single gun and crew, to hold the lines while the rest marched away. Then these eventually joined the march and were replaced by cavalrymen of Chambiss's and Robertson's brigades. A light rain, plus smoke from the campfires, helped to mask the withdrawal. One of Rodes' men said that the turnpike "was so blocked up with troops that we did not get on very fast, and when we got to Williamsport we found it crowded with soldiers."[23]

Ewell's artillery was supposed to cross first, but that would take so long that Lieutenant Colonel James L. Corley of Lee's staff decided to send Ewell's artillery down the C&O Canal's towpath to Falling Waters, accompanied by Hays's Brigade for protection, to be followed across the bridge by Longstreet's and Hill's guns. Corley then ordered Ewell's wagons to cross the ford at Williamsport and three other fords farther upstream. Some of the wagons were caught by the current and swept down the river. Meanwhile, Ewell's infantrymen waited. "We had to stand and wait an hour or more," the same soldier recorded, "for there was no place to sit down as the streets were ankle deep with mud and water. Finally we moved on down towards the river, but every few yards the column would halt – so that we were just creeping along at a most fatiguing pace."[24]

The infantrymen had first to wade the aqueduct that carried the C&O Canal over the mouth of Conococheague Creek, because the wagons were using the towpath, then they entered the river in pairs, holding onto each other to resist the current. "It was very dark, raining, and excessively muddy," General Rodes later reported. "The men had to wade through the aqueduct, down the steep bank of soft and slippery mud, in which numbers lost their shoes and down which many fell. The water was cold, deep, and rising; the lights on either side of the river were dim, just affording enough light to mark the places of entrance and exit; the cartridge-boxes of the men had to be placed around their necks; some small men had to be carried over by their comrades; the water was up to the armpits of a full-sized man. All the circumstances attending the crossing combined to make it an affair not only involving great hardship, but one of great danger to the men and company officers; but be it said to the everlasting honor of these brave fellows, they encountered it not only promptly, but actually with cheers and laughter. We crossed without the loss of a single man, but I regret to say with the loss of some 25,000 or 30,000 rounds of ammunition, which were unavoidably wetted and spoiled. After crossing, I marched, by orders, a short distance beyond Falling Waters, and then bivouacked; and there ended the Pennsylvania campaign, so far as this division was concerned."[25]

Jed Hotchkiss, the 2d Corps' cartographer, reported that 8,000 pairs of shoes were lost during the crossing. One private wrote home on the fourteenth, "Our clothes, blankets (partly) & haversacks all got wet, which increased our load & made it very disagreeable marching after crossing. The banks were muddy & on this side so steep & slippery that it was difficult to scuffle up it. We were very tired & confidently expected to stop directly after getting over the river, but on we went without stopping. . . . At 6 or 7 O'clock this morning we came to a halt. After being on our feet the whole night – marching on a sloppy pike, & stopped to rest only once (5 or 10 mins.) during the whole trip. Oh! It was a killing march. It beggars description."[26] It was midnight by the time Johnson's Division reached Williamsport, and dawn on the fourteenth by the time Early's Division began crossing. Ferguson's cavalry were the last to cross.

Scouts brought word to General Kilpatrick at about 3 a.m. on 14 July that the Rebel pickets on his front were retiring, and he immediately ordered his men to quietly mount up and find out where the enemy had gone, but he doesn't seem to have forwarded the information to other units. The 5th Michigan Cavalry of Custer's brigade led the way, capturing a few stragglers along the road, and a few minutes before 6 a.m. reached the last hills overlooking Williamsport. The Federals charged through the town, driving the last few Confederates into the river, about fifty of whom drowned. A couple of dozen wagons were swept away by the current as they struggled to escape, and Custer's attached battery of horse artillery exchanged shots with Rebel guns across the river, killing a few men in Ferguson's 14th Virginia Cavalry. But the bulk of the Rebels were safely across the river. "I cannot describe my feelings of disappointment and discouragement," the 5th Michigan's commander wrote. One Rebel cavalryman said the Confederates had crossed just in time, "for in a few hours after we got over[,] the River was not fordable. The Yankees came up on the other side and seemed very much provoked at our giving them the slip."[27] However, civilians soon informed Kilpatrick that other Confederates had taken the road to Falling Waters, some four miles downstream. Leaving the 5th Michigan to hold Williamsport and round up Rebel stragglers, the rest of the brigade soon headed for Falling Waters, a single squadron of the 6th Michigan leading, with Kilpatrick and Custer just behind them, then the rest of that regiment, and then the other two regiments.

At about the same time that Rodes' Division began its march from the army's left, McLaws' Division of Longstreet's 1st Corps started to withdraw from the entrenchments on Lee's far right, followed by Hood's Division. They took the Hagerstown-Downsville Road and then turned onto the Falling Waters Road. There were large bonfires where the two roads met, and Lee sat his horse there for a while, watching the columns pass, before moving on to the bridge. These roads were not paved. "The mud," one of McLaws' men wrote, "was almost knee deep and about as thick as corn meal batter. We waded through it like horses, and such a squashing you never heard. I believe I had over fifteen or twenty pounds of mud clinging to my shoes and pants."[28]

Lee had placed General Longstreet at the floating bridge to oversee the crossing of the wagons there. "The route to the bridge was over a new road," Longstreet later wrote; "at the ends of the bridge were green willow poles to prevent the wheels cutting through the mud, but the soil underneath was wet and soggy under the long season of rain, and before night rain again began to fall. . . . The rain fell in showers, sometimes in blinding sheets, during the entire night; the wagons cut deep in the mud during the early hours, and began to 'stall' going down the hill, and one or two of the batteries were 'stalled' before they reached the bridge. The best standing points were ankle-deep in mud, and the roads halfway to the knee, puddling and getting worse. We could only keep three or four torches alight, and those were dimmed at times when heavy rains came. Then, to crown our troubles, a load of the wounded came down, missed the end of the bridge, and plunged the wagon into the raging torrent. Right at the end of the bridge the water was three feet deep, and the current swift and surging. It did not seem possible that a man could be saved, but every one who could get through the mud and water rushed to their relief, and Providence was there to bring tears of joy to the sufferers. The wagon was righted and on the bridge and rolled off to Virginia's banks. The ground under the poles became so puddled before daylight that they would bend under the wheels and feet of the animals until they could bend no farther, and then would occasionally slip to one side far enough to spring up and catch a horse's foot and throw him broadside in the puddled mud. Under the trials and vexations every one was exhausted of patience, the general and staff were ready for a family quarrel as the only relief for their pent-up trouble, when daylight came, and with it General Lee to relieve and give us opportunity for a little repose."[29]

When they reached the floating bridge, the infantrymen had to wait for the wagons and artillery to cross first. A private in the Texas Brigade remembered that it rained all night, and said, "We could hear the distant rumbling of an electric storm far away to our left and see the incessant glimmering of the lightning as it played along the lofty summit of old South Mountain."[30] By the time the Texans reached the bridge, it was daylight, although there was a fog on the river and in the valley. The same private saw General Lee there, after he had relieved General Longstreet. "He had always appeared to me before that morning as a model of elegance. On that gloomy occasion he looked pale, haggard, and old, but sat old Traveller as knightly as a Chevalier Bayard. He was bespattered with mud from the spurs on his boots to the gold cord on his black Kossuth hat. Old Traveller, whose original color was a light iron gray, on that memorable morning was a veritable claybank."[31]

Hill's 3rd Corps was the last to move and had the longest route. Anderson's Division, followed by Pender's, withdrew from their positions near the army's center, took the road south towards Downsville, turned west onto the Williamsport-Boonsborough Road, south on a crossroad, and finally west on the Falling Waters Road. Heth's Division, in the corps' center, came last, making it the rear guard of the entire army. Hampton's Brigade of cavalry, still commanded by Colonel Baker, took over Hill's trenches after the infantry and artillery left. It took all night for Anderson's column to march five miles, and it was still three miles from Falling Waters. It was daylight when it came to a halt at the rear of Hood's Division. By the time that Heth's Division set out, the rain was falling in sheets, the night was pitch black, and the roads had been made even worse by the latest rain, the wheels of all the preceding wagons and guns, and the thousands of marching feet that stirred the water and soil into gooey mud. It took twelve hours for Heth's column to march seven miles. Two guns had to be abandoned when they became so mired in the mud that the exhausted teams could not extricate them.

It was already daylight on the fourteenth when Heth's Division came to the ridge where Lee's engineers had prepared a final defensive line, about a mile and a half from the floating bridge. "Tired, foot-sore, wet, hungry, and literally frazzled out," a lieutenant later wrote, "our division lay down in the old field in the edge of which was an apple orchard."[32] General Hill ordered Heth to place his division in the entrenchments on both sides of the road, but the gun emplacements could not be filled, as all the artillery was ordered to cross the river as rapidly as possible. "Did you ever hear of a rear guard of a retreating army without artillery?" General Pettigrew asked Heth.

Pettigrew, with his own brigade and Archer's, filled the trenches on the left of the road; Brockenbrough's and Davis's brigades were to the right, or south, of the road. Pender's Division, still under General Lane, formed a reserve on lower ground about 200 yards closer to the bridge. Anderson's Division was still waiting to cross the bridge, then filled with Hood's troops, guns and wagons. Along the road, long columns of division wagons and many stragglers continued to move towards the bridge, and somewhere back up the road, Heth assumed, were some of Fitz Lee's cavalry, screening the army's rear. So Heth ordered his men to stack muskets, lie down, and get some sleep. Pettigrew took it upon himself, however, to send out pickets in front of his half of the division.

Jeb Stuart, in his report, stated that his cavalry was supposed to cross the river at Williamsport, following Ewell's corps, except that Fitz Lee's brigade, "should he find the pontoon bridge clear in time, was to cross at the bridge; otherwise to cross at the ford at Williamsport.... General Fitz Lee, finding the bridge would not be clear in time for his command, moved after daylight to the ford, sending two squadrons to cross in rear of the infantry at the bridge. These squadrons, mistaking Longstreet's rear for the rear of the army on that route, crossed over in rear of it."[33] In other words, the cavalry had crossed ahead of Hill's corps without Harry Heth being aware of it, so that when Union cavalry appeared he thought, at first, that it was the expected Confederate horsemen.

But the approaching cavalry was, in fact, the head of Kilpatrick's column. "The march from Williamsport to Falling Waters was a wild ride," Captain Kidd later wrote. "For the whole distance the horses were spurred to a gallop. Kilpatrick was afraid he would not get there in time to overtake the enemy, so he spared neither man nor beast. The road was soft and miry, and the horses sank almost to their knees in the sticky mud. For this reason the column straggled, and it was not possible to keep a single troop closed up in sets of fours." Soon the rest of the column had fallen behind the leading squadron, which was commanded by Major Peter Weber. "On nearing Falling Waters," Kidd said, "the column turned to the right through a wood, which skirted a large cultivated field. To the right and front, beyond the field, was a high hill or knoll on which an earthwork had been thrown up. Behind the earthwork a considerable force of Confederate infantry was seen in bivouac, evidently taking a rest, with arms stacked. . . . On sighting this force, Custer ordered Weber to dismount his men, advance a line of skirmishers toward the hill and ascertain what he had to encounter. Kilpatrick however ordered Weber to remount and charge the hill. At that time no other portion of the regiment had arrived so as to support the charge."[34] Weber's command consisted of only 57 men, but he had recently stated that his greatest ambition in life was to lead a saber charge, and so his wish was fulfilled.

Generals Heth and Pettigrew were conferring when they first spotted the horsemen approaching through the fog, but neither could tell whether they were Federals or Confederates. They carried stars-and-stripes company guidons, but their uniforms were dirty and faded to the point that they looked more gray than blue. Concluding that the flags were captured, Pettigrew prepared to arrest the cavalry's commander for displaying them so incautiously. Some officers ordered their men to open fire, but Heth countermanded the order. The fact that the squadron came on in column and at a leisurely pace "confirmed all," one Rebel recorded, "in the belief that they were our own cavalry. Suddenly they deployed into line and rushed upon the division."[35] A member of Archer's Brigade said the horsemen came to within thirty yards of the Confederate line before wheeling into line and charging. "They struck the head of our column yelling, cutting right and left, and riding over our men while asleep," he said, "breaking arms and legs and trampling some to death."[36]

Most of the Federals cut diagonally right through Heth's line, yelling for the Confederates to surrender. Many did raise their hands while others fell to the ground, out of the reach of the swinging sabers as the horsemen rushed past. Pettigrew, with one bad hand and the other arm in a sling from wounds picked up at Gettysburg, lost control of his mount when it reared at the sudden noise and confusion. The horse fell on him, but he managed to get to his feet and run to a fence near where the road penetrated his line. He ordered his men to about-face and fire into the Federals' rear, while Pender's Division fired on their front and extended its line to block their access to the bridge. Major Weber ordered his men to turn back and cut their way out, catching many Confederates before they could reload. "The men clubbed their guns and knocked the Yankees off of their horses," one Rebel remembered. "One man knocked one off with a fence rail and another killed a Yankee with an ax."[37]

Pettigrew spotted an unhorsed Union corporal firing from behind a nearby barn and ordered some of Archer's men to shoot him. They fired but missed, so the general drew his revolver and walked through a garden to take a shot himself. The cavalryman fired first, his bullet passing through the base of Pettigrew's spine. Surgeons who rushed to his aid said he should not be moved farther than to the barn; his only hope of survival was to be left to the care of the enemy. Pettigrew, who had been wounded and captured the year before at Seven Pines, refused, saying, "I would die before I would again be taken a prisoner."[38] Meanwhile, one of his North Carolinians knocked the Federal trooper to the ground and killed him with repeated blows from a large rock.

Major Weber was killed by a bullet to the head; one of his troop commanders was also killed, and the other was wounded and captured. Only about half of his troopers got back to rejoin their regiment. "In the meantime," Kidd later wrote, "just as Weber's command was repulsed, the other squadrons of the regiment began to arrive, and were hurried across the field to the foot of the hill, and there dismounted to fight, dressing to the left as they successively reached the alignment and opening fire with their Spencers at once. But having disposed of the two mounted troops, the Confederates filled the earthworks, and began to send a shower of bullets at those already formed below."[39] Just as Kidd brought up his own troop he was hit in the right foot, "making what the surgeon in Washington afterwards said was the 'prettiest wound I ever saw.'"[40] Three months later he returned to the regiment, promoted to major to take Weber's place. He would end the war in command of the Michigan Brigade.

Kilpatrick "directed General Custer to send forward one regiment as skirmishers," as he later reported. "They were repulsed before support could be sent them, and driven back, closely followed by the rebels, until checked by the First Michigan and a squadron of the Eighth New York."[41] The latter unit was from Buford's Division, just coming up. A color-bearer in Brockenbrough's Brigade ran forward yelling, "Come on, boys, it's nothing but cavalry," and Colonel Brockenbrough ordered his whole brigade to follow, although he personally continued to retreat. Led by Brockenbrough's aide, Captain Wayland Dunaway, the Virginians collided with the dismounted 8th Illinois Cavalry of Gamble's brigade, but Dunaway soon noticed another cavalry regiment forming in the woods and that the rest of Heth's Division was falling back. "All of a sudden it flashed through my mind that we could neither fight nor run," he later wrote. "Further resistance was vain; escape, impossible."[42]

The "nothing but cavalry" charged and gobbled up most of the little brigade. Two sergeants of the 1st Michigan Cavalry captured sixty men of the 44th Virginia, plus its major and its battleflag. Two privates of the same regiment captured the flag of the 47th Virginia while their regiment rounded up 56 men and 5 officers of that regiment. Altogether, the 1st Michigan claimed one cannon, two caissons, and 500 prisoners. The 7th Michigan also claimed the capture of a gun, and one of its squadrons, totaling only 77 men, charged into the 55th Virginia and came away with 400 prisoners, as well as that regiment's colonel and its battleflag. In all, Kilpatrick claimed the capture of 2 guns, 3 battleflags, and upward of 1,500 prisoners, but this probably included the fight at Williamsport, stragglers picked up along his route, and a large number of wounded Confederates who had been left behind under the care of their own surgeons.

Pettigrew was carried on a stretcher over the bridge, and his brigade was the last major unit to cross there. An entire battalion of Lee's artillery, plus various other batteries, lined the West Virginia side, and their fire discouraged any Union attempt to follow too closely. Engineers, and men from the 4th Alabama of Hood's Division, cut the bridge loose from the Maryland bank and used cables to pull it to the other side, where it could be disassembled. Skirmishers from the 4th Alabama were the last Confederates to cross the river, being poled over in pontoon boats. Then, as one Texan said, the Rebels "plodded on in rags and hope, believing we were right and would finally win."[43]

Although Kilpatrick's cavalry had discovered the Confederate withdrawal at 3 a.m., the rest of the Union army had not been notified and did not detect it so early. At dawn, a soldier in the Union 3rd Corps discovered that the Rebel entrenchments were empty. Word was passed up the chain of command, and orders came back down for the division's pickets to advance as far as they could go. They moved through the darkness to within a mile of Williamsport, capturing 21 Confederate stragglers. Brigadier General Horatio Wright, commander of the 1st Division of Sedgwick's 6th Corps, said, "Lee's retreat was admirably managed and evinced great forecast. My own pickets – not 200 yards from his main line did not discover the retreat till day light."[44] Wright "at once ordered the skirmishers forward, proceeding with them some 2 miles beyond the enemy's intrenchments, when I ordered the advance of the division and proceeded with it to Williamsport, where it was found that the enemy's forces had crossed the Potomac River some hours before, and that farther pursuit was impracticable, owing to the depth of the river, which was rapidly rising and then too deep for fording."[45] "There is no picket in our front at all," a 6th Corps officer complained, "and so we quietly fall in and march six miles to Williamsport, for what purpose? God knows! It's plain we're not going to cross at Williamsport and its plain we'll have to march back again."[46]

Meanwhile, Meade and his staff were just mounting up at 7 a.m. when a courier arrived with a message General Howard had written at 6:35, some three and a half hours after Kilpatrick's cavalry started out: "My brigade commander in Hagerstown reports the works in his front evacuated." Word from the 6th Corps evidently arrived not long thereafter, for at 7:40 a.m. Chief of Staff Humphreys wrote a reply to a message from Sedgwick, saying, "The major-general commanding desires me to say that the facts you communicate render the movement ordered last night still more necessary, and directs that you continue it until the position of the enemy is ascertained, supporting the reconnoitering force with your whole corps, if necessary, and following that up, if required, by the First and Eleventh Corps."[47] Throughout the morning there was a flurry of communications between Meade's headquarters and the various corps, as they struggled to catch any part of Lee's army that had not yet crossed the river – all much too late. It was, for instance, 8:20 a.m. before General Pleasonton sent orders to Huey's cavalry brigade to move up the Williamsport pike in search of the enemy. (Later in the day, Huey was sent to rejoin Gregg's division.)

At 8:30, Meade finally ordered a general advance of his army. It was an impressive sight. "Upon advancing beyond the Antietam, the army moved in battle array," wrote the historian of the 5th Corps, "each corps in line, each brigade in columns of regimental front, and as the ground marched over consisted of open cultivated fields, the whole line could be seen, with its colors proudly floating in the breeze and bayonets by the tens of thousands gleaming in the sunlight." He added that, "The fields were groaning with the yellow ripened grain, and when the army had passed everything bore the appearance of having a tornado pass over it. Hardly a stalk of grain was left standing in the fields."[48] It was all for nought, of course, as the Confederates were long gone, and many of the men were bitter and frustrated, feeling that all their hard marching and fighting had been wasted.

Noah Brooks, the correspondent for a Sacramento, California, newspaper who had known Lincoln back in Illinois, had come up, with a pass from Lincoln, to witness the pending battle, only to discover that Lee had escaped, and he reached the field of the rearguard action not long after the fighting ended. "Turning my horse's head in the direction of Meade's headquarters," he wrote long afterwards, "I looked across the swollen and turbid Potomac where I could see the smoke of rebel camps rising in the thick Virginia woods on the other side of the stream. It is impossible now to describe – almost impossible to recall – the feeling of bitterness with which we regarded the sight. Lee's Army was gone. In spite of warnings, expostulations, doubts, and fears, it had escaped, and further pursuit was not even to be thought of. I remember the anxiety, almost anguish, with which Lincoln had said before I left Washington that he was afraid that 'something would happen' to prevent that annihilation of Lee's Army, which, as he thought, was then certainly within the bounds of possibility. But the last hope of the Confederacy had not failed them yet. The desperate venture of an invasion of Pennsylvania and Maryland had failed, it was true. But the fatal blow which seemed to hang in the air when I left Washington did not fall. As I rode down the hill and through the undulating fields beyond, the blue-coated soldiers, jolly and *insouciant*, greeted the solitary civilian horseman with jocose remarks about the 'Johnny Rebs' who had so cunningly run away from them. Many of these men had enlisted 'for the war,' and when I stopped to exchange salutations, they good-naturedly said, 'Well, here goes for two years more.'"[49] They weren't far wrong, for the war would last another 22 months. That night another thunderstorm drenched the soldiers again.

At 11 a.m. Meade reported to Halleck: "On advancing my army this morning, with a view of ascertaining the exact position of the enemy and attacking him if the result of the examination should justify me, I found, on reaching his lines, that they were evacuated. I immediately put my army in pursuit, the cavalry in advance. At this period my forces occupy Williamsport, but I have not yet heard from the advance on Falling Waters, where it is reported he crossed his infantry on a bridge. Your instructions as to further movements, in case the enemy are entirely across the river, are desired."[50] At noon Meade's headquarters issued a circular, saying: "The commanding general, having reason to believe that the enemy has crossed the river, directs that corps commanders, as soon as they are satisfied that his whole force has crossed, halt their commands and report their positions."[51]

Halleck replied to Meade at 1 p.m.: "The enemy should be pursued and cut up, wherever he may have gone. This pursuit may or may not be upon the rear or flank, as circumstances may require. The inner flank toward Washington presents the greatest advantages. Supply yourself from the country as far as possible. I cannot advise details, as I do not know where Lee's army is, nor where your pontoon bridges are. I need hardly say to you that the escape of Lee's army without another battle has created great dissatisfaction in the mind of the President, and it will require an active and energetic pursuit on your part to remove the impression that it has not been sufficiently active heretofore."[52] He followed this up an hour and a half later with another telegram: "Should you cross at Berlin, or below Harper's Ferry, your supplies for the time can be sent by the Baltimore and Ohio Railroad. General Meigs will, therefore, recall General Haupt and the Railroad Brigade to repair the Manassas road, so that supplies can meet you by Thoroughfare Gap or Warrenton, should you require them there. Telegraph condition of things."[53]

Meade was offended and disgusted by Halleck's first message and had turned to his chief quartermaster and said, "Ingalls don't you want to take command of this army?" To which Ingalls replied, "No, I thank you. It's too big an elephant for me." Meade said, "Well, it's too big for me, too."[54]

So, at 2:30 p.m., Meade wired Halleck: "Having performed my duty conscientiously and to the best of my ability, the censure of the President conveyed in your dispatch of 1 p.m. this day, is in my judgment, so undeserved that I feel compelled most respectfully to ask to be immediately relieved from the command of this army." A half-hour later he told Halleck: "My cavalry now occupy Falling Waters, having overtaken and captured a brigade of infantry 1,500 strong, 2 guns, 2 caissons, 2 battleflags, and a large number of small arms. The enemy are all across the Potomac." After another half-hour, he added, "The difficulty of supplying the army in the Valley of the Shenandoah, owing to the destruction of railroad, has decided me to move by Berlin. I shall pursue and harass the retreat of the enemy with my cavalry."[55]

In the meantime, a Federal pontoon bridge had been completed at Sandy Hook, another one was being ordered at Berlin, and the railroad bridge at Harper's Ferry had been repaired to the extent that infantry could cross it. At 2:15 p.m. General Naglee wired General Humphreys: "One of my regiments occupies Bolivar Heights and the town of Harper's Ferry."[56]

That same day, a division commanded by Brigadier General George H. Gordon, composed of regiments that had formerly belonged to the 4th Corps down in the Department of Virginia (including two that had just been temporarily assigned to the 1st Corps), was assigned to Howard's 11th Corps. Halleck, meanwhile, told General Heintzelman, commanding the Department of Washington, to stop forwarding units to Meade, but to hold them in depot. They could be sent from there directly to Virginia.

At 4:30 p.m. Halleck responded to Meade's request to be relieved: "My telegram, stating the disappointment of the President at the escape of Lee's army, was not intended as a censure, but as a stimulus to an active pursuit. It is not deemed a sufficient cause for your application to be relieved."[57] Evidently mollified, Meade made no further comment. At 8:30 p.m. he reported: "My cavalry have captured

500 prisoners, in addition to those previously reported. General Pettigrew, of the Confederate army, was killed this morning in the attack on the enemy's rear guard. His body is in our hands. A division of my cavalry crossed the river at Harper's Ferry to-day, who will pursue and harass the retreat of the enemy and give me information of his movements. General Kelley, with an infantry force, and Averell's cavalry, have reached Williamsport. Am I authorized to detain him here to watch the Potomac while I move to Berlin?" Meade was misinformed about Pettigrew, who had been carried across the pontoon bridge and did not die until the morning of the seventeenth. Halleck replied the following afternoon: "General Kelley has been ordered to cross the Potomac and act on Lee's right flank, in order to prevent raids into West Virginia. It is hoped that he may be able to do the enemy some harm there."[58]

Generals Ingalls, Meigs, and Haupt exchanged several messages that day about how to change the Army of the Potomac's supply line, now that it would be returning to Virginia. Haupt wired Meigs at 5:30 p.m.: "Construction corps will be ordered back immediately to Alexandria. This movement is precisely as I expected and predicted. I did not see how we could prevent the enemy from crossing. It is now of the greatest importance to occupy the gaps of the Blue Ridge, and push forces ahead to secure from destruction any bridges on the Orange and Alexandria Railroad that may still remain."[59]

However, there were many soldiers of both armies who would never return to Virginia. At 6 p.m., Dr. Henry Janes, the surgeon in charge of the wounded at Gettysburg, wrote to Meade's medical director: "Five thousand eight hundred Union and 1,500 Confederates have been sent from here, besides 4,000 supposed to have gone from Littlestown and Westminster. I think about 3,000 Union and 6,000 Confederates remain. Probably 3,000 cannot be moved.... Have selected a fine site for the camp. Am anxiously awaiting the tents."[60]

At 9 p.m., Meade wrote to General Couch, saying: I am about moving down the river to cross at Berlin, and move down the Loudoun Valley. I wish to take every available man with me now with my army. At the same time I think Hagerstown ought to be occupied and the river watched, till we know what has become of Lee. If you can do this with the forces under your command, you will render me an essential service. I have directed General Smith to report to you for instructions, as the time of his men is so nearly out."[61]

That afternoon, Ewell's Corps, at the head of Lee's army, entered Martinsburg. Hill's Corps followed, then Longstreet's. Union sympathizers among the residents were jubilant over the Rebels' misfortunes, and Confederate sympathizers correspondingly sad. The Union prisoners that Lee had brought back from Pennsylvania marched through Woodstock and Edinburgh that day and camped for the night about seven miles north of Mount Jackson.

President Lincoln, meanwhile, wrote a long letter to Meade that day: "I have just seen your despatch to Gen. Halleck, asking to be relieved of your command, because of a supposed censure of mine. I am very – *very* – grateful to you for the magnificent success you gave the cause of the country at Gettysburg; and I am sorry now to be the author of the slightest pain to you. But I was in such deep distress myself that I could not restrain some expression of it. I had been oppressed nearly ever since the battle at Gettysburg, by what appeared to be evidence that yourself, and Gen. Couch, and Gen. Smith, were not seeking a collision with the enemy, but were trying to get him across the river without another battle. What these evidences were, if you please, I hope to tell you at some time, when we shall both feel better. The case, summarily stated is this. You fought and beat the enemy at Gettysburg; and, of course, to say the least, his loss was as great as yours. He retreated; and you did not, as it seemed to me, pressingly pursue him; but a flood in the river detained him, till, by slow degrees, you were again upon him. You had at least twenty thousand veteran troops directly with you, and as many more raw ones within supporting distance, all in addition to those who fought with you at Gettysburg; while it was not possible that he had received a single recruit; and yet you stood and let the flood run down, bridges be built, and the enemy move away at his leisure, without attacking him. And Couch and Smith! The latter left Carlisle in time, upon all ordinary calculation, to have aided you in the last battle at Gettysburg; but he did not arrive. At the end of more than ten days, I believe twelve, under constant urging, he reached Hagerstown from Carlisle, which is not an inch over fiftyfive miles, if so much. And Couch's movement was very little different.

"Again, my dear general, I do not believe you appreciate the magnitude of the misfortune involved in Lee's escape. He was within your easy grasp, and to have closed upon him would, in connection with our other late successes, have ended the war. As it is, the war will be prolonged indefinitely. If you could not safely attack Lee last Monday, how can you possibly do so South of the river, when you can take with you very few more than two thirds of the force you then had in hand? It would be unreasonable to expect, and I do not expect you can now effect much. Your golden opportunity is gone, and I am distressed immeasurably because of it.

"I beg you will not consider this a prossecution, or persecution of yourself. As you had learned that I was dissatisfied, I have thought it best to kindly tell you why."[62]

However, Lincoln never signed nor sent the letter, but merely filed it away in his desk. Having vented his feelings in writing it, he evidently decided to spare Meade's feelings and not send it. Nevertheless, he was still upset about Lee's escape. According to the diary of John Hay, one of Lincoln's secretaries, Lincoln's oldest son, Robert, then home from Harvard, reported that his father had said, "If I had gone up there, I could have whipped them myself." And Hay added, "I know he had that idea."[63]

Down in Mississippi, Sherman was writing a long report to Grant about his operations since leaving the Vicksburg area with most of the latter's army. After describing his march to Jackson in some detail, and his early operations there, he said: "Having invested the place, I ordered Colonel [Cyrus] Bussey, chief of cavalry, with his cavalry force, numbering about 1,000 effectives, to proceed to Canton and destroy the cars, locomotives, railroads, and machine-shops there, and proceed on to the Big Black River Bridge [north of Canton] and destroy that. He has returned, having found Canton occupied by a force too large for him to attack, and he did not go to the bridge at all, as he deemed it unsafe to pass so considerable a force by the flank, but he destroyed 2 locomotives and 14 box cars at Calhoun Station.

"At the same time the cavalry force attached to General Ord's corps were dispatched south. This party has also returned, having burned five bridges on the road out for 15 miles. We have also in our possession here about 20 platform cars, which will be completely burned, and two brigades are kept on daily duty burning the railroad ties and iron north and south, with orders to completely destroy it for 10 miles each way, so that a very fair beginning has been made toward the destruction of this railway; but I am determined that it shall be so effectually destroyed that it cannot be repaired during the war."

Farther down in his long letter, he said: "Our foraging parties now go out about 15 miles, but are invariably guarded by a regiment of infantry. We are absolutely stripping the country of corn, cattle, hogs, sheep, poultry, everything, and the new-growing corn is being thrown open as pasture fields or hauled for the use of our animals. The wholesale destruction to which this country is now being subjected is terrible to contemplate, but it is the scourge of war, to which ambitious men have appealed, rather than the judgment of the learned and pure tribunals which our forefathers had provided for supposed wrongs and injuries."[64]

That evening, Sherman replied to Grant's message of

the day before, saying: "All is well with us. I think I have troops enough. . . . I do not think Johnston is receiving reenforcements; at all events, he has manifested no intention to rally, and has permitted us to surround him with parapets. A brigade is breaking railroad both ways, and as soon as I know our ammunition train is coming I will send a good brigade and artillery and cavalry to complete the destruction of Canton and Big Black River Bridge; also cavalry party to Brookhaven, south."[65] He also wrote to Rawlins, Grant's chief of staff, asking for "the fate of Lee's army the moment you hear," and saying, "I think we are doing well out here, but won't brag till Johnston clears out and stops shooting his big rifle guns at us. If he moves across Pearl River and makes good speed, I will let him go. By a flag of truce to-day, I sent him our newspapers of 7th and 8th; that, with our cannon tonight, will disturb his slumbers."[66]

From Fort Monroe, Virginia, the Union agent for the exchange of prisoners, Lieutenant Colonel William H. Ludlow, replied that day to the notice he had received from his Confederate counterpart, saying that he declined to agree to the exchange of the generals and some colonels captured at Vicksburg, saying that because the Rebels, in violation of the cartel on exchange of prisoners, were holding in close confinement and refusing to exchange certain officers (by which he meant those captured while in command of black troops), officers could only be exchanged by special agreement, and he declined to so agree in this case until the two agents could meet face to face, and pointed out that he had not yet even received the paroles of those officers from General Grant. "Please, therefore, notify the officers named by you that their exchange cannot be recognized by our authorities until the declarations be united in by me. . . . To settle all difficulties connected with exchanges of officers I again invite you to a return to the cartel, and if you refuse I again ask you why such refusal?" In a postscript, he added that Ould already owed him some 8-900 men. "Please make no more declarations until we meet."[67]

In riot-torn New York City that day, Tuesday, 14 July, a black man, probably a cook from some vessel in the Hudson River, came ashore at the foot of Leroy Street, on the Lower West Side, about 6 a.m., carrying a bag and a basket, and approached several boys and some white laborers to get directions. "A man named Edward Canfield came out of Jones's liquor store and asked the colored man what he wanted," young Edward Ray, a schoolboy, later testified. "He answered that he wanted a grocery store." At that, Ray said, without a word, Canfield knocked the man down, kicked him, jumped on him, and "kicked his eyes out," while leaning on another man for support and others shouted encouragement. Another man tried to stick a knife in the fallen man's chest, but it failed to penetrate. A neighbor of Ray's dropped a flagstone the size of a man's head on the fallen man's chest several times, and then three other men took turns jumping on the man's chest. Finally, they all retired to Jones's liquor store, swearing "vengeance on every nigger in New-York."[68] A crowd of women and children gathered around the fallen man, and a group of firemen came by and looked at the victim, who was still alive, but did nothing to help him. Police eventually arrived, placed him in a wagon, and sent him to a hospital, where he died two hours later.

Black men were targeted all over the city that second day of the riots. Joel Headley said that "it became a regular hunt for them. A sight of one in the streets would call forth a halloo, as when a fox breaks cover, and away would dash half a dozen men in pursuit. Sometimes a whole crowd streamed after with shouts and curses . . . If overtaken, he was pounded to death at once; if he escaped into a negro's house for safety, it was set on fire . . . If he could reach a police station he felt safe; but, alas! If the force happened to be away on duty, he could not stay even there." Headley said there was a corpse of a black man at Seventh Avenue and 27th Street, "stripped nearly naked, and around it a collection of

Irishmen, absolutely dancing or shouting like wild Indians."[69] In black neighborhoods, a grocery, a barbershop, and several boarding houses were burned down.

Black refugees by the hundreds fled to police stations, police headquarters, and the arsenal. Others fled to the rivers, where some drowned, some swam to ships, and some hid under the piers until their pursuers gave up and went away. Workers at a brickyard near the Hudson put one refugee into a rowboat, and he escaped to New Jersey. Another made it safely to the Canal Street ferry just in time to escape his pursuers. All the ferries were packed with black refugees getting off of Manhattan. Some went to Brooklyn – still a separate city in those days – but were not safe there either, especially since over a hundred policemen had been sent from Brooklyn to New York, as had many Marines and 300 sailors armed with cutlasses and revolvers. And the forces that remained in Brooklyn were mostly concentrated on defending the Navy Yard.

Manton Marble, editor of the New York *World*, continued to focus his editorials on the initial grievance that had started the riots, writing that day that "although the community generally condemns the plundering and cruelty perpetrated by some hangers-on of the mob, yet there is an astonishing deal of public and private sympathy expressed in public places with the one idea of resistance to the draft. The laboring classes say that they are confident that it will never be enforced in the city, and that any new attempt will meet with still more serious opposition. They believe that no force, military or civil, will be able to enforce this unpopular measure." Marble blamed it all on the Lincoln administration, its Emancipation Proclamation, and its suspensions of *habeas corpus*. "Will they now believe that Defiance of the Law in rulers breeds Defiance of the Law in the people? Does the doctrine proclaimed from the Capitol that in war laws are silent please them [when] put in practice in the streets of New York?" The people, he said, supported war for "the Union and the Constitution," but not for abolition of slavery.

"Does any man wonder that poor men refuse to be forced into a war mismanaged almost into hopelessness, perverted almost into partisanship?"

William Cullen Bryant's *Evening Post* charged that the *World* had been "for weeks endeavoring to arouse the mob spirit in this city," and said it was trying to "inflame the passions of ignorant readers, and incite such to violence."[70] Anna Dickinson went even further, saying, "It was absurd and futile to characterize this new reign of terror as anything but an effort on the part of Northern rebels to help Southern ones at the most critical moment of the war, with the state militia and available troops absent in a neighboring commonwealth and the loyal people unprepared. These editors and their coadjutors, men of brains and ability, were of that most poisonous growth – traitors to the government and the flag of their country – renegade Americans."[71]

Parts of Manhattan were quiet enough that morning that many shops and factories were opened for business, but the streets in the heart of the city were again filled with rioters. However, now, on this second day, the authorities were better prepared. General Wool consented, early that morning, to put General Brown back in charge of the Federal troops, and Brown immediately concentrated over 700 men at the Central Office of the police, where he could coordinate with Commissioner Acton, who had gathered most of his own mobile forces there. General Sandford called for all troops to gather at the 35th Street arsenal, but it had no telegraph link to police headquarters, so Brown ignored the order, saying it pertained only to militia. About 400 civilians had been issued badges and clubs and sworn in as Volunteer Specials, and these men were put on guard duty, freeing the veteran policemen to move to wherever needed.

Information was received at 9:15 a.m. that a mob was burning buildings at 34th Street and Second Avenue. Acton put Inspector Carpenter and 300 men on Third Avenue street cars, and they sped north. They came upon a mob of some 10,000, including many who were just onlookers. A Catholic priest was urging them to maintain the peace, but the sight of the Metropolitans made them more belligerent. Rioters who had taken to upper windows and rooftops showered bricks and paving stones down on the policemen, seriously injuring two of them, while others closed in behind them, and for a moment it seemed that the police would be overwhelmed. But the officers used their revolvers to end the shower of missiles; Carpenter sent 50 men to drive the rioters from the houses; and the rest charged and drove back the crowd in front of them, then turned about and dispersed those behind them. The street and gutters were soon filled with bodies.

Before long, the police were joined by Colonel H. T. O'Brien with 150 infantrymen and two cannon manned by 25 artillerymen. O'Brien lived in this area and had been in the process of raising a regiment of volunteers for the war when the rioting broke out the day before. When the mob regrouped and again blocked the policemen's way, O'Brien ordered the artillerymen to fire blank cartridges at it, and the infantrymen to fire live rounds over the mob's heads. The rioters fled, but the soldiers' bullets killed seven people, including two children, who had been watching from windows of nearby houses. This killing of innocent bystanders only further enraged the rioters, who, of course, blamed the soldiers, not themselves.

Meanwhile, at about 10 a.m., General Brown sent Lieutenant Thomas Wood with 130 soldiers into the industrial slums on the Lower East Side, where they found 5,000 rioters, who not only refused to disperse but attacked the soldiers with clubs, stones and bricks. The soldiers opened fire, killing 14 and wounding 17, then scattered the rest with a bayonet charge. A few blocks away these troops were again confronted by a mob, but this time just the menace of the bayonets and a threat to open fire was enough to clear the street.

There was also a mob near the East River at the gates of a factory that made ironclads for the Navy. The local precinct called the Central Office for help, and Acton forwarded the request to General Sandford via another precinct near the arsenal, but Sandford sent no help. Brown sent troops to patrol Grand Street, but rioters there just waited for the soldiers to pass by, then looted a gun store. Just north of Grand Street a mob refused to give way even after being fired upon, and this time the soldiers had to retreat.

Still insisting on keeping to his routine, Horace Greeley took a streetcar past burning buildings and barricades and then walked through the mob to the *Tribune*. There he discovered that the building had been converted in his absence into a fortress. "What are these, Mr. Gilmore?" he asked, pointing to some cannon shells stashed near a window. "Brimstone pills for those red ragamuffins down there on the sidewalk," Gilmore said. "But I wanted no arms brought into the building," Greeley complained. "Oh, yes; but that was yesterday," Gilmore replied. "Take 'em away, take 'em away!" Greeley ordered. "I don't want to kill anybody, and besides they're a damn sight more likely to go off and kill some of us!"

Greeley went off to write his editorial, and Gilmore ignored the order. He and Sidney Gay had decided in the early hours of the morning that the *Tribune* "must arm itself to the very teeth, and, looking for no outside aid, resist the rioters to the last extremity." The first thing they had done, of course, was to look for outside aid. Gilmore had gone to the Brooklyn Navy Yard and asked Rear Admiral Hiram Paulding for weapons. With a gleam in his eye, Paulding had loaded him up with bombshells and hand grenades, saying, "I'll give you enough of both to send ten thousand of those rascals to the devil to-night." True to his word, he gave Gilmore two wagonloads of these explosives and told him that if he used every one of them "there will never be another riot in New York."[72]

By the time Gilmore had returned with his explosives, the *Tribune* employees were being organized by an Army colonel, the broken doors and windows were barricaded with bales of paper saturated with water, and a hose had been attached to the boiler that powered the presses, ready to spew scalding steam at a moment's notice. There was a loaded cannon at windows on both the second and third floors, and proper ammunition had been acquired for the muskets, which were loaded and ready at other windows. Gilmore deployed his bombshells on the fourth floor. By using five long wooden troughs that the admiral had given him, they could be launched from a window far enough out so that, when they exploded in the street below, they would not damage the building. The staff of the nearby *Times* was also well armed, with a pair of Gatling guns in their front entrance, and it had been agreed that Gilmore's launching of a bombshell would be the signal for the staffs at both papers to open fire with everything. Friends tried to get Greeley to leave the building, not only for his own safety but because his presence incited the mob to attack. He said he would go when he was finished with what he was writing, which seemed to be taking all afternoon.

At noon a mob gathered outside the Union Steam Works, one block north of the armory at Second and 25th that they had attacked the day before. Inside it were some 4,000 carbines, which the rioters wanted. The streets all around were filled for blocks with angry men, while the women and children of the neighborhood looked on. Encouraged by Francis Cusick and other leaders, the mob drove off the police guard, broke into the building, started seizing the carbines, and prepared to turn the sturdy brick building into a fortress. At 2 p.m. 200 Metropolitan policemen, led by Inspector George Dilks, arrived, closed ranks, and began clearing rioters from the street in front of the building with their clubs.

One of the mob's leaders fell against an iron gate and was killed when one of its pickets pierced his jaw. When the police later removed his body it was found that he was wearing a fine linen shirt and a costly vest under his workman's clothing. This fueled suspicion that wealthy Copperheads were behind the riots, but his body was later carried off by other rioters, and so he was never identified. The New York *World* noted that one or two men in each crowd "of better appearance and apparel than the rest" were seen inciting the rest to violence, though they disappeared when the fighting actually started.[73]

Having cleared the streets, Dilks sent a detachment into the building, which fought its way up stairs into the main room on the second floor, causing many rioters to jump from windows, to their injury. Those who managed to escape were clubbed by other policemen waiting in the streets. A mob of women attacked the police with bricks and rocks and refused to disperse when ordered to do so. The police opened fire with their revolvers and killed more than a dozen. Then, leaving a small contingent to guard the building and the remaining carbines, they loaded as many of the carbines as possible into a large wagon and, carrying others, took them to police headquarters. Along the way, people came out of their houses to cheer the policemen.

Meanwhile, at about noon, a large crowd had gathered around the *Tribune* building, where it was being urged by one its leaders to sack the place, when shouts of "Governor Seymour, Governor Seymour" arose, and the crowd made off for City Hall Park. Horatio Seymour, governor of the state of New York, was a prominent member of the peace wing of the Democratic Party. He had been visiting relatives in New Jersey until that morning, when he had met with Mayor Opdyke at the Saint Nicholas Hotel. Just before noon, these two had walked down Broadway, without guard or escort, to City Hall. There, as the crowd gathered, they both, along with District Attorney A. Oakey Hall and the city's Democratic Party leader, William "Boss" Tweed, mounted the front steps, and Seymour made a speech. Addressing the crowd as "My friends," he called on them to maintain law and order, ". . . for your salvation depends on this. Anarchy will be ruin. If the conscription law will not bear the test of the courts and the Constitution, it will not be enforced, but if upheld by the courts, then the state and city authorities will combine for the purpose of equalizing the tax and making it bear proportionately on the rich and the poor."[74] This drew loud cheers of approval.

After the speech, Seymour and Opdyke met with other local officials and the military leaders, and said they would only ask for martial law as a last resort. No doubt politics played its part in this. Martial law would put the Republicans of the Federal government in charge of the city, until now a Democratic stronghold. Instead, the governor issued a proclamation placing himself in command of enforcing the law in New York City. The proclamation also called on all citizens to return to their homes and jobs and promised that the rights of every draftee would be protected by the state courts.

Later Seymour and Tweed toured the city in a carriage and the governor made speeches on Wall Street and on the upper West Side. He then established his headquarters in the Saint Nicholas Hotel, where he conferred with General George McClellan and other prominent Democrats, many of whom he dispatched to various parts of the city to persuade mobs to disperse. Businessmen also addressed various crowds, promising to oppose the $300 clause, and Catholic priests also tried to calm the mobs. Two of them saved the home of Columbia College President Charles King, which the mob wanted to burn, because he was rich and a Republican.

At 2 p.m. General Halleck wired General Couch, at Chambersburg: "You will immediately detach two regiments of New York militia, and send them by railroad to New York, to report to General Wool." Halleck also telegraphed General Schenck, in Baltimore, and Colonel Ed Schriver, at Frederick: "The Seventh New York Militia will be immediately sent to New York by rail to report to General Wool."[75]

Also at around 2 p.m., Colonel O'Brien, whose men had accidentally killed some bystanders earlier in the day, made the mistake of returning to his neighborhood alone, probably to check on his family, not knowing that they had escaped to Brooklyn and that his house had been sacked. Coming out of a drugstore he was confronted by a crowd. When he drew and cocked his revolver a woman threw a rock at him. He fired into the ground or street to intimidate the mob, but the bullet ricocheted up and hit the woman in the knee, whereupon the mob knocked him down and beat him senseless. Three or four men then dragged him into the street by his hair. When the druggist tried to give him water the crowd looted his store. After torturing the unconscious colonel for several hours, they dragged him into an alley, and whenever groans indicated that he was still alive they would smash his head on the pavement. An Irish priest tried to intervene, but the torturing carried on for a few more hours. The priest did manage to give him the last rites just before he died.

Also at about 2 p.m., a mob gathered in front of several Fifth Avenue mansions in the 46th Street area. General Brown dispatched Captain H. R. Putnam of the 12th U.S. Infantry with his company of 82 men, along with some 60 policemen under Captain George Walling, and they found a mob of some 2,000 people burning and destroying property. At the top of his lungs, so that the rioters would be sure to hear him, Walling yelled, "Kill every man who has a club!" then ordered a charge.[76] With women on the edges of the crowd calling on their men to stand and fight, the melee lasted about five minutes, then the rioters broke and fled in several directions, leaving about 40 dead and wounded behind. Several soldiers were also injured, two of whom were badly beaten, and one of those had to be hospitalized.

Meanwhile, the small garrison that had been left at the Union Steam Works had been overwhelmed, and rioters had reoccupied the building, fighting off an attempt by police from the local precinct to evict them. So, at about 2:30 p.m., a large force of police, some Volunteer Specials, and a few soldiers were sent to recapture the place. Wielding their clubs and making liberal use of their revolvers, the policemen, under Captain John Helme, charged the building, and within ten minutes had rescued the garrison that had been left behind by Dilks and scattered the rioters. They then commandeered a wagon and loaded it with nearly a thousand carbines, but by the time this was done they were surrounded by a large and infuriated mob, soon reinforced by the rioters who had murdered Colonel O'Brien, who pelted them with stones and occasional bullets.

However, Inspector Dilks then showed up with 150 policemen and 100 soldiers under Captain Walter Franklin, who charged into the crowd from the rear. The mob fell back, but continued to throw rocks and fire muskets. "The crowd grew more insolent and increased the firing as we advanced," Franklin said. "I halted the company, and fired by sections, allowing each section to fall to the rear to load as fast as it had fired." This tactic cleared the street, but the rioters took to the houses and rooftops and continued to pelt the soldiers and policemen with rocks and bullets. However, Franklin's men soon made it "dangerous to show a head anywhere." The police and soldiers then marched off down Second Avenue with their wagon full of carbines, but the rioters followed them. "They were allowed to get quite close to us," Franklin said, "when I faced the rear section about, and fired one or two volleys, which must have been very effective, as they dispersed, and did not give us any further trouble."[77]

Many rioters were killed or wounded, as were, also, according to the *World*, many innocent bystanders, including women and children. People gathered on street corners to discuss the situation, and one woman admonished one of the larger crowds for not standing their ground, saying they ought to be ashamed of themselves for running away from a smaller force. One man said that all they needed was a leader, and, volunteering for the position himself, tried to lead them back to Fifth Avenue to punish the rich, but he couldn't muster more than a few dozen men and boys and so gave up the effort. The general consensus was that they would all meet that night to make further plans.

At 2:40 p.m., E. S. Sanford of the Military Telegraph Service wired Secretary Stanton: "You may judge of the capacity at headquarters here when every effort cannot extract any more information than I have forwarded. Excuse me for saying that this mob is testing the Government nearly as strongly as the Southern rebellion. If you cannot enforce the draft here, it will not be enforced anywhere. The example will prove contagious, and similar events transpire in every large city. If you send sufficient force here to demonstrate the power of the Government, its effect will reach every part of the country, and one settlement answer for the whole. Immediate action is necessary, or the Government and country will be disgraced."[78]

After an hour or two of rest, Captain Franklin and his men were sent out again, this time to Eighth Avenue and 29th Street, where a mob was looting the home of prominent abolitionists James and Abby Gibbons. Abby and her daughter Sally were down South, nursing wounded soldiers, and James had gone out to buy a newspaper, but daughters Julia and Lucy, and cousin Sarah Powell, expecting trouble, had packed a few things and gone over the rooftops to their uncle's house. At about 5 p.m. there was a sudden uproar in the street. Watching through the shutters, the girls saw rioters break into their house with axes and ransack the interior, throwing valuables out the windows for the mob in the street to fight over. James came home and, not being recognized by the looters, made his way to his desk to recover his revolver, but seeing that the place was overrun by the mob, didn't use it and made his way out again.

Just then the police arrived and charged into the house, clubbing looters and driving them out into the courtyard, where other policemen clubbed them again. Then Franklin and his troops arrived, some of whom fired without orders, wounding several policemen, one of them mortally. The soldiers drove the looters away, Lucy later recalled, and "returned and drove away the mob a second time, and then marched away. As they disappeared one way, the mob returned in full force by another and the looting went on." Someone in the crowed cried, "Shame! Don't you know what Mrs. Gibbons did for the 69th Regiment?"[79] (The 69th New York was a famous Irish regiment in the Army of the Potomac.) But the looting went on. Soon smoke poured out of the windows, but some of the neighbors carried water over the roofs and down into the house and put out the fires.

That evening the rioters began to form barricades in the streets, using wagons, carts, telegraph poles, lampposts, furniture, barrels, and crates, often lashed together with telegraph wires. A police telegrapher who had helped man the barricades in Berlin during the revolts of 1848 saw this effort to seal off portions of the city as an ominous sign that things were escalating from rioting to revolution. Captain Walling of the police was ordered to clear six blocks of Ninth Avenue, and he asked General Brown for reinforcements from the Army. The Regulars arrived at 6 p.m., but militia that Brown had requested from General Sandford never showed up.

Walling's policemen were fired upon by rioters on the rooftops, as well as behind the barricades as they approached, but most of the shots missed. The policemen stepped aside and let the soldiers through to fire several volleys, which drove the mob back to their next barricade, a block north. Rioters on the rooftops continued to fire down on the policemen as they worked to dismantle the first barricade, but the soldiers began to pick off these snipers and then drove the mob from the second barricade and on until they had eliminated every obstruction. When the rioters scattered, the soldiers broke ranks to pursue them, which was a bad mistake, as they soon found themselves pelted by a shower of brickbats from the rooftops. At this the soldiers marched back to Police Headquarters, as it was then almost dark.

At 6:55 p.m., Secretary Stanton wired Mayor Opdyke: "Five regiments are under orders to return to New York. The retreat of Lee having now become a rout, with his army broken and much heavier loss of killed and wounded than was supposed, will relieve a larger force for the restoration of order in New York. Intelligence has just reached here of the auspicious commencement of General Gillmore's operations against Charleston. All but one fort on Morris Island have been captured, and that will be speedily reduced, after which Sumter must follow."[80]

At the *Tribune*, Gilmore finally convinced Horace Greeley to leave the building at about 8 p.m., telling him, "A hundred and fifty of us are risking our lives to defend this building, and you have no right to add to our danger." Greeley said he would take a streetcar home, but Gilmore pointed to the mob gathered outside and said he'd never make it to a streetcar, and convinced him to slip out the back and into a closed carriage. The old man who had rowed Gilmore over to Governor's Island the night before saw him then and asked to be allowed to help defend the building. Instead, Gilmore sent him to mingle with the crowd and spread the word that Greeley had gone home, that the building was "so thoroughly armed that the first discharge from it would slay a thousand of the rioters."[81] This ploy evidently worked, for while the mob continued to besiege the building, it never attacked.

That night two tenements on Roosevelt Street where blacks lived were burned to the ground, and a row of tenements in Greenwich Village was only saved because a company of firemen happened to be passing by on its way to another fire uptown. A mixed couple was attacked in their apartment on Worth Street. The black husband escaped, thinking the mob would not molest his white wife or their children, but the rioters attacked their son with an ax and a club. The mother managed to save the boy by shielding him with her own body. When a nearby grocer admonished the men for abusing the boy and his mother they threatened to hang him, but he produced a pistol and was soon reinforced by German neighbors, and the rioters went off looking for easier prey. The mother died two months later from her injuries.

At 8:40 p.m., Secretary Stanton received another message from E. S. Sanford: "We are expecting momentarily that our Southern wires will be cut, as the rioters are at work in their immediate neighborhood. It seems very important for the United States Government to define its position immediately in this city, and, if not done immediately, the opportunity will be lost. . . . The police so far report themselves as having been successful in every fight, of which they have had many, but they say they are exhausted, and cannot much longer sustain the unequal contest. Not less than 10,000 good native soldiers ought to be here this moment to restore and enforce order."[82]

By 10:30 p.m. the mob had returned to the Union Steam Works. Since they had not been able to take it and hold it, this time they set it on fire, then proceeded to do the same to a police station, where the four officers on duty barely managed to escape by knocking the bars out of a cell window. Around midnight rioters attacked an African American church on 30th Street between Seventh and Eighth, trying to chop it down rather than burn it, so as to spare neighboring houses that belonged to their friends. Captain Walling's policemen mingled unnoticed with some firemen who happened to be passing by and surprised the vandals but were soon met by shots from nearby alleys and houses. Walling said that his men used their revolvers then for the first time that day, but mainly cracked heads with their clubs until the area was cleared and the church was saved.

Throughout this second day, as the first, General Sandford confined his militia and those units of Regulars who had been sent to him to merely hold the arsenal at 35th Street and Seventh Avenue, without doing anything to quell the rioting. That night Commissioner Acton sent Seth Hawley, clerk of the police commission, to see Governor Seymour, who was Sandford's superior. The governor said he knew nothing of what was going on at the arsenal because Sandford didn't keep him informed. Hawley asked him to send a messenger to the general to order him to release the Regulars to General Brown. When Seymour said he had no one to send, Hawley volunteered to carry the order, which he was careful to deliver not to Sandford himself but to his adjutant.

After watching their home being looted from their uncle's house, Julia and Lucy Gibbons had been taken by carriage to a cousin's home. That night, excited and unable to sleep, they eventually got up and stood by the window. "The dead silence of the night was dreadful," teenaged Lucy later remembered. "Once we heard a faint cry, three times repeated, far away: "Murder! Murder! Murder!"[83]

∽ Endnotes ∽

1. McCreary, "Morgan's Raid Comes to an Inglorious End," *B&G*, 682.
2. *OR*, I:23:I:659.
3. *OR*, I:23:II:531. Both messages.
4. Ibid., I:26:I:231.
5. Ibid., I:26:I:232.
6. Ibid., I:24:III:1001-2.
7. Ibid., I:24:I:246.
8. Ibid., I:24:III:507-8.
9. Ibid., I:24:III:508-9.
10. Basler, ed., *The Collected Works of Abraham Lincoln*, VI:326.
11. *OR*, II:6:113.
12. Ibid., I:23:II:908. In his article about the Chickamauga campaign (*B&L* III, 638), written long after the war, Hill said that Davis came to see him on 13 July and proposed sending him to Bragg's army – not Johnston's – to replace corps commander Lieutenant General William J. Hardee, who would be sent to Mississippi, and that Hill had pointed out that one of Hardee's division commanders, A. P. Stewart, outranked him as a major general, but that Davis had said he could cure that by promoting him to lieutenant general, which was the appropriate rank in the Confederate Army for a corps commander. However, this order, and a subsequent one which will be quoted at the appropriate point, show that Hill's original assignment was to Mississippi and then changed to Tennessee the next day. So the promotion was not due to Hill being outranked by Stewart. In fact, Hill outranked Stewart as a major general by more than a year. Stewart was also outranked by Hardee's other division commander, Major General Patrick Cleburne, but Hill outranked Cleburne as well. Also, Hill's promotion to lieutenant general was dated 11 July, not 13 or 14 July. Such are the vagaries of memory long after the fact.
13. Ibid., I:27:III:677.
14. Ibid., I:27:III:678. Both messages.
15. Ibid., I:27:III:681.
16. Ibid., I:27:I:91-2.
17. Wittenberg, Petruzzi and Nugent, *One Continuous Fight*, 266.
18. *OR*, I:27:II:705.
19. Wittenberg, Petruzzi and Nugent, *One Continuous Fight*, 268.
20. *OR*, I:27:I:92.
21. Ibid., I:27:III:675.
22. Ibid., I:27:III:676.
23. Brown, *Retreat from Gettysburg*, 329.
24. Ibid., 329-30.
25. *OR*, I:27:II:558-9.
26. Wittenberg, Petruzzi and Nugent, *One Continuous Fight*, 276.
27. Ibid., 280.
28. Brown, *Retreat from Gettysburg*, 333.
29. Longstreet, *From Manassas to Appomattox*, 429-30.
30. Brown, *Retreat from Gettysburg*, 333.
31. Ibid., 341-2.
32. Ibid., 337.
33. *OR*, I:27:II:705.
34. Kidd, *A Cavalryman with Custer*, 110-11.
35. Wittenberg, Petruzzi and Nugent, *One Continuous Fight*, 285.

36 Ibid., 286.
37 Brown, *Retreat from Gettysburg*, 347.
38 Ibid.
39 Kidd, *A Cavalryman with Custer*, 112.
40 Ibid., 113.
41 *OR*, I:27:I:990.
42 Wittenberg, Petruzzi and Nugent, *One Continuous Fight*, 293.
43 Brown, *Retreat from Gettysburg*, 349.
44 Wittenberg, Petruzzi and Nugent, *One Continuous Fight*, 299.
45 *OR*, I:27:I:667.
46 Wittenberg, Petruzzi and Nugent, *One Continuous Fight*, 300.
47 *OR*, I:27:III:683.
48 Wittenberg, Petruzzi and Nugent, *One Continuous Fight*, 300.
49 Brooks, *Washington, D.C., in Lincoln's Time*, 91-2.
50 *OR*, I:27:I:92.
51 Ibid., I:27:III:690.
52 Ibid., I:27:I:92.
53 Ibid., I:27:I:93.
54 Wittenberg, Petruzzi and Nugent, *One Continuous Fight*, 323.
55 *OR*, I:27:I:93, all three messages.
56 Ibid., I:27:III:690.
57 Ibid., I:27:I:93-4.
58 Ibid., I:27:I:94, both messages.
59 Ibid., I:27:III:696.
60 Ibid., I:27:III:699-700.
61 Ibid., I:27:III:698.
62 Basler, ed., *Collected Works of Abraham Lincoln*, VI:327-8.
63 Ibid., VI:329n.
64 *OR*, I:24:II:526.
65 Ibid., I:24:II:524-5.
66 Ibid., I:24:II:527.
67 Ibid., II:6:116.
68 Schecter, *The Devil's Own Work*, 172.
69 Ibid., 172-3.
70 Ibid., 174-5, both quotes.
71 Dickinson, "Anna Dickinson Sees the Draft Riots in New York City," in *B&G*, 719.
72 Schecter, *The Devil's Own Work*, 178.
73 Ibid., 180.
74 Ibid., 186.
75 *OR*, I:27:II:914, both messages.
76 Schecter, *The Devil's Own Work*, 190.
77 Ibid., 191.
78 *OR*, I:27:II:888.
79 Schecter, *The Devil's Own Work*, 194, both quotes.
80 *OR*, I:27:II:916.
81 Schecter, *The Devil's Own Work*, 196, both quotes.
82 *OR*, I:27:II:889.
83 Schecter, *The Devil's Own Work*, 200.

CHAPTER 24
"Let There Be No Compromising"
14 – 16 July 1863

As E. S. Sanford had warned Secretary Stanton, news of the riots in New York was fanning the flames of resistance to conscription in other cities across the North. In one of Sanford's telegrams to Stanton that afternoon he said: "It is reported from Boston that at 3 o'clock this afternoon a large body of armed men had assembled in North street to resist the draft. No details of the situation were received."[1] In fact, a mob of about a thousand had attacked an armory in Boston, throwing rocks and bricks through its windows and breaking the door open. When their warnings were ignored, the soldiers inside fired a cannon loaded with canister, killing four or five rioters and wounding a dozen others, then scattered the rest with a bayonet charge. Other rioters broke into gun shops and stole weapons, but the mayor and chief of police soon stationed policemen and troops at key points to prevent further rioting in that city.

But other places were also simmering. Captain J. S. Newberry, the provost marshal of the First Congressional District of Michigan, in Detroit, wrote to his superior that day saying that leading men of the city were warning him that there was an organized body of men there – some said up to 5,000 strong – armed and ready to resist the draft. The captain said he doubted that there were more than 1,500, and doubted that they were organized, "but there is doubtless a large number of disaffected persons who have threatened violence, and who would instantly join any attempted outbreak having for an object the obstruction or prevention of the draft. This feeling has become intensified to an alarming degree by the successful violence in the city of New York, compelling the draft to be deferred. A spark here would explode the whole and bring it into the most violent action." He said they had already had a race riot there within the last few months that had controlled the city and burned some 30 houses, and had only been quelled by the arrival of the 27th Michigan Infantry. Therefore, he said, "it would be the height of folly to attempt the drawing or the enforcement of the draft without a strong military force to protect the office and papers. . . . A strong force should be ordered to this city at once."[2]

Newberry's letter was forwarded to the provost-marshal-general's office in Washington with an indorsement by his superior, Major B. H. Hill, which said, in part: "There is in this city but a single company of provost guards and a few men of the Invalid Corps. There are about 100 men (recruits) of the regiment of sharpshooters at Dearborn, but these men will be required to afford protection to the arsenal there. . . . I must say that unless the present mob is put down most summarily in New York the attempt to execute a draft here will lead to similar violence unless supported by a strong military force."[3]

The provost marshal at Kingston, N.Y., wrote to Provost-Marshal-General Fry that "it will require a force of 500 armed men to protect this office if the draft takes place."[4] A captain at Elmira, N.Y., reported that he expected a riot there and recommended that "500 or more well-disciplined men" be sent there.[5] A provost marshal in Maryland wrote to Fry that day that he had asked General Schenck for three companies of cavalry. "For want of such a sustaining force, the intimidation is such that I am unable to procure the services of enrolling officers in some localities."[6]

The assistant provost-marshal-general for Vermont wrote to Fry that day that "It is reported to me from various quarters that men are leaving this State and neighboring States in large numbers to evade the draft. Yesterday on my way from Brattleborough to [Burlington] the conductor of the train informed me that he had some thirty men on the train from Massachusetts whom he felt sure were going to Canada to evade the draft. The provost-marshal of the First District reports that the Irish laborers in the disaffected region in his district are leaving in large numbers. Reports from various parts of the State are of the same character."[7]

An officer in Philadelphia wired Fry that day that, although the mayor wanted the draft to be suspended there for a week, unless Fry ordered to the contrary it would take place in one district the next day. "I think it had better go on, being satisfied that I can quell a riot."[8] But by Fry's order of that day, the draft was temporarily suspended in Buffalo. A mob broke the windows in the home of a provost marshal in Newark, N.J., and the windows of the *Mercury* newspaper there, and, according to an informant of Secretary of State William Seward, "The city authorities did nothing to prevent these outrages. The citizens are at the mercy of ruffians."[9]

Morgan's raiders were now in southwest Ohio, bypassing well-defended Cincinnati on an all-night ride, the men and horses exhausted. The night was extremely dark, the roads numerous, crossing in a confusing patchwork, and men often took a wrong turn or wandered off half asleep. Major McCreary said they "rested by capturing a train of cars on the Little Miami and a considerable number of prisoners."[10]

At about 2 a.m. on the 14th, the head of the column approached the Cincinnati, Hamilton & Dayton Railroad at Glendale. Burnside could easily have sent troops there by rail from either Cincinnati or Hamilton to head them off. But no, a train carrying a battery of artillery had passed through about a half-hour before, but no troops had been sent to defend the railroad. The Rebels had threaded the needle. At Sharonville, at first light, Morgan spread his troops out to forage for horses, food and plunder. The general was fed breakfast on the porch of a house in East Sycamore, being warned not to enter the house, as there was a child bedridden with smallpox lying within. Actually, a family of escaped slaves and two fine horses were hidden in the parlor and never discovered. Morgan wasn't the only one who could pull off a ruse.

One final obstacle remained: Camp Dennison. Named for a former governor of the state, this was a 1,700-acre facility that had been built at the beginning of the war for mustering and training new units, and it now held one of the country's largest military hospitals. It was commanded by Lieutenant Colonel George W. Neff, a 30-year-old native of Cincinnati, who knew the area 'round about very well. He had only about 600 soldiers, most of them new recruits and convalescents, and only enough arms for about 400 of those, but he was determined to hold his post. Throughout the day he received reinforcements of 1,400 militiamen, but no additional arms.

The day before, he had sent out four companies of the 11th Ohio Cavalry to patrol all the roads leading into the camp, and he had sent two officers with 50 able-bodied men to dig rifle pits on a hill overlooking an intersection of three roads on the west side of the camp, and then 150 convalescents to man these works. At 4:30 a.m. on the 14th, a civilian brought him word that Morgan was only five miles away. He sent 50 more armed convalescents to the rifle pits and 100 militiamen with axes to fell trees across the roads to their front. Just after 6 a.m., the head of Morgan's column reached this barricade, and the defenders drove them back with a volley. Morgan had Johnson's brigade dismount, and his skirmishers advanced to this abatis, but rifle fire alone could not dislodge the defenders, so he brought up a couple of howitzers, which shelled the defenses for half an hour, but still the defenders refused to budge. Not wishing to lose any more time in fighting, Morgan backtracked and then moved to ford the Little Miami River at Porter's Mill.

His scouts placed a barrier on the Little Miami Railroad to protect the column's flank as it crossed the tracks, which was fortunate for the Rebels, for a troop train soon came around a bend. When the Confederates fired on it, the engineer increased his speed and failed to see the barrier in time. The engine and tender jumped the track, and the 115 militiamen in the cars were captured and paroled. At about 7:30 a.m., Morgan's scouts surprised some of the Ohio cavalrymen that Colonel Neff had sent out, captured one of them and all eight of their horses, and the bridge carrying the Madisonville Turnpike over the Little Miami River. However, just beyond Miamiville, they found the pickets guarding the Little Miami Railroad bridge more alert and weren't able to take it.

Two hundred militiamen had just reached Neff, along with a supply of arms and ammunition, so Neff dispatched them and a young artillery officer about a mile up the road to defend the bridge. They arrived just in time to save it. Colonel Duke had sent some men across the river to turn the right flank of the Union cavalrymen, had driven them off and were preparing to burn the railroad bridge when the Union reinforcements arrived. The militiamen charged the Rebels and drove them to the safety of some trees lining the far side of the river. Then Lieutenant William H. H. Smith, the artillery officer, took charge, rallied the cavalrymen, and formed them and the militia into a line centered on the bridge, after which the battle devolved into a fire fight across the river.

Morgan soon arrived and ordered his section of two 10-pounder Parrott rifles to open fire, then rode off to hurry on the rest of his column, but even this failed to dislodge the defenders, and at about 10:30 a.m. Colonel Neff arrived with a reinforcement of 20 convalescents from the Invalid Corps, an organization of veteran soldiers still fit for light duty but not for field service. A few minutes later, most of the men who had been defending the barricade on the other side of the camp also arrived, and they soon captured the bridge. Colonel Duke decided that the bridge wasn't worth the time it was taking and ordered his men to withdraw. Neff chose this moment to lead his convalescents in a bayonet charge over the bridge, which caught some of Duke's rear guard by surprise. Several Confederates were bayoneted and some were captured, including two scouts and a lieutenant who was pinned under his fallen horse. By 11 a.m. the fight was over. The mounted Rebels soon outdistanced any pursuit on foot. In a rare bit of cosmic justice, six days later, Neff was promoted to full colonel.

Although the fight had saved the bridge, it had also given Morgan time to get his division over the Little Miami River, which was very low because the area had had a dry summer so far. And the raiders soon rode into Mulberry, near which they found a small supply depot called Camp Shady, with 50 brand-new wagons and the horses and mules intended to pull them. They took what supplies they wanted, and, of course, the animals, and burned the wagons and what supplies they didn't want. At about 4 p.m. the head of the column came to Williamsburg, where Morgan finally let them go into camp and get some rest. His all-night march and a few skirmishes had cost him another 60 men, but he had safely by-passed the Union's largest city west of the mountains.

Hobson's weary pursuers continued to follow the raiders' trail, their spirits lifted by an even larger than usual turnout of cheering citizens and ladies with all kinds of home-cooked food for them. One Federal described his ride as "Six hundred square miles of fried chicken."[11] That night they camped near Mulberry.

The Richmond government changed newly promoted Lieutenant General D. H. Hill's orders that day, sending him to Bragg's Army of Tennessee instead of Johnston's army in Mississippi. Hill would replace Lieutenant General William J. Hardee, one of Bragg's corps commanders, who was sent to Mississippi instead. Hill was succeeded in command of Confederate forces in North Carolina by Major General W. H. C. Whiting, until then the commander of the Military District of Wilmington.

Down on Morris Island, on the South Carolina coast, both sides continued to strengthen their positions, and

Union ironclads bombarded Battery Wagner frequently. (Colonel Charles Olmstead, whose Georgians had joined the garrison, said that at first his men were not impressed by the monitors, they being small and rather insignificant-looking – until one fired a 15-inch shell at them.) General Beauregard had sent the defenders two 32-pounder howitzers, four 12-pounder howitzers, and a new commander, Brigadier General William Booth Taliaferro (pronounced TAH-liver), a veteran of Stonewall Jackson's campaigns. Taliaferro wanted to know what the Federals were up to, down the island, so in the early hours of 14 July he sent out about 150 men of the 7th South Carolina Battalion to find out. These Confederates advanced some three-quarters of a mile before discovering a line of Union rifle pits, and the Federals opened fire even before their own pickets had scrambled out of the way. The Rebels returned fire, but when Union artillery joined in the fight, they fell back. However, once back at Battery Wagner, their commander discovered that 27 men were missing, so he took a small search party back down the island, found 24 of his missing men, discovered that the rifle pits had been abandoned, and captured two Federals. From them he learned that heavy guns and mortars were being mounted so as to bear on Wagner.

Simon Cameron, former Secretary of War and an important Pennsylvania Republican, wired President Lincoln the evening of the fourteenth from Harrisburg: "I left the Army of the Potomac yesterday, believing that the decision of General Meade's council of war on Saturday night, not to attack the rebels, would allow them to escape. His army is in fine spirits and eager for battle. They will win, if they get a chance. General Couch has a fine army between Carlisle and Greencastle, but will move no farther south without orders, under the strong belief that his duty is to guard the Susquehanna. In my opinion, the Susquehanna needs no guard. I have urged him from the beginning to join Meade. I hope to God you will put forth your authority, and order every man in arms between the Susquehanna and the Potomac to unite with Meade, so that he may have no reason to delay in giving battle before the falling of the flood allows Lee to escape."[12]

Lincoln replied the following day, the fifteenth: "Your dispatch of yesterday received. Lee was already across the river when you sent it. I would give much to be relieved of the impression that Meade, Couch, Smith, and all, since the battle of Gettysburg, have striven only to get Lee over the river, without another fight. Please tell me, if you know, who was the one corps commander who was for fighting, in the council of war on Sunday night."[13]

That day, Noah Brooks later wrote, having returned from his visit to the Army of the Potomac, "according to the President's request, I reported to him all that I had seen and heard. It is enough to say that although he was not so profoundly distressed as he was when Hooker's Army recrossed the Rappahannock after the battle of Chancellorsville, his grief and anger were something sorrowful to behold."[14]

In southern Ohio on the fifteenth, Morgan's raiders took to the road at 3 a.m. after the longest rest they had had in almost a week. Having thrown a great scare into Indiana and Ohio, all they needed to do now was get back to Kentucky and, eventually, Tennessee. Morgan sent his brother Dick with a large detachment to reconnoiter near the river for fords. Dick Morgan took the road through Georgetown, where General Grant had grown up, and then headed for Ripley on the Ohio River, a town full of abolitionists whose ford had featured in the novel *Uncle Tom's Cabin*. But he rejoined Morgan at Winchester with bad news. Not only was there a large body of militia, complete with a cannon, at Ripley, but there were gunboats in the river. So the General decided against trying to cross the river there, and instead headed due east, toward Buffington Island in Meigs County, where the river was said to be only two feet deep, and thus, of course, too shallow for the gunboats.

Hobson's pursuing Federals had been taken five miles out of their way through the ignorance of their guide, but they plodded on, and were joined that day by a small brigade under Colonel W. P. Sanders, consisting of parts of the 8th and 9th Michigan cavalry regiments and a section of the 11th Michigan Battery. These units had been brought up the Ohio River on steamboats and off-loaded at Cincinnati. Sanders (West Point, 1856), who had been born in Kentucky and raised in Mississippi, was a cousin of Jefferson Davis, but, as a young officer in the Army, he had remained loyal to the Union. He was now the colonel of the 5th Kentucky Cavalry, and Burnside had put him command of the two Michigan regiments to replace their previous commander, who had failed to reinforce the 20th Kentucky down at Lebanon. General Judah, with more cavalry, had also been shipped up the Ohio, and spent that day at Cincinnati receiving fresh horses.

Down in Mississippi, Sherman still besieged Joe Johnston in the city of Jackson with most of Grant's army, and Herron's division still occupied Yazoo City. However, Grant wrote to Herron that day: "The enemy's cavalry, 4,000 strong, have crossed Pearl River, 14 miles above Jackson, evidently with the intention of getting in the rear of Sherman, to operate on his wagon trains. Whilst it is necessary for you to keep a force at Yazoo City, move eastward with all the force not necessary to leave back, so as to attract the attention of this cavalry. It will only be necessary for you to go eastward about 20 or 25 miles, on to a point east of Black River, where, if you hear of this cavalry, you can threaten them. The entire object of this move is to protect Sherman's wagon train from the rebel cavalry. You will, therefore, be governed in your movements accordingly. You need not stay out to exceed four or five days."[15] This is a good example of the clarity and precision of all Grant's orders. It clearly states the enemy to be dealt with and the mission to be accomplished, indicates a general course of action, and leaves the particulars to the officer in the field.

The same day, Grant wrote to Sherman: "If the enemy's cavalry have crossed to this side of the river, can you throw a force to the east side and destroy their trains?"[16] In a separate message, Grant told Sherman that information from paroled Rebel officers indicated that Jackson would be abandoned the next day or the day after. "May not Johnston's sending his cavalry this side of the river mean a retreat, and, by adopting this course, to cripple you? To prevent, Herron is ordered eastward toward Canton from Yazoo City, but I fear he will be too late to interrupt Johnston's cavalry." Sherman, meanwhile, warned the colonel commanding a brigade at the Big Black River Bridge east of Vicksburg about the Rebel cavalry. "Be sure to see that the large [wagon] train [sent] up is escorted by the brigade left for that purpose at Champion's Hill, and that they are cautioned against this cavalry. I will send infantry to the north to cut off this cavalry."[17]

Sherman was already preparing an expedition, consisting of most of his cavalry and a brigade of infantry, to march north to Canton again the next day, destroying the railroad along the way, with the cavalry to go on alone another twelve miles to destroy the railroad bridge over the upper reaches of the Big Black River. He was also preparing a smaller, all-mounted, raid from Ord's 13th Corps to do the same to the south again, going as far as Brookhaven, halfway to the Louisiana line. Johnston telegraphed President Davis that day: "The enemy is evidently making a siege which we cannot resist. It would be madness to attack him. The remainder of the army under Grant at Vicksburg is beyond doubt on its way to this place."[18]

Also on the fifteenth, General Hurlbut, still in command of Grant's garrisons in West Tennessee, was writing to ask for the return of one of his 16th Corps divisions, saying that his cavalry, although successful in a recent skirmish at Jackson,

Tennessee, was overworked, and saying, "... the duty is enormous, and the line of country is too heavy for the force I have."[19]

General Halleck wrote on the 15th to Colonel William H. Ludlow, the Federal agent for the exchange of prisoners of war, telling him that the President directed him to immediately place in close confinement, under a strong guard, Confederate Brigadier General W. H. F. Lee and another officer to be selected by Ludlow, not below the rank of captain, and to inform his Rebel counterpart that if the Confederates carried through their intention of hanging two Union captains drawn by lot from those in Libby Prison "or any other officers or men in the service of the United States not guilty of crimes punishable with death by the laws of war," that these two Rebel officers would be hanged in retaliation. This Lee, better known as "Rooney," was the second son of General R. E. Lee and had commanded a brigade in Jeb Stuart's cavalry. He had been wounded at the battle of Brandy Station and captured on 26 June, while recuperating, by Union cavalry who came across him during a raid on the Confederate railroads near Richmond. The other officer, chosen by Ludlow, was Captain William Sidney Winder, son of Brigadier General John Henry Winder, commander of Libby Prison and its counterpart in Richmond for Union enlisted men, Belle Isle. The Federal captains were not executed.

Lee's army moved on up the Shenandoah Valley that day. Hill's and Longstreet's corps reached the town of Bunker Hill that night, Hill's corps camping west of the town and Longstreet's on the east, both along Mill Creek, and Ewell's corps camped along Middle Creek. Lee was avoiding the town of Winchester, a little farther up the road, because the presence of numerous sick and wounded soldiers being housed there had led to an outbreak of typhoid fever.

The mortally wounded General Pettigrew was taken to one of the finer homes in the area, where he was visited by Lee, Longstreet, Hill, and many other high-ranking officers, all of whom knew as well as he did that he would never recover.

Governor A. G. Curtin of Pennsylvania wired Secretary Stanton that same day, Wednesday, 15 July, saying that Lee's retreat across the Potomac would probably allow his state's militia to be discharged and pointing out how important it was that they should all be paid at the time of being mustered out. "While the prompt performance of this duty will operate favorably to the draft, and be an inducement to many to enter the three-years' service of the Government, it will also be an encouragement to the militia to volunteer readily should any future exigency require them. This is an important consideration, for I have felt the non-payment of the militia called out by the President last fall has been used against the Government during the calls recently made."[20] The same day, General Brooks, at Pittsburgh, complained to General Halleck that, out of three Pennsylvania militia regiments he had ordered to West Virginia the previous week, one regiment and a company of another had refused to go. He had ordered the single company to turn in its arms and equipment and said that, while the reluctant regiment had boarded the railroad cars and departed, over 100 of its men had left the cars along the way.

Meanwhile, the Army of the Potomac was still preparing to cross its namesake river. The men's spirits were low. "When we were chasing the rebs," a surgeon in the 154th New York wrote home that day, "the boys, although barefooted and ragged and half fed, were cheerful on their forced marches, but today they feel chagrined and humbugged. They are silent and morose and what little they say is damning the foolishness and shortsightedness of their officers. They are right, for they have endured everything, braved everything for the sake of success, and success bountiful and lasting was within their grasp – but lost by the imbecility of commandery. Our army is an anomaly," he told his wife, "it is an army of Lions commanded by jackasses!"[21]

In accordance with orders issued the day before, the 2nd and 12th Corps moved on the fifteenth by way of Downsville and Sharpsburg to encamp in Pleasant Valley, near Harper's Ferry; the 1st and 5th Corps moved via Jones's Crossroads and Keedysville to Berlin; and the 6th and 11th Corps via Funkstown, Boonsborough and Middletown to Berlin, with the Artillery Reserve joining them on the road and marching between them. Meade's headquarters was at Berlin that night. Chief Quartermaster Ingalls told the depot quartermaster at Washington, that day, "I think the army will not all be over the river under four days from to-day."[22] An officer of engineers reported to General Humphreys that morning that a raft of 52 pontoon boats had started from Washington for Berlin at 9 a.m., via the C&O Canal, and that another 32 boats would start at noon. And at 2 p.m. General Warren wired Humphreys that the bridge at Sandy Hook "will now let troops pass into the Shenandoah Valley. It will take us till morning to repair the bridge over the Shenandoah. We are at it. I am patching up boats, so as to get, if I can, the number of boats necessary for the bridge at Berlin, even if the boats do not arrive from Washington by to-morrow night."[23]

The depot quartermaster at Gettysburg wired Ingalls that day that tents had finally arrived for the hospitals there and were being put up. He said provost marshals were bringing in many horses that farmers had taken away but that 100,000 pounds of hay he had received was all rotten and useless. He was ordering another 100,000 pounds.

Cavalry Corps headquarters warned General Gregg, now at Shepherdstown, that Averell's cavalry, from the Department of West Virginia, would cross the Potomac at Williamsport that day and follow the Confederates on their flank. General Kelley reported to Halleck that evening that he hoped to cross part of his infantry and artillery the next day. He said that Jenkins' Confederates were camped near North Mountain Station on the B&O Railroad but he should be able to drive them from there soon. However, other Rebels were threatening his garrison at Beverly, so he would have to send it some reinforcements. "As soon as I can possibly get my force across, I will follow the range of North Mountain, and annoy the enemy's flank all I can."[24]

Meade's headquarters published an order that day relieving Baldy Smith's division of militia from further service with the Army of the Potomac and returning it to Couch's command, with thanks for their efforts. Couch told Smith to remain at Hagerstown and to watch the river. The same order assigned Colonel McReynolds and his 1st New York Cavalry, who had reported to Meade for orders, to the job of watching the Potomac from Harper's Ferry to Williamsport, or to such point as would connect him with Kelley's forces from West Virginia, with special attention to Falling Waters. The same order also ordered the 8th U.S. Infantry Regiment and a battery of the Regular Army to proceed to New York City and report to General Wool for temporary duty there.

However, Wool would not be the officer to receive them. Complaints against Wool's inactivity were reaching Washington, along with several calls for a new commanding general, including several for Benjamin Butler to be put in his place. Butler, a Massachusetts War Democrat, had earned a reputation for sternness (and corruption) as Banks' predecessor in the Department of the Gulf. However, with many of the troops of Dix's Department of Virginia having been sent to the Army of the Potomac and/or about to be discharged at the end of their enlistments, Dix, the second-most senior active officer of U.S. Volunteers, no longer had a command worthy of his status. Moreover, Dix had been a prominent Democrat in New York before the war. Therefore, his department was combined with the Department of North Carolina, which consisted of a number of Union lodgments along the coast of that state, and Dix was ordered to New York to take command of the Department of the East, replacing Wool, who at age 79, would retire.

General Keyes, commander of the 4th Corps in Dix's former department, had gone north with the troops being sent to Meade, but his units had been used to fill up other corps, leaving him without a command, and Dix had not wanted him back (blaming him for a weak showing down on the Pamunkey), so Keyes was assigned that day to a retiring board. By the same order, Brigadier General E. R. S. Canby, an assistant adjutant general in Washington (who had, earlier in the war, successfully defended New Mexico Territory from a Confederate invasion), was ordered to repair to New York City and report to Dix, to become the commanding general at the city and harbor of New York.

The authorities in Washington and elsewhere were bombarded again on the fifteenth with alarms from other parts of the country about resistence to the draft. The provost marshal in Denver, Colorado Territory (then in the midst of a gold rush), warned his superior that day that "There is a strong secession element almost throughout this Territory, and hundreds who are arriving here from the Border States weekly are nearly all Southern sympathizers. In several counties threats have been made that the Government should not enroll in the county. . . ." He said he had arrested several men for making such threats and made them take the oath of allegiance and post bonds and was holding one man for threatening to shoot any officer who tried to conscript him. "I have, however, no fears of being able to enroll in every part of this Territory as soon as the surgeon and commissioners are appointed, and to enforce the draft when ordered."[25] A provost marshal at Ironton, Missouri, wired his superior at St. Louis that "there are several counties in this district in such a condition that in my judgment renders it useless to appoint a deputy provost marshal for each one. A considerable military force would be required to enable them to do anything. . . ."[26]

The governor of Iowa, Samuel J. Kirkwood, an ardent supporter of the Lincoln administration, wired Secretary Stanton that day: "The enforcement of the draft throughout the country depends upon its enforcement in New York City.

If it can be successfully resisted there, it cannot be enforced elsewhere. For God's sake let there be no compromising or half-way measures."[27] A telegram to Lincoln that was signed by several Iowa officials, simply said, "Suspension of draft in New York as suggested by Governor Seymour will result disastrously in Iowa."[28]

The acting assistant provost marshal general for New Jersey wired Colonel Fry that day: "There is much excitement in the State, and organizations are forming to resist the draft. I have no means of enforcing it, when ordered, at my disposal." Fry replied, "Troops have been sent to New York, and when the riot is quelled there [,] will be available for New Jersey, and opposition will be put down. The draft will not be ordered in New Jersey until we are prepared to enforce it."[29]

The officer in charge of the draft in western New York state wrote to Fry that it was proceeding quietly in some districts and had been delayed in others because of mistakes in the allotments, for which he was not sorry since it gave him an excuse to hold off. "There is much talk of combination and resistance, and if the Government puts down the riot in New York by yielding to it in whole or in part by showing any disposition to compromise with the rioters, as Governor Seymour seems to propose, then I expect the resistance to be universal."[30] He said that the commandant at Elmira had asked for 500 men, and that Buffalo would need the same, and he had armed 100 new recruits with weapons taken from the Invalid Corps.

There was some good news as well: Colonel William D. Whipple, military governor of Philadelphia, in Couch's department, wired Fry: "Draft completed in one enrollment district to-day without trouble."[31] However, Colonel Richard Rush of the 6th Pennsylvania Cavalry (Rush's Lancers), son of a prominent diplomat, and descendant of a founding father of the country, wrote to Fry that day that "as a Philadelphian, I have means of hearing from various sources what has caused me to believe that there will be serious resistance to the draft in that city, and under pretext of that the mob will endeavor to take possession of the U.S. property in that city.... I have seen the telegram in which Colonel Whipple thinks he can carry out the draft with the force he has. I beg leave to differ with him, and would strongly urge that the draft be not attempted in Philadelphia until the resistance to it elsewhere has been put down by force, and then execute it in Philadelphia under the presence of an efficient force of 1,500 to 2,000 reliable troops."[32]

Meanwhile, neither the new commanders nor any more troops had reached New York by the morning of Wednesday, the fifteenth, which was the hottest day of the year there, in more ways than one. Commissioner Acton promised his policemen quail on toast as soon as the riot was put down, but his men and many of the soldiers were approaching exhaustion. Some sixty buildings had been burned, the mob continued to wreak havoc on black neighborhoods, and people of all colors were fleeing the city by every means possible, which did not include the railroad because rioters had broken the tracks leading out of town.

The efforts of Governor Seymour and Tammany Hall Democrats had succeeded in quieting some neighborhoods, but residents of three areas of tenements and factories on the East Side were setting up barricades, patrolling their streets, and searching buildings for any hidden policemen or soldiers. Meanwhile, General Brown and Commissioner Acton broke up their reserve at the Central Office into four groups, placing two uptown on the East Side, one downtown at City Hall, and one at the northern tip of the island.

The Common Council of the city, that day, instructed the city's counsel to challenge the constitutionality of the draft law in the courts and decided to create a fund of $2.5 million to pay the $300 commutation fees for any drafted New Yorkers who could not afford to pay it themselves. The money would be raised by floating bonds that would pay up to 7 percent interest. Mayor Opdyke refused to sign the bill, saying it would amount to bowing to the dictates of the mob. Instead, that afternoon he issued a proclamation, claiming that "What now remains of the mob are fragments prowling about for plunder."[33] He asked for citizens to form volunteer associations to protect their own neighborhoods, urged people to go back to their jobs, and the street cars, railways and telegraphs to resume services.

Meanwhile, the city's numerous newspapers warred upon each other with editorials, the Republican papers accusing the Democrats of encouraging the riots in order to help the Confederacy, and the Democratic papers accusing the Republicans of causing the riots by favoring the draft and by demonstrating, as the *Evening Post* put it, "such intense sympathy with the negro, at the expense of white men, that the Northern sentiment has been naturally embittered toward the unfortunate race. . . ."[34]

Colonel Nugent met with Governor Seymour, Mayor Opdyke, and others that afternoon. Seymour asked, as Nugent later reported to Colonel Fry, ". . . if I had any instructions from Washington in relation to the suspension of the draft in New York and the other Congressional districts, to which I replied that I had received instructions as far as regards New York and Brooklyn, but that I was not at liberty to publish them without express authority from you." Fry had specifically forbidden Nugent to publish Fry's order to suspend the draft, for fear that it would encourage the rioters to know that they had accomplished that much. However, pushed by these authorities, and "as they considered that it would have the effect of allaying the excitement to have the fact made known, I did so over my own signature."[35] That afternoon, Secretary of State William Seward, a former governor of New York, wired Henry J. Raymond, publisher of the N.Y. *Times*, and a Republican: "The draft in New York was suspended by mob force, which rendered its execution for the moment impossible. No directions have been given respecting it beyond the period when order shall be restored."[36]

Nugent wrote to Fry that day, saying, in part, "I would suggest that when an adequate force is sent here, the draft should be resumed in one district at a time, and rigidly enforced there. . . . The mob spirit must be put down by the strong arm of the military power. There is no use in trying to conciliate it or reason with it. It has now assumed the character of an organized mass of plunderers, and the public generally have lost all sympathy for it; so that now is the time to crush out rebellion. This can be easily done, if the proper force is placed at our disposal."[37]

Meanwhile, the rioting had continued. At about 6 a.m. a black shoemaker named James Costello was chased down West 32nd Street by William Mealy, a white shoemaker who possibly resented Costello's competition. Costello turned and shot Mealy with a pistol, but a mob of 200 or 300 soon gathered, chased Costello down, dragged him out into the street, pummeled him with fists and rocks, and hanged him from a tree with a rope provided by the owner of a nearby stable. Not content with killing him, the mob mutilated his body, then went on to burn the house he had tried to escape into and a row of tenements behind it, which someone said was full of black families, and then went on a looting spree. A heavy rain was falling when General Brown sent troops under Lieutenant B. Franklin Ryer to the area, and the rioters scattered without the soldiers having to fire a shot. The soldiers cut down Costello's body but left it behind when they proceeded to the Seventh Avenue arsenal.

They were soon sent back to 32nd Street, however, for the mob had returned there and was attacking a house in which several black families were hiding. Again the rioters scattered, and the soldiers escorted fourteen people to the safety of the armory. A mob followed them, but Lieutenant Ryer deployed a platoon across Seventh Avenue at 32nd and had it fire two volleys, which drove the mob back with losses of at least 23 people, including some women and children. Meanwhile, another lieutenant at the arsenal had received a tip that rioters had a large collection of weapons in a house at 32nd and Broadway. He attacked the house with fifteen soldiers and captured 73 British-made Enfield rifles and brought them to the arsenal. A troop of cavalry was dispatched to 33rd Street, where a mob was chasing a black man named Augustus Stuart. In confusion, Stuart fired a pistol at the soldiers, one of whom then wounded him mortally with his sword. As soon as all these soldiers were gone, the mob strung Costello's body back up again.

Similar treatment was meted out to Abraham Franklin, a black coachman who stopped to see his mother at Seventh Avenue and 28th. A mob broke down his mother's door, beat Franklin with fists and clubs, dragged him out into the street, and hanged him from a lamppost while setting his mother's house on fire. Soldiers scattered the crowd, and Franklin still showed signs of life when they cut him down, but he was left on the street when the soldiers moved on, and the rioters returned, strung him up again, cut up the body, and then dragged it through the streets.

Blacks were not the only ethnic group targeted. Two different groups of Irish Catholics threatened Josiah Porter and his wife that day, not only because he was a Republican, but because he was an Orangeman – that is, a Protestant Irishman. Porter managed to escape, but his wife was warned that she had two hours before they would return to burn down her house. When they returned they found her still there, and several Catholic neighbors as well, one of whom warned the men that they "were laying themselves liable to the law," but the leader of this group replied that "there was no law in New York."[38] He and another man then set the house on fire.

At about 4 p.m. General Sandford sent Lt. Ryer out again, with 50 men, to help policemen who were fighting a mob of some 2,000 rioters who were setting fire to buildings near Tenth Avenue and 42nd Street. The soldiers were met with a shower of bricks and rocks, as well as shots from windows and roofs of nearby buildings. Ryer ordered the mob to disperse, and when it failed to do so he had his men fire five or more volleys into the crowd. The rioters in the streets fled, but shots were still coming from the nearby houses, so Ryer dispatched another lieutenant with ten men to clear them, and they soon returned with two prisoners. The soldiers headed back to the armory, but, as before, they were followed by a mob, which charged them from behind. Again Ryer faced a platoon about and had it give the pursuers two more volleys, after which the soldiers were able to proceed unmolested. However, not long afterwards a Tammany judge appeared at the arsenal wanting to arrest the officer who, he said, had killed women and children on Tenth Avenue. General Wool claimed not to know who had been in charge there.

Sometime that evening General Couch wired Halleck that he was sending eleven New York militia regiments to New York by rail. Halleck replied that only two regiments had been so ordered. "Why have eleven regiments been sent there, and by what authority?" Couch answered that "New York regiments are going home because their time is out – two were ordered by General Smith, after consultation with General Meade, by way of Frederick. Those in my command are marching to Shippensburg, thence by rail. The [order] can still be countermanded, if desired."[39] And Halleck did tell him to countermand the order and send only the two regiments he had asked for.

At 6 p.m., Mayor Opdyke wired Secretary Stanton: "Thus far the day has passed off more quietly than yesterday, but at present the demonstrations are reported threatening. Neither of the regiments ordered here from the field has yet arrived, nor have we yet received any military aid from any quarter outside of the city. The police and military force here have been very effective, but their duties have been so arduous that they are greatly exhausted."[40] Commissioner Acton, for instance, had not slept since taking direct control of the Metropolitan Police three days and nights before.

Also at about 6 p.m., Wool responded to reports of a large mob gathering on First Avenue between 18th and 19th by sending Colonel Cleveland Winslow of the 5th New York (Duryee's Zouaves), a famous 2-years regiment that had recently been discharged and was in the process of being re-formed from recruits and veterans, and Major Edward Jardine, a veteran of the 9th New York (Hawkins' Zouaves), with two howitzers. Like Ryer's smaller force, earlier, they were met not only by a mob in the streets but shots and showers of bricks from surrounding rooftops. The howitzers fired several rounds of canister, killing some thirty rioters and/or bystanders, but some rioters waited around corners of buildings until the artillerymen fired, then popped out to fire at them as they reloaded. The *Times* later reported that the mob was well organized and that someone was giving orders when to fire. Instead of sending troops to clear the houses, as Lt. Ryer had done, Colonel Winslow ordered a retreat, leaving dead and wounded soldiers, including Jardine, behind. Winslow went to the Saint Nicholas hotel and told Governor Seymour what had happened, and Seymour sent him to General Brown to get help.

At 9 p.m., Brown dispatched Captain H. R. Putnam with 150 Regulars and one artillery piece to find Jardine and escort him and the other wounded men to safety. But Jardine, who had a broken leg, and some of his wounded men had found refuge in the home of a friendly family, where his regimental surgeon dressed their wounds. They were given civilian clothes so that they could pose as rioters wounded in the fighting. Those who could walk escaped over the roofs while Jardine, the surgeon, and the worst wounded were hidden in the basement. However, rioters came to the door saying that they knew soldiers were in the house and demanding that they be brought out. Two women of the family tried to deny them entrance, but part of the mob burst in, made a search, and found the soldiers, and were not fooled by their civilian clothes. However, they hesitated when Jardine asked to see a priest, not sure that they wanted to kill a fellow Catholic.

The two women had meanwhile befriended the sentry that the rioters had left at the door and persuaded him to pretend that he knew Jardine and to say that he was no soldier. The leaders of the mob were convinced, and even offered to leave a sentry to prevent any further searches. Eventually, long after midnight, a member of the family was able to lead Putnam's Regulars to their home, who escorted the wounded soldiers and the family to the Central Office of the police. The women were then taken to the Saint Nicholas hotel and given comfortable rooms, though they were still too excited to sleep.

Some working men took advantage of the general lawlessness to take revenge for other grievances. Shortly after 11 p.m. the Atlantic Dock Basin was attacked by about 200 men who had formerly shoveled grain there, because it had hired strike-breakers against them the previous summer. They burned down two huge grain elevators and a scow.

Late that night, Secretary Stanton wrote a private message to Thurlow Weed, Republican political boss in New York state: "We have this evening official report by General Banks of the unconditional surrender of Port Hudson. The agreement for surrender was made on the 8th, and possession taken on the 9th. Prisoners estimated at 12,000. Four great victories – Gettysburg, Helena, Vicksburg, Port Hudson – in eight days. We have taken over 55,000 prisoners, and the rebel loss in killed, wounded, and prisoners is about 84,000 men. Every rebel army has been captured or is in flight; every rebel stronghold is beleaguered. Gillmore's official report, received to-night, shows thus far unexpected success against Charleston, and Banks' dispatches come by the Mississippi, now free to New Orleans. Our success within so brief a period since the first of this month is unexampled in military history. The rebel disasters are greater than ever befell any belligerent – the command of the Mississippi! Has New York no sympathy for these achievements won by the valor of her own sons? Shall their glory be dimmed by the bloody riots of a street mob?"[41]

At about 5 p.m. seven companies of the 65th New York State National Guard, a militia regiment sent from General Couch's department, reached the city, with a battery of three howitzers from another regiment attached. "On arriving in New York," the 65th's Colonel, William F. Berens, later reported, "I immediately marched my command to headquarters, reporting in person to General Wool. On the way from the dock, a large mob gathered about, and attempted to get possession of two negroes who were serving as cooks with the artillery company of the Eighth New York National Guard. I protected them from harm by placing them amidst the battery, and protecting the same by a company thrown on either flank. Upon reporting to General Wool, I was ordered to take quarters at Centre Market, and to report to General Harvey Brown, which I did. Pursuant to orders from General Brown, the same evening I sent two companies to guard the treasury buildings, on Wall street . . . and two other companies, along with some United States troops, to restore order in the vicinity of Union Square. . . ."[42]

This regiment was followed later by the 152nd New York and the 26th Michigan, two volunteer regiments from Dix's old Department of Virginia. And, at about 4:30 a.m. on the 16th, the 7th New York National Guard., an elite regiment that had been used to put down riots many times in New York's stormy past, disembarked at the foot of Canal Street, some 600 strong, following a brief stay in Maryland as part of Schenck's Middle Department, its third stint of Federalized service during the war. In the early morning light, the 7th marched up Broadway to the Saint Nicholas Hotel to report to Governor Seymour. One of the women who had helped to save Colonel Jardine saw it there. "Loud cheers brought us to the window to see the glorious returning 'Seventh' marshaled before us," she wrote, "and with all our hearts and voices we joined in the welcome which greeted them."[43]

Nevertheless, the violence still continued on Thursday, the sixteenth. Some fifty rioters chased Samuel Johnson, a black man, to the 34th Street ferry, beat him up, and threw him into the East River, where he drowned. William O. Stoddard, one of Lincoln's personal secretaries, who was in New York recovering from typhoid, said that black people were hiding "in cellars and garrets, hardly daring to venture out for food." Many fled to police stations, which were often overflowing with such refugees, but Commissioner Acton told them to "Refuse nobody."[44]

Through the newspapers, Mayor Opdyke called on residents to return to work. Some of the streetcar lines tried to resume business, but a mob of about 100 men stopped the cars on Second Avenue at 23rd Street and forced them to turn back, and on Fourth Avenue the conductor and passengers were robbed. On First Avenue the cars were allowed to proceed because the owner was said to be a staunch Democrat.

At around 7 a.m., General Brown sent Colonel Berens and the remaining three companies of his 65th National Guard plus his attached howitzers to guard factories on the East Side that made weapons and ammunition. Berens left one company and one howitzer at the Hotchkiss shell factory, on 24th Street, and proceeded to Seward's shell factory, on 17th. Along the way they were threatened by a mob, but there was no violence, and he left another company and another howitzer at Seward's. Then he took his one remaining company and last howitzer up Avenue A, heading for Jackson's shell factory on 28th, where he intended to make his headquarters.

"On arriving at the corner of Avenue A and Twenty-second street," he later reported, "I was fired into by the mob. I wheeled my men into line to return the fire, and the mob skedaddled. I then passed on a block farther, to the corner of Twenty-third street, when the mob gathered in upon my company from both directions on Twenty-third street, and commenced at once to fire upon us. I returned the fire, and kept up the street, firing, until I arrived at Twenty-eighth street. Finding my small company of only 28 men, besides the men serving the howitzer, too small to disperse so large a mob as had collected, I dispatched Quartermaster Flack to headquarters, on Mulberry street, for re-enforcements. The mob seemed to be very generally armed. I then fought my way through the mob to the factory. One of my men was wounded, and several of the crowd were killed and wounded by our fire. On arriving at the factory, we found the door closed. I forced the door, and took possession. The mob gathered heavily around the factory and fired upon us. We returned their fire, and afterward sallied out upon them and drove them up Twenty-eighth street, as far as the corner of First avenue, and dispersed them. At 2 p.m. Quartermaster R. Flack arrived with Companies A and D."[45]

A reporter for the *Times* said that the rioters demanded that the soldiers turn over to them the four policemen who were with them. Only then would they disperse. "The committee stood at a respectful distance while delivering their message," he wrote, "and took to their heels, on an intimation to do so or they would be shot."[46]

"At about 5 p.m." Berens reported, "a priest came to me as a commissioner from the riotous populace, and urged me to quit the factory and return, stating the people agreed that if I did so the factory should not be injured. He stated further that the crowd threatened that if we did not leave they would burn us out. He implored me to accept the proposal, saying that he feared the worst consequences; that the mob was about 4,000 strong – altogether too large for my weak force to resist – and that he could not control or restrain them. I reported the offer made to me by the priest to General Brown. His answer was, to hold the place at all events, and to disperse the assemblage about me at the point of the bayonet, if necessary. Previous to the receipt of this response from General Brown, however, having refused the offered compromise, and the priest having retired beyond the reach of harm, and the crowd gathering heavily around the building we occupied, I found it necessary to open fire upon them, which was kept up until our assailants were driven back behind the corners of the neighboring streets."[47]

That afternoon, along with a state senator and the judge who had wanted to arrest the commander of the soldiers who had fired on civilians, called on Governor Seymour to suggest keeping all troops out of the 18th Ward and letting the middle-class residents there keep order themselves. Seymour liked the idea and wrote a letter supporting it, which they took to Commissioner Acton. He turned them down, telling them, "We have been fighting a week, and are going to keep on until every man, white or black, can go anywhere on this island in perfect safety." General Brown agreed, saying, "I'll not move a man unless Mr. Acton tells me to."[48]

Meanwhile, the New York newspapers continued to blame each other for the rioting. The *World* wrote that "Negroes are cruelly beaten in New York because mock philanthropists have made them odious by parading them and their emancipation as the object to which peace first and the Union afterward [–] with the lives of myriads of Northern men [–] are to be sacrificed." Henry Raymond, editor of the *Times* who normally took a moderate stance, came to the defense of the more radical *Tribune* and *Evening Post*, saying, "The *World*, with an eager ferocity which finds its proper counterpart in the ranks of the mob, seizes the opportunity to denounce those journals which support the Government as responsible for the riot, and to point them out to the mob as proper objects of its vengeance." He said that opposition to the draft was what started the riots and asked, "Who stimulated that opposition? Who has day after day devoted time and talent and strength to denunciation of the law – long after it had been placed upon the statute book, and when criticism had thus become utterly unavailing for any purpose consistent with the public good?"[49]

The national authorities at Washington received mixed messages from the local authorities at New York that day. At 1:25 p.m. Stanton's office received a telegram from Governor Seymour that said: "There is great disorder here. It is important to have the New York and Brooklyn regiments sent home at once." And at the same hour Quartermaster General Meigs received a telegram from the quartermaster in New York saying: "The aspect of affairs is unchanged. The mob is becoming better organized, hence more formidable, while our forces are not arriving fast enough. The mob will be put down, but the longer delayed the more difficult it will be. Five thousand good troops should arrive to-day. The Seventh Regiment arrived this morning. I should be telegraphed promptly as each regiment leaves, so as to have boats in readiness."[50] However, Mayor Opdyke wired Stanton that evening: "We had but little disturbance in the city last night, and none this morning. I think the riot is at an end for the present. Andrews, one of the chief leaders, is arrested."[51]

Indeed, four detectives had entered John Andrews' house on 11th Street that day, finding him in bed with his mistress, a black prostitute and madam. They took him to the Central Office, where he was shackled and transferred to Fort Lafayette, near Brooklyn. A special order was requested and received of Secretary Stanton to have the commander there hold him and any other prisoners arrested for participation in the riots. Andrews seems to have been more connected to the criminal element of the city than to the Copperheads, but the *Tribune* denounced him as one who had "roused the fierce passions of the mob, and turned men into incarnate devils." While the *World* was more appalled by his having a black mistress, calling him a "practical amalgamationist."[52]

Stanton replied to Seymour at 4:40 p.m.: "Eleven New York regiments are relieved and are at Frederick, and will be forwarded to New York as fast as transportation can be furnished them. Please signify to me anything you may desire to be done by the Department. Whatever means are at its disposal shall be at your command for the purpose of restoring order in New York."[53] Stanton must have overruled Halleck, who had told Couch not to send those troops. Couch had informed Halleck at 9 a.m. that "The movement of New York troops, via Frederick, was suspended last night by telegraph. Those men were dissatisfied at having to march into Maryland. It will be better to keep faith as to term of service, if possible. The emergency men of this State [Pennsylvania] say that their time is up. Please inform me if the War Department will decide when those, as well as the militia, are to be discharged."[54]

Mayor Opdyke was a bit premature in saying that the riot was at an end, as there was one more major fight to be had. A force of about 80 cavalrymen, reconnoitering eastward on foot along 22nd Street from Gramercy Park, was ambushed that afternoon between Second and Third by snipers firing from windows and roofs of barricaded houses while being confronted by rioters in the street. The cavalry retreated rather hastily, leaving behind the body of a sergeant. Their colonel hurried to police headquarters to report the incident to General Brown, who angrily ordered him back to his regiment and, at about 6 p.m., sent Captain Putnam, who had rescued Colonel Jardine the night before, with 160 infantry and artillerymen and a few policemen, to the area. The infantry drove snipers from houses at Gramercy Park, and Putnam informed the women living there that if they allowed their homes to again be used by snipers the houses would be leveled by his artillery.

Proceeding eastward on 22nd, Putnam's men soon recovered the body of the cavalry sergeant, but when he ordered the keeper of a livery stable to hitch his horses to a carriage and bring the body along, the man refused, saying the mob would kill him if he did. Putnam told the man that he'd kill him if he didn't, which proved to be sufficient motivation. However, Putnam's men now came under fire from nearby houses. "If they had been cool and steady," Putnam later wrote, "they might have done us great harm. As it was, they fired wildly, running to a window and firing, and then retreating back out of danger." He deployed skirmishers in the street whose fire forced the snipers away from the windows, and sent the rest of his infantry to clear the houses, taking a few prisoners, but killing most of them. Then he marched his force eastward again, then northward up Second Avenue, driving the rioters before him, as far as 31st Street, where the mob was reinforced and more snipers opened fire. This time he had his artillery open fire on the rioters in the street while his infantry again cleared the houses of snipers. "Some of them fought like incarnate fiends," he wrote, "and would not surrender. All such were shot on the spot."[55] His men captured several large revolvers and one ancient blunderbuss. Then, with his prisoners, Putnam marched his men back to the Central Office, where they were greeted as heroes. "The loss of the rioters was great," said Commissioner Acton, "and seemed for the first time to break down the desperate spirit of the mob."[56]

And there was still some sporadic fighting left to do. The 7th National Guard mopped up the East Side between 14th and 35th Streets and also received some sniper fire. One of the most determined snipers used a woman as a shield while he loaded and fired, but he was eventually brought down by two members of the 7th who had also taken to the rooftops. Another sniper was Martin Moran, a suspected ringleader, who was captured and nearly hanged on the spot before officers could restrain their men. He was turned over to the police. "About 10 p.m.," one member of the 7th wrote, "we formed a strong force and with a howitzer in front patrolled the neighborhood and met with no resistance."[57] By midnight the city was quiet. At 2 a.m., Commissioner Acton finally got some sleep.

In Ohio, Morgan's raiders were becoming more desperate on the sixteenth. "Today we find the first obstruction in our way, consisting of felled trees," Colonel McCreary recorded. "The enemy are now pressing us on all sides, and the woods swarm with militia. We capture hundreds of prisoners, but a parole being null, we can only sweep them as chaff out of our way. Today we crossed the Scioto to Piketon, and, as usual, destroyed the bridge. Thence we moved to Jackson."[58] To obtain a guide to a ford over the Scioto River, some of Morgan's men shot and killed a militiaman in order to intimidate the rest of his company, which had surrendered only after a brief fight and had refused to guide them. They looted the town of Jasper and burned several buildings there, as well as bridges and boats on the Ohio and Erie Canal. They reached Jackson at about 10 p.m.

General Hobson later reported that, "As I found great difficulty in bringing my artillery forward, owing to the horses having broken down, and the impossibility of procuring fresh ones on the road, I separated my command, ordering Colonel [August V.] Kautz to move forward with his brigade, composed of the Second and Seventh Ohio Regiments, and to make every endeavor to overtake Morgan, attack, and compel him to make a stand, and I would support him with Colonel Sanders' brigade, while the balance of my command would follow as fast as their jaded condition would permit. In some places the road had been partially obstructed, but not so as to cause the enemy any serious delay. At Jasper, Morgan burned the bridge over the canal, causing some delay to my advance, but it was speedily rebuilt, under the direction of Colonel Kautz."[59]

Kautz (West Point, 1852), who would later command a cavalry division in Virginia and serve on the military commission that tried the conspirators in the assassination of Lincoln, was in familiar territory; although born in Germany, he had been raised in Georgetown, Ohio, where General Grant, six years his senior, had also spent most of his youth. His two regiments had also been raised in this area, so they wouldn't have to depend on civilian guides. Kautz later reported that his brigade reached Jasper at 11 p.m. and that it took five or six hours to repair the bridge there. But, while thus delayed, he sent a lieutenant with a few men north to Chillicothe, where they took the railroad to get ahead of Morgan and block the crossings of the Hocking River.

In the meantime, light-draft gunboats of the Navy patrolled the river, trying to keep all fording places covered, and General Judah's Union cavalry was brought up the river from Cincinnati on steamboats. "I reached Portsmouth, on the Ohio River, on the afternoon of the 16th instant," he later reported, "disembarked, procured supplies for men and horses, and transportation, and at 9 p.m. I marched for Fair Oaks and Portland, 30 miles distant."[60]

In Mississippi, Grant was writing to General Banks,

saying that the sick and wounded Confederates left in the hospitals at Vicksburg had been so troublesome that he had consented to send them either west to Monroe, Louisiana, or east to Mobile, Alabama, and that he was sending the first batch down the river that day with hopes that Banks would transfer them to suitable vessels and send them along the Gulf coast to Mobile.

Unknown to Grant, or even to Sherman, Joe Johnston withdrew from Jackson that night. "On the 16th of July," Johnston later reported, "information was received that a large [wagon] train from Vicksburg, loaded with ammunition, was near the enemy's camp. This and the condition of their batteries made it probable that Sherman would on the next day concentrate upon us the fire of nearly two hundred guns. It was also reported that the enemy [Herron] had crossed Pearl River in rear of their left flank. The evacuation of Jackson that night was therefore determined on. Our withdrawal was effected on the night of the 16th. All public property, and the sick and wounded, except a few not in a condition to be moved, had been previously carried to the rear. The right wing retired toward Brandon by the new Brandon road and the left wing by the old Brandon road. The cavalry remained to destroy the bridges over Pearl River and observe the enemy. The evacuation was not discovered by the enemy until the next day."[61]

That same sixteenth day of July, a civilian steamer from the North reached New Orleans – the first to do so in more than two years.

～ Endnotes ～

1 *OR*, I:27:II:888-9.
2 Ibid., III:3:488.
3 Ibid., III:3:488-9.
4 Ibid., III:3:490.
5 Ibid., III:3:491.
6 Ibid., III:3:492.
7 Ibid.
8 Ibid., III:3:491.
9 Ibid., III:3:489.

10 McCreary, "Morgan's Raid Comes to an Inglorious End," *B&G*, 683.
11 Mowery, *Morgan's Great Raid*, 98.
12 *OR*, I:27:III:700.
13 Ibid., I:27:III:703.
14 Brooks, *Washington, D.C., in Lincoln's Time*, 94.
15 *OR*, I:24:III:513.
16 Ibid.
17 Ibid., I:24:III:514. Both messages. No indication could be found in the records that a large Confederate cavalry force had moved as reported.
18 Ibid., I:24:I:246.
19 Ibid., I:24:III:518.
20 Ibid., I:27:III:707.
21 Wittenberg, Petruzzi and Nugent, *One Continuous Fight*, 319.
22 *OR*, I:27:III:703.
23 Ibid., I:27:III:701.
24 Ibid., I:27:III:708.
25 Ibid., III:3:494.
26 Ibid., III:3:495.
27 Ibid., III:3:494.
28 Ibid., III:3:495.
29 Ibid., III:3: 496. Both messages.
30 Ibid., III:3:497.
31 Ibid.
32 Ibid., III:3:499.
33 Schecter, *The Devil's Own Work*, 216.
34 Ibid., 215.
35 *OR*, I:27:II:901-2.
36 Ibid., I:27:II:924.
37 Ibid., I:27:II:988.
38 Schecter, *The Devil's Own Work*, 210.
39 *OR*, I:27:II:920-1. All 3 messages.
40 Ibid., I:27:II:920.
41 Ibid., I:27:II:921.
42 Ibid., I:27:II:253.
43 Schecter, *The Devil's Own Work*, 223.
44 Ibid., 225. Both quotes.
45 *OR*, I:27:II:253-4.
46 Schecter, *The Devil's Own Work*, 226.
47 *OR*, I:27:II:254.
48 Schecter, *The Devil's Own Work*, 229. Both quotes.
49 Ibid., 228. Both quotes.
50 *OR*, I:27:II:925. All three messages.
51 Ibid., I:27:II:926.
52 Schecter, *The Devil's Own Work*, 226. Both quotes.
53 *OR*, I:27:II:926
54 Ibid., I:27:II:925.
55 Schecter, *The Devil's Own Work*, 230.
56 Ibid.
57 Ibid., 231.
58 McCreary, "Morgan's Raid Comes to an Inglorious End," *B&G*, 683.
59 *OR*, I:23:I:660.
60 Ibid., I:23:I:656.
61 Ibid., I:24:I:246.

AFTERWORD

The events of that summer of 1863 overlapped in such a way as to prevent me from neatly wrapping up every thread of this narrative without extending too far beyond the climax. Primarily, I had to leave Morgan and his raiders north of the Ohio, increasingly harried on their desperate ride. But by the time that ended, on 26 July, the fight for Charleston Harbor had heated up again and Lee and Meade were sparring again in Virginia. Let us leave it here for now. In my previous works I covered about fourteen months of the war in four volumes, or something over three months per volume. But this present trilogy covers slightly less than four months, or a bit more than one month per volume. It was a busy time.

A very great deal had already been written about the battle of Gettysburg before I began this present volume, and still other works appeared while it was in progress. No doubt more will come out before you read these words. One of the interesting things about history is that there is never any final word on such great events. I have done my best to understand the complex events on that field on those three days, and their aftermath, and to help the reader to do so. I certainly learned a few things about it that I had not realized before. Perhaps foremost among them was Lee's fixation on taking Cemetery Hill, or trying to.

Many works I have read assumed that Lee's focus on 2 July was on Meade's left flank and the two Round Tops. In the course of my research, however, it became apparent to me that, yes, he was focused on Meade's left, but he did not understand where that flank really was. He thought Meade's line ran along the Emmitsburg Road, and thought that Longstreet could do to Meade there what Stonewall Jackson had done to Hooker's right flank at Chancellorsville – then roll up the Union line and finally take the key high ground of Cemetery Hill that Ewell had failed to take the night before. He was not interested in the Round Tops.

Sickles' advance to the area of the Peach Orchard just happened to place his 3rd Corps right on the ground where Longstreet was supposed to form for his attack. This move did not, as Sickles and his supporters always claimed, save the Union army; instead it nearly wrecked his corps, as well as several units sent to his aid. However, it did disrupt Lee's plan and did enough damage to Longstreet's two divisions that Longstreet begged off using them in the next day's attack. Meanwhile, in the course of the second day's fight, still searching for the Union flank so he could turn it, division commander Sam Hood sent his brigades off to the east before a wound took him out of the equation. A fight for Little Round Top eventually ensued, but it had not been the original target.

I believe this present volume might be the first to pair an account of the battle of Gettysburg with a fairly detailed look at Lee's retreat to, and finally escape across, the Potomac. Over the years, beginning with President Lincoln, and/or Meade's own men, Meade's pursuit has often been criticized as being too timid. That officer had many problems, it is true, but I have to agree, on the whole (with 20-20 hindsight), that he should have been more aggressive. First, he wasted too much time trying to figure out where Lee was and what he would do. It should have been obvious that Lee could not remain north of the Potomac after the losses his army had suffered at Gettysburg, nor be able to live off the country in the face of Meade's army and the forces of Couch's department. All he could do was try to return to Virginia.

I think Meade was right not to attack Lee's entrenched position between Hagerstown and the Potomac, at least not with a frontal assault. But once it was obvious that a rise in the river would prevent Lee from crossing immediately,

I cannot fathom why neither Meade, nor Halleck, nor, evidently, anyone else in the Union high command, thought to get sizable forces south of the river themselves, so as to prevent Lee from crossing. Also, as Wilson Greene has pointed out, Meade's plan for a reconnaissance on 14 July to begin at 7 a.m. can be faulted for wasting two hours of daylight.[1] Had it kicked off at first light, sizable parts of Lee's army would have been caught still on the Maryland side of the Potomac.

These three volumes began with two brilliant Union plans. Grant's turning of Vicksburg in the West, and Hooker's turning of Lee's Fredericksburg position in the East. One succeeded; the other did not. Much of the difference lies in the personalities of the two Union generals. Grant had well-deserved confidence in himself; Hooker, for all his boasting, did not. And much lies in the qualities of the opposition. Just as Hooker was no Grant, neither was Pemberton, or even Joe Johnston, a Lee. Lee's bold refusal to retreat, as Hooker expected (and as one must assume that Johnston, Pemberton, or almost any other general would have), caused Hooker to hesitate while Lee responded with his own brilliant maneuvering, on a more limited scale, that soon hustled Hooker back across the Rappahannock.

Lee then followed up with his own long-delayed invasion/raid into Pennsylvania, which began brilliantly, clearing the Valley and capturing much of Milroy's division, but in the end it accomplished only a few weeks of respite for war-torn Northern Virginia and the gathering in of a huge quantity of badly needed supplies, but at the cost of serious damage to his own army. (Lee argued that had he remained in Virginia he would have had to fight there and probably have taken just as many losses; and there is some validity to that argument.) But he did not in any way loosen Grant's hold on Vicksburg and Pemberton's army, and the Army of the Potomac's success did much to raise the morale of its troops and of the folks back home. As General Warren observed in a letter to his bride of less than a month: "Terrible has been the ruin of the rebels' hopes, as I told you it would be, if they invaded the North." However he had to add that "we have not yet destroyed Lee's army; and the campaign must go on. We shall follow their retreat, and you must live without me, and I without you."[2]

Between those two theaters, Rosecrans had also devised and executed a brilliant campaign that cleared the Confederates out of Middle Tennessee by the beginning of July. It was his misfortune that rains similar to those that almost trapped Lee against the flooded Potomac had slowed his own columns sufficiently for Bragg to just manage to escape across the Tennessee River. And, as he somewhat justifiably complained (one of his major talents), because his campaign did not involve so much bloodshed as those to the east and west of him, he received much less credit at the time. However, Bragg's army had escaped to fight another day, as Lee's had escaped Meade and Johnston's had escaped Sherman, each putting a river between them and any pursuit. But Pemberton had not escaped Grant, who now stood out as the Union's most successful general.

Health (so far, so good) and time permitting, I will soon resume the narrative and proceed to examine the late summer and autumn of 1863, where the primary focus will be, of course, the Chickamauga and Chattanooga campaigns and the long-sought, much-delayed, liberation of East Tennessee.

Endnotes

1   A. Wilson Greene, "Meade's Pursuit of Lee: From Gettysburg to Falling Waters," in *The Third Day at Gettysburg and Beyond*, Gary W. Gallagher, editor.
2   Wittenberg, Petruzzie and Nugent, *One Continuous Fight*, 319.

THE ARMIES

★ UNITED STATES ARMY: ★
Commander-in-Chief – President Abraham Lincoln
Secretary of War – Edwin M. Stanton
General-in-Chief – Major General Henry Wager Halleck
Adjutant General – Brigadier General Lorenzo Thomas
Quartermaster General – Brigadier General Montgomery Meigs

DEPARTMENT OF THE EAST (N.J., N.Y. and New England):
Commanding General – Major General John E. Wool

MIDDLE DEPARTMENT (8th ARMY CORPS – Md. and Del.):
Commanding General – Major General Robert Schenck

    1st Provisional Brigade: Brigadier General Daniel Tyler
    2nd Separate Brigade: Brigadier General William W. Morris
    3rd Separate Brigade: Brigadier General Henry S. Briggs
    Annapolis, Md.: Lieutenant Colonel George Sangster
    Fort Delaware: Brigadier General Albin Schoepf

    French's Division: Major General William H. French
    Maryland Brigade: Brigadier General John R. Kenly
    3rd Provisional Brigade: Brigadier General William H. Morris

    Elliott's Command: Brigadier General Washington L. Elliott
    1st Brigade: (Brigadier General Washington L. Elliott)
    3rd Brigade, French's Division: Colonel Benjamin F. Smith

DEPARTMENT OF WASHINGTON (22nd ARMY CORPS):
Commanding General – Major General Samuel P. Heintzelman
    Military Governor, Alexandria, Va.: Brigadier General John P. Slough
    Military Governor, Washington, D.C.: Brigadier General John Martindale
    Fort Washington: Colonel Charles S. Merchant
    Camp Convalescent and Paroled Prisoners: Lt. Col. Samuel McKelvy
    Provisional Brigades: Major General Silas Casey
    Cavalry: Colonel Percy Wyndham
    Artillery Camp of Instruction: Brigadier General William F. Barry

Defenses North of the Potomac: Lieut. Col. Joseph A. Haskin, ADC
1st Brigade: Colonel Augustus A. Gibson
2nd Brigade: Colonel Lewis O. Morris
3rd Brigade: Colonel Alexander Piper

Defenses South of the Potomac: Brig. Gen. Gustavus A. De Russy
1st Brigade: Colonel Thomas R. Tannatt
2nd Brigade: Colonel Leverette W. Wessells
3rd Brigade: Colonel Henry L. Abbot
4th Brigade: Colonel Henry H. Hall

ARMY OF THE POTOMAC:[1]
Commanding General – Major General George Gordon Meade
Chief of Staff – Brigadier General Daniel Butterfield
Assistant Adjutant General – Brigadier General Seth Williams
Chief Quartermaster – Brigadier General Rufus Ingalls
Chief of Artillery – Brigadier General Henry Hunt
Chief Engineer – Brigadier General Gouveneur K. Warren
Provost Marshal General – Brigadier General Marsena B. Patrick

Provost Marshal's Brigade: (Brig. Gen. Marsena B. Patrick)
Engineer Brigade: Brigadier General Henry W. Benham

1st ARMY CORPS: Major General John F. Reynolds

1st Division: Brigadier General James Wadsworth
1st (Iron) Brigade: Brigadier General Solomon Meredith
2nd Brigade: Brigadier General Lysander Cutler

2nd Division: Brigadier General John C. Robinson
1st Brigade: Brigadier General Gabriel R. Paul
2nd Brigade: Brigadier General Henry Baxter

3rd Division: Major General Abner Doubleday
1st Brigade: Brigadier General Thomas A. Rowley
2nd (Bucktail) Brigade: Colonel Roy Stone
3rd (2nd Vermont) Brigade: Brigadier General George J. Stannard

Artillery Brigade: Colonel Charles S. Wainwright

2nd Army Corps: Major General Winfield Scott Hancock

1st Division: Brigadier General John C. Caldwell
1st Brigade: Colonel Edward E. Cross
2nd (Irish) Brigade: Colonel Patrick Kelly
3rd Brigade: Brigadier General Samuel K. Zook
4th Brigade: Colonel John R. Brooke

2nd Division: Brigadier General John Gibbon
1st Brigade: Brigadier General William Harrow
2nd Brigade: Brigadier General Alexander Webb
3rd Brigade: Colonel Norman J. Hall

3rd Division: Brigadier General Alexander Hays
1st Brigade: Colonel Samuel S. Carroll
2nd Brigade: Colonel Thomas A. Smyth
3rd (Harper's Ferry) Brigade: Colonel George Willard

Artillery Brigade: Captain John G. Hazard

3rd Army Corps: Major General Daniel E. Sickles

1st Division: Major General David B. Birney
1st Brigade: Brigadier General Charles K. Graham
2nd Brigade: Brigadier General J. H. Hobart Ward
3rd Brigade: Colonel P. Regis de Trobriand

2nd Division: Brigadier General Andrew A. Humphreys
1st Brigade: Brigadier General Joseph B. Carr
2nd (Excelsior) Brigade: Colonel William R. Brewster
3rd Brigade: Colonel George C. Burling

Artillery Brigade: Captain George E. Randolph

5th Army Corps: Major General George Sykes

1st Division: Brigadier General James Barnes
1st Brigade: Colonel William S. Tilton
2nd Brigade: Colonel Jacob B. Sweitzer
3rd Brigade: Colonel Strong Vincent

2nd Division: Brigadier General Romeyn B. Ayres
1st (Regular) Brigade: Colonel Hannibal Day
2nd (Regular) Brigade: Colonel Sidney Burbank
3rd Brigade: Brigadier General Stephen H. Weed

3rd (Pennsylvania Reserve) Division: Brig. Gen. Samuel W. Crawford
1st Brigade: Colonel William McCandless
3rd Brigade: Colonel Joseph W. Fisher

Artillery Brigade: Captain Augustus P. Martin

6th ARMY CORPS: Major General John Sedgwick

1st Division: Brigadier General Horatio G. Wright
1st (New Jersey) Brigade: Brigadier General A. T. A. Torbert
2nd Brigade: Brigadier General Joseph J. Bartlett
3rd Brigade: Brigadier General David A. Russell

2nd Division: Brigadier General Albion P. Howe
2nd (Vermont) Brigade: Colonel Lewis A. Grant
3rd Brigade: Brigadier General Thomas H. Neill

3rd Division: Major General John Newton
1st Brigade: Brigadier General Alexander Shaler
2nd Brigade: Colonel Henry L. Eustis
3rd Brigade: Brigadier General Frank Wheaton

Artillery Brigade: Colonel Charles H. Tomkins

11th ARMY CORPS: Major General Oliver Otis Howard

1st Division: Brigadier General Francis C. Barlow
1st Brigade: Colonel Leopold von Gilsa
2nd Brigade: Brigadier General Adelbert Ames

2nd Division: Brigadier General Adolph von Steinwehr
1st Brigade: Colonel Charles R. Coster
2nd Brigade: Colonel Orland Smith

3rd Division: Major General Carl Schurz
1st Brigade: Brigadier General Alexander Schimmelfennig
2nd Brigade: Colonel W. Krzyanowski

Artillery Brigade: Major Thomas W. Osborn

12th Army Corps: Major General Henry W. Slocum

Attached Brigade: Brigadier General Henry H. Lockwood

1st Division: Brigadier General Alpheus S. Williams
1st Brigade: Colonel Archibald L. McDougall
3rd Brigade: Brigadier General Thomas H. Ruger

2nd Division: Brigadier General John W. Geary
1st Brigade: Colonel Charles Candy
2nd Brigade: Brigadier General Thomas L. Kane
3rd Brigade: Brigadier General George S. Greene

Artillery Brigade: Lieutenant Edward D. Muhlenberg

Cavalry Corps: Major General Alfred Pleasonton

1st Division: Brigadier General John Buford
1st Brigade: Colonel William Gamble
2nd Brigade: Colonel Thomas C. Devin
Reserve Brigade: Brigadier General Wesley Merritt

2nd Division: Brigadier General David M. Gregg
1st Brigade: Colonel John B. McIntosh
2nd Brigade: Colonel Pennock Huey
3rd Brigade: Colonel J. Irvin Gregg

3rd Division: Brigadier General Hugh Judson Kilpatrick
1st Brigade: Brigadier General Elon J. Farnsworth
2nd (Michigan) Brigade: Brigadier General George A. Custer

1st Brigade, Horse Artillery: Captain James M. Robertson

2nd Brigade, Horse Artillery: Captain John C. Tidball

Artillery Reserve: Brigadier General Robert O. Tyler

1st Regular Brigade: Captain Dunbar R. Ransom
1st Volunteer Brigade: Lieutenant Colonel Freeman McGilvery
2nd Volunteer Brigade: Captain Elijah D. Taft
3rd Volunteer Brigade: Captain James F. Huntington
4th Volunteer Brigade: Captain Robert H. Fitzhugh

DEPARTMENT OF THE SUSQUEHANNA (Eastern Penn.):
Commanding General – Major General Darius N. Couch

    Bloody Run, Pa.: Colonel Lewis B. Pierce
    Camp Curtis, Pa.: Colonel James A. Beaver
    Fenwick, Pa.: Brigadier General Charles Yates
    Harrisburg, Pa.: Colonel Charles M. Prevost
    Mount Union, Pa.: Colonel Joseph W. Hawley
    Philadelphia, Pa.: Lieutenant Colonel William D. Whipple
    York, Pa.: Colonel William B. Thomas

    1st Division: Brigadier General William F. "Baldy" Smith
    1st Brigade: Brigadier General Joseph F. Knipe
    2nd Brigade: Brigadier General Philip St. George Cooke
    3rd Brigade: Brigadier General Jesse C. Smith
    4th Brigade: Brigadier General John Ewen
    5th Brigade: Colonel William Burbank
    6th Brigade: Colonel Jacob G. Frick

DEPARTMENT OF THE MONONGAHELA (Western Penn.):
Commanding General – Major General W. T. H. Brooks

DEPARTMENT OF WEST VIRGINIA:
Commanding General – Brigadier General Benjamin F. Kelley

    Averell's Brigade: Brigadier General William W. Averell
    Campbell's Brigade: Colonel Jacob M. Campbell
    Mulligan's Brigade: Colonel James A. Mulligan
    Wikinson's Brigade: Colonel Nathan Wikinson

    Scammon's ("Kanawha") Division: Brig. Gen. Eliakim P. Scammon
    1st Brigade: Colonel Rutherford B. Hayes
    2nd Brigade: Colonel Carr B. White

DEPARTMENT OF VIRGINIA:
Commanding General – Major General John A. Dix

    4th ARMY CORPS: Major General Erasmus D. Keyes

    1st Division: Brigadier General Rufus King
    1st Brigade: Brigadier General Hector Tyndale
    2nd Brigade: Colonel George E. Church
    3rd Brigade: Colonel Charles Kleckner

2nd Division: Brigadier General George H. Gordon
1st Brigade: Colonel William Gurney
2nd Brigade: Colonel Burr Porter

Reserve Artillery: Captain James McKnight

Independent Brigade: Colonel Robert M. West

7th ARMY CORPS: (Major General John A. Dix)

Provisional Brigade: Colonel David W. Wardrop
Wistar's Brigade: Brigadier General Isaac J. Wistar
Spinola's Brigade: Brigadier General Francis B. Spinola
Norfolk, Va.: Brigadier General Egbert L. Viele

1st Division: Brigadier General Michael Corcoran
1st Brigade: Brigadier General Henry D. Terry
2nd Brigade: Brigadier General Robert S. Foster
3rd Brigade (Irish Legion): Colonel Mathew Murphy
Artillery: Captain Frederick M. Follett

2nd Division: Brigadier General George W. Getty
1st Brigade: Colonel Samuel M. Alford
2nd Brigade: Brigadier General Edward Harland
3rd Brigade: Colonel William h. P. Steere

DEPARTMENT OF NORTH CAROLINA (18th ARMY CORPS):
Commanding General – Major General John G. Foster

District of Beaufort: Brigadier General Charles A. Heckman

District of the Albemarle: Brigadier General Henry W. Wessells

District of the Pamlico: Lieutenant Colonel Joseph M. McChesney

1st Division: Colonel Thomas J. C. Amory
1st Brigade: Captain Luther Day
2nd Brigade: Colonel Horace C. Lee
Jourdan's Brigade: Colonel James Jourdan
Cavalry Brigade: Lieutenant Colonel George W. Lewis

DEPARTMENT OF THE SOUTH (10th ARMY CORPS) (S.C., Ga., E. Fla.):[2]
Commanding General – Brigadier General Quincy A. Gillmore

Folly Island, S.C.: **Brigadier General Israel Vogdes**
1st Brigade: Colonel Haldimand S. Putnam
2nd Brigade: Colonel Joshua B. Howell

Port Royal Island, S.C.: **Brigadier General Rufus Saxton**

Seabrook Island: **Brigadier General Thomas G. Stevenson**

Saint Helena Island, S.C.: **Brigadier General George C. Strong**

Hilton Head Island, S.C.: **Colonel John Chatfield**

DEPARTMENT OF THE OHIO:[3]
Commanding General – Major General Ambrose E. Burnside

District of Ohio: Brigadier General Jacob D. Cox

District of Illinois: Brigadier General Jacob Ammen

District of Indiana and Michigan: Brig. General Orlando B. Willcox

23rd ARMY CORPS: Major General George L. Hartsuff

1st Division: **Brigadier General Samuel D. Sturgis**
1st Brigade: Brigadier General Samuel P. Carter
2nd Brigade: Colonel Samuel A. Gilbert
3rd Brigade: Colonel August V. Kautz

2nd Division (District of Kentucky): **Brig. General Jeremiah Boyle**
1st Brigade: Brigadier General James M. Shackelford
Munfordville, Ky.: Colonel Charles D. Pennebaker
Bowling Green, Ky.: Colonel Cicero Maxwell
Lebanon, Ky and other points: no commander listed

3rd Division: **Brigadier General Henry M. Judah**
1st Brigade: Brigadier General Mahlon D. Manson
2nd Brigade: Brigadier General Edward H. Hobson
3rd Brigade: Colonel Joseph A. Cooper

4th Division: **Brigadier General Julius White**
1st Brigade: Colonel Daniel Cameron
2nd Brigade: Colonel Samuel R. Mott

DEPARTMENT AND ARMY OF THE CUMBERLAND:[4]
Commanding General – Major General William S. Rosecrans
Chief of Staff – Brigadier General James A. Garfield

Pioneer Brigade: Brigadier General James St. Clair Morton

14th ARMY CORPS: Major General George H. Thomas

1st Division: Major General Lovell H. Rousseau
1st Brigade: Colonel Benjamin F. Scribner
2nd Brigade: Colonel Henry A. Hambright
3rd Brigade (Regulars): Brigadier General John H. King
Artillery: Colonel Cyrus O. Loomis

2nd Division: Major General James S. Negley
1st Brigade: Brigadier General John Beatty
2nd Brigade: Colonel William L. Stoughton
3rd Brigade: Colonel William Sirwell
Artillery: Captain Frederick Schultz

3rd Division: Brigadier General John M. Brannan
1st Brigade: Colonel Moses B. Walker
2nd Brigade: Brigadier General James B. Steedman
3rd Brigade: Colonel Ferdinand Van Derveer
Artillery: no commander listed

4th Division: Major General Joseph J. Reynolds
1st (Lightning) Brigade (mounted): Colonel John T. Wilder
2nd Brigade: Colonel Albert S. Hall
3rd Brigade: Brigadier General George Crook
Artillery: no commander listed

20th ARMY CORPS: Major General Alexander M. McCook

1st Division: Brigadier General Jefferson C. Davis
1st Brigade: Colonel P. Sidney Post
2nd Brigade: Brigadier General William P. Carlin
3rd Brigade: Colonel Hans C. Heg
Artillery: no commander listed

2nd Division: Brigadier General Richard W. Johnson
1st Brigade: Brigadier General August Willich
2nd Brigade: Colonel Joseph B. Dodge
3rd Brigade: Colonel Philemon P. Baldwin
Artillery: Captain Peter Simonson

3rd Division: Major General Philip H. Sheridan
1st Brigade: Brigadier General William H. Lytle
2nd Brigade: Colonel Bernard Laiboldt
3rd Brigade: Colonel Luther P. Bradley
Artillery: Captain Henry Hescock

21st ARMY CORPS: Major General Thomas L. Crittenden

1st Division: Brigadier General Thomas J. Wood
1st Brigade: Colonel George P. Buell
2nd Brigade: Brigadier General George D. Wagner
3rd Brigade: Colonel Charles G. Harker
Artillery: Captain Cullen Bradley

2nd Division: Major General John M. Palmer
1st Brigade: Brigadier General Charles Cruft
2nd Brigade: Brigadier General William B. Hazen
3rd Brigade: Colonel William Grose
Artillery: Captain William E. Standart

3rd Division: Brigadier General Horatio P. Van Cleve
1st Brigade: Brigadier General Samuel Beatty
2nd Brigade: Colonel George F. Dick
3rd Brigade: Colonel Sidney M. Barnes
Artillery: Captain Lucius H. Drury

RESERVE CORPS: Major General Gordon Granger

Artillery Reserve (Nashville): Captain Warren P. Edgarton
Camp Spears (Nashville): Colonel Alvan C. Gillem
Clarksville, Tn.: Colonel Sanders D. Bruce
Gallatin, Tn.: Colonel Benjamin J. Sweet

1st Division: Brigadier General Absalom Baird
1st Brigade: Colonel Smith D. Atkins
2nd Brigade: Colonel William P. Reid
3rd Brigade: Colonel Henry C. Gilbert
Artillery: no commander listed

2nd Division: Brigadier General James D. Morgan
1st Brigade: Colonel Robert F. Smith
2nd Brigade: Colonel Daniel McCook
3rd Brigade: Colonel Charles C. Doolittle
Artillery: no commander listed

3rd Division: Brigadier General Robert S. Granger
1st Brigade: Colonel William P. Lyon
2nd Brigade: Brigadier General William T. Ward

CAVALRY CORPS: Major General David S. Stanley

1st Cavalry Division: Brigadier General Robert B. Mitchell
1st Brigade: Colonel Archibald P. Campbell
2nd Brigade: Colonel Edward M. McCook

2nd Cavalry Division: Brigadier General John B. Turchin
1st Brigade: Colonel Robert H. G. Minty
2nd Brigade: Colonel Eli Long

DEPARTMENT AND ARMY OF THE TENNESSEE:
Commanding General – Major General Ulysses S. Grant
Chief of Staff – Lieutenant Colonel John Rawlins

Unattached Cavalry (brigade): Colonel Cyrus Bussey

Herron's Division: Major General Francis J. Herron
1st Brigade: Brigadier General William Vandever
2nd Brigade: Brigadier General William W. Orme

9th ARMY CORPS: Major General John G. Parke

1st Division: Brigadier General Thomas Welsh
1st Brigade: Colonel Henry Bowman
3rd Brigade: Colonel Daniel Leasure

2nd Division: Brigadier General Robert B. Potter
1st Brigade: Colonel Simon G. Griffin
2nd Brigade: Brigadier General Edward Ferrero
3rd Brigade: Colonel Benjamin C. Christ

13th ARMY CORPS: Major General Edward O. C. Ord

6th Division: Brigadier General Peter J. Osterhaus
1st Brigade: Colonel James Keigwin
2nd Brigade: Colonel Daniel W. Lindsey
Artillery: Captain Jacob T. Foster

10th Division: Brigadier General Andrew Jackson Smith
1st Brigade: Brigadier General Stephen G. Burbridge
2nd Brigade: Colonel William J. Landram

12th Division: Brigadier General Alvin P. Hovey
1st Brigade: Brigadier General George F. McGinnis
2nd Brigade: Colonel James R. Slack

14th Division: Brigadier General Eugene A. Carr
1st Brigade: Colonel David Shunk
2nd Brigade: Brigadier General Michael K. Lawler

15th ARMY CORPS: Major General William Tecumseh Sherman

1st Division: Major General Frederick Steele
1st Brigade: Colonel Bernard G. Farrar
2nd Brigade: Colonel Charles R. Woods
3rd Brigade: Brigadier General John M. Thayer

2nd Division: Major General Frank P. Blair
1st Brigade: Colonel Giles A. Smith
2nd Brigade: Brigadier General Joseph A. J. Lightburn
3rd Brigade: Brigadier General Hugh Ewing

3rd Division: Brigadier General James M. Tuttle
1st Brigade: Colonel William L. McMillen
2nd Brigade: Brigadier General Joseph A. Mower
3rd Brigade: Colonel Joseph J. Woods
Artillery: Captain Nelson T. Spoor

DETACHMENT, 16th CORPS: Major Gen. Cadwallader C. Washburn

1st Division: Brigadier General William Sooy Smith
1st Brigade: Colonel John M. Loomis
2nd Brigade: Colonel Stephen G. Hicks
3rd Brigade: Colonel Joseph R. Cockerill
4th Brigade: Colonel William W. Sanford
Artillery: Captain William Cogswell

4th Division: Brigadier General Jacob G. Lauman
1st Brigade: Colonel Isaac C. Pugh
2nd Brigade: Colonel Cyrus Hall
3rd Brigade: Colonel Amory K. Johnson
Artillery: Captain George C. Gumbart

Provisional Division: Brigadier General Nathan Kimball
Engelman's Brigade: Colonel Adolph Engelman
Richmond's Brigade: Colonel Jonathan Richmond
Montgomery's Brigade: Colonel Milton Montgomery

17th ARMY CORPS: Major General James B. McPherson

3rd Division: Major General John A. Logan
1st Brigade: Brigadier General Mortimer D. Leggett
2nd Brigade: Colonel Manning F. Force
3rd Brigade: Brigadier General John D. Stevenson
Artillery: Major Charles J. Stolbrand

6th Division: Brigadier General John McArthur
1st Brigade: Brigadier General Hugh T. Reid
2nd Brigade: Brigadier General Thomas E. G. Ransom
3rd Brigade: Colonel Alexander Chambers
Artillery: Major Thomas D. Maurice

7th Division: Brigadier General John E. Smith
1st Brigade: Colonel John B. Sanborn
2nd Brigade: Colonel Green B. Raum
3rd Brigade: Brigadier General Charles L. Matthies
Artillery: Captain Henry Dillon

District of Northeast Louisiana: Brigadier General Elias S. Dennis
Detached Brigade: Colonel George W. Neeley
African Brigade: Colonel Isaac F. Shepard
Post of Milliken's Bend: Colonel Hiram Schofield
Post of Goodrich's Landing: Colonel William F. Wood

District of Eastern Arkansas: Brig. General Benjamin M. Prentiss
Cavalry Brigade: Colonel Powell Clayton

13th Division, 13th Corps: Brigadier General Frederick Salomon
1st Brigade: Colonel William McLean
2nd Brigade: Colonel Samuel A. Rice

16th ARMY CORPS (West Tenn. & Ky.): Maj. Gen. Stephen A. Hurlbut

District of Memphis (5th Division): Brig. General James C. Veatch
1st Brigade: Colonel Charles D. Murray
2nd Brigade: Colonel William H. Morgan
3rd Brigade: Colonel John W. Fuller
4th Brigade: Colonel David Moore

District of Columbus (6th Division): Brig. Gen. Alexander Asboth
Cairo, IL: Brigadier General Napoleon B. Buford
Columbus, KY: Colonel George E. Waring
Paducah, KY: Colonel James S. Martin
Island No. 10: Captain John A. Gordon

Left Wing, 16th ARMY CORPS: Major General Richard J. Oglesby

3rd Brigade, 3rd Division: Colonel James M. True

District of Corinth (2nd Division): Brig. Gen. Grenville M. Dodge
1st Brigade: Brigadier General Thomas W. Sweeny
2nd Brigade: Colonel August Mersy
3rd Brigade: Colonel Moses M. Bane

Cavalry Division: Colonel John K. Mizner
1st Brigade: Colonel Lafayette McCrillis
2nd Brigade: Colonel Edward Hatch
3rd Brigade: Colonel Florence M. Cornyn
4th Brigade: Lieutenant Colonel Bazil D. Meek

DEPARTMENT OF THE GULF (19th ARMY CORPS):
Commanding General – Major General Nathaniel P. Banks

Weitzel's Brigade: Brigadier General Godfrey Weitzel
Corps d'Afrique: Brigadier General Daniel Ullman
Cavalry: Brigadier General Benjamin H. Grierson

1st Division: Major General Christopher C. Augur
1st Brigade: Colonel Charles J. Paine
2nd Brigade: Colonel Nathan A. M. Dudley

2nd Division: Brigadier General William Dwight
1st Brigade: Colonel Thomas S. Clark
3rd Brigade: Brigadier General Frank S. Nickerson

3rd Division: Colonel Hawkes Fearing, Jr.
1st Brigade: Colonel Samuel P. Farris
2nd Brigade: Major John H. Allcot
3rd Brigade: Colonel Oliver P. Gooding

4th Division: Brigadier General Cuvier Grover
1st Brigade: Colonel Joseph S. Morgan
2nd Brigade: Colonel William K. Kimball
3rd Brigade: Colonel Henry W. Birge

Defenses of New Orleans: Brigadier General William H. Emory
2nd Brigade, 2nd Division: Colonel Thomas W. Cahill

District of Key West and the Turtugas: Br. Gen. Daniel P. Woodbury

District of Pensacola: Colonel Isaac Dyer[5]

Ship Island: Colonel Nathan W. Daniels

DEPARTMENT OF THE MISSOURI:
Commanding General – Major General John M. Schofield

District of Central Missouri: Brigadier General Egbert B. Brown

District of Northeastern Missouri: Colonel Odon Guitar

District of Northwestern Missouri: Brig. General Willard P. Hall

District of Rolla: Brigadier General Thomas A. Davies
1st Brigade: Lieutenant Colonel John T. Burris

District of Saint Louis: Brigadier General William K. Strong

District of Southeastern Missouri: Brig, General John W. Davidson

Cape Girardeau, Mo.: Colonel John B. Rogers

1st Cavalry Division: (Brigadier General John W. Davidson)
1st Brigade: Colonel Lewis Merrill
2nd Brigade: Colonel John M. Glover

District of Southwestern Missouri: Colonel William F. Cloud
Springfield, Mo.: Colonel John Edwards

District of Colorado: Colonel John M. Chivington

District of the Frontier: Major General James G. Blunt

District of Nebraska: Brigadier General Thomas J. McKean

Enrolled Missouri Militia, Eighth District:
    Brigadier General Thomas J. Bartholow

DEPARTMENT OF THE NORTHWEST:
Commanding General – Major General John Pope

    District of Wisconsin: Brigadier General Thomas C. H. Smith

    District of Minnesota: Brigadier General Henry H. Sibley

    District of Iowa: Brigadier General Benjamin S. Roberts

    District of Dakota: Brigadier General Alfred Sully

DEPARTMENT OF NEW MEXICO:
Commanding General – Brigadier General James H. Carleton

DEPARTMENT OF THE PACIFIC:
Commanding General – Brigadier General George Wright

★ CONFEDERATE STATES ARMY ★
Commander-in-Chief – President Jefferson Davis
Secretary of War – James Seddon
Adjutant and Inspector General – General Samuel Cooper
Quartermaster General – Colonel Lucius B. Northrup

ARMY OF NORTHERN VIRGINIA:
Commanding General – General Robert E. Lee
Chief of Artillery – Brigadier General William N. Pendleton

    Northwest Virginia (mounted) Brigade: Brig, General J. D. Imboden

    1st ARMY CORPS: Lieutenant General James Longstreet

    McLaws Division: Major General Lafayette McLaws
    Kershaw's (S.C.) Brigade: Brigadier General James B. Kershaw
    Semmes' (Ga.) Brigade: Brigadier General Paul J. Semmes
    Barksdale's (Miss.) Brigade: Brigadier General William Barksdale
    Wofford's (Ga.) Brigade: Brigadier General William T. Wofford
    Artillery Battalion: Colonel H. C. Cabell

Hood's Division: Major General John Bell Hood
Law's (Ala.) Brigade: Brigadier General Evander M. Law
Robertson's (Tex. & Ark.) Brigade: Brigadier General J. B. Robertson
Anderson's (Ga.) Brigade: Brigadier General George T. "Tige" Anderson
Benning's (Ga.) Brigade: Brigadier General Henry L. Benning
Artillery Battalion: Major M. W. Henry

Pickett's Division: Major General George E. Pickett
Garnett's (Va.) Brigade: Brigadier General Richard B. Garnett
Kemper's (Va.) Brigade: Brigadier General James L. Kemper
Armistead's (Va.) Brigade: Brigadier General Lewis A. Armistead
Artillery Battalion: Major James Dearing

Artillery Reserve: Colonel J. B. Walton
Alexander's Battalion: Colonel E. Porter Alexander
Washington (La.) Battalion: Major B. F. Eshleman

2nd ARMY CORPS: Lieutenant General Richard S. Ewell

Early's Division: Major General Jubal A. Early
Hays' (La.) Brigade: Brigadier General Harry T. Hays
Smith's (Va.) Brigade: Brigadier General William "Extra Billy" Smith
Hoke's (N.C.) Brigade: Colonel Isaac E. Avery
Gordon's (Ga.) Brigade: Brigadier General John B. Gordon
Artillery Battalion: Lieutenant Colonel H. P. Jones

Rodes' Division: Major General Robert E. Rodes
Daniel's (N.C.) Brigade: Brigadier General Junius Daniel
Iverson's (N.C.) Brigade: Brigadier General Alfred Iverson
Doles' (Ga.) Brigade: Brigadier General George Doles
Ramseur's (N.C.) Brigade: Brigadier General Stephen D. Ramseur
O'Neal's (Ala.) Brigade: Colonel E. A. O'Neal
Artillery Battalion: Lieutenant Colonel Thomas H. Carter

Johnson's Division: Major General Edward "Allegheny" Johnson
Steuart's (Va., N.C. & Md.) Brigade: Brig. Gen. George Steuart
Nicholl's (La.) Brigade: Colonel J. M. Williams
Stonewall (Va.) Brigade: Brigadier General James A. Walker
Jones' (Va.) Brigade: Brigadier General John M. Jones
Artillery Battalion: Major J. W. Latimer

Artillery Reserve: Colonel J. Thompson Brown
First Virginia Artillery: Captain Willis J. Dance
Nelson's Battalion: Lieutenant Colonel William Nelson

Attached Cavalry:
Jenkins' (Va.) Brigade: Brigadier General A. G. Jenkins
35th Virginia Cavalry Battalion: Lieutenant Colonel Elijah V. White
1st Maryland Cavalry Battalion: Major Harry Gilmor

3rd ARMY CORPS: Lieutenant General Ambrose Powell Hill

Pender's Division: Major General William Dorsey Pender
1st (S.C.) Brigade: Colonel Abner Perrin
2nd (N.C.) Brigade: Brigadier General James H. Lane
3rd (Ga.) Brigade: Brigadier General Edward L. Thomas
4th (N.C.) Brigade: Brigadier General Alfred M. Scales
Artillery Battalion: Major William T. Poague

Heth's Division: Major General Henry "Harry" Heth
1st (N.C.) Brigade: Brigadier General J. Johnston Pettigrew
2nd (Va.) Brigade: Colonel J. M. Brockenbrough
3rd (Ala. & Tenn.) Brigade: Brigadier General James J. Archer
4th (Miss. & N.C.) Brigade: Brigadier General Joseph R. Davis
Artillery Battalion: Lieutenant Colonel John J. Garnett

Anderson's Division: Major General Richard H. Anderson
Wilcox's (Ala.) Brigade: Brigadier General Cadmus M. Wilcox
Wright's (Ga.) Brigade: Brigadier General A. R. "Rans" Wright
Mahone's (Va.) Brigade: Brigadier General William Mahone
Perry's (Fla.) Brigade: Colonel David Lang
Posey's (Miss.) Brigade: Brigadier General Carnot Posey
Sumter (artillery) Battalion: Major John Lane

Artillery Reserve: Colonel R. Lindsay Walker
McIntosh's Battalion: Major D. G. McIntosh
Pegram's Battalion: Major W. J. Pegram

Cavalry Division: Major General James Ewell Brown "Jeb" Stuart
Hampton's Brigade: Brigadier General Wade Hampton
Fitz. Lee's (Va.) Brigade: Brigadier General Fitzhugh Lee
W. H. F. Lee's (Va. & N.C.) Brigade: Colonel John R. Chambliss, Jr.
Jones's (Va.) Brigade: Brigadier General William E. "Grumble" Jones
Robertson's (N.C.) Brigade: Brigadier General Beverly H. Robertson
Stuart Horse Artillery: Major R. F. Beckham

Valley District: Maj. Gen. Isaac Trimble (traveling with 2nd Corps)

DEPARTMENT OF WESTERN VIRGINIA:[6]
Commanding General – Major General Samuel Jones

1st (Va.) Brigade: Brigadier General John Echols
2nd (Va.) Brigade: Brigadier General John S. Williams
3rd (Va.) Brigade: Colonel G. C. Wharton
4th (Va.) Brigade: Colonel John McCausland
Cavalry (Va.) Brigade: (most of it transferred to Lee, under Albert Jenkins)

DEPARTMENT OF RICHMOND:
Commanding General – Major General Arnold Elzey

Wise's (Va.) Brigade: Brigadier General Henry Wise
Corse's (Va.) Brigade (of Pickett's Division): Br. Gen. Montgomery Corse

DEPARTMENT OF NORTH CAROLINA:[7]
Commanding General – Major General Daniel Harvey Hill

Ransom's (N.C.) Brigade: Brig. General M. W. Ransom (at Richmond)
Jenkins' (S.C.) Brigade: Brig. General Micah Jenkins (at Richmond)
Cooke's (N.C.) Brigade: Brig. General John R. Cooke (at Richmond)
Colquitt's (Ga.) Brigade: Brig. Gen. A. H. Colquitt (at Kinston, N.C.)
Clingman's (N.C.) Brig.: Br. Gen. T. L. Clingman (near Wilmington, N.C.)
Martin's (N.C.) Brig.: Br. Gen. J. G. Martin (guarding the Weldon railroad)
Moseley's Battalion (artillery): Major E. F. Moseley
Boggs' Battalion (artillery): Major F. J. Boggs
Branch's Battalion (artillery): Major J. R. Branch

District of Cape Fear: Major General W. H. C. Whiting

DEPARTMENT OF SOUTH CAROLINA, GEORGIA & FLORIDA:[8]
Commanding General – General Pierre Gustave Toutant Beauregard

1st Military District: Brigadier General Roswell S. Ripley
1st Sub-division (James Island): Colonel Charles H. Simonton
2nd Sub-division (Sullivan's Island): Colonel Lawrence M. Keitt
3rd Sub-division (Morris Island): Colonel Robert F. Graham
4th Sub-division (Charleston & forts): Colonel Alfred Rhett

2nd Military District: Brigadier General Johnson Hagood

3rd Military District: Brigadier General William S. Walker

4th Military District: Brigadier General James H. Trapier

District of Georgia: Brigadier General Hugh W. Mercer
Taliaferro's (Ga.) Brigade: Brigadier General William B. Taliaferro
Fort McAllister: Major G. W. Anderson, Jr.
River Batteries: Colonel E. C. Anderson

District of East Florida: Brigadier General Joseph Finnegan

District of Middle Florida: Brigadier General Howell Cobb

TRANS-MISSISSIPPI DEPARTMENT:
Commanding General – Lieutenant General E. Kirby Smith

District of Arkansas: Lieutenant General Theophilus H. Holmes
Fagan's Brigade: Brigadier General James Fagan
Walker's (Cavalry) Brigade: Brigadier General Lucius "Marsh" Walker

Price's Division: Major General Sterling Price
The Missouri Brigade: Brigadier General Mosby Parsons
the Arkansas Brigade: Brigadier General Dandridge McRae

Marmaduke's (Cavalry) Division: Brig. General John Marmaduke[9]
Carter's Brigade: Colonel George W. Carter
Burbridge's Brigade: Colonel John Q. Burbridge

Defenses of the Lower Arkansas: Brig. General Daniel Marsh Frost
1st Brigade: Colonel John B. Clark, Jr.

District of Western Louisiana: Major General Richard Taylor
Tappan's Brigade: Brigadier General James C. Tappan
Green's (Cavalry) Brigade: Brigadier General Thomas Green
Mouton's (Cavalry) Brigade: Brigadier General Alfred Mouton
Major's (Cavalry) Brigade: Colonel James P. Major

Walker's Texas Division: Major General John G. Walker
McCulloch's Brigade: Brigadier General Henry E. McCulloch
Hawes' Brigade: Brigadier General J. M. Hawes
Randal's Brigade: Colonel Horace Randal
Cavalry Brigade: Colonel Frank A. Bartlett

District of the Indian Territory: Brigadier General William Steele

District of Texas, New Mexico, and Arizona: Maj. Gen. John Magruder

☆ **DEPARTMENT OF THE WEST** ☆
Commanding General – General Joseph E. Johnston

ARMY OF RELIEF:
Commanding General – (General Joseph E. Johnston)

Loring's Division: Major General William W. Loring
1st (Miss.) Brigade: Brigadier General Lloyd Tilghman
2nd (Miss.) Brigade: Brigadier General Winfield Scott Featherston
3rd (mixed) Brigade: Brigadier General Abraham Buford

Breckinridge's Division: Major General John C. Breckinridge
Adams' (La. & Ala.) Brigade: Brigadier General Daniel W. Adams
Helm's (Ky. & Ala.) Brigade: Brigadier General Ben. Hardin Helm
Preston's (Fla. & N.C.) Brigade: Brigadier General William Preston

Walker's Division: Major General William Henry Talbot Walker
Ector's Brigade: Brigadier General Matthew D. Ector
McNair's Brigade: Brigadier General Evander McNair
Gregg's Brigade: Brigadier General John Gregg
Walker's Brigade: commander unknown

Jackson's (Cavalry) Division: Brig. General William H. "Red" Jackson
1st (Miss.) Brigade: Brigadier General George B. Cosby
2nd (Tex.) Brigade: Brigadier General John W. Whitfield

DEPARTMENT OF MISSISSIPPI AND EASTERN LOUISIANA:[10]
Commanding General – Lieutenant General John Pemberton

Stevenson's Division: Major General Carter L. Stevenson
1st Brigade (Ga.): Brigadier General S. M. Barton
2nd Brigade (Ga.): Brigadier General Alfred Cumming
3rd Brigade (Ala.): Brigadier General Stephen Dill Lee
4th Brigade (Tenn.) Colonel A. W. Reynolds
Waul's Texas Legion: Colonel T. N. Waul

Forney's Division: Major General John H. Forney
Hebert's (Ms. & La.) Brigade: Brigadier General Louis Hebert
Moore's (Ala., Ms., Tx.) Brigade: Brigadier General John C. Moore

Smith's Division: Major General Martin Luther Smith
Baldwin's (La. & Ms.) Brigade: Brigadier General W. E. Baldwin
Vaughn's (Tenn.) Brigade: Brigadier General J. C. Vaughn
Shoup's (La.) Brigade: Brigadier General Francis A. Shoup
Mississippi State Troops: Brigadier General John V. Harris

Bowen's Division: Major General John S. Bowen
1st (Mo.) Brigade: Colonel Francis Cockrell
2nd (Ark.) Brigade: Colonel T. P. Dockery

River Batteries: Colonel Ed. Higgins

Dist. of Eastern Louisiana (Port Hudson): Maj. Gen. Franklin Gardner
Left Wing: Colonel I. G. W. Steedman
Center: Brigadier General William N. R. Beall
Right Wing: Colonel William R. Miles
Cavalry: Colonel John Logan

DEPARTMENT No. 2 and ARMY OF TENNESSEE:
Commanding General – General Braxton Bragg
Chief of Staff – Brigadier General William W. Mackall

District of Tennessee: Brig. Gen. John K. Jackson (infantry brigade)

District of Northern Alabama: Col. Philip D. Roddey (cavalry brig.)

Forrest's Cavalry Division: Brigadier General Nathan B. Forrest
1st Brigade: Brigadier General Frank C. Armstrong
2nd (Tenn.) Brigade: Colonel George G. Dibrell

1st ARMY CORPS: Lieutenant General Leonidas Polk

Cheatham's Division: Major General Benjamin F. Cheatham
Maney's (Tenn.) Brigade: Brigadier General George E. Maney
Wright's (Tenn.) Brigade: Brigadier General Marcus J. Wright
Smith's (Tenn.) Brigade: Brigadier General Preston Smith
Strahl's (Tenn.) Brigade: Colonel Otho F. Strahl

Withers' Division: Major General Jones M. Withers
Anderson's (Miss.) Brigade: Brigadier General J. Patton Anderson
Walthall's (Miss.) Brigade: Brigadier General Edward C. Walthall
Manigault's (Ala.) Brigade: Brigadier General Arthur M. Manigault
Deas' (Ala.) Brigade: Brigadier General Zachariah C. Deas

2nd ARMY CORPS: Lieutenant General William J. Hardee

Cleburne's Division: Major General Patrick Cleburne
Wood's (Ala.) Brigade: Brigadier General Sterling A. M. Wood
Liddell's (Ark.) Brigade: Brigadier General St. John R. Liddell
Churchill's (Tex. & Ark.) Brigade: Brigadier General T. J. Churchill
Polk's (Tenn. & Ark.) Brigade: Brigadier General Lucius E. Polk

Stewart's Division: Major General Alexander P. Stewart
Johnson's (Tenn.) Brigade: Brigadier General Bushrod R. Johnson
Bate's (Tn., Ga., Ala.) Brigade: Brigadier General William B. Bate
Brown's (Tenn.) Brigade: Brigadier General John C. Brown
Clayton's (Ala.) Brigade: Brigadier General Henry D. Clayton

Cavalry Corps: Major General Joseph Wheeler

Wharton's Division: Brigadier General John A. Wharton
1st (Ga. & Ala.) Brigade: Colonel C. C. Crews
2nd (Tx., Tn., Ky.) Brigade: Colonel Thomas Harrison

Martin's Division: Brigadier General Will T. Martin
1st (Ala.) Brigade: Colonel James Hagan
2nd (Ala.) Brigade: Colonel A. A. Russell

Morgan's Division: Brigadier General John Hunt Morgan
1st (Ky. & Tenn.) Brigade: Colonel Basil W. Duke
2nd (Ky.) Brigade: Colonel Adam R. Johnson

Artillery Reserve: Colonel James Deshler

DEPARTMENT OF EAST TENNESSEE: Maj. Gen. Simon Bolivar Buckner[11]

1st Brigade: Brigadier General William Preston
2nd Brigade: Colonel Robert C. Trigg
3rd Brigade: Brigadier General Archibald Gracie, Jr.
4th Brigade: Brigadier General A. E. Jackson
5th Brigade: Brigadier General J. W. Frazer
1st Cavalry Brigade: Brigadier General John Pegram
2nd Cavalry Brigade: Colonel John S. Scott

DEPARTMENT OF THE GULF:
Commanding General – Major General Dabney H. Maury

Slaughter's (Ala.) Brigade: Brigadier General James E. Slaughter
Powell's (Ala.) Brigade: Colonel W. L. Powell
Eastern Division (brigade size): Brigadier General James Cantey

∽ Endnotes ∽

1. As of 1 July 1863
2. As of 30 June 1863
3. As of 30 June 1863.
4. As of 30 June 1863.
5. As of 31 March 1863. Someone named Holbrook listed in the summary of returns for June in *OR* I:26:I:610.
6. As of 31 May 1863
7. As of 30 June 1863.
8. As of June 1863, based mostly on Wise, *Gate of Hell*, pp. 222-5.
9. As of 20 May 1863. *OR* I:22:II:845.
10. As of 4 July 1863. *OR* I:24:II:326.
11. As of 31 July 1863. *OR* I:23:II:945.

BIBLIOGRAPHY

Books

Alexander, Edward Porter. *Military Memoirs of a Confederate: A Critical Narrative.* New York, 1907.

Archer, John M. *Fury on the Bliss Farm at Gettysburg.* Gettysburg, 2012.

Basler, Roy P., editor. *The Collected Works of Abraham Lincoln.* Vol. 6. New Brunswick NJ, 1953.

Boatner, Mark Mayo III. *The Civil War Dictionary.* New York, 1959.

Bowden, Scott and Bill Ward. *Last Chance for Victory: Robert E. Lee and the Gettysburg Campaign.* Conshohocken PA, 2001.

Brooks, Noah. *Washington, D.C., in Lincoln's Time.* (Originally titled *Washington in Lincoln's Time*). New York, 1895. University of Georgia paperback edition.

Brown, Kent Masterson. *Cushing of Gettysburg.* Lexington KY, 1993.

-------- *Retreat from Gettysburg: Lee, Logistics, and the Pennsylvania Campaign.* Chapel Hill NC, 2005.

Carhart, Tom. *Lost Triumph: Lee's Real Plan at Gettysburg – and Why it Failed.* New York, 2005.

Carter, Samuel III. *The Final Fortress: The Campaign for Vicksburg 1862-1863.* New York, 1980.

Catton, Bruce. *Never Call Retreat.* Garden City NY, 1965.

Coco, Gregory A. *A Strange and Blighted Land – Gettysburg: The Aftermath of a Battle.* Gettysburg, 1995.

Coddington, Edwin B. *The Gettysburg Campaign: A Study in Command.* New York, 1968.

Coffin, Howard. *Nine Months to Gettysburg: Stannard's*

Vermonters and the Repulse of Pickett's Charge. Woodstock VT, 1997.

Commager, Henry Steele, editor. *The Blue and the Gray: The Story of the Civil War as Told by Participants.* Indianapolis and New York, 1950. Cited in notes as *B&G*. Individual articles quoted in the text are listed below.

Cunningham, Edward. *The Port Hudson Campaign 1862-1863.* Baton Rouge, 1963.

Dana, Charles A. *Recollections of the Civil War.* Collier paperback edition, New York, 1963.

Doubleday, Abner. *Chancellorsville & Gettysburg.* New York, 1908.

Douglas, Henry Kyd. *I Rode With Stonewall.* Chapel Hill NC, 1940, Mockingbird Books paperback edition, Atlanta, 1961.

Dowdey, Clifford, editor. *The Wartime Papers of R. E. Lee.* New York, 1961.

Early, Jubal A. *Autobiographical Sketch and Narrative of the War Between the States.* Philadelphia, 1912.*

Faust, Patricia L., editor. *Historical Times Illustrated Encyclopedia of the Civil War.* New York, 1986.

Fishel, Edwin C. *The Secret War for the Union: The Untold Story of Military Intelligence in the Civil War.* Boston and New York, 1996.

Freeman, Douglas Southall. *Lee's Lieutenants* (Volume 3). New York, 1944.

-------- *R. E. Lee* (Volume 3). New York, 1935.

Gallagher, Gary W. *The Third Day at Gettysburg & Beyond.* Chapel Hill NC, 1994.

Gottfried, Bradley M. *The Maps of Gettysburg: An Atlas of the Gettysburg Campaign, June 3 – July 13, 1863.* New York, 2007.

Grant, U. S. *Personal Memoirs of U. S. Grant.* (Volume 1.) New York, 1885.

Hall, Jeffrey C. *The Stand of the U.S. Army at Gettysburg.* Bloomington IN and Indianapolis, 2003.

Harman, Troy D. *Lee's Real Plan at Gettysburg.*

Mechanicsburg PA, 2003.

Haskell, Frank A. *The Battle of Gettysburg.* Boston and Cambridge MA, 1958.

Hassler, William Woods. *A. P. Hill: Lee's Forgotten General.* Richmond VA, 1962.

Herdegen, Lance J. and William J. K. Beaudot. *In the Bloody Railroad Cut at Gettysburg.* Dayton OH, 1990.

Hessler, James A. *Sickles at Gettysburg: The Controversial General Who Committed Murder, Abandoned Little Round Top, and Declared Himself the Hero of Gettysburg.* New York, 2009.

Hoehling, A. A., and the editors, Army Times Publishing Company. *Vicksburg: 47 Days of Siege.* New York, 1969.

Horan, James D. *Confederate Agent: A Discovery in History.* New York, 1954.

Imholte, John Quinn. *The First Volunteers.* Minneapolis, 1963.

Johnson, Robert Underwood, and Clarence Clough Buel, editors. *Battles and Leaders of the Civil War.* Four volumes. New York, 1888 (Castle Books edition, New York, 1956). Cited in notes as *B&L*. Individual articles quoted in the text are listed below.

Jordan, David M. *Happiness Is Not My Companion: The Life of General G. K. Warren.* Bloomington IN and Indianapolis, 2001.

Kidd, J. H. *A Cavalryman with Custer.* New York, 1991. An abridged edition of *Personal Recollections of a Cavalryman*, New York, 1908.

LaFantasie, Glenn W. *Twilight at Little Round Top: July 2, 1863 – The Tide Turns at Gettysburg.* Hoboken NJ, 2005.

Longacre, Edward G. *The Cavalry at Gettysburg: A Tactical Study of Mounted Operations during the Civil War's Pivotal Campaign, 9 June - 14 July 1863.* Lincoln NB, 1986.

Longstreet, James. *From Manassas to Appomattox.* Mallard Press edition, New York, 1991.

McClellan, H. B. *I Rode with Jeb Stuart: The Life and*

Campaigns of Major General J. E. B. Stuart. Bloomington IN, 1958.

Mowery, David L. *Morgan's Great Raid: The Remarkable Expedition frm Kentucky to Ohio.* Charleston SC, 2013.

Newton, Steven H. *McPherson's Ridge.* Cambridge MA, 2002.

Nichols, Edward J. *Toward Gettysburg: A Biography of General John F. Reynolds.* New York, 1958.

Pfanz, Harry W. *Gettysburg – Culp's Hill and Cemetery Hill.* Chapel Hill NC, 1993.

------- *Gettysburg – The First Day.* Chapel Hill NC, 2001.

------- *Gettysburg – The Second Day.* Chapel Hill NC, 1987.

Pullen, John J. *The Twentieth Maine: A Volunteer Regiment in the Civil War.* New York, 1957; Fawcett paperback edition, 1962.

Ramage, James A. *Rebel Raider: The Life of General John Hunt Morgan.* Lexington KY, 1986.

Rollins, Richard, editor. *Pickett's Charge: Eyewitness Accounts at the Battle of Gettysburg.* Mechanicsburg PA, 1994.

Roske, Ralph J. and Charles Van Doren. *Lincoln's Commando: The Biography of Commander W. B. Cushing, U.S.N.* New York, 1957.

Sandburg, Carl. *Abraham Lincoln: The War Years, 1861-1864.* New York, 1954. Dell paperback edition, 1959.

Schecter, Barnett. *The Devil's Own Work: The Civil War Draft Riots and the Fight to
Reconstruct America.* New York, 2005.

Schultz, Duane. *The Most Glorious Fourth: Vicksburg and Gettysburg, July 4, 1863.* New York and London, 2002.

Sears, Stephen W. *Gettysburg.* Boston and New York, 2003.

Sherman, William T. *Memoirs of General William T. Sherman.* New York, 1875. One-volume Da Capo Press paperback edition, 1984.

Shultz, David, and David Wieck. *The Battle Between the Farm Lanes: Hancock Saves the Union Center, Gettysburg, July 2, 1863.* Columbus OH, 2006.

Southern Historical Society Papers. Richmond, 1876-1930, 47 volumes. Cited in notes as *SHSP.* Individual articles quoted in the text are listed below.*

Starr, Louis M. *Bohemian Brigade: Civil War Newsmen in Action.* New York, 1954.

Stewart, George R. *Pickett's Charge: A Microhistory of the Final Attack at Gettysburg, July 3, 1863.* New York, 1959; Fawcett paperback edition, 1963.

Urwin, Gregory J. W. *Custer Victorious: The Civil War Battles of General George Armstrong Custer.* East Brunswick NJ, 1983.

U.S. War Department. *War of the Rebellion: Official Records of the Union and Confederate Armies.* Washington, 1889. Cited in notes as *OR,* with series, volume, and part, if any).

Wert, Jeffry D. *From Winchester to Cedar Creek: The Shenandoah Campaign of 1864.* Carlisle PA, 1987.

--------- *Gettysburg: Day Three.* New York, 2001.

Whelan, *Libby Prison Breakout: The Daring Escape from the Notorious Civil War Prison.* New York, 2010.

Wheeler, Richard. *Witness to Gettysburg.* New York, 1987.

Williams, Kenneth P. *Lincoln Finds a General: A Military Study of the Civil War.* Five volumes. New York, 1950.

Wittenberg, Eric. *Protecting the Flank: The Battles for Brinkerhoff's Ridge and East Cavalry Field, Battle of Gettysburg.* Celina OH, 2002.

-------, *Gettysburg's Forgotten Cavalry Actions: Farnsworth's Charge, South Cavalry Field, and the Battle of Fairfield, July 3, 1863.* Revised edition. New York and El Dorado Hills CA, 2011.

------- , J. David Petruzzi, and Michael F. Nugent. *One Continuous Fight: The Retreat from Gettysburg and the Pursuit of Lee's Army of Northern Virginia, July 4-14, 1863.* New York and El Dorado Hills CA, 2008.

Articles

Alexander, E. Porter. "The Great Charge and Artillery Fighting at Gettysburg." In *B&L* III.

-------- "Letter from General E. P. Alexander, Late Chief of Artillery, First Corps A.N.V." In *SHSP* IV.*

Alston, Robert. "Morgan's Cavalrymen Sweep Through Kentucky." In *B&G*.

Bicknell, L. E. "Repelling Lee's Last Blow at Gettysburg, IV." In *B&L* III.

Early, J. A. "Leading Confederates On the Battle of Gettysburg." In *SHSP* IV.*

Greene, A. Wilson. "Meade's Pursuit of Lee: From Gettysburg to Falling Waters," in *The Third Day at Gettysburg & Beyond*. Gary W. Gallagher, editor.

Heth, Henry. "Letter From Major General Heth, Hill's Corps, A. N. V." In *SHSP* IV.*

Horowitz, Tony. "Mapping the Past." *Smithsonian* magazine, October 2012.

Hunt, Henry J. "The Second Day at Gettysburg." In *B&L* III.

--------- "The Third Day at Gettysburg." In *B&L* III.

Imboden, John D. "The Confederate Retreat from Gettysburg." In *B&L* III

Kershaw, J. B. "Kershaw's Brigade at Gettysburg." In *B&L* III.

Long, A. L. Letter quoted in "Causes of Lee's Defeat at Gettysburg." In *SHSP* IV.*

Longstreet, James. "Lee's Right Wing at Gettysburg." In *B&L* III.

McCreary, James B. "Morgan's Raid Comes to an Inglorious End." In *B&G*.

McLaws, Lafayette. "Gettysburg." In *SHSP* VII.*

Meade, George G. "A Letter from General Meade." In *B&L* III.

Pfanz, Harry W. "The Gettysburg Campaign After Pickett's Charge." In *The Morningside Notes: An Occasional Publication of Morningside Bookshop, Division of*

Morningside House, Inc. No issue number given. Copyright 1981 and '82.

Rice, Edmund. "Repelling Lee's Last Blow at Gettysburg, I." In *B&L* III.

Smith, James Power. "General Lee at Gettysburg." In *SHSP* XXXIII.*

Trimble, Isaac R. "The Battle and Campaign of Gettysburg." In *SHSP* XXVI.*

Youngblood, William. "Unwritten History of Gettysburg Campaign." In *SHSP* XXXVIII.*

∽ DVD-ROM ∽

The Complete Civil War DVD-ROM: The Official Records and more. Oliver Computing LLC.

* Books and articles marked with an asterisk were consulted only on the DVD-ROM listed here. The *Official Records* were consulted both on the DVD and (primarily) in the American Historical Society reprint.

Index of Names

A

Acton, Thomas 653, 655, 658, 659, 666, 700, 701, 711, 730, 734, 738, 739, 740, 743
Alexander, E. Porter 155, 156, 172, 173, 184, 219, 227, 228, 236, 237, 238, 264, 275, 279, 348, 353, 354, 367, 368, 369, 376, 384, 385, 386, 387, 391, 393, 424, 426, 435
Allen, Joe 500
Alston, Robert 322, 450, 534, 535, 536
Ames, Adelbert 90, 92, 93, 97, 98, 99, 100, 112, 200, 289, 290
Anderson, Richard 11, 13, 49, 88, 116, 130, 148, 155, 166, 171, 175, 184, 242, 251, 256, 257, 258, 259, 357, 420, 421, 424, 426, 434, 462, 463, 464, 513, 521, 541, 553, 683, 684
Anderson, Thomas G. "Tige" 185, 195, 217, 218, 220, 221, 222, 224, 225, 226, 234, 235, 241, 251, 360, 432, 621, 622
Andrews, George L. 595
Andrews, John 649, 650, 655, 656, 661, 741
Archer, James J. 13, 16, 17, 19, 23, 25, 27, 29, 30, 31, 35, 80, 82, 86, 104, 122, 344, 358, 394, 616, 684, 685, 686
Arnold, William 399, 409
Ashby, Turner 428
Averell, W. W. 529, 628, 693, 726
Avery, Isaac 89, 97, 100, 101, 102, 117, 274, 289, 291, 292, 293
Aylett, William 556, 558
Ayres, Romeyne 144, 160, 198, 232, 233, 235

B

Bachelder, John B. 1
Baker, Lawrence S. 440, 509, 558, 683
Balder, Christian 430, 431
Baldwin, Briscoe 454
Banks, Nathaniel 307, 314, 323, 326, 477, 479, 492, 533, 573, 574, 575, 582, 594, 595, 596, 614, 632, 633, 634, 635, 646, 670, 671, 673, 727, 736, 744, 745
Barksdale, William 183, 184, 191, 219, 228, 229, 230, 231, 233, 236, 238, 240, 242, 243, 251, 254, 279, 280, 351
Barlow, Francis 51, 52, 57, 58, 89, 90, 91, 93, 94, 98, 99, 100, 101, 112, 138, 296, 452
Barnes, James 144, 160, 199, 202, 216, 217, 221, 222, 225, 234, 235, 236, 239, 240
Baxter, Henry 44, 62, 63, 64, 66, 67, 68, 69, 78, 108
Bayly, Mrs. Joseph 138
Beauregard, P. G. T. 170, 336, 337, 451, 565, 582, 608, 611, 638, 672, 720
Bell, R. H. 256
Belo, Alfred H. 36, 39
Benham, Henry W. 506, 605
Benning, Henry L. 185, 194, 195, 196, 222
Berdan, Hiram 165, 166, 167, 178, 180, 197, 242, 452
Berens, William F. 736, 738, 739
Beveridge, John L. 16
Bickley, George 639
Biddle, Chapman 81, 82, 84, 87, 102, 107, 401
Bird, W. H. 30
Birney, David 95, 129, 159, 162, 165, 166, 167, 179, 180, 181, 188, 190,

195, 216, 222, 223, 232, 242, 244,
  249, 250, 252, 297, 298, 465, 542,
  548, 605
Blackford, Eugene 345
Black, John Logan 360, 432, 555, 556,
  557, 558
Blair, John A. 36, 39
Blair, Montgomery 467
Bliss, William 145, 154, 167, 249, 256,
  257, 347, 348, 349, 369, 371, 397,
  405, 452
Bowen, Edward R. 228, 230
Bowen, John S. 324, 325, 326, 327,
  577
Boyd, William 466, 567, 568
Boyle, Jeremiah 579, 596
Bragg, Braxton 316, 317, 447, 448,
  449, 451, 601, 631, 632, 719, 750
Breckinridge, John 309
Brewster, William R. 181, 190, 245,
  250, 254, 255
Bright, Robert 394, 420
Briscoe, Joseph 165, 166, 167
Broadhead, Sally 371
Brockenbrough, John 13, 30, 78, 80,
  85, 106, 394, 395, 396, 405, 406,
  407, 684, 687
Brooke, John Rutter 224, 225, 233
Brooks, Noah 690, 721
Brooks, W. H. 487
Brooks, W. T. H. 568, 569, 590, 725
Brown, G. Campbell 49, 50, 63, 119,
  271, 272, 439, 440
Brown, Harvey 658, 664, 700, 701,
  702, 706, 709, 711, 730, 732, 735,
  737, 738, 739, 740, 742
Brown, J. Thomson 276
Brown, T. Frederick 191, 401, 402
Bryan, Abraham 397, 398, 399, 410
Bryan, Goode 623
Bryant, William Cullen 700
Buckner, Simon Bolivar 447, 449,
  601, 631
Buell, Augustus 109
Buford, John 5, 7, 11, 14, 15, 16, 18,
  19, 21, 22, 23, 24, 26, 29, 51, 57, 58,
  62, 74, 94, 97, 103, 113, 114, 152,
  159, 160, 212, 270, 335, 360, 429,
  459, 470, 526, 527, 528, 552, 553,
  555, 556, 557, 558, 559, 566, 567,
  569, 571, 584, 585, 586, 604, 607,
  620, 621, 623, 624, 625, 644, 676,
  687
Buhrman, C. H. 472, 473, 499
Bunce, Francis 609
Burbank, Sidney 232, 233, 235
Burling, George C. 181, 195, 216, 218,
  227
Burnside, Ambrose 304, 318, 449,
  450, 466, 492, 536, 537, 596, 598,
  632, 633, 641, 670, 716, 722
Burns, John 73, 74, 81, 86
Burr, Chauncey 613, 614
Bussey, Cyrus 614, 696
Butler, Benjamin 648, 727
Butterfield, Dan 46, 47, 123, 126, 128,
  129, 130, 141, 167, 296, 297, 298,
  349, 403, 447, 452, 458, 459, 461,
  504, 505, 506, 509, 526, 543, 547

C

Cabell, Henry C. 184
Caesar, Julius 210
Caldwell, John 146, 154, 159, 167,
  190, 223, 224, 225, 232, 233, 234,
  239, 247, 250, 252, 259, 279, 397,
  423
Caldwell, (telegraph operator) 351,
  461
Calef, John H. 18, 19, 23, 26, 32, 41,
  42, 62
Cameron, Simon 720
Canby, E. R. S. 728
Candy, Charles 287, 288, 338, 340
Canfield, Edward 698
Carpenter, Daniel 659, 660, 663, 665,
  666, 700, 701
Carrington, Henry 613
Carr, Joseph B. 181, 190, 254

Carroll, Samuel S. 293, 397, 400, 405
Carter, Thomas H. 63, 65, 368
Cavada, Frederick 228, 230
Chalmers, James 671
Chamberlain, John 200
Chamberlain, Joshua Lawrence 200, 201, 207, 208, 209, 210, 211, 212, 213
Chamberlain, (Major) 73, 74
Chamberlain, Tom 200
Chambliss, John R. 362, 363, 364, 377, 378, 379, 380, 440, 509, 510, 511, 541, 553, 559, 607
Chase, Salmon 530, 573
Christiancy, Henry 229, 245
Clark, Atherton 200
Clarke, John J. 148
Clayton, Powell 481, 483
Cline, Milton 168, 169, 336
Clingman, Thomas 611
Coan, Elisha 200
Cobham, George 287, 288
Cole, H. A. 524
Colgrove, Silas 342, 343
Colquitt, Alfred 611
Colvill, William 253, 254
Cooke, John R. 496
Cooke, Philip St. George 496
Cooper, Samuel 170, 451
Corley, James L. 441, 603, 679
Corse, Montgomery 170, 583
Costello, James 732, 733
Coster, Charles R. 100, 101, 102, 293
Couch, Darius 125, 351, 352, 438, 439, 451, 466, 507, 518, 524, 545, 547, 549, 550, 565, 567, 568, 571, 588, 590, 591, 604, 605, 619, 625, 627, 644, 652, 674, 676, 694, 695, 705, 720, 721, 727, 729, 734, 736, 741, 748
Cowan, Andrew 402, 413, 414, 448
Cram, George C. 429, 430, 431, 572
Crawford, Samuel 127, 160, 210, 235, 241, 435
Creasman, W. B. 671

Cribben, Henry 206
Cross, Edward 223, 224, 225
Culp, John Wesley 344
Curtin, A. G. 725
Cushing, Alonzo 346, 347, 397, 399, 400, 402, 405, 412, 421, 422, 437
Cushing, Howard 399
Cushing, William 399, 437
Cusick, Francis 650, 651, 703
Custer, George Armstrong 9, 206, 267, 268, 269, 270, 361, 362, 364, 365, 376, 377, 379, 381, 383, 399, 433, 461, 472, 473, 500, 501, 502, 511, 558, 559, 586, 643, 680, 681, 685, 687
Cutler, Lysander 25, 31, 32, 33, 35, 42, 44, 62, 66, 69, 78, 109, 111, 113, 134, 286

D

Dahlgren, John A. 475, 476, 477, 552, 609, 610
Dahlgren, Ulric 168, 169, 171, 336, 447, 470, 515, 516, 553, 554
Dana, Charles A. 306, 309, 310, 327, 329, 330, 491, 492, 532, 538
Dana, Edmund L. 77, 78
Dana, N. J. T. 619, 627, 674
Daniel, Junius 61, 64, 68, 69, 70, 74, 75, 76, 77, 78, 79, 275, 295, 300, 337, 340, 341, 342, 344, 503, 541, 545
David, James L. 535
Davis, Jefferson 169, 170, 314, 319, 337, 380, 443, 447, 449, 451, 454, 455, 467, 498, 563, 582, 604, 615, 616, 618, 636, 642, 672, 684, 722, 723
Davis, Joseph R. 14, 19, 23, 25, 26, 31, 35, 36, 39, 40, 80, 394, 395, 396, 397, 405, 406, 410, 495, 519, 556
Davis, William J. 640
Davis, William S. 77, 78
Dawes, Rufus 34, 35, 36, 37, 38, 39, 40, 41, 111

Day, Hannibal 232, 235
Dearing, James 420
Decker, John 656, 661
de Forest, Othneil 604
Delony, William 557
de Trobriand, Phillippe Regis 128, 180, 183, 191, 194, 195, 216, 217, 221, 222, 223, 605
Devin, Thomas C. 15, 16, 25, 97, 555, 556, 558, 566, 584, 585, 607, 621, 623, 624, 644
Dickinson, Anna 658, 700
Dilger, Hubert 65, 100
Dilks, George 703, 704, 706, 707
Dix, John A. 320, 321, 467, 497, 530, 582, 626, 727, 728, 737
Dodge, Grenville 577
Doles, George 60, 61, 64, 90, 91, 97, 98, 99, 100, 275, 294, 295, 408, 545
Dooley, John 388
Doster, William 551, 552
Doubleday, Abner 20, 21, 22, 27, 29, 31, 32, 34, 42, 43, 44, 52, 54, 56, 59, 61, 69, 71, 73, 81, 84, 87, 93, 102, 103, 104, 108, 109, 113, 114, 115, 116, 124, 129, 130, 174, 260, 262, 393, 397, 401, 402, 417, 506
Douglas, Henry Kyd 117, 118, 121, 289, 299
Duke, Basil 579, 580, 596, 670, 718
Dunaway, Wayland 687
Dungan, Robert 284
Dunn, William M. 491
Dwight, Walton 75, 77

E

Eagan, John 651
Early, Jubal Anderson 6, 7, 9, 10, 11, 16, 63, 88, 89, 91, 97, 100, 117, 118, 120, 121, 122, 131, 132, 133, 155, 156, 274, 289, 292, 294, 295, 300, 339, 353, 354, 409, 443, 462, 522, 523, 541, 553, 678, 680
Eckert, Thomas 461

Elliott, Washington L. 546, 570
Ellis, Theodore 348, 349
Emack, George M. 471, 499, 501, 502, 512
Emory, William H. 478, 533, 575
Eustice, George 81
Evans, William 40, 41
Ewell, Richard 6, 7, 8, 9, 10, 11, 13, 16, 24, 46, 48, 49, 50, 57, 59, 62, 63, 88, 116, 117, 118, 119, 120, 121, 122, 124, 125, 131, 132, 133, 134, 138, 147, 148, 149, 151, 152, 153, 154, 156, 157, 185, 186, 264, 265, 267, 268, 269, 271, 272, 274, 275, 276, 279, 282, 283, 299, 300, 336, 337, 345, 352, 353, 359, 362, 363, 372, 408, 409, 427, 439, 440, 444, 454, 456, 457, 464, 466, 505, 512, 513, 516, 522, 528, 541, 545, 559, 560, 564, 617, 642, 676, 678, 679, 684, 694, 724, 748

F

Fagan, James 480, 482, 483, 484, 485, 486, 487
Fairfax, (Colonel) 186
Farley, Porter 206, 210
Farnsworth, Elon J. 9, 269, 270, 360, 361, 431, 432, 433, 434, 472, 499, 604
Farragut, David 307, 533, 646
Ferguson, Milton J. 362, 363, 364, 509, 510, 511, 512, 541, 553, 555, 559, 585, 586, 607, 617, 620, 621, 622, 680, 681
Ferry, Noah 378
Field, Charles W. 13
Finley, G. W. 392, 409, 412, 413
Fisher, Joseph 235
Fiske, Samuel 374, 375
Flack, R. 738, 739
Foley, Shadrack 457, 458
Foster, Robert S. 494, 495, 496, 582
Fowler, Edward B. 25, 27, 37, 39, 286,

287
Franklin, Abraham 733
Franklin, Walter 707, 708
Fremantle, Arthur 156, 258, 275, 420, 427
Fremont, John Charles 54, 55
French, William H. 349, 350, 351, 457, 458, 459, 507, 510, 518, 524, 525, 526, 527, 528, 546, 561, 568, 569, 570, 592, 605, 616, 644, 646, 677
Fry, Birkett 80, 358, 359, 394, 395, 397, 406, 407, 410, 412
Fry, James B. 560, 648, 715, 716, 729, 731
Fuger, Frederick 346, 399, 402

G

Gamble, William 15, 16, 18, 25, 41, 81, 84, 86, 97, 103, 104, 105, 555, 556, 557, 558, 584, 585, 586, 607, 621, 623, 624, 687
Gardner, Alexander 525
Gardner, Franklin 575, 594, 595
Garlach, Anna 111
Garnett, John 109
Garnett, Richard "Dick" 358, 359, 387, 388, 391, 392, 393, 394, 412, 413, 421, 583
Garrard, Kenner 210
Gay, Sidney 661, 663, 702
Geary, John 114, 144, 145, 152, 161, 279, 281, 282, 284, 287, 288, 299, 336, 337, 338, 339, 340, 341, 342
Georg, Kathleen 3
Getty, George W. 320, 467, 494, 496, 497
Gibbon, John 47, 115, 129, 130, 145, 146, 147, 154, 168, 190, 245, 246, 247, 250, 255, 260, 262, 293, 297, 298, 299, 346, 354, 355, 373, 375, 388, 393, 397, 399, 400, 401, 403, 411, 412, 421, 423, 435, 436, 438, 643

Gibbons, Abby 708
Gibbons, James 708
Gibbons, Julia 708, 711
Gibbons, Lucy 708, 711
Gibbons, Sally 708
Gillmore, Quincy Adams 475, 476, 477, 552, 575, 607, 608, 610, 611, 709, 736
Gilmore, James 649, 661, 664, 665, 702, 703, 709, 710
Glenn, James 108
Godwin, Archibald 294
Goode, Robert W. 512
Gordon, George H. 692
Gordon, John Brown 89, 95, 96, 97, 99, 100, 117, 118, 121, 122, 274, 289, 293, 294, 345, 522, 523
Goss, Warren 137
Graham, (Captain) 368
Graham, Charles K. 180, 181, 187, 227, 228, 230, 231, 242, 296, 334, 335
Grant, Fred 488
Grant, Lewis A. 624
Grant, Ulysses S. 144, 170, 305, 306, 307, 308, 309, 310, 312, 313, 314, 318, 324, 325, 326, 327, 328, 329, 330, 399, 479, 480, 481, 488, 489, 491, 492, 493, 532, 533, 538, 569, 573, 574, 575, 576, 577, 587, 593, 594, 596, 597, 614, 615, 632, 633, 634, 635, 636, 646, 647, 648, 671, 672, 673, 696, 697, 721, 722, 723, 744, 745, 749, 750
Gray, George 379
Greeley, Horace 578, 656, 660, 661, 702, 703, 709, 710
Greene, George S. 281, 282, 284, 286, 287, 290, 338, 341, 342
Greene, Wilson 749
Greenough, George 457, 458
Green, Thomas 533, 671
Gregg, David McMurtrie 160, 270, 271, 272, 273, 283, 361, 362, 363, 364, 376, 379, 381, 383, 384, 470,

472, 514, 587, 604, 624, 678, 689, 726
Gregg, J. Irvin 271, 272, 361, 364, 377, 470, 514, 551, 552, 565
Grierson, Benjamin 594, 615, 647
Griffin, Charles 217
Griffin, Thomas 251, 363
Grover, Cuvier 671
Guild, Lafayette 442

H

Hall, A. Oakey 704
Halleck, Henry W. 6, 124, 181, 296, 305, 317, 334, 335, 350, 352, 360, 438, 447, 448, 449, 453, 461, 464, 467, 468, 470, 478, 507, 524, 525, 526, 527, 529, 532, 539, 546, 560, 561, 568, 569, 570, 571, 573, 575, 587, 588, 589, 591, 593, 606, 615, 620, 626, 627, 631, 632, 633, 645, 670, 674, 675, 677, 690, 691, 692, 693, 694, 705, 724, 725, 726, 734, 741, 749
Hall, James A. 25, 32, 33, 34, 35, 40, 42, 52
Hall, Norman 190, 255, 401, 403, 404, 411, 414, 415, 416
Hampton, Wade 264, 265, 266, 267, 269, 360, 362, 363, 364, 379, 380, 381, 383, 440, 462, 509, 547, 555, 558, 621, 683
Hancock, Winfield Scott 46, 47, 48, 54, 93, 103, 112, 113, 114, 115, 116, 123, 124, 125, 128, 129, 144, 146, 159, 161, 167, 168, 189, 190, 223, 229, 245, 246, 247, 249, 250, 251, 252, 253, 254, 257, 259, 260, 261, 279, 285, 293, 296, 297, 298, 335, 352, 354, 373, 375, 385, 397, 410, 412, 415, 416, 417, 422, 423, 434, 436, 438, 634, 643
Hanson, Charles S. 534, 535, 536
Hardee, William J. 719
Harman, Amelia 17, 18, 82, 83

Harman, John Alexander 444, 462, 500, 603
Harman, Troy D. 3
Harney, George 32, 33
Harris, Andrew 289, 290
Harris, Avery 74
Harris, Edward P. 257
Harrison (spy) 10
Harrison, Walter 1, 2, 3
Harrow, William 146, 246, 247, 252, 255, 401, 404, 414, 415, 416, 423
Hartsuff, George L. 450, 596
Haskell, Frank 262, 352, 373, 374, 375, 387, 398, 401, 403, 404, 412, 414, 416, 422, 423, 436
Haskell, John Cheves 174
Haupt, Herman 335, 468, 469, 508, 560, 592, 607, 619, 691, 693
Hauschild, Henry 58
Hauser, John 40
Hawley, Seth 711
Hay, John 560, 695
Hays, Alexander 144, 145, 161, 249, 257, 347, 348, 349, 397, 398, 399, 403, 406, 407, 410, 422, 438, 643
Hays, Harry 89, 97, 100, 101, 102, 117, 274, 289, 290, 291, 292, 293, 294, 345, 679
Hazard, John 347, 438
Hazlett, Charles E. 203, 204, 205, 206, 210
Headley, Joel Tyler 649, 650, 654, 655, 660, 698
Heath, Francis 247, 249
Hebert, P. T. 671
Heckman, Lewis 101
Heintzelman, Samuel 526, 692
Helme, John 706
Herbert, Hilary 425
Herron, F. J. 596, 614, 615, 636, 671, 672, 722, 723, 745
Heth, Henry "Harry" 11, 12, 13, 14, 16, 18, 19, 22, 23, 31, 40, 50, 61, 78, 80, 83, 84, 87, 104, 105, 109, 116, 344, 353, 355, 356, 357, 384, 396,

463, 519, 520, 521, 547, 556, 616, 683, 684, 685, 687
Higginson, Thomas 611
Hill, A. P. 10, 11, 12, 13, 24, 46, 49, 50, 57, 59, 60, 62, 63, 70, 74, 77, 80, 88, 94, 103, 104, 116, 117, 118, 124, 133, 151, 152, 153, 154, 156, 157, 159, 166, 171, 186, 232, 242, 248, 258, 275, 279, 346, 351, 353, 355, 356, 358, 367, 369, 370, 371, 395, 409, 420, 439, 440, 521, 522, 541, 559, 617, 678, 679, 683, 684, 694, 724, 725
Hill, B. H. 715
Hill, D. H. 170, 321, 565, 674, 719
Hines, Tom 579, 669
Hobson, Edward H. 318, 319, 536, 537, 538, 579, 581, 596, 598, 612, 640, 641, 669, 719, 722, 743
Hoke, R. F. 89, 274, 289, 293
Hollinger, Jacob 40
Holmes, Theophilus 314, 479, 480, 481, 482, 484, 485, 486, 487
Hood, John Bell "Sam" 149, 151, 153, 155, 158, 172, 173, 174, 183, 184, 185, 186, 187, 191, 192, 193, 198, 217, 219, 355, 360, 436, 462, 521, 541, 556, 558, 622, 681, 683, 684, 688, 748
Hooker, Joseph 6, 7, 8, 55, 125, 126, 128, 160, 163, 249, 304, 634, 721, 748, 749
Hotchkiss, Jed 680
Howard 20
Howard, Charles 58, 103
Howard, Oliver Otis 22, 47, 48, 51, 52, 54, 55, 56, 57, 58, 59, 90, 91, 92, 93, 94, 95, 100, 102, 103, 111, 112, 113, 114, 115, 124, 125, 126, 128, 130, 139, 142, 277, 286, 293, 297, 298, 336, 362, 385, 423, 438, 465, 506, 542, 544, 548, 572, 586, 626, 643, 646, 677, 689, 692
Howe, Albion 623, 624
Huey, Pennock 470, 472, 511, 552, 620, 624, 644, 678, 689
Humphreys, Andrew A. 129, 130, 159, 168, 179, 180, 181, 190, 198, 228, 229, 242, 243, 244, 245, 246, 247, 250, 254, 262, 588, 625, 645, 689, 692, 726
Hunter, David 476
Hunt, Henry 130, 139, 141, 142, 144, 153, 154, 163, 164, 165, 167, 178, 179, 180, 189, 220, 248, 346, 369, 371, 372, 375, 385
Hurlbut, Stephen A. 577, 632, 723

I

Imboden, George W. 462
Imboden, John D. 120, 428, 429, 440, 441, 442, 444, 454, 455, 457, 461, 462, 463, 466, 510, 511, 513, 514, 515, 516, 517, 518, 520, 551, 555, 556, 557, 558, 559, 560, 565, 568, 571, 584, 602, 603, 675
Ingalls, Rufus 143, 144, 335, 468, 469, 591, 618, 691, 693, 726
Irvin, William J. 580
Iverson, Alfred 60, 61, 63, 64, 65, 66, 67, 68, 69, 70, 71, 77, 275, 294, 295, 408, 464, 471, 502, 503, 521, 554, 616

J

Jackson, Allan H. 101
Jackson, Thomas J. "Stonewall" 11, 55, 59, 65, 91, 118, 121, 243, 249, 440, 720, 748
Jacobs, Michael 122
James, Robert 245, 246, 248
Janes, Henry 693
Jardine, Edward 735, 737, 742
Jenkins, Albert G. 138, 265, 271, 272, 362, 363, 364, 440, 511, 547, 726
Jenkins, Charles 652
Johnson, Adam R. 597, 670, 717
Johnson, Bushrod 601

Johnson, Edward "Allegheny" 48, 49, 117, 118, 121, 122, 133, 134, 148, 149, 155, 271, 273, 274, 276, 277, 278, 283, 288, 289, 294, 299, 300, 337, 339, 342, 344, 350, 408, 426, 443, 444, 462, 541, 553, 678, 680

Johnson, Samuel 737

Johnston, Joseph E. 308, 309, 310, 312, 324, 326, 327, 328, 331, 447, 448, 449, 451, 478, 491, 494, 533, 538, 578, 593, 596, 614, 615, 632, 633, 634, 635, 636, 647, 648, 672, 673, 674, 697, 719, 722, 723, 745, 749, 750

Johnston, Samuel R. 148, 149, 150, 152, 153, 154, 157, 158, 160, 173

Jones, Abram 518, 519, 520, 549

Jones, John M. 283, 284, 285, 337, 338

Jones, Samuel 604, 618, 628, 631, 642

Jones, W. E. "Grumble" 265, 428, 429, 430, 431, 440, 471, 472, 501, 502, 504, 509, 513, 517, 541, 553, 559, 567, 584, 586, 607, 617, 675

Jones, William 662

Jordan, Lewis 580, 597

Jordan, William 208, 212

Judah, Henry M. 318, 319, 322, 536, 538, 596, 722, 744

K

Kane, Thomas 287, 288, 338, 340

Kautz, August V. 538, 744

Kelley, Benjamin F. 465, 528, 568, 569, 589, 590, 604, 606, 619, 627, 675, 693, 726, 727

Kelly, Patrick 225, 226, 233

Kenly, John R. 570, 587, 618, 626

Kennedy, John 639, 651, 652, 655

Kershaw, J. B. 174, 182, 183, 184, 191, 219, 220, 221, 222, 225, 226, 227, 228, 229, 233, 235, 238, 239, 241, 623

Keyes, Erasmus 320, 321, 497, 727, 728

Kidd, J. H. 380, 381, 382, 383, 461, 472, 501, 684, 685, 686, 687

Kilpatrick, Hugh Judson 9, 160, 266, 268, 269, 270, 275, 360, 361, 362, 364, 376, 383, 431, 432, 433, 434, 436, 470, 472, 473, 499, 501, 502, 503, 504, 509, 510, 511, 512, 522, 552, 553, 558, 559, 566, 584, 585, 586, 604, 620, 624, 626, 643, 676, 680, 681, 684, 685, 687, 688, 689

Kimball, Nathan 672

King, Charles 705

Kirkwood, Samuel J. 728

Klingle, Daniel 181, 190

Knipe, Joseph 551, 591

Krzyzanowski, Wladimer 97, 98, 99, 101, 293

Kurtz, L. B. 644

L

Lane, James H. 104, 105, 259, 294, 356, 359, 395, 406, 408, 410, 426, 684

Lang, David 244, 247, 251, 254, 255, 259, 261, 262, 357, 424, 425, 426

Latimer, Joseph W. 276, 277, 278, 283

Lauman, (General) 636

Law, Evander 151, 158, 185, 192, 193, 194, 195, 197, 198, 207, 208, 360, 432, 433, 436, 622

Lee, Custis 54

Lee, Fitzhugh "Fitz" 265, 362, 363, 364, 377, 379, 381, 382, 440, 463, 509, 514, 551, 552, 558, 559, 565, 621, 622, 684

Lee, Robert E. 2, 3, 6, 7, 8, 9, 10, 11, 12, 13, 15, 17, 20, 24, 31, 46, 48, 49, 50, 57, 61, 63, 70, 74, 80, 83, 88, 102, 109, 110, 117, 118, 119, 120, 121, 130, 131, 132, 133, 134, 139, 141, 147, 148, 149, 150, 151, 152, 153, 154, 155, 156, 157, 159, 160, 163, 166, 169, 170, 171, 173, 174, 175, 183, 184, 185, 186, 187, 216, 219,

242, 243, 258, 264, 265, 268, 274, 278, 279, 282, 283, 296, 297, 298, 299, 300, 301, 304, 305, 316, 318, 319, 320, 321, 324, 334, 336, 337, 350, 351, 352, 353, 354, 355, 356, 358, 359, 360, 362, 363, 368, 369, 370, 386, 387, 409, 420, 426, 427, 428, 429, 432, 434, 435, 436, 437, 438, 439, 440, 441, 442, 443, 447, 448, 449, 451, 454, 455, 456, 457, 458, 459, 460, 461, 462, 463, 464, 465, 466, 467, 475, 480, 496, 505, 507, 508, 509, 510, 512, 515, 517, 518, 520, 521, 522, 523, 524, 526, 527, 528, 529, 541, 542, 545, 546, 548, 549, 551, 554, 555, 559, 560, 563, 564, 565, 566, 567, 568, 569, 571, 572, 573, 578, 582, 583, 584, 586, 587, 589, 590, 592, 593, 597, 601, 602, 603, 604, 606, 607, 615, 616, 617, 618, 619, 620, 624, 626, 628, 629, 634, 641, 642, 643, 645, 646, 652, 672, 673, 674, 675, 676, 677, 678, 679, 681, 682, 683, 688, 689, 690, 691, 692, 693, 694, 695, 697, 709, 721, 724, 725, 747, 748, 749, 750
Lee, Samuel P. 467, 539
Lee, W. H. F. "Rooney" 170, 320, 362, 364, 724
Leggett, M. D. 489
Leigh, B. Watkins 342
Lincoln, Abraham 6, 21, 55, 72, 127, 304, 305, 306, 317, 319, 459, 467, 475, 525, 529, 530, 539, 560, 573, 574, 590, 628, 673, 690, 694, 695, 699, 720, 721, 728, 729, 737, 744, 748
Lincoln, Mary 460
Lincoln, Robert 695
Lincoln, Tad 530
Livermore, William 206
Livingston, Manning 248
Lockwood, Henry H. 161, 279, 280, 337, 339

Logan, John A. 489, 492
Long, Armistead L. 120, 151, 152, 156, 258, 353, 642
Longstreet, James 2, 10, 11, 12, 42, 48, 49, 80, 94, 118, 119, 120, 124, 130, 132, 133, 141, 147, 148, 149, 150, 151, 153, 154, 155, 156, 157, 158, 171, 172, 173, 174, 175, 181, 182, 183, 184, 185, 186, 187, 191, 219, 241, 243, 265, 267, 274, 275, 299, 300, 301, 320, 337, 348, 351, 353, 354, 355, 356, 357, 358, 359, 360, 367, 368, 369, 370, 384, 386, 387, 392, 394, 395, 409, 418, 420, 421, 431, 436, 440, 455, 463, 521, 522, 541, 545, 551, 559, 603, 616, 617, 621, 642, 644, 676, 678, 679, 681, 682, 684, 694, 724, 725, 747, 748
Lowrance, W. Lee 359, 395, 406
Ludlow, William H. 539, 540, 697, 724
Lufman, William 219
Lyon, Nathaniel 577

M

Mackenzie, Ranald 198, 543, 547, 645
Madill, Henry 231
Magennis, (unknown) 451
Mahone, William 258, 259, 420
Manierre, Benjamin 654
Mann, William 379
Marble, Manton 699
Marmaduke, John 480, 482, 483, 486, 487, 633
Marshall, Charles 133
Marshall, James K. 394, 395, 396, 406, 410
Martin, Augustus P. 203
Mayo, Joseph 414
Mayo, Robert M. 394
McArthur, John 647, 672
McCabe 540
McClellan, Carswell 242
McClellan, George 127, 144, 304, 532,

559, 560, 587, 705
McClellan, Henry 265, 363, 382
McConnell, Charles H. 83, 85
McCreary, Albertus 123
McCreary, James B. 596, 612, 613, 640, 641, 669, 670, 716, 743
McCredie, Robert 654
McDougall, Archibald 336, 344
McGilvery, Freeman 220, 238, 239, 240, 248, 251, 259, 280, 354, 392, 393
McIntosh, John B. 270, 272, 362, 364, 376, 377, 379, 382, 470, 545, 548, 619, 627
McKeen, H. Boyd 224
McLaws, Lafayette 119, 149, 150, 151, 152, 153, 155, 158, 171, 172, 173, 174, 175, 183, 184, 185, 186, 187, 191, 192, 193, 219, 233, 243, 299, 355, 436, 521, 541, 622, 623, 681
McLean, William 481, 483
McPherson, James B. 330, 492, 532, 538, 576, 593, 634, 636, 647
McRae, Dandridge 482, 484, 485, 486, 487
McReynolds, Andrew T. 350, 457, 727
Meade, George G. 6, 7, 9, 10, 12, 15, 19, 20, 22, 24, 42, 44, 45, 46, 47, 48, 50, 51, 52, 57, 93, 103, 112, 115, 123, 124, 125, 126, 127, 128, 129, 130, 134, 139, 140, 141, 142, 143, 144, 145, 146, 147, 154, 155, 158, 159, 160, 162, 163, 164, 167, 168, 178, 181, 182, 187, 188, 189, 190, 198, 205, 232, 249, 250, 259, 260, 261, 262, 267, 268, 270, 274, 278, 279, 280, 281, 282, 296, 297, 298, 299, 300, 313, 334, 335, 336, 344, 349, 350, 351, 352, 358, 360, 361, 362, 373, 375, 385, 403, 412, 422, 423, 434, 435, 436, 438, 439, 447, 449, 452, 453, 454, 461, 463, 464, 465, 466, 468, 470, 504, 506, 507, 508, 509, 518, 523, 524, 526, 530, 542, 543, 544, 545, 546, 547, 548, 549, 550, 551, 560, 561, 563, 565, 566, 567, 569, 570, 571, 572, 573, 574, 578, 584, 585, 586, 587, 588, 589, 590, 591, 592, 593, 604, 605, 606, 615, 617, 619, 620, 624, 625, 627, 633, 634, 643, 644, 645, 646, 673, 674, 675, 676, 677, 678, 689, 690, 691, 692, 693, 694, 695, 720, 721, 726, 727, 728, 734, 747, 748, 749, 750
Meade, George G.? 126
Meade, George Jr. 130, 158, 161, 260
Mealy, William 732
Meigs, John R. 592, 606
Meigs, Montgomery 335, 468, 469, 591, 592, 607, 618, 691, 693, 740
Melcher, Holman 211, 212
Meredith, Solomon 27, 35, 73, 85, 102
Merritt, Wesley 160, 360, 429, 430, 431, 432, 433, 434, 470, 527, 528, 555, 556, 557, 558, 584, 585, 621
Meysenburg, Theodore 51, 52, 57
Miller, Anderson 311
Miller, Dora 311
Miller, William 382
Milroy, Robert 352, 550, 674, 749
Montgomery, L. M. 325, 327
Moore, Orlando 450
Moore, William Roby 84
Moran, Martin 743
Morgan, Charlton 535
Morgan, Dick 537, 580, 597, 721
Morgan, John Hunt 317, 318, 319, 321, 322, 450, 451, 534, 535, 536, 537, 538, 578, 579, 580, 581, 596, 597, 598, 612, 613, 640, 641, 669, 670, 716, 717, 718, 719, 721, 743, 744, 747
Morgan, Joseph S. 671
Morgan, Tom 535
Morrill, Walter G. 201, 207
Morton, Oliver P. 596, 612, 613
Mosby, John Singleton 8
Mower, Joseph 672

Muhlenberg, William 654
Mulholland, St. Clair 372, 373, 375
Mull, Daniel 516
Murphy, (Captain) 451
Murphy, W. B. 40

N

Naglee, Henry M. 587, 588, 606, 645, 692
Neff, George W. 717, 718, 719
Neill, Thomas 543, 544, 545, 548, 565, 572, 590, 605, 617, 619, 627
Nelson, Alanson 230
Nevin, David 236, 241
Newberry, J. S. 714, 715
Newton, John 115, 260, 297, 298, 299, 373, 438, 452, 465, 506, 542, 543, 544, 548, 643, 645
Nugent, Robert 652, 654, 655, 664, 731

O

Oates, William C. 192, 193, 194, 196, 197, 200, 208, 209, 211, 212, 213, 433, 434
O'Brien, Henry 421
O'Brien, H. T. 701, 705, 706
Oglesby, Richard 577
O'Kane, Dennis 413
Olmstead, Charles 611, 720
O'Neal, E. A. 61, 63, 64, 65, 66, 67, 68, 70, 88, 275, 295, 300, 337, 338, 339, 340, 344, 408, 502, 503
Opdyke, George 653, 656, 657, 659, 661, 664, 704, 705, 709, 730, 731, 734, 738, 741
Ord, E. O. C. 326, 492, 539, 614, 636, 696, 723
O'Rorke, Patrick 205, 206
Osborn, Thomas 112, 278, 385
Ould, Robert 467, 540, 673, 697

P

Pace, Thomas 487
Page, R. C. M. 65
Paine, William 130, 139, 160, 188
Parke, John 326, 492, 614
Parsons, Henry 433
Parsons, Mosby 482, 483, 484, 485, 486
Parton, James 660, 661, 662, 663
Passegger, Franz 518, 519, 520
Paulding, Hiram 702
Paul, Gabriel 44, 66, 68, 69, 78, 296
Pegram, William 12, 16, 19, 258
Pemberton, John 308, 312, 313, 324, 325, 326, 327, 328, 329, 330, 331, 488, 489, 491, 493, 532, 538, 576, 577, 593, 615, 635, 648, 673, 749, 750
Pender, Dorsey 13, 24, 49, 50, 54, 80, 87, 88, 104, 105, 106, 109, 116, 118, 257, 259, 294, 295, 348, 353, 355, 356, 357, 359, 395, 408, 409, 426, 434, 462, 463, 520, 521, 547, 683, 684, 686
Pendleton, Sandy 118
Pendleton, William N. 109, 110, 152, 160, 171, 367, 368, 371, 386, 490
Pennington, Alexander 365, 376, 377, 378, 472, 501, 502, 511
Perrin, Abner 104, 106, 107, 109, 408
Pettigrew, J. Johnston 11, 12, 13, 14, 80, 82, 85, 86, 87, 104, 355, 357, 358, 359, 384, 387, 393, 394, 395, 396, 397, 403, 405, 407, 408, 409, 410, 420, 421, 422, 436, 519, 616, 683, 684, 685, 686, 688, 693, 725
Pfanz, Harry 63
Pickett, Charles 420
Pickett, George 2, 3, 120, 149, 151, 170, 243, 296, 300, 301, 320, 354, 355, 356, 357, 358, 359, 367, 369, 370, 371, 384, 386, 387, 388, 391, 392, 393, 394, 395, 396, 397, 403, 404, 405, 409, 411, 414, 416, 420,

421, 422, 424, 425, 426, 429, 434, 436, 441, 521, 522, 541, 556, 564, 583, 602, 616, 626
Pierce, Lewis B. 351, 352, 466, 518, 550, 568, 590, 591, 619
Pleasonton, Alfred 159, 160, 169, 188, 267, 268, 270, 278, 334, 361, 362, 373, 429, 465, 470, 507, 508, 523, 545, 547, 561, 565, 585, 623, 645, 646, 678, 689
Pope, John 55
Porter, David 330, 487, 573
Porter, Josiah 733
Posey, Carnot 256, 257, 258, 259, 347, 420, 421, 452
Powell, R. M. 460
Powell, Sarah 708
Powell, William 663
Prentiss, Benjamin 480, 481, 482, 483, 485, 487, 615
Prescott, G. L. 221
Preston, Addison 499, 500, 511
Preston, William 631
Price, Sterling 480, 482, 483, 484, 485, 486, 487, 577, 633
Putnam, H. R. 706, 735, 736, 742
Pye, Edward 37

Q

Quirk, Tom 319

R

Ramseur, Dodson 61, 68, 70, 71, 77, 110, 275, 294, 295, 408, 502, 616
Randall, Francis 260, 261, 404, 416, 417
Randol, Alanson 376, 377, 381
Randolph, George E. 158, 189, 228
Ransom, T. E. G. 671
Rawlins, John 330, 331, 697
Ray, Edward 698
Raymond, Henry J. 731, 740
Reid, Whitelaw 142

Reynolds, Gilbert 43
Reynolds, John F. 15, 18, 19, 20, 21, 22, 23, 24, 25, 26, 27, 29, 30, 35, 42, 44, 45, 46, 47, 51, 52, 56, 94, 95, 124, 126, 128, 174, 335, 406
Rice, Edmund 388, 411, 416
Rice, James 199, 200, 201, 205, 210
Rice, Samuel 481, 483
Richardson, (Major) 367
Richmond, Nathaniel 472, 499, 511, 553, 554, 559, 585, 604
Ricketts, R. Bruce 292, 293
Riddle, William 52
Riggin, (Colonel) 635
Robertson, Beverly 185, 192, 193, 194, 195, 217, 265, 428, 429, 440, 472, 509, 513, 541, 553, 554, 559, 584, 617, 679
Robinson, John C. 43, 44, 62, 67, 68, 69, 71, 108, 109, 111, 145, 260, 587
Rodes, Robert 49, 59, 60, 61, 62, 63, 64, 65, 70, 74, 80, 84, 88, 89, 90, 91, 97, 107, 109, 116, 117, 118, 120, 121, 122, 131, 132, 133, 155, 275, 289, 292, 294, 295, 300, 337, 353, 354, 357, 395, 408, 409, 426, 434, 443, 444, 462, 464, 471, 501, 502, 541, 545, 616, 678, 679, 681
Rodman, Daniel 636, 637, 638
Roebling, Washington 198, 205
Rogers, Peter 245, 261, 393
Root, Adrian 69
Rorty, James M. 259, 401, 405, 414
Rosecrans, William S. 316, 317, 447, 449, 573, 601, 631, 632, 633, 634, 670, 750
Rowley, Thomas A. 43, 81, 84, 86, 87, 111, 116, 129, 401
Ruch, Reuben 96, 97
Ruger, Thomas H. 279, 280, 282, 288, 336, 339, 342, 344, 453
Rummel, John 365, 377, 378, 380
Rummel, Sarah 365
Rupp, John 345
Rushling, James 530

Rush, Richard 432, 729
Ryer, B. Franklin 732, 733, 734, 735

S

Salomon, Edward 59
Salomon, Frederick 480, 481, 487
Sanders, W. P. 722, 744
Sandford, Charles 653, 657, 658, 664, 666, 700, 702, 709, 711, 733
Sanford, Edward S. 666, 707, 710, 714
Sawyer, Franklin 405, 406, 407
Scales, Alfred M. 104, 105, 106, 107, 359, 395, 462
Schenck, Robert 527, 592, 606, 705, 715, 737
Schimmelfennig, Alexander 56, 57, 58, 90, 92, 93, 94, 96, 97, 99, 100, 111, 286, 452
Schriver, Ed 705
Schurz, Carl 52, 55, 56, 57, 58, 59, 63, 90, 92, 93, 94, 97, 98, 100, 101, 102, 103, 111, 112, 113, 116, 145, 286, 293, 396, 452, 586, 604, 626
Scott, Winfield 148
Seddon, James A. 321, 628, 642
Sedgwick, John 46, 123, 124, 129, 280, 297, 298, 465, 505, 506, 507, 509, 522, 523, 524, 542, 543, 544, 545, 546, 547, 548, 623, 625, 634, 643, 688, 689
Seeley, Francis W. 245, 246
Semmes, Paul 183, 191, 219, 220, 225, 226, 227, 241, 622
Seward, William 467, 529, 716, 731
Seymour, Horatio 658, 704, 705, 711, 729, 730, 731, 735, 737, 739, 740, 741
Seymour, Truman 476, 609
Shackelford, James M. 318, 538
Shaler, Alexander 341
Sharpe, George Henry 168, 296, 297, 300
Shaw, George 648
Shepard, S. G. 410

Sheridan, Philip 448
Sherman, William Tecumseh 27, 306, 308, 309, 324, 326, 327, 328, 331, 491, 492, 493, 533, 538, 578, 593, 596, 614, 615, 634, 635, 636, 647, 672, 696, 722, 723, 745, 750
Sherrill, Eliakim 399
Shotwell, Anna 660
Sickles, Daniel 20, 22, 52, 57, 94, 123, 124, 126, 128, 129, 130, 145, 152, 158, 159, 160, 161, 162, 163, 164, 165, 167, 168, 175, 178, 179, 180, 181, 185, 187, 188, 189, 190, 198, 205, 216, 222, 223, 231, 232, 242, 249, 296, 334, 354, 459, 530, 570, 605, 748
Sigel, Franz 55
Sinclair, Samuel 661
Slocum, Henry W. 57, 92, 93, 103, 114, 115, 124, 125, 126, 128, 129, 130, 134, 140, 142, 144, 160, 279, 280, 281, 282, 296, 297, 298, 299, 341, 342, 344, 403, 404, 453, 464, 465, 506, 524, 548, 620, 625, 644
Smith, A. J. 326, 327, 636
Smith, E. Kirby 314, 319, 323, 477, 478, 479, 480, 487, 533, 576, 615
Smith, James E. 179, 180, 194
Smith, James Power 118
Smith, Martin Luther 635
Smith, Orlando 111
Smith, T. Kilby 574, 594, 635
Smith, W. F. "Baldy" 9, 351, 466, 504, 505, 547, 549, 550, 551, 565, 567, 571, 590, 591, 604, 617, 619, 627, 644, 645, 676, 694, 695, 721, 727, 734
Smith, William "Extra Billy" 89, 97, 117, 118, 119, 120, 121, 275, 300, 339, 343, 344, 615
Smith, William H. H. 718
Smyth, Thomas A. 257, 348, 349, 398, 399, 402, 410
Sorrel, G. Moxley 157
Spangler, Joseph 142, 243, 287, 288,

338, 358, 365, 367, 397
Spear, Ellis 200, 208, 209, 210, 212
Spear, Samuel 494, 495, 496
Spinola, Francis 627
Stannard, George 116, 145, 260, 397, 401, 404, 416, 417, 425, 426
Stanton, Edwin 306, 310, 317, 327, 329, 449, 450, 451, 467, 468, 469, 523, 529, 530, 532, 560, 569, 590, 626, 648, 658, 666, 707, 709, 710, 714, 725, 728, 734, 736, 740, 741
Starr, Samuel "Paddy" 429, 430, 431
Steele, Frederick 539
Stephens, Alexander 319, 467, 529, 530, 539
Steuart, George "Maryland" 283, 285, 286, 288, 336, 337, 338, 339, 340, 341, 342
Stevens, Greenleaf 43, 112, 113, 142, 277, 290, 291
Stevens, Thaddeus 133
Stoddard, William O. 737
Stone, Roy 42, 43, 62, 70, 71, 72, 73, 74, 75, 76, 77, 78, 80, 85, 106, 110
Storrs, Charles 266, 267
Stratton, Franklin 496
Streight, Abel 497
Strong, George 608, 609, 610, 636, 637, 638
Strong, George Templeton 664
Stuart, Augustus 733
Stuart, J. E. B. "Jeb" 8, 9, 10, 12, 49, 50, 54, 63, 120, 168, 169, 264, 265, 266, 267, 268, 269, 270, 271, 272, 304, 320, 335, 362, 363, 364, 365, 376, 377, 378, 379, 381, 382, 383, 384, 427, 428, 440, 463, 496, 509, 510, 511, 512, 513, 517, 525, 541, 553, 555, 564, 584, 585, 586, 607, 617, 619, 620, 621, 622, 624, 642, 676, 684, 724
Sweitzer, Jacob 217, 221, 234, 235, 236
Sykes, George 126, 127, 134, 160, 174, 188, 198, 199, 205, 210, 217, 223, 224, 232, 235, 280, 298, 435, 438, 505, 506, 523, 525, 643, 644

T

Taliaferro, William Booth 611, 612, 720
Tate, Theodore 272
Taylor, Richard 314, 477, 478, 479, 533, 615
Taylor, Sam 669
Taylor, Walter 13, 120, 642
Taylor, Zachary 314
Terry, Alfred 608
Thomas, Edward L. 104, 408
Thomas, Evan 168, 247, 250, 252
Thomas, George H. 573, 634
Thomas, Lorenzo 168, 451, 590, 619
Thom, George 645
Thompson, Benjamin 346
Thompson, Richard 347, 348
Thompson, "Widow" 133
Tidball, John 259, 260
Tilton, William 217, 220, 221, 239
Timberlake, John 580
Tippin, Andrew 231
Tremain, Henry E. 178, 187, 188, 228, 229, 232
Trimble, Isaac 121, 156, 357, 359, 393, 395, 397, 403, 406, 407, 408, 409, 410, 422, 436, 443, 547
Trowbridge, Luther 462
Turnbull, John 245, 248, 250, 254, 255
Tweed, William "Boss" 704, 705

V

Veazey, W. G. 425, 426
Venable, A. Reid 63
Venable, Charles S. 148, 156, 355
Vincent, Strong 199, 200, 201, 202, 203, 204, 205, 206, 210, 216, 232, 235
von Gilsa, Leopold 90, 91, 95, 96, 97, 98, 99, 289, 290, 291, 292

von Steinwehr, Adolph 57, 112, 290, 293

W

Wade, Virginia "Jennie" 345
Wadsworth, James 21, 22, 23, 25, 26, 27, 31, 32, 33, 34, 35, 40, 41, 42, 51, 52, 56, 59, 62, 82, 84, 102, 108, 111, 113, 144, 286, 336, 645, 646
Wainwright, Charles 21, 42, 43, 62, 84, 108, 110, 112, 277, 290, 437
Walker, James A. 273, 283, 342
Walker, John G. 323, 478, 533, 575
Walker, Lucius "Marsh" 480, 482, 486, 487
Walker, R. Lindsay 151, 152, 156, 157, 171, 368
Wallace, Lew 612, 639
Waller, Frank 40
Walling, George 706, 709, 711
Ward, Hobart 165, 180, 183, 191, 194, 195, 196, 199, 216, 217, 222
Wardrop, David W. 494, 496
Warren, Gouverneur 112, 128, 130, 141, 160, 163, 188, 190, 198, 203, 204, 205, 296, 297, 465, 505, 523, 547, 571, 572, 644, 645, 646, 726, 749
Watie, Stand 315
Watson, Joseph 580, 581
Watson, Malbone 240
Watts, N. G. 593
Webb, Alexander 191, 255, 346, 400, 401, 402, 404, 411, 412, 413, 414, 415, 416
Weber, Peter 685, 686, 687
Webster, Daniel 21
Weed, Stephen H. 198, 205, 210, 232
Weed, Thurlow 736
Weikert, George 139, 199, 241
Weir, Gulian 246, 247, 248, 249, 259, 261
Welles, Gideon 467, 529, 539, 573
Welsh, Warner 471, 503

Wheeler, Joe 317
Wheeler, William 100
Whipple, William D. 729, 730
White, Julius 321
White, William W. 622, 623
Whiting, H. A. 408
Whiting, W. H. C. 608, 611, 719
Wiedrich, Michael 117, 291, 292
Wilcox, Cadmus M. 130, 148, 166, 167, 171, 172, 242, 243, 244, 246, 247, 248, 251, 252, 253, 254, 258, 357, 391, 420, 424, 425, 426, 427
Wilkerson, Bayard 91, 97, 100
Willard, George 161, 167, 249, 250, 251, 252, 253, 254, 279
Williams, Alpheus 114, 118, 125, 140, 144, 152, 160, 279, 280, 281, 288, 297, 298, 299, 336, 337, 342, 453
Williams, Jesse 283
Williams, J. M. 315, 316
Williams, Lewis 391
Williams, Seth 45, 46, 95, 336, 466, 542, 543, 544, 565, 604, 619, 626, 627
Winder, John Henry 724
Winder, William Sidney 724
Winkler, Frederick 101
Winslow, Cleveland 734, 735
Winslow, George 218, 222
Wister, Langhorne 73, 76, 77, 81
Witcher, Vincent 364, 365, 377, 378, 620, 621, 623
Wofford, William T. 183, 191, 229, 231, 233, 235, 239, 240, 241, 354, 355
Wolford, Frank 538
Wood, Benjamin 656
Wood, Fernando 639
Woodruff, Charles 518, 519, 520
Woodruff, George "Little Dad" 374, 398, 399, 405, 438
Wood, Thomas 701
Wool, John E. 591, 653, 657, 658, 661, 664, 666, 700, 705, 727, 734, 737
Wright, Ambrose Ransom "Rans"

    248, 249, 255, 256, 257, 259, 260,
    262, 370, 400, 420, 421, 464, 521
Wright, Horatio G. 465, 505, 688

Y

Young, Anna Mary 58, 123, 131
Young, Louis B. 12, 13

Z

Zeilinger, Hetty 473
Zook, Samuel 223, 225, 226, 233, 296

Printed in Great Britain
by Amazon